750

Twenty-Two Caliber Varmint Rifles

By

CHARLES S. LANDIS

Author of

.22 CALIBER RIFLE SHOOTING
HUNTING WITH THE TWENTY-TWO

A Samworth Book on Firearms

Published by

SMALL ARMS TECHNICAL PUBLISHING COMPANY

GEORGETOWN, SOUTH CAROLINA

U. S. A.

Printed in the United States of America
By
THE TELEGRAPH PRESS
Harrisburg, Pennsylvania

CONTENTS

TWENTY-TWO CALIBER
VARMINT RIFLES

By CHARLES S. LANDIS

INTRODUCTION

THIS BOOK has been written and published for the purpose of acquainting gunmakers, sportsmen, and riflemen with the extraordinary possibilities of the .22 caliber rifle as a hunting arm and for target work and testing.

Its preparation and publication had no connection with any firearms, ammunition, rifle sight, powder manufacturer, or custom gunsmith. It is the combined work of an author and a publisher, both of whom are experienced hunters and riflemen, who have taken this means of providing shooters and rifle cranks with a practical work on the .22 varmint rifle and its ammunition, such as never before has been attempted.

The data and material for this and its two companion works, to follow, has been developed over a period of eight years. When finally collected this book was then written and is right up to date as of late spring of 1948. In this compilation between 2,000 and 3,000 letters and communications referring specifically to these works passed back and forth. This may give some idea of the thoroughness with which this material has been assembled and placed in book form.

No attempt has been made to list in this book or to describe *every* experimental or individual gun or rifle crank's ideas or cartridge. Those logical rifles, cartridges and loads have been chosen which appeared most efficient ballistically, and best adapted to the needs of the greatest number of riflemen distributed throughout the whole of North America. The inclusion, mention, or the omission of the name or product of any person, custom gunsmith, manufacturer, or of any rifle, cartridge, primer, propellant, or of any other component, should not be construed as reflecting in any manner upon that person, article, or ammunition constituent. The sole purpose of this work has been to provide the shooting public with a book on .22 caliber varmint rifles and their ammunition which shall be instructive, practical and interesting. We trust that we have accomplished that purpose.

It should also be put forth that the material in this book is the product of the minds and experiences, and has actually been made possible by the cooperation of hundreds of riflemen, custom gunsmiths and experimenters. Each has contributed his bit. Many have worked with the author over a period of months, and even years, in compiling their data and putting it down in understandable form and then checking and re-checking the information, loads and statements. Hence, this publication can be accepted as the product of many who have spent a lifetime acquiring a definite degree of mastery in the making, loading and shooting of .22 caliber wildcat rifles. Therefore, the reader, particularly the beginner, should read closely and heed carefully the suggestions and cautions contained herein; because the statements in this book are the actual result of the experience of skilled riflemen, experimenters and craftsmen who, since their youth, have above all else loved the .22 caliber rifle.

It should be mentioned too that almost without exception, these modern .22 caliber wildcat cartridges are definitely the product of the minds and experiments, and of the experiences in the field, of the shooters themselves. They are not commercial creations. The fact that we riflemen have cooperated, exchanged facts and experiences, and have developed, tested and described these modern cartridges which today are sweeping the boards, is of itself significant. A man must make his living where he can, but only a rifleman really loves a rifle. Consequently, it takes riflemen to develop rifles and cartridges to the point where they make better than one minute of angle groups consistently within their accuracy range. Within this work you will see the proof of this!

The author has endeavored to make this a book which the rifle crank and the varmint hunter will find of such interest that he will keep it in his shooting library throughout his lifetime—in other words that he will regard it as his .22 caliber varmint rifle Bible, and hand it down to the next of line in his family as a true record of what was possible with .22 rifles and cartridges during *his* lifetime. As stated, the .22 caliber rim fire rifle will be treated in another volume.

Before we plunge too avidly and too deeply into the many subjects connected with .22 varmint rifles and their shooting, there are a few things in general which the reader should think over.

The facts stated and the suggestions or recommendations made in this book are based on careful research and experiment *and are believed to be correct.* They have been checked and re-checked and have been compiled from what are believed to be the most accurate available sources and from the personal experience of reputable persons. No *guarantee* of their accuracy is made, however, and both the author and the publisher suggest that riflemen make their own tests to determine the suitability of any rifle, cartridge or load for their particular purposes. They recommend that all full charges as well as those which are not quite maximum charges, but which nevertheless may develop considerable pressure, possibly in a new rifle and regardless of the size or name of the cartridge, be developed gradually, beginning always with 0.5 to 2.0 grains below the normal full charges, and with even a greater reduction if the rifle appears to have been chambered very closely or throated very short. The amount of decrease of the charge when starting to experiment, should be greatest with large cartridges and also with those having very sharply tapered shoulders.

Furthermore, the subject of primers, most particularly different makes and lots of the more recent and powerful non-corrosive primers, must at all times be given the most careful attention. Neither author nor publisher assume responsibility for the use of non-corrosive primers, especially to ignite charges which have been developed for use with other types of primers or priming mixtures. Especial care should be used when loading high intensity cartridges with less powder capacity or sharper shoulder slope and different neck length, or when loading bullets of heavier weight, thicker, tougher bullet jacket, or having a longer bearing surface. Unusual care should be employed, also, not to overload when firing at temperatures of 30 to 70 degrees below Zero, Fahrenheit, or above 110 degrees Fahrenheit.

Also, the author and the publisher assume no responsibility when the reader may fire cartridges in chambers of different length, diameter, or design; for the purpose of reforming cartridge cases for firing in a new, larger or longer type of chamber. They assume no responsibility if the reader may feel impelled to fire a powerful, high-intensity, high pressure cartridge in a rifle, action, or with non-bushed firing pin, all or any of them not sufficiently strong or of proper material or design to handle such ammunition. The author and publisher have done everything humanly possible to provide readers with an interesting, instructive and complete book on the .22 varmint rifle, its cartridges, and its shooting. But their responsibility stops there.

The degree of excellence of the workmanship of various custom gunsmiths may vary over the course of years, or in proportion to the skill of workmen they may employ. We can, of course, assume no responsibility for such workmanship or the moral or financial responsibility of gunsmiths or manufacturers.

Nothing in this book should be construed as reflecting upon any patent right or as suggesting the use of any patent illegally, or improperly, or for personal gain. It could be remembered though, by the reader, that within a certain period of years, patents automatically expire.

Possibly it should be said that this and the accompanying volumes on the .22 rifle are presented without apology to further popularize and dignify the .22 caliber rifle, both rim and center fire, including the commercial and wildcat calibers, as serious sporting rifles of almost unlimited possibilities and accomplishments. Those who scoff at the .22 rifle quite obviously have never really become skilled in the use of the .22 varmint rifle. With an accurate arm of this type, and proper ammunition, the time has come when literally you can cross your "t's" and dot your "i's" with bullets.

The author hopes that the reader will enjoy the .22 rifle as he has enjoyed it through nearly 50 years of practical field shooting experience. If this work serves to acquaint you with the real possibilities of the vast number and types of .22 varmint rifles and cartridges, bullets and loads, and most particularly if it helps to induce the large commercial manufacturers to standardize and bring out some of the best models of these cartridges in modern, sufficiently large and sufficiently strong and *heavy* precision-made varmint rifles to satisfy the needs of *riflemen,* it will have served its purpose. The development of .22 caliber varmint rifles from now on should have a very bright future.

It is entirely possible that one of the .22 varmint rifles described herein will give you a new understanding and meaning of the word accuracy. Those who know this best have made possible this volume.

CHARLES S. LANDIS,

April, 1948.   Wilmington, Delaware.

Chapter 1

THE HISTORY OF .22 CALIBER VARMINT RIFLES

A QUARTER of a billion years ago, when the planet which we call the Earth, was still young, varmint hunting had its inception. Varmints were then hunting each other. One hundred to one hundred and fifty million years ago, man arrived on earth. He appears to have had the intellect of a moron but the physique of a heavy-weight wrestler. Life for him probably had few comfortable days and few safe moments. Probably no dull ones. The saber-tooth tiger, many lions, leopards, tigers, tremendous lizards, reptiles and saurians of enormous size, were probably all classed with the varmints in those days. Size and strength, longevity (if not killed), and ferociousness, were outstanding characteristics of most of the mammals and reptiles of those periods. The earliest known man, who probably left his skull and bones on Java, was more than likely killed by a varmint. Men who followed, even for centuries, lacked the use of fire, steel, iron, copper and other essentials needed for the making of even the crudest effective weapons against beasts of the plains or the forest, the marsh or the rocky cliffs.

Because man's weapons were of the crudest, and lacked range, they were of little effect upon varmints in prehistoric times. Obviously, the .22 caliber varmint rifle of great accuracy and flat trajectory was not then known to hunters. If you wish you had lived in those times, remember you would have been faced by many ballistic problems impossible of solution by the use of modern tools because these were then non-existent. In this instance, you might well be thankful you were a few years too late. It is unfortunately all too true, that the varmint hunter, down through the ages, usually had plenty of targets and no rifle, or plenty of rifles and few targets in the hunting field. Yet there always seemed to be plenty of varmints every place upon the globe on which animals or reptiles could sustain life. But it is probable that we may safely assume that in the earlier

1

days few men were confirmed varmint hunters. Edible game was of all sizes and usually abundant. It was good to eat and safer to hunt.

For various good reasons, such as lack of definite information, and limited space we will skip over a few million years and start you in the 1890's when metal-cased bullets and smokeless powder came in. A well known early experimenter told the author he had accurate shooting rifles around 1894 and 1895, yet it was not until some time in 1906 that he really got interested in the .22 caliber wildcat rifle. A great many other riflemen, who eventually became expert with special .22 or .25 caliber wildcat rifles, started their active varmint shooting about that time.

Harvey Donaldson's first accurate rifle for the use of metal-cased bullets was made up from suggestions and ideas inspired by letters from the late Dr. Franklin W. Mann, the rifle enthusiast and ballistic authority who inspired much of the early work of so many of us, the author included. The author had voluminous correspondence from Dr. Mann, Dr. Henry A. Baker, and some from A. O. Niedner, as had Donaldson, back in those days.

When Niedner was living in Malden, Massachusetts, Donaldson had him make up a special rifle on a Stevens single shot action. The case was the .32-40 necked down to .22 caliber (bottle-neck) but the mouth of the case was made *smaller* than bullet diameter. He used the Mann base band bullet in this rifle, which was one of the very earliest .22-32/40 varmint jobs and placed the bullet in the breech of the rifle, inserted a loaded cartridge (which did *not* contain a bullet) back of it, and then closed the action, thus seating the bullet firmly in the rifling. The author recalls distinctly receiving letter after letter from Dr. Mann on identically the same subject, which to Mann was then most important.

With this ammunition, the woodchuck hunter would carry his loaded and primed cases which contained the powder charge, a wad, and of course the primer, but no bullet. The loaded cartridge acted as a bullet seater, and incidentally, as a very good bullet seater. They used the Mann base band bullet. In chuck hunting the riflemen carried these cases with a special wad on top, to keep the powder from bouncing out due to the loosening of the usual type wad from extended hunting.

The bullets were early metal cased .22's, made from a lead core and empty .22 caliber Short copper cartridge cases, which had been fired and retrieved, and each bullet was seated snugly in the barrel. Dr. Mann used this combination extensively in the field, and also in his 200-yard testing range. Niedner, Dr. Baker, and quite a number

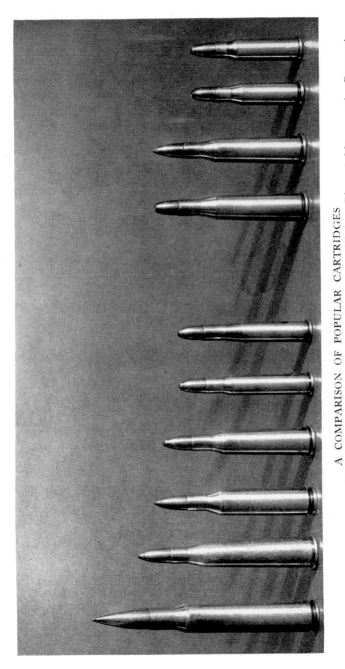

A COMPARISON OF POPULAR CARTRIDGES

Left to right: .30-1906, .224 Lightning, .22 Niedner Rimless Magnum, .22 Niedner Rimmed Magnum, the R-2, and .22/3000 Lovell, .219 Zipper, .22 Niedner Rimmed Magnum, .218 Bee and .22 Baby Niedner.

of others shot woodchucks with such "loose" ammunition and rifles.

Assuming the gunner had his empty rifle in hand, when he saw an object at which he wished to fire, like a crow or a woodchuck, he would open the breech block, tip the muzzle downward, drop a bullet carefully into the chamber, point forward of course, raise the muzzle a bit and then insert the charged cartridge and close the breech. The bullet was thus seated in the lands and the rifle was ready to fire. In accuracy, it was really a "bumble bee" rifle.

In this era, Charles Newton had his start as a rifle and cartridge designer, and experimenter. Much of this field work was carried out in the West by a Colorado rifleman about whom we will talk a bit later. Newton and the author had much correspondence and exchange of ideas. Particularly on the .22 and .250/3000 Newton. Newton was not merely a reloader; he was a ballistics expert and a designer. Professionally, he was lawyer. He was not a practical rifle manufacturer, nor a successful one, unfortunately, as he designed cartridges which were at least 10 to 20 years ahead of his time. They deserved better rifles.

For some years Donaldson did much of the actual testing and experimenting on many of Newton's early varmint rifles and the cartridge loading, while out West C. E. Howard shot the Newton single shot .22 H. P. rifles with base band bullets, on gray wolves, coyotes, jack rabbits, antelope and deer.

Just past the turn of the Nineteenth century, by a few years, Donaldson made up what might well have been called the first varminter. It used a Donaldson design case and he tried to get the Savage Arms Corporation to adopt this caliber in place of the .22 Savage H. P. cartridge, but they would not do this because they were already tooled up for the .22 Savage H. P. and to have a second cartridge would hurt the sale of rifles for the other, and for that combination they already had tools, which always are expensive to make. In long past years the author has also had correspondence with manufacturers in which a .22-250/3000 was suggested, by merely necking down the .250/3000 to .22 caliber. Others probably suggested or thought of the same thing.

A cartridge very similar if not identical to Gebby's .22 Varminter Junior was used many years ago by Mann, Niedner, and numerous others. It was made by necking down the .32-40 case (or some other of similar head size), to .22 caliber, as is the Gebby, and was then loaded with .22 caliber base band bullets which were metal-cased and often made from .22 Short cartridge cases, either fired or new copper metal.

Harvey Donaldson began experimenting with smokeless small caliber cases about 1893. One of the first black powder cases he tried to convert was the .22-10-45 Maynard single shot rifle cartridge; others used it also. This small case used the No. 0 primer. With black powder the .22 Maynard C. F. was difficult to clean, both case and rifle barrel. Shotgun smokeless was used to overcome this difficulty, but the cartridge case was not sufficiently strong at the head to stand the pressures; the primer pocket expanded, and then the primer would drop out. He next became interested in the .22-13-45 W.C.F. and also used and shot the .25-21, .25-25, and .28-30 rifles, a .32-40 Ballard, a very accurate .32-35 Stevens, a cartridge slightly shorter and somewhat less powerful than the .32-40 but nevertheless, extremely accurate. The author seriously contemplated getting a fine Stevens for it at one time.

About this time Leopold broke into the circle of .22 rifle experimenters. E. A. Leopold was a telegraph operator and special station agent at Norristown, Pennsylvania, and both Donaldson and the author corresponded with Leopold quite extensively over a considerable period. This took in the subjects of .22 and .25 caliber rifles, cartridges and bullets. The time was back in the period when Eastern railroads most magnanimously paid graduates of Yale, Princeton and Harvard, around $40.00 a month when employed in clerical positions and to others not so well educated, certainly no more, and this meant that two to three months salary was needed to purchase a good Stevens Ideal Target rifle, for those employed in white collar jobs. Doctor Mann and Harry Pope generously cooperated with Leopold who had considerable success, as had Herrick, with the .22-15-60 Stevens cartridge. Leopold was a good penman and a rather prolific correspondent. He designed most excellent paper-patched bullets in .22 and .25 calibers and sent samples to Donaldson, the author, and others. I then exchanged targets and an occasional rifle with Doctor Mann, and was probably the one to convince Doctor Mann that the .22 Long Rifle would really shoot in those days. I shot numerous 30-shot tests for him in Central Pennsylvania, and then sent him my best .22 rifle, a fine Stevens Schuetzen for test on his indoor range, with a lot of its best ammunition, and the rifle promptly duplicated its Pennsylvania test groups in Massachusetts, being the first .22 rim fire to do this for the Doctor. It had an uncanny ability to score a 99 or an occasional 100 on the first target at 50 yards, and 99's were not too common with .22's in those days, shooting outdoors.

That winter was abnormally cold and snowy all over the New

England and the Middle Atlantic States. We had one snow storm and blizzard after another, a tremendous migration of crows and hawks occurred through Central Pennsylvania and my best shooting .22 was iced-in on the 200-yard covered range at Milford, Massachusetts, the Doctor could not get out to his range for a period of about six weeks, so many a crow and hawk owed its safety to that unfortunate circumstance.

Meantime, Leopold became even more interested in bullet design. He was a crow, hawk and woodchuck shooter. He had a rather small circle of friends but among them he was a most interesting correspondent. His design of .22 paper-patched bullet was so effective that in recent years Donaldson has used the same form of bullet, in *metal-cased* style, in his most recent cartridges like the .219 Donaldson-Wasp. He has mentioned this himself, to the author.

Donaldson, at one time, had a bullet mould made up by the Ideal Company to cast a long, slim-pointed bullet of the Leopold design, and quite recently still had some of these bullets on hand. He mentioned that the metal-cased bullets for which he had a swage, and which are of the Leopold point contour, certainly *shoot*. In other words, Leopold's design of cast bullet, laid out 40 years ago, is just as practical in a metal-cased bullet as when it was used in the making of Leopold's paper-patched bullets for the .22-15-60 Stevens single shot rifle before the days of Theodore Roosevelt as President. The design as made up, cast a slug which was noted principally for having a point or tapered portion materially longer than that of the Sisk five or six diameter metal-cased bullets, and yet was much thicker or "fatter" than the forward portion of the Morse 8S bullet, the final design of which Donaldson mentioned to the author that he (Donaldson) had developed.

Consequently we may assume that there have been at least *three* general shapes of .22 cased or metal-jacketed bullets, in addition to the Herrick flat-point 60-grain lead-alloy bullets for the .22-15-60 Stevens, each capable of giving exceptional accuracy when properly formed. These included the 8S, the Leopold and Leopold-Donaldson, and the one best typified by the 63-grain Sisk bullet. Mannen has a bullet of approximately the same weight, and just as good lines as the 63-grain Sisk, or the Sisk-Niedner. This gives us sharp point, pencil point bullets; long, sharp pointed bullets but having a nose thicker and more rounded at the base of the nose, not the base of the bullet; and still another design which is common to the Sisk bullets. The Hill bullets are quite similar also. We also have another very old and very accurate but lighter bullet, the 45 or 46-grain .22 Hornet bullet with the blunted point, which originated as the Niedner-Shelhamer design of bullet in the .22 Koshollek and was baptized then as the "Baby Niedner," the bullet having been taken up practically "in toto," according to report, by Winchester in their original and very accurate .22 Hornet cartridge —four general styles in all, all more or less alike in accuracy, and all widely different in shape and ranging ability. Donaldson mentioned that in his opinion each has its critical velocity for maximum accuracy, and these velocities are not the same, and in this he is very likely entirely correct. However, these same bullets would probably shoot just as well at 700 f.s. lower velocity and 700 f.s. higher velocity—the latter if the jackets would provide sufficient insulation for the core to prevent melting of the core of the bullet.

So much for a most important subject in the history of the .22 varmint rifle, the designs of its best bullets.

Donaldson wrote the author February 11, 1946: "For years I used the round nose, soft point bullets as designed by Sisk for use in the .22 Hornet and the .22 Niedner-Magnum, and about which I have often written. It was only when we got better long range varmint rifles—better because of flatter trajectory—such as the Swift, and my own .22-250/3000 design, my own R-2, the .22/4500 Krag, and the .219 Donaldson Wasp, that we were better able to appreciate the 8S pointed bullet that would carry up and *maintain* its velocity out at 250 and 300 yards; it was then that we turned to the 8S design."

"Sam Clark, of Oakland, Maine, will tell you that I can obtain just as great accuracy at 100 yards with any of the .22 bullets regardless of point design. It is simply a matter of *knowing* the particular velocity each design requires to give the best accuracy. I have worked out a formula for this."

The long pointed bullets only come into their own, really, out at long range where they carry up better, being able to maintain a higher percentage of their initial (or muzzle) velocity. There is even a limit in this direction. The 90-grain bullet has been used in the .22 Newton and a quicker twist was necessary. The quicker twist and faster rate of spin of the bullet reduced the velocity. Donaldson reported that he had experimented with different experimental bullets from Charles Morse swages that form .22 caliber bullets of 60, 65, 70, 75 and even 80-grain. The 60 to 65-grain weight of a .22 bullet is *ideal,* in Donaldson's opinion, because any bullets of a longer length and greater weight than 63 to 65-grains require a quicker twist of rifling which of itself reduces the velocity out where the chuck is sitting. Muzzle velocity does not mean too much, in fact, Donaldson claims it does not "mean a thing"—comparatively speaking— in .22 varmint rifles and that his own shooting will prove and has proved that a *well designed* case will drive a 50-grain bullet *faster* with the same powder charge than a 45-grain bullet in the same rifle.

The author would like to add that this is particularly true with the coarser I.M.R. powders like 4320 and 4064, more so than with 4198, and it may also be true in some instances with 3031, because a heavier bullet is required to make the coarser I.M.R. powders burn completely in the smaller and shorter and lower and medium capacity cases and definitely so in the large capacity .22 caliber necked down cases. If the pressure is not up to the working pressure of the powder, and for which that powder was designed or found to work best, then complete combustion cannot occur within the cartridge case and the breech portion of the barrel. There is nothing to make it happen; nothing can but sufficient pressure. Pressure does not build up in time before the gas column lengthens excessively as the bullet passes up the barrel at a lower than maximum or desirable velocity.

The present placing of 10 shots within a 1″ group at 100 yards, time after time, as has been done with certain medium size .22 wildcat cartridges, is due to the most excellent combustion of the powder in these cartridges plus proper bullet design and jacketing for the velocity attained.

Now for some Western experimental work in .22 cartridge development.

High velocity .22 caliber varmint rifles, mostly on Stevens 44½ and Winchester Hi-Side actions, were made up by the late Charles Newton and also by A. O. Niedner, around 35 to 40 years ago, possibly even earlier.

In the Spring of 1910, the late C. E. Howard, of North Park, Colorado, purchased from A. O. Niedner, then in Massachusetts, a Winchester Hi-Side single shot rifle equipped with a 26″ barrel. It used a cartridge made from the .32-40 B & M. case and necked down to .22 caliber. It was loaded with 60-grain metal jacketed bullets made by taking .22 Short cases from the machines before being headed-up and placing these over lead cores, much as the R.C.B.S. bullets are made today, and swaging the two together. Verily there is not so much new under the old sun!

These 60-grain Niedner bullets, which were supplied by him, were driven by 25.0 grains of Lightning No. 1 powder. The muzzle velocity was estimated to be approximately 3,300 f.s. Remember that was with a 60-grain bullet and not with a 35 or 41-grain bullet, in which instance the muzzle velocity might have been around 3,800 f.s.

In the winter of 1910-11, according to the late Mr. Howard's records and recollection, he killed 60 coyotes and some gray wolves with this .22-32/40 rifle. The first 20 were shot and killed without a miss. Imagine anyone killing 20 straight on coyotes today! The average shot was claimed to have been 278 yards for the first 45 coyotes shot. By that time the survivors probably began to "wise up" and to conclude that probably the "guvment" was after them!

The bullets for this .22-32/40 rifle had a pointed, bare lead tip, were of *base band* style, and sat in the neck of the cartridge case but 0.07" and the front of the bullet projected up into the rifling so that the lands touched the band of the bullet. This combination gave 4" groups at 200 yards. This rifle also killed a number of deer and antelope.

A condition common to almost all rifle shooters is that regardless of how good the results which are being obtained, the rifleman always hopes that on the morrow he will do just a bit better. Usually this takes the form of getting another and higher velocity rifle.

Shortly after 1911, Charles Newton, then in his heyday as an experimenter, made up another rifle for C. E. Howard, using a .22 case made from the .30-40 Krag cartridge, the load being a 70-grain jacketed bullet and 32.0 grains of Lightning No. 1 powder. This was seven grains more of Lightning and the new cartridge therefore threw a 17% heavier bullet which was being pushed along by 28% heavier powder charge. The muzzle velocity was but 3,276 f.s.; however, this was imparted to a 70-grain bullet. Compare that with the .22 Savage H.P. of today!

This rifle was made up on the Stevens 44½ action, was fitted with a Stevens .22-15-60 barrel rifled 0.001" deeper than normal, and it shot numerous groups reproduced in *Arms & The Man* of that period, which clusters measured from 4½" to 3¼" in diameter at 200 yards. Not bad, considering that this was about 35 years ago and the bullets of those days were not modern bullets.

The coyotes and the gray wolves of North Park sat out on those bare snow-swept hillsides and howled worse than ever when they heard that this .22-30/40 had been imported to Colorado especially for their benefit. Literally, Woe had come to them!

C. E. Howard, Charles Newton and A. O. Niedner received a great deal of publicity along about 1910-12, on .22 high powers of special design but they were not monopolizing the magazines. Dr.

Franklin W. Mann had a few .22 high powers using base band bullets before 1910. He made his own bullets. He manufactured machines commercially for the grinding of poultry foods, and apparently was rather ingenious mechanically.

Hervey Lovell made up his first .22-32/40 rifle in 1912, and Niedner again pushed this type of rifle about 1922, as the author had correspondence at that time to prove it; so had others.

The Development of the .22 Hornet

There have been numerous claims as to the originator of, and the principal developers of the .22 Hornet cartridge, bullets and rifle. The original .22 Hornet cartridge, which was not like the .22 Hornet of today was apparently developed back in the early '90s by none other than Reuben Harwood, the celebrated "Iron Ramrod," most famous writer on small bore center fire rifles in the old *Shooting and Fishing* and *Arms & The Man* magazine.

Years later, Hervey Lovell imported .22 Hornet rifles and ammunition from Continental Europe and sold them here through advertisements in *The American Rifleman* and *Field & Stream*. I personally saw the advertisements and apparently the rifles and ammunition were accurate.

Shortly thereafter, G. B. Crandall, gunsmith of Woodstock, Ontario, began relining .22 rifles with Parkerifled (British) tubes and in addition to .22 Long Rifle barrels relined numerous ones for the .22 Hornet cartridge as well. These rifles shot well and were rather widely used in Canada, especially in Southern Ontario.

A group of four men in the Ordnance Department then took up experimental work and publicity incident to the popularizing of the .22 Hornet cartridge. They were Al Woodworth, ballistic engineer at Springfield Arsenal, or proof house foreman, as they were usually called; Capt. G. A. Woody; Capt. G. L. Wotkyns; and Lt. Col. Townsend Whelen. Al Woodworth and Woody did most of the bullet experimental work and design, Woodworth having a bullet which was rather sharp pointed which gave good accuracy. Wotkyns gave the Hornet cartridge considerable publicity and shooting and developed a standard load of Hercules 2400 Powder for it. Whelen, with his usual enthusiasm, gave it still more publicity as a small bore development and a hunting cartridge par-excellence in its velocity range.

The author has recommended it for years, through his columns, as the most center fire cartridge for the money, in accuracy and killing power, for small game and varmint shooting, above the .22 Long

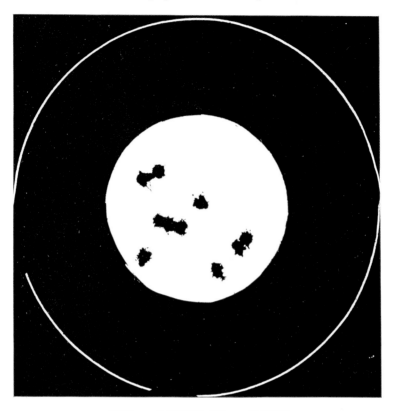

THE .22 HORNET AT 200 YARDS

This target was shot at 200 yards, bench rest, July 4, 1937, by J. Bushnell Smith, using a .22 Hornet Winchester single shot Schuetzen rifle.
Barrel was by Charles C. Johnson and has a 14″ twist. Lyman Targetspot, Jr., 10 X. Load 10.0 grs. of No. 2400 and 55-gr. Sisk Hornet bullets.
This is a 10-shot group, measuring 1¼″ center to center.

Rifle in power. His son, Charles S. Landis, Jr., the most successful
rifle shot on hawks the author has ever seen in action, developed and
experimented with many loads of 2400, 1204 and various other powders and both of us shot many of them at hawks with real success.
Inside 175 yards, there is no equally good factory load for such
shooting, and few which are better in hand loads.

The important feature of the .22 Hornet cartridge is the remarkable and uniform accuracy of the factory ammunition universally
supplied for it. No other small caliber commercial center fire cartridge equals this accuracy.

The .22/3000 Rifles

To Hervey Lovell should go the credit for the design and development of the early .22/3000 gentle slope Lovell. This, and the sharper slope (12° to 12° 30′ in most instances, although a few run up to 17° or more) which originally came out through the efforts of Harvey Donaldson and M. S. Risley—who made up the dies and

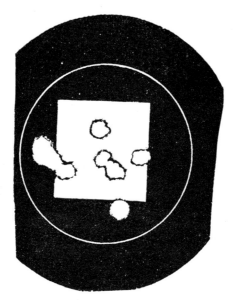

R-2, .22/3000 AT 100 YARDS

This target was made at 100 yards, with R-2, .22/3000 Gebby-Martini rifle and Lyman 6X Targetspot, Jr., scope. Fired from bench rest by J. Bushnell Smith. Load 15.0 grs. IMR No. 4227 and 50-gr. 8S Morse bullets.

tools—and which cartridge had variations in shoulder slope by Charles C. Johnson, Robert U. Milhoan, and others; all performed well. Nearly all of these .22/3000 rifles shot unusually well, especially the original with HiVel No. 3, and the sharper shoulder jobs with the two smaller granulations of the duPont I.M.R. powders.

When the dense powder HiVel No. 3 was taken off the market, Hervey Lovell came out with his present 15° shoulder slope .22/3000 Lovell which today shoots best with Sisk 55-grain Niedner, 55-grain Express, and 55-grain Morse 8S bullets, according to Lovell, and

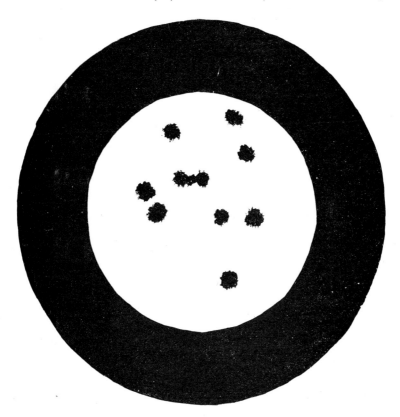

Target shot at 200 yards, measured, by A. R. Weeks using Charles C. Johnson heavy barrel on Winchester Hi-Side S.S. action. Caliber R-2 .22/3000 and a load of 16.0 grs. 4227 with matched 45-grain 8S bullets, R primers and G & H cases. Ten shots in $1\frac{11}{16}''$ group and nine shots in $1\frac{1}{4}''$. This "bumble bee" barrel lasted for 6,600 rounds and with it Weeks killed hundreds of crows annually, for many years.

which are the three bullets he usually uses in testing his rifles as they are prepared for shipment to a customer.

In the opinion of most of our custom gunsmiths, the various .22/3000 cartridges were definitely over-exploited, too many excessive claims were made for them, as compared with the larger, more powerful, flatter shooting, and equally or even more accurate cartridges such as the .22 Chucker and .22 Super-Chucker Lindahl cartridges; the .219 Donaldson-Wasp; the .22-303 Crandall Varmint-R, at least four of the Jake Pfeifer jobs, and the faster and equally accurate cartridges made from the R-2 cases, the .22 Maximum Lovell and the Kilbourn K-Lovell cartridges. The work of G. B. Crandall and Lysle Kilbourn should not be forgotten in relation to each of these cases they helped perfect.

Fred Ness, when he was Dope Bag Editor of *The American Rifleman*, undoubtedly gave more publicity to the .22/3000 cartridges than probably anyone else, so much so in fact that it is prob-

COMMERCIAL, SPECIAL AND EXPERIMENTAL

Left to right: .218 Bee; .22 Winchester C. F.: .22 Hornet, .22/3000 original; .22/3000, R-2; .220 Swift; .22 Newton High Power, original case, reloaded .22 H.P. Bullet; .22/300 H&H and .22-275 H&H, two types of experimental cartridges, discarded after they proved them too large; .22 Savage High Power; .22 Varminter as now-standardized, 8S bullet, 50-gr.; .219 Zipper; .22 Niedner-Magnum; .22-10-60; .22 C. F. Maynard.

ably unfortunate that he did not have, at the proper periods, more access to Lindahl Chucker rifles, Pfeifer .22 (short-length) .30-40 neckdowns, and especially to the close grouping .219 Donaldson-Wasp cartridges.

Between the dates of 1932 and 1939, the .22/3000 Lovells of different sorts, and the R-2 made the headlines in greatest force, and it was during this period that they saw their greatest popularity and development.

The K-Hornet

Lysle Kilbourn, who by re-chambering jobs priced at $3.00 to $10.00, depending upon what was done, has made more varmint rifle shooters out of chaps in very modest circumstances and others who had little to spend for firearms changes, than any other custom gunsmith, was responsible, with G. B. Crandall, of Woodstock, Ontario, for the design and perfection of the K-Hornet cartridge.

This is today, a more practical cartridge—due to greater ease of obtainment of empties for reloading,—the .22 Hornet cases being much easier to obtain than the .25-20 S.S. Stevens cases, for which few new rifles have been made for the last 15 years, or the .218 Bee cases from which the .22/3000 cases may also be made.

Henry E. Davis, of Florence, South Carolina, who is today the outstanding writer on shooting wild turkeys with rifles, and on turkey hunting, has done much of the field work and accuracy testing of K-Hornet loads. This K-Hornet cartridge is about the maximum in power for wild turkeys because flatter shooting and more powerful charges like the R-2 full loads tear up the turkey if within 150 yards, and besides they crack louder and the report carries farther in the woods, especially in damp weather or when there is high humidity.

For settled communities, and those not so settled but still inhabited by considerable numbers of persons scattered here and there, the K-Hornet cartridge, for which rifle chambering is done very inexpensively by Kilbourn, is just about ideal. It is fine for crows inside 225 yards or so, and good on crows at 275 yards.

Also the ammunition is very small, easily carried, loose or in boxes of 50 cartridges; it is comparatively light in weight, and it is one of if not the very best when comparing results—accuracy, uniform shooting, sufficient power, reasonably flat trajectory, in relation to the amount of powder used per cartridge and in relative cost and wear on the rifle. A K-Hornet rifle should outwear a .22/3000 or a .22 Maximum Lovell, because the powder charge is smaller and the heat developed in the chamber portion of the barrel, less, and is also less than in other good .22 varmint cartridges of small or medium size excepting the still lower powered ones, the .22 Hornet and the .22 K-Hornet Jr.

The author firmly believes that the K-Hornet represents the best value today, in a *hand-loaded* varmint rifle of small cartridge size, accuracy, killing power, low cost of ammunition and flatness of trajectory, barrel life, all considered. It will also shoot the .22 Hornet factory ammunition with reasonably good accuracy, and sometimes with fine accuracy. But it is illogical to expect that it will equal a good custom made .22 Hornet job in accuracy alone, when using factory loaded Hornet ammunition, other things being equal, but the K-Hornet is probably fully equal to the .22 Hornet in accuracy and superior at long range or on windy days, when using its own carefully hand-loaded ammunition.

With the .219 Donaldson-Wasp, the latest at this writing to receive extensive public acclaim, we will start to close this section and refer you to the various chapters in this book in which each gunsmith or each cartridge is discussed at much greater length than such subjects can be covered in a history of .22 varmint rifles and cartridges.

J. Bushnell Smith
Photo courtesy of Don Fellows

The .219 Donaldson-Wasp is a development by Harvey Donaldson and his co-experimenters and reloaders, varmint rifle shooters and others who have cooperated with Donaldson in the field in testing and load development and the bullet making for this very accurate medium size .22 varmint cartridge. These co-experimenters included Vaughan Cail of New Haven; Samuel Clark, Jr., of Oakland,

Maine; Mr. Clark's father, Samuel Clark, Sr., who made up some of the most accurate R.C.B.S. bullets for it; a chambering expert by the name of Morgan; and Charles Morse, the co-designer and maker of the Morse 8S bullets. Al Marciante of Trenton, New Jersey, did some of the chambering of .219 Wasp rifles.

In 1945 and 1946, this cartridge was making as many as *eight* consecutive 100-yard (or their 200-yard equivalent) *10-shot* groups, 1″ or better in diameter of circle, measured center to center, and that, reader, is *shooting*. Ballistic Laboratory testing of loads for velocity and pressure, was performed by Merton Robinson's crew at Winchester. A complete story of this will be given in the section devoted to the .219 Donaldson-Wasp.

The .22/250 and .22 Varminter cartridges are the other outstanding larger size cartridges. These are really .22 caliber adaptations of the .250/3000 Savage H.P. cartridge, a Charles Newton development at its start.

Jerry Gebby, J. Bushnell Smith, and such other custom gunsmiths as Parker Ackley, Lovell, Vickery, and others have had a hand, as had Grove Wotkyns in the earlier .22-250/3000 developments with J. B. Sweany.

These are all outstandingly accurate but slightly larger and slightly greater capacity cartridges than the .219 Donaldson-Wasp, and generally speaking, came out at a somewhat earlier date.

The .219 Zipper Improved, both original Ackley and later Ackley designs; the very accurate incorporations of this cartridge by W. F. Vickery, of Boise, Idaho, who acquired a national reputation for very fine shooting original-design maximum charge .219 Zipper-Improved rifles; and the Eastern designs of this cartridge, the No. 7 Hervey Lovell cartridge, the most accurate of his magnum cartridges, a 33-grain case, with the Kilbourn K-Zipper; and the Hervey Lovell Nos. 8 and 9 cartridges made from .22 H.P. and .25-35 cases, are outstanding .22 varmint cartridges.

There are a legion of others, most of the good ones having come along since about the 1934-36 development era, and many since 1940. Read the book and you will find most of them discussed under the appropriate heading on custom gunsmith comment and development.

However, as we sit thus and consider that America has had a phenomenal development in .22 varmint rifles and cartridges, that almost all of this development and popularity has accrued through the workmanship, experiment, private shooting, publicity, experimental design and patience of men who were at least during some part of their life *riflemen* rather than large commercial manufacturers, we must not lose sight of the work which has been done in England, Germany, Canada, and other countries by experimenters who also loved the small bore rifle, but who by the accident of birth did not happen to be delivered into this world on the same shores, or in the same states or communities.

As we stand today, on the threshold of the atomic age, which can revolutionize the life of man, or which can destroy mankind, depending upon the type of people who control and operate the development of atomic energy *liberation,* and as we stand also upon a point at which the financial future of our land is being seriously jeopardized by reckless and ill-advised spending of the finances and resources of the nation, we as riflemen, can congratulate ourselves that the future of rifle shooting and of hunting is being materially helped by the destruction or at least the control of varmints which throughout 365 days in the year, often prey upon one of our country's most precious heritages, our native wild game.

The experimental development of the .22 caliber varmint rifle, its cartridges, and its super-accurate loads, has been brought about, not by militarists, politicians, crackpots or damn fools, but by those rugged individualists, the experimental small bore rifleman-hunters to whom America is still a land peopled by *Americans* who like to hunt America's game.

To each of these men and women, to whom there is no sweeter sound than the crack of the .22 caliber, super-accurate, high velocity hunting rifle, this book is addressed, dedicated, and presented. Read it through carefully and with the idea that since the birth of man, no more accurate, efficient, enjoyable and useful rifle has been invented than the .22 caliber center fire varmint rifles and cartridges described in these pages.

Who knows, maybe the history of the .22 Varmint rifle has just begun. By remembering and putting into practice some of the ideas and developments set forth here, *your* part in the history of .22 caliber Varmint rifles can begin.

George Schnerring offered the following comment upon the early history of the .22 high velocity rifles:

"I have looked over the early reports of the .22 wildcats and have prodded memory, and believe that the last Schuetzenfest held in the East (there were later ones in Iowa—Author) was held at Union Hill, New Jersey, in 1911. Several members of the Philadelphia Rifle Association attended. We were there for several days and shot through the matches. The group included Major Claude Goddard, Nathan Spering, Dr. Dubbs and myself.

"In these matches Adolph Niedner and another shooter companion, perhaps it was Harvey Donaldson, shot .22 caliber high powers. As I remember it, they used a rimmed case necked to take the 70-grain Savage jacketed bullet. They got remarkable results. One of them made a score of 72 x 75 on the 3-shot Honor Target, which as you know was difficult. If my memory serves me right, that was the high score. All this shooting was standing, on both feet, and offhand.

"They had the powder charges weighed out in small, corked vials. The cases were loaded in the shooting house, a la Schuetzen style. I still do not see why the light .22 bullets, up to 55-grain (and I have fired many of them in my tests of the .22/4000 and also the .220 Swift) should be less affected by wind than say, an 100-grain or even an 87-grain .257 Roberts or the .250/3000 cartridges at 2,800 to 3,100 f.s. muzzle velocity.

"I know of course that the long heavy, target type barrel will give finer accuracy than the conventional hunting, or as Winchester calls them the 'standard' type barrel. The Wasp, as loaded with about 33.0 grains of Nos. 3031 or 4320 will probably give 3,800 f.s. velocity in a long barrelled rifle with bolt action.

"In my .25 caliber barrels mounted on Model 70 actions the .25-35 will outshoot the .250/3000, both loaded with the same powder (but not the same charge) and using the same Western 100-grain bullets.

"The .250/3000 at approximately 2,800 f.s., which is developed by 35.0 grains and the 100-grain bullet, and the .25-35 with a load of 32.0 grains of 3031, which develops 2,650 f.s. muzzle velocity, are both grand shooting rifles. In my own battery, the .250/3000 is a standard barrel 24″ Model 70, while the .25-35 has a 24″ barrel also, but it is a very heavy, straight-taper tube of the Target Barrel type.

"I would again enjoy shooting offhand in the Schuetzen game, with any one of a number of the small caliber, high velocity, varmint rifles, were it possible for us to all turn back the calendar.

"The .22 and .25 caliber high velocity varmint rifles were accurate many years before the average reader realizes. The passing of 10, 20 or 40 years has seen the coming of numerous new and very accurate cartridges and loads but, except for the greater perfection of metal cased bullets in the smaller calibers, there has, comparatively, been but little change—in the all-important question of accuracy."

There are numerous .22 varmint cartridges of outstanding design and merit, some of which have attained a popularity throughout the whole of North America, and consequently rifles are chambered for them by many celebrated custom gunsmiths. Other .22 varmint cartridges are of equally good and often definitely superior design but for one reason or another, sometimes because they are more powerful than is necessary for most Eastern varmint shooting, or because they have not been taken up by some widely known firm and then bally-hooed across the nation, they are as yet but little known to many who could profit by acquaintance with them.

A number of such cartridges are discussed here. Some are note-worthy for an exceptionally high degree of ballistic efficiency; great accuracy and high velocity are developed in proportion to the powder charge consumed. Others are much larger, have consequently, a lower degree of ballistic efficiency per grain of powder burned, and are more expensive to shoot in cost of load and in relative barrel life when such cartridge is used. But they are noteworthy in that each is of outstanding good design and has a high degree of accuracy and efficiency within the limits of its usual range.

From this list you can choose cartridges that are effective for any varmint or game shooting, from squirrels and woodchucks to goats and sheep. It is a good plan to choose a cartridge of such power and range that it will be effective on your average shot, with about a 25% margin, or factor, of safety, or of excess efficiency, but which, at the same time, does not produce such an excessively sharp and piercing report that you will soon become persona non grata on your favorite shooting grounds.

One of the very important factors in the choice of a cartridge is that the necessary cartridge brass be available for forming the empty cases when you need them. Do not choose a cartridge made from a larger cartridge which is no longer generally popular and widely available and for which sporting rifles are no longer being produced by the larger commercial manufacturers.

Among the .22 varmint cartridges which have proved exceptionally satisfactory in their different fields are the K-Hornet, .22/3000, R-2, .22 Maximum Lovell, .219 Improved Zipper, Lindahl .22 Chucker, .22 Lindahl Super-Chucker, .219 Donaldson Wasp, .22/4000 Sedgley Schnerring and .220 Wilson Arrow. A number of these are described specifically in this section, the others in the chapters devoted to the line of .22 varmint cartridges turned out by the custom gunsmith who produces rifles chambered for them.

In either case, you can determine what game such cartridges are adapted to shooting, the best loads to use in them, and who makes rifles which safely and effectively handle these cartridges.

The reader should understand that most .22 varmint cartridges are definitely high intensity and high pressure loads, as compared with most commercial .22 cartridges, particularly those commonly used in lever action rifles.

These special cartridges should in every case be used on a strong rifle action, carefully stocked, well sighted with first-class sights, properly head spaced and breeched, with firing pin bushed and of proper size for the cartridge used. Maximum loads should not be attempted with any cartridge until you have become skilled in small caliber, high intensity cartridge loading and until you have frequently tried lower pressure loads in your own rifle and have had opportunity to discover whether such rifle is probably suited to handle a charge of higher intensity. Even so, go slowly; increase your charge but a few tenths of a grain at a time; do not change primer, bullet bearing length, weight or diameter and powder charge all at one time. Make but one change in components at a time and be careful when you make that variation. Your future pleasure in rifle shooting will depend largely upon having no accidents which are serious and in doing nothing which in any manner could injure your eyesight.

The "by gosh and by guess" expert should not attempt to load high intensity rifle ammunition *of any caliber!* He should not try to increase or improve upon the charges that more skilled and more careful men have developed, and when using .22 varmint calibers of the larger sizes he should remember that the loads which are recommended here are quite effective at 50% greater range than he is at all likely to kill consistently; so why experiment further on the high-side? Those who know something about what they are doing and who possibly may have had a few minor mishaps along the way, have wisely decided to stop at a reasonably safe limit, even with perfect loading components.

There are no rifles in America that are more accurate than those described in this book. You would not expect a tinsmith to oil, adjust and repair a very expensive, veri-thin, highest grade Hamilton, Gruen, Elgin or Bulova watch and do so successfully; consequently, in the loading and design of .22 varmint rifles of great range, power and super accuracy, be satisfied with the recommendations of men who have cut their eye teeth in this particular field and who have had ample opportunity to make proper deductions from the experiences of hundreds of skilled riflemen customers who do know how to load, design and use successfully small caliber, high intensity, super-accurate varmint rifle ammunition.

It is a big world, and those who get the most enjoyment due to living in it do so by sensible, thoughtful and scientifically-perfect methods of conducting the sports in which they find the most enjoyment. There is a great deal more personal enjoyment in the firing of 5,000 shots carefully and without overstepping the bounds of safety, than in firing 10 shots and holding your breath for every shot because you do not know what is going to happen each time the rifle announces its over-loading by producing an ear-splitting and high pitched crash.

The zenith of rifle shooting enjoyment comes when your rifle, ammunition, sight and shooter are so tuned one-to-all-the-others that you are definitely astonished and dismayed each time you miss *anything*. Kite your load 10% or 20% and you immediately break up that superb combination.

Remember that the super-accurate varmint rifle shoots X's like a belt or rivet punch drills holes. Why pick on that sort of rifle? It is seldom given to one man to own another.

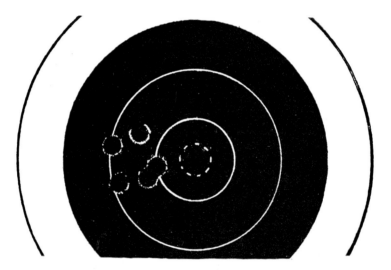

Jerry Gebby has always claimed that he could hit a house fly at 100 yards if it would stay there for three shots. This group, made with his famous Varminter, proves that statement.

Chapter 2

THE .22 NEWTON, .22/4000 SEDGLEY-SCHNERRING AND .220 ARROW

The .22 Newton Cartridge

This is one of the earlier of the .22 center fire cartridges of long range, flat trajectory and great power. The case was designed several years back by the late Charles Newton, and was made by swaging and necking down the 7mm Mauser cartridge, one of the most widely used and accurate cartridges ever placed upon the market.

There is a certain similarity between the .22/4000 Sedgley-Schnerring cartridge and the .22 Newton; both come from the same case but they are not of the same shape and they were not designed for the same purpose.

The .22 Newton cartridge was loaded with a 90-grain bullet to develop 3,103 f.s.m.v.—which is quite a velocity with a 90-grain bullet in a .22. It would then have 2,891 f.s. left at 100 yards, 2,689 f.s. at 200 yards and 2,496 f.s. at 300 yards. The trajectory over 100 yards—height taken at 50 yards—was 0.48″; at 100 yards, when firing at 200 yards, was 2.076″; and the height at 150 yards, when shooting at 300 yards, 5″. A 90-grain bullet driving along with a 2″ trajectory over 200 yards and only 5″ over 300 yards was not to be sneezed at as a coyote, wolf and antelope load.

The .22/4000 Sedgley-Schnerring, on the other hand, used from 45 to 55-grain bullets, giving a materially higher muzzle velocity but not the long range striking power and trajectory of the .22 Newton; remember that the Newton was developed in the days when modern powders were as yet unknown.

Today, or at least recently, 90-grain bullets for the .22 Newton have been practically unobtainable, and the cartridge had never been in wide use, and was not likely to be, as the Newton rifle never became commercially important, and those which were made were mostly in the .30-1906 and .256 Newton calibers with a few in the .30 Newton.

23

As it was easier to obtain 70-grain bullets intended for the .22 H.P. Savage cartridge than 90-grain bullets for the .22 Newton, and as the twist of rifling would handle the 70-grain bullets to advantages, these were more often used in the .22 Newton. This bullet with 35.0 to 36.0 grains of No. 3031 or No. 4320 was reported to have given groups as small as 4.5″ to 5″ at 500 yards. The author does not question this, as he has seen most excellent shooting done at 600 yards, in a fair side wind, with 87-grain bullets in a .25 Niedner H.P., and also very consistent shooting with it from group to group; this was on the Frankford Arsenal Ballistic Station official testing range.

W. F. Vickery, gunsmith, of 123 Peasley St., Boise, Idaho, who is a specialist on single shot varmint rifles, is credited with having made some rifles for the .22 Newton cartridge. However, Mr. Vickery had a somewhat different slant on the matter. His comments, to the author on April 15, 1945, follow:

"It was several years ago that I made up a rifle to try out the .22 Newton, or, to be exact, I took the 7mm Mauser cartridge and necked it down to .22 on its original shoulder slope. I had one .22 Newton cartridge as a sample and, as I remember it, this necked down 7mm .22 was an exact duplicate of the case size and shape, with the exception that I used a .22 Long Rifle Springfield barrel and Sisk 0.2225″ diameter bullets.

"As this rifle turned out to be a failure, *in regard to the purpose for which it was intended,* I gave it up. Since this case had more powder capacity than the .220 Swift case, I thought it would handle the 55-grain bullet at higher velocities for long range chuck shooting than could be expected with the .220 Swift. After experimenting with many loads, some of which *raised belts* around the rear and of the cases resembling those regularly found on the .300 Holland and Holland Magnum cartridges, I found that this case (in the barrel used, of course), would handle exactly the same load as the Swift with the 55-grain bullet and give good accuracy; the load was 40.0 grains of No. 4064 powder and the 55-grain bullet, which gave 0.875″ groups at 100 yards. My experiences were that no other loads would shoot worth a whoop in this cartridge in the matter of extreme accuracy of grouping, although some of them apparently gave higher velocity. They would spread out to 6″ clusters at 100 yards.

"Lawrence Ramsey, of Clear View Farms, Lebanon, New Jersey, obtained a .22 Newton barrel from the late Charles Newton, put it on a Springfield action and did considerable chuck shooting with the combination and, as I recall, he told me that he used bullets up to 70-grains weight."

Mr. Vickery then added comment which possibly should be included here as it is so applicable. Meanwhile, we should bear in mind that the .22 Sedgley-Schnerring cartridge was a .22 of large capacity made up from the 7mm cartridge, and tested with a wide variety of loads and George Schnerring, who did the development and testing work, was Frankford Arsenal's most experienced ballistic man. He has tested possibly more .30-1906 National Match and International Match ammunition than any other man living. He is not the type to develop and put out other than a thoroughly practical, accurate and safe-pressure cartridge.

Mr. Vickery says he has found and adds that Mr. Ackley says he has also found, that the 0.224″ diameter .22's will not handle the heavier bullets of more than 60-grain weight, successfully. These heavier bullets of 70 to 90-grain weight, require a groove diameter of 0.228″ or more, or that they be started at a muzzle velocity of not more than 3,000 f.s. Actually it would seem, and Mr. Vickery is of this opinion, when a rifleman desires a bullet of 70-grain weight, the .25 calibers or probably the .240 British type barrel should be used as these give a greater cross section, a larger area, and not such a long bearing of the bullet in proportion to the caliber. Another method of handling the matter would be, as Mr. Vickery suggests, that the barrel either be free-bored, or that a flash tube be used in the case to start the bullet easily and quickly.

Mr. Vickery says that his reason for suggesting this is that the bullet "sets back" in the barrel, increasing the bearing length of the bullet and thereby raising the pressure considerably. He has examined Sisk 55-grain bullets fired in the .220 Swift with 40.0 grains of No. 4064 powder and then picked them up in soft dirt with the bullet unmarked at 800 yards, and has found that the bullet point had set back far enough to increase the bearing length of the bullet almost 0.125″. He says: "When this happens with a 55-grain bullet you can imagine what occurs with 70-grain, or more, weight."

Possibly we should recall here that Charles Newton designed the .22 Newton cartridge to be used with, and for, powders made *before* the present Nos. 4064 and 3031 series of powders was produced, and obviously he did not know they were coming along. He also designed it as a big game load, in .22 caliber, as well as a varmint charge. The .22 Newton is essentially a long range, big game cartridge—for wolves, coyotes, eagles, et cetera. A barrel *rifled* to handle 90-grain bullets obviously could not be expected to shoot 40,

41, 45 and 50-grain bullets with equal success especially at full speed for the latter bullets.

At the time the .22 Newton cartridge was designed it appeared to have great possibilities. This was at the time riflemen were trying out .25-30/1906 cartridges and had not as then found out that smaller cases were better for both .22 and .25 caliber cartridges necked down for varmints. They had too much powder room, burned a lot of powder needlessly in many cases and had a loud and carrying report that was undesirable in many areas. They had also, much erosion, but at that time, few if any, had shot such cartridges often enough to have found this out. It was too, before riflemen had designed and tried out something like a few hundred different shoulder slopes, neck lengths and what have you! The author has not shot the .22 Newton but one of his friends at one time shot the .256 Newton with all sorts of loads, as often as several times a week, in his company, and he himself, has shot the .30-1906 Newton rifle, with National Match ammunition, and always had a very excellent opinion of Charles Newton's cartridge designs.

Unfortunately, Newton was active before the later powders came along. Had he been active in designing and shooting 10 to 20 years later, he might have done considerable in the developing and perfecting of some of the smaller and later cartridges like the .22 Chucker, the .22 Zipper Improved and others. As it was, his experiments with the smaller .22's were mostly with such cases as the .32-40 necked down, and the like and the larger ones with .30-40, 7mm and .30-1906 cases, in .22 and .25 calibers.

Some day the .22 Newton may *yet* be developed to its full, given still more improved powders for *such* cases, and stronger, heavier jackets and better bullets to stand the pressures developed. But, as Mr. Vickery and Mr. Ackley have suggested, the 0.228″ bore would be the better selection.

As a general proposition, it does not pay to overload a rifle, a motor, an engine, or any other contrivance for the purpose of transmitting energy or power. A powerful charge of high explosive will fail to move a burden if the charge is not of sufficient size to move that quantity of rock, even though the velocity of detonation of a single stick or of the whole charge is the same.

Rifle experimenters should be taught that merely enlarging the powder capacity of a cartridge is not always an "improvement"; that changing the neck length, the shoulder slope, or shortening the cartridge, may none of them be an "improvement" unless, with the powder and bullet being used, greater accuracy, lower pressure, less erosion, a more desirable degree of killing power (which may be either more or less), are thus attained. Magnum cartridges are like magnum battleships or magnum cannon; they may appear more deadly, especially at extreme ranges, but you always pay heavily for this one way or another.

The .22 Newton was one extreme in the .22 field. For most shooters, a much smaller, cheaper to shoot and handier .22 cartridge like the 3,500 f.s.m.v. Chucker, Zipper Improved and Varminter Junior, will be found better.

The .22/4000 Sedgley-Schnerring Cartridge

The .22/4000 Sedgley-Schnerring cartridge was designed by George Schnerring, of Folsom, Delaware County, Pennsylvania, who for most of his life and ballistic experience, was Proof House Foreman (corresponding to Ballistic Engineer) of Frankford Arsenal. He made this cartridge for R. F. Sedgley for use in a Sedgley bolt action varmint sporting rifle. It was made by swaging down the very accurate 7mm Mauser case to .22 caliber and loading it with Winchester or Sisk metal-cased expanding hunting bullets and duPont No. 3031 and No. 4064 powders. He also made it up from the .257 Roberts case, necked down from .25 to .22 caliber, and this made just as good a case. The author likes the looks of this cartridge a great deal better than either the .220 Swift, the .22 Gebby-Varminter Senior or the .220 Arrow cartridge. For one thing, he has a very good opinion of George Schnerring's ballistic experience and ability and his conservatism in developing loads and in keeping down pressures to *safe* limits.

Schnerring has tested more .30-1906 Springfield ammunition than probably any man living—at least he had charge of the testing of more of it—and it was not an honorary title. He was a very practical rifleman and once held the offhand rifle championship of this country, won at Camp Perry, Ohio, where he shot on one of the earliest Dewar teams. He used the Springfield military rifle in tournaments most of his life and shot it well; he has developed a number of excellent .25 caliber woodchuck loads and a host of .22 and .25 caliber charges, and he has worked them up with a pressure rifle as well as the chronograph. Consequently, the .22/4000 Sedgley-Schnerring cartridge is not at all likely to develop freakish characteristics. Its designer does not go in for that sort of thing. There is nothing offside about the 7mm case or its loads, and when necked down to .22 caliber the reduction is not sufficient to cause unnecessary sharp slope of the shoulders or much cutting off of the

THE .22/4000 SEDGLEY-SCHNERRING

PHYSICAL SPECIFICATIONS

Cartridge	Head Diam.	Shoulder Diameter	Shoulder Slope	Length to Shoulder	Case Length	O. A. Length
.22/4000 Schnerring	0.473" Theoretical 0.471" Actual	0.431" 0.432" Actual	25°	1.75"	2.24"	2.70"

COMPARISON OF SIZES AND CAPACITY

Cartridge	Shoulder Slope	Head Diam.	Shoulder Diameter	Length to Shoulder	Length Case	O. A. Length	Neck Length
.22-250 Sweany-Lovell	28°	0.473"* 0.471"†	0.4128"	1.50"	1.92"	2.44"	0.24"
.220 Wilson Arrow	28°	0.473"* 0.4685"†	0.402"* 0.401"	1.74"	2.25"	2.70"	0.30"
.22/4000 Schnerring	25°	0.473"* 0.471"†	0.431"* 0.432"†	1.75"	2.24"	2.70"	0.35"
.22 Ackley Magnum	28°	0.473"* 0.4695"†	0.445"* 0.445"	1.68"	2.21"	2.88"	0.25"

* Theoretical
† Actual

neck. In other words, you can just go neck it down and you have a good cartridge right there. People who had good sense ballistically and also brains designed and developed the 7mm. This .22/4000 Sedgley-Schnerring can be used in the Model 54, Model 70 bolt actions, the 30-S or 720 Remingtons, the 1917 and the .30-1906 Springfield, possibly with slight changes, or small magazine alterations, if the bullet point happens to be very long and sharp. The cartridge is rimless and of the proper head size and shape.

This cartridge has a moderately short shoulder and moderate shoulder slope but it has an abnormally long neck, 0.35″, which is 0.10″ longer than most of the long-necked wildcats of .22 caliber.

It looks very much like an overgrown or Super Varminter; in fact surprisingly so, although I doubt very much that Schnerring had seen the .22-250 before he designed the .22/4000 Sedgley-Schnerring. The principal differences are that the case is approximately 0.22″ longer up to the beginning of the shoulder; the case is about 0.17″ larger in outside diameter *at* the shoulder and slopes a little less sharply from head to shoulder; but this difference in slope is more pronounced when you "mike" both of them than when you merely stand them up side by side and look at the pair. The cartridge heads are presumably the same theoretical size, but actually the micrometer when set for the .22-250 case head will not take the .257 case head of the cartridges here before me, the .22 Varminter cartridge actually miking 0.466″ and the .22/4000 measuring, with the same mike, 0.471 head diameter. Other cases may not show as much or any difference. The principal visual differences between the two cases—the .22 Varminter and the .22/4000 Sedgley-Schnerring—are the greater body length of the Schnerring and the 0.10″ longer neck.

Of course the Schnerring case holds the most powder and will burn coarser powder more efficiently, which normally appears to be an advantage in obtaining accuracy. Powder capacity is an advantage, of course, in flatness of trajectory and in range, in coyote and woodchuck shooting at a distance. This Schnerring cartridge is as large and as long as the author believes will normally be found really efficient in a .22 caliber case. By that I refer to obtaining velocity with ballistic efficiency and evenness of shooting in proportion to the quantity of powder burned. Ackley has written quite a bit to the author on this subject and also on the matter of excessive claims for certain cartridges, particularly those of the size of the .22/3000.

We can expect some difficulty in obtaining full ballistic efficiency

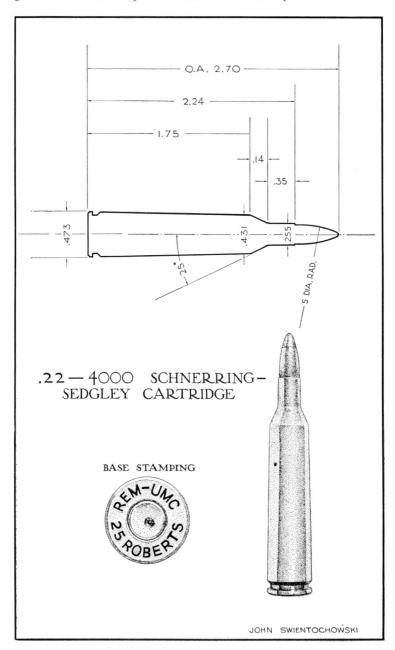

.22—4000 SCHNERRING—
SEDGLEY CARTRIDGE

BASE STAMPING

JOHN SWIENTOCHOWSKI

in *.22 caliber* center fire cartridges of a larger case or capacity than
the .22 Zipper Improved type, the .22 Lovell Hi-Power Improved
with the *shorter* up-to-the-shoulder length of 1.58″ and case length
of 2″ with an 0.30″ length of neck. The No. 10 or .22 Super
Lovell Hi-Power is 1.70″ up to the shoulder and the .22 Marciante
Blue Streak much the same as the Super.

The .22/4000 Sedgley-Schnerring, or vice versa, is so almost
exactly the case size of the .220 Wilson Arrow, except that the
Schnerring is larger in diameter at the shoulder—0.432″ as compared with 0.401″—being more along the lines of the Kilbourn cases
and similar in being straighter in main body contour and with less
taper from head to shoulder. The .228 Ackley Magnum is very
similar to the Schnerring, which antedated it, except that it is still
larger—0.445″ in diameter as compared with 0.432″ for the Schnerring and 0.401″ for the Arrow. To show the remarkable but
accidental similarity of the three cases, and also the smaller size but
general similarity of the .22-250 Sweany-Lovell, and of course, the
Gebby, Ackley and Epps cartridges of the .22-250 persuasion, that
is also included in a comparison.

The over-all length superiority of the Ackley .228 Magnum is due
largely to its having been loaded with a very long, very pointed
bullet, which of necessity sticks farther forward. That point does
not bear on the barrel.

The .220 Arrow differs from the others in being relatively considerably smaller in diameter at the shoulder—being thus more
tapered—for a long cartridge and one of good capacity.

The .22/4000 Sedgley-Schnerring appears to have an average accuracy life, before much erosion appears in the throat, of 1,500 to
2,000 rounds. Many others are practically gone at 750 rounds or
less. I am referring now to cartridges of comparable size and powder
capacity.

The reason the .22/4000 Sedgley-Schnerring—a most excellent
design, in fact, a really splendid design—has not been pushed
stronger, was that it was discovered that the .220 Swift cartridge
could be placed in the Schnerring chamber and *fired,* at which point
fireworks could be expected immediately, as the case had the same
head diameter, but at the forward portion of the straight part of
the cartridge it measured 0.402″ in outside diameter and it would
be in a chamber measuring about 0.434″ to 0.436″ in diameter—
which is just 0.030″ to 0.032″ too large—causing, with Swift pressure, a prompt case rupture of complete proportions and the possible immediate wrecking of the rifle. There are, in this country,

numberless people who just love to shoot a smaller cartridge in a larger chamber, merely to see whether "it can be done." You also can lay your hand gently on the rapidly revolving teeth of a large band saw in a sawmill. This proves you can lay your hand on the saw, and it also proves that the saw teeth are nice and sharp and will cut, but the poor old hand—just not so good from there on. Winchester was marketing the .220 Swift ammunition and rifles in quantity and as Mr. Pugsley, of Winchester, and the late Mr.

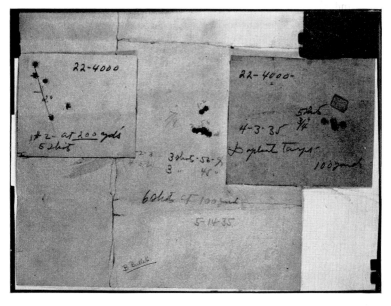

TARGETS MADE WITH .22/4000 SEDGLEY SCHNERRING

Here are some targets made with Dr. Given's .22/4000 (7 mm case necked down) Sedgley-Schnerring woodchuck rifle.

Group on Left. A 2″ five-shot group at 200 yards. Those in center, all at 100 yards. Upper holes made by 45-gr. and lower by 56-gr. bullets. Same sight setting for both. The six shots measure ⅞″ center to center. Group on Right: A five-shot, ¾″ group at 100 yards.

Sedgley, of R. F. Sedgley & Co., were very close friends and neither wished to run the risk of burst rifles or of complaints of ammunition not fitting (there are people who will try to shoot anything they may have in any sort of rifle in which it can be chambered) the .22/4000 Sedgley-Schnerring rifle was not actively pushed after the .220 Swift was well advertised and came on the market in some quantity.

It is possible to blow up a .30-1906 Springfield by carelessly inserting a .35 Remington rimless cartridge in the magazine, closing the bolt and pulling the trigger—according to Emil Koshollek, the custom gunsmith—and no doubt a .32 Remington rimless would do nearly as good a job if so used. However, neither .30-1906 Springfields or either of the two Remington cartridges were taken off the

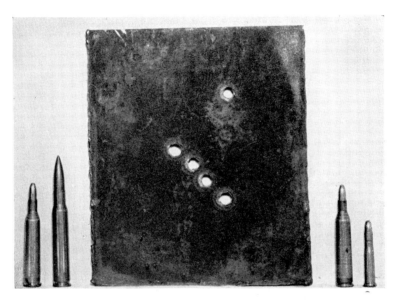

HIGH SPEED BULLET PENETRATION IN STEEL

Left to Right: The .22/4000 Sedgley Schnerring with open point, jacketed bullet. The Springfield service cartridge. ¼″ armor plate showing holes made by .22/4000 soft point bullet. Splotches between one hole and four holes, made by .22 cal. lead bullets.

On right side: .22/4000 cartridge and .22 Hornet.

market due to that possibility, and no such accidents have occurred insofar as the author has been advised. We all know that today many of the .22 wildcat cartridges are made available to reloaders by being "blown up" from smaller cases in a larger chamber, examples including the .22 Maximum Lovell and Kilbourn's K-Lovell from the R-2 and the Improved Zippers from factory full load Zippers. Sedgley personally told the author that about 50% of the .220 Swift factory loads would burst badly if fired in a .22/4000. This was no fault of the rifle nor of the design of the .22/4000 cartridge. It was simply because the .220 case was about 0.032″ to 0.034″ smaller than the forward part of the main body of the chamber wall of the .22/4000. There were no chamber walls close by to support the case when the powder charge was ignited by the primer. With a lower pressure cartridge results might not have been too serious—factory Zippers probably being 30,000 to 38,000 pounds pressure—but with the .220 Swift, it was a different pressure level; probably 20,000 pounds higher. Both Schnerring and Dr. Given found the .22/4000 Schnerring very effective on woodchucks.

Edward S. Burrell, of Philadelphia, made the following report on the work of a .22/4000 Sedgley Springfield Sporter, on big game in Maine:

"The Hi-Power 46-grain bullet was used to kill two black bear. The first one was shot back of the ears at approximately 50 yards. The hole of entrance was about 2″ in diameter and the skull fractured into small fragments under the skin; no exit could be found. This was a large male cub and the one shot, of course, was sufficient.

"The second bear was a female not quite fully grown. This bear was broadside at about 65 yards and the bullet entered back of the right shoulder. The entrance hole was about 2″ in diameter and showed definite signs of blow back. The right shoulder was badly pulped and the tip of the left shoulder blade was fractured. A few small pieces of jacket about 0.125″ in size were found in the meat around the hole. This shot killed the bear instantly without any thrashing around on the ground."

In full loads, this .22/4000 is definitely a black bear and deer cartridge and a long range woodchuck load. Lighter charges should be used for shooting smaller varmints and small game.

For the 4,000 f.s.m.v. type of loads in the .22/4000 rifle, Sedgley and Schnerring suggested the Sisk 46-grain, 5-diameter, soft point bullet with 7% antimony core. The Sisk 55-grain, 4-diameter point, 7% antimony core bullet at 3,856 f.s.m.v., was more effective at longer ranges than the 46-grain. Both bullets at maximum velocity give fine accuracy in this cartridge, and are claimed to develop safe pressures for .30-1906 Springfield action, Mauser and Model 54 and of course for the Model 70 and the 1917 Enfield. Lead bullets can be used in the .22/4000 rifle if not speeded up over 1,700 f.s.m.v.

Muzzle velocities are 100 f.s. higher, than at 53 feet, and 125 f.s. higher (approximately) than at 78 feet, as given in the following table:

CHARGES FOR
THE SEDGLEY-SCHNERRING .22/4000 CARTRIDGE

Powder	Charge	Bullet	Mfg. by	Vel.	At	Over-all Length
D-3031	43.5 Gr.	46-Gr.	Sisk	4,012	53 ft.	2.74″
D-3031	42.0 Gr.	46-Gr.	Sisk	3,890	53 ft.	2.74″
D-3031	40.0 Gr.	46-Gr.	Sisk	3,750	53 ft.	2.74″
D-3031	41.0 Gr.	55-Gr.	Sisk	3,658	78 ft.	2.78″
D-3031	42.0 Gr.	55-Gr.	Sisk	3,778	78 ft.	2.78″
D-4064	44.0 Gr.	55-Gr.	Sisk	3,783	78 ft.	2.78″
D-4064	45.0 Gr.	55-Gr.	Sisk	3,862	78 ft.	2.78″
D-4064	45.0 Gr.	46-Gr.	W. R. A.	4,000	78 ft.	2.58″
D-4064	44.0 Gr.	46-Gr.	W. R. A.	3,910	78 ft.	2.58″
D-3031	42.0 Gr.	46-Gr.	W. R. A.	3,826	78 ft.	2.58″
D-3031	40.0 Gr.	46-Gr.	W. R. A.	3,657	78 ft.	2.58″
D-3031	38.0 Gr.	46-Gr.	W. R. A.	3,450	78 ft.	2.58″
D-3031	36.0 Gr.	46-Gr.	W. R. A.	3,335	78 ft.	2.58″
D-3031	34.0 Gr.	46-Gr.	W. R. A.	3,180	78 ft.	2.58″
D-3031	32.0 Gr.	46-Gr.	W. R. A.	3,025	78 ft.	2.58″
D-3031	30.0 Gr.	46-Gr.	W. R. A.	2,850	78 ft.	2.58″
D-3031	28.0 Gr.	46-Gr.	W. R. A.	2,686	78 ft.	2.58″
D-3031	26.0 Gr.	46-Gr.	W. R. A.	2,518	78 ft.	2.58″
D-3031	24.0 Gr.	46-Gr.	W. R. A.	2,341	78 ft.	2.58″
D-4064	43.0 Gr.	56-Gr.	W. R. A.	3,687	78 ft.	2.70″
D-3031	39.0 Gr.	56-Gr.	W. R. A.	3,633	53 ft.	2.70″
D-3031	37.0 Gr.	56-Gr.	W. R. A.	3,513	53 ft.	2.70″
D-3031	35.0 Gr.	56-Gr.	W. R. A.	3,393	53 ft.	2.70″
D-3031	33.0 Gr.	56-Gr.	W. R. A.	3,230	53 ft.	2.70″
D-3031	32.0 Gr.	55-Gr.	Sisk	3,070	78 ft.	2.78″
D-3031	30.0 Gr.	55-Gr.	Sisk	2,908	78 ft.	2.78″
D-3031	28.0 Gr.	55-Gr.	Sisk	2,740	78 ft.	2.78″
D-3031	26.0 Gr.	55-Gr.	Sisk	2,581	78 ft.	2.78″

As the firm of R. F. Sedgley discontinued custom rifle work shortly after the death of Mr. Sedgley; and as Mr. Schnerring is getting well along in his shooting career due to age; and as this cartridge has never, to the author's knowledge, been patented in name or form, there seems no good reason (except that .220 Swift ammunition can be exploded in the rifle chamber) why it should not be tried, further developed and used by other experimental riflemen and woodchuck hunters desiring a large and very long-ranged .22 wildcat cartridge, for good loads have been developed. The author considers it one of the best *large* .22 wildcats ever designed.

The *Wilson-Wotkyns .220 Arrow*

The .220 Arrow wildcat cartridge is a powerful, high velocity, high pressure, very flat shooting, long range .22 caliber case made by very slightly shortening the .220 Swift case and making the shoulder taper considerably sharper.

It appears to have been a mutual development and promotion of L. E. Wilson and Capt. G. L. Wotkyns. The author knew L. E. Wilson in the heyday of his match shooting experiences at Camp Perry, Ohio, and was present when "L. E." was the first man to win the Small Bore Rifle National Championship at Perry in 1920. He shot a Winchester 52 of serial number 53. He was at that time a particularly close and hard holder and also a cool, determined and calm rifleman, with little to say.

Wilson has developed quite a reputation as a maker of fine precision produced gages, cartridge case trimmers, inside neck reamers, head space gages, bullet seaters, cartridge case gages, primer pocket reamers, resizing and forming dies and special cutters and reamers often required by riflemen and custom gunsmiths.

At last reports he was so tied up with work making gages that he was able to spend very little time on commercial work or .22 wildcats, but should get around to this later. His sons, who formerly helped him at 104 Division St., Cashmere, Washington, were still in the services. One had been flying a B-24 and the other piloting a P-51 Mustang fighter.

Wotkyns, now deceased, is the same man who helped advertise the .22-250 rifle, the case of which was originally developed by J. B. Sweany, of Winters, California, and which case, the .250/3000 Savage, was a product of the genius of the late Charles Newton.

Normally, L. E. Wilson does all kinds of rifle chambering and eventually will have a full line of .22 Long Rifle head space gages which will be added to his present lines.

The 0.224″ barrel for the .220 Swift is a good selection for the .220 Arrow. This is made with 14″ twist. The same type barrel will do nicely for the .219 Zipper, .22 Varminter and .22 Niedner Magnum and would also do for various Juniors or shortenings of these cases, but if light bullets are used in the latter, bullets of 45 to 40-grains, then the 16″ twist would be preferable.

Among recommended loads for the .220 Arrow are Sisk 55-grain bullet with 36.5 to 37.0 grains of No. 4320. A rifleman was reported to have made less than 1″ groups at 105 yards with this cartridge, using the W-M 8S 55-grain bullet. He also obtained

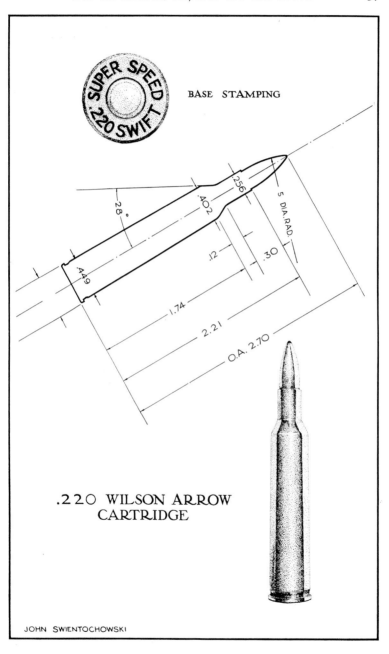

BASE STAMPING

.220 WILSON ARROW
CARTRIDGE

JOHN SWIENTOCHOWSKI

about as satisfactory results with 25.0 to 30.0 grains of No. 3031 and the Sisk 55-grain bullet, getting some groups under 1″.

C. C. Carpenter, of Staunton, Virginia, using a .220 Arrow and 38.0 grains of No. 4064, in a 28″ barrel rifle, with W-M 8S 55-grain cadmium-plated bullet, obtained a 5-shot group at *400 yards* of slightly less than 2″. The total drop has been given by Fred Ness as 9.55″ over 300 yards.

Hosea Sarber, of the Alaskan Game Commission, Petersburg, Alaska, who before he went with that department, did a lot of guiding and varmint shooting, has been using these .220 rifles. He reported excellent long range work on both big game and eagles, many of which he collected for scientific study, as well, years ago, as bounty producers. Eagles in Alaska, especially the golden eagles, are definitely a curse to game, according to many practical woodsmen and hunters. In particular have they been destructive to live salmon, foxes and various fur bearing animals which normally are raised in quantity along the Alaskan coast. Eagles gorge themselves upon salmon on their runs. For years the Alaskan Legislature paid a bounty of a dollar per pair on eagle's feet and a long range, accurate, flat shooting rifle would make money for its owner, as well as help game.

Alaskan Experiences with the .220 Arrow Cartridge

Few riflemen in the United States can have an accurate conception of the amount of varmint shooting obtainable in Alaska. During the 29 years during which the author of this book has handled the firearms correspondence of *Rod & Gun* in Canada he has had a fair Alaskan, Yukon Territory and British Columbia clientele. He has met and talked with various hunters, trappers and miners who have lived and hunted in Alaska. Two of his close friends were William B. Meetch and Harry W. Meetch, who hunted in Alaska and on one trip there killed eight Kodiaks. He has sat on the skin and skull of the largest of these (they brought all of the skins home) and has talked over shooting conditions there by the hour.

In time you will be able to fly from Boston, Philadelphia, New York, Cleveland, Chicago and Detroit to Fairbanks or any place on the Alaskan highway, in five to nine hours. Today, no place on the globe is more than 22 hours by air from any other place on earth. You can hunt woodchucks in New York or Ontario one day and a very short time later be busy shooting eagles or bear in Alaska.

Having thus shown you something of a varmint hunting field, largely hitherto untouched by white men, and when hunted, not by outsiders, we will now open the pages to Hosea Sarber, Wild Life Agent, The Alaskan Game Commission, to hear some of his experiences in Alaska with three different .220 Arrow varmint rifles.

THE .220 ARROW CARTRIDGE

By Hosea Sarber

From Petersburg, Alaska, April 15, 1945, Mr. Sarber wrote the author as follows: "The .220 Arrow cartridge as chambered by L. E. Wilson, of Cashmere, Washington, is the finest and most versatile all-round .22 caliber varmint hull I have ever found, both as to accuracy with a wide variety of components and in flexibility in loading. It is simply the .220 Swift case given a much sharper and more abrupt shoulder slope, the case body remaining the same in length and case taper. It uses Swift loads and delivers, as near as I can tell in field shooting, Swift velocities or a bit more. In its killing effect upon varmints and small game its performance is the same as the Swift and Varminter type rifles.

"To begin with, the Swift case is the best and heaviest piece of brass of any of our commercial cartidges, and the sharpening of the shoulder of this fine hull prevents the brass from stretching or flowing forward in firing, thus eliminating the necessity of repeated case trimming and the danger of weakened cases from stretching. I have fired many .220 Arrow cases 25 to 30 times or more with full charge loads without any stretching and these cases are still giving good service. Full length sizing is usually necessary after about four to six firings to prevent slight sticking in the chamber but the cases do not stretch in length.

"One of the chief characteristics of this hull is its extreme flexibility in loading. It delivers the finest accuracy with any of the Swift or Varminter bullets that are first class and uses perfectly duPont powders Nos. 4320, 4064, 3031 or 4350—the only powders I have tried. It also uses efficiently any of the regular large size rifle primers.

"I have obtained extreme accuracy with the W-M 8S bullets in 50, 55 and 60-grain weights and with the Sisk Express 55 and 60-grain bullets. The Sisk-Niedner 55-grain bullet has given the finest accuracy with proper loads, which must be *reduced* slightly with this bullet because it will not stand the velocity of full charges in this caliber.

"With the W-M 8S 55-grain or the Sisk Express 55-grain bullets my standard load is 38.0 grains of either duPont Nos. 4064 or 4320 with the Winchester 120 primer. Either of these loads properly assembled, will shoot well into one minute of angle (1″ per 100 yards approximately). I have repeatedly made 10-shot groups with them of less than 1″ at 100 yards and inside 2″ at 200 yards. These loads will actually *average* better than 1″ at 100 yards and this is the finest accuracy I have ever gotten from

Two fancy .220 Wilson Arrow caliber Model 70 Winchester heavy sporters owned by Hosea Sarber of Alaska Game Commission, Petersburg, Alaska. Custom stocks on these rifles inletted and fitted by A. L. Knight of Fort Worth, Texas, and completed by Hosea Sarber. Note particularly handsome checkering and pistol grips.

Both rifles will shoot 1″ groups at 100 yards, although one of them has been fired 1,800 rounds. They have killed hundreds of head of Alaskan varmints, some big game, seals and coyotes. The .220 Arrow is the Swift with sharp shoulder, shoots very flat over 300 yards and cartridge cases can be reloaded 20 to 30 times.

any rifle. The Varminter will deliver the same accuracy only with certain loads and special bullets while the .220 Arrow will handle anything that is good.

"I have also used 35.0, 36.0, 37.0 and 37.5 grains of these powders with the same bullets and have obtained similar results in accuracy.

"With the Sisk-Niedner 55-grain bullet I have settled on 36.0 grains of No. 4064 as a top load for this bullet, using the No. 120 primer. The regular load of 38.0 grains gives too much velocity for this pill and it will blow on about one-half of the shots. With this load of 36.0 grains, however, it shoots beautifully and will stay right at 1″ or less at 100 yards. This load is right at the peak of velocity for this bullet, and it is all the bullet will stand, apparently. With the Remington No. 8½ primer a shot, now and then, will blow, as this primer with the load mentioned apparently increases velocity slightly. Or pressure?

"Other amazingly good loads in this caliber are the W-M 8S 60-grain bullet and the Sisk Express in the same weight; with these projectiles I have used both 39.0 and 40.0 grains of No. 4350 powder and the No. 120 primer. Both of these loads gave splendid accuracy, and the velocity, judging from the field shooting, is apparently that of the regular 55-grain bullet loads. They make the best long range varmint and game loads of any that I have tried in the .220 Arrow cartridge.

"I (Sarber) have now been using this caliber over a period of some two years and have shot it in *three* different rifles—two of my own and one belonging to a friend. All three rifles have shot exactly alike with all loads tried. These rifles were all the Model 70 Winchester in Target Grade, using .220 Swift barrels rechambered by L. E. Wilson. With this cartridge I have killed hundreds of hair seals and eagles in my regular collecting work with perfect results. Its killing effect is superb on all sorts of varmints, up to and including coyotes. I have also shot a great many hawks and ravens with it and one gray wolf. It killed the wolf instantly with the W-M 8S 55-grain load, with a shot in the neck at 250 yards, although I believe this is about the largest of animals that should be shot regularly with it.

"On a number of occasions I have taken black bears with this caliber, and while such rifles will kill big game animals of the black bear and deer size amazingly well on certain shots, they are, in my opinion, inadequate for such game. My experience with this and such calibers as the .220 Swift and the .22 Varminter has been such that I would not recommend them for any type of big game. They are ideal for all varmints of such sizes up to coyotes and possibly wolves, at medium ranges, but their use on game should be restricted to such shooting. On eagles, seals and all smaller varmints, the .220 Arrow kills like a streak of lightning.

"There are several peculiarities about this caliber—the .220 Arrow—that should be brought out in its description. It seems to shoot equally well with any of the standard primers; it groups its shots in all loads the closest to a common center of impact of any caliber I have ever shot. Another characteristic is that it will *not* handle graphite wads regularly used in many similar calibers; at least it will not use them here in Alaska. To use such wads will destroy the accuracy in all loads I have tried.

"Apparently, however, wads are not needed in this caliber as barrel life and accuracy are excellent without them. In one of my barrels I have now fired some 1,800 rounds of full charge loads and the barrel still shoots as well as ever. The last test groups fired were still less than 1″ in diameter at 100 yards. It is not yet showing the "smoked" or rough appearance ahead of the chamber common to barrels showing visibly the effects of erosion, although the lands are beginning to lose their sharp edges.

"One thing should be mentioned, it seems to me, in describing fine accuracy: we riflemen often rant and brag about shooting and the splendid accuracy we obtain as if this were all the work of the man behind the rifle. But let no man think he will obtain such accuracy without a lot of effort on the part of the stocker and others who make such rifles. It requires a perfect job of inletting and bedding the rifle in its target type stock—the type of work performed by such artists as Alvin Linden, Knight, Steagall and others. The stock work these men turn out is near perfection. Also the chambering work and dies that L. E. Wilson turns out is nothing less than perfection itself.

"The two rifles being shown in an accompanying photograph, were inletted and bedded by A. L. Knight, of Fort Worth, Texas, the remainder of the stock work having been done by myself (Sarber). The target a seal presents on the water is only the head, or more often about one-half of the head, showing above water as he swims out anywhere up to 300 yards, which is as far as they can usually be hit. A small photo sent shows three eagles taken in regular collecting work for stomach analysis in research work. The Arrow will take such game very nicely to and beyond 300 yards if conditions are favorable.

"To maintain such accuracy, as described above, it is necessary, usually after the rifle has had considerable shooting, to touch up the bedding here and there, particularly to refit and shim the recoil shoulder. Every detail must be perfect, if 2″ or less average groups at 200 yards are to be held. The .220 Arrow will deliver such accuracy if kept tuned up, and, riflemen, that is really *shooting.*"

The .220 Arrow is just as applicable to long range woodchuck, hawk, buzzard, crow or similar shooting in the Middle Atlantic and New England states, and in Southern Ontario, as was found

in Alaska. Such calibers are often unnecessarily powerful and loud
in report for much Eastern shooting. On the other hand, they
have range and power when that is needed to reach away over
on the far hill and tap the varmint.

Remember, this cartridge is in the same general class as to trajectory, range, energy and killing power, as the .220 Swift, .22
Varminter Senior, .22/4000 Sedgley-Schnerring and similar charges
and cartridges.

It does its best work in heavy rifles, with long, straight, fairly
heavy barrels and, of course, when fitted with an effective telescope
sight. It is not well adapted to brush shooting, to short carbine
style rifles, to short barrelled rifles of any size, due to sharp muzzle
report, and a good length of barrel being necessary to obtain
maximum velocity, and it is not adapted to small game hunting,
except with very much reduced loads, because all full charge loads
—or even mid-range loads—will blow small game like cottontail
rabbits, grouse and squirrels to pieces and even to bits.

This is a most excellent caliber for plains shooting on coyotes,
for long range pot shots at Arctic owls, barred owls, eagles, destructive hawks of all kinds—especially the large and wilder varieties—
and to crow shooting on the snow at extreme ranges. It should do
well at target group shooting, especially at more than 100 yards;
also for use at quarter of beef, turkey, chicken and trophy shoots
in which small groups are required. It seems to shoot not only
consistently, but to a very small vertical zero and to the same zero,
day after day. Such are the necessary requirements for a long
range, powerful and deadly varmint rifle and cartridge.

CHAPTER III

COMMERCIAL VARMINT .22 CARTRIDGES

The .22 Hornet Cartridge

THE .22 Hornet is the center fire, commercial cartridge which in dollar and cents value in retail price, accuracy, killing power and flatness of trajectory, is really to be compared with the unusual value contained in the .22 Long Rifle cartridge.

The original .22 Hornet cartridge was developed by the outstanding rifleman-writer of his time, none other than the famous "Reuben Harwood" famous in Shooting and Fishing and in Arms & The Man. Reuben Harwood lived in Somerville, Massachusetts, in 1893 and 1894 when he developed the original ".22 Hornet" which he loaded with a 48-grain type-metal bullet and duplex powder load of duPont No. 1 Rifle Smokeless and FFG semismokeless which gave 1,900 f.s. m.v. It also gave over 1,750 f.s. m.v. with a 55-grain bullet. Harwood also had another charge in 1894, consisting of duPont No. 2 Rifle Smokeless and F.F.G. Semismokeless and a 48-grain bullet which developed 2,000 f.s. m.v. This information was confirmed by Ned Roberts, who dug up correspondence he had with Reuben Harwood in 1893-94, and which he had preserved. This information was mentioned by Roberts in *American Rifleman* during the year 1942.

At this writing therefore, the .22 Hornet cartridge, or at least a .22 Hornet cartridge has been in existence at least 52 years and many, many years in advance of the first experiments with later ".22 Hornet" cartridges which were thought or claimed by some to be the first experiments or developments with a .22 cartridge of that name.

A ".22 Hornet" cartridge was listed and described with its loads, in the old No. 6 Ideal Handbook, which cartridge the author definitely recalls.

German developments of the .22 Hornet were not only described in *American Rifleman* by Hervey Lovell, but Lovell imported these cartridges and bullets for them into this country, many, many years ago, before anything definite was done in the working up of such a charge in this country. This German development of the .22 Hornet was known as the 5.6 x 35 R Vierling, and was loaded with various full metal jacketed, soft point flat nose, soft point round nose and lead bullets in approximately 39, 40 and 46-grain. The author definitely and distinctly recalls the Lovell paid advertisements which usually were of about 1″ depth of space, but some larger, in magazines such as *Field & Stream* and *American Rifleman*.

Some time later, four officers and employees of the Ordnance Department, including Al Woodworth, Woody, Townsend Whelen and G. L. Wotkyns, worked out many special loads and special bullets for a .22 Hornet developed from the .22-13-45 Winchester S.S. case as a basis. These were of much the same general characteristics ballistically, as the Lovell importations from Continental Europe, but the Springfield experimenters' bullets were mostly different. Lovell, I believe, used some full metal-cased bullets swaged to proper diameter from the 5.5-mm Velo Dog cartridge; some of these bullets were reversed by being swaged wrong end to, to make a soft point hunting bullet.

In the old days, a number of cartridges were available to play with in development of more modern loads, among them being the .22-13-45 W.C.F. in which Winchester then became interested, and developed their .22 Hornet cartridge. There was also the .22-15-60 Stevens, the .22-15-45 Stevens, the .22-10-45 Maynard C.F., among others.

R. B. Sisk, of Iowa Park, Texas, has had much to do, as had Niedner Rifle Corporation, with more modern bullets for the .22 Hornet. Sisk made up his own designs. Shelhamer made many thousands of bullets for the Niedner Rifle Corporation. Woodworth and Woody made various types and designs. Harvey Donaldson made metalcased bullets for .22 center fires, but mostly of larger size cartridge case designs, from shortly after 1900. But not commercially. The Niedner .22 Hornet bullet design was closely followed by Winchester in their early .22 Hornet ammunition, according to Shelhamer. Niedner developed the .22 Hornet type bullets for use in the .22 Baby Niedner cartridge which in turn was simply the .22 Koshollek but with a Niedner design bullet of more rounded ogive and which, they thought, shot better. The Koshollek bullet was quite pointed and weighed 49-grains.

Winchester Repeating Arms Co. first catalogued the .22 Hornet commercial cartridge in 1932, according to Edwin Pugsley, although work had been going on in its development by Winchester since about 1930. Since 1932 this wonderful little cartridge, which was also brought out in very accurate form about that time by Peters Cartridge Co., and by others, has become very widely known. Earlier Remington .22 Hornet ammunition did not seem to quite equal some others, but later lots shot splendidly. At least that was our experience with it.

The author's favorite center fire rifle is one of the early Winchester 54's in .22 Hornet caliber, this one being serial No. 40581A, and it is the most deadly rifle, with the first shot fired, of any center fire hunting rifle he has ever used for varmint shooting. Winchester pioneered the .22 Hornet in the Model 54 bolt action, and later in the Model 70 bolt action which contains a number of minor improvements of design, but none of which is essential to the .22 Hornet cartridge.

The Savage Arms Corporation brought out their Sporter model of bolt action rifle to handle the .22 Hornet commercial ammunition, and due to the very moderate retail price of the Savage .22 Hornet when first manufactured and its most excellently designed and splendidly fitting stock and good balance this rifle became very popular almost from its introduction. Savage also put out a somewhat heavier barrel model in .22 Hornet, which was fitted with what could be called a light, target-weight barrel and this had some advantages in steadiness of shooting, and a local friend, Edgar Burkins still uses one of these as his favorite woodchuck rifle, but it did not sell in the same numbers as the regular Savage .22 Sporter Hornet model. Stevens also catalogued a very few .22 Hornet rifles in one or two of their more recent heavy singleshot, drop lever action rifles but this caliber was very shortly thereafter discontinued by Stevens. The cartridge was probably too high-pressure for that action.

In Canada, very early in the .22 Hornet development, individual rifles custom made, in .22 Hornet caliber were turned out by G. B. Crandall, who also made up quite a few of these singleshot .22 Hornets with relined barrels. He had good orders for these until the .22 Hornet rifles made commercially by Winchester and Savage became common on the market. The British, also, have developed a few .22 Hornet rifles. Some of these have been made up on Farquharson or Martini actions, and others on bolt actions. They also have some few .22 wildcats. Such firms as W. W. Greener, Webley & Scott, B.S.A. through Parker-Hale, and the Imperial Chemical Industries, the British ammunition trust, through their Eley affiliate or branch, would all be interested. A. G. Banks, probably the most prominent British shooting writer, made extensive experiments with the .22 Hornet and the .22 Long Rifle standard velocity cartridges, firing at 100 yards in approximately 10-15 miles per hour side winds, shooting first in one direction, then in the opposite, and taking the mean of the wind drift as average, found that the .22 Hornet gave 69% as much wind drift as the .22 Long Rifle standard velocity cartridges. So much for the development of the various .22 Hornet rifles and cartridges, here and abroad, from 1893 up to the present era. This with the though of giving credit to as many as possible and taking credit away from the efforts of none. Those who have experimented with, and loaded special charges for the .22 Hornet rifles are legion.

The present .22 Hornet cartridge has a standard head diameter of .350″ but usually measures somewhat smaller on the rim. It has an over-all length loaded, with the usual blunt-point bullet of 1.69″ to 1.71″, and the case itself is 1.39″ in length. It has an outside diameter, at the very moderately sloped shoulder, of .278″, and a shoulder slope of but 5° 38′ which means the shoulder slope extends for quite some length up the case. This compares with 11° 30′ to 17° for most of the R-2 and .22/3000 Lovell cartridges of wildcat type put out by custom loaders and gunsmiths and with the 20° shoulder slope for the Crandall .22 K-B Hornet and with 35° shoulder slope for the .22 Kilbourn K-Hornet. This K-Hornet is a lengthened and expanded custom Hornet fired in a special chamber and which gives materially higher velocity to the .22 Hornet or other .22 metal-cased bullets which are used in it. This K-Hornet has the highest degree of ballistic efficiency for the charge used, of probably any of the .22 wildcat cartridges and is probably a higher efficiency cartridge than any .22 commercial center fire cartridge. Regular .22 Hornet cartridges may be used in either of the K-Hornet chambers at a loss in velocity of probably 150 f.s.

The .22 Hornet has the smallest head diameter of any of the standard modern .22 commercial center fire cartridges of today. It therefore delivers the least number of total pounds pressure against the face of the bolt or of the breech, for a given pressure expressed in pounds per square inch. The pressure in pounds delivered by the cartridge against the face of the breech is found by multiplying the pressure in lbs./sq. in. by the area of the cartridge head, in square inches. Actually, the area is a small fraction of a square inch.

Reloading the .22 Hornet

In ordinary times, Remington, Western, Winchester and Peters all load commercial ammunition of great accuracy for the .22 Hornet cartridge. It is sold through the usual hardware and sporting goods dealers, Custom hand-loaders also put out hand loads for this cartridge. Sisk, and other bulletmakers provide bullets, as do the various ammunition factories and these bullets are normally, extremely accurate at Hornet velocities or a bit above.

Suggested Hand Loads for the .22 Hornet

In *Better Loads for Better Shooting,* published by E. I. duPont de Nemours & Co. in 1936, they suggested the following loads of I.M.R. powders for the .22 Hornet:

Bullet	Powder	Charge	M.V.
45-gr. S.P.	4227	8.8 grs.	2,045 f. s.
45-gr. S.P.	4227	10.8 "	2,410 f. s.

Charges from Other Sources

Bullet	Powder	Charge	M.V.	
35-gr. Sisk	4227	10.0 grs.	2,250 f. s.	
35-gr. Jacketed	2400	11.6 "	3,020 f. s.	
40-gr. "	2400	10.5 "	2,670 "	
40-gr. "	2400	11.2 "	2,860 "	
45-gr. "	4227	8.8 "	2.045 "	
45-gr. "	4227	10.8 "	2,410 "	
45-gr. "	2400	9.5 "	2,400 "	WRA
45-gr. Peters H.P.	80	4.0 grs.	....	No 116 Pr.
45-gr. W.R.A. S.P. ..	80	4.0 "	....	"
45-gr. Peters H.P.	1204	10.5 grs.	2,400	"

(This last is C. S. Landis, Jr.'s woodchuck load.) With this charge he killed 42 woodchucks in one week and 30 crows and 33 hawks in five weeks.)

SPECIAL LOADS FOR THE .22 HORNET
These are mostly short range and medium range hunting loads

Bullet	Powder	Charge	M.V.	Recommended by
40-gr. Sisk O. P.	duPont Smokeless shotgun	4.5 grs.	1,400-1,500	J. B. Smith

This charge above was designed particularly for Pennsylvania gray and black squirrel hunting for Dr. Ellis E. W. Given.

43-gr. Loverin G. C. No. 80 (Bullet 225438)		5.5 grs.		Guy Loverin
39-gr. Loverin flat base No. 80 (225438)		5.5 grs.		"

These later Loverin bullets are rather light and sharp at the point and are well balanced, giving 1½″ to 2½″ groups at 100 yards.

SPECIAL LOADS FOR THE .22 HORNET
These are mostly short range and medium range hunting loads

Bullet	Powder	Charge	M.V.	Recommended by
46-gr. H.P.	duPont Smokeless shotgun	4.8 grs.	1,600 f. s.	J. B. Smith

Squirrel Loads for .22 Hornet—recommended *years ago,* by duPont Ballistic Station to C. S. Landis, Jr.

				Former rec.
45-gr. Hornet	1204	7.0	1,590	by duPont
45-gr. Hornet	80	4.0	1,350	"
45-gr. Hornet	80	5.2	1,680	"
45-gr. Lead	80	3.7	1,470	"
45-gr. Lead	80	4.7	1,620	"

This last load should not be as accurate as the preceding one. Would suggest 4 grains.

Faster Hunting Loads for .22 Hornet

45-gr. F.M.J. .... 4227 10.8 2,400 J. B. Smith

This one was suggested by J. Bushnell Smith for wild Turkey shooting.

55-gr. Sisk .... 2400 10.0 2,450 est.

This load was reported as giving 1½″ ten-shot groups at 200 yards in a Charles C. Johnson .22 Hornet barrel with 14″ twist. Pressure of this load is close to service pressures. Another load is 9.3 grs. of 2400 with same bullet.

				Former rec.
45-gr. Hornet	1204	8.3	1,850	by duPont
45-gr. Hornet	1204	9.6	2,115	"
45-gr. Hornet	1204	10.5	2,300	"
40-gr. Sisk	1204	10.5	2,295	"
40-gr. Sisk	1204	11.0	2,442	"
45-gr. Sisk	1204	11.2	2,495	"
45-gr. F.M.J. Sisk	1204	11.2	2,481	"

The last load given is a wild turkey load, and for shooting red, cross and gray foxes where you do not want to tear the hide.

Following Loads were supplied C. S. Landis, Jr., Years ago, by duPont Ballistic Station as Guidance in Developing Woodchuck and Crow Loads for .22 Hornet rifles

Bullet	Powder	Charge	Instrumental Velocity	Rec. by
Ideal 225438 44-gr. ..	1204	7.0	1,822	*duPont*
Same	1204	10.0	2,303	"
Ideal 225415 48-gr. ...	1204	7.0	1,856	"
Same	1204	10.0	2,275	"
45-gr. S.P.*	1204	10.5	2,400	"
55-gr. Sisk	1204	8.0	1,845	"
55-gr. Sisk *	1204	10.0	2,209	"
45-gr. Hi-Speed *	1204	10.5	2,406	"

Loads Marked * moderately high pressures. Do not exceed.

Add 40 f.s. to 60 f.s. to above velocities for muzzle velocities. The lighter bullets require the greater additions.

Ballistic information, .22 Hornet, supplied author by Edgar Beugless, duPont Ballistic Station, May 1937, while same was still being supplied.

SPECIAL LOADS FOR THE .22 HORNET
These are mostly short range and medium range hunting loads

Bullet	Powder	Charge	M.V.	Recommended by
45-gr. Hornet S.P. ...	4227	6.0	1,450	duPont
45-gr. Hornet S.P. ...	80	5.5	1,470	"
45-gr. Hornet S.P. ...	80	7.0	1,810	"

Above are squirrel, rabbit and pheasant loads. For varmints up to foxes and woodchucks, at moderate ranges.

Above loads also suitable for experiment in K-Hornet Crandall and Kilbourn re-chambered custom rifles. Maximum loads should be developed carefully for K-Hornet, which has a longer, larger capacity case but also a very much sharper shoulder taper, which latter increases speed of burning of powder charge, raising pressure. The K-Hornet is a high intensity, very efficient cartridge, made by firing .22 Hornet cartridge is longer K-Hornet chamber. Result is a case with greater length to shoulder and greater powder capacity, but with then a different burning speed of charge. Rifles should have bushed firing pin and strong action, for K-Hornet caliber.

.22 Hornet Loads

The following were Hercules Ballistic Station recommendations for .22 Hornet rifles, with charges of Hercules 2400, a dense, double base powder, which gives good accuracy in small cartridges but which should be handled very carefully in good rifles only, in heaviest charges mentioned below.

Charges marked with an asterisk* give pressures slightly exceeding 40,000 lbs. per sq. inch and should be cut down when used with non-corrosive primers in very *cold* weather. All the other charges listed below for 2400 give very moderate pressures.

Charges of 2400 exceeding 11.0 grains with 35-grain bullet, 10.8 grains with 40-grain bullet, 8.9 grains with 55-grain bullet, or 9.8 grains with 45-grain bullet should be developed very carefully, particularly with non-corrosive priming, and especially for cold weather use. If your rifle shows evidence of high pressures before reaching the charges given above and below, stop right there, reduce your charge slightly, and then try to preserve uniformity of loading from cartridge to cartridge.

HERCULES 2400
.22 Hornet

BULLET	Powder Charge (grains)	Muzzle Velocity (f.s.)	Seating Depth (in.)
35-Grain Sisk	7.0	1,900	.099
35-Grain Sisk	9.5	2,540	.099

BULLET	Powder Charge (grains)	Muzzle Velocity (f.s.)	Seating Depth (in.)
35-Grain Sisk	11.6	3,020	.099
40-Grain Sisk	7.0	1,870	.155
40-Grain Sisk	9.5	2,460	.155
40-Grain Sisk	11.2	2,860	.155
55-Grain Sisk	6.0	1,580	.274
55-Grain Sisk	6.0	1,580	.274
55-Grain Sisk	9.3	2,340	.274
45-Grain H. P.	5.0	1,475	.229
45-Grain H. P.	8.0	2,100	.229
45-Grain H. P.	10.3	2,605	.229
45-Grain S. P.	6.0	1,665	.196
45-Grain S. P.	8.0	2,100	.196
45-Grain S. P.	10.4	2,640	.196

Cull's Hand Loads for the .22 Hornet

John L. Cull, of Toronto, Ontario, Canada, made the following comments on reduced loads in the .22 Hornet, as reported in *Rod and Gun*:

"In addition to the factory loaded cartridges, with soft nosed or hollow pointed 45-grain bullets, I have used many hand-loaded reduced charges, such as the 39-grain lead bullet with 4.5 grains No. 80, to approximate the .22 Long Rifle high speed; the 48-grain flat nosed gas-check bullet with 5.5 grains No. 80, and a 35-grain sharp pointed, copper-cased bullet with 11.5 grains No. 1204, which gave an estimated velocity close to 3,000 f.s. at the muzzle.

"The 39-grain lead bullet was found very satisfactory for squirrels and small game as it killed cleanly without tearing; even on anything so small as a blackbird, the point of exit was no larger than the entrance. Similarly the 35-grain copper-cased bullet with 9.0 grains of 1204 made a wonderful charge for small game, giving a trajectory so flat that one need make practically no allowance for distance up to 100 yards.

"The flat-nosed gas-check bullet was found to tear rather badly, being probably more suitable for game larger than a rabbit. A crow struck by the 35-grain soft-nosed bullet travelling at 3,000 f.s. or so, was completely torn apart, little more than a shell of the body being left, and a centre hit seemed to distintegrate the crow as completely as a 45-grain load. A squirrel struck with the 35-grain bullet, either soft point or solid point was reduced to a mangled mass of fur. A chuck collapsed in his tracks, when hit right.

"With any of these fast loads a chuck's performance depends upon his position and his attention. If he is broadside on and engaged in feeding, the impact of the bullet makes him wilt in his tracks. If, however, he is on top of a stone pile or boulder watching the shooter, with muscles tense, he jumps into the air a foot or so, to collapse without a kick.

"This cartridge has been used on woodchucks at all ranges from 50 yards up to an estimated 200 yards, and in no case where a hollow point bullet was used, did the bullet go through the chuck, but stayed inside to expend all its energy in the animal. A soft-nosed bullet on the contrary, would almost always go through, mushrooming well and tearing a good sized hole at the point of exit. Those who use the Hornet find it a most satisfactory load from the standpoint of efficiency, economy and lack of noise."

Milhoan Loads for the .22 Hornet

Robert U. Milhoan, gunsmith, of R.F.D., Elizabeth, W. Va., made the following recommendations to the author for exceptionally accurate loads in the .22 Hornet. Eleven grains of 2400, Winchester soft point 45-grain Hornet bullet with Winchester No. 116 primer and Winchester cases. This load gave 1″ 40-shot group at 100 yards. Author estimates this charge would develop close to service rifle pressures, in a closely-chambered custom rifle.

Second Milhoan load: 45-grain jacketed bullet, 10.3 grains of 2400, Winchester 116 primer and Winchester cases. This is described as a very accurate load. This charge is listed as giving 2,605 f.s. m.v. in a booklet printed some years back, by Hercules. Pressures in the neighborhood of those developed in the Krag.

Third Milhoan load: A squirrel and small game load: 35-grain F.M.C. Sisk bullet and 7.0 grains of 2400; Winchester No. 116 primer and Winchester cases. Gives ⅝ groups at 50 yards. A group of that size would give a brain shot practically every time on gray, black or fox squirrels. This charge gave 1,900 f.s. m.v. and a breech pressure so low, it is extremely safe to shoot, assuming the powder is uniform. One hundred yard trajectory would be about 1 1/5″ or less. The cases should reload very easily as the pressures are so low.

This load, with soft point or H. P. bullets, especially the former, which expand easier and quicker with low velocity loads, would be satisfactory for shooting woodchucks at short and medium ranges, if aim be taken at butt of ear, high on shoulder, or to smash through both shoulder joints.

If used with soft point, expanding bullet, would also be a fine hawk or crow load for shooting from a car, or in woods or fields close to town where minimum report and moderate range are desirable characteristics. Shots often average 75 to 125 yards in such circumstances, in which instance, such charge is entirely adequate.

Without question the .22 Hornet set a new standard of accuracy with .22 commercial, factory loaded ammunition. These loads have close to the accuracy of the .30-1906 International Match load at 100 yards, and which charge had a muzzle velocity of 2,250 f.s. using HiVel No. 2 powder. That powder is not suitable for the .22 Hornet cartridge.

The .22 Hornet, with various charges, dozens of which are listed in this chapter, covers perfectly every variety of small game shooting from red or pine squirrel, through gopher, gray squirrel, black squirrel, fox squirrel, red fox, gray fox, grouse, jack rabbit, and moderate range woodchuck and coyote shooting. It is probably the best factory load for wild turkeys ever put out. The careful reloader can provide charges for each variety of game as enumerated above, by selecting the proper charge from the listings given in this chapter. You require no special hand-made loading or bullet seating tools, no swaged down, hand-prepared cartridge cases, no fire-formed cases, you are not hung up for ammunition, a new barrel or this and that, if someone dies, goes out of business, or takes up some new caliber of cartridge. There is nothing "special" about the .22 Hornet rifle or its ammunition except a degree of accuracy at 100 to 200 yards that will make your eyes pop. The author believes the .22 Hornet to be the most generally useful, factory loaded varmint cartridge on the commercial market.

.22 HORNET
Ideal Cast Bullet Loads—Ideal Handbook No. 34

Bullet	Powder	Charge	M.V.	Primer
224450 — 47-gr.	4227	10.0	2,400 f. s.	
225438 — 43-gr.	80	5.0	1,540 Est.	
225438 — 43-gr.	2400	7.5	1,950 f. s.	
225438 — 43-gr.	4227	10.0	2,250 Est.	
225415 — 48-gr.	4227	8.8	2,000 Est.	
225415 — 48-gr.	4227	10.8	2,410 f. s.	
— 48-gr. G.C.	4759	7.5	1,910 f.s.	

The .22 Hornet is an ideal cartridge to use around settled districts where nearly all shots are taken under 200 yards, where report of rifle cannot be too loud, and where ricochets are not desired. In this particular soft point .22 Hornet bullets go to pieces very much better on earth, sod, gravel, sand, stones, hard knots, dead trees, etc. They also kill better on varmints, if both they and H.P. bullets have the same muzzle velocity, assuming they then have similar or equal coefficient of form.

At very high velocity for the .22 Hornet, sometimes desirable, but frequently undesirable, the H.P. bullet holds its form better, it carries better without deforming in a rifle magazine, or in the pocket, but it is not always as certain to expand promptly and completely at low and moderate velocities. In game, the H.P. bullet is likely to retain more of the jacket from the front end of the bullet. On the other hand, it may smash up badly and even turn end for end in shots in the skull of a woodchuck, coyote, dog, wolf, or similar animal.

The .218 Bee

The .218 Bee is a short, sharply bottle necked, squatty, but quite powerful little cartridge, greatly resembling the original .22 Koshollek cartridge, which branched out a bit later as the .22 Baby Niedner cartridge when fitted with a different shape of bullet from the Koshollek. The same style of rounded ogive bullet was then used in the very accurate .22 Hornet cartridge. The .218 Bee develops 2,860 f.s. m.v. with 46-grain hollow point expanding bullet, or with a 45-grain soft point projectile. Each gives a muzzle energy of over 800 ft. lbs. It has a 50-yard trajectory of 0.7″ when firing at 100 yards, and 3.5″ at 100 yards when shooting at 200. This is about the same as with the .30-1906 Springfield service load. Over 300 yards the .218 Bee develops a 10½″ trajectory which is good for a small hunting load.

The .218 Bee cartridge has a standard head diameter of .408″, as compared with the much smaller .350″ of the .22 Hornet and the much larger .506″ for the .219 Zipper, the .22 Savage H.P. and the .25-35 case. The .218 has an outside diameter of .3334″ at the beginning of the shoulder which has a slope of 15°. In comparison, the Savage .22 H.P. has a shoulder slope of 14° and the Zipper 12°. The muzzle velocity of the .218 Bee is almost double that of the old .25-20 and .32-20 cartridges and about 30% higher than the Hi-Speed and Super-Speed type of .25-20, but the bullet is proportionately shorter and lighter.

The .218 Bee case contains a groove just in front of the head, which is both wider and deeper than in the .219 Zipper cartridge. This gives a good bite for the extractor if the case sticks in the chamber.

When we compare the .218 Bee cartridge directly with the .22 Hornet and the R-2, we find a cartridge about 200 f.s. faster than the .22 Hornet and 200 to 500 f.s. less than most of the charges for the .22 Lovell. Obviously, the pressures had to be kept down for the lever action Model 65 Winchester rifle. Reports of accuracy of the .218 Bee have varied considerably. Winchester boosts it, which is natural, and compared with the other short, light cartridges for lever action rifles, it probably shows up well, except for the .22 Hornet which is considerably more accurate. Arthur Hubalek once told the author—after he had rebarrelled a good many rifles like Hi-Side Winchester singleshots, for the .218 Bee that it will not quite equal the .22/3000 R-2 Donaldson type cartridges, but that it can be made to average about 1¾″ groups at 100 yards, in a fairly heavy target style barrel. This would mean in a barrel ¾″ to ⅞″ in diameter at the muzzle.

One should not regularly expect equal accuracy in a light barrel lever action sporting rifle, although occasional rifles of that type, will at times give groups almost as close as those obtained from match barrels.

The Winchester barrels for the .218 Bee are rifled with a right hand twist, one turn in 16″, but Hubalek used 1 turn in 17″ which he thought gave improved accuracy. At one time Gebby had relined a dozen or more singleshot Winchester and Winchester or Marlin .25-20 and .32-20 repeaters for the .218 and advised: "They have more power than the Hornet (which of course was obvious), less than the .22/3000, (which was equally obvious to both of us), and not over one-half the accuracy of either." He made up two solid barrels in heavy weight style for Smith's Custom Loads, on a Krag action. Smith used this for .218 hand-loaded ammunition testing and reported much better accuracy than factory figures. He concluded the cartridge was underloaded and proceeded to speed it up a little. The groups closed up—in other words, gave better accuracy. The cartridge appeared to Smith to be loaded with No. 4227. When the charge was increased so that the velocity developed was 3,000 to 3,100 f.s the accuracy was excellent but these loads were suited only to bolt actions or Hi-Side singleshot actions having a bushed firing pin.

Comment was that the loads average 14.0 to 14.5 grains of 4227 with Hornet 45-grain bullets. He also used 50-grain Lovell bullets with better accuracy, and also obtained good accuracy with some of the early 8-S bullets for the .22 Varminter. This in the Krag-Bee and not in the .218 Winchester Bee.

Another gunsmith, very well known, but who would in this instance, probably prefer to remain anonymous, reported to the author that his experience with this cartridge was that it only averaged about 2½″ groups at 100 yards, and his other .22 varmint rifles did so much better in the way of accuracy that so far he had refused to build rifles for the .218 Bee caliber.

Consequently, we find a general situation of having in the .218 a cartridge and rifle of which in normal times, both rifles and ammunition are readily available, at a very moderate price everything considered, and that it is a cartridge which will kill coyotes and woodchucks at 250 yards and less with fair regularity, but not always score brain shots. It just doesn't have the accuracy for brain shots at anything beyond 150 yards as a normal expectancy. It is a good jack rabbit cartridge, most excellent in fact, especially for running shooting on jacks. It is, in fact, probably the best rifle on the market in lever action, for running jack rabbit shooting, price of ammunition considered.

Factory loads are entirely too powerful for squirrel shooting, including fox squirrels; for squirrels you should try head shots, and expect to miss your share of them. It is much too powerful for cottontail rabbits, prairie chickens and ruffed grouse. It is a good clean killer on tough ringnecked cocks, but also mangles them. On turkeys, it will be a first class cartridge at moderate ranges, with a tendency to mangle the turkey if shot so that the feathers mat and the bullet slashes through so that it tears across the breast, or goes in the rump and comes out through the center of the breast meat. A shot through the butts of the wings from the side, is the best shot on wild turkeys with any cartridge of this type. If you hit the exact butt of the wing however, so that the bullet follows along the wing bone to the shoulder and shatters it, which it will, with its high velocity, you may find quite a few bone fragments in the breast, or shoulder meat near where the bullet struck. Look out for such bone fragments when using a high velocity bullet, as they can cut like leg bone fragments from a cottontail rabbit when killed with No. 4 shot.

Safety of the .218 Bee Ammunition

The Winchester folks played safe by designing the .218 Bee too fat to go into the .22/3000 Lovell, Kilbourn and Ackley chambers; it is much too large in both case diameter and head size, to go into the .22 Hornet or K-Hornet chambers, and is too small in head diameter by almost .10″ to fit in the .219 Zipper chamber, so the owner of a .218 Bee has got to shoot .218 Bee ammunition in it. This will be an awful disappointment to a great many owners of .218 Bee rifles, because it is surprising how many people write to Gun Editors asking whether they can't shoot .38-40's in the .44-40, .30-30 in the .32 Special, or some other misfit. The boys who really go to town are those who own some of the older black powder rifles and cannot get proper ammunition these days. At times they report with considerable glee that they have rigged up a special contrivance which permitted them to discharge the cartridge, and one or two have even claimed to have killed game at close range, with such "sub-caliber" loads. Another reason for the Bee being shaped like it is, can be traced to the condition that .22/3000 Lovell, R-2, L-17 and similar wildcats are too high pressure, when fully charged, for the Winchester lever action, and the chap who insisted on using something else would be unpleasantly surprised.

The .218 will supplant the .25-20 and .32-20 calibers in many instances because the trajectory is much flatter, and it is as accurate or more so. The very finest .218 Bee rifles will be the heavy custom built jobs, put out by such firms as Charles C. Johnson, Hubalek, Parker O. Ackley Company and the like, Sukalle, and other Western gunsmiths, and chambered in some instances somewhat more closely than the lever action factory rifles. Such custom rifles will reload much better than the lever actions, which will require cartridges to be resized the full length, if shot previously with full charge factory ammunition. Be sure to differentiate between .218 Bee loads for the lever action and for the custom singleshots.

Reloads for the .218 Bee Winchester

There are certain ballistic and mechanical difficulties to overcome in successfully reloading for best results in the .218 Bee cartridge, when the ammunition is to be used through the Winchester lever action repeating rifle.

Sharply pointed bullets are not suitable for use in the magazine of this rifle, consequently they are only suggested for use in bolt action rifles fitted with .218 Bee barrels. The pointed bullet of a cartridge might easily explode the primer of the cartridge directly in front of it in the magazine. Another difficulty is that pounding in the magazine, due to carrying the rifle in the hand, on the shoulder, in an auto, or in a scabbard on horseback, might jam the bullet back into the case and set up high pressure when fired, or even cause the spilling of powder if jammed right down into the case past the bearing point. Consequently the standard open-point bullet for the factory cartridge is the only one to use in the lever action Bee, because this is at present the *only* cannelured or deeply grooved bullet in the .22 clan and you need this cannelure for proper crimping of the bullet into the case to be used in lever actions.

Bushnell Smith has suggested a number of loads for the .218 Bee cartridge, tested in his .218 Bee barrel on a Krag action. These could also be used in Winchester Model 70 or Model 54 actions fitted with a Bee barrel. Or in a Bee fitted to a High Side Winchester singleshot action.

.218 BEE

The first two of these loads are for special rifle only

Bullet	Powder	Charge	Rec. by
50-gr. Sisk-Lovell	HiVel No 3	15.5 grs.	J. B. Smith
50-gr. Sisk-Lovell	IMR 4227	14.0 grs.	J. B. Smith
These are both full charge loads.			
45-gr. Winchester F.M.C. ..	duPont Shotgun	6.0 grs.	J. B. Smith
45-gr. Winchester F.M.C. ..	IMR 4227	14.0 grs.	J. B. Smith

The first of these last two charges is for squirrel shooting except in those states where full metal-cased bullets are not permitted by the game laws, in which instance you will have to use a soft point or hollow point bullet. The second is recommended for shooting foxes and other furred game. You can use the 45-grain H.P. or soft point bullet for turkeys, hawks, crows, and coyotes. This load will shoot with approximately the factory sighting.

Smith suggests that these latter two loads can both be used in the Winchester repeater but if so used, and are loaded with full metal-cased bullets, can only be used in the chamber, using the rifle as a singleshot. The remedy is to carry one such cartridge in the chamber and factory loads in the magazine.

Willard L. McEwen kindly made the following suggestions from loads that he had compiled, mostly, I believe, from Fred Ness' Dope Bag.

One was 15.0 grains of IMR No. 4198 and the 45-grain Remington Hornet bullet which shot well in the Winchester lever action rifle. This seems to have been one of the few loads recommended for that rifle.

Another bunch, all primed with Winchester No. 6½ primers, were shot successfully in a Model 54 Winchester fitted with a .218 Winchester barrel.

Bullet	Powder	Charge	Primer
40-gr. Lovell	IMR 4227	14.5 grs.	6½ W.R.A.
45-gr. Rem. S.P. ..	IMR 4198	15.0 grs.	6½ W.R.A.
50-gr. Lovell	IMR 4198	15.0 grs.	6½ W.R.A.

In the same Model 54 rifle with .218 Bee barrel, the following charges did well with Western No. 6½ primers.

Bullet	Powder	Charge	Primer
50-gr. Lovell	IMR 4227	13.5 grs.	West. 6½
55-gr. Lovell	IMR 4198	15.0 grs.	West. 6½
40-gr. Lovell	IMR 4227	14.5 grs.	West. 6½

Special Heavy Loads for Heavy Singleshot or Bolt Action .218 Bee Rifles Only

Fred Ness reported the following loads as developing pressures believed to be high for his own light singleshot Winchester but that he felt they were O.K. for use in Model 54 Winchester or other bolt action rifles of somewhat similar type, or for heavy Sharps-Borchardt singleshot actions. They should be satisfactory with High-Side, heavy barrel singleshot Winchester actions with bushed firing pin, likely also for Farquharson actions and Remington-Hepburn and Remington bolt actions of the 720 type, when properly gunsmithed to handle the .218 Bee cartridge.

Bullet	Charge	Powder	M. Velocity
40-gr. 8-S	15.0 grs.	2400	3,330 f. s.
45-gr. Hornet	15.0 grs.	2400	3,227 f. s.
45-gr. Hornet	15.0 grs.	4227	3,040 f. s.
45-gr. Hornet	16.0 grs.	4227	3,166 f. s.
50-gr. 8-S	15.0 grs.	4227	3,081 f. s.
Standard Reloads for .218 Bee rifles including the Lever Action Repeater			
Ideal 47.5-gr. No. 224450	12.0 grs.	2400	2,200 f. s.
Ideal 48-gr. No. 225415 ..	7.0 grs.	80	
W-M 8-S 50-gr.	12.5 grs.	2400	2,800 f. s.
S.P. Hornet 45-gr.	13.5 grs.	2400	2,900 f. s.
45-gr. jacketed Hornet ..	15.0 grs.	4198	2,800 f. s.
50-gr. jacketed	13.5 grs.	4227	
55-gr. jacketed	15.0 grs.	4198	

General Comment

The primary reason for the .218 Bee is to provide a high-speed load in .22 caliber, with a 300-yard trajectory about that of the .30-1906 service charge, which can be used in a short-receiver type, lever action rifle which can be carried conveniently in scabbard, on the back seat or the floor of an auto, a farm wagon or a sled, uses light recoil and moderately inexpensive ammunition suitable for the use of cowboys, sheepherders, and ranchers needing a hunting rifle with light weight but reasonably powerful ammunition and which will cover the varmint and game field up to and including an occasional shot at deer or coyotes. Or, in the East, at woodchucks.

It is not a small game rifle because it is too powerful. It is not a real big game rifle. Yet it can be used with moderate success for a great many kinds of field shooting. It is light, convenient and easy to carry and pack. It is a good trail rifle. Ammunition is of a price that the average busy man will not attempt to reload it.

But for the crank shooter, the K-Hornet, the .22/3000, the .22 Maximum Lovell, the .22 Rimmed Lindahl Chucker and the .219 Donaldson-Wasp or Lindahl Super-Chucker are all better catridges and can all be used in better bolt action or singleshot rifles. But, every one of them is a hand-loading proposition. The .218 Mashburn-Bee is a sharper-shoulder private adaptation of the same cartridge and the author does not care for this shape design, being much more in favor of the longer, slimmer, more accurate developments in .22 wildcats. The .218 Mashburn-Bee loaded ammunition is *not* intended to be used in .218 Winchester factory barrels without re-chambering.

Here is a cartridge and rifle in which the factory load is the one you better buy and stick to. The combination is not a reloader's dream of heaven. However, it is almost certainly the most generally useful and generally satisfactory of the .22 Winchester center fires larger than the very accurate and uniform shooting .22 Hornet. The author prefers the .22 Hornet in the bolt action Winchester.

The .219 Zipper

This cartridge is supplied for the Model 64 Winchester lever action rifle which is practically the '94 Model with different stock. The cartridge is important because it is one of the longest ranged and flattest shooting .22 center fire cartridges for use in this type of action.

The 46-grain H.P. bullet has been chronographed at 3,390 f.s. m.v. and the 56-grain charge at 3,050 f.s. m.v—these velocities being 10 f.s. and 50 f.s. less than those originally given out. The free recoil is but 1.6 ft. lbs. and 2.2 ft. lbs. in each instance, which is a good reason why this rifle will be popular with many who like high velocity rifles with a very light recoil in proportion to killing power developed. Recoil is largely a function of mass and weight of bullets, not of velocity. The muzzle energy developed is between 1100 and 1200 ft. lbs. and fortunately the trajectory is extremely flat over 300 yards, being 2½″ over 200 yards and 7″ over 300 yards for the lighter bullet and 8″ for the heavier. At 50 yards, when firing at 100 yards, the trajectory heights are respectively .4″ and .6″, or averaging .5″.

This cartridge is a very pleasant shooting charge, with fairly sharp report, which is not particularly unpleasant with the 26″ barrel of the Winchester but it does very much better shooting and is more uniform in grouping in a heavier barrelled singleshot with bushed firing pin, or in a good bolt action rifle, than in lever actions which are repeaters. With such there are complaints of excessive verticals and failure to hold zero.

This .219 Zipper cartridge has been the base of a number of the most superbly accurate .22 wildcat cartridges ever designed. Lovell, Kilbourn, Ackley, Vickery, Donaldson, and others have made up wonderful shooting rifles from improved Zippers and Lindahl has two different lengths made from this case, a standard Chucker and a Super-Chucker. The Zipper case is made of good heavy brass, with a strong head and has the following standard factory dimensions: Diameter of rim, 506″. The outside diameter of case is .3649″ while that of the Savage .22 H.P. case is .369″, and the .25-35 case is .3715″. From this it can be seen that it is tapered a good deal more, rim to shoulder. The three have the same size rims. The shoulder has a 12° slope. Most of the Improved Zippers made by custom gunsmiths have the cartridge fire-formed or blown out and maybe trimmed before reloading and shooting, and then we have a case with a much sharper shoulder and sometimes a larger forward-end-of-case diameter.

The net result in the case of the Improved Zipper wildcats is that one gets a cartridge which will now and then make 10-shot 1″ groups or less at 200 yards in a good heavy bolt action or heavy barrel singleshot rifle, which very definitely one should not expect with a lever action, light repeater.

Creighton Bradford of Bradford & Cameron, of Owen Sound, Ontario, wrote the author in 1939 that he had a singleshot .219 Zipper with which he had been doing most surprising shooting. He had killed 36 crows within a few weeks in the Spring of that year, when crows are not too numerous in Ontario, and at ranges up to 250 yards, but averaging about 175 yards. With a 2½″ trajectory over 200 yards this would not be too difficult.

George Schnerring advised the author that he had experimented extensively with this cartridge and that the most uniformly accurate load was the 45-grain Hornet bullet .224″ in diameter,

24.0 grains of Government Pyro D.G. (or duPont No. 20) powder, which gave approximately 3,500 f.s. m.v.

In 1937, when they were still giving out velocities and pressures, Edgar Beugless of E. I. duPont de Nemours & Co.'s Ballistic Station at Carney's Point, N. J. gave the author the following loads for the .219 Zipper in lever action rifles:

Bullet	Powder	Charge	Muzzle Velocity
46-gr. H.P.	3031	21.0 grs.	2,535 f. s.
46-gr. H.P.	3031	28.0 grs.	3,200 f. s.
46-gr. H.P.	4320	22.0 grs.	2,510 f. s.
46-gr. H.P.	4320	29.5 grs.	3,150 f. s.
46-gr. H.P.	4064	22.0 grs.	2,505 f. s.
46-gr. H.P.	4064	29.0 grs.	3,155 f. s.

Cartridge length, when loaded, 2.25″. Rifle barrel length, 26″. Think of the .219 Zipper as a .25-35 necked down to .22 caliber, and loaded so as to shoot much flatter over 150 yards, and with materially less recoil, even, than the .25-35, and you have a good mind picture of the .219 Zipper. Reloaders who still have some No. 80 on hand, will likely find 8.0 to 13.0 grains of No. 80, to give satisfactory results for short range shooting.

Cartridges of about this power will kill well when properly handled. The various .219 Zipper Improved cartridges, which nearly all are longer and some are larger in diameter at the front end of the main part of the case, have made quite a reputation as woodchuck rifles.

Additional Loads for .219 Zipper

Bullet	Powder	Charge	Muzzle Velocity
56-grain	4064	26.5 grs.	2,816 f. s.
56-grain	3031	25.6 grs.	3,100 f. s.
46-grain	4064	29.0 grs.	3,072 f. s.
46-grain WRA	3031	27.5 grs.	3,420 f. s.
43-gr. Lyman cast.	80	8.5 grs.	

Caution

I want to caution readers, particularly those with comparatively little or no reloading experience, to *not* use, or try to use, loads recommended anywhere for .219 *IMPROVED* wildcat cartridges in the factory .219 Zipper cartridge described here. A few of the .22 Improved Zippers are shorter in the body of the case, than the factory job but most of them are longer, have a much sharper shoulder slope, and some are enlarged by firing, to a greater diameter at the shoulder. Consequently *such* cartridges, the greater capacity ones, are adapted to a materially heavier load than the factory cartridge. Be sure you are trying charges for factory cartridges and not for some special cartridge put out by a custom gunsmith.

For the wildcat Zipper Improved cartridges, use only the charges recommended for them, not those above.

The .220 Swift Cartridge

The .220 Swift is the flattest shooting and the most powerful .22 caliber center fire cartridge put out commercially in the United States. The two Winchester rifles so far produced for it, the Models 54 and 70—both bolt actions, have both been made in sporting and target weight.

The three commercial .220 Swift cartridges made so far include the 48-grain soft point cartridge at 4,140 f.s. muzzle velocity, but the bullet drops to 3,490 f.s. at 100 yards. This bullet gives a 0.3″ trajectory height over 100 yards, 1.50″ over 200 yards and 3.50″ over 300 yards. It gives the same 300-yard trajectory height as most other varmint rifles give over 200 yards.

This will shoot through 0.50″ of mild steel at 50 yards, and it makes a hole 0.50″ in diameter in penetrating that steel plate. The metal flows back toward the shooter as well as out on the far side of the plate. This is the only cartridge which has shot clear through the hard steel plate on our local outdoor rifle range, although Springfields, Krags, .257 Roberts and many other calibers have been fired upon it.

Two additional factory charges were normally provided for the .220 Swift. One is a 46-grain H.P. bullet at 4,140 f.s. and the 56-grain H.P. bullet at 3,690 f.s. The trajectories over 100, 200 and 300 yards are the same, approximately, as with the first-mentioned load, except for 0.50″ to 1″ or less differences, even at the mid-point for 300 yards.

My own 54 Winchester, which is equipped with a medium-sized gold bead front and Lyman 48 receiver peep sight, and is .220 caliber, has shot quite a number of 5-shot and 10-shot groups for me at 50 yards, which measured 0.8″ to 1.25″ in diameter, while sighting at the 4″ bull of the 100-yard scope target. The gold bead covers more space at 50 yards than this bullseye. These groups were with Winchester and Western 48 and 46-grain loads. In the field, however, this rifle has not been satisfactory. Frankly, with the same loads, on the first shot fired, with either iron sights or the 4 power Fecker hunting telescope, it can not be depended upon to hit anything and I think it often vaporizes the first bullet fired.

The .220 Swift cartridge is the .236 Lee straight pull case fitted with a .30-1906 head, to fit the 54 and 70 bolt face. The cartridge case is strong and heavy, and needs to be. In size and general shape it resembles the .257 Roberts more than most other cartridges, but the .220 Swift has a much narrower cannelure at the head. It is really a semi-rimless affair with a small, clearly-felt rim. The cartridge is almost 0.03125″ shorter than the .257 Roberts, and is of about the same length up to the end of the sharply necked down portion of the case. The loaded .220 is within 0.1875″ of being the same over-all length as the .257. However it lacks the accuracy of a *good,* well broken in .257, and is not as accurate as the .22 Hornet at 100 yards.

The .220 Swift is not a settled district cartridge. It is not a small game charge. It is primarily a very high velocity, small caliber, flat shooting, light recoil cartridge for open country shooting on deer and black bear, wolves, coyotes, and for long range shots on buzzards, eagles and similar targets. Crows, hawks, jack rabbits, cottontails, grouse, will all be badly blown to pieces and even to small shreds when struck. Particularly is this so if shot at ranges of 40 to 75 yards. A crow shot on the ground will be shattered, and its remains, legs, feathers, head, will be scattered over 50 to 75 feet—blown out from the common center where it stood when struck. A hawk or crow sitting on a limb will be blown into a great whirling burst of feathers, wings, legs, shreds of flesh and even the "caw" may not all come down in one squawk—as one fellow put it.

The shattering effect of the bullet, especially of the 48-grain soft point bullet, must be seen to be believed. Of course this is much greater at 50 to 125 yards than beyond, but anything hit with this bullet is, as that chap also remarked, "blown to Hell in an awful hurry!"

I recall one instance in which two men fired simultaneously at two birds the size of large turkeys, at approximately 150 yards, as they fed on a bare field on the ground. They were in plain sight and the exact effect of the bullets as they landed could be observed. One was using the .22 Hornet and did not quite center his bird, which rolled around a bit and then lay over and died. But the big tough bird shot with the .220 Swift had the far side simply blown out, it was suddenly deflated like a bladder that had been punctured, it settled to the ground and never even moved, and not a feather on it blew in the wind—even though the wind was blowing rather strongly across the field—it died that instantly; life was simply exploded out of it. The only thing I ever saw killed so instantaneously was a white rooster that once ran across the road in front of a large, fully loaded White truck. That rooster was smashed so very flat even its feathers had no substance and cessation

FACTORY AND EXPERIMENTAL C. F. CARTRIDGES

Left to right: .22-15-60 Stevens; .22 Niedner Magnum rimmed; .219 Win. Zipper; .22 Varminter; .250/3000 Savage; .22 H.P. Savage; .220 Swift; .22 Newton H.P.; .22 C. F. made from necked down .275 Holland and Holland Magnum.

of all movement was instantaneous. Sometimes you get the same result with a bird shot with a .220 Swift bullet. Even the muscles scarcely twitch. Heart, brain, lungs, and everything all seem to let go at once. Hydraulic action is apparent in addition to the blasting effect.

Fred Ness got the idea this cartridge would be very effective on deer and also, most likely to shut off possible criticism on recommendations from the Big Bore clan, he printed a questionnaire in

the November 1936 *American Rifleman,* asking for results and
gave the resume of the data from big game hunters, in the March
1937 issue. Excerpts from his conclusions follow—these being the
most complete and painstaking reports of their kind on the Swift:

"We received complete detailed reports on 26 deer killed with
the .220 Swift during the 1936 season. These included 17 white
tail, 6 black tail, and 3 mule deer—from widely scattered localities.
* * * The distances over which these kills were made ranged from
20 yards to 500 yards. Eight were killed beyond 200 yards, and of
the other 18, eight were killed beyond 150 yards. Five were killed
under 100 yards. * * * There were two paunch shots, one being
a grazing or skin hit which, none the less, knocked the animal down.
This one was finished with a neck shot. There was one chest shot
from above. One shot through the brisket from directly in front.
Only three were neck shots, with but one head shot, between the
eyes from in front. One was a diagonal flank shot. Of the remaining 17 shots, 5 were shoulder hits and 12 struck behind the shoulder
or behind the front leg.

"Thirteen, or 50% were dropped and killed instantly, there being
no visible movement after the animal left its feet. An additional
nine were also practically instant kills, but having been shot when
running, made a jump or two before losing all motion. Another
one ran 35 yards before dropping dead. This means 23 quick
kills out of 26 shots at all ranges. * * * The record stands 100%
bagged on the first shot, 96% killed cleanly and quickly; 90%
were stone dead within 50 feet; 96% were dead within 40 yards.

"No caliber or cartridge has a better record. * * * The consensus
of opinion among the hunters and observers represented is that the
.220 Swift is a dependable deer slayer but unnecessarily and undesirably destructive."

But its bullet may be quite easily exploded or deflected by brush.
Thirteen of the hunters used Winchester 48-grain, soft point loads;
one Winchester 46-grain H.P., and 12 used various handloads, six
being Smith's Custom Loads.

C. F. Holmes, of Little Rock, Arkansas, writing in *Hunter,
Trader, Trapper* of June 1937, on the .220 Swift on varmints—
meaning hawks and crows, in this instance, made the following
comments:

"We go hawk shooting here, once a week. * * * We always get
10 to 25 hawks a day. My longest shot on a hawk was 435 long
steps. A man 6' 9" tall, stepped the distance. * * * I was using a
48-grain Swift bullet with 39.5 grains of duPont No. 3031, and *no*

graphite wad. I keep my scope sighted for a 200-yard center kill. I held just 2″ over his head and squeezed off the trigger and to my surprise the hawk fell out of the tree. When I picked up this hawk his head was crushed to a soft mess, like an egg-shell is crushed. That is what you might call a freak shot.

"Last week Mr. W— and I went hawk shooting on the prairie. Together we bagged 23 hawks with 54 shots. The average distance the hawks were killed was 180 yards, some were as close as 90 yards, several well over 300 yards. Some of the hawks were blown to pieces. Bear in mind that this barrel of mine had been fired over 7,000 times. The reason we had such good luck on the prairie was that the wind was not blowing at all. The load I was using was 38.0 grains duPont No. 3031 powder, a graphite wad, and the 55-grain Sisk pointed bullet. This is the most powerful load I used."

Speaking of another shooting trip, in which five men took part, Mr. Holmes wrote in "H. T. T.":

"'The first shot that was offered was at a hawk 280 yards off. Tom took the shot. He held the crosshairs on the middle of the hawk, killing him without a flap of his wings. Tom stepped off the distance back to the car and it was 327 long steps. * * * We had not driven more than half a mile, when all at once a big hawk flew up on a telegraph pole about 75 yards off. This hawk was then blown to pieces. The bullet drove every bit of blood out of him. When struck, the bullet landing on the bird's feathers made a sound like that when taking a blown up paper bag in one hand and whacking it on the other and it bursts!

"Before the day was over, we had killed 30 hawks and two buzzards. One of the buzzards shot, which was about 75 yards distance, was killed instantly. The bullet blew feathers and pulverized meat for 20 yards. This buzzard exploded completely. The .220 Swift seems to blow up buzzards worse than hawks. * * * The average distance at which these 30 hawks were killed was 203 yards."

This is the most favorable comment upon the Swift and its cartridge the author has seen. The author's varmint shooting experiences with the .220 Swift, spread over years, have not been satisfactory. For some reasons, both with a Fecker game scope, and with the factory iron sights, there have been a tremendous number of misses, unexplainable ones. Sometimes the bullet was seen to strike. Other times there was a blast and a mist and nothing whatever could be found of a striking bullet mark. In some such instances, the bullet might have gone to pieces in the air. I recall in particular a very large crow fired at while standing on the ballast of a railroad switchback. I had a perfect hold. Not a thing happened to that crow, and while dust seemed to blow up from everywhere thereabouts, the crow was only half stunned and no bullet mark or hole could be seen anywhere. That bullet hit everywhere and nowhere! The crow then got up and staggered off and flew. Repeated trips back to a rifle range for a re-sighting at 100 yards, have never shown anything much out of the way. At times the zero was off a little, but usually the rifle either was shooting into and close around the 10-ring or could soon be brought there. The rifle fits splendidly, the trigger pull is fine—better than on my Hornet of the same model—and the 26″ barrel seems in perfect condition. The Fecker scope has repeatedly shot loose on the mount bases in five to eight shots, yet the recoil, while very quick and sharp, is only four pounds or so, as compared with 15 to 18 foot pounds for the .30-1906 Springfield sporter. Iron sight shooting as mentioned previously, has been no better on varmints. I would kill five times as many things with a .22 Hornet as with my .220 Swift and I have not as yet solved the riddle.

Reloading the .220 Swift

J. Bushnell Smith wrote thus of the .220 Swift: "The chap who 'knows all the answers' in reloading any other cartridge is just like a baby learning to walk, when he tackles the .220 Swift. He has a lot of crawling to forget and a lot of new steps to learn. The Swift is the most finicky cartridge to reload in the world. *Everything* must be right. * * * The smallest irregularity in load may jump the pressures 5,000 to 15,000 pounds per square inch, and without a bit of warning."

One complaint on the Swift, is that after two shots or so, of full loads, the case both lengthens and thickens in the metal of its neck. They lengthen as much as 0.002″. That is equal to the usual clearance in the .220 Swift chamber. Next time the cartridge is reloaded it may not enter the chamber or may swage down some when so entering and thus the chamber pressures are raised, when the cartridge is fired.

Mr. Smith wrote the author: "Good reduced loads are difficult in the Swift, but one load that has given good results in the 55-grain F.M.J. bullet at approximately 2,000 f.s. and at 3,000 f.s. is accurate, and should make a long range fox load. With the 55-grain F.M.J. bullet use 12.0 grains duPont shotgun bulk, for approximately 2,000 f.s. and 17.0 grains for the heavier 3,000 f.s. charge.

"In firing low pressure loads in rimless cartridges, the very powerful non-fouling rifle primers have a tendency to drive the cartridge away from the bolt face and against the chamber shoulder. This sometimes *shortens* the case, giving excess head space when this cartridge is again reloaded. Loads developing less than 75% of the normal full load pressure should use less powerful primers. Large size pistol primers work well with the very light loads."

C. F. Holmes used graphite wads with *all* the following loads in the .220 Swift:

45-gr. Rem. S.P. and 30.0 grs. No. 3031 duPont.
45-gr. Rem. S.P. and 39.0 grs. No. 3031.
45-gr. S.P. and 16.0 grs. No. 80.
48-gr. Swift S.P. and 39.5 grs. No. 3031.
55-gr. Sisk pointed and 38.0 grs. No. 3031.
55-gr. Sisk pointed and 32.0 grs. No. 3031.
55-gr. Sisk pointed and 30.0 grs. HiVel No. 2.
55-gr. Sisk pointed and 36.0 grs. HiVel No. 2.

Holmes generally uses the 45-grain Remington Hornet bullet because he can get them for about one-half the price of the 55-grain Sisk bullets, but he prefers the latter for hawks, crows and targets as it bucks the wind better than the 45-grain bullet.

He reports getting some 1.25″ and 1.50″ groups at 100 yards, with his reloads. Holmes has also used short range loads of No. 80, for smaller stuff and shorter range target shooting.

Loads for the .220 Swift, suggested to the author in 1937, by Edgar Beugless, of duPont:

Bullet	Powder	Charge	M.V.
48-gr. S.P.	No. 80	10.0 grs.	1,960 f.s.
48-gr. S.P.	No. 80	13.0 grs.	2,245 f.s.
48-gr. S.P.	No. 80	16.0 grs.	2,500 f.s.
			Most accurate load
48-gr. S.P.	No. 4198 duPont	23.0 grs.	2,900 f.s.

The reports on the Swift to date do not appear to be anything like as common as those on the smaller center fire .22 varmint cartridges. Most likely this is due to several causes: ammunition costs between two and three times as much as that of the .22 Hornet, in factory loads, when available; loads are too powerful for small game shooting; and reloading is not generally as successful, with greatly reduced loads, as with the smaller .22 center fire cartridges.

The author's experience with factory loads in the .220 Swift, as compared with factory loads in two .257 Roberts rifles—a Remington 30-S and a heavy barrel 54 .257—is that the Roberts cartridge peels a good deal more brass from the rim of the head than does the .220. Many times these brass shavings drop into the well of the chamber and cause jams or hard-sticking cases which are difficult to seat and may raise pressures. This was more noticeable with earlier and heavier loaded Remington-Roberts .257's than with later issues, in which pressures were lower. This is one advantage for the .220 Swift.

The Swift of today can be described as a wonderfully fine coyote and wolf rifle, if mangled pelts are no drawback and you have reliable ammunition. If the pelt must be preserved without mutilation, full metal-cased bullets, or slower loads for the Swift, are the only solutions. It is a clean-killing deer rifle, but as a reloading proposition stands almost at the foot of the list among modern high powers, and the tyro had better cut his reloading eye-teeth on some other cartridge.

Mr. Holmes, who shot on the Oklahoma State Military Rifle Team some years ago, has shown that accurate and effective hand loads may be produced for the .220 in both full charges and greatly reduced loads. Do not get the idea however, that it is the perfect all-around cartridge for squirrels, woodchucks, coyotes, hawks and crows, simply by changing powder or bullet. It is really a specialist's cartridge in the super-velocity field.

Dr. Mann got better than 4,000 f.s. muzzle velocity around 30 years ago, with Lightning, HiVel and such powders, and much higher with very light bullets; the German Halger rifle, a two-diameter proposition, was better than 5,000 f.s., so the Swift is not unique, merely a rather practical commercial version of high intensity loading. Its two real advantages are very flat trajectory and very light recoil in proportion to killing power. With the 48-grain bullet there is little need to worry about ricochets, but with 0.375″ to 0.50″ penetration in steel plate at 50 and 100 yards, and considerable at 400 to 500 yards, it does pay to be careful on a line shot.

Normally, the most important thing to watch, with the Swift and all other 3,500—4,000 f.s. rifles is to keep the ear drums away from the rifle muzzle when firing, and under no circumstances to walk right out in front of, or beside the muzzle of a companion's

Swift rifle when he is about to fire. Never shoot such high intensity rifles *indoors,* nor from the inside of a closed room—always stick the muzzle out of a door or a window. The muzzle blast will be ear-splitting.

In conclusion, the Swift amazes the neophyte and disgusts the real veteran rifleman and reloader. There are occasional accurate Swifts but the average one is not very satisfactory and will not be until better bullets are developed, bullets which are insulated against melting of cores.

George Schnerring, Proof House Foreman of Frankford Arsenal for many, many years, wrote the author in October, 1942, and has not changed his mind since on the .220:

"Your experience on the .220 Swift checks with my own. I shot out a 54 standard barrel Swift and it did not take long to do it. I tried all weights of bullets and all makes and all charges of duPont powders,—3031, 4320, 4064 et cetera from 30.0 to 38.0 grains, according to the granulation—and never could duplicate good 5-shot groups at 100 yards.

"Then I tried a 14″ pitch tube and while I had some fair results, still I never could depend upon it. I also missed chucks and crows galore, and finally put a .30-1906 barrel on the 54 action and sold it.

"Before I played with the Swift, I designed and developed the .22/4000 cartridge. This case has practically the same velocities as the Swift, in fact about 50 to 75 feet higher. I found that the breech soon eroded, the lands shot out at the bullet throat after 600 rounds of high velocity ammunition. With such a short bullet the gas gets past the base of the projectile as soon as it leaves the case, and then the accuracy suffers.

"I shot out at least two Winchester barrels, heavy 1″ diameter tubes, in making my tests, therefore had some experience with .22 caliber ultra-high velocity cartridges.

"There may be heavy jacketed bullets made soon that will stand that velocity. That is what is necessary with a very high velocity bullet. A heavy *jacket* and a core that will not melt.

"Charles Newton found that out over 30 years ago, and he made some bullets that had the core insulated (the author remembers this, it was written up in the original *Outdoor Life* or else in *Outer's Book),* and this insulation was paper. It prevented the vaporizing of the core. If you will shoot through a paper screen set up at say, 50 feet from the muzzle, and another at 75 and at 100 yards, you will probably get bullet holes that show a comet on the right side of the bullet hole. If you examine it closely you will see it is vaporized lead. That bullet will not be accurate.

"Or, get someone to fire the Swift, and stand directly back of the shooter. You will probably see a puff of what looks like smoke traveling down the range. Normally you can see it at about 50 yards from the muzzle."

The comment varies as much as this. What is one man's favorite is another man's disappointment. The .220 Swift needs better bullets and some changes in cartridge design to make it more like the .220 Wilson Arrow which has a sharper shoulder slope that helps prevent cartridge expansion forward.

Mr. Holmes is the only man who has claimed a very long barrel life for a Swift, to the author's knowledge. Normally, the accuracy life is between 600 and 1,500 or 2,000 rounds. Some improvements in barrel steel or bore treatment may improve this figure.

Feb. 10, 1938—195 yards

Model 70 Win. Target .220 Swift Scope sight—10X Targetspot 37.5 grs. I.M.R. 4320—55-gr. Express bullet. Fired from bench rest by J. Bushnell Smith.

CHAPTER 4

HERVEY LOVELL

AND HIS LINE OF TWELVE .22 WILDCATS

FEW CUSTOM gunsmiths with a hand in the development of
.22 center fire, high velocity varmint cartridges have received
greater praise and more gratuitous and deserved advertising in riflemen's magazines than Hervey Lovell.

Lovell formerly lived at 3345 N. Gale Street, Indianapolis,
Indiana. His shop was about eight miles from the center of the
city and was sufficiently rural so that he had a pet fox squirrel
which came to the shop to be fed. He says that someone badly
spoiled that fox squirrel; guess who?

Hervey waited quite a long time to take Horace Greeley's advice to "Go West, young man," but finally at the turn of the year
into 1946 he said goodbye to the pet fox squirrel—and that probably
went tough—boarded a Pullman and when he rubbed the dust out
of his eyes he was gazing at an arm of the Pacific Ocean—at
Port Townsend, Washington.

At last accounts Lovell was located at 925 Water Street, Port
Townsend, Washington. He writes: "We use a cabin cruiser for
trolling for food fish; cod, perch, flounder, sea bass and other
varieties can be caught from my back door. Bluebills and mallards
are all around us. We picked up a rare small goose under the
shop dock and are feeding her now with the chickens; she was all
covered with oil. No squirrels here but wildcats, sea lions and
seals are the varmints. Kids kill them with .22's, using the .22
Long Rifle. There is a $3.00 bounty on seals. One chap got eight
with his new .22, paid for the rifle and 1,000 rounds of ammunition
before they slid off their rock.

"Men with big rifles shoot sea lions at long range, but the elk
are the real big game here. Deer come in town and sometimes
are killed by autos.

"Police picked up a doe and took her back to the woods. She

was eating grocers' lettuce and is an old offender. They usually book her for petty larceny. Imagine that doe telling the other deer: 'One more head of lettuce and I would have been *arrested;* in fact girls, I almost went *to jail.'* "

Turkey matches are in vogue all over that Washington State section. Lovell says that there is one really crack 52, and one .257 caliber Model 70 that are hot. The latter uses 28.5 grains of 4320 and the 117-grain bullet, the Western boattail. It gives 1½" groups at 200 yards, according to Western comment, when its owner is in top form. The real competition will start when the .219 Zipper Improved Lovell rifles, which use his No. 7 cartridge, become common in that section of Washington. These give the same, or a slightly improved standard of accuracy.

The author first met Hervey Lovell at the National Matches at Camp Perry, Ohio, about 25 years before this chapter was written. At that time he was with an Indiana State Military Rifle Team, which, a bit earlier, had among its members the late Capt. Herbert W. McBride, who wrote *A Rifleman Went to War,* the outstanding book on sniping.

Even at the time of Lovell's early trips to Perry he was a most expert gunsmith on the fitting of Ballard rifle actions. He had with him then the closest fitted Ballard the author has ever examined. Today, Lovell is probably best known among shooters for his work in developing and introducing rifles for the original .22/3000 Lovell cartridge, with approximately 5° shoulder angle. Also, for his present .22/3000 Lovell with 15° shoulder angle, made later to properly burn the I.M.R. line of powders after HiVel No. 3, which was so successful in the original case, had been taken off the market by its manufacturers.

Lovell has repeatedly mentioned that the most accurate of his early .22/3000 rifles were the first ones with shoulder angle less than the R-2 (which has 12° shoulder slope, approximately) yet steeper than the standard early .22/3000 Lovells. This set-up has been most accurate with 14.0 grains of duPont No. 1204 and 14.5 grains of duPont No. 4227. It was not practical to load it much beyond the 3,000 f.s. of the original design. He calls this rifle the "Bell Rifle." About a dozen of them were made with Springfield M-1 barrels on Krag actions, and Savage .2235" blanks fitted to Sharps-Borchardt actions. Henry E. Davis has one of these rifles and this is the one he speaks so highly of as a hawk and crow rifle in his comments in the author's companion work *Hunting with the Twenty-two.*

Lovell has advised the author that his shooting partner had an M-1 barrelled Krag, chambered with the Bell reamer (which long ago wore out) and that this rifle put 8 shots out of 10 under a nickel at 200 yards. This in a breeze that blew two of the 45-grain bullets out for a 2″ group with only a ¾″ vertical. Groove size of barrel, .2235″.

In the summer of 1946 Lovell had a line of 12 different .22 wildcats, which assortment would permit almost any desirable type and size of .22 cartridge for which a customer might have need. With such diversity of designs, a shooting enthusiast trying to make the one best selection might find himself in much the same position as Eliza in the following story. It is said that Eliza had mothered 12 youngsters, who, when washed, slicked up and carefully arranged in a straight line, from smallest to largest, so much resembled one another, that strangers were often unable to tell 'tother from which. Eliza always claimed she could name each instantly and correctly.

One day, when showing them off, something distracted her attention for a moment, and Angelina and Parsnip suddenly swapped places, without its having been noticed. Eliza started to call off their names, in the usual manner and of course named two incorrectly.

When taken to task she exclaimed indignantly, "Angelina, you is allus No. 7 and Parsnip is allus No. 8. If any of you gits out 'er line on 'de day of Jedgment it'll make St. Peter so all-fired mad he'll send 'dis whole fambly straight into de mouf of de roarin' furnace."

To prevent anything so catastrophic happening to the 12 .22 Lovells, the author had them all labeled neatly, photographed in line and sent the print to Hervey for positive re-check. The description of each is given in the following copy, with some of his best loads, so that you may have this information compiled as accurately as voluminous but often divergent correspondence makes possible.

No. 1—Lovell K-Hornet

This is Hervey Lovell's K-Hornet (Kilbourn-Hornet) type cartridge. It should be remembered that Lovell imported and advertised .22 Hornet rifles and ammunition from abroad, long before they were sprung on the public here as a new discovery, the remarkable little cartridge evolving from the .22-13-45 C.F. Winchester, now known generally as the ".22 Hornet." The author personally saw many of those advertisements many years ago and also had correspondence about them.

THE HERVEY LOVELL LINE OF .22 WILDCAT CARTRIDGES

Left to right: No. 1, K-Hornet; No. 2, R-2 (Risley—2) with 12° shoulder; No. 3, The .22 Lovell, with 15° shoulder; No. 4, a short-neck version of .22/3000 Lovell; No. 5, another short-neck version of the .22/3000 Lovell; No. 6, The .22 Maximum Lovell—claimed by Lovell to be most efficient cartridge per grain of powder burned.

No. 7, .22 Lovell-Zipper, with 30° shoulder; No. 8, Love .22 High Power, with 24° shoulder angle; No. 9, .22-25/35 case, 30° shoulder angle. No. 10, .22-224 Lovell, F. W. Mann design. From .25-35, .30-30, or .32-40 cases. No. 11, .22-250 Lovell with 28° shoulder. Sweany design. No. 12, is .22-224-30; 1906 case. Doering-McCrea-Lovell design.

No. 8 has flattest trajectory; No. 7, .22 Lovell Improved Zipper is most accurate of lot, and best one for Hi-Side Winchester S.S. and Krag action for 1″ groups or better, at 200 yards. Comments by Lovell, for guidance of riflemen wishing cartridges with certain individual characteristics.

This No. 1 present day cartridge is the smallest of the Lovell line. It uses the same charges as given for Lysle Kilbourn's K-Hornet, itemized in another chapter. Probably the most accurate load for the K-Hornet is 12.0 grains of 4198, with 50-grain expanding bullet and Western No. 1½ primers in Winchester Super Speed cases. It also has a long case life. Another good load is 12.0 grains of 4227, which is finer and faster, and gives 2,950 f.s. in the Winchester cases and 2,850 in the Remington cases. For the 45-grain bullets they use 12.5 grains of the same powders.

Normally, this K-Hornet Lovell is moderately faster than the .22 Hornet at 2,650 f.s. muzzle velocity. Body of case is longer, shoulder is much more abrupt. It should, therefore, burn the coarser types of powders to better advantage than the standard Hornet, but not some of the faster powders.

No. 2—Lovell R-2

This is an illustration of the Risley-2 adaptation of the Lovell. This design gained its greatest popularity about 1936-1938, since which time cartridge brass of that size (.25-20 S.S. necked down) has been more difficult to obtain and later and stronger cartridges came on the market, and many of them are listed here in the Lovell line. During 1945 Lovell was not making up rifles for the R-2 case as he had, for a long time previously, concentrated on the small cases, upon his later 15° shoulder slope cartridge which is his No. 3 cartridge, called today the .22/3000 Lovell.

Loads suitable for the R-2, however, were just one grain *more* powder than for the early, gentle slope 5° Lovell. The R-2 loads are given for 1945 as 16.5 grains of 4198 and 50 or 55-grain Sisk bullet, or up to 16.5 grains of 4227 and the same bullet, or slightly lighter weight bullet, as the 4227 is faster than 4198.

No. 3—Lovell .22/3000

This is the latest .22/3000 Lovell, with 15° shoulder taper. At one time Hervey credited this with 70% of his business. It is however, no longer so popular, for the good reason that .25-20 single shot rifles have not been made for quite a number of years and not in heavy quantity for a time before that, and the demand for .25-20 *single shot* loaded and empty cartridge cases was gradually decreasing, therefore they were harder to obtain for necking down.

Another reason for changing to other cartridge brass sources is that many of the larger and more powerful commercial cartridges are made with thicker and tougher brass of advanced design, and that of course is safer to load. However, it should be clearly understood that the .22/3000 with 15° slope is just as effective, as deadly, as inexpensive to load and shoot and so long as you can get cartridge brass for it, which is quite difficult at present, it will prove just as satisfactory and as accurate as ever, because the 15° case is properly proportioned to burn 4198 or 4227.

.22/3000 Favorite Loads

Lovell recommends 15.5 to 16.0 grains of 4227 with 50-grain Sisk-Lovell bullet. Another good load is 16.5 grains of 4198 with 55-grain Sisk bullet. Or, 17.0 grains with 50-grain Sisk-Lovell bullet. A very fine load is 16.5 grains of duPont No. 4227 and 41-grain Sisk-Lovell bullet. This is a very flat shooting load for 150 to 200 yards or less which makes it a good crow and hawk load for settled communities in which you want to avoid shooting over or under crows or hawks at moderate ranges, thus making nearly every shot a kill, and with a light weight bullet that will disintegrate on almost any sort of soil or rock, if you do miss or after it penetrates the varmint. Such load avoids setting loose a sharp rifle report without hitting anything and thus attracting attention to your gunning, with no result to show for it. It is not a very good wind-bucking load, due to the light bullet. The author is definitely sold on the proposition of shooting only when you expect to make a kill, using a bullet which goes to pieces so as to avoid a whining ricochet, and of using a charge which does not give too loud a report. In open, little-settled districts, and in backfield woodchuck pastures, this is not so important, but within a 600-yard radius around farm buildings and woods of one to five acres extent, located on intensively cultivated farms, this matter of shooting and hunting without annoying the farming brethren is definitely advantageous. The .22/3000 is about the top limit and certainly nothing faster than the Kilbourn Magnum *Junior* cartridge should be used in *such* areas.

Another good .22/3000 load is 15.5 grains of 4227 and 46-grain Hornet bullet. Normally, such bullets are inexpensive and easy to obtain; they are accurate, many of them being closely designed following an early Niedner .22 bullet design; and there are numerous sources of supply, a great advantage to the rifleman; Western, Winchester and Remington make Hornet bullets.

All these loads are based on .224″ groove diameter and .224″ bullets. Also, upon a 2⅛″ or 2.125″ over-all cartridge loading

length. Bullet must *not* show land marks cut into ogive of bullet. Be
sure to remember this. Lovell calls particular attention to it, to avoid
blowing primers, primer pockets, or puncturing primers. For some
reason it seems to direct abnormal pressure to the rear at the beginning of ignition of the charge. By loading the bullet a little farther
back into the case, the bullet seems to develop a certain amount of
momentum—it has started from a state of rest and is now *moving*
toward the throat when it strikes the rifling, thus can enter the throat

A RIFLEMAKER AT WORK

Hervey Lovell testing very handsome, high wall, engraved, .219 Zipper
Cal. Winchester single shot rifle on homemade machine rest. Forearm
removed and heavy barrel resting in V Blocks. Note hand-made pistol
grip stock with cheek piece.

and the rifling with lower pressure than if started from a state of
rest directly against the rifling grooves, in which case it would have
no momentum, at the instant of starting, to help drive into the rifling
without immediately having the pressure pile up against the base of
the bullet where the gases would be roiling and churning around.

This is just an old principle of physics applied to rifle cartridge
loading and shooting—that it is much easier, and requires far less

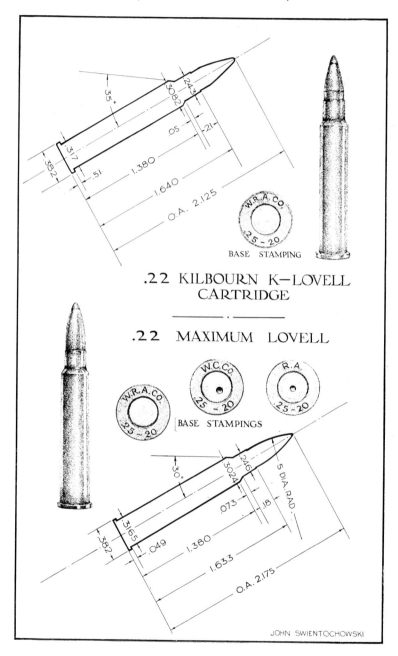

BASE STAMPING

.22 KILBOURN K—LOVELL
CARTRIDGE

.22 MAXIMUM LOVELL

BASE STAMPINGS

JOHN SWIENTOCHOWSKI

effort to keep a bullet or any other object *moving,* after it is once started from a state of rest, than to *start it* from that state of rest.

Also, as the bullet starts to move forward, the powder chamber immediately lengthens, and the powder gases start to move in the direction in which the powder chamber is enlarging its volume, and the faster that length of gas chamber increases the lower will be the chamber pressure. Some powders, too, as for instance No. 80, have a tendency in certain cartridges to develop a lot of pressure back against the head of the case, especially if the bullet is relatively heavy and hard to start forward, so we avoid much of that type of difficulty with 4198 and 4227 and similar powders by *not* loading the bullet out so that it seats into the rifling, as is done in much .30 caliber match ammunition. Much of that ammunition, too, develops quite a bit of recoil, and this is probably one of the reasons; the starting of the bullet, from a state of rest, while jammed into the throat against the end of the rifling grooves.

No. 4 and No. 5 Lovells

These were short-neck versions of the .22/3000 Lovell, with the sharper slopes. Such cases are easy to load with 17.5 grains of 4198 with *light weight* bullets, or 16.5 to 17.0 grains 4198 with 50-grain bullet. A later letter from Lovell suggests 17.5 grains of 4198, with the *short neck* and the *long case,* these being 15° shoulder taper jobs, with the long neck. This latter letter suggested 16.5 grains 4227 and the 46-grain Hornet bullet as another desirable combination.

No. 6—Maximum Lovell

This cartridge is claimed by Hervey Lovell to be the most efficient of all the .22 Lovells, as made from the .25-20 S.S. cases, necked down to various lengths and sizes, and in the instance of the Maximum Lovell then blown up to full length by shooting cases necked to R-2 shape in a Maximum Lovell chamber.

The Maximum Lovell has the flattest trajectory of any of these *small* .22 wildcat cartridges. The trajectory is not as flat, of course, as that of the many larger cartridges, most of which give higher muzzle velocity if loaded to or near the case capacity.

The .22 Maximum Lovell has an actual total drop over 200 yards of 11″, according to a letter from Remington Arms Co., which means a trajectory measured above the bore of the rifle of 2.75″ over 200 yards. The trajectory above the line of sight of the rifle, when fitted with scope sight, would be about 1¼″ at 100 yards, with 200 yards

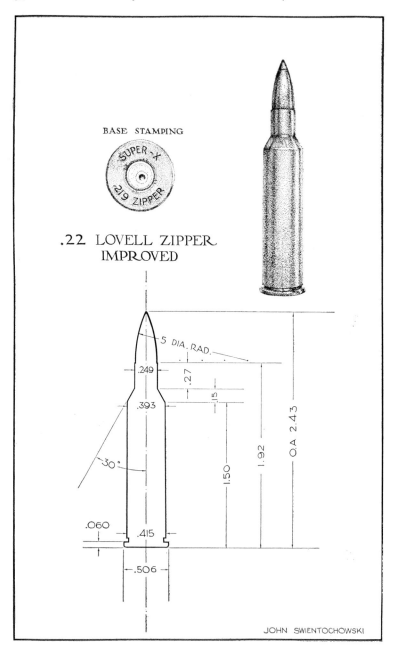

BASE STAMPING

.22 LOVELL ZIPPER
IMPROVED

5 DIA. RAD.

.249

.27

.15

.393

30°

.060

.415

.506

1.50

1.92

O.A. 2.43

JOHN SWIENTOCHOWSKI

zero sighting. As a matter of practical comment it could be inserted here that it is almost impossible for the average rifleman to get his rifle zeroed *exactly* at 200 yards, because the area of dispersion, plus wind drift, plus light changes, plus variations due to humidity changes and temperature corrections, is considerable. At 100 yards it is much easier to obtain a range which is more nearly completely protected from wind and light difficulties and you can come closer at 100 yards to a perfect sight setting.

Case Shape of Maximum Lovell

The Maximum Lovell has a long, fairly straight shape, with little taper from head to shoulder, and is designed to hold all the powder it is possible to load into a .22 caliber case made from the .25-20 cartridge. It has a sharper shoulder angle—of 30° slope, to burn 18.3 to 18.5 grains of 4198 with 55-grain or 50-grain Sisk bullet as a maximum charge in a 16″ twist barrel with .224″ groove measurement. Kilbourn gives his Maximum Lovell cartridge as having a 35° shoulder.

For the shooter who must economize in powder charge, wants to obtain all the velocity possible, and the highest possible accuracy, in a *small* cartridge, and without developing too sharp a report, this is one of the best selections. It does not require a reamed case mouth or special bullets. Lovell does not appear to have worked up any special loads using W-M 8S bullets.

Normal charge is 18.2 to 18.3 grains of 4198. You can use a finer powder if you wish, in which instance, stick to lighter weight bullets, like 41 to 46-grain. This is one of the best looking sharp shoulder cartridges of small size on the market. For a more powerful cartridge, or one giving better results over 250 to 350 or 400 yards, try the No. 7 Lovell, next following.

No. 7—Lovell Improved Zipper

This is the super accurate 200-yard H. Lovell cartridge. It has a shoulder angle of 30° and is made from the .219 Zipper cartridge case. The reformed case has a diameter at shoulder of .393″ and uses 36.5 to 36.6 grains of 4320 with 50-grain bullets, with No. 115 primer or, it does well with 33.0 grains of 4064 and 55-grain bullets, according to Lovell's experience. Notice that as the case is increased in size they go to the longer, heavier bullets, as they have plenty of powder to drive them and sufficient case capacity to keep down pressures.

A number of gunsmiths, including P. O. Ackley and W. F. Vickery have done well with "improved" .219 Zippers. It is a good heavy brass case of moderate size, made originally from the .25-35 case necked down, has rather pleasing lines, and the sharper shoulder wildcats seem to shoot much better than the gentle slope factory load. Had it appeared in the Model 70 and 720 rifles the Zipper might have established a much better reputation for accuracy. This .22 Lovell Zipper is a good sensible selection for an all-around wildcat cartridge. The fact that his clientele is obtaining better accuracy in this one form, than any other Lovell wildcat, should commend it to every fox, woodchuck and coyote hunter, also the long-range crow shooter who has plenty of space out in front of him and wants a rifle of medium power and range to ring the bell shot after shot.

No. 8—Lovell .22 Hi-Power Improved

This is the .22 Hi-Power Savage case with re-vamped 24° shoulder angle, .370″ shoulder diameter. The empty case is 2.00″ long, 1.58″ up to the shoulder, as measured by the author, using a fine engineer's scale. In comparison the No. 7, the Zipper Improved, is 1.92″ overall and 1.50″ up to the shoulder. The case is therefore 0.08″ longer to the shoulder, and is also 0.023″ *less* in diameter, at the shoulder. This means that it is a longer, more evenly contoured case with different case taper. *All* the Lovell cartridges have *rimmed* cases except No. 11 and No. 12.

Both No. 7 and No. 8 are well-proportioned, good looking cartridge designs, both are made of tough, thick brass, and other wildcat specialists have had excellent results with cartridges made very much like them.

For No. 8 the .22 Hi-Power Improved, Lovell recommends 31.0 grains of 3031 or 32.0 grains of 4064 with 50-grain Sisk bullet. This projectile is .224″ in diameter. Hervey claims this cartridge gives the flattest trajectory of any of his 12 Lovells. That it has shown drops of ¾″ and ⅞″ at 200 yards below the 100-yard point of impact. This, of course, means when fired in a telescopically sighted rifle with line of sight about 1⅝″ above the bore, therefore making the bullet climb about 2½″ in 100 yards. It is said this cartridge and load will drive a 45-grain Hornet bullet through ½″ of steel at 100 yards, using 31.0 grains of 4064.

The Lovell .22 Hi-Power is used in a rifle with 16″ twist, .224″ groove diameter. It is suitable for a Krag action or a Hi-Side Winchester single shot, or any other action equally strong and adequate for rimmed cases.

The .22 Hi-Power cases are formed by firing a light load in each in the chambered rifle and this can be done nicely and inexpensively by using 25.0 grains of salvaged Pyro D.G.

N. 9—.22-25/35 Lovell Improved

The original case was made by necking down the .25-35 cartridge case, making the outside shoulder diameter 0.393″, with 30° slope of shoulder, and to hold 34.0 grains of 4064. The ammunition situation being what it is, and knowing the .22 Hi-Power case was made originally by necking down the .25-35 to .22 caliber, the author was not surprised when he received this case actually made from the .22 Hi-Power case. Angelina and Parsnip probably got fidgety and swapped places again, but no matter.

The rifle for this case is chambered by using the reamer ordinarily used to chamber for the Zipper Improved cartridge No. 7 on the list, but running it in farther, for a case ⅛″ longer. The case holds two grains more powder and is rather straight with very gradual taper up to the shoulder.

The No. 8 Lovell case is 2.03″ over-all and measures 1.580″ up to the shoulder, which is rounded rather gently. The Nos. 7, 8 and 9 look much alike in a photo, showing only slight difference in outline and capacity, but Lovell claims the No. 7 has made more groups of five shots each, less than 1″ in diameter, at 200 yards, in a number of different rifles of that Lovell caliber, than any other on the list.

No. 10—.22 Mann-Lovell; Called the .22 Super Lovell

This usually is made from the .25-35, .30-30 or .32-40 case but the one sent the author was made from the Savage .22 Hi-Power case, necked to hold the .224″ bullet. It uses 31.0 grains of 3031 with 50-grain bullet which charge develops 3,900 f.s. ± velocity on J. Bushnell's Smith's chronograph. It is based on moderate taper of case, chamber made with Brown & Sharpe #3 taper, ½″ taper per foot. Lovell's Zipper is ¼″ taper per foot, standard taper pin. This number is Dr. Franklin W. Mann's design in which he used 19.0 grains of Hercules Lightning, with 60-grain home-made .227″ base band bullets. Grooves in those days—around 1910—were .227″. The barrels were cut with 14″ twist, were .22 W.R.F. nickel steel No. 3 barrels, according to Lovell, and the velocity produced was 3,400 f.s., giving ½″ trajectory at half-way over 100 yards.

Lovell's first rifle for this Mann case design was made around 1912, and was mounted on a Stevens 49 action which he used for

300-meter matches. After the First World War, he used a 70-grain Savage bullet and 27.0 grains of duPont No. 18 powder. This was a finer grain propellant than No. 16 or 17. Cases were never resized to reload.

Lovell commented that recently Marciante, Gebby and McCrea had designed similar cases under the names of Marciante Blue Streak; Jr. Varminter, (Gebby); and McCrea's Super .22 Hi-

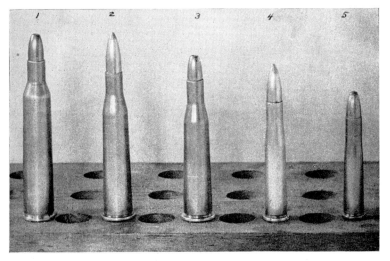

A FEW LOVELL LOADINGS

L. to R.: .220 Swift, reported not more accurate than .219 Zipper or .22 Savage H.P. when all used in equally good rifles—but has flatter trajectory; Long body .22 Hi-Power, 50-gr. Sisk bullet, 31 grs. 3031. Est. M.V. 3,600 f.s.—body length ⅛" greater than Zipper; .219 Winchester Zipper with 56-gr. O.P. bullet—accurate in heavy single shots; .22/3000 Lovell with 50-gr. Sisk bullet ahead of 16.2 grs. 4198—3,200 f.s.; .22 Hornet.

Power. Lovell made six rifles for this old timer, using one himself on a Tell action. The only drawback, he says, was extraction when the long body of this taper shows pressure near the base as most all *long* cases do when loaded to full capacity.

This gun maker commented, also, that the shorter case and better brass of the Zipper (and Improved Zipper) holds and uses more powder with resulting better accuracy. The Improved Zipper is an outstanding cartridge among all the wildcats. It appears to be Lovell's favorite today, although the .22 Super-Lovell, or whatever you want to call it, made from the .22 H.P. Savage case, was his favorite some years ago before he began to play with the .219 Zipper case. The Improved Zipper can be used in a Krag action. It can also be used very successfully in the Hi-Side Winchester single shot action, and makes an ideal crow and woodchuck caliber, where report is permissible. Lovell says himself that the .22 Lovell Improved Zipper cartridge is more accurate than any .22/3000 Lovell R-2 and he also claimed, in letter of May 15, 1945 to the author, that it gave more accurate results than the Varminter or the .22-250 cartridges. The load is the Improved Zipper case full—level full—of 4064 and the 50-grain bullet. He says this makes a perfectly balanced load in this caliber. That it is the first caliber with which he could make 1" groups at 200 yards rest, and that several of his customers had made smaller than 1" groups at 200 yards, with this cartridge.

Makes All These Calibers

Lovell stated that as of May 15, 1945, he was making rifles for all 12 of the Lovell cartridges, in about equal numbers, but he prefers to make the calibers that are most accurate for the customers—easy for a beginner to load best and with the longest case and rifle bore *life*. The case which comes in factory loaded form, ready to shoot and form in the chambers, is what he prefers.

No. 11—Lovell .22-250

This Lovell case, the No. 11 on the list, is the .250/3000 Savage case necked first in .22 caliber, 28° shoulder. It was first developed by Sweany, the California gunsmith, and one of the best experimenters, in Lovell's judgment, in the United States.

This cartridge is now called the .22-250, while it and the .22 Varminter are often called the Wotkyns .220 West of the Rockies. All Red Elliott fine chambering reamers for this caliber sold out West are stamped, according to Lovell, "Wotkyns .220 Swift."

In Lovell's opinion, the .250 Savage case is not as good brass and bridge (web) as the 7mm, .220 Swift or .30-1906, when cut to 1 15/16" length of the .250. Lovell claims that a shoulder angle of 30° shows more uniform accuracy than the original 28° shoulder angle usually made by dozens of shops. The standard load for this case is given by Lovell as 36.6 grains of 4320 and a 50-grain cased bullet, which, he says, gives higher velocity and better accuracy in the Improved Zipper case, which is suitable for Krags and for Hi-Side Winchester single shots. He comments that the Wilson .220 Arrow-altered Swift case will shoot flatter with equal or better accuracy, but the .250 necked to fit and hold the .224″ bullet received most of the ballyhoo and buildup. This is given as a gunsmith's comment and as giving his reactions and beliefs as of this period, when, as a matter of fact he probably would just as soon build one as the other, insofar as financial returns are concerned.

We must all remember that everyone is entitled to his own views; that there is always some feeling, unfortunately, between competitive makers of most anything from mouse traps to tanks, and that this must be borne in mind when considering any set of claims and comments. Everyone sees the matter from where he sits, from his own experience and that of his customers in whom he has most confidence.

The average sporting goods dealer thinks his competitor up the street is not all the law should insist upon, and competitive manufacturers and retailers, large and small, are at times liable to agree that their closest competitor is not exactly endowed by heaven, or is at all sure of eventually going there.

After all, there is good and bad in almost every design and in every person. There are even points about many so-called scientific theories which appear largely contrary to fact, or which do not always seem to work out 100% in daily life. It is unfortunate for us all that such conditions occur but we must bear these in mind when coming to any general set of conclusions. It is well to hear all sides, weigh one against the other, and finally pick your choice when necessary with every possible viewpoint and determination in mind. Practically every wildcat specialist or gunsmith wants to see riflemen properly outfitted; he wants to help them where and whenever he can and it is a stupid man who does not heed the suggestion of those who have had opportunity to draw conclusions from many men and many cartridges.

No. 12—.22-30/1906 Lovell

This is a Doering-McCrea-Lovell design. It is the .30-1906 cartridge case cut off, necked down to hold .224″ bullets and to use the same loads as the .22-250 or the .22 Varminter. The reason for this one appears to be that of .30-1906 cases being comparatively easy to obtain, and also being tough and strong, and heavy-weight stock.

The .30-1906, .270 W.C.F., 7mm, 7.9mm and .257 Remington-Roberts can all be used to make these cases, as they all have the same, or approximately the same head diameter, and they all contain good weight stock.

The empty or the loaded cartridge of this caliber feels quite heavy, singly or a box of them, as the cartridge case is heavy as compared with previous numbers in the Lovell series. The case has very little body taper from head to shoulder. The .22-30/1906 case measured 0.473″ at the cannelure and 0.440″ at the shoulder. The result is a cartridge with very little taper of case. It could extract hard if loaded heavily and shot in a chamber which has been allowed to rust even slightly; on the other hand, the case was nicely polished and most gun cranks clean and oil, regardless of ballyhoo.

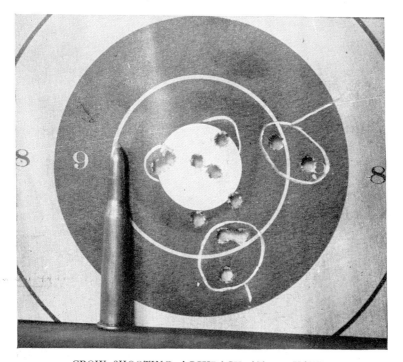

CROW SHOOTING ACCURACY AT 200 YARDS

Hervey Lovell's .22 H.P. bolt action Mauser heavy barrel rifle shot these at 200 yards. 55-gr. Sisk bullet and 29 grs. 3031, est. velocity. 3,400 f.s.

The neck of the cartridge is 0.25″ long, the shoulder is drawn in at a very flat slope and very sharp angle and is also drawn in a great distance, because we have here a large .30 caliber cartridge necked down sharply to a neck of .224″ inside diameter and thus without the usual degree of case slope on the sides.

To the author, this case does not have as good lines, from the shoulder forward, as the others in the Lovell series. However, it provides one with a more certain method of getting cartridge case brass.

Lovell advises that he sent Doering the first barrel of this type which McCrea then stocked in the Bull-Pup style. McCrea has one now but Lovell does not as yet have his own rifle of this caliber finished. He says there is too much work connected with cutting, necking and reaming cases in a lathe chuck, with a third sizing die, and if orders come in for this one, in volume, "I won't be home." The butler will draw himself up in his best English butler's manner and say "the mawster is *out!*" He will then close the gunshop door, gently but firmly, and you will have to go back to your car, with your rifle action, stock and ideas and you will likely become huffed and *slam* the car door hard! Maybe very hard!

A rifleman with a pet idea he insists upon putting into wood and steel may not always be correct in his ideas or fair in his demands. While the above was intended as a pleasantry, sometimes the gunsmith or his assistants are at fault and feeling develops. After all, it is the customers money which is being spent. A fair and reasonable attitude is needed on both sides.

Considering everything; the present scarcity of .25-20 single shot cases to neck down; the condition that .25-20 single shot rifles have not been made for some years and not in large quantities for a good many seasons; and that .25-20 repeater cases are not suitable; and the further fact that .30-1906 cases are excessively large for a .25—and certainly too large for a .22—and must be cut off to be necked into any reasonable size and powder capacity; the preference of Lovell and others for cartridge cases which are between these two extremes is easy to fathom.

One of the better loads for the .22-30/1906 Lovell case is 36.6 grains of 4320 and the 50-grain Sisk bullet.

The Nos. 7, 8 or 9 cases would seem better selections today, unless some firm should make quantities of .22/3000 Lovell cases (Winchester did make .22/3000 cases for a while) and factory loaded cartridges, or the R-2, or the Maximum Lovell case, as a regular large scale proposition. And that, incidentally, would be a splendid thing for riflemen and would help the game very materially; and would also give such firm a new, exclusive and very accurate and most efficient cartridge. Some of the best cartridge cases on the market have been rifle crank designs.

So much has been said about the .22/3000 Lovell cartridge—the original gentle slope Lovell—that numberless people think that Hervey Lovell does not and has not produced and supplied any other .22 wildcat cartridges. Such is far from the case. The small .25-20 case .22/3000 Lovell has not been *his* favorite cartridge since about 1938 or 1939.

No more skillful class of riflemen exist on this planet than those who use .22 and .25 caliber wildcat cartridges in special heavy, field shooting rifles for woodchuck and similar shooting. No more difficult-to-please aggregation of men exist anywhere in the shooting game. Therefore, what *they* consider good and what the gunsmiths who cater individually to these riflemen think are best, as a result of the combined experience of their customers and themselves, is likely to be the *most accurate* and most effective type of cartridge and rifle obtainable today in North America.

A gunsmith or a firm of custom rifle makers, providing but one, two or three cartridges of such type, may be both experienced and skillful and they might be quite honest and sincere, but it is obvious that they are limited to only those very few cartridges they provide. When they supply 10 or 12 cartridges, however, or rifles built for them, and have therefore, a clientele which covers a larger and more diversified field, it is more probable that their own recommendations would more accurately fulfill your real requirements, if you will state them clearly, than in the case of those who have fewer rifle cartridges from which a limited selection may be made. It would appear to the author, therefore, that a gunsmith like Lovell should be able and would be inclined to make a practical selection from his various cartridges if you will tell him the exact type and varieties of game and varmints you expect to hunt and, most particularly, if you will advise the average *range* at which you expect to shoot and the type of country in which the shooting is to be done. This should always include information as to whether the *report* of the cartridge is liable to cause you to lose your shooting rights, if too sharp. As a general rule any small bore cartridge which is really effective on woodchucks and coyotes or hawks, at 300 to 400 yards, will have a very sharp report and it will also be a high pitched and piercing report. Any cartridge which is really effective on the average shot at 225 to 250 yards, will have a moderately sharp report. In the woods, on damp days, it will carry quite far. If the average shot is not beyond 75 to 150 yards then the .22 Hornet, the K-Hornet or the .22/3000 Lovell is plenty of cartridge and you will merely risk being run out oftener than necessary by using a rifle of greater powder capacity and sharper report. It is not so much the volume of sound which annoys landowners as the high pitched crack.

The recoil is not a factor with any normal wildcat of .22 caliber if your rifle and scope together weigh from $8\frac{1}{2}$ to $10\frac{1}{2}$ pounds or more, for the reason that it will not be more than 1 to $4\frac{1}{2}$ foot pounds. Consequently, the factors of accuracy, range, barrel life, report, difficulty and expense of obtaining components are the important factors to keep in mind in choosing the cartridge. Lovell should be able to give you practical and sensible advice on all of these subjects.

A rifleman should always remember two things: if he cannot take the time or give the study and skill necessary to loading *good* hand-loaded wildcat ammunition he should buy a rifle for which factory ammunition can readily be obtained in normal times. Do not buy a rifle for a cartridge for which brass cases cannot be secured readily or just because the rifle is cheap. There is usually a reason for the low price in these days.

If you select a rifle too powerful for the game or varmint you are hunting, you are worse off than shooting an arm just a trifle too weak in power or too short in range. The 4,000 to 5,000 f.s. sounds wonderful in the catalog or sporting magazine's Gun Department but in practice you are then shooting a cartridge delivering the kinetic energy of a deer rifle and the bullet is traveling so fast the energy of the speeding bullet is delivered to the body of the object shot in such a small fraction of a second that all soft parts of the bird or small animal are shredded, distributed over 25 to 400 square feet, and when picked up it has the appearance of having been blasted. A wild turkey will be badly shattered by such a bullet, even of .22 caliber.

Unless you can average at least 95 per cent on the small bore prone target at 100 or 200 yards and in addition are a real good offhand shot, or when aiming along the side of a tree trunk or over the top of a fence post, do not dally too much with the idea that you require a rifle that will enable you to kill woodchucks at 400 yards. Your limit of reasonably consistent hits may be about 125 yards and anything over an R-2 is wasting energy.

If you are considering ordering a Lovell barrel-chambering job, loading tool and .22 Lovell wildcat cartridge, be guided largely by what this book suggests or what he tells you. Over the last 30 or 40 years he has learned a good bit about woodchuck rifles and cartridges.

Remember that the stamp of an expert rifleman, in the field, is that of a man who walks along quietly looking over the country; he chooses his places to sit and watch for shots with due regards to dens, feeding grounds, woodlots, men working in fields, livestock and a safe background for his bullet. He may not fire more than half a dozen shots in a day, but four or five of these should be clean kills; on exceptional days, all six. If game is plentiful he should fire 12 or 15 shots, but rarely will he shoot more than once or twice an hour. He soon learns the normal effective range for his rifle and cartridge, and seldom shoots at anything much beyond that. You will find that he is much more concerned with making a clean kill on every shot than in taking pot shots at everything in sight or in firing at a woodchuck 400 yards away on yonder hill just to see the dust fly.

Rarely are farmers, landowners and ranchers annoyed by the presence of a rifle shot in whose judgment, skill and careful methods of hunting and shooting they have come to have confidence. They invite such a rifleman back to kill off the excess woodchucks. They are glad that every now and then he shoots a crow, a game-destroying variety of hawk, or a coyote.

This book is intended to get you interested in knowing more about that kind of rifle, cartridges and rifle shooting. This chapter, and those which follow, discuss the output of men and firms which have specialized in the design and making of the most accurate and specialized kinds of high velocity, super-accurate .22 caliber rifles, cartridges, bullets, loads and the equipment needed to put such ammunition together.

By comparing the output of different concerns and then picking a cartridge which appears, from the comment given, to meet the conditions which *you* will face in the hunting field, you should be able to select an outfit or a number of them which will serve you well, serve you efficiently and which, with care, should last you the rest of your lifetime.

Most of the Lovell cartridges are .22 caliber, are of small or medium size, well designed, accurate, easily loaded and flat shooting. All of them are too powerful, in full loads, for red, gray and fox squirrels or ruffed grouse but, when loaded with a 35 to 45-grain bullet and 3.5 to 6.0 grains of a powder like No. 80 or Unique, they can be made to do for such shooting. Essentially, they are crow, hawk, woodchuck and coyote cartridges. They comprise one of the most accurate and efficient lines of special cartridges on the market, and any of them from the .22/3000 on up, will do deadly work on deer in the hands of a man who can qualify as both a hunter and a rifleman.

CHAPTER 6

THE LYSLE D. KILBOURN .22-K WILDCAT
CARTRIDGES

LYSLE D. KILBOURN, of Whitesboro, New York, a town
lying between Albany and Syracuse, is a woodchuck shooting
gunsmith who prices his services in line with the quaint idea there
are many more men prepared to spend a moderate amount of
money to convert a favorite rifle into a .22 high velocity wildcat
than are in a position to spend much greater sums. This is so
unusual among custom gunsmiths that the author felt that it
merited special announcement at the head of this chapter. There
are today many who need better rifles but many less who are
prepared to pay enough to purchase them. Kilbourn's re-chambering
will help some, for this reason.

The whole Kilbourn line of .22 wildcats is quite obviously designed for economical shooting and easy carrying. He provides a
small, powder-saving cartridge, or, if you prefer, a whole line of
six cartridges with a seventh on special order, which in size step
up in regular procession.

From smallest to largest, in regular order, they follow:

Cartridge	Shoulder Angle	Diameter at Shoulder
1. .22 K-Hornet Junior	35°	.2915″
2. .22 K-Hornet	35°	.2885″
3. .22 K.-Lovell (About same as Maximum Lovell)	35°	.3082″
4. .22 K-Zipper	25°	.4075″ to .4085″
5. .22 K-Magnum Rimless	25°	.4075″ to .4085″
6. .22 K-Hi-Power	25°	.407″ to .4075″
7. .22 K-Magnum Junior	25°	.4019″

94

The first four, and the sixth, are *rimmed* cartridges. The first two are formed from .22 Hornet cartridges; the third from the .25-20 S.S. Stevens cartridge formed in R-2; the fourth from the .219 Zipper; the fifth from the .30 Remington Rimless—it can also be made from the .25 Remington Rimless or the .32 Remington Rimless; the sixth from the .22 Savage Hi-Power; the seventh from the .25 Remington Rimless.

All of these are of small or of medium, center fire type. None is abnormally large or long, thus requiring too much forming or cutting of brass, nor are any especially fat and squatty. Most are made with little taper. It should be understood that the Kilbourn cartridges made from the .219 Zipper, .30 Remington Rimless and .22 Savage Hi-Power cartridges have much *stronger* cases than the three smaller cartridges. Also, they each hold a good deal more smokeless power.

The .22 K-Hornet Junior

This is a short, stubby cartridge that Lysle Kilbourn produced for safe use in Low-Side single shot Winchesters and for other single shot rifles such as the 44½ Stevens Ideal, and those lower number Ideals having the 44½ action, which he assumed were scarcely of the proper frame and action strength to successfully handle the normal pressures of the .22 Hornet cartridge. Anyway, the Junior accomplishes this by supplying insufficient chamber length for insertion of the regular Hornet cartridge. This of course precludes the use of factory Hornet ammunition in the .22 K-Hornet Junior—you just can not close the breech.

On the other hand, the .22 K-Hornet Junior *can* be reloaded into the usual pressure range of the regular .22 Hornet factory ammunition, and when so loaded, is no safer in light action and with light breech mechanisms than the regular standard .22 Hornet ammunition. It is, of course, probably safer then than the regular .22 Hornet ammunition would be if *that* be overloaded.

Kilbourn's idea was to confine the K-Hornet Junior to 2,000 f.s. loads, a very good idea in *most* settled localities.

Ness reported that a rifle Kilbourn had chambered for the K-Hornet Junior gave better accuracy when *overloaded* than when normally loaded. This, of course, would have the tendency to encourage overloading, thus destroying the theoretical usefulness of the cartridge, at least in the hands of many riflemen. Most shooters have a tendency to shoot maximum normal loads, to obtain greater killing power and flatter trajectory, and most of our so-called "improved" wildcats are nothing more than a normal cartridge either made longer and of greater powder capacity, or made with a sharper shoulder slope to step-up pressures with many of the later duPont powders, which, in some cases, seems to improve burning qualities in small cartridges particularly. Small, that is, for the larger-grained powders of these types, normally made mostly for larger calibers.

Ness reported the Junior Kilbourn to have the following maximum powder capacity: 10.5 grains of 2400; 9.5 grains of 4227; 8.8 grains of 4198; or 6.7 grains of 4759 powder. The first is a Hercules brand, the others duPont.

Kilbourn's favorite load for the Kilbourn Hornet Junior is a cast, gas-check 43-grain bullet and 8.5 grains of No. 2400 Hercules, which he gives as producing about 2,200 f.s.m.v. This load is also good, so he reports, for 35-grain jacketed bullets.

Fred Ness developed a favorite load for it—a 44-grain lead alloy bullet and 8.5 grains of 4227. His best load was the 45-grain Sisk bullet for the .22 Hornet rifle (a metal-cased bullet) and using 6.7 grains of 4759. Another Ness load was 10.5 grains of 2400 and the 35-grain Spitfire bullet. Other loads were given as 44-grain gas-check alloy bullet with 8.0 grains of 2400, or 8.5 grains of 4227. His best load of this type was quoted as being 6.7 grains of 4759 and this lead bullet, using Remington pistol primers. Also, 9.5 grains of 2400 and 40-grain Spitfire bullet, which did well at 100 and 200 yards.

The .22 K-Hornet Junior has a case length of 1.065″. This was given by Ness as the mouth of the K-Hornet Junior just reaching the shoulder of the regular K-Hornet. This is not quite accurate with the ammunition sent the author by Kilbourn. The length of case is correct but the K-Hornet shoulder is higher; it is opposite the front end of the straight portion of the bullet in the Junior. The comparison he probably actually meant was that the mouth of the K-Hornet was just opposite the shoulder of the .22 K-Lovell, which is a still larger cartridge, approximately the same size as the .22 Maximum Lovell.

The author is not especially intrigued by the shape or appearance of the Kilbourn Junior Hornet. He would rather have a rifle made for the regular .22 Hornet cartridge. However, the Hornet Junior may have possibilities.

Today we *do* need a .22 center fire cartridge of more modest ballistic possibilities than the present 2,650 f.s. Hornet charge. The author believes this can be obtained by underloading the present .22 Hornet, in which case any charge can be obtained, as required,

between that and the maximum. It should be brought out here, that
no standard factory load of *any* caliber, has ever made a reputation
for accuracy with a load giving between 1,575 f.s.m.v. and 1,900
f.s.m.v. This would include at least 200 consecutive shots. It is an
area of velocities which it appears desirable to avoid. In it, you obtain
a desirable degree of killing power for the larger small game, but
you do not appear to also obtain the desired high degree of accuracy.

There seem to have been but very few Kilbourn Hornet Juniors
made. Ness reported a degree of accuracy for this cartridge of 1¼″
to 6″ at 100 yards—and there may have been worse targets not
mentioned. No one else appears to have tested it extensively. As
there is no factory loaded ammunition available for the Hornet Junior, and no likelihood of such, at least soon, the standard Hornet
cartridge appears more desirable. The author is not prejudiced
against this cartridge, but he has never seen *any* cartridge of this size
and shape which *did* give a high degree of accuracy, in either .22 or
.25 calibers. Were it possible to supply a design apparently suited to
a much higher degree of accuracy and a still lower average muzzle
velocity, yet materially above that of the .22 Long Rifle H.V., or
the .22 W.R.F. H.V., such cartridge should be popular. As the
matter stands he considers all of the other five Kilbourn cartridges
superior in ballistic design.

.22 K-Hornet (35° Shoulder Slope)

This cartridge is generally known as the .22 Kilbourn-Hornet. It
is formed by firing regular standard .22 Hornet factory cartridges
in a rifle chambered for the K-Hornet cartridge. The standard .22
Hornet Winchester factory cartridge has a long, very gentle slope of
shoulder, and a bullet stop ring crimped around the case, just below
the bullet base. The length of the case above this cannelure is 0.25″.
When this case fills out in the elongated chamber of the K-Hornet
rifle, we have a straight portion, or with a very straight taper, 1.13″
long, then a very sharp abrupt shoulder, of 35° slope, which is *short,*
and a neck about 0.22″. The over-all length of the K-Hornet empty
case is apparently just the same as that of the factory Hornet. The
case sent the author measures 1.39″ over-all, and the loaded cartridge,
1.88″ over-all, when containing a metal-cased bullet having a long,
nearly straight-taper ogive.

The K-Hornet is claimed to be the fastest and most efficient cartridge of *its size* yet developed. The shoulder on this cartridge was
designed largely on the ideas suggested by G. B. Crandall, gunsmith,
of Woodstock, Ontario, and Mr. Kilbourn wishes to have this

JOHN SWIENTOCHOWSKI

· BASE STAMPING ·

· .22 KILBOURN K — HORNET ·

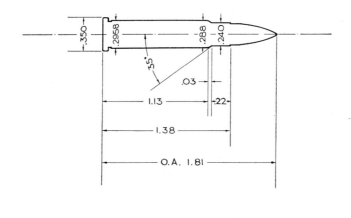

brought out in appreciation of Mr. Crandall's design. It is very inexpensive to have a Hornet rifle re-chambered by Kilbourn for the K-Hornet cartridge and this re-chambering gives a cartridge which can be normally loaded to give approximately 20% to 25% higher velocity, and thus increases the effective range of the .22 Hornet by 50 to 75 or even 100 yards, depending upon the size of the game.

Various riflemen, experimenters and gunsmiths, including Mr. Crandall, describe the K-Hornet and the K-Lovell (or Maximum Lovell) cartridges as giving the most in killing power, range, accuracy, flatness of trajectory in proportion to the money invested in the rifle, in ammunition, and in cheapness of shooting; especially in using a very small amount of powder and not too expensive a bullet, to get results on such game and varmints as woodchucks, hawks, owls (including the very large owls), buzzards, crows, gophers and similar targets at ranges up to about 250 yards or slightly beyond. Furthermore, the report, while sharp, is not too loud and piercing, is more like the .22 Hornet report than like the .220 Swift, which is noisy and penetrating and is likely to cause complaints from farmers and owners of estates, on which shooting is done, sometimes without too much previous discussion. One way to get a little shooting these days is to be quiet, use a low-report rifle, and keep your mouth closed about what you are doing or have done. Sometimes it *does not* pay to advertise. You are pretty sure to be doing a good, old-fashioned, practical, game-saving piece of work. Neither Simon Kenton nor Daniel Boone went around advertising in advance when they were going to fire at something or where, neither did they feel impelled, always, to ask someone whether they "oughter." A man can sometimes do his daily good deed, in shooting, alone and in silence. You may have observed this and profited thereby. And so does the game in your vicinity!

Recommended Loads for the .22 K (Kilbourn) Hornet

The most recent loads recommended to the author by Kilbourn, as being his *best* loads, as determined by field shooting and chronograph testing:

A 50-grain jacketed bullet and 12.0 grains of No. 4198, with No. 1½ primer; m.v. not given. Probably about 2,800—2,900 f.s. depending upon carrtidge case used. This load was primed with Western No. 1½ primer. Kilbourn reports Remington No. 1½ primers appear to give different results and do not work as well. He says this charge of 12.0 grains of 4198, 50-grain bullet and Western No. 1½ primers is *very* accurate and gives long cartridge case life.

LOADS OF #4227 FOR IMPROVED KILBOURN-HORNET

Bullet Weight Jacketed	Powder Charge	Win. SS Ctg.	Rem. Ctg.
50-grain	12.0	2950	2850
45-grain	12.5	3050	....
45-grain	13.0	....	3000
40-grain	12.5	3100	3000
40-grain	13.0	3150	3050

Loads as low as 11.5 grains with 40-grain bullet, and as high as 13.5 grains with 40 and with 45-grain bullets, and up to 14.0 grains in Remington cases, *only*, with 40-grain bullet, have been tested by Kilbourn, but above *recommended* loads gave better results.

RECOMMENDED LOADS OF 2400 FOR IMPROVED KILBOURN-HORNET GIVEN AS MOST DESIRABLE LOADS, BY LYSLE KILBOURN

	Charge	W.R.A. Cases	Rem. Cases
45-grain bullet	11.5	3150	3050
40-grain bullet	12.0	3250	3150
40-grain bullet	13.0	....	3250

Kilbourn suggests Hercules No. 2400 powder for 35 and 40-grain bullets in the K-Hornet. Crandall uses 11.5 grains of No. 2400.

Additional loads have been tested, including one of 11.5 grains with 50-grain bullet, and heavier loads with the lighter bullets, but above loads recommended by Kilbourn gave better results.

Hornet loading tools that neck-size only, such as Belding & Mull and Ideal No. 3, can be used as is for K-Hornet. Kilbourn checks head space and can correct same, when desired and needed. He makes re-cut Hornet die and bullet-seaters for K-Hornet and checks bedding of barrel if whole rifle is shipped. He has told the author he makes his own chambering reamers.

Normal speed of the K-Hornet is given as 3,300 f.s. with 40-grain bullet, if loaded to full capacity; 3,100 f.s. with 45-grain bullet and 2,850 f.s. with 50-grain bullet. This is sufficient to disintegrate bullet when striking stones, sand, earth, or rock and will do fair wind bucking.

The author likes the contour of this cartridge, but would expect some case loss in expanding if brass is not annealed properly. Regular Hornet loads can be used on close-in woodchuck shooting when merely expanding cases.

The .22 K-Lovell (35° Shoulder Slope)

The .22 K or Kilbourn Lovell is Lysle Kilbourn's "Maximum Lovell" size cartridge. It is made from the .25-20 Stevens single shot cartridge. It is a very good looking and well proportioned case and is probably just about as powerful and effective a design as can safely be made from this design of case.

The case—that is the .22 K-Lovell case—is 1.625" long. The main or straight taper part of the cartridge, as re-formed, is 1.38" long, including the head, and the neck is 0.225" long. Shoulder is very abrupt, 35° slope, same as K-Hornet. The over-all length of the loaded cartridge will, of course, vary with the length and contour of the bullet used, but the one at hand, with a long, soft-point 8S type of bullet, measures 1.65" with the bullet seated.

When a .22 K-Lovell and a K-Hornet cartridge are stood on end, side by side, the mouth of the K-Hornet just comes up to the shoulder of the K-Lovell. There is rather substantial increase in powder capacity over the K-Hornet and the case, if anything, is a trifle better looking although both give a good impression of chamber design.

Kilbourn's favorite load for the K-Lovell, he says, is 17.0 grains up to 18.5 grains of 4198, the exact load used varying with different rifles, and whether using 45-grain, 50-grain or 55-grain bullets, the heavier bullets using less powder for corresponding pressures. The longer, heavier bullets always give the higher pressures *anyhow*.

Speeds are normally from 3,300 to 3,500 f.s.m.v., at least with the light bullets.

Kilbourn uses the long drop tube for 18.2 grains and regular drop tube for 17.5 grains, thrown with Ideal powder measure.

Fred Ness reported ⅝" to ¾" five-shot groups made at 135 yards and reported to him by Kilbourn. These were shot by the 40-grain 8S bullet ahead of 17.3 grains of 4198 in a Low-Wall Winchester single shot, using No. 6½ R.A. primers.

Cartridges fired with a test load of 18.2 grains of 4198 held for an average of 10 reloads per case. Groups were reported as having been three, five-shot groups with the 40-grain 8S bullet and 17.3 grains of 4198 which measured 13/16" and 11/16"; one, six-shot group of 1¼"; five shots with 17.8 grains of 4198 and No. 116 W.R.A. primer and 50-grain bullet measured 1¼"; with the 41-grain bullet, six shots in seven measured ⅞"; the 47-grain bullet did about the same with six shots in seven; five shots, then at 100 yards, with the last load, gave a 1⅛" group; the 50-grain Sisk bullet was tried for six shots and gave a round group of 1¼" for 100 yards; using a load of 50-grain Sisk-Lovell bullet and 18.2 grains of

4198, in a scope sighted rifle, the group measured 1.15″ at 100 yards and the same five-shot group was 3.56″ at 200 yards and striking 1″ high at 100 yards and 3″ low at 200 yards. Remember this is not the trajectory of the bullet above the bore, but the bullet flight in relation to the line of sight, which is the practical field trajectory in hunting.

A charge of the 55-grain S.N. bullet, with 17.5 grains of 4198, had a point of impact 1″ high at 100 yards and just under 2″ low at 200 yards, measured from the sighting line of the rifle telescope.

This rifle had a Farquharson action and apparently had an original R-2 Lovell barrel—re-chambered for the K-Lovell case by Kilbourn. The arm had apparently been shot considerably before re-chambering from the K-2 to the R-2 Lovell cartridge.

C. F. Hober, of Belmont, New York, is reported to have killed 74 woodchucks up to 260 paces with a K-Lovell, using a charge of 17.0 grains of 4198 and the Hornaday 45-grain bullet. He re-forms his cases by firing 15.0 grains of 4227 the first time, using it on close-in chucks, under 100 yards or so. Report by Fred Ness: Rifle was a Hi-Wall Winchester single shot converted from the R-2 by Kilbourn. Rifle is fitted with an 8-X Lyman Targetspot Junior scope, with ¾″ Lee Dot; rifle zeroed for 1″ high at 100 yards. Both Kilbourn and Hober reported ease of extraction and normal case life, according to Ness. Fred reported that he had similar experience in regard to case extraction and case life, both very important these days with ammunition shortages, and empties becoming more increasingly valuable and more difficult to obtain.

When compared, side by side, with the Jerry Gebby .22 Varminter Junior cartridge, made by necking-down the .32-40 Ballard & Marlin cartridge, the K-Lovell has an over-all length of 1.625″ while the Gebby Junior is 1.70″ to the shoulder and 2.03″ in case length and is very definitely of much greater powder capacity. So that, whether a case is called a Maximum Lovell, a K-Lovell or a Gebby Varminter Junior, is not likely, of itself, to prove very illuminating as to its relative size or as to its actual size. You must first either measure it or compare it with something of which you know the dimensions.

The Maximum Lovell and the K-Lovell may be compared visually as being roughly half the size of the .22 Gebby Varminter Junior and of much the same case shape up to the shoulder, except the Kilbourn case is materially the straighter, but the Kilbourn shoulder is very short and very much more abrupt, having a 35° slope while the neck lengths are about the same. Consequently, Maximums, Standards, Juniors and Peewees, or what have you, mean very little *unless* you know what cartridge case they have been made out of and the approximate powder capacity.

Today we need a very accurate, effective .22 Peewee Pifflepoop, firing a 35-grain metal cased bullet at about 1,500 f.s. and another pair of loads, throwing 40-grain metal-cased bullets at 1,550 and 1,950 f.s., a great deal more than we have *ever* needed another .22/4000 Super-Duper. We have more .22 and .25 wildcats now than we know what to do with but we have *never* had a perfect *small game* cartridge in .22 caliber. They are all either too weak or they shoot too hard.

Lysle Kilbourn has told the author that the principal reason he brought out the .22 Kilbourn-Lovell case design was to enable shooters to use duPont I.M.R. No. 4198 powder more effectively in a small .22 caliber cartridge. The shoulder was made abrupt to create greater confinement and churning around during the burning of the powder, thus permitting a rise in pressure with more complete consumption of the smokeless propellant.

When Hercules Hi-Vel No. 3 was available, the .22/3000 Lovell and the R-2 cases were very effective, but after Hi-Vel No. 3 was discontinued (it may have a successor shortly) the riflemen found they could not use 4198 with maximum anticipated success in these small cases with gradual shoulder taper, because that was not the condition under which 4198 performed to maximum advantage and because they could not get enough 4198 in such cases to develop sufficient pressure to cause perfect burning of the propellant. They swung to 4227, which burns more rapidly, being cut finer and this is what many users of the .22/3000 Lovell and also the R-2 use, but this powder is a bit too fast for best results.

Kilbourn says that he then designed the Kilbourn (or K-Lovell), and due to its larger capacity, greater length and sharper shoulder slope, it confined a larger charge of 4198 and burned it to much better advantage. He claims it proved the theory. This seems to be so. The sharper shoulder held back the gases at moment of ignition and the combination worked to perfection.

Kilbourn says he has found the Maximum or K-Lovell is not a critical case. It will accept the case full of 4198, just scooping it full, and with 40, 45, 50 or 55-grain bullet one will attain very fair accuracy and also closer points of center of impact with different bullets and weights of bullets than is generally the case. Thus he considers it an easy case to load, and one with which shooters are unlikely to have trouble. The conclusion seems plausible and the theory sound.

The .22 K-219 Zipper—Usually Known as .22 K-Zipper
(25° Shoulder Slope)

This Lysle Kilbourn cartridge is made by firing factory loaded .219 Zipper cartridges in K-chambered Zipper barrels. In the same manner the K-Lovell ammunition, or rather empties, are made by firing K-2 Lovell cartridges in the K-Lovell chamber.

This cartridge, in case you do not recall, is a *rimmed* cartridge. After being turned into a K-Zipper it is an even 1.50" up to the shoulder. The length of the empty cartridge is probably intended to be 1.90". The one in my possession actually measures 1.91". The loaded cartridge will, of course, be of varying lengths depending upon the length and depth of seating of the bullet, but the one at hand, with a long pointed bullet, is just 2.50" in over-all length. Length of neck is 0.23". Shoulder taper is reasonably sharp—25°— yet not excessively so.

It is a cartridge with most of its length in the main body of the case. It contains a good weight of metal. It is a good looking cartridge and should shoot accurately with a fairly wide range of powders yet probably not excessively so with any of them. In other words, the general design of the cartridge suggests that it is not extreme in any one particular. It is just a good looking, medium sized, *rimmed* center fire cartridge.

How do these measurements compare with the factory loaded .219 Zipper cartridge? The Winchester Super-Speed factory cartridge with 56-grain blunt hollow point, metal cased bullet, measures 1.36" up to the shoulder; in comparison the K-Zipper is 1.50" for the same dimension. The shoulder is long and very gradual in slope in the factory charge. The factory case has a 0.30" neck, as compared with 0.23" for the Kilbourn. Over-all length of the factory cartridge with 56-grain stubby bullet is 2.25". These are actual measurements taken with an engineer's scale.

Remember, the .219 Zipper factory cartridge was made for a lever action rifle in which breech pressures had to be kept down. The K-Zipper was designed for use in a High-Side Winchester single shot action, or one of similar strength, with bushed firing pin.

Kilbourn's loads for the .22 K-Zipper follow: 31.0 grains of 4320 with 55-grain bullet, velocity 3,250 f.s. to 3,600 f.s.; then 34.0 grains 3031 with 50-grain bullet gives 3,400 f.s., according to Kilbourn. These are the loads he has used personally. He says frankly he has comparatively little shooting dope on this cartridge.

As a comparison the Lindahl Rimmed Chucker cartridge is very much shorter in the main body of the case and is just a trifle shorter over-all, than the .22 K-Lovell cartridge. However, it is (the Lindahl Rimmed Chucker) the finest finished job of precision ammunition making of all the wildcats, which have been sent to this author. The Lindahl measures a scant 1.20″ up to the shoulder as compared with 1.50″ up to the shoulder for the Kilbourn K-Zipper—a difference of 0.30″. The Kilbourn burns a good deal more powder as it has more powder capacity but the Chucker is a 3,500 f.s. cartridge just the same.

In some ways the K-Zipper reminds one a bit of the .257 Roberts case and cartridge in appearance. The Chucker looks a good deal like the rather short, stubby but extremely efficient (ballistically) German 7.9mm carbine cartridge which is away ahead of our .30 carbine cartridge, ballistically.

The Kilbourn K-Zipper looks like a good selection for a 3,500 f.s. rifle. It is easily and inexpensively made and so is its ammunition. It should outshoot the .219 Zipper loads considerably in both accuracy and velocity. It is the sort of case design which will produce in both .22 and .25 calibers in *varmint type* rifles.

The .22 K-Magnum Rimless (25° Shoulder Slope)

This Kilbourn development was intended as an "improvement" upon the old .22 Niedner Magnum Rimless and to hold about seven grains more powder than the Niedner. It also holds a grain or two more powder than the .22 (Standard) Varminter, or than the .22-250 cartridges. It should drive the bullet a trifle faster for that reason.

The standard load for the .22 K-Magnum is 35.0 grains of 4320 with a 55-grain bullet to develop 3,700 f.s.m.v. This cartridge will also give good results with the 45-grain, 47-grain and 50-grain W.M. 8S bullets. The shorter and lighter bullets will use a bit more powder to advantage, the weight and shorter bearing surface of the bullet permitting more powder. The long, rather sharply pointed W.M. bullets permit the holding of velocity somewhat better than normal, although that shape of bullet is rarely as good a killer in the field as the more conventional types such as the Sisk, Sisk-Lovell and Sisk-Niedner.

Cases for the .22 K-Magnum are made by necking down the .30 Remington rimless case. They can also be made similarly from the .25 Remington rimless or the .32 Remington rimless. He necks them down and then fires in the K-Magnum Rimless chamber to re-form the shoulder and to put it farther forward.

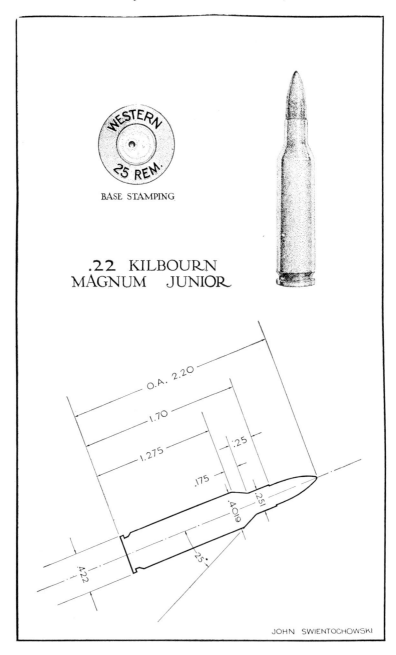

BASE STAMPING

.22 KILBOURN
MAGNUM   JUNIOR

JOHN SWIENTOCHOWSKI

Ballistics of .22 Kilbourn-Magnum

Tests by J. Bushnell Smith of .22 Kilbourn-Magnum cartridge and rifle: Load was 34.0 grains of 3031, 50-grain Morse cadmium bullet, range 100 yards. One, two-shot and two, five-shot unselected groups; muzzle velocity of charge 3,735 f.s.

Two-shot group measured 0.21" and one five-shot group measured 0.87" vertically x 0.40" horizontally and the other 0.45" x 1.03", center to center.

Kilbourn also has a .22 K-Magnum Rimless *Junior* case, but at the time of last report he had made but one or two rifles for that one, which is very *similar* in size and powder capacity to the Lindahl Rimless Chucker. He has never advertised this one and does not push it as he prefers the longer, larger powder-capacity cartridge. He feels the longer, larger case is preferable, possibly because he lives in the part of New York state where woodchucks are likely to be seen and shot at now and then at very long ranges. He is also sold on the idea of a longer case.

Measurements of .22 K-Magnum Rimless Junior Cartridge

Sample of this cartridge came to hand in June, 1945. June 1, 1945, was quite a memorable day in Wilmington, Delaware. It snowed slightly at midday and there was a long parade honoring the only living Delaware recipient of the Congressional Medal of Honor. The author sawed up a big rock-maple log for a fire in his furnace and used it right afterward. Thus, quite a number of unusual events occurred.

That morning the Kilbourn-Magnum Junior arrived. The author does not share Kilbourn's reticence in regard to pushing this cartridge. It appears to the author like a thoroughly practical medium range woodchuck cartridge; one for use up to 250 or 300 yards.

The .22 K-Magnum Rimless Junior is almost a dead-ringer for the Lindahl Rimmed Chucker. Kilbourn had almost certainly never seen the latter. The only apparent difference is that the Kilbourn Junior is a trifle longer in the body of the case; the shoulder appears to be a trifle more gradual in slope; the necks are the same length and it will shoot anything the Chucker will handle, plus 1.0 grains to 1.5 grains more powder. No. 3031 and the 45 or 47-grain W.M. 8S should do splendidly in this cartridge although Kilbourn uses the Sisk bullets. The case at hand appears to be loaded with 50-grain Sisk bullet.

This Kilbourn Junior measures a scant 1.70" over-all when empty and 2.20" from case head to bullet point when loaded. Length up to the shoulder is 1.275" and the Lindahl Chucker 1.20". The Kilbourn Junior is, therefore, 0.075" longer up to the shoulder.

The .22 Kilbourn Rimless Junior cartridges are made from the .25 Remington rimless cartridges cut off and necked down, and can also be made from the .30 Remington rimless or from the .32 Remington rimless.

While it is, of course, true that the longer cases could develop as much velocity with somewhat lower pressures but, while burning more powder, nevertheless, this cartridge is just the right length to carry well in the pocket without too much weight and without too much rattling around. The author has never objected to long, heavy rifles for woodchuck and varmint hunting, but he does object to lugging long, heavy *cartridges,* particularly the few he would carry loose in his right pants pocket. Loose wildcat cartridges, if long and heavy, are annoying in wearing holes in pockets.

This cartridge is particularly adapted to shooting 45, 47 and 50-grain bullets and at average full charge load velocities of 3,250 f.s. to 3,550 or 3,600 f.s.m.v. It will probably do 3,700 to 3,800 f.s. with the 41-grain Sisk bullets and it should be thoroughly suited with 3031 and any light bullet of .224" diameter, jacketed to stand the pressures needed to develop 3,200 to 3,600 f.s.m.v.

The report should be rather sharp, yet not too piercing, like that of the .220 Swift and the .220 Arrow, the .22/4000 Schnerring-Sedgley cartridge and similar charges. It should be a good selection for moderately open-farming-community woodchuck shooting and be a first-class 200 to 300-yard cartridge for shooting buzzards, eagles, the large barred owls, larger hawks and even coyotes at moderate ranges. Sighting should be 1" high at 100 yards above line of cross-hairs. That would drop you 1" or 2" low at 200 yards, below the Lee Dot.

A 2,000 f.s. load should work in this case; a 1,350 f.s. squirrel load should be practical and a 2,700 to 2,750 f.s. load should turn out to be quite accurate, very low recoil and very moderate report and the pressures up to 3,000 f.s. should be quite moderate. This is *not* a 3,800 to 4,000 f.s. cartridge with 45, 47 and 50-grain bullets; it does not have enough case room.

I would expect it to be superbly accurate at 3,250 f.s. and 3,550 f.s. with 45 and 47-grain bullets. Cartridge cases should be tough and long wearing and erosion moderate. Due to the moderate slope of shoulder it will likely be found shooting better with 3031 than with 4198. The Maximum Lovell is a *trifle* shorter cartridge but its shoulder is about 1/10" higher and its powder capacity is by no means as large. The .22 K-Magnum Rimless Junior is definitely a larger diameter, stronger, tougher case than the .22 K-Lovell or the .22 Maximum Lovell cases, the brass is easier to obtain today and will likely be easier to obtain in future years.

It strikes the author as being a *safer* selection because of the added strength of the cartridge case. This cartridge, in either rimless or rimmed head form, should be a thoroughly practical choice for wood-chuck shooting in country that is fairly open and hilly, where the farmers and neighbors are not too fussy and yet where the ranges are not so long that you are continually passing up shots at chucks so darned far off they are safe and *know it*.

This is the Eastern adaptation of the Lindahl Chuckers; the .25 Remington rimless is the best brass from which to make it; the case is the most conveniently re-formed to this size; and anyone who is not satisfied with this much cartridge could get his rifle re-chambered for the regular full length .22 K-Magnum Rimless at any time he wanted to. This latter operation would give him then a new barrel, to all practical purposes, because it would then have the old lead (or leade) cut out and the erosion area would be removed by the chambering reamer. Maybe this is an idea for Lysle Kilbourn to keep in mind. Partly shot-out barrels, chambered for shorter cases, should be good for another 2,000 rounds by re-chambering for the longer case and by cutting a quarter inch or so off the muzzle and carefully chamfering the new muzzle. Both ends of the barrel would then present different surfaces to the entrance and exit of the bullet.

Measurements of .22 K-Magnum

The over-all length of the loaded cartridge with long, pointed bullet, is 2.56"; length up to shoulder 1.65"; case neck length 0.23"; shoulder slope 25°. As a comparison, the Lovell cartridges of somewhat similar size and shape use 30° shoulder angles on the Zipper Improved and the .22 Hi-Power job, and both of which have a .393" forward end of case diameter and a 24° slope on the .22 Hi-Power job which is slimmer and has a .370" similar diameter. The three Gebby jobs have 25°, 28° and 30° by measurement of cases at hand and most of the .22-250's use a 28° shoulder. This Kilbourn case, therefore, has a very gentle slope, comparatively. But it is 10° to 13° sharper slope than the various .22/3000 and R-2 cartridges, which are smaller and have much less powder capacity, being .25-20 conversions.

The .22 Kilbourn Magnum Rimless considerably resembles the .22 Rimless Chucker made from the .25 Remington rimless case, as may be commented upon elsewhere, but it is very much larger in the main body of the cartridge. The Kilbourn-Magnum measures 1.65″ up to the shoulder which is 0.45″ more than the Lindahl Chucker—nearly half an inch. What this extra 0.45″ of case capacity permits is that it turns the cartridge into one preferring a powder like 4320 instead of 3031 like the Chucker, and it handles the 55-grain bullet to splendid advantage, while a cartridge like the Chucker or the Kilbourn Magnum *Junior* would do better with 3031 and 45, 47 or 50-grain bullets.

As a general proposition these longer cases keep the pressures down; on the other hand, not having as much case slope up to the shoulder like the .22 Standard Varminter, or the .22-250's, they should be used in a bolt action or single shot rifle with a good strong extractor. Then too, with these longer cases, one had better stick to empties fired in his own rifle, unless completely re-sized for their full length. The author once had a .30-1906 Springfield star gaged military rifle which was a wonderful shooting rifle and with which he took fifth place in the Members Match at 600 yards, and placed very well up near the top in both the Wimbledon Cup and the Marine Corps Cup Matches the same year at Perry, and made a long run and finished about seventh or so in the Western Cartridge Company's Match at 900 yards the following year. This rifle had a tight spot in the chamber—it was chambered *very closely* at that point, about ½″ to 1″ up from the head of the case, but the rest of the chamber was not abnormally tight and sometimes cases came out pretty hard, or else had a tendency to split longitudinally, right at that spot, and at least 75% of the empty cartridges just fired in other star gaged Springfields of that approximate date of manufacture would not go in that chamber at all unless completely re-sized.

Very few of these Kilbourn Magnums have been made but it is a good looking, moderately long case, of medium capacity and I am merely telling you what to look out for with such a case without suggesting in any way that you should expect trouble. A short, stubby case is likely to—and generally does—produce higher pressures when loaded to capacity than the longer case with a moderate charge, and the moderate length with a fairly sharp taper to the body of the case, like the .22-250's, will extract smooth as silk but they will set back harder against the face of the breech block than the straighter cases, particularly if the cartridge case or the chamber itself is oiled, clean, bright and free of rust. There is nothing to keep it from setting back; it does not grip the sides of the chamber like the straighter cases.

Every shape has its practical advantages; every shape has its practical disadvantages. They are never the same in all cases. Always expect to find such differences when re-loading ammunition and when shooting it. Every factory, every gunsmith, and every experienced rifleman ought to know this. Knowing what to expect often saves a man difficulties or enables him to partly overcome them, by loading accordingly and by choosing a rifle action suited to handling that shape and size of cartridge you want to use.

The .22 Standard Varminter or the .22-250 is capable, in Kilbourn's opinion, of developing as much velocity as a .220 Swift. The author feels that it will probably be 50 to 100 feet less with most bullets, but at any rate, the difference will be very slight. Acting on this premise Kilbourn believes that his .22 K-Magnum Rimless will develop about the same velocity as the .22 Varminter but with less pressure.

The .22 K-Magnum is 0.15" longer from head of case to rear of shoulder than the .22 Varminter and the .22-250 and is somewhat more straight in taper in the main body of the case. The case length is 1.90". Its cartridge head is heavier back of the cannelure, on the edge where the extractor grips it, than the .22 Varminter case which is made from the .250/3000 Savage case, which in this respect is a trifle lighter in brass stock.

So, if this rather straight case needs more pull to get it started out of the chamber when maximum loads are used, the extractor should not ride over the rim. The importance of the extractor not jumping the comparatively small half-rim, as it were, of a so-called rimless case must not be overlooked.

In a comparison with the .22 Varminter and the .220 Arrow, the Arrow (a Wilson-Wotkyns development) made from the .220 Swift case measures 1.72" up to the shoulder as compared with 1.65" for the Kilbourn Magnum. The .220 Arrow is also somewhat longer in the neck. Except for the admitted somewhat easier extraction of the .22 Varminter, the author likes the looks of this .22 Kilbourn Magnum Rimless about as well as anything for use in long range .22 wildcat rifles.

It is sufficiently sharp in neck taper, compared with the size of the case at the shoulder, to probably not expand in length when fired three or four times, as happens with the .220 Swift. Makers of the Model 70 and 720 rifles could, with profit to themselves possibly, examine this case design for a cartridge of .22 center fire caliber to use in those rifles.

The fact that so far lighter bullet loads have not been extensively developed is no drawback. Anything from 41-grain to 55-grain should work satisfactorily and 60-grain as well, or 63-grain if the pitch is adequate. Remember that Kilbourn's business is chambering barrels and essentially that of chambering *existing* barrels. The cost is usually between $3.00 and $6.00, plus whatever else may need to be done, such as a bit of fitting of the barrel into the forend, looking to the bedding of recoil shoulders, proper size or bushing of firing pin and such matters having to do with making the rifle really shoot

COMPARISON OF LYSLE KILBOURN'S CARTRIDGES

Left to Right: W.R.A. .22 Hornet and .219 Zipper: Then: Kilbourn .22 K-Hornet Junior; Kilbourn .22-K Hornet; Kilbourn .22 K-Lovell (about same as Hervey Lovell's Maximum Lovell); Kilbourn .22 K-Zipper; and Kilbourn .22 K-Magnum Rimless.

Not in group: Kilbourn .22-K Hi-Power and .22 K Magnum Junior. (This latter cartridge is shown on page 106).

with the new cartridge and at a price that either the Office Boy or the Company President—minus Federal taxes, minus state taxes, minus city taxes, minus county taxes, minus a ten-spot for a new hat for the wife so there will be no complaint from *that* quarter—can *then* afford to spend.

The arms industry and the gunsmithing trade is full of people with things to sell, in normal times, but not all of them offer quality rifle work at a price which is definitely within the reach of everyone. Kilbourn seems to be offering wildcat rifle cartridge quality at a very moderate price.

Recent Loads for .22 K-Magnum

The Kilbourn .22 K-Magnum is made with a body taper of 0.01″. The capacity of the case is 39.0 grains. This puts it in the class of the real long range woodchuck cartridges. It is just as suitable for shooting foxes, coyotes, gray wolves, eagles (in places like Alaska), hawks, crows, buzzards, wild turkeys and for similar-sized game and varmints.

Kilbourn's favorite load is, as mentioned elsewhere, 32.0 grains of 4320 with 55-grain pointed Express bullet. Kilbourn has been reported to have shot more chucks at real long range—300 to 450 yards—with this cartridge than with any others. Very little erosion of the bore has been observed after 2,800 rounds in one barrel examined. Kilbourn does not use graphite wads with this cartridge; incidentally, most ballistic engineers frown on this practice.

Tests made with J. Bushnell Smith's ballistic pendulum gave the following results for the Kilbourn Magnum:

Bullet	Powder	Charge	Velocity
45 R. A.	4320	32.0	3,320 f.s.
45 R. A.	4320	33.0	3,500
45 R. A.	3031	33.0	3,620
45 R. A.	4320	34.0	3,520
55 Sisk	4064	31.0	3,245
55 Sisk	4320	31.0	3,232
55 Sisk	4320	32.0	3,290
55 Sisk	4320	33.0	3,600
55 Sisk	4064	33.0	3,500
55 Sisk	4064	34.0	3,453

.22 K-Hi-Power (25° Shoulder Slope)

This is a *rimmed* cartridge of Lysle Kilbourn design made from the .22 Savage Hi-Power cartridge. It looks very similar to the K-Zipper except that it is 0.125″ (or ⅛″) longer.

Of course, this gives it more powder room and the load to use will naturally be somewhat larger than those used in the K-Zipper. One can *start in* with those loads and develop charges, increasing the charge not to exceed .2 grains of powder at a time and do not change *two* components when working up a load. For instance, do not change *both* powder charge and bullet, or do not increase both powder charge and change primer at the same time, particularly if the new primer might happen to be *stronger* than the previous one used.

The .22 K-Hi-Power is adapted to Hi-Wall Winchester single shots with bushed firing pin; Sharps-Borchardt and such strong bolt actions as *might* take a rimmed cartridge successfully. Remember, the 54 and the 70 both take the Hornet cartridge, which is a rimmed case.

The .22 K-Hi-Power is not a cartridge to choose for use around wealthy estates, or generally in thickly settled communities, especially those in which the "recent rich" reside. This type is inclined to become *extremely* exclusive all of a sudden and in such localities you will find yourself able to shoot occasionally over a course of years with a .22 Hornet, a K-Hornet or a K-Lovell where you might find yourself talking earnestly to the State Police within the half hour if you over-stepped the permissible rifle *report* limit.

The .22 K-Hi-Power has many of the ballistic characteristics of the Marciante Blue Streak. For long range shooting the K-Hi-Power will be found to have merit, much merit, I believe. Its maximum range with long pointed, metal jacketed bullet and maximum charge, is probably between three and three and one-half miles if fired so as to give maximum elevation. Just bear this in mind when tempted to convert a crow on a tree into a bursting cloud of black feathers. You could miss!

At such speed, bullets which *hit* usually disintegrate into very small fragments which, normally, have only a short distance to travel after making a kill.

Physical Measurements of the .22 K-Hi-Power

Samples of this cartridge could not be obtained until June, 1945. The empty case measures just 2.00″ long. It is 1.60″ up to the shoulder from the case head. The shoulder has a 25° slope as mentioned and neck of the case is 0.26″ long. The over-all length of the loaded cartridge containing a long, jacketed bullet is 2.56″.

One-tenth inch back of the shoulder the case is 0.40″ in diameter. At the shoulder it is 0.38″. It looks to this author like a cartridge that will pack quite a wallop, shoot very flat over 300 yards, and the case sides are quite straight. It should make a good long range cartridge for Hi-Side Winchester single shots. The cartridge case made from the Winchester Super-Speed .22 H.P. case has a good heavy head and seems to be made of excellent brass. I would expect few split necks with this cartridge; and moderate pressures, considering the large charge it will hold, the rather moderate and pleasing shoulder slope and the general lines. The case is sufficiently straight to hug the chamber walls. It is somewhat straighter and is a bit longer

than the .22-250 cartridge. Gebby's .22 Standard Varminter is
0.07″ shorter at the neck, and 0.08″ approximately, shorter, over-all
than this Kilbourn .22 K-Hi-Power. The .22 Standard Varminter
and the .22-250 cases have a little more case taper than the Kilbourn
cartridge, but the .22-250 is rimless and the other a good heavy stock,
rimmed cartridge of rather reddish brass that looks strong structurally and tough in material.

For the boys who like to reach right out and smack them and want
to have an existing rifle chambered inexpensively, this Kilbourn .22
K-Hi-Power should be a fine woodchuck and wolf cartridge up to
350 or 400 yards.

I am giving herewith a number of examples of target and field
shooting with various loads in Kilbourn-chambered rifles:

Comment on .22 Kilbourn Magnum

This from L. J. Burkett, of 204 Wilson avenue, DuBois, Pennsylvania:

"I am enclosing two groups, both witnessed, which I shot recently
over a sand bag rest. Rifle was your K-Magnum using the necked
down .25 Remington case. This one you chambered for me has it on
anything I ever saw from 100 to 400 yards, and I have been using a
variety of wildcats for eight years.

"My sons and I have had eight different .219 Zippers and .22
wildcats and have shot thousands of rounds experimenting with them.

"These groups, which should speak for themselves, were shot with
34.5 grains of 4320 and 55-grain Sisk-Niedner bullets. The 100-
yard, five-shot group measured 0.45″ center to center and the 200-yard
five-shot group 0.95″ x 1.05″ center to center. The first was shot
6/21/1944 and the latter 7/18/1944.

"This rifle you made for me last year has a Charles Diller barrel
with 14″ twist. The one that is on the rifle of my son is also a Diller.

"I have just received a new Unertl 1¼″ scope, and I sent it right
on to T. K. Lee for the pair of dots. This Unertl is a dandy. I am
no expert rifleman, but am an old woodchuck hunter."

Comment Upon Work of .22 K-Magnum Rimless Junior

This from R. W. White, of 450 W. Main St., Geneva, Ohio, in
a letter which was forwarded to the author:

"I wrote to Mr. Kilbourn in February, 1944 requesting that he
convert my M-70 Winchester .22 Hornet to a K-Lovell but raised
an objection to the Lovell—short life of the cases—as I only had a
few cases. Mr. Kilbourn suggested then the .22 K-Magnum Junior.

Having seen several of Mr. Kilbourn's conversions, I had faith in his ability to produce good results, so I told him to proceed.

"The last of April, 1944 the rifle arrived with 50 .32 Remington cases necked to .22 caliber, and loaded, and a bullet seating die. Mr. Kilbourn suggested 26.0 grains of 4320 behind a 55-grain Wotkyns-Morse bullet. This load put 10-shots in 1¾" at 100 yards, which was very good, all things considered: dull day, medium 9 o'clock breeze, blowing in light gusts. But only had 100 Wotkyns-Morse bullets and this small supply was too soon exhausted before I had an opportunity to try it on chucks and crows.

"A shift was then made to .22 Hornet Super-X, 45-grain soft point bullet and after many different loads with 2400 and 4320; the best group with the 2400—some 21.5 grains—gave 10 shots in 1⅝" at 100 yards; 30.0 grains of 4320 produced 1½" group for 10 shots. So I settled on this load and by October 1, had killed 50 woodchucks and many crows. I did not count the number of crows shot—only the woodchucks. Only one chuck was shot at a distance of less than 100 yards, and it was a complete mess—one shoulder and a part of its head gone. Of the 50 chucks, not one lived long enough to get into its den, despite the fact that some were hit in the paunch at distance ranging from 100 to 300 yards. The longest shot was measured 351 yards. This chuck was hit in the head and some of the brain came out of the far side with the bullet. My opinion is that the bullet did definitely expand at this distance. Incidentally, this hit was the sixth shot fired with the crosshairs of the scope resting on top of the chuck's head but no daylight showing underneath. As near as can be ascertained the 100 yard trajectory is about 2⅝" with the 45-grain Hornet bullet. Load was 30.0 grains of No. 4320.

"In testing cases for durability one case was fired 17 times with 28.0 grains of 4320 and 55-grain Western Cartridge Company's bullet. The case was only neck-sized after each shot and showed no ill effects after the 17th shot. Another case was fired 15 times with 18.0 grains of 2400 and 55-grain Western Cartridge Company's bullet and this case showed no ill effects. Both cases are still in service. The case is easily made by re-forming .32 Remington or .25 Remington auto rifle cases (and also .30 Remington cases as well; Author). They are very strong and do not seem to stretch at all.

"One item that is desirable to some shooters is the fact that there is no noticeable recoil. The report is sharp, but in no manner can it be compared with the lusty bellow of the .220 Swift. This announces to all and sundry farmers that action is going on in their pastures."

Kilbourn inserted here the comment that: "The process of expanding a .25, .30 or .32 Remington case that has been necked down to .22 caliber to a K-shoulder is the same as firing factory Hornet, Zipper or .22 Hi-Power in a K-chamber and the action is the same."

Chapter 6

THE LINDAHL CHUCKERS

ABOUT the year 1940, Leslie M. Lindahl, of Central City, Nebraska, designed a pair of .22 center fire high velocity cartridges which have proved to be of exceptional accuracy and ballistic merit.

Protracted shooting by Mr. Lindahl and other users of these two cartridges appears to indicate no appreciable difference in accuracy between the Rimmed and Rimless versions of the Chucker cartridge. They are identical in shape and capacity and the same set of loading dies will handle either or both cartridges. Only one, of course, can be used in a given rifle because a rifle will handle either a rimmed case or a rimless case, but not both.

The necks of all these cases are precision line-reamed in a special die to insure uniform neck-wall thickness. This permits closer chambering tolerance in the neck of the chamber and is a contribution to accuracy. The bullet seat, or throat, is cut with special throating reamers with pilots fitting the bore diameter to 0.0001"-0.0002" tolerance.

Cartridge Cases

The standard cases which Mr. Lindahl uses for forming the .22 Chucker cartridges, are the .219 Zipper case to make the Rimmed Chucker and the .25 Remington rimless case to form the .22 Rimless Chucker. A number of other rimmed cases can be used to form the Rimmed Chucker including, I understand, the .30-30 case. Mr. Lindahl has built special tools and reamers for forming these cases and, in normal times, expects to be in a position to supply the formed and line-reamed cases to other gunsmiths as well as to his own customers. At the time of writing this, customers will have to supply empty .219 Zipper or .25 Remington cases to Mr. Lindahl for such forming. This gunsmith told the author in a letter Feb. 8, 1945,

118

that he (Lindahl) would not object—that "any other gunsmith who wishes to do so is free to go ahead and make up reamers and tools for the 'Chucker' caliber, but I (Lindahl) will not supply or make up any reamers or forming tools for other gunsmiths."

Twists Used

Mr. Lindahl, of the Lindahl Gun Co., has used a number of barrels with 14″ twist and they gave excellent accuracy with these cartridges. However, he believes in using the slowest twist that will give the required accuracy. His regular twist for the .22 Lindahl Chuckers is 1 turn in 16″. Pressures are lower and velocity higher with the slower twist. Also, chances of stripping bullets or tearing thin jackets are less.

Barrels Used

Leslie Lindahl has used different makes of barrels as available. These included Winchester, Remington, Savage, Stevens, Diller, Sukalle, Buhmiller and other makes. He does not bore any of his own barrels. He chambers them and provides cases.

Actions Used

Lindahl says that he has secured fully as good accuracy from single shot Chucker rifles as from the Model 70 Winchester bolt action Chucker. The single shot with a barrel tightly fitted to receiver and properly bedded forend has given superb accuracy.

Bushed Firing Pins

Breech blocks of the single shot rifle such as the Winchester High Sidewall S.S.; Stevens 44½—45 47, 49, et cetera with *44½ action;* and Sharps-Borchardt are taken care of by first boring out the firing pin body hole, then counterboring the hole for the bushing with use of a counterbore, fitted with a close-fitting pilot. Bushings are held in place in the block either with cross pins through the block or with two 3/48″ flat-head screws into the face of the blocks; the head of the screws fitting into a counterbored or recessed hole of about 0.050″ depth. Firing pins are altered by cutting off the original tip or point, drilling a hole of required size to a depth of ¼″ to ⅜″ into firing pin body. This hole is drilled 0.001″ undersize and the firing pin point of Malin spring steel wire is pressed in. Pressing the Malin spring steel wire point into the 0.001″ undersize hole firmly holds the point in place. Sweating or soldering them in destroys the temper of the spring steel point. For the Winchester action Lindahl can use points of 0.075" diameter, although one can use firing pin points of diameters up to 0.091" if desired, according to Mr. Lindahl. For the Stevens 44½ style actions he uses points of 0.063" to 0.075" in diameter. Bushings are made of tool steel, hardened and tempered.

Loads for the Chucker Cartridges

Best loads for the standard Chucker cases, according to Mr. Lindahl, and judged from results announced by his various customers, include 24.0 to 25.0 grains of duPont No. 3031, with W-M (Wotkyns-Morse) 8S R-2 bullets of 45, 47 and 50-grain weight. The W-M 8S bullets have given the best accuracy of any so far tested in these cartridges, according to Mr. Lindahl. Very fine accuracy has also been secured with 41-grain Sisk Super-Lovell and 50-grain Lovell bullets.

Ten-shot groups at 100 yards were reported as averaging about 1.00". One user of the Chucker, Austin C. Taylor, of 1312 Chestnut St., North Syracuse, New York, reported groups to Lindahl of ⅝" to ¾" for 10 shots at 100 yards. His rifle was a Model 70 Target weight. It formerly was chambered for a .22 Lovell cartridge, according to report. This was a Rimless Chucker. His shooting partner, C. A. Kyle, also uses a Rimless Chucker. They are both reported to have credited the Chucker with better accuracy than given by former .22 wildcat rifles they had used.

Velocity Tests

Velocity tests of the Chucker have been made on a comparison basis, using a home-made pendulum type chronograph. These tests indicated that the Chucker has 300 f.s. higher muzzle velocity than the Lovell (probably the R-2 with 15° shoulder) with same weight of bullet. Using Hornet and Lovell rifles with loads giving known velocities, comparison tests were made on the home-constructed pendulum chronograph and from results obtained the conclusion reached was that velocity obtained was right at the 300 f.s. faster level, with 45, 47 and 50-grain bullets.

Lindahl believes that the Chucker develops 3,500 f.s.m.v. with a load of 25.0 grains of No. 3031 and the 45-grain W-M 8S bullet. Lighter charges, of course, are practical, right down the line, and in many, many cases and situations would be preferable. It could be remembered in this regard that one of the most accurate charges so far developed for the .22 Varminter cartridge, which is a larger, more powerful and higher maximum velocity cartridge, gives 3,250 f.s.m.v. The author has shot that charge.

Pressures Developed

Pressure rifles for this cartridge, in either type of case, have apparently not so far been constructed. Pressures are said to be "moderate," conclusion based on ease of extraction, flatness of primers, expansion of the cases, and the fact that the cases last almost indefinitely as they do not lengthen to appreciable extent. In the .220 Swift caliber this can be a very annoying feature of continued shooting, using full charges in reloaded cases.

One condition which would help such a conclusion may be due to the most excellent and very high grade of workmanship shown in the making and forming of the .22 Chucker cartridge cases. They are beautiful jobs of precision workmanship.

Primers Used

For Winchester and Western cases, Lindahl uses No. 115 primers. For Remington cases the No. 8½ Remington appears best. He has also used the Winchester No. 120 and Remington No. 9½ primers. He cannot see that there is very much difference in the results obtained. Remember, these conclusions have been reached without the aid of a pressure gage. However, when a rifle is shooting around a 1.00″ average at 100 yards for 10-shot groups, measured center to center of bullet holes farthest apart, any pronounced change in velocity or pressure is almost certain to immediately enlarge the group or show fliers, or shots printing around a different center of impact. Results apparently were very good with all of them.

Shoulder Tapers of the Chucker Cartridges

This is often regarded of supreme importance, especially in getting good burning with certain types of powders. One powder will give best results with a given slope of chamber shoulder, another powder with a sharper or a more gentle slope shoulder.

Lindahl feels that a shoulder taper of 28°, on the Chucker is sufficient to insure efficient combustion and that little, if anything, is gained by the use of a more abrupt chamber or case shoulder slope.

The taper of the body of the Chucker cases is .015″. The original design used 0.040″ taper. However, the later and improved design with the 0.015″ body taper for its length gives easier extraction and a more efficient cartridge, in Lindahl's opinion. The short, stubby case, with husky shoulder, handles No. 3031 powder "beautifully," according to his expression for results obtained. Other experimenters and users of short and stubby .22 wildcats have, according to Leslie Lindahl, also found No. 3031 powder to give a proper burning rate and superb accuracy in such cases.

General Comments

Leslie Lindahl's gunsmithing work has been confined in the past few years to the fitting and chambering of barrels for different .22 wildcat rifles and also some of the standard .22's like the Hornet and the .218 Bee. He has done considerable experimental work with different versions of the .22/3000 Lovell cartridge. A number

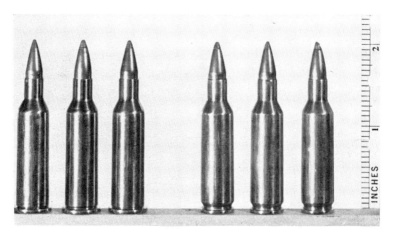

.22 LINDAHL "CHUCKER" CARTRIDGES

Left to Right: Three different loads in .22 Lindahl "Chuckers" *rimmed* cartridge-made from .219 Zipper case; cartridges on right, three different loads in .22 Lindahl "Chucker" *rimless* cartridge—made from .25 Remington rimless case. No difference in ballistics or accuracy between the two styles. These are all 3,500 f.s. charges. even in these short cartridges. This is very fine, precision-made wildcat ammunition.

of years ago he made up reamers and tools for a sharp-shouldered Lovell, using a neck length of 0.250" and a shoulder taper of 25°. Body of the case was about 0.005" to 0.006" larger at the shoulder than the R-2 type of cartridge. He has also made up Lovells with neck lengths of ⅛" and 3/16", thus giving them maximum powder capacity. However, he found that by increasing the capacity much if any, over the standard Lovell case, nothing was gained. Too many users overloaded the Lovell R-2 case, according to Lindahl. It is not too strong a case, being revamped from the .25-20 single shot Stevens case, which was not a high pressure smokeless case to begin with when designed back in the previous century.

Lindahl feels that the standard Lovell R-2 or his own L-4 type, with 25° shoulder and ¼″ length neck, are, either of them, amply large enough in powder capacity, considering the inherent strength of the case.

Leslie Lindahl's mail order powder business takes up a good deal of his time. Consequently, his gunsmithing work at the time of writing was being confined to Chucker caliber re-chambering and fitting of barrels, mounting of telescopic sights and shotgun chokes. He does not do any barrel boring or rifling. Only the fitting of barrels, chambering, milling of extractor slots, bushing of breech blocks on the single shots, and similar work. He makes up re-loading tool dies of different types for the Chucker. He does no restocking.

Bore and Land Diameters

Lindahl has found that the most suitable barrel dimensions for the Chucker barrels are a bore diameter of 0.218″-0.219″; with a groove diameter of 0.223″ to 0.224″, and the 16″ twist as previously mentioned.

He does not do any gunsmithing or chambering work on .22 rim fires except for himself. So far, during the last five years, he has made up just about twice as many Rimmed type of Chuckers as the Rimless type, which means that most of them have been made up on single shot actions, to which the rimmed type of case is much better suited. At the time of writing he had about 17 rifles in process or in the shop and was in position to supply about one re-chambered rifle a week. This could, of course, be increased or decreased according to other business and demand.

In general, Lindahl seems to represent a rifle crank who first made up the Chucker and other wildcats for his own use and shooting and then took up fine gunsmithing of this type as a side line. He was originally the owner and operator of a wholesale and retail oil business, in addition to his mail order business in scopes, chokes, shooting books, reloading tools and such. He sold the oil business in the fall of 1944, built a larger warehouse for supplies and at last accounts was devoting his full time to reloading supplies and work on the Chucker caliber of rifles.

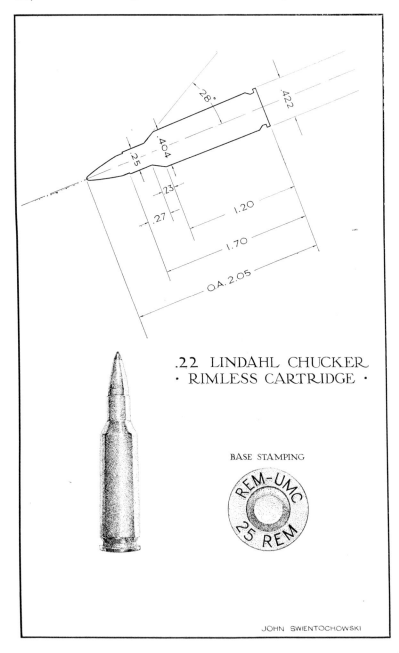

.22 LINDAHL CHUCKER
· RIMLESS CARTRIDGE ·

BASE STAMPING

JOHN SWIENTOCHOWSKI

The author is considerably and favorably impressed with the quality, finish and shape of this Chucker ammunition. It shows quality workmanship and good design. In velocity and ranging power, trajectory and exterior ballistics in general, the Chucker cartridges are between the Hornet, Kilbourn-Hornet, .22/3000 gentle slope Lovells, R-2 Johnson and similar cartridges at the bottom, and the larger and faster and greater capacity cartridges like the .22-30/1906, .22-30/40, .22-303 British, .220 Swift, .22/4000 Sedgley, .22 Varminter and similar wildcats. It is similar to the Kilbourn K-Magnum Junior, but holds slightly less powder.

The .22 wildcat family is large, runs quite a gamut of sizes, shapes, neck and shoulder sizes and ballistics.

These Chuckers are both good strong cartridge cases. Not so large as to be heavy to carry, nor so long as to be powder "eaters" or hard to extract for that reason, nor so flimsy as to be dangerous from that cause, even with ordinary full charges, and to possess great promise for the rifle crank who wants a middle-of-the-road rifle and cartridge, which is well designed and thoroughly well made.

As a woodchuck cartridge, it can be classed as a 200 to 250 yard cartridge. It can be used successfully at greater ranges, but it is not a 400-yard load or case. On the other hand, neither is it such a cannon that the user is likely to be run out of most neighborhoods simply on the grounds of making a nuisance of himself due to shooting "too much rifle" for that area.

Lindahl uses this cartridge for shooting prairie dogs, crows, probably some hawks, jack rabbits and similar stuff which is all that is to be found around that part of Nebraska. It is not a squirrel cartridge except with considerably reduced loads in which case it should be loaded with about a grain of powder more than the R-2 type of cartridge. For general Eastern shooting, it should be found a nearly perfect cartridge, except on the long bare hills of Central New York state, which are often bare and windswept for 500 or 600 yards, dotted with chuck holes and now and then a head. In such cases, noise is not often too important and range is imperative. It will do just as well on close in and medium range shots in such areas, as anywhere else, but the longer and more powerful .22 wildcats will outrange them there. In the edges of estates and in more settled areas, generally, it will be found at least as noisy and powerful and long range, with full charges, as one would care to use, and sometimes too long-ranged. In which case, the owner should use slightly more than mid-range charges, which are quite practical in a 28° chamber shoulder. About 75% of the full load is a good selection for such shooting, provided, of course, the powder being used burns properly with the bullet weight chosen, at that loading. If it does not, use a quicker burning powder, adapted to short, sharply bottlenecked cases. We will add comment obtained from other users of the .22 Chuckers to conclude this chapter.

In general, the Chuckers are 20 to 25-grain cartridges. This compares with 14 to 17-grain for the Lovells. With 16″ twist, they will do best with bullets of 35 to 50-grains weight. As wind-drift cartridges they should show better results than the Lovells and the Hornets, the Kilbourn-Hornet and similar, and show more drift than the larger cases with the longer, heavier bullets in one instance or the same weight bullets as above but at still higher velocities. Barrel life should be from 4,000 to 6,000 rounds as the top limit, and down to 2,500 to 3,000 in less fortunate cases. This judgment is based on what is known of barrel life as found to be average for cartridges which are both slower and faster and of much the same shoulder taper.

The recoil will be found low, probably two to three foot pounds in most instances or less. Muzzle report, moderately sharp, rather high pitched but not excessively painful or too long ranged in carrying power. The superb accuracy of such cartridges and ammunition provides the type of hitting and killing which appeals to the real rifle crank and to the engineer or professional man who wants top results without too extreme velocities, barrel worry or having to pay too much attention to farmers, passersby and farm, ranch and estate owners, and how they may react to your shooting of a Chucker.

There seems to be no sensible reason for having a Chucker made too heavy. It is a sporting cartridge, the case of which may be reloaded indefinitely and through a very wide range of charges with medium and light weights of bullets   It is reasonably flat shooting over 250 yards and very flat shooting over 175 yards. Beyond 300 yards, watch your high and low shots and try to shoot when your game is presenting the maximum mark in a vertical direction. Sketches, photos and groups will give you a good visual idea of what it will do and what you may expect to be able to obtain with a well-made .22 Chucker rifle, properly sighted and substantially stocked. The standard weight of barrel, or the medium heavy barrel, is plenty of tube to put on a rifle of the .22 Chucker caliber. Any first class hunting or target telescope sight should take its mild recoil indefinitely.

For a sporting stock, select the round, baseball bat shape of forearm and do not have the comb or pistol grip too massive. This rifle should be built so as to be quick in handling, yet deliberate in holding ability and easily carried all day, for practical hunting. For an all-around small game and varmint rifle it is one of the very best selections for everything up to foxes, woodchucks, coyotes and hawks. For match shooting or group shooting for turkeys, quarters of beef, ducks, geese, chickens or cash, within a range of 200 yards, it will be found one of the very best. Such cartridges hold their elevation well and the bullet is only moderately affected by windage, within the practical medium range of the outfit.

It is strictly and entirely a hand loading proposition. There is no factory ammunition. It uses standard diameter, metal-cased, expanding bullets; however, it can be loaded with cast bullets for reduced loads, but will be found giving its greatest accuracy and best results with 75% to 100% of the full charges as recommended by the maker. For such a rifle, you should pick the very best barrel you can obtain, or the gunsmith can buy, and then have it re-chambered, firing pin bushed if not already so adjusted, and see that the stocking has been very carefully done.

You should then have a real "bumble bee" rifle. The author would be inclined to select the rimless case, if your rifle action will handle it. For single shots, invariably choose a rimmed cartridge.

This is a precision job all the way through and should be regarded accordingly. Clean and take care of such a rifle. Keep the chamber carefully greased or oiled when not in use. Such a rifle makes up well in a weight of 9½ to 10½ pounds, with 24" to 28" barrel. Choose 24", 25" or 26" on a bolt action, 27" to 30" on a single shot; No. 2 or No. 3 barrel on the single shot actions. A speed action and handwork in adjusting the trigger pull will be a great help in getting better than 1 minute of angle accuracy.

Further Information on "Chucker" Ammunition

In the late winter and early spring of 1945 the author received so much mail and so many telephone calls regarding the purchase of second hand rifles; inability to obtain high speed .22 caliber woodchuck rifles; difficulty to obtain small caliber rifle ammunition; that at that time he asked Mr. Lindahl to go into some further detail on the matter of cartridge cases which could be sized down for the two Lindahl cartridges, and also to supply some additional information which is incorporated in the following data:

To date, and particularly in the East, especially in the woodchuck districts of the Middle Atlantic and New England States, comparatively few .219 Zipper rifles or cartridges had been sold, or were available in the hands of dealers, or of shooters, and not very many .25 Remington cartridge cases were available in any form, anywhere; consequently, it was most advisable to know definitely and *accurately* how many other empty rifle cartridges of different calibers—including most especially calibers which had been in much greater use throughout the woodchuck and deer hunting districts, than had the .219 Zipper and the .25 Remington cartridges—could be used for "Chuckers." Empty rifle cartridges of such calibers as the .30-30 Winchester, .32 Special, .32-40 Ballard & Marlin, .30 Remington and .35 Remington, would be far easier to pick up here and there, simply because tens of thousands of these had been sold where hundreds of the others mentioned had been fired. After some consideration and cartridge head checking, the following information was made available:

Lindahl's charge for complete re-forming of cartridge cases, to either of the Chucker cartridges is 4¢ each for the .219 Zipper and the .25 Remington, plus the cost of new empty cases. Therefore, the cost when *he* supplies the cases, will run approximately 8¢ each. Where the customer supplies the cases the cost would be 4¢ each for re-forming, line-reaming the necks, chamfering the mouth of the neck inside and out, and neck sizing.

As suggested previously, the .219 Zipper is the best and strongest case for the Rimmed Chucker. It is the easiest case to re-form. The .22 Savage High Power case, .25-35, .30-30, .32 Winchester Special and the .32-40 Ballard & Marlin cases have the same base and head diameter, or very close to it, *and can be used*. This, of course, is extremely important to anyone who cannot get the .219 Zipper cases, and needs sized cases for the Rimmed .22 Chucker. It should be understood that the Chuckers are not "improved" or lengthened .219 Zippers but are shortened Zippers with *less* powder capacity.

In the Rimless version of the Chucker, the .25 Remington case is best, but the .30 Remington, .32 Remington and .35 Remington cases *can be used*. It is necessary to run these large cases through several dies and to neck them down progressively.

The smaller caliber cases make up into the best Chucker cases and it is, of course, easier to re-form them than cases like the .30-30, .32 Special, and .32 and .35 Remington. Quite a little more work is involved in re-forming these calibers and the cost for having Lindahl do this work is 5¢ to 6¢ each.

The .250/3000 Savage, 6.5mm Mannlicher and 7mm Mauser cases *can not be used*. They have a larger body diameter at the base than the .25 Remington cases. Regarding different calibers of cases adaptable to the Rimmed versions of the Chucker, Lindahl has found the .30-30 cases manufactured 1943-45 inclusive to have a rather wide variation in thickness of head—as much as 0.005″. Also there is a variation in head width of the different calibers that could be used. This makes it advisable, *when possible,* to use the .219 Zipper case exclusively for the Rimmed version.

Lindahl makes up precision-built seating dies to the proper size to fit the Pacific Tool for $5.00 each; Sizing dies $5.50; Straight-line adjustable hand type seating dies, with anvil and seating plunger, precision-chambered for $7.00. These prices should be helpful in estimating costs for somewhat similar tools for other cartridges.

Short Range Loads for the Chuckers

The shooter who might wish to use a Chucker rifle for shooting squirrels, for killing trap bait, for exterminating small winged varmints or nuisances like blue jays, magpies, small hawks, starlings and the like, or for shooting grouse for the pot, would be in need of light, non-mangling and comparatively short ranged reduced loads. Mr. Lindahl has not been particularly interested in these, not being located in a district where such are a problem, nor where tree game is important. He feels that such loads defeat the purpose for which he designed the Chucker, that of a fairly powerful, extremely accurate, and flat shooting varmint cartridge. However, he expects to develop such loads as time goes on.

In general, it may be said that reduced loads containing 1.0 to 3.0 grains more reduced load powders than those for the .22 Hornet, .22 Lovell and .22 R-2 Risley cartridges, and similar, could be used with expectation of obtaining accurate and satisfactory results.

Trajectory Tests with Hunting Rifle

Varmint shooting in Nebraska is mostly at crows and prairie dogs and most kills are made at 100 to 200 yards, with the average shot about 150 yards. When using a Lyman Super-Targetspot telescope and standard Lyman target mounts and a load of 24.5 grains of No. 3031 duPont powder with 45-grain W-M 8S bullet, the drop between 100 and 200 yards will average right at 2½″ with the 100 yard group centered on the point of aim. If rifle was sighted to shoot 1″ high at 100 yards the drop below point of aim at 200 yards would be probably ½″, or practically centered on the target.

With the rifle sighted to center at 100 yards, and aimed at a level of the eye of a crow or a hawk at 200 yards, the bullet should strike about the point of the shoulder, if proper windage is taken.

EXPERIMENTS AND EXPERIENCES WITH .22
LINDAHL RIMLESS CHUCKER

(As told the author by Austin C. Taylor, 312 Chestnut St.,
North Syracuse, New York)

Austin C. Taylor and his friend, Charles Kyle, are both very
enthusiastic users of the .22 Lindahl "Chucker" rifles. They have
used these rifles extensively for quite sometime for woodchuck and
crow shooting in Central New York State and have very kindly
placed their experiences and experiments in loading and shooting at
command of the author, even going to the extreme of supplying the
loose leaf sheets from Mr. Taylor's "Score Book and Game Log" in
the author's hands for unlimited examination, although they are
accustomed to having this Game Log with them when hunting for
the very valuable data which it contains.

Quoting Mr. Taylor, (letter to the author March 2, 1945):
"I never try to get closer to a woodchuck after I spot him and so
far I have had very, very few misses with my Chucker rifle. I am
sending you with this letter all of my woodchuck and crow-shooting
data, which I keep in the little book that I carry with me at all
times when shooting woodchucks. After I found the most accurate
load for this rifle I quit experimenting with different loads, as I
see no point in using any other load after a thoroughly satisfactory
charge is obtained.

"I use a Model 70 bolt action rifle in Target Grade fitted with
J. W. Fecker 8 x 1⅛" scope equipped with T. K. Lee floating dot
reticule. The dot covers ⅝" at 100 yards, and the scope has ½
minute clicks. This rifle is chambered for the .22 Lindahl Rimless
cartridge—known as the Chucker.

"I sight in my rifle so that the point of impact is 1" high at
100 yards. The bullets are then just cutting the top of the 10-ring
of the usual 100-yard small bore target, and the point of impact,
with that sighting is about 2" low at 200 yards."

(Author's note: This does not mean that the bullet has a 1"
trajectory over 100 yards, or that it has a 1½" trajectory with a 6"
total drop over 200 yards. It means that with the line of sight
1½" to 1⅝" above the line of the bore, the practical hunting
trajectory—which is an entirely different thing than the trajectory
figured from the line of projection from the bore of the rifle—is 1"
high at 100 yards and 2" low at 200 yards. This is measured
entirely from the line of sight through the telescope. If the axis of
the telescope is exactly parallel to the long axis of the rifle barrel,

which could only occur if the center of the scope barrel is *exactly* the same distance above the center of the bore, directly above the rear mount base, as it is above the center of the bore directly above the front mount base. In which case, this shooting indicates the actual trajectory of the bullet above the bore of the rifle is about 2½″ to 2⅝″ over 200 yards, and the total drop of the bullet below the prolongation of the long axis of the bore of the barrel is about 10″; that of the .30-1906 with 150-grain service load is about 14″; that of the .220 Swift with either 48-grain or the 55-grain factory bullets, 6″; that of the .270 Winchester with very fast 3,540 f.s. 110-grain hunting bullet, 6″. This will give a direct and practical comparison. Either the .220 Swift or the .270 W.C.F. will give a practical hunting trajectory over 200 yards, with scope sight the same distance above the bore of practically shooting into the same group at 50, 100 and 200 yards.)

"At 300 yards, when shooting at woodchucks, a raise of elevation of two clicks on my scope mount, or one minute of angle is enough. I have shot but two chucks as you will note from the Data Book sent you, at ranges of 400 yards and both times I raised scope mount reading three clicks and both times the chucks were feeding, not sitting up. Consequently, the target presented was small in a vertical direction. However, neither chuck moved a muscle after being struck except to wave his tail.

"I tried four clicks raise on one chuck at 400 yards and shot right over him, so since then have never raised the scope more than three clicks.

"I talked with Kyle this A.M. (March 5, 1945) and he said he was up on our range yesterday. He sighted in his Chucker rifle to zero at 200 yards getting a fine 1½″ group. He then shot a group at 100 yards and was just 1½″ high (remember the line of sight was about 1½″ above the line of bore—Author). I shot a crow yesterday, holding dead center at 150 yards, and the bullet hit dead center and my rifle has the same identical sighting as I used on it all last summer, when it was sighted to group 1″ high at 100 yards. It has not changed its point of impact, although it has stood in my gun cabinet all winter. It sure is a real rifle.

"The Chucker is the most deadly and the most accurate cartridge I have ever seen or used and it is real pleasant to shoot for the report is real 'polite' and not at all like the sharp crack of the Hornet or Lovell, and the recoil, using my heavy rifle, is just a cozy little push.

"I am using the Rimless .22 Chucker with .25 Remington auto cartridge necked down, and I also have a No. 44½ Stevens rifle at

Lindahl's now to be chambered for the Rimmed .22 Chucker, but at present have no dope on that combination.

"I have had an R-2 Lovell and used it quite a good deal with many different loads and then had Johnson re-chamber it for his J-19 Lovell cartridge which has a sharp shoulder and short neck. I never was quite satisfied with the accuracy, nor the killing power of either one, and the cartridge cases would not stand a real good load. Primer pockets stretched so that the primers dropped out when you got a load up to the point where it really worked and from my experience and also Mr. Kyle's who went through the same thing as I—that is, the Hornet, Lovell, then Chucker—the Lovell did not work well unless it was loaded to the full capacity of the case and the powder was pressed down by the bullet.

"I use 24.5 grains of No. 3031 powder and the 45-grain Wotkyns-Morse bullet. The over-all length of the loaded cartridge is 2.050".

"All powder is carefully weighed on a Voland & Sons balance and is weighed to about 1/50th grain. Bullets are seated by me with straight-line seater made by Mr. Lindahl and this is a real precision instrument for it fits the cartridge perfectly and bullets will not fall into place but have to be pushed down through the bore of the tool into the case so they are really seated straight-in-line.

"I have tried this rifle in all different positions, with tight sling, loose sling, and with no sling, by shooting out of the car window, over the car hood, when leaning up against the car or the trunk of a tree with cold rifle barrel, hot barrel, and in all positions from prone to standing and have never had any appreciable change of impact. I have never used a chuck *rest* and all shots are made without rest of any kind.

"Charley Kyle is as enthusiastic about his rifle as I am about mine and our experiences are much the same. In fact *are* the same. His rifle is a Winchester Model 54 with Target Grade weight barrel and he uses 24.5 grains of No. 3031 powder and the 47-grain W-M bullet. Results with his load are almost identical with mine.

"Neither of us has had a cartridge case give out so far, although they are re-sized full length each time they are reloaded."

Mr. Taylor's Data Book Notes

A Score Book, a Dope Book, a Game Log or a Game Record Book are all small books of great interest and value to the keeper of same, but rarely supply quotations which are particularly smooth reading, and in most instances anyone other than the man who kept such book, and compiled its data, must search and figure out what each bit of material and each page of notes actually means.

The following quotations from Mr. Taylor's Data Book are concerning a number of different cartridges and rifles, but are lumped here under one heading, because of their general interest. Please note that the first few of these do not refer to the Lindahl Chucker rifles:

"Rifle—Winchester Model 70 Target Grade, chambered for Johnson J-19 Lovell cartridge. A sharp shoulder cartridge made from the .25-20 Stevens single shot cases, necked down. Load tests: 17.5 grains No. 4227 with 47-grain W-M bullet. This load shows too much pressure; primers blow out; 16.3 grains No. 4227, N.G.; 16.2 grains No. 4227, also N.G.; 16.0 grains No. 4227, also N.G.

"Same cartridge and rifle: 15.5 grains No. 4227 and 47-grain W-M bullet, J-19 Johnson Lovell cartridge; this load is very good; 15.7 grains and same bullet, this load is also very good; 16.5 grains No. 4198 and Remington bullet, O.K. Shot four starlings with it without a miss!; 16.7 grains No. 4198 and the Remington bullet, tested April 30, 1943, was O.K., in fact, very good; 'Dave' (Taylor's son) shot four starlings; 17.0 grains No. 4198 is *fair;* it has possibilities; 17.0 grains of No. 4227, tested same date, is fair and can be developed.

"Model 70 rifle shipped back to Winchester factory for new stock—original stock showed crack in forearm. Rifle tested by Jack Lacy (of Quinnipiac Rifle Club, of New Haven); 17.0 grains of No. 4227 and 48-grain Remington bullet gave less than 1″ groups."

Then came notes about shooting a bunch of starlings, four crows and four chucks. This rifle was now fitted with the Chucker-chambered barrel. On September 19, 1943, with Chucker, he killed crows at 160, 156, 75 yards and woodchucks at 117 and 270 yards. Note: "Longest shot yet made and a bullseye—some rifle!" Then followed some shooting just over 100 yards—a mixed bag.

Notes about groups made by rifle just after, or, when received from Lindahl, as follows:

"5-shot group, 100 yards 0.60″; 8-shot group, same range 0.80″; 10-shot group, same range 0.65″ x 0.85″. Load, 24.5 grains No. 3031, W-M 45-grain bullet, Remington primers. Tried 24.5 grains No. 3031 and 48-grain Remington bullet, Remington primer; results 'fair'; 24.0 grains No. 3031 and 48-grain Remington bullet and Remington primers; good results; then 23.5 grains No. 3031 and 48-grain Remington bullets with Remington primers; results fair; then results not good.

"Next, 23.8 grains No. 3031, 48-grain Remington bullet with F.A. No. 70 primers; results fair; with 24.2 grains No. 3031 and 48-grain Remington bullet and F.A. No. 70 primers; N.G.

"October 24, 1943: two 5-shot groups with 24.5 grains of No. .3031 and W-M 45-grain bullets, measuring 0.224″, gave 7/16″ and 11/16″; Remington No. 8½ primers; day was windy.

"Further shooting November 21, 1943: 24.5 grains No. 3031 with W-M 45-grain 0.222″ diameter bullets; group at 100 yards was 1 7/16″ and printed at 7 o'clock; very good; windy; Remington primers used. Ten-shot group with 25.0 grains No. 3031, with Remington 48-grain bullet and group also printed at 7 o'clock, measured 1½″; very good; Remington primers for that one.

"Next tested 25.0 grains No. 3031, with 48-grain Remington bullets and F.A. No. 70 primers; very good results. Then tried with Remington No. 8½ primers and got 10 shots in 1⅞″; eight in 1 5/16″ and seven in 1″; very good.

"November 25, 1943: tested 24.5 grains No. 3031 with 45-grain W-M bullets; Remington No. 8½ primers; bullets measured 0.224″; obtained a 5-shot group at 100 yards, measuring 9/16″; day was windy.

"Then came a group with 24.5 grains of No. 3031, 45-grain W-M bullets which measured but 0.222″ in diameter. The 10-shot group at 100 yards measured 1 7/16″. The same No. 8½ type Remington primers were used. This group looks larger than the other, but one group is not indicative of a load just because it happens to be exceptionally small, and one group was but five shots and the other 10. A large, badly scattered group, however, may suggest a load which is definitely inaccurate, due to excessive pressures, poor bullet fit, unequal burning of the powder charges because the pressures are too *low* or other causes. It is often difficult to tell too, much about any load without firing at least three 10-shot groups. The next 10-shot group measured 1½″ at 100 yards and with six in 1 5/16″. This rifle apparently shot well with either 0.224″ or 0.222″ bullets with chances normally favoring the 0.224″ bullets.

"A slightly heavier load of 25.0 grains of No. 3031 and 45-grain W-M bullets measuring 0.222″, charge fired by Remington No. 8½ primers, gave 1½″ group at 100 yards; windy, as usual.

"November 28: a charge of 24.5 grains of No. 3031, 45-grain W-M 0.224″ bullets and Remington No. 8½ primers, although shot in a gusty, fishtail wind, gave a group 1 5/16″ wide and only ⅝″ high for the 10 shots. Then, 25.0 grains of No. 3031, 48-grain

Remington bullet, Remington No. 8½ primers, gave a group of 2⅝" for 20 shots."

That is good shooting—20-shot groups nearly always contain at least three bad flyers, compared with the remainder of the group, and the group size is materially larger than for 5-shot or for 10-shot groups.

Small Variations in Weight of W-M Bullets Noted

The author cannot recall having seen anything published anywhere about the variations in *weight* of W-M 8S bullets for .22 caliber wildcats. Mr. Taylor carried in his notebook the following record of a test of so-called "45-grain" W-M bullets, weighed on a balance, accurate to 1/50th grain:

45.-grain; 44.7, 45.0-, 45.3, 45.3, 45.2, 45.2+, 45.3, 45.3- 45.3-, 45.0, 45.0+, 45.1, 45.5, 45.4.

Conclusions by Author: For 15 bullets the average weight was 45.2-grains. Extreme variation only 0.8-grain—eight of the projectiles varied only 0.1-grain from the mean.

Two were 0.3-grain heavy; one 0.2-grain heavy; two were 0.2-grain light; one 0.5-grain light. Extreme variation actually but 1%. More than 50% of the bullets varied but two-tenths of 1%.

May 14, 1944, Mr. Taylor shot a group at 100 yards of 9/16" and a 200-yard group of ⅞". Number of shots in each group were five; load 24.5 grains of No. 3031, 45 gr. W-M bullets; No. 8½ *Western* primer. The primer designation is emphasized here to differentiate it from the No. 8½ Remington primers previously used. The small variations from the mean weight will give an idea of the degree of uniformity of bullet manufacture necessary to obtain such very small groups at 200 yards. In using Western primers in Remington cases, primer pockets must be cleaned out carefully so each primer will seat to the bottom of primer pocket or primer will protrude and may be dangerous or cause trouble when closing bolt.

Woodchuck Shooting with Super-Accurate Ammunition

After all, what a rifle will do in the field is what interests the real rifleman. Ballistics and tables, groups and figures, are nice to mull over to while away cold winter evenings. However, when the woodchuck season opens, what the rifleman lives for then is the moment when he makes a spectacular long range shot and then carefully looks through his glass to see if that chuck's tail is waving frantically back and forth like the "swabbo" flag on a rifle range.

If the tail waves frenziedly all is well and Mr. Chuck has gone to join his honorable ancestors.

March 26, 1944 was very early in the season, especially of a cold winter like that of 1943-44, for chuck shooting in New York State. But, try keeping a couple of confirmed woodchuck hunters indoors *then*. The doctor must pronounce it pneumonia or a compound fracture to keep the real cranks at home safe in bed!

Sometimes a rifleman is not safe even in bed. I recall one instance when they had the author exactly where they wanted him —in bed with a case of bronchitis. It was Friday the 13th and very icy on the streets and it *did* seem better to stay there. Along about 10 A.M. the hot water boiler next door, and situated almost directly under the author's bedroom, *exploded,* blew things around, filled their house and our's with steam, everyone rushed wildly to the street, children next door were screaming and yelling for help, so the author got up, dressed and went out. It sounded too dangerous to stay home!

Fred Gates and Mr. Taylor probably felt much the same, that March day, so they went woodchuck hunting near Apulia. First blood was at 150 yards; next at 200 yards; third was offhand at 50 yards; then the hunters started to look farther away from the car and Taylor bagged a pair at 200; meantime, Gates cut tails on four chucks and bagged a crow.

This kept their temperature *up* for another two weeks after which they sallied forth again. Same grounds; chucks were bagged by Taylor at 300, 175, 150, 200, 150, 75, 225 and 200 yards. Gates bagged six chucks, two with Taylor's "Chuckers." They shot two with a Hornet—both getting in the dens; must have been poorly placed shots. All chucks shot with the Chucker reported as not moving after being knocked over.

One week later, April 16, notes give results of some further test of 24.5 grains of No. 3031 with 45-grain W-M bullets and No. 8½ Western primers; 5-shot group 3/16″ wide and ⅝″ high at 100 yards; over-all length of cartridge 2.050″.

By April 23 the party expanded to three—Gates, Charley Kyle and Taylor went to Perryville. Kyle drew first blood at 150 yards; then Taylor at 125; Gates a pair at 100 and 130 yards; Kyle dropped one at 200; Taylor one at 150 and a cat at 75 yards—all nine lives snuffed out just like that! This sort of unnerved someone, because just then Kyle lost a chuck in a hole mouth at 150 yards; Gates bagged a pair at 75 and 100 yards; Taylor one at 150 and another offhand at 50 yards; Kyle then shot a chuck from the kneeling position at 50 yards. So, off to bed and happy dreams.

May 7, 1944 the party increased to four; included was Fred Gates' daughter, Avis, a fine rifle and pistol shot, who was then 15. This time they went to Apulia and Pompey. First a chuck was shot at 50 yards; then Gates lost one in its den at 125 yards; using a Hornet; Gates killed one offhand at 175 yards with the 44½ Stevens-Lovell—which *is* a shot! Kyle bagged two at 185; Taylor another at 180 and two more at shorter ranges; Kyle stopped one at 75 yards; then Gates scored at 150 yards; Kyle a pair at 75 and 151 yards; Gates two at 75 and 50 yards; Gates another at 137 and a fourth at 50 and Avis Gates one at 75.

Taylor killed a chuck which raised its brush at 150 yards and flagged! Then Gates took two at 75 and 120 yards; Taylor one at 150 yards and Gates cleaned up three at 130, 200 and 175 yards. A happy crowd motored home.

But luck changes! May 21, 1944 Gates and Kyle went to Camillus, where the pastures looked greener from a distance, but failed to produce chucks! Kyle killed one at 250 yards and Taylor one at the same distance. Total to date, as of notebook, 103 chucks. Then came three at 50, 50 and 200 yards; one from sitting position at 75 yards and three long range kills at 235, 400 and 250 yards. Note that one was killed that day at 400 yards—a record for this party.

Next trip was to Apulia where the chucks started to dive in as soon as they saw the car. Getting educated—and suspicious of this bunch of shooters. Taylor bagged two at 300 and 350 yards which made him feel good; Gates took another pair at 250 and 250 yards; then Taylor killed at 250 and Kyle one at 100 yards; Avis Gates bagged four chucks and the score was up to 120.

This is average shooting for open hillside country, and some alfalfa fields, in North Central New York State, which is often a combination of bare hillsides and meadows and alfalfa. Chucks are smaller on the hills; fat in the alfalfa; better feeding also in the meadows.

The author has not been in exactly this general area, yet he has photographed chucks, chuck dens, pheasants, et cetera, time and again, around Sherburne and Greene, New York, in Lysle Kilbourn's general area; has been in Ilion, Utica and a week in and around Rochester; out on the lake, down in the hilly ravines around Watkins Glen; over along the Hudson River by Poughkeepsie, in George Sheldon's old district; at Kingston and Port Ewen on the west bank of the Hudson; so is generally familiar with much of the chuck hunting country of Central New York State. Also, he has been almost eaten alive by skeeters at Canandaigua, and has been in the sandy hill country of North Central Pennsylvania, which has some woodchucks but not at such long ranges, generally, as there is more cover than in the regions somewhat farther north.

To continue: They had a day in Apulia; Kyle stopped one at 100 yards; Taylor three at 200, 250 and 200 yards, which was nice shooting with the Chucker; and Fred Gates took one by the tail after killing it at 200 yards. Then they motored to Plainville, New York, and found chucks rather scarce. Gates bagged one at 100 yards; Taylor a crow at 200, a large winged varmint at 250 yards; Gates three crows at 200 each; and Kyle two chucks at 200.

Over at Otisco Lake. Most of the shots that day at 100 yards. Nine kills; most unusual being two crows at one shot by Charley Kyle; range 150 yards.

Visit to Oneida, on July 16, 1944, netted 21 kills. Kyle started the ball to rolling with a kill on a woodchuck at 225 yards; then Taylor shot one from the sitting position at 225 yards; another from the same position at 250 yards; Kyle killed a crow at 225 yards; Kyle bagged a chuck at 200 yards; Taylor a chuck at 225 yards; all the others were fairly easy shots.

July 30, 1944, Taylor and Gates went to Redwood and made 14 kills. Best of these was a kill at 225 yards by Taylor; another right after it at 400 yards by Taylor, who, by that time probably felt like a million dollars, and then celebrated by killing one standing at 100 yards. He also shot a crow standing at 75 yards. Other shots were mostly around 100 yards, but they had enough *long* and difficult kills that day to make it a noteworthy hunt. Also, to show just what a Chucker rifle will do when *held*. The score was then up to 169 kills and increasing with every trip.

The author is giving considerable space to this .22 Chucker dope for two reasons; three in fact. Comparatively little has been said in print about the Chucker cartridges, as compared with the .22/3000 Lovell and the R-2 Lovell and J-19 Johnson cartridges. The Chucker cartridges are made of brass from cases made much *heavier* and *stronger* than any of the .25-20 cases, which are necked down for the .22/3000, the R-2, the J-19 and are heavier and stronger than any of the K-Hornets. This makes the Chucker cartridges *safer* with non-corrosive primers which often give higher pressures, at least with some load combinations.

They are also safer for nitroglycerin powders with non-corrosive primers when shot in extremely cold climates and in cold snaps when the thermometer bulb shows extremely low readings, yet in which hawk and crow shooting is at its very best and at a time where pressures may be high, in some combinations. They are safer in very hot weather in woodchuck shooting, where temperatures are away up, and we have the other extreme of normal loads giving somewhat higher pressures.

Remember, that nearly all of the wildcat cartridges, especially the very sharp shoulder wildcats, are high pressure load combinations. The thing that saves the shooter is that the pressures are computed in pounds per square inch, and not in excessive total poundage of pressure on the face of the bolt. The cartridge heads of most of the wildcats are small in diameter, and, therefore, small in area of bearing surface against the bolt. Hence, even with 55,000 pounds pressures, total pressure upon the bolt face is not as high as in the case of cartridges with larger area heads like the .30-1906, the .30-40, the .348 Winchester, et cetera, necked down to .22.

Also, Central New York State provides the longest-ranged average shooting at woodchucks of any place between North Carolina and Ontario, except around Troy, New York, which also is bare, as is the area in some parts, around Lake Champlain, both the New York State and the Vermont sides, and in various areas in Vermont, Massachusetts, New Hampshire and Connecticut. But in Connecticut the stone fences give the chucks more protection, when they have no other cover, and riflemen can slip up closer quite frequently. Consequently, in New York, a cartridge and rifle is likely to find harder going due to longer ranged shots than in any other Eastern State, due to general conditions of topography and terrain. While New York has plenty of brush in the Catskills and the Adirondacks, yet out in the Mohawk Valley and in other open areas, there are many long, bare hillsides which give 500 to 600-yard shots in some instances, if a man had the equipment and wanted to risk them.

But, back to the Taylor shooting: August 13, 1944, Taylor, Kyle and Gates made another trip around Apulia. They shot seven chucks and a crow. Taylor had one kill at 225 yards and Kyle one at 230 yards; others were at 150 yards or less.

August 20, 1944, Erieville was hunted and again on September 3. First time Taylor, Kyle and one other shooter bagged 13. Earl Matteson was the other rifleman on those two trips. Taylor and Kyle each bagged a chuck at 200 yards, other shots being 75 to 150 yards. Second hunt in that area produced 12 kills, of which two were crows, the remainder chucks. The last three kills were at 200, 275 and 225 yards.

The whole summer's bag totaled 201 woodchucks and 22 crows—
a few scattering. Considering the number of riflemen this was not
particularly large, yet most of the shots were at moderately long
range on days in which they appeared to be in best form. Exceptionally long kills were few. Apparently they shot at or shot
few, if any, hawks. There was no mention of shooting snakes,
turtles, foxes, buzzards or similar targets which often fall to the
lot of the rifleman who is out and finds something he feels merits
a bullet, or merely provides a convenient target. Evidently they did
not make any close kills along the roadside at chucks feeding in
meadow land, in pastures, denned under stumps or in dewberry
thickets close to the road, or sticking their heads out of den mouths
along roadside fencerows. Also, they may have passed up all shots
under 50 yards as being without too much sporting chance. The
author understands they usually drove on a short distance, stopped
the car, then fired.

In no instance did it appear that chucks were especially plentiful
in the areas hunted. Some places equally good shooting could have
been done with a .22 Hornet, a K-Hornet, or a .22/3000 Lovell—
or just about as good, ranges considered—and also on the condition
that most of the country is fairly open. On the other hand, at ranges
of 200 yards and over, the cartridges beginning with the .22 Chucker
and including the .22 Varminter, .22-250, .22 Marciante Blue
Streak, .220 Arrow and the .22-303, would be still more effective,
due to greater range and flatter trajectories—but possibly needless
for most of the shooting obtained.

This is not a .22 hunting book. For that read *Hunting with the
Twenty-two*. On the other hand, any book devoted to .22 rifles and
.22 cartridges should contain material amounts of specific examples
of what the various rifles and cartridges discussed therein can and
will do in the field when handled by good rifle shots and keen hunters.
The author would have liked to include also something about woodchuck shooting east and north of Troy, New York, by someone like
his old-time friend J. A. Van Wie, of the New York State Civilian
Rifle Team, who used to shoot chucks in that area when woodchucks
were thicker than flies in the rather open and den-dotted country
thereabouts. For some reason they had a scarcity of woodchucks a
bit later on and it is doubtful that woodchuck shooting around Troy
is as good now as it was 30 to 15 years ago, although the conditions
there favor very flat shooting and not too loud .22 wildcat rifles.

Chuck shooting in New York State is in general the closest to
coyote shooting on the plains of the West, of any varmint shooting

in the East, and it is the only shooting we have, except crow and hawk shooting which requires small caliber rifles of comparable velocity, range and flatness of trajectory. In the East it is especially desirable that the varmint rifle shatter its bullet into minute fragments in case of a miss, and if the rifle and bullet are of such types that the bullet will strike with very high velocity and then go to pieces in the woodchuck, rarely showing complete side to side penetration, and never end to end penetration—*that* rifle is the safest type rifle which can be shot at such game. Obviously, the .22 rifle throws smaller fragments, and a smaller, unmutilated bullet, than any larger caliber. In fact, it throws just under 50% as much jacket and lead core as the .25's of 87-grain and over. It is not as safe to shoot off into space as the .22 Long Rifle but it is much safer to shoot against earth, ice, sand or stones, because the .22 Long Rifle is more likely to give a whining ricochet with the full weight pellet sailing off into space.

The .22 Chucker rifle cartridge is about as high as one can go in the scale of .22 wildcats without having a real sharp and piercing report. Its own report is sharp enough in most areas.

The owner and user of the super-accurate, medium power, flat shooting small caliber woodchuck rifle has in his possession possibly the most superb light sporting rifle the world has seen. Due to its very light recoil, it can be shot more accurately and more deadly on game, by the average rifleman, especially the average technically trained rifleman, than any other rifle suited for such shooting. It is in every way a weapon of precision and its ammunition is *precision ammunition.*

However, in its use, it should be remembered that *brains* go right along with using a woodchuck rifle; particularly in shooting over the top of the nearby hill. If just *one* person is hit accidentally, every one of the other half dozen woodchuck hunters in the neighborhood will then be under suspicion and have trouble in hunting with a rifle in local fields, even though all of these be extremely careful riflemen and not at all at fault. Hence, the suggestion is offered here: look before you shoot and then *think.* You will almost always have ample time in which to kill the game. The Chucker is a real rifle and not a BB gun.

Rifles like the Chucker are so extremely accurate at 200 yards that shooting chucks is like dotting the exact spot you want to mark on an engineer's tracing; you make a dot on it with a pen point— just a dot—and that dot is right where you want it to be. This assumes that you are enough of a wind-doper to hit the inner ring at 150 yards in the first stage of the Small Bore Palma with a .22

Long Rifle bullet, and if you can do that you ought to be able to hit a woodchuck's head at 150 to 250 yards with a Chucker rifle.

Finally, what is the best *sighting* for the .22 Chucker? As suggested previously, Mr. Taylor, and most others, sight their rifle to group just 1″ high at 100 yards. Then the bullets center about 2″ (Lindahl gave it ½″) low at 200 yards. Anyone with normal common sense and some elementary rifle shooting experience ought to be able to figure out where to hold on a shot any place inside 225 yards. He suggests also that some who have sighted in for 200 yards with the Chucker, and therefore, grouped high at 100 yards, will have trouble shooting over at shorter ranges, most trouble between 75 and 130 yards, for there the bullet is above the point of aim. Enough above to cause misses on woodchuck heads, and frequently on crows, and, of course, also on small hawks.

The author is very definitely of the opinion that it is *always* a mistake to sight a rifle to shoot point blank at extreme range, or even at 75% of extreme range. You want your rifle to shoot *right on the dot,* or very slightly above center, on the *average* shot, and on a shot just a bit beyond *average* range. One nearly always has more time in which to judge hold-off on a 200-yard or a 300-yard shot than on a shot inside 125 yards. Most chucks, crows and hawks glimpsed at less than 150 yards are definitely on the alert and you do not have time to stop and calculate how many inches *low* to aim. I never did like to have to aim *low* on game. Holding over a bit does not bother me but holding *low* always has. Sight *any* .22 wildcat to shoot 1″ high at 100 yards when using a scope sighted rifle and you will not be so very far wrong for most Eastern shooting. With 4,000 f.s. rifles and over, ½″ high at 100 yards will be better.

The author believes that rifles of the .22 Chucker type are sufficiently powerful and sufficiently flat shooting for most varmint shooting other than the *dangerous* varmints, and that unless you need a rifle with a softer report, so that you can shoot in very thickly settled areas, or those containing many wealthy estates, you will find it difficult to make a wiser selection. A well made rifle of this caliber should have an accuracy life of 3,000 to 6,000 rounds. The one best load to shoot in such rifle is the charge which gives the smallest groups and particularly the smallest daily variations in center of impact. In such instance you will have a tack-driving rifle!

The most important feature of sighting that rifle is that it be sighted carefully to deliver the *first shot fired from a cold barrel* 1″ above the line of sight at 100 yards. Tighten the mounts and let them alone; keep a careful record of these readings in a small notebook or card which you will carry with you while hunting. Keep your tang screws tight. Keep the scope sight base screws *tight*. Be *very* careful of the condition of the chamber and bore of your rifle and clean your scope sight lenses with soft tissue—never a rough, cheap handkerchief; or use the fine, soft paper sold for cleaning high grade camera lenses. Treat your rifle and your scope like an engineer handles a transit or a Wye-level and your outfit should outlast you, and shoot just as well five to 10 years from now as when you first

This is C. R. Larson and Leslie Lindahl, of Central City, Neb. looking properly serious over a good bag of prairie dogs shot with .22 Lindahl Chuckers in the level prairie country of Nebraska. The Lindahl Chuckers were the most beautiful precision jobs of ammunition manufacture the author has seen of all the .22 wildcats he examined in preparing manuscript for this book.

unpack it. You can always tell the characteristics of a rifleman by the looks and condition of his rifle. Having such a rifle, the two important things in getting results in the field are calmness and patience. Anyone of fair experience, having those characteristics, will usually pick his shots with care and will fire at the right time. The result, with a rifle of the average accuracy of the Chucker, should be a pinwheel!

Always, for safety, look once *into the distance,* then make a final judging of the direction and velocity of the wind, note if the light has changed materially, then *shoot.* Get that shot off perfectly and *expect* to make a certain kill. *Confidence* in your ability to make that kill will go far to prevent flinching! Woodchuck hunting and squirrel hunting are the two sports which will test your mettle as a rifleman. Strive to learn how to and then *make* long runs of consecutive kills. There is nothing else in the whole game of rifle shooting which will quite equal the thrill that comes when you have made your first 10, 15 or 20 straight *kills.* The two absolute essentials are care in making the stalk, so as to be in position to shoot at the *right time* and then getting off the shot with a perfect straight-to-the-rear pressing of the trigger. It comes instinctively with practice; and with skill comes confidence.

In chuck shooting the important thing is to be at the right place, in the right shooting position, at the right instant. A well-made "Chucker" or similar .22 will very largely take care of the rest of it! The instantly deadly shots are: 1. In the brain pan. 2. Directly into the sticking place from in front. 3. High up, through both shoulders. 4. An inch or two below the butt of the ear from the side, so as to break the spine in the neck, or cut the carotid artery or the jugular vein. 5. A shot through both lungs. If it also strikes the heart so much the better; keep this shot well forward if the animal is feeding, and well up if standing and listening. 6. A shot into the spine, from either back or front—any place in the spine from the lungs upward. Do not aim at any other *spot* on the woodchuck. You would not like it if you were the woodchuck. Remember, you never aim merely *at* the woodchuck; you pick out a definite, *vital* area and then attempt to hit it! That is expert rifle shooting; no other method of hunting and shooting will give you long runs of consecutive kills.

A Note About A. C. Taylor

The author feels that the readers are entitled to a bit of comment about Austin C. Taylor, of North Syracuse, New York, who has so kindly supplied much interesting and valuable first hand field-testing data about the .22 Lindahl Chucker rifles.

Mr. Taylor lives in a woodchuck country of North Central New York State which is, in large measure, a sandy loam chuck district containing some long, bare hills, grassy meadows and a fair number of stands of alfalfa. This gives a variety of conditions. In the latter cover woodchucks grow much larger and fatter than on the bare hillside ranges.

As to Mr. Taylor's shooting skill; at the National Small Bore Rifle Matches of 1941, at Camp Perry, O., he took third place in the American Dewar Match with 395, but he made the highest number of X's scored in the match. He was one of three shooters who tied for first and was ranked in second place on X's, with a score of 398 x 400 in the difficult R.W.S. Match. Targets supplied with his material, but which are not shown in the book, are in keeping with his Camp Perry results.

A woodchuck at 200 to 300 yards is no more difficult to a skilled and experienced small bore target shot than is the 10-ring at 50, 100 or 200 yards. Kills may be expected with a super-accurate flat-shooting woodchuck rifle with the same average consistency that X's are scored in important National Small Bore competitions.

It is hoped that this chapter may be helpful in showing you the way to greater success in the field with rifles of the type of the .22 Rimless Lindahl Chucker, the .22 Rimmed Lindahl Chucker and the .22 Kilbourn Magnum Junior, which are quite similar in range and ballistics.

As a sort of after-thought to his previous communications, along came a note from Mr. Taylor in June, 1945, saying that he and a friend had taken a week's fishing trip but it had rained and the conditions were unfavorable, so they went chuck hunting instead. They killed 40 woodchucks and a wildcat; that should have been more fun than the fishing!

The Lindahl Super-Chucker

In the late summer of 1945 Leslie Lindahl completed the design of his .22 Lindahl Super-Chucker. Final dimensions came to hand just before going to press. The author suggested the powder charges for the cartridge so that, of course, decided the size of the cartridge cases.

The .22 Rimless Lindahl Super-Chucker

This is made from the .25 Remington Rimless case. Over-all length of cartridge case 1.820"; length of case, face to shoulder, 1.420"; length of neck 0.250"; shoulder slope 28°; diameter at shoulder, an even 0.400"; taper for full body length 0.015". Charges recommended by Lindahl: 31.0 to 32.0 grains of duPont No. 3031 with 45-grain bullets; the 50 and 55-grain bullets will hold right at 35.0 grains of No. 4320 and 33.0 to 33.5 grains of No. 4064.

Lindahl advises that in his opinion Hi-Vel No. 2 should not be used in any of these .22's like his Super-Chuckers, the Varminter or the .220 Swift; reason being that it eventually leaves a deposit in the bore and the rifle is spoiled because the deposit is difficult to remove when using present-day primers. That is not found with the larger calibers. Hi-Vel No. 3 is not available any longer, so that narrows the choice down to the duPont powders, at present, for the Super-Chuckers.

The .22 Rimmed Lindahl Super-Chucker

This one is made from the .219 Zipper case. The case is 1.820″ long; length, face of head to shoulder, 1.420″; this is greater than the corresponding length for the .219 Wasp but less for some of the other .219 Zipper improved cartridges; shoulder slope is 28°; neck length 0.25″; taper for body length 0.015″. Charges recommended by Lindahl: 31.0 to 33.0 grains of No. 3031 for 45-grain bullet; and for 50 and 55-grain bullets suggested charges are 33.0 to 33.5 grains of No. 4064 or 35.0 grains of No. 4320.

Measurements of the new cartridge indicate it is 0.10″ to 0.12″ shorter from rear face of head to shoulder than the No. 7 Lovell Improved Zipper and also the K-Zipper of the Kilbourn line. It is 0.007″ greater in diameter at the shoulder than the Lovell cartridge and 0.008″ smaller in diameter at the shoulder than the Kilbourn job. It has exactly the same diameter at the shoulder as the Ackley and as the Ackley-Vickery Improved Zippers and is 0.10″ and 0.14″ respectively, shorter to the shoulder than these. It is 0.0045″ smaller in diameter at the shoulder, but is 0.12″ longer to the shoulder than the .219 Donaldson-Wasp. It has very slightly less shoulder slope. In other words, it is a middle-of-the-road cartridge designed to combine, as much as possible, the advantages of each with the disadvantages of none, if that be possible. A middle-of-the-road policy in design, which is either as good as other middle-of-the-road policies, or else no middle-of-the-road policy is worth a whoop.

A first class match cartridge is usually the result of eliminating all of the "bugs" which can be removed by discarding all of the abnormalities and poor fits and striking a mean which seems to produce more even pressures, shot after shot, and more uniform delivery of the bullet into the bore, than other designs. Also, the bullet, velocity and twist are perfectly balanced.

I have an idea that one turn in 15″ will be found to be about a perfect twist for this cartridge, especially with 50 and 55-grain bullets.

A cartridge of this length, shoulder diameter and taper, should shoot well and with great accuracy very slightly reduced loads of No. 3031; about 29.5 to 30.5 grains of No. 3031 with 45-grain bullets, or 47-grain 8S bullets or the 45-grain Sisk. Be good charges too, so long as they are large enough to burn evenly, for the chap who has not reloaded too many cartridges to begin with, for he would have less likelihood of getting into trouble if he happened to make a slight mistake and over-charged accidentally. Sometimes, with charges a few grains under full charge, shots string up and down a bit, but on the other hand, with some rifles a slight under-load gives super-accuracy with very pleasant pressures and long cartridge-case life.

Hervey Lovell's load for his .219 Zipper Improved, which is 0.08″ longer in the barrel of the case and 0.007″ smaller in diameter at shoulder, is 36.5 to 36.6 grains of No. 4320 with 50-grain Sisk bullet and 33.0 grains of No. 4064 with 55-grain Sisk bullet. This suggests that the case will burn a little more No. 4064 and a little less No. 4320 to advantage than the Lovell Zipper, assuming that so far Lindahl has his loads exactly balanced as to bullet, powder, twist and case capacity—something not easy to do first crack out of the box with a new cartridge. Rifles vary one from the other, and some handle a heavy load well, others a slightly smaller charge, due in part to slight differences in chambering, boring, throating or bedding, stocking, head-spacing or whatnot. Remember, that people cannot all take the same dose of medicine to best advantage.

These .22 Lindahl Super-Chucker cartridges are long range coyote, woodchuck, crow and hawk cartridges. They are not needed for most 250 yard shots, the regular Lindahl cases being sufficiently powerful for most 200 to 250 yard shots on woodchucks.

The Lindahl cartridges are not made to hold (although they could be used with) IPCO wads. Lindahl says that he does not use wads or grease of any sort. He does not feel that they are of any value unless one is doing a lot of test shooting and the barrel is heating up. He doubts the value of graphite under pressure and heat (Lindahl used to be in the gas and oil business). He suggests that if one must use a lubricant it would be better to use a grease wad without graphite. He uses a very short throat taper in his rifle chambers. Just enough to taper off the lands and prevent any undue tearing of bullet jacket and to help in lining up the bullet with the rifle bore. He line-reams the case necks so that all are of uniform neck-wall thickness and that helps to give uniform pressures. This results in improved accuracy and more uniform pressures, shot to shot.

Chapter 7

ACKLEY RIFLES AND CARTRIDGES

THIS CHAPTER contains a great deal of general information about different .17 and .22 wildcat cartridges and about the rimless and the rimmed .228 Magnums. The .17 caliber Ackleys are the smallest caliber cartridges and throw the least amount of mass of bullet of any low velocity or high velocity cartridge on the American market. Where ricochets are a real problem, and dangerous; where you must shoot at very long range for small game, without much in the way of hills or a substantial backstop; they should be found the safest loads to shoot outdoors.

There is much information in this chapter about the building of .22 wildcat rifles; about chambering; cartridge variations; relative strength of different rifle actions which may be available for use; about cartridge neck variations due to difference in thickness of brass; the fire-forming of cartridges; wildcat cartridge tapers; shoulder slopes; reduction of muzzle velocity of factory charges when fired in longer wildcat chamber; excessive head space and its dangers and possibilities; possible injury to rifle chambers by burst cases; and wartime bullets and their variations. These, and many other problems of the rifleman and the gun builder are discussed in this chapter. The comparison of Springfield, Enfield and the various Mauser actions is a most interesting feature.

The .228 Magnums, made in three lengths and sizes in both rimmed and in rimless cases, supplement the .224 Ackley Magnums. All of these are discussed as big game loads in this chapter as is their suitability for other uses. The full line of 18 Ackleys plus their many special chambering jobs are set forth here. For variety of comment this is the most elaborate chapter in the book. It will be just as interesting to those having little or no interest in Ackley cartridges as to those who do and the thanks of the shooting folk are due P. O. Ackley for so readily supplying all this oft-times hard-to-get technical data.

148

The P. O. Ackley .22 Wildcats

The most extensive and complete line of .22 center fire wildcat rifle cartridges in the Rocky Mountain States area is produced by P. O. Ackley and Company, of 160 Elm St., Trinidad, Colorado.

Ackley spent five or six days in chronograph testing in getting together special loads for this chapter because both he and the author are inclined to be conservative in the matter of claimed velocities and both wanted to be sure of results with some of the loads.

Ackley barrels have established a good reputation for themselves, not only in the Rocky Mountain and far Western trade, but are imported into Canada in considerable numbers where they are being re-chambered or mounted as chambered by G. B. Crandall and Ellwood Epps, both of whom have reported privately to the author upon the excellence of these tubes.

The Ackley line of wildcats is even more extensive than the Hervey Lovell line. There are 12 cartridges regularly made at present, and the last two of these are also each being made in three different lengths, which actually adds up to 16 different Ackley .22 wildcats, if we include the two sizes of .17 caliber Ackleys as "Baby .22's"; there are also two specials. For your convenience and guidance each of these will be described in some detail, with loads suitable for each, and with special information concerning shoulder tapers; cartridge case lengths from end of case head to shoulder; length of case; and, in many instances, over-all length of loaded cartridge. The latter distance, however, will often vary, both with the length of bullet used and especially with the length and ogive of the bullet point; on that dimension, length was given for the samples on hand.

First we will describe each cartridge with its loads and ballistics. After that will come general descriptive matters in relation to putting together rifles or ammunition of these types and what may be expected of them.

The .17 Caliber Ackleys

Gather round and listen intently to the comment upon the .17 caliber Ackley Pee Wee and .17 caliber Super-Pee Wee Specials because some day these .17 caliber Pee Wee's may develop into super-squirrel and crow cartridges, particularly in shooting in settled communities where you want to keep the noise to the minimum, reduce bullet fragments to the irreducible minimum and eliminate ricochets insofar as that be physically possible. There is no possible way to distribute 45 to 100 grains of lead around the landscape if the bullet only weighs 20 to 26 grains when held in the loaded cartridge. There is no possible way to splatter Farmer Yonson's choice Guernsey heifer with a chunk of lead and copper the size of a marble if the minute bit of metal-jacket bullet is no larger than the diamond in a $9.99 engagement ring. That is what you have in the .17 caliber.

No. 1—.17 Ackley Pee Wee

The cartridge is made by necking down and re-forming the .300 Carbine service cartridge or the .218 Winchester Bee center fire cartridge; either will do.

SPECIFICATIONS OF .17 ACKLEY PEE WEE

Shoulder Taper	Outside Diameter at at Shoulder	Length to Shoulder	Length Case	O.A. Length
28°	.350″			

For all practical purposes this is the .218 Bee in .17 caliber and the result is that you start off these tiny .17 caliber bullets which are of regular type, and metal-cased with soft points or expanding points just like those in .22 cartridges, but traveling along at speeds equalling the .22/3000 to almost up to the .220 Swift.

LOADS FOR .17 ACKLEY PEE WEE

Bullet	Powder and Charge	Muzzle Velocity
20-grain	13.5 grains 4198	3,803 f.s.
26-grain	13.0 grains 4198	3,314 f.s.

In case this does not look like a practical cartridge, just remember that the very best air rifles are made in .177 caliber, they are more effective than any .22 air rifles so far attempted, and their waisted projectiles in either air rifles or air pistols are accurate within their accepted range.

This cartridge holds considerably more powder than the .22 Hornet, at least 75% as much as either the .22/3000 Lovell or the R-2 cartridges and quite as much as was normally used in grouse, squirrel, rabbit and other pot-meat loads for the .30-40 and the .30-1906 cartridges. When this charge is burned and the powder gases funneled down a sharp shoulder into a long, thin tube which is the neck of the .17 Ackley, you have a situation in which considerable pressure can be brought to bear upon the base of that minute .17 bullet. It is blown up the barrel and out into space, like a cork out of an applejack demijohn; "phoopppp ! ! !"—like that ! It goes up the range like one of those big red biting ants up a Major General's pants leg and when it connects there may be a General Uproar! Just like that! Remember, an elephant is more afraid of a mouse than of a rhinocerous, so don't ridicule this idea of a .17 caliber cartridge just because it is "smaller than a .22."

Parker O. Ackley trying out a new load.

The author is of the opinion that the safest and quietest flat shooting 250-yard hawk, squirrel and crow load of the future may be a .17 caliber Pee Wee or something like it. Here is a field in which you Super-Duper ballistics students and engineers can start to work.

No. 2—.17 Ackley Super-Pee Wee

A Super-Pee Wee was once described as a circus midget on the outside of three shots of bay rum plus a chaser of lemon extract; in such condition he proposes to the fat lady and is immediately accepted!

The P. O. Ackley Super-Pee Wee case is formed by slightly shortening the main part of the body of a .219 Zipper cartridge case or a .25-35 case if a rimmed cartridge be desired, and by performing the same operation on a .25 Remington Rimless cartridge case if a rimless case is on order. The new case is made with a long, tiny neck, the neck alone being 0.35″—(not many of the .22 wildcats of reputation have a neck more than 0.25″ long)—and a fairly sharp shoulder of 28° taper—the same taper as that used for a .22 Varminter and for the .22-250 cartridges but it is relatively sharper because it comes down from a .405″ cartridge case diameter to one sufficiently small to hold a .17″ bullet, and then the extra long neck makes the assembly look like a copper pin in a long-necked brass bottle. Yet it has ballistic possibilities.

SPECIFICATIONS OF .17 ACKLEY SUPER-PEE WEE

Shoulder Taper	Outside Diameter at Shoulder	Length to Shoulder	Length Case	O.A. Length
28°	.405″	1.30″	1.85″	2.225″

In other words, the loaded cartridges are about 2¼″ long and hold 26.0 grains of No. 3031 powder readily, so that behind this 20-grain bullet is as much or more 3031 as is loaded behind a 45 to 47-grain bullet in the .22 Rimless Lindahl Chucker, the .22 Rimmed Lindahl Chucker or the .22 Kilbourn Magnum Junior cartridges, all three of which are fine woodchuck cartridges at 250 yards.

What happens ballistically is that the 20-grain metal-cased soft point Sisk bullet is started in life at 4,309 f.s. by chronograph test, which is 200 f.s. faster than the .220 Swift and nearly as fast as T. K. Lee's .22 Gebby Varminter Senior cartridge made from the .257 Remington Roberts case necked to .22 caliber.

About three or four years ago a writer burst forth with quite a bit of publicity on a .170 cartridge and barrel giving something like 6,000 f.s.m.v., or so it was claimed at that time in the press. Ackley commented on that matter in a letter to the author June 28, 1945, in which he suggested that this writer probably did that "in a taper-bored barrel unless he used extremely light bullets." As he understood it, this writer reached nearly 7,000 f.s.m.v. with a .22 bullet in a *bore tapering .30 caliber to .22* and using a 40-grain bullet.

Such results are not too practical today, as yet, because of difficulties of manufacture of both barrels and bullets and to date there has been no jacketed bullet that would stand speeds much over 4,000 f.s. without running into trouble with melted cores (even if paper insulated) and other mishaps. It should be comparatively easy to reach 6,000 to 7,000 f.s. with a solid alloy bullet with compressible fins which could be fired through a tapered-bore. A 40-grain bullet with a .30 caliber base which could be reduced to .22 as it passes up the bore could be driven to terrific speed.

Do not forget Germany's 75-mile Paris gun, and the Haiger rifle, and some of the German guns that shelled London and others which were almost ready to shell it and which were found in the Krupp works ruins had tremendous bores, and would have been much more effective and long-ranged. We are today merely on the threshhold of ballistic development. Unfortunately, German engineers often beat us to it, and we do not wake up as often as we should, until we land over our heads in a world-engulfing war, and about the time the war is over we are just getting caught up with ballistic developments of the enemy, except in the matter of exaggerated ballyhoo in which we need take no back seat to anyone (Ackley seconds this comment).

The .17 caliber today is by no means a ballistic unknown. It may very well prove to be a favorite squirrel cartridge of 1960.

LOADS FOR .17 ACKLEY SUPER-PEE WEE

Bullet	Powder and Charge	Muzzle Velocity
20-grain	26.0 grains 3031	4,309 f.s.

The trajectory of such a cartridge and bullet over 100 yards is bound to be extremely flat and while a 20-grain bullet will not be too much of a windbucker, nevertheless, in woods shooting wind is seldom a factor of much account in making calculations. The author predicts that the .17 or even a .15 caliber rifle may some day be more of a serious competitor of the modern .22 than is the .25

caliber today.   Of course, a bore of such small diameter is difficult
to clean from the breech because of the large chamber as compared
with the small bore, and the very small patch which must be
exactly centered on the tip of a round or flat-tip cleaning rod.   Such
patch will quite easily puncture.   But such bore and chamber can
be adequately cleaned with a slotted rod of copper, using a small
rectangular patch.   With non-corrosive priming, cleaning is not
today as much of a chore nor is sweating out as much of a problem
as 15 or 20 years ago.

Today, rifles like the .220 Swift, .220 Arrow, .220 Swift Improved and .22-348 caliber are sufficiently difficult to clean from
the breech with a straight rod with flatted tip.   Never buy and use

Upper: Ackley .228 Magnum.

Lower: Ackley Imp. Zipper Winchester.

such a rifle without first supplying yourself with a good strong,
practical cleaning rod adapted to such shape of .22 chamber.   With
a .17 rifle this matter of cleaning rod purchase before rifle purchase
becomes even more important.   It pays sometimes to buy the cart
before the horse, because the horse without the cart is of not too
much practical use.

Ackley seems to largely control the field on the manufacture of
.17 caliber rifles in the United States; once the public becomes impressed with the capabilities of the cartridge it may have a good
sale.   Remember, that Ackley can make practical .17 caliber rifles
using as a source of brass the .300 Carbine case, the .218 Bee, the
.219 Zipper, the .25-35, the .22 Savage H.P. and he could also
use the .25 Remington rimless for bolt actions or the .25-36 Marlin
for Hi-Sides.

No. 3—.22 Ackley Improved Hornet

This cartridge is made by expanding the .22 Hornet case in length by shooting in a .22 Ackley Improved Hornet chamber. The resultant brass is then reloaded with any of the following charges:

Bullet	Powder	Charge	Muzzle Velocity
45-grain	2400	12.0 grains	3,000 f.s.
50-grain	2400	11.0 grains	2,700 f.s.

SPECIFICATIONS FOR .22 ACKLEY IMPROVED HORNET

Shoulder Taper	Outside Diameter at Shoulder	Length to Shoulder	Length Case	O.A. Length
30°	0.290"	1.18"	1.375"	1.80"

Case neck length 0.16"

Other loads about same as for K-Hornet chambered by Lysle Kilbourn and described in another chapter.

No. 4—.22 Ackley Improved .218 Bee

Velocities and loads for this Ackley cartridge are just about the same as those for the R-2 type .22/3000 Lovell. Incidentally, Ackley mentions that the reamers which they make themselves for the R-2 Risley-Donaldson .22/3000 cartridge are made with and are ground for a 12° 30′ shoulder slope. That compares with 12° for C. C. Johnson and various others and 15° at present for Hervey Lovell .22/3000 rifles. It should be obvious that you can use a sharper slope in a given chamber, but not a cartridge with a more gentle slope, if the breech block is head spaced very closely, assuming the chamber is very closely fitted to the cartridge for which the rifle was intended.

In theory, at least, .218 Bee cartridge brass can be obtained today more readily than .25-20 brass, but on the other hand, certainly the .218 Bee case is no knockout for fine design, neither has anyone set a record for accuracy with it. It is just a good modern, strong, little case made to be used in a comparatively short-receiver, lever-action rifle of around seven pounds.

Develop charges for this cartridge carefully. The author would prefer a different selection simply because the Lovell, Kilbourn and Ackley lines have received greater advertising, and well-deserved advertising, in most instances, on other calibers, and in case you want to sell a rifle anytime, it is advisable that it be of a caliber the public holds in good favor, in fact, that the public holds in *highest* favor. Such brings a better price when second hand. No one knows when he may want to try another new wildcat.

No. 5—.22 Ackley Improved Lovell

This cartridge brass is made by blowing up (shooting) R-2 cartridges in a .22 Ackley Improved Lovell chamber. Loads and velocities are approximately 5% greater; velocities in proportion to the increase in charge. Charge can sometimes be increased by as much as 2.0 grains of powder over the recommended R-2 loads, if using 4198, but without changing primer and without increasing the bullet weight. Recommended R-2 standard loads will give close to the same velocity and are much easier to load in this case. It has a sharp shoulder and a long, fairly straight body taper. This is a cartridge giving maximum results for each grain of powder burned —a boon to you Scotsmen, as nothing goes to waste.

SPECIFICATIONS FOR .22 ACKLEY IMPROVED LOVELL

Shoulder Taper	Outside Diameter at Shoulder	Length to Shoulder	Length Case	O.A. Length
30°	0.300″	1.38″	1.60″	2.13″

It is a small, light, easily carried, very efficient little case which uses approximately the same charges as the Lovell and Kilbourn cartridges of very similar design and name. Remember, that a more gentle slope shoulder gives lower pressures and a sharper slope shoulder higher pressures, than when burning the same powder in another cartridge of the corresponding size but slightly differing diameter taper or shoulder slope.

Hervey Lovell mentions that it is extremely difficult to exactly fit many .22 wildcats with charges from a given table. The charge may need to be jockeyed this way and that until you get exactly the right pressure and velocity to work in that rifle. While doing so you will have no pressure gage and no chronograph to lead your venturesome feet; so go slow and take things easy.

No. 6—.22 Ackley Improved .219 Zipper

This is one of the most promising .22 wildcat cartridges in the whole Ackley line. You may recall that in the Lovell chapter it is pointed out that Lovell has found the No. 7 cartridge in his line— the .22 Lovell Improved Zipper, or Zipper Improved—to be the most accurate cartridge in his whole list of 12 at the range of 200 yards,. That one made numerous 1″ or smaller groups at 200 yards, and was the only cartridge with which he, himself, could make 1″ groups at 200 yards, yet he had two others very similar in shape and size.

SPECIFICATIONS OF .22 ACKLEY IMPROVED .219 ZIPPER

Shoulder Taper	Outside Diameter at Shoulder	Length to Shoulder	Length Case	O.A. Length
28°	0.400″	1.50″	1.92″	2.38″

W. F. Vickery, gunsmith, of Boise, Idaho, who has made a specialty of Improved Zipper rifles for Hi-Side single shots, wrote the author June 26, 1945:

"I make up only the original Ackley Improved Zipper and as far as I know, Ackley makes up only the shortened version of this Improved Zipper. Ackley said there was about 0.040″ difference in the length from head to shoulder. The reamers for both of us were made up by Red Elliott and Ackley had Elliott grind his back 0.040″ at the shoulder, so Elliott told me.

"In connection with these Zippers and in fact all Zippers, something else has come up and that is that the brass in the later Zipper cases, as purchased during 1944, is about 0.002″ thicker in the neck of the case. This cuts down neck clearance in Zipper Improved chambers and I found that chambers with a fairly close fit in the neck for the earlier Zipper cartridges would sometimes refuse to chamber this later Zipper cartridge until the neck of the chamber was cut out an additional 0.002″."

From this it will be seen by readers that loads, and loaded ammunition, and re-loading tools which are made with very close tolerances should be carefully developed.

Another thing is that the over-all loading length—the length of case and such part of the seated bullet as projects from the neck—

A scene in the barrel turning and barrel boring department of the Parker O. Ackley factory in Trinidad, Colorado.

will vary with different lengths and shapes of bullet point. The long, pointed bullets will either stick out farther, or else the bearing part of the bullet will have to be seated much deeper in the case and the same charge then might and likely *would* not be right for both types of bullet. The one with the longer bearing or which was seated deeper in the case, thus leaving less air space between bullet base and powder charge, and the deeply seated or long bullet, could not be safely loaded ahead of as much powder as the shorter bearing bullet.

Also, the tight fit of necks in chambers will immediately raise breech pressures materially and, unless freed, this will necessitate a reduction in charge; and if it is freed then if the rifleman obtains another lot of Zipper cases with thinner necks, his cases will fit very loosely in the chamber opposite the neck, as compared with the heavier brass cases, and this will probably cause increased erosion by more gas shooting up along the walls of the bullet before being fully seated in the lands. Hence, the troubles which a re-loader must watch for are legion and often serious and annoying. It is like trying to make the same automobile seat or office chair fit a dozen or even two people of widely different physical build; it is impossible—it will fit some but not the others.

Accurate varmint rifle shooting is possible only after these various "bugs" are eliminated. It is not a case of merely throwing 35.0 grains of No. 3031 into a case and putting a 40-grain bullet in and seating same and then hoping for the best; the best may turn out to be *worst,* simply because some one thing does not suit that rifle.

LOADS FOR THE .22 ACKLEY IMPROVED .219 ZIPPER

(Other Improved Zippers may require slightly more, or slightly less powder, to give the very finest accuracy at 200 to 300 yards)

Bullets	Powder and Charge	Muzzle Velocity
40-grain	38.0 grains 4320	4,097 f.s.
40-grain	35.0 grains 3031	4,213 f.s.
45-grain	33.0 grains 3031	3,952 f.s.
45-grain	34.0 grains 3031	4,048 f.s.
50-grain	37.0 grains 4320	3,913 f.s.

All of these bullets, of course, were soft point or hollow point metal-cased hunting bullets intended for heavy charges and moderately high pressures.

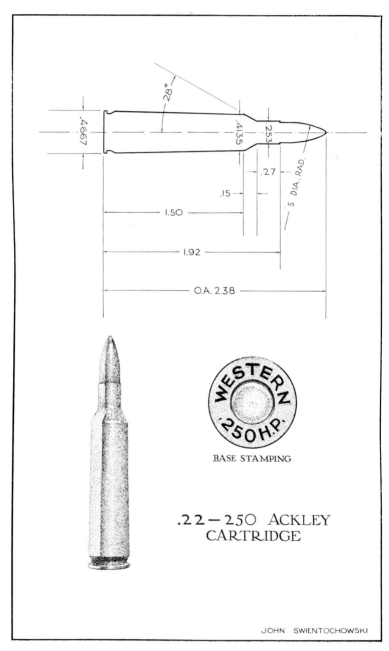

BASE STAMPING

.22 – 250 ACKLEY
CARTRIDGE

JOHN SWIENTOCHOWSKI

Charges of lesser weight, giving about 3,750 and 3,250 f.s.m.v. may be found as accurate, or more accurate, than these faster loads. Charges of such velocity nearly always shoot very accurately in 14″ and 16″ twists in .22 caliber rifles.

This Ackley cartridge looks very similar in size and shape to the .22-250 and the .22 Standard Varminter cartridges, except that the Zipper Improved cartridge is a rimmed case and the others are rimless cartridges. According to George Schnerring, the rimmed cases of such type are about 20 per cent stronger at the head than the rimless cases, which must be cut away more for the extractor groove.

No. 7—.22 Ackley Improved .22 Hi-Power

This has the same shoulder taper and the same diameter of case at the beginning of the shoulder as the previous .219 Zipper Improved cartridge. However, both of them are 0.020″ smaller in outside diameter, at the shoulder, than the Ackley .22-250 cartridge (which also has a 28° shoulder slope) and are 0.030″ smaller at the shoulder, in outside diameter, than the .220 Ackley Improved Swift. Yet visually you can scarcely notice the difference.

It should be stated here that other custom gunsmiths have brought out at least three lengths of .22 Improved .22 Hi-Powers which may vary as much as ⅛″ in length, consequently, the loads which are given here are for the .22 Ackley Improved .22 Hi-Power only, and for such others of that caliber as may have approximately the same or slightly larger cases.

This .22 Hi-Power case, with a fairly steep shoulder, and various lengths of case and straight portion of same, seems to have done well in almost every instance. It can be made from the .22 Savage Hi-Power cartridge brass, from the .25-35 from which the .22 Hi-Power was originally necked down, and from various other cases of nearly the same size and *of* the same head size—all rimmed, of course.

No. 8—.22-250 Ackley

We can think of this Ackley job as being almost identical with the .22 Ackley Improved .219 Zipper, except that it is rimless and is made for use in bolt action rifles like the Models 54 and 70 Winchester, the Models 30-S and 720 Remington, the Mauser, also any of the Savages which handled the .250/3000; but in lever action Savages the pressures must be kept down to not over the usual lever action limits.

The .22-250 is made, as you know, by necking down the .250/3000 Savage Rimless cases. The Ackley shoulder taper is 28° which is the same as Gebby uses in the .22 Varminter. He also uses that taper in many other Ackley jobs as you will observe and those which have different shoulder tapers are all 30° except the .228's which are necked down from .30-1906 brass.

SPECIFICATIONS OF .22-250 ACKLEY

Shoulder Taper	Outside Diameter at Shoulder	Length to Shoulder	Length Case	O.A. Length
28°	0.420″	1.50″	1.92″	2.38″

Use same loads as for .22-250 Standard Varminter.

No. 9—.220 Ackley Improved Swift

Everyone that "improves" the .220 Swift makes it with a sharper shoulder to keep the cases from lengthening, or at least from lengthening so much so that re-loading is impossible without re-sizing and then cutting off the neck of the case. The .220 Improved Ackley is made with 30° shoulder taper; it is fairly fat in front; the case is long and with comparatively little case taper. The .219 Improved Zipper is 1.50″ up to the shoulder and 1.92″ in case length. The .22-250 is also 1.50″ up to the shoulder and 1.92″ in case length, measured on different cases. The .220 Ackley Improved Swift, on the other hand, is an extra 0.010″ in diameter at the shoulder, is 1.73″—(or 0.23″ longer)—up to the shoulder slope than either of the others, and is 2.18″ in case length, or 0.26″ longer over-all, before loading. This gives more "boiler room," it holds more powder, it has greater length to hold down pressures, and if pressures build up they are likely to be around the rim, near the head, which is where pressures build up in long, comparatively straight cartridge cases.

SPECIFICATIONS OF .220 ACKLEY IMPROVED SWIFT

Shoulder Taper	Outside Diameter at Shoulder	Length to Shoulder	Length Case	O.A. Length
30°	0.430″	1.73″	2.18″	2.625″

Case neck length 0.28″

Part of the stocking department in the Ackley factory.

Loads

Increase of 2% to 3% over .220 Swift loads and an approximate increase of 100 f.s.m.v. The Swift can be helped more by using a bullet that does not buck the wind so poorly, which means by a sharper ogive on the nose. However, there is always the danger of a long, sharp bullet setting back at the nose, if not very heavily jacketed and hard in the core. Remember, the .220 Swift sometimes turns its bullets into spray, especially in the instance of a dry bullet out of a clean, cold barrel.

No. 10—.228 Ackley Medium

This cartridge is also made in 0.224" groove and bullet diameter and is then known frequently as the .224 Ackley. It should be distinctly understood by readers that 0.224" bullets cannot be used successfully in 0.228" barrels, and very definitely 0.228" bullets should not be used in 0.224" barrels, nor in cases made for the other size, because the small case will not hold the large diameter bullet without bulging badly, and the smaller bullet is not large enough in diameter to fit tightly in the 0.228" inside diameter case. Also, 0.004" is a good deal of difference in diameter in a .22 caliber rifle; it makes a lot of difference in bullet base, because areas are to each other as the square of like dimensions—the square of the diameter—which means you step up nicely with the 0.228" in area and volumes compare as the cube of similar dimensions.

The whole reason for using a 0.228" diameter in this cartridge was to get greater bullet diameter and greater bullet length and weight, and also to prevent using .22 Hornet and similar bullets not made for such velocities as the 0.228" produces. The 0.228" diameters are long range, 60 to 70-grain bullet cases and are apparently not so good for the light weight bullets as the 0.224" jobs. On the other hand, you need a 0.228" diameter to get best results with a bullet over 55 or 60-grains. Particularly if anyone gets the idea of using an 80 or a 90-grain bullet. In both 0.224" and 0.228" jobs this case is rather short and squatty.

SPECIFICATIONS .228 ACKLEY SHORT

Shoulder Taper	Outside Diameter at Shoulder	Length to Shoulder	Length Case	O.A. Length
35°	0.440"	1.38"	1.78"	2.40"

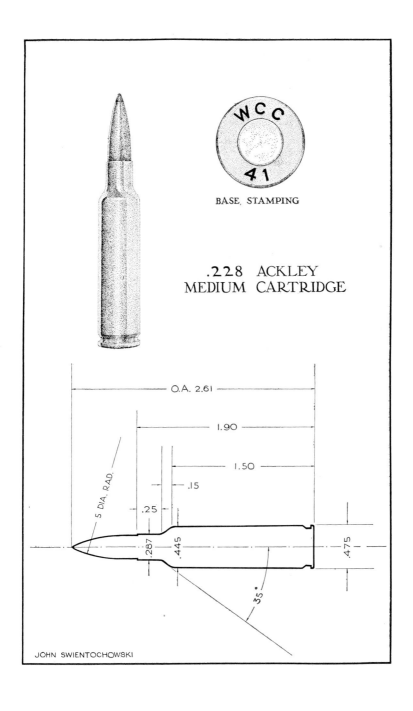

BASE, STAMPING

.228 ACKLEY
MEDIUM CARTRIDGE

O.A. 2.61

1.90

1.50

.15

5 DIA. RAD.

.25

.287

.445

.475

35°

JOHN SWIENTOCHOWSKI

No. 11-.228 Ackley Magnum

This cartridge brass is made by necking down and cutting off .30-1906 cases. The case is made in three lengths, giving the customer the choice of the short, the medium or the long, .228 Ackley cartridge. Ackley will also make his Improved Zipper in different lengths to suit the customer and as short as to hold 20 grains of powder. The .228 however, should have greater capacity than that. The three Ackleys measure 2.40", 2.61" and 2.88" in overall length.

Ackley supplies special forming dies which are easy to use and which insure proper head space, so, it is claimed, with the cases that you make up from the .30-1906 brass. It is assumed that he is prepared to size down, cut off and otherwise prepare such cartridge cases for your .228 if you do not want to bother doing this yourself, or do not feel that you are a close competitor of Willie Westinghouse Smith Jones.

The .228 Ackley is intended for a long range rifle in .22 caliber, for big game shooting, in the two larger sizes, or rather, longer lengths and in tests made by Ackley over 600 yards gave only one-half as much bullet drop as the .30-1906, 172-grain pointed, match cartridge. However, this improvement was much more noticeable past 500 yards than at shorter ranges and apparently did not begin to show up much under 300 yards. The wind bucking qualities of this cartridge are claimed to be much better than the .220 Swift with factory loads, or rather, with factory bullets.

The .228 Ackley Magnum is claimed to have killed well on deer and has been used also on elk, usually effectively. It is a better load for lung and paunch shots, however, than for shots through the shoulder. A very fast bullet of this type would give instant pole-axe effects on shots in the spine of the animal from ear to shoulders. Particularly if the bullet happened to hit in a joint between two vertebrae.

The .228 Medium is the better looking of the three and the long case is the one to pick for plains shooting at coyotes, lobo wolves and at antelope or deer in open country. The author would not suggest any .22 high velocity cartridge for deer hunting in brush. There is too much chance that the bullet will explode and fly to pieces on tough brush and twigs between you and the deer. Much timberland surveying has shown the author that in most Eastern mountain country, in early deer season when most of the trees still have some of their leaves on the branches, that in second growth, and in fairly close timber under 30 to 50 years of age, it is difficult to see for 100 feet clearly, without using an axe to cut away brush between the telescope sight of the transit, and the brilliantly painted red and white range pole or the Wye-level rod. Consequently, flat shooting is not so necessary in brush as knock-down-and-keep-'em-down qualities of a cartridge like the .35 Remington or heavier.

SPECIFICATIONS OF .228 ACKLEY CARTRIDGES

Shoulder Taper	Outside Diameter at Shoulder	Length to Shoulder	Length Case	O.A. Length
.228 Ackley Medium:				
35°	0.445"	1.50"	1.90"	2.61"
.228 Standard Ackley Magnum:				
28°	0.445"	1.68"	2.21"	2.88"

LOADS .228 ACKLEY MAGNUM

(Tests of 6-23-45, Ackley's Chronograph)

Bullet	Powder and Charge	Muzzle Velocity
70-grain	40.0 grains Hi-Vel No. 2	3,600 f.s.
60-grain	42.0 grains Hi-Vel No. 2	3,980 f.s.
60-grain	43.0 grains Hi-Vel No. 2	4,000 f.s.
	(Tests of 6-27-45)	
70-grain	46.0 grains No. 4350	3,700 f.s.
70-grain	35.0 grains No. 3031	3,230 f.s.
70-grain	35.0 grains Hi-Vel No. 2	3,250 f.s.
70-grain	46.0 grains No. 4350	3,700-3,750 f.s.
70-grain	44.0-45.0 grains No. 4350	3,600 f.s. (recommended Load)

No. 12—.228 Ackley Magnum Rimmed

Same as the standard .228 Ackley, except cases are made from .30-40 Krag cases; better for Hi-Side Winchester S.S., Stevens 44½, Farquharson and Sharps-Borchardt actions. Probably best to use loads for medium length, .228 Ackley Rimless, or else cut down the others somewhat, as you are not working with a bolt action.

Canadian shooters should have their .228 Ackleys made from .303 British cases, necked down and cut off, in appearance something like the most excellent design of G. B. Crandall which he calls his .22-303 Varmint-R. Canadians find it easy to obtain plenty of .303 cases as compared with most all other sizes except the .30-30 Winchester, which is also a rimmed cartridge.

Loads for these rimmed cases should be developed gradually, carefully and keeping in mind the probable strength of the rifle action you are using, whether the firing pin is properly bushed, hammer is lightened, and hammer throw is short or long; all this has an effect upon ignition.

All of the loads mentioned in this chapter, for all of the .22 Ackley wildcat cartridges, were primed with Winchester No. 115 primers. If other primers, either weaker or stronger, are used the loads will have to be proportioned to the primers.

Variations in Measurements of Chambers and Cartridges

Many readers will imagine that it is possible and practical to make up 10 reamers or 100 reamers for cutting .22 wildcat chambers, or for finishing them, and that if they are made to the same set of blue prints all of these reamers will be identical in size, contour and shape.

However, it does not always work out that way. P. O. Ackley says of duplicating measurements: "These measurements can vary slightly either way. When new tools are made sometimes they are not exactly the same as the old ones." That refers to cartridges and loading tools, also.

Hervey Lovell has never apparently been able to exactly duplicate the first chambering reamers with which he cut the "Bell" rifles which was the designation of the super-accurate .22/3000 Lovells with slight shoulder slope, (somewhere between 5° and 15°), he made up some 10 or 15 years ago. Very recently he paid $100.00, so he mentioned rather bitterly to the author, to have a number of chambering reamers re-sharpened, and all of them came back re-cut to the wrong dimensions. Obviously, they would cut beautiful chambers but not to the dimensions desired; they might even make more accurate rifles than if cut to the given measurements but they would not duplicate the exact results Lovell hoped to obtain. In running a gunshop, one man cannot do everything. Anyone who has been in the manufacturing game during World War II knows from bitter personal experience that you are exceedingly lucky to get anything done right and you have to ask the government whether you can make it, have to get permission for the materials, and have to fill out enough forms to choke an ox, before you can even try. Life just is not what it used to be!

Free-Boring of Ackley Rifles

A good many readers of shooting magazines assume, incorrectly, that all or at least most of the Ackley barrels are free-bored with all rifling bored out and the barrel cylindrical and smooth inside for a portion of its length from chamber toward the muzzle—this to cut down pressures, increase muzzle velocity, permit the use of more powder in the cartridge, therefore, give the rifle a greater range and a flatter trajectory to the bullet. Actual facts are different from this belief.

P. O. Ackley on June 28, 1945, wrote the author: "Just received a letter from W. F. Vickery on the subject of Free-Boring. Vickery thinks that with lighter bullets the pressures are materially reduced but with the heavier bullets it seems to make little difference. Whether this is true, or whether it merely appeared to act that way, would be a question for prolonged experimentation. I always felt that the main value of free-boring is for the rejuvenation of old barrels. When an old barrel is badly eroded in the throat, it happens sometimes that if free-bored for 1½" to 2" from the throat forward toward the muzzle, accuracy will again be satisfactory for a while. Some gunsmiths who have done quite a bit of this type of work say that it pans out about 50 per cent of the time. I free-bored a .219 Zipper a few days ago and accuracy seems to be good in this particular barrel but I could see no difference in the pressures, although so far I have not loaded this one to the top. In fact, we never have any pressure trouble with the Improved Zipper if any sort of really normal and reasonable loads are used.

"I have always regarded free-bored rifles about as you do and it seems that this might be a quick way to wear the barrel to its finish. On this basis the main value would be in the restoration of shooting qualities in a damaged or rusted old barrel—one ruined or badly gone near the breech. This could be a result of erosion, corrosion, or of burring of lands due to poor cleaning methods; free-boring would remove this metal."

Capt. A. F. Laudensack, the man who designed and built the first of the Model 52 Winchester match rifles, told the author in the Winchester plant upon one occasion that he had free-bored a 52 rifle for 10" ahead of the chamber and the rifle still shot well. However, he made no claim that this free-boring improved the shooting qualities of the rifle, either as to accuracy or velocity.

P. O. Ackley wrote in a letter June 4, 1945 to the author "We do not *regularly* free-bore our Magnums. We get quite a

few orders for this system and the ones we have done from time
to time, on special orders, work out all right. I do not use the
free-boring in my own rifle but that does not mean that it is not
a good idea. As you will probably notice, we are not inclined to
crack up any particular idea too much. We have done about as
much experimenting as most, but even the more radical riflemen
usually go back to the more conservative designs in the end. We
free-bore rifles when the customer wants them cut that way, but
not otherwise."

Fire-Forming Cases

Comment by Ackley: "In regard to gas leaking or gas leakage,
when fire-forming cartridge cases in lengthened chambers of the
'Improved Zipper' type; if any break occurs, it is always up at the
shoulder and for some reason nothing happens at the rear. There
is never any leakage except if a head breaks off, but a solid head
is unlikely to break off and if this occurs in any chamber it has no
connection with fire-forming. In fact, I never had a head come
loose while fire-forming a cartridge; I believe this is the experience
of all the other experimenters who have been using fire-forming
methods. I have fired the .219 Improved Zipper sometimes with
Remington ammunition when practically every case would blow
out at the shoulder. There never seemed to be any escaping gas
coming to the rear. There seemed to be no trouble with inaccuracy
or gas. This apparently indicates that the chamber is thoroughly
sealed before any break occurs at the shoulder. None of these
blow-outs ever resulted in injury to the chamber. It has been our
experience that it takes a good stiff load to really fire-form the
case correctly and if good heavy loads are used much less loss of
brass will occur.

"If a reduced load be used to fire-form, according to our experience, a very high loss of brass will occur; this seems to be the
experience of others."

Wildcat Body Tapers

Ackley commented to the author June 4, 1945: "At the time I
started using the designs (the Ackley cartridge designs), most
gunsmiths were using excessive body tapers. Now the most radical
have gone to the other extreme and have hardly any body taper to
their cartridge cases. We have continued to steer a middle course
as we still think it is the best practice."

Action Strength for .22 Wildcats

Ackley says in this regard: "We have been extremely careful of the actions we fit to .22 wildcats, and other calibers of wildcats. We turn down many orders which call for actions we consider on the border line. Sometimes we are criticised a bit for not fitting barrels to actions that we consider unsafe, but we feel it is better to stay on the safe side and use the actions we are sure of. We simply refuse to use any of the super calibers on the old earlier actions of the Springfield line; we select the Mauser or Enfield as always good for a larger head space."

Shoulder Slopes or Tapers

P. O. Ackley again is quoted: "Most of our own .22 cases, such as the .228 Ackleys, the Improved Zippers, the .17 caliber, are all 28° shoulder. We can see very little difference in small changes of shoulder angle. We have tried the 45° shoulders but did not like the results; we can see no increase in efficiency over the 30° or even the 28° but with the too-sharp angles the head space is hard to maintain. That is, the first shot or two will expand the cases slightly, which causes the bolt to turn down tremendously hard, due to the fact that there is little taper on the shoulder and the case can not be pushed (wedged) into the chamber as easily as with the more tapered design. This necessitates the setting of the head space with full length sizing which I do not like to do. This is also in complete agreement with Ashurst, Gipson and Lovell; they all agree that the 28° and 30° shoulder slopes are the best for satisfactory results." Ackley is now making up rifles also for the .170-250/4500 Ambrose-Landis cartridge with 30° shoulder slope, m.v. 4935 feet.

Reduction of Velocity of Factory Charge in Fire-Formed Case

"Any fire-formed case shows a reduction in velocity with factory loads. A factory load fired in a Kilbourn case or in our Improved Zipper would show a very definite reduction in velocity as compared with the factory chamber. The increase in velocity claimed is only given and realized when the increased hand loads are used and the improvement is entirely due to the fact that increased loads can be used without raising the pressure to an undesirable or dangerous level. The chamber is longer, the sharper slope of shoulder causes the powder to burn satisfactorily, regardless, and we obtain the results usual otherwise only with a larger cartridge in a standard chamber.

"None of our cartridges or loads are what is considered dangerous. We feel that the possibilities of many of the special cartridges on the market, particularly some of the smaller ones, have been over-stressed but we have always preferred to give out only conservative figures and use loads with which the riflemen could duplicate claims made. This seems to be the better plan and many other custom gun-smiths probably find this the better policy. We give velocities which the rifleman should obtain in the field."

Readers may find many of these suggestions helpful and useful in answering questions they have often asked themselves and for which a ready answer was not always available.

Supplementary Ackley Cartridge Data and Comment

When the original Ackley cartridge data was obtained for this book there were some gaps due to lack of samples of some of the cartridges for examination and measurement. There are 17 or more regular .22s and .17s in this line and some others made only upon order. Some loads obviously also required checking at Trinidad. When this was attended to and the gaps were filled this gave Ackley a better idea of exactly what was wanted, and he came through with a lot of general suggestions and comments, many of which are most useful to almost everyone interested in .22 caliber wildcat cart-ridges and even to those not interested in the Ackley line. As this came to hand just as the manuscript had to be shipped to the pub-lisher the only thing to do if much of it were to be included was to add some of it as an addenda to the chapter which has been done.

Attention is called particularly to the discussion and comments upon the relative desirability of the different makes of Mauser actions for use in rebuilt rifles. Thousands of these actions have been shipped into the United States and Canada by returning soldiers and others. It is well to know which are the better ones because you want a *good* action as the basis of your pet .22 varmint rifle.

You will find much other information on the following pages— most of which the average rifleman has not even guessed. Now for the additional Ackley comments:

Excessive Head Space

"Possibly heretofore we have failed to bring out clearly just what our experience suggests does happen when excessive head space exists. The trouble has probably never occurred seriously, in rifles such as the Krag or the single shots, because practically always the head space is adjusted when the new barrel is fitted or when the conversion is made. However, it sometimes happens that we convert Model '99 Savages which have already been barrelled for the standard Zipper or .22 Hi-Power and which have perhaps 0.010″ or 0.012″ or more head space. If these chambers are converted without any change being made in the head space a tremendous loss in the brass takes place by splits or by the separation of the cartridge heads. This must indicate that the head must be tight enough so that there is no give in that portion of the case. If all of the movement in the brass takes place in the forward direction there is no trouble but if some of the movement can take place in both directions a separation is likely to follow. I have never had any detrimental effects from such breaks in these actions; there seems to be no backward rush of gas which would prove injurious to the shooter and this may be due to good gas protection in these actions. However, it is essential that the head space be minimum for best results when fire-forming *rimmed* cases. For some reason head space does not seem to affect *rimless* cases as much as rimmed so far as this particular trouble is concerned.

Possible Injury to Rifle Chambers

"Now with respect to injury to chambers. There have been two or three instances brought to my attention which gave chamber injury. In each case this was the PMVF (Powell-Miller-Venturi Free-bored). The damage, if it may be called that, occurred at the shoulder. As you know the PMVF requires a tremendous amount of fire-forming. The capacity of the case is increased a great deal and in a very radical manner as far as shoulder angle is concerned. In these cases, using such a tremendous powder charge for such a small bore capacity, when a rupture occurs at the shoulder the unburned powder apparently rushes through the breach in the brass and sand blasts (gas cuts) a portion of the shoulder, exactly corresponding in shape to the break itself, at the shoulder of the chamber. These are usually elliptical in shape. However, with smaller capacity cases such as our .250 Magnum or the Zipper, I have fired as many as 25 old mercuric brass cases in a row, *all* of which ruptured in this manner and none of which gave any effect upon the chamber at all. It must follow that this chamber damage would occur (would be more likely to occur—Author) only with very large capacity cases where so much of the unburned powder (or gases, or partly burned powder and part gases—Author) could rush out and come in contact with a small portion of the chamber.

This comment is not made with the idea of criticising any particular design or maker; it is made simply to illustrate the effect of excessive powder capacities and their effect upon the chamber when fire-forming.

Choosing the Better Mauser Actions

"As to the selection of action—we do not use *all* Mauser actions; it so happens that I prefer the Mauser to all other existing designs (as does Hervey Lovell—Author), for several reasons, but it does not follow that we recommend all Mauser actions, because there is a great deal of difference between Mauser actions obtained from different sources. We consider the Erfurt only suitable for the lowest pressure range of modern calibers. I usually refuse to re-barrel the Erfurt with anything larger and higher pressure than the 7mm or any other caliber of higher pressure than the 7mm or 257. In other words, I would not want to use one of these Erfurt actions with the .220 Swift, the .22 Varminter or .22-250 on it and I would not want to use anything higher than the standard .30-1906 military load.

Later Issue Mausers

"The late issue Mausers are apparently O.K. (for rebarrelling) when in good condition. However, we select only the better makes of these Mauser actions.

"The better Mausers are the Oberndorf, Haenel and Sauer for the 'hottest' calibers, with the exception of the late issue ones and then we grade them on down as we think best. Berlin, Danzig and such are always good actions when in good condition and are perfectly all right to use with any reasonable loads.

The Enfield Action

"The Enfield action is recommended more highly for calibers giving considerable breech pressure than most other actions. I (Ackley) do not hold to this opinion. I think it is a good action and perfectly satisfactory for any of the larger calibers and this also applies to the Model 70 Winchester and the *nickel steel* Springfield actions. The Springfields I really discriminate against are the so-called re-heat treated ones and the old hard, low number Springfields. I especially do not like the re-heat treated ones because in many cases they have been re-heat treated by someone who does not know the score and there has been more damage done to the receiver than anything else.

"We have tested these old hard Springfield receivers after they have been fitted with late issue bolts of nickel steel type and found them to be reasonably strong. In fact, standard blue-pill tests loads do not hurt them at all. Recently we blew an Enfield action completely to pieces. We have now selected a 1944 late Mauser action with which we are going to try to do the same thing (with overloads—Author). If I can get this accomplished within a reasonably short time I will give you a detailed report of what happens and will try to explain in sufficient detail so that you can get the idea across to your readers, explaining and showing the reaction to overloads of the different design of actions.

Number of Different Ackleys Which Can be Made Up

"Dealing with the number of .22 calibers, it happens that we have a great many special reamers and can make up any special reamer according to the dreams of the experimenter or the enthusiast. We do not make an excessive charge for helping these experimenters with their designs and problems; we are always glad to make up the special tools provided they will give us the time so that this special work does not hold back regular work and take our time when their work should have preference to purely experimental work.

"With almost any cartridge it is possible to give any length or capacity to the case (up to a normal maximum) that the customer may want. If a short case is desired the reamer would not be run in as far. We can vary the standard .22-250 design to suit almost anyone using some combination of reamers that we would be bound to have on hand. The same applies to a good many other calibers. For instance, we can furnish all of our .228 series for use with 0.224″ bullets, or 0.230″ bullets or 0.240″ bullets. We can supply the .240 Magnum in almost any length or bore from .22 on up.

Flexibility of Different .22 Wildcats

"Regarding the flexibility of the various different .22 cartridge cases, I, personally, think this angle has been overworked, and that almost every caliber is going to require that proper loads be worked out for it. We feel that too much propaganda has been put out by individuals concerning only individual rifles. This has the detrimental effect of giving the impression to the layman that certain calibers are practically fool-proof and that they will shoot with any load in anyone's hands; that 1″ groups are practically automatic with such caliber or rifle. I have seen a good many groups smaller than ½″ at 100 yards. I am not able to shoot them very consistently and so do not think that many barrels will *consistently* do it. One sees the groups that are hung up in prominent places but he does not see the many more groups that have been thrown away. I would be more interested in knowing how many groups it took to get the abnormally good group. I imagine you are pretty much of the same opinion—having gone through the mill for so many years in the target game.

Variation in Neck Thickness of Cartridges

"Wartime ammunition has shown such a rather wide variation in both rim thickness and neck thickness that more head space trouble has developed throughout the war than any period heretofore. It seems to be necessary, at the present time, to widen the tolerances very slightly for the reason that so many kinds and thicknesses of brass are now being used to make cases for the various calibers. The Improved Zipper, for instance, will accept brass made from cases of various calibers (including the .219 Zipper, .25-35 and .22 Savage H.P.—Author). This includes also brass made over a period of a good many years and just about every variation in the book will be found under such conditions. This comment also applies to wartime bullets.

Wartime Bullets and Their Variations

"In addition to the few custom bullet makers whom we had before the war, like Sisk, Barnes and others, there have been a great number of dies developed for every conceivable kind of press or tool and every shooter and his brother has started making .22 caliber bullets. The RCBS equipment works out fairly well for the average .22 shooter but the big trouble is that every illogical as well as every conservative idea has been developed, so that it is almost impossible to throat a barrel to suit them all. In the old days they would tell us to throat them for the Sisk bullets and that about covered the subject. Now we have so many kinds and shapes of bullets that you almost have to free-bore a barrel for ¼″ to accommodate some of the newer style bullets. For instance, we have a bullet on display that is a full 0.2245″ diameter at the base of the 8S ogive and from there back it tapers to 0.223″ or a butt which is 0.0015″ *smaller* in diameter and leaving a very sharp angle at the largest point of the bullet.

"This means that you have to throat the barrel with a very special type of throat if it is going to be throated according to the ideas of the shooter. Imagine how it will fit the regular style bullets? You can imagine how many such ideas have been developed and the difficulties of gunsmiths who have to put these ideas into steel and get results. We have no quarrel or argument with these new ideas; this one mentioned shoots very well. We do not object to making up such designs, but it takes time and patience and if the design does not work out will the designer blame the custom gunsmith or the design? The necessity of making such bullets through the war will probably result, eventually, in getting some pretty good bullet designs before the experimental work dies down and regular commercial bullets of really first class average accuracy are again available from many sources and in needed quantity.

Thick Case Necks and the Troubles They Bring

"The condition of excessively thick necks has perhaps been worse in the .22-250 and the .22 Varminter (standard) than in some others. Everyone has made Varminter or .22-250 cases and so have all of his uncles and cousins and from every conceivable type of brass that would lend itself to this design. Different lots of brass give different neck thicknesses and, primarily, they give different powder capacities to the re-formed case. This affects accuracy and pressure and sometimes affects it materially. A change in interior shape and powder capacity changes the ballistic characteristics of the whole cartridge. There is no remedy for such a present condition because of the scarcity of cartridge brass in the hands of the shooter and the gunmaker alike. A rifleman uses what he can obtain; he can do nothing else! The difficulties you have yourself outlined in these particular paragraphs are some of the reasons why it is not always possible to guarantee the accuracy of a barrel. There are simply too many conditions beyond the control of the custom gunsmith after the barrel leaves his hands. Sometimes a lack of shooting ability of an outfit is due to poor stocking or the swelling of the walnut wood, due to absorption of moisture by the pores of the wood, as I understand you are outlining elsewhere in your books.

"In three instances I have seen rifles which did not perform well in one way or another, and I found that they had been stocked so that the bolt closure was being held up by the wood at least one-third of the lug seating distance. One Mauser in particular, with a .250 Magnum chamber (it could just as well have occurred with a .22 wildcat) was not utilizing much over 50% of the locking surface and the bolt itself had set back easily 1/32″ (or 0.03125″ expressed decimally). This rifle had been stocked by a supposedly good stocker. In two other instances, both of them .250 Magnums on Model 70 actions, the bolts were engaging not over 66 2/3% of their area or surface. The firing pins in each instance happened to be placed sufficiently low so that the rifles could be fired. In both instances I found the trouble before the shooters lost their heads from an explosion caused by a partly unlocked rifle promptly blowing open. These poor fits could have caused serious accidents— with the cause probably laid to the custom gunsmith doing the chambering!"

(The stocking of a high intensity rifle should be watched very carefully to see that the recoil shoulder bears properly against the wood; that the wood of the tang, on top, does not bind—and then split, ruining the stock; and that the wood does not protrude or bind so that the bolt handle cannot be lowered to its full travel).

Factory Cartridges Can be Used in .22 Improved Zippers

"As you have noticed by our catalog we can furnish any length Zipper or similar case wanted and for any reasonable powder capacity. However, the standard design is made as standard, so that it will accept factory loaded commercial ammunition. To many, in fact to the majority, this is a very favorable feature; I feel that any wildcat that will accept a variety of factory ammunition will be infinitely more satisfactory to the average shooter than special wildcats that necessitate forming the cases before any shooting whatever can be done.

"With such calibers as the .22 Improved Zippers very good accuracy is obtained with factory ammunition even though they show a reduction of *200 f. s.* in velocity. (P. O. Ackley has his own chronograph and can test this easily, or confirm it—Author). If the rifleman has no way at the moment to reload his empties, he can always, in normal times, buy a box or two of factory loads and go about his business."

(However, he will have to re-sight his rifle, except at very short ranges, as that drop of 200 f.s.m.v. and a corresponding reduction at all other ranges, will cause a change in muzzle flip of the barrel, and will also cause the bullet to strike lower all along the path of its flight; consequently, the rifle will almost certainly shoot materially lower and with possibly ½″ to 2″ change in horizontal zero at 100 yards. A change in sighting or rather in normal zero, of the rifle, is of much more importance to the hunter than most people imagine. Always remember, that when a .22 rifle like the Zipper is made into an "Improved Zipper" by enlarging or lengthening its chamber, or changing the slope of the forepart of the chamber, you have automatically changed the ballistics results to be expected from factory ammunition shot in that chamber. Any variation from this result is of an individual rifle only, is good at only one range and can not be expected to be the same but will vary at other ranges—Author).

"We can also make the .22 Improved Ackley Zipper or the .22 Hi-Power using the .25 Remington case and furnish this for actions requiring *rimless* cases"

(It should be obvious here that such rimless cases could not be used successfully in chambers intended for Rimmed Zipper or .22 Savage H.P. cases—Author).

Other Cases Used for .22-250 Ammunition

Ackley says that they can furnish the .22-250 in two other versions. One is called the .22-06 (made from the .30-1906 cartridge brass) and is slightly greater in capacity than the regular .22-250, but gives a man plenty of cases who has .30-1906 empties to convert, but has no .250/3000 Savage cases to neck down. This feature has been mentioned elsewhere regarding other .22-250's made from .30-1906, or other larger cases made from .30-1906 empties. The .22-06 Ackley is almost identical with the medium size .228 Ackley. It will accept standard .250 brass necked to .22 but is fire-formed to give approximately a 35° shoulder angle somewhat venturified and with slightly greater case capacity due to the removal of the excessive case body taper.

The .22-250 Ackley is also made up in a different version with mostly a straighter body taper. Some are ordering this version because it extracts better. However, were it not made with a very sharply shaped shoulder it would not extract easier. The straighter sides make that shoulder considerably larger in area and that is like butting the end of a 30″ log against a side of a building; it will not stick—it will tend to rebound. Ackley claims there is no change in accuracy but loads can be increased appreciably and Swift ballistics can be duplicated, or nearly so, with either of these versions, which it is not quite possible to do with the standard .22-250. In this regard it might better be mentioned here that the .220 Swift is fairly sharply tapered *to* the shoulder.

The Improved Swift

The Ackley Improved Swift is another Ackley wildcat which will accept factory ammunition. When so used, the factory ammunition does not show the considerable reduction in velocity given by the .219 Zipper in its wildcat. The change by fire-forming is much less radical. On the other hand, with the .220 Swift the pressure is a great deal higher than with the .219 Zipper. It might be well to insert here a caution because of the great concern felt by Messrs. Pugsley and R. F. Sedgley in the firing of .220 Swift factory ammunition in the .22/4000 Sedgley-Schnerring cartridge chamber as pointed out elsewhere by the author; the .22/4000 being made up from either the 7mm or the .257 Roberts cases. The .22/4000 had a good large diameter at the shoulder. Ackley claims that his improved Swift is one of the best of the Super .22's. He feels this is so in bolt action rifles, but the semi-rimmed design may give some trouble in rifles not properly altered to handle it.

The Real Use of the .228 Ackley Magnum

P. O. Ackley has talked quite a bit to the author about the best uses for the various rimless and rimmed versions (three of each) of the .228 Ackley cartridges. He never recommends this caliber for purely varmint shooting except for *very* long range woodchuck and coyote shooting—this when the shooter gets an especial thrill out of making an abnormally long hit. He feels that its real use is as a deer cartridge, or for soft skinned African hoofed game of not much larger than deer size where it would be effective. He says that he has never seen a better killing cartridge for deer. In fact, he claims he has never seen its equal for that purpose based on his own observation and reports from users in the field. He has had a great many such reports and but one mentioned having to hit the deer more than once; the average shot producing a kill as if electrocuted, from shock transmitted to the brain and the nerve centers, hydraulic action on the brain and heart, lungs, and intestinal area.

On elk an entirely different effect was obtained. In no case have they ever recovered a bullet from an elk. Expansion is very good on deer, but on heavier bodied elk, for some reason, bullets showed very little expansion, the bullet passed right through the animal, was not recovered and the wound of exit was very small. He suggests that this would indicate they have a lot of work ahead of them in developing bullets suitable for elk in the .228.

Sisk was really bearing down on this problem as was mentioned at last reports. He has a number of .228 rifles on order for this experimental work and for next Fall's hunting. Ackley and Sisk are working together to some extent, so it is reported, on the production of a solid alloy bullet with the exception of the soft point, which is expanding. They have done a good deal of game shooting with this rifle and get very even expansion, so Ackley mentions; it expands on Western ground squirrels yet does not blow up on deer. Usually the 70-grain bullet, which has a very long point, will maintain at least 75% of its weight on a hit on game, which means the butt of the bullet still holds together to the extent of 49 or 50 grains. It usually just about shoots through the animal. These bullets are made of pure copper with a specially designed soft point.

The author would like to caution here what they are talking about is mostly Western deer hunting, which normally is a whole lot more open and long range than Eastern deer shooting in dense choppings. In this, the light recoil, light weight of ammunition and the very flat trajectory would be of great advantage to many hunters. Women can shoot such a rifle without fear of recoil, the flat trajectory makes it possible to hit over 300 yards when shooting through a small opening in undergrowth, without danger of an unseen twig being cut above the line of aim and thus deflecting the bullet. On the other hand, such a smaller caliber bullet is definitely not *likely* to hold together when striking young hickory, scrub oak, jack pine, chestnut or black oak limbs, twigs and brush, which one is very likely to hit between you and the game, at least a third to one half of your shots, when shooting at *running* or moving deer. As deer move through brush in bounds and do not run along in a fairly level line, and as they move irregularly and fast, a man just does not have time to pick out nice open places in the scrub to shoot through on most chances; occasionally he can do so but not always.

Even when two or three men are hunting together, one on the track, the other on the uphill side and maybe somewhat ahead of the tracker, usually the first thing that either knows that the deer has jumped in front of them is a crash in the brush and when they look up there goes the deer's back side and flag over the nearest heap of trash, or maybe he is sneaking along with his head down and circling around back of the tracker. You are too busy trying to see whether it has horns, instead of merely long ears which look like horns, how many points are on each horn and whether it is *legal* to begin firing, to look at every nook and cranny to see whether that it the best place to shoot through, so your bullet gets to the game instead of flying to pieces or being deflected on a hard twig about the size of your thumb that you did not see when you touched off.

Western deer shooting is generally much more open, across a ravine, or up or down a fairly open draw, maybe on the point of a hill or some place where one can often use flat trajectory and quick shooting to advantage. They, of course, have thick brush here and there, but the soil on most Western range country is not of sufficient depth or fertility to support a heavy stand of vegetation of any kind. When a deer gets up you can see it and you can see it plainly at several hundred yards. The places where the author has found the most deer and black bear and where he has been nearly run down by both, was in such thick brush that half the time one was down trying to crawl through it; or else as quietly as possible moving the brush to the side with the hands. Suddenly the brush starts to erupt deer, bear or what have you. You see brush moving but if you actually see anything but the rear end of a deer you are lucky. The only direction in which you can see anything for distances greater than 30 to 75 feet is straight up or else across a ravine on another brushy hillside which itself may be just as thick.

At 200 yards a .22 Newton shooting a long shell and plenty of powder behind a 70 to 80-grain bullet will have more than twice the energy of the old .22 Savage H.P. and 36% more than the .250/3000. It will have almost as much energy remaining at 300 yards as both the .22 H.P. and the .25/3000 Savage combined or about the energy of the .405 Winchester. At all ranges beyond the muzzle it has more energy than the .30-40 Krag. This is why the .228 Ackleys are deer cartridges, rather than charges to knock off a pine squirrel across a ravine. Crows, hawks, buzzards, turkeys, sod poodles and the like are simply "blasted" within 50 to 100 yards and the remains "erupt" and come floating down for 10 or 15 yards around, or may even be blown into or flattened on the ground. You pick up a leg here and a wing there. Such blasting effect is simply not required on small varmints. And very definitely it is not desired on grouse, wild turkeys, geese (where you can shoot them with a rifle), cottontail rabbits or anything which you expect to use for food.

A Choice Between Various Ackley Cartridges

P. O. Ackley commented in mid-summer of 1945 to the author: "Ballistic laboratory tests show that the standard .219 Zipper case will give the 55-grain bullet 3,200 f.s.m.v. using 26.5 grains of 3031 with a breech pressure of a bit over 40,000 pounds per square inch. The same muzzle velocity may be obtained with 18.0 grains of 4198 in the R-2 but the breech pressure will be upwards of 50,000 pounds per square inch. The same comparison applies to the standard Zipper and the Improved Zipper. The velocity can be improved better than 400 f.s. with pressures remaining approximately the same or possibly a few thousand pounds higher. The powder charge must necessarily be increased but the pressure level remains much the same.

"As we go up with the size of the case and powder charge for a given bullet the pressure level will not be greatly increased and sometimes not at all, but if this increase plus the velocities fall off in comparison to the increase in capacity and charge this is the reason we say that the Improved Zipper case or a case of that size is about the best all-around cartridge for the .224 bore. The general all-around over-all efficiency is not as great per grain of powder as the R-2 and related cases, but it is very much greater than with the .22-60 and .22-348 and is an all-around compromise so that the .219 Zipper or related designs are just about tops so far as general utility is concerned. They cover a wide variety of shooting without being materially lacking in any particular except that they are fairly noisy.

"The general utility feature has also been found true of the .228. As we increase the capacity of powder charge over that of the standard .228 or the largest .228 Magnum things begin to happen next day in the wrong direction. Velocities do not increase anything like the increase in powder charge or in capacity. Pressures do not give trouble, but the efficiency—the ballistic efficiency of the cartridge—comes down as the size goes up after leaving a certain size and powder capacity. This ballistic efficiency is reduced for any given bore diameter or caliber as soon as a certain point is passed. The perfect cartridge is the one which is designed to be exactly at this point. If of good sensible shape, as well, it should be both accurate and highly efficient ballistically and it should also be quite flexible in loading."

Chapter 8

THE GEBBY .22 WILDCAT CARTRIDGES
THE .22 VARMINTER

THE NAME ".22 Varminter" (patented by J. B. Gebby), suggests a cartridge designed for shooting varmints such as lobo wolves, coyotes, woodchucks, foxes, hawks, crows, prairie dogs and similar animals and birds. They are frequently difficult to spot and kill, due to cover, range and the small size of the vital areas. Extreme accuracy and very flat trajectory are therefore important in long-range shooting at such game.

Many persons have experimented with .22 cartridges made by necking down and possibly shortening or lengthening .250/3000 Savage cases. Obviously, different case lengths, shapes, capacities and bullet diameters, weights and designs, could have been employed. Often experimenters spring up in different sections of the country and bring out new cartridges about the same time. Each feels that he is the originator. Many such riflemen correspond and exchange ideas or suggestions. Quite frequently someone takes a cartridge design in common public use, or used by some private experimenter 20 to 40 years previously, and changes the shoulder slope, the length of straight part of the case, the neck, lightens the bullet or uses a different design of the bullet, makes a different chamber throat, or whatnot and out he comes then with a new and special cartridge. Some of the ideas may be new; others may have been old long before his time. All deserve credit.

About the year 1934 the author of this work was deluged with a mass of targets, groups, and a number of manuscripts and suggestions on a .22-250 cartridge by the then Capt. Grosvenor L. Wotkyns, writing from California. Grove, as he was known to his friends, passed away in the Spring of 1945. These letters and manuscripts were quite enthusiastic and credited this cartridge then to J. B. Sweany, the gunsmith, which credit is confirmed by Hervey Lovell, but Wotkyns handled the correspondence, which was extensive, he contributed ballistic ideas, some quite practical but not all of which may have been original as the .250/3000 Savage cartridge was a Charles Newton design and development originally, put out to fit the 1899 Savage action, and nearly everything made from it seems to shoot well.

The author visited Captain Wotkyns in his office and at his home and was a guest in his quarters while Grove was stationed at Frankford Arsenal, Bridesburg, Pa., and lived on the arsenal grounds. This was probably about 1925-1928. Wotkyns was quite anxious to have this cartridge put out commercially, at that time, but unfortunately for everyone concerned, including the shooting public, and especially the .22 rifle cranks of varmint hunting type, it came along at a time when manufacturers were beginning to reduce the number of cartridges rather than to increase them or add better ones.

The original .22-250 Sweany-Wotkyns cartridge used bullets of a different and smaller diameter than the .22-250's of today. When the .22-250/3000 or, as it is officially called by Gebby, the .22 (standard) Varminter cartridge, was put out by Jerry Gebby and J. Bushnell Smith, the boring measurement was increased from 0.2225″ or 0.223″ to the more recent 0.224″ barrels which most excellent blanks were bored and rifled by C. A. Diller or J. R. Buhmiller, both making them at various times for the Ohio Rifle Barrel Co., which was the Gebby or the Gebby-Smith outlet. Gebby fits the barrels, throats and chambers the barrel—which he claims is the principal feature in barrel accuracy—turns down the barrel if necessary, and blues it. He also beds the barrel into the forearm.

It may be that Gebby, or Gebby and J. B. Smith, or J. B. Smith independently, experimented with a .22-250 rifle and case, much earlier than many heard of it, and not wishing to deprive anyone of credit where credit is due, this thought is brought forward here. The important thing is, what is available and where is it available at present?

The firm supplies three cartridges of .22 wildcat type, but these will be commented upon later, while the .22-250, or .22 Varminter, will be discussed here in the preliminary portion of this chapter.

The .22 Varminter, being a sharply necked case, according to its promoters, handles "rather large and the medium I.M.R. powders better than some more gradually necked cases of somewhat similar powder capacity." The reason is obvious—the pressure builds up quicker.

No one, except possibly a few small custom loaders, provides loaded ammunition of .22 Varminter, or of .22-250 caliber today as this is being written, however, before World War II, Smith's Custom Loads, of which J. B. Smith, of Middlebury, Vermont, is proprietor (and associate of Gebby in promoting the .22 Varminter) was prepared to do so, and I believe, is again loading ammunition since leaving the Naval Service.

This or a very similar cartridge will probably be supplied commercially by one or more of the large ammunition companies, one of these days—possibly before this appears in print—and if so supplied, should then be a very popular and very efficient and effective varmint commercial cartridge, especially if put out in a rifle like the 70 Winchester or the 720 Remington with good weight of both stock and barrel and proper attention to snug bedding of the recoil shoulder or shoulders into the stock.

Rifles which would best handle the .22 Varminter, or the .22-250 as well, would include the short Mauser, the .250/3000 Savage bolt action, the 70 Winchester, 720 Remington, as above mentioned, the Sauer-Mauser or Waffenfabrik Mauser rifles, probably with slight alterations, which would come under the head of Mauser actions, and similar types suitable for high intensity and high pressure military and sporting ammunition. This, of course, includes the .30-1906 Springfield and the 1917 Enfield.

As may have been mentioned briefly in other copy some years ago, a 16-pound, very long and heavily stocked Springfield .22 Varminter rifle was sent around to various Gun Editors with many claims as to super-accuracy of performance. Actually, it showed no such traits while here with the author; in part due to having the stock too long and the scope set so far forward that a stockily built man, with wide shoulders and broad chest could not get up close enough to the scope to see more than a pin point of light through the scope—a condition ideally adapted to giving a wild shot and some eyestrain. But it did give accuracy about equal to a good standard weight military Springfield.

It did not, at some other places, it is reported, do as well as many other .22 Varminters. My son, shooting in my presence, scored 99, 98 and 99 at 100 yards on the regular 100-yard small bore targets with 2″ 10-ring and I had a 98 and a 97 at the same time, both in mid-winter, in real gusty wind conditions, and cool, although the best day for a month or more, as it was a bad winter. We were, obviously, not in a position to either cut off the stock or to mount another scope block closer to the eye on a loaned rifle. But why anyone should desire a rifle of those proportions is beyond this author. The sensible proportions of a .22 Varminter bolt action rifle for hunting are a weight of 8½ to 10½ pounds, plus scope, and with 24″ to 26″ barrel.

In our local tests of this rifle, using J. Bushnell Smith's loaded ammunition, we had no difficulty whatever with sticking cartridges, locked bolt, burst necks, shaved rims, excessively long cases or appearances of excessive pressure on primer or bolt head. The loads were 3,250 and 3,750 f.s. charges and in a rifle built to suit a man weighing 150 to 180 pounds should have been much better.

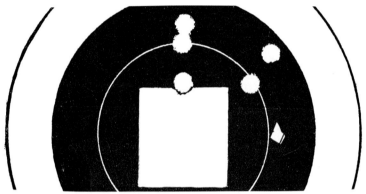

IMR. 3031 IN .22 VARMINTER

This 1.0″ group at 100 yards, was put on with 30.0 grs. duPont No. 3031 and Sisk-Niedner 55-gr. bullets at 3,250 f.s.

The following loads have been suggested by Gebby or Smith, or both, for the *standard* .22 Varminter cartridge, made from the .250/3000 Savage case necked down.

These were supplied before Smith entered the services and any more recent ones will be included in copy a bit later in this chapter. However, they are very complete. They could be used, with such *modifications* as may be required due to any difference in bullet fit, weight or cartridge and chamber dimensions and twist of rifling used, in .22-250 rifles. The reader should begin with reduced loads from these, when making such trials, if he does not have loads suggested for those calibers of rifles. Twist, diameter of rifling and grooves, diameter and bearing length of bullet, seating depth, closeness of throat to bullet, temperature and similar conditions all affect breech pressures and should be borne in mind at all times when working up a load, or when taking data from one set of suggestions and using it as a basis of experiment in another which may vary in one, two, three or more essential conditions.

This .22 Varminter standard cartridge rifle has a very light and not at all obnoxious recoil, consequently, the rifle can be built in practical length, size and weight, and a bull gun with super-stock and barrel is not at all necessary.

.22 VARMINTER LOADS

Loads recommended by J. Bushnell Smith or Jerry Gebby

Bullet	Powder	Charge	M.V.	Rec. By
50-gr. 8S (Morse)	duPont 4320	38.0 gr.	3,890 f.s.	J. B. Smith
50-gr. 8S	4320	36.0 gr.	3,760 f.s.	J. B. Smith
			(Standard charge)	
50-gr. 8S	4320	39.0 gr.	4,070 f.s.	J. B. Smith

The above loads for deer, antelope, sheep, wolves, coyotes, long range shots at woodchucks et cetera.

Bullet	Powder	Charge	M.V.	Rec. By
55-gr. Sisk-Niedner	duPont 3031	30.0 gr.	3,250 f.s.	J. B. Smith
40-gr. 8S	....	......	4,190 f.s.	J. B. Smith
			(Woodchuck load)	
50-gr. 8S	4198	25.0 gr.	3,250 f.s.	J. B. Smith
			(Woodchuck load)	
55-gr. F. M. J.	4198	25.0 gr.	3,000 f.s.	J. B. Smith
			(Foxes or turkeys)	
45-gr. F. M. J.	4198	22.0 gr.	3,000 f.s.	J. B. Smith
			(Foxes or turkeys)	
45-gr. F. M. J.	duPont Bulk Shotgun Smokeless 8-10.0 gr.		1,700-2,000 f.s. (Squirrels, foxes, rabbits, large grouse—head shots, and where little tearing is desired.)	J. B. Smith
45-gr. F. M. J.	duPont Shotgun Bulk 8.5-9.0 gr.		1,800-1,900 f.s. (Fox, gray and black squirrels.)	Gebby
45 or 46-gr. S. P. or H. P.	duPont No. 80 5-6.0 gr.		1,300-1,550 f.s. (Squirrels in Pennsylvania where FMP bullets may not be used on game.)	

LOADS CHRONOGRAPHED AT KINGS MILLS IN .22 VARMINTER,

28" BARREL, 0.224" GROOVE DIAMETER, 14" PITCH

Bullet	*Powder*		*Charge*	*M.V.*
	duPont			
46-gr. Hornet	4227		8.5 gr.	1,792 f.s.
46-gr. Hornet	4227		10.0 gr.	1,980 f.s.
46-gr. Hornet	4227		12.5 gr.	2,268 f.s.
46-gr. Hornet	80		8.0 gr.	1,786 f.s.
46-gr. Hornet	duPont	Shotgun	8.0 gr.	1,780 f.s.
50 gr. Sisk	4198		15.0 gr.	2,296 f.s.
50-gr. Sisk	4198		18.0 gr.	2,555 f.s.
50-gr. Sisk	4198		22.0 gr.	3,140 f.s.
50-gr. Sisk	3031		22.5 gr.	3,044 f.s.
50-gr. Sisk	3031		27.5 gr.	3,218 f.s.
50-gr. Sisk	3031		35.0 gr.	3,884 f.s.
50-gr. Sisk	4320		35.0 gr.	3,629 f.s.
50-gr. Sisk	4320		36.0 gr.	3,767 f.s.
50-gr. Sisk	4320		37.0 gr.	3,785 f.s.
50-gr. Sisk	4320		38.0 gr.	3,889 f.s.
40-gr. Express	4320		40.0 gr.	4,441 f.s.
55-gr. Express	4320		35.0 gr.	3,599 f.s.
55-gr. Express	4320		36.0 gr.	3,701 f.s.
55-gr. Express	4320		37.0 gr.	3,749 f.s.

A Comparison of the Three .22 Varminter Gebby Cartridges

This is a frank and candid comparison of the three .22 Varminter cartridges—the .22 Varminter, the .22 Senior Varminter and the .22 Junior Varminter—their physical characteristics and loads. Such comparison is necessary to prevent riflemen readers from becoming confused between the various ones and to eliminate likelihood of using a load in one intended for either of the others.

Jerry Gebby, of 298 Springbrook Blvd., Dayton 5, Ohio, markets rifles for all three cartridges, and may, in time, see the advisability of having arms for one or two *smaller* cases, which give less report and are not so powerful, for use in thickly settled communities. However, any of the three calibers mentioned can be underloaded successfully with lighter charges than the full loads.

Mr. Gebby has declined to supply the author with standard chamber or cartridge dimensions, as he has declined to supply same to others, but he has in past given the Varminter standard shoulder slope as 28° and for comparison the author has carefully measured all three loaded cartridges, as supplied to him by Mr. Gebby or by T. K. Lee, so that you will be able to recognize any of them and make practical and sensible comparisons. The author believes that a policy of frankness with the public is best, as anyone skilled with a

J. E. Gebby milling extractor groove in a Varminter barrel.

micrometer and an engineer's or draftsman's scale can, within a few minutes, find out the dimensions of any rifle cartridge and with a sulphur cast get the exact chamber dimensions likewise.

The name ".22 Varminter" as a sales slogan has been copyrighted by Mr. Gebby, but that does not appear to have interfered, so far, with the marketing of rather similar .22-250 cartridges and some day we may have a commercial .22-250 cartridge of rather familiar lines marketed as the ".22 Insect" something or other; which will be a fine thing for all those accustomed to having a .22 Varminter or a .22-250 standard caliber rifle, because factory loaded ammunition will then appear which may be used; and empty cases made available which may be re-loaded with little or no re-forming, except possibly a neck re-sizing before loading.

The availability of commercial ammunition would avoid the necessity of an explosives license, magazine, re-loading work when time is unavailable and everyone would benefit. Gebby was for four years, it is said, superintendent of the barrel plant of the Frigidaire unit of General Motors—Frigidaire being reportedly the largest manufacturers of .50-caliber Browning machine guns in the United States. He has been a .22 target shot of note and this, with his mechanical bent, is helpful in turning out .22 varmint rifles.

The .22 Standard Varminter is made from the .250/3000 Savage case as stated. This, a rimless case, is of moderate size, powder capacity and brass thickness.

The .22 Senior Varminter is made from the .257 Remington-Robert Rimless cartridge case. This is a larger and stronger cartridge. It (the .257) was originally designed by N. H. Roberts; Gebby has made a .22 out of it.

The .22 Junior Varminter is made from the .32-40 Ballard & Marlin and can also be made from the .32-40 Winchester case, practically the same. A cartridge very similar to the Junior Varminter was produced, probably before 1910, by Dr. Mann. It was made at least as early as 1910 by A. O. Niedner—was made up commercially by him then; by Hervey Lovell in 1912; and was pushed by Niedner again around 1922. A resumé of these early .22-32/40 rifles is given just below for your information. All three Gebby calibers are made with 1 turn in 14″ of rifling, right hand twist, 0.224″ diameter barrels for 0.224″ diameter bullets. The first two for the Springfield, Mauser, Winchester Model 70, Remington 720, 30-s, the 1917 Enfields and others as mentioned. These cartridges have real merit for long range varmint shooting.

The Earliest .22-32/40 Rifles

Such rifles were made up by Charles Newton many, many years ago. They were also designed and manufactured by A. O. Niedner, as just mentioned, as early as 1910 and probably at a still earlier year. The author corresponded with the late Charles Newton as early as about 1905.

In the Spring of 1910, as described in *Hunting With the Twenty-two,* the late C. E. Howard, of North Park, Colorado, purchased from A. O. Niedner a Hi-Side Winchester S.S. rifle equipped with 26″ hard steel barrel. He equipped this with a 4-power Sidle scope, later removing this and putting on a 6-power Malcolm.

The .22-32/40 by Niedner was a full-capacity cartridge of that day, was loaded with a 60-grain metal-cased bullet made by using .22 Short cases taken from the machines before being headed-up and placing these over lead cores and swaging the two together. The 60-grain bullet was driven by 25.0 grains of Lightning No. 1 powder.

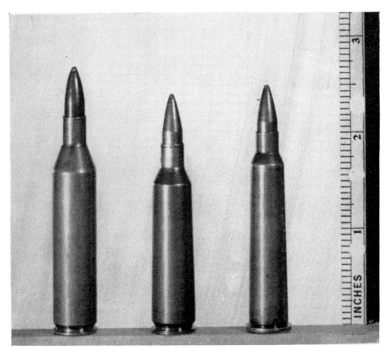

THE JERRY GEBBY "VARMINTER" CARTRIDGES

Left to right: .22 SENIOR Varminter—made from .257 Remington-Roberts cartridge; next, .22 (Standard) Varminter—made from .250/3000 Savage rimless case—this one is the most widely used and is most versatile of the three—will use widest variety of loads; and, on right, .22 JUNIOR Varminter, made from .32-40 Ballard & Marlin case. Maximum velocities of these three are 4,500 to 3,800 f.s., left to right. The Junior is for Hi-Side single shot actions, the other two for bolt action rifles.

The muzzle velocity was estimated to be 3,300 f.s. Remember, that was with a 60-grain bullet and not with a 41 to 45-grain bullet, which would have given much higher muzzle velocities but would not have retained the velocity as well and would have given greater long range wind drift, quite undesirable in Colorado coyote shooting.

In the winter of 1910-11, according to Howard's records and recollection, he killed 60 coyotes with this .22-32/40 rifle by Niedner. The first 20 were killed without a miss. The first 45, of which a record was kept in a shooting log, were shot at ranges of 50 to 616 yards, the average being 278 yards; 10 taken as they came being at 250, 250, 110, 200, 150, 300, 300, 230, 320 and 550 yards. He also killed quite a number of the large, gray lobo wolves with the same rifle.

The bullet for this rifle had a pointed, bare lead tip, was of base band style and sat in the case about 1/16″ only, and the front of the bullet projected up into the rifling so that the lands touched the band of the bullet. This cartridge and load gave 4″ groups at 200 yards in good weather. It had about 100 yards additional effective range over a .25-36 Marlin they used at the time. They (he and his brother) had also used a number of .25-20 Marlins for coyote shooting, one of which was extremely accurate, as was the .25-36 Marlin, which was a very accurate cartridge and apparently handled cast bullets better than the .25-35 rifle.

The .22-32/40 Niedner rifle owned by C. E. Howard, he has told the author, was chambered very closely, the cases did not expand appreciably and no re-sizing was necessary. The bullet of this rifle was a good killer and was just right for coyotes but tore them up pretty badly on close-in shots. Howard killed a number of deer with this rifle, mostly at close range while hunting coyotes. He considered 200 yards or less a close shot in Colorado in those days. He also killed one large grizzly bear with this rifle and an eagle at approximately 500 yards.

All this would suggest that the .22-32/40 case rifle would be very effective today on coyotes, woodchucks, eagles, hawks, crows and all similar varmints.

Shortly after 1911, Charles Newton made up a rifle for Howard, from the .30-40 Krag case, the load being a 70-grain bullet, 32.0 grains of Lightning No. 1 powder which gave a muzzle velocity, according to Newton, of 3,276 f.s. Remember, this was with a 70-grain bullet. This rifle was written up in *Arms & The Man* about 1911-1912 and they reproduced groups at 200 yards of 4½″ down to 3¼″ for 10 shots. The barrel was made from a Stevens .22-15/60 barrel, rifling 0.001″ deeper than normal, thus being a 0.2235″ or 0.224″ barrel, and mounted on a 44½ Stevens action. We can see, therefore, that the original cartridge for both the .22-32/40 and the .22-30/40 cases, which were probably very similar if not practically the same as the .22 Gebby Varminter Junior and the .224 Krag, were in actual use in Colorado around 1910 to 1912, according to best records today. They proved that these cartridges were both practical and effective, with Lightning powder, at least 33 to 35 years before this was written. They are even better today.

VARMINTER TARGET AT 100 YARDS

Here is a 1.1″ group at 100 yards, shot with .22 Varminter and 8-X Targetspot, Jr., Load 36.0 grs. No. 4320, giving, 3,760 f.s. muzzle velocity to 50-gr. 8S Morse bullet.

How the Various .22 Varminters Compare

The present Gebby Varminters are not made for base band bullets but for modern commercial bullets, and principally for bullets of lighter weight at higher muzzle velocity, around 20 per cent of which is normally lost in the first 100 yards by cartridges of this type—the high speed, light projectile .22's.

The .22 Junior Varminter is for use in Hi-Side Winchester S.S., 44½ Stevens actions in 45 to 54 grades, the Farquharson, Sharps-Borchardt and similar strong actions with *bushed firing pin*.

The .22 Standard Varminter is the most flexible of the three, can be used with the widest variety of loads, and both the Standard Varminter and the Senior Varminter are for use in proper bolt actions intended to handle rimless cases.

The Senior will give velocities up to approximately 4,500 f.s. with 45-grain and 4,200 f.s. with 55-grain bullets. The regular Varminter up to 4,100 to 4,200 f.s. with 45-grain bullets, so Gebby claims, and 4,550 f.s. with 40 or 41-grain short, light bullets. The 40-grain bullet gave 4,320 f.s. at Kings Mills about eight years ago. In any .22 wildcat, maximum loads should, in all cases, be built up gradually, to see what your rifle is doing in more moderate loads with the components used.

The Junior Varminter will develop up to 3,800 f.s.m.v. with short, light, tough-core metal-cased bullets. The author prefers the lines and appearance of the Standard Varminter and the Junior Varminter although the Senior Varminter has possibilities. It is designed for more powder room and a long, sharp shoulder.

How to Measure the Shoulder Angle

Possibly it is in keeping here to mention that the author has had 15 years of active drafting and engineering experience, in railroad, timberland, farm, state highway survey, sewer design and construction, high explosives and smokeless powder plant design, layout and equipment, and, therefore, should know how to read a scale and suggest how to check the shoulder slope of your pet wildcat or standard commercial cartridge. With many of the very sharp and very short shoulders in use today it is very easy for two experienced men to measure a shoulder angle and obtain as much as 2° to 5° difference in reading, simply because chambers and cases vary and also the difficulty of accurately determining the angle of such a very short line, which, incidentally, slopes on a curve at both ends.

Draw a *horizontal* line 8″ to 12″ long. Make a small dot in the center of it. From this point, using a protractor (an angle measuring scale), lay off to the left angles of 5°, 15°, 25°, 35°. Take another sheet of white paper or Bristol board, and repeat the process, laying off angles of 10°, 20°, 28°, 30°, 40°, platting them upward from the horizontal. From the small dot in the center of each line, and using a very sharp-pointed draftsman's pencil, (about 3H or 4H in hardness) draw very fine lines to the left, out to wherever you wish to draw your encircling arc. If you have a ruling pen, and the blades of it are clean and sharp, use black India ink and ink in these lines. The reason for using two sheets of Bristol board is that if all lines are drawn on one board, even with care, the ruling lines will run together at the center dot and it will be almost impossible for you to read off the angle correctly to which your shoulder slope most closely corresponds. The angle of each line

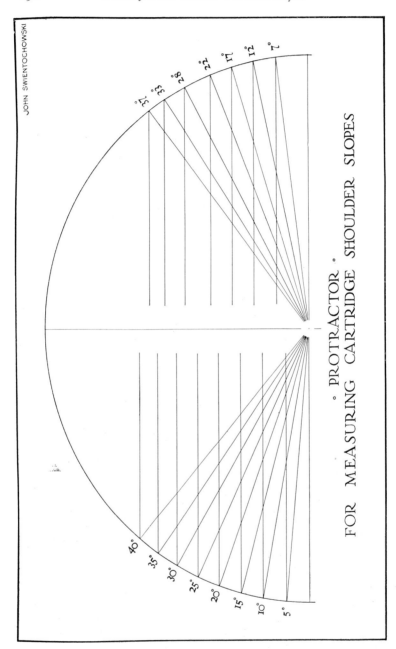

should be lettered out on the arc at the extremity of the line. Draw these lines along the edge of a smooth triangle; a ruler is not sufficiently smooth in surface along the edge. A straight line is the shortest distance between two points, and in theory has but one dimension—length—but a line must actually have some width, or you cannot see it. Draw your lines thin, even, and regular in outline.

When the drawings are finished and *dry*—India ink dries slowly in wet or damp weather—lay your cartridge along the base line, slide it along the base until the shoulder slope exactly or almost coincides with one of these lines, preserving always the imaginary line joining the bullet's point and center of primer pocket, directly above your *base line*. That too, while looking down directly onto the cartridge from above it. Then, read off the degree of line *closest* to the line of slope of the cartridge shoulder. This is approximately the slope of your cartridge shoulder.

This should be done with half a dozen cartridges, if possible, and the mean, or average reading taken as the determination.

Gentle slope cartridges will nearly all have between 3° and a 15° shoulder slope, and fairly steep cartridge slopes will fall between 25° and 36°—often from 25° to 30°.

Use a magnifying glass or a reading glass if you need it, but remember to keep both bullet point and center of primer pocket *directly* over your base line, or your reading will be incorrect.

If you prefer to draw the angle lines to the right instead of the left, then reverse the position of the cartridge, swapping ends, base and nose, and the results will come out identical, unless the light is coming in from a distinct angle.

Remember, in this regard, that you take all measurements from a line drawn through the longitudinal axis of the cartridge; not from a vertical line.

Of course some wise lug will rise up and say: "Your readings are incorrect; the real reading is so and so instead of thus and so, as you have made it." In that case, tell him to go bite his nails, because cartridges will not only vary in shape after being fired, but also before being shot, one from the other, and all gunsmiths and tool makers have trouble making a dozen chambering reamers *exactly alike*. Some of the best known have had trouble to exactly duplicate a chamber which originally gave remarkable results; possibly they forgot what angle and length had been used; possibly they did not ever know until later measurements gave such approximate measurements. You can be certain that your measurements are very

close to the theoretical, if carefully taken and averaged. This as
sumes the rifle was chambered exactly as its theoretical design or
chamber called for. If it were chambered with a set of reamers
cut to a slightly different shoulder, that is not your fault and does
not prove your measurement to be wrong. You simply measure the
angle to which the case was expanded.

Readings of "actual" measurements of head and case, and readings
of diameter outside of case at beginning of shoulder, were taken
with a brand new Brown & Sharpe micrometer with no plus or
minus reading on its zero; and of loaded Varminter cartridges
supplied by Jerry Gebby, cartridge length with engineer's scale;
other head or rim measurements are factory standards.

Length of case necks: Senior Varminter 0.27"; Varminter 0.24";
Junior 0.21". Length shoulder: Senior Varminter 0.25"; Varminter
0.18"; Junior 0.12"; as measured.

Gebby's Loads

.22 Senior Varminter: 47.0 grains of No. 4064 with 45-grain 8S
bullet, 4,500 f.s.m.v.; 47.0 grains No. 4350 with 55-grain bullet,
or, 43.0 to 44.0 grains No. 4064 with 55-grain W-M 8S bullet
4,200 f.s.m.v.

.22 Varminter (standard): 36.5 grains of No. 4320 with 50-grain
W-M 8S bullet, or, 35.0 grains No. 3031 with 55-grain W-M 8S
bullet—latter giving up to 3,550 f.s.m.v. For a squirrel or grouse
load, or for cotton-tail rabbits, 5.0 grains of duPont shotgun smokeless, with 45-grain bullet, giving 1,150 f.s.m.v. It is claimed that
20.0 to 30.0 grains No. 4759 with 45-grain, 47-grain and 50-grain
W-M 8S bullets will shoot well. Best and most accurate loads within
these extremes to be determined by test-firing with individual rifles,
the larger powder charges to be used with the lighter bullets if loading to maximum pressures.

.22 Junior Varminter: 28.0 to 34.0 grains of No. 3031 or No.
4320 or No. 4064 with 50-grain to 55-grain W-M 8S bullets, with
velocities of fastest loads up to 3,800 f.s.m.v.

Jerry Gebby's best load for the Junior Varminter cartridge has
been reported as 34.0 grains No. 4064 and 55-grain W-M 8S
bullet; 1" groups at 100 yards are claimed for it.

All of the above loads tested and made up with No. 115 primers,
in Western Cartridge Company's cases, 0.33" IPCO wad over
powder. Barrels all 0.224" to 0.2245" groove diameter and, with as
stated, 14" right hand twist.

Fred Ness reported best load tested for Junior Varminter was 34.0 grains No. 4064 with 55-grain W-M 8S bullet. This load gave 1″ groups at 100 yards.

Manufacture and Chambering of Gebby Barrels

Gebby barrels have been mostly of C. A. Diller or J. R. Buhmiller manufacture. Gebby claims that if the barrel borers hold specifications to within 0.0005″ he devotes full time to cutting chamber and bullet seat as he feels these are the most important specifications and considerations. Gebby did not state who makes his chambering tools.

General Comment

The largest demand for the three .22 Varminters, by far, is said to be for the .22 Varminter Standard cartridge. This is easily understood—it has received 90 per cent of the advertising; also most of what might be termed "ballyhoo."

The .250/3000 Savage case, either as it is made, or when necked to .22-250 is accurate in almost any well designed arm. This cartridge seems to require no breaking in of the barrel or "shooting it in."

There have been very few heavy barrel, bolt action .250/3000 rifles made, consequently the public has never realized what a good-shooting little cartridge that is, with either full loads or squirrel loads. Clarence Held, the well-known small bore rifle shot of the Bear Rock Rifle Club, of Germansville, Pennsylvania, but who in commercial life has been for years the "Gun Man" in the principal sporting goods store in Allentown, Pennsylvania, has a .250/3000 woodchuck rifle which shoots like a house afire. The .22 Standard Varminter is the same thing with case necked to .22 and the 0.224″ bullets and barrel.

Hervey Lovell suggests that a .22-250 rifle shoots more accurately if the shoulder slope be changed from 28° to 30°, which has the effect, of course, of making the powder gases churn around more, holds them back a bit while charge is burning, and thus raises the breech pressures somewhat higher—maybe a fair bit with the heavier bullets and No. 3031 or similar granulations of powders. But on the other hand, the 57 varieties of gunsmiths who make .22-250's all make them with 28° as standard. What some of them actually turn out to be in shoulder slope may be something else, because there are in this country persons chambering rifles and making chambering reamers who, in some instances, are not as skilled tool makers and barrel men as you could find in some plants where they have done just this and nothing else for the past 20 or 30 years, hour after hour, week after week. You do not always pick up the fine points of working in steel in the first two weeks of effort. On the other hand, there may be a few veteran barrel men who have reached an age and condition of eyesight where they do not see quite all they think they see.

The .22 Junior Varminter

To the author's eyes the .22 Junior Varminter is a better looking cartridge than either of the others, except that the case is a trifle long. Just as good a case, most likely, could be made and it might be less liable to stick in a close chamber, when over-loaded if made 1.75″ long instead of 2.00″ to 2.03″ long and by moving the shoulder back 0.25″. This one would then hold 3.0 to 6.0 grains less powder and develop 3,500 to 3,700 f.s. top velocity but it would be quite powerful and sufficiently flat shooting for most woodchuck hunting. It would then extract easier, and that, for closely chambered Winchester single shots with a lever that is not too robust, would be helpful. The author has bruised the palm of his hand time and time again, opening the sticking finger lever of a .22 Hornet rifle in Hi-Side Winchester S.S. type, because it was very closely chambered and would stick with factory ammunition. Schnerring had an exactly similar rifle which did the same thing.

Speaking of cartridge brass, you can obtain good cases from the .25 Remington, .30 Remington or .32 Remington rimless cases, for .22 rimless cartridges and good rimmed cases from the .25-35, .219 Zipper, .22 H.P. and .32-40 for the medium size rimmed .22 wildcats. So, one is not stuck for brass to neck down, just because the empties do not happen to be on hand which old Doctor Neckerdown wrote down on his prescription pad.

Some need to be cut off and trimmed; others blown up by firing in a new and longer and differently shaped chamber. Those mentioned all need to be necked down. The number of calibers which can be made to do is often surprising, unless one is familiar with the number which have the same diameter of head. Sometimes the case head must be trimmed off a trifle on the perimeter, or trimmed thinner on the inner edge, to make a more perfect fit. All this obligates one to a certain amount of whittle and try, and putting the old right eye down behind the striker or hammer, when firing the first few, does not strike this commentator as being something that wise old Solomon would have done.

The .22 Senior Varminter

This cartridge has been popularized largely by T. K. (Tackhole) Lee. Lee's is probably the first one of its type. It is a very long range and powerful .22 cartridge but the *need* for such a case is not too heavy in most communities.

It should be noted that Lee has had quite a reputation as a hard holder of small bore rifles, and at one time was unquestionably the most noted home range, small bore rifle expert shooting in N.R.A. matches. When hunting alone or with a few chosen companions, in small parties, where one of his keen and rather high strung mentality is not bothered by others to any marked extent, he would be able to extend himself in the field with a .22 varmint rifle so that the very best that is possible in such form of shooting could be demonstrated. The small game and varmint shooting that a man of his keenness of mind and hard holding ability *can* do must be seen to be appreciated. The average shot, or even a real good rifle shot, will never in this world possess such ability and therefore cannot either see or experience it.

Most Recent Gebby Activities

As Jerry Gebby appears rather hard to contact quickly, and as the Dayton postoffice apparently does not forward his mail from a previous address in that city, it may help readers to jot down the following information if interested in any of the .22 Varminters.

Jerry Gebby, whose address in the summer of 1946 was 298 Springbrook Blvd., Dayton 5, Ohio, converts .22 Hornets, other than .22 Savage Hornets, to the R-2 and the other rifles in .220 Swift caliber to .22 Varminter or .22 Senior Varminter. That means the Models 70 or 54. He converts single shot Hornets to R-2, or, as he refers to it, 2-R and if they have solid (not re-lined) barrels, he changes Hornets and 2-R single shots into the .22 Junior Varminter caliber, upon order.

He does blueing upon all of his work and inlets heavy barrels into the wood of the forearm when necessary. No other stock work is done in his shop. Apparently he is entirely a worker in metal. He does *not* make loading tools of any kind or caliber; Pacific makes tools and dies for all of his cartridges. In more normal times he installs rifle sights and formerly supplied complete Model 70 Winchester rifles re-barrelled for the two .22 rimless Varminters. He expects to again do this when more ormal manufacturing conditions exist in this land.

.22 VARMINTERS—CARTRIDGE SPECIFICATIONS AND MEASUREMENTS—JERRY GEBBY .22 AMMUNITION, HAND LOADED

Cartridge	Shoulder Slope	Rim or Head Diam.	Diam. at Shoulder	Length to Shoulder	Case Length	O.A. Length
.22 Senior Varminter (.257 Roberts)	25°	0.473"* 0.473"†	.4695"	1.66"	2.20"	2.73"
.22 Varminter (.250/3000)	28°	0.473"* 0.467"†	.4155"	1.50"	1.92"	2.43"
.22 Junior Varminter (.32-40 B. & M.)	30°	0.4905"†	.359"	1.70"	2.03"	2.50"

* Theoretical
† Actual

CHAPTER 9

THE .22 MARCIANTE BLUE STREAK

THIS IS A long, large capacity case, with a gradual body taper, a very short neck with 25° shoulder angle, and is made from the .22 H. P. Savage case but has greater powder capacity. The over-all length of the loaded cartridge, with 55-grain bullet, is about 0.10″ greater than the length of an empty .30-1906 cartridge case—which will give you an easy method of comparison with something you may have handy.

Now something about the story of Al Marciante, of 1216 Princeton Ave., Trenton, New Jersey, and you can better visualize the layout and how this cartridge came about and its degree of development and its possibilities.

Al Marciante had a shooting father. Marciante says that he inherited his love of firearms and shooting from his parent. In addition, he early had a craze for learning to be a skilled machinist. But this was not too easy to accomplish in his area, where most machine shops were interested in turning out their own products, but not in letting a young rifle crank fool around with their lathes, drill presses, shapers, planers and whatnot.

However, when Al got married things started to happen, as they often do, but in this case not as you might imagine. His mother presented him with a South Bend lathe as a wedding present— probably one of the very few such ever presented as a wedding present—and right there is where Al Marciante went to work to learn to be a machinist, and eventually a gunsmith.

Most of Marciante's early rifles were worked over in one way or another to make them better woodchuck rifles. This was done on the "wedding present" lathe with various hand tools, such as are found in most small machine shops. For some time, prior to April, 1941, he had been using a rifle that he had made up himself from a Hi-Side Winchester S.S. action. This rifle was fitted with a Savage

203

four-groove barrel, of the type that they made up for their Hornet cartridge. Marciante chambered this with tools that he made himself for the standard .22 Hi-Power Savage cartridge, but necked sufficiently tight to hold 0.224″ metal-cased bullets. This rifle, with Lyman 5-A scope, made a rather good little woodchuck and crow outfit, and, at that time, the best he had tried for this sort of shooting.

He had used a fine .25-20 Winchester S.S., Sharps-Borchardt combination, which gave him excellent results, but it lacked range, and also it lacked flatness of trajectory.

As Marciante had no velocity figures then and no pressure data he went along cautiously and carefully with his early rifles. One evening two friends of his, whom he named as Ernest Baldwin and Robert Miller, came over with the idea of having him change their .22 Hi-Powers, which Marciante had made up similar to his mentioned above, made from the Winchester action and the Savage .22 barrel. All three had accounted for woodchucks, a few of which were paced out as having been shot up to 300 yards, but most of these were counted largely accidental.

The idea was born of changing over the .22 Hi-Power case so that it would have a larger powder capacity and a different shoulder angle. The suggestion was to make the case with a 28° shoulder angle, which was to be pushed farther forward, towards the mouth of the case. But they soon discovered that this would allow the powder to burn in the throat of the barrel, instead of inside the case, and then up in the barrel, so they changed the shoulder angle to 25°, and found that burned the powder to better advantage.

With the shoulder slope decided upon Marciante went to work to make chambering reamers so that they could re-chamber their rifles to take the new, enlarged and greater powder capacity .22 Hi-Power cartridge. Read this description very carefully, because some day you may wish to make up chambering reamers to make a Smith-Jones-Green-Thompson .22 wildcat for yourself, and after you have gotten through with all of the studies of mathematics, chemistry, the action of water and gases flowing under pressure through nozzles of different shapes, and find out what you can of the burning characteristics of different powders you may want to use, you are about to go to it. Your big problem then will likely be chambering reamers.

A chambering reamer is nothing more or less than a duplicate, (with small tolerances) of the case desired. These reamers are made of steel drill rod, slabbed to exactly half their diameter, all leading

angles relieved to form the cutting edge. Reamers are then hardened
and tempered to a light straw color. Marciante found that they
worked fine in barrels that were not too tough cutting, but in the
chrome alloy barrels they did not hold up too long. Apparently
Hervey Lovell and many others found the same difficulties in their
early experiments from what some of them have said.

Marciante has chambered a good many barrels with reamers made
in just this way. The three Trenton experimenters soon found that
this new type case had some merit, for in the two rifles which
Marciante chambered for Messrs. Baldwin and Miller, they obtained
what he says was "much more velocity." The question was now how
much more and how to prove these velocities were being developed.
Accuracy did not seem to suffer by the re-chambering. Marciante
then re-chambered his own rifle for the same case. When a rifle
crank and machinist gets around to the point where he re-chambers
his *own* pet rifle, rather than merely those of his friends, you can
bet on it that *he* has been converted. But not before! Up to that time,
however, so Marciante says, the cartridge had not as yet been
named for any bird, bee, beast, reptile or insect. Truly it was still
duly swathed in its three-cornered pants because the first thing they
do with a .22 wildcat is to combine the tactics of the negro mammy
in naming her 12 children, beginning with Geranium and ending
with Eucalyptus. They add all the Bees, Hornets, Wasps, Yellow
Jackets and Dragon Flies they can think of, tack on 4,000 to 6,000
f.s. (always being liberal in such matters) and finally, the newcomer is born; almost always—*almost* always, I was careful to add
—the inventor modestly adds his own name, as we all might do
under similar temptation.

Then the wildcat is sprung on a public that too often is dis-
tressingly callous and unsympathetic, as well as slightly bored, but
not as yet interested in buying a new gun and another Westinghouse-
Edison looks out on a Blue Monday and a dull morning, wondering
whether it was all worthwhile. Nevertheless, he *perseveres*—rifle
cranks all being that way—and finally after he has found a deeply
sympathetic and receptive Gun Editor the world is told about it,
and often, possibly from widely scattered and far away places, converts write, telegraph, telephone or they pour gas in the old jallopy
and call in person on the inventor; and whenever a wildcat inventor
or specialist hears a very violent throwing-on of brakes, rattling of
tinware and thumping of horn, out by the watering trough, he knows
that another rifleman has arrived, all out of breath, but thirsting
and hungering to see the *new development*.

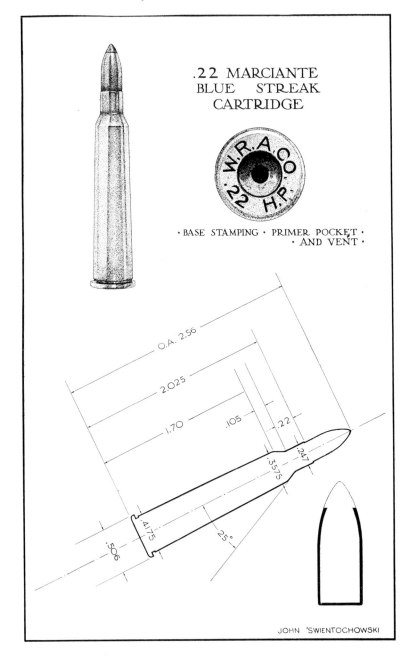

.22 MARCIANTE
BLUE   STREAK
CARTRIDGE

· BASE STAMPING · PRIMER POCKET ·
· AND VENT ·

O.A. 2.56

2.025

1.70

.105

.22

.247

.3575

.4175

.506

25°

JOHN 'SWIENTOCHOWSKI

But to get back to Mr. Marciante: While testing out different rifle loads one evening, it was discovered that a very distinct blue streak was to be noted following in the path of the bullet when the rifle was fired. Mr. Miller, it is said, suggested that they call the cartridge the *Blue Streak.* The name stuck, for it was noted later that this blue streak was noticeable in almost all weather conditions.

Another gent in their clan had a .220 Swift caliber rifle with a Mauser action and a Sukalle barrel. They shot this rifle against the Blue Streak for comparison tests for penetration and soon found, as they claimed, they were getting velocities that were apparently much the same, as this unbaptized, but quite effective "Swift" was producing. Naturally, this aroused their curiosity, also imagination, and so Marciante made a trip to see J. Bushnell Smith, at Middlebury, Vermont. Bushnell Smith has had many visitors in his time, most of them bent on much the same errand and probably to be sure they would find the right gent in a metropolitan center like Middlebury he had a photo made up showing himself posed in an agreeable humor on the front porch of the shop or whatisit; some rifle cranks call it their "Den," others "The Shop"; larger concerns refer to it as "The Ballistic Laboratory." Generally, the larger establishments are noted principally for the lack of real rifle cranks therein, but in the small places there is pretty sure to be a simon-pure rifle crank with a compelling urge to find what makes it tick, domiciled on the premises. It may be someone who, like Harry Pope, locked the door so that he could get some work done, and it may be the other extreme, the hangout of the local and visiting rifle nuts, but whatever it is, *there* is where the cavalcade comes to a halt.

So, when a visitor drives up at 90 miles an hour, in a cloud of dust and sweat and disembarks with a determined look on his face, one can be reasonably certain it is either a shooter with something on his mind which is quite pressing and needs immediate discussing, or else a *customer* has arrived. In the latter case, he will likely have but one rifle; in the first instance maybe three or four.

In this instance, after a long trip, Marciante arrived at Middlebury, and, as he says, after a very lovely trip through the beautiful state of Vermont introductions were made and they got right down to business.

They chronographed the Blue Streak with various loads. It is reported that Smith asked Marciante to chamber him a rifle for the same cartridge even before testing was completed. A bit farther on chronographed results for the Blue Streak are given in this chapter. On the way home Marciante called to see "Shiff, The Gunman," at North Woodstock, New Hampshire, and had a fine time there. Mr. Shiffer opened about every case that contained guns and they really and literally "went to town." It was described as "an education" visiting "Shiff, The Gunman"; others have made the same comment.

In October of the same year, 1941, Marciante made another trip to see Bushnell Smith to have Blue Streak loads chronographed. Results were very similar to those obtained the previous April on the same range.

Since then, numerous rifles have been re-chambered for the .22 Blue Streak Marciante cartridge. Among those for whom Marciante has re-chambered rifles are said to be Colonel Whelen, Ned Roberts, Allyn Tedmon, Harvey Donaldson, Al Barr and various others.

One of the things which had better be mentioned here is that Marciante now makes his chambering reamers with six flutes for the finishing reamers and four flutes for the roughing reamers. He has also made himself a dividing head for use with milling attachments for his South Bend lathe. This latter equipment or attachment is for fluting the reamer blanks.

Al Marciante has made up a considerable number of named and unnamed wildcats, known and unknown specials and has re-chambered for a goodly number of these, including the very latest long cartridge .219 Donaldson-Wasp. He says that he finds that given a good barrel, and by this he means a barrel that is *not* too tight in the bore and groove diameter for the 0.224" bullets, plus a good rifling job, and decent chambering and they will *all shoot fine,* regardless of the design of case. He says he realizes that he may be laying himself open to criticism, but it is a fact, as he sees it, and if it is not a fact then why is it that good results have been obtained with so many different wildcat designs that their number truly is legion. Some may give high pressures, others may give very short barrel life, due to directing the super-heated powder gases on to the butt ends of the lands in the rifle throat, by poor cartridge case design, but all of them shoot when in good, new condition. Some, of course, excel others and how any one case burns a given powder may depend upon its shoulder slope, its case length up to the shoulder slope, and also to some extent upon the length of the neck. Extraction will depend, in considerable measure, upon outside case slope up to the shoulder, the smoothness of chambering, the leverage and strength of the extractor and whatnot.

Marciante comments that we all know that cases vary in their flexibility, some being more adaptable than others, in ability to handle different combinations and loads, but all of them are capable of producing *very fine accuracy*. Given, of course, a barrel rifled with the proper twist for the load and bullet used, and good components.

At the present time he is doing a lot of chambering for the Blue Streak, the .219 Wasp and for the .22-250 cartridge. This .22-250 is a very flexible cartridge. It seems to handle a variety of loads to advantage. This has been found true by many riflemen and experimenters and gunsmiths. Capt. Paul Wilcox thinks Marciante's workmanship is absolutely "tops."

The .22 Marciante Blue Streak, incidentally, is a *rimmed* cartridge, suitable for single shot rifles of the Hi-Side Winchester S.S. type, and such bolt actions as will handle a rimmed case of this length and have sufficient strength of action to handle given pressures.

Ballistic data from J. Bushnell Smith's chronograph follows:

CHRONOGRAPH TEST 4/24/41 AL MARCIANTE'S BLUE STREAK

Bullet	Powder Charge	Velocity at 25 ft. (— 60 f.s.)
50-gr. 8S	31.5 grs. 3031	4,001 f.s.
55-gr. Sisk-Express	31.0 grs. 4064	3,526 f.s.
55-gr. Sisk-Express	30.0 grs. 3031	3,780 f.s.
		at 200 yds. 2,763 f.s.
40-gr. Sisk-Express	30.0 grs. 4198	4,295 f.s.
40-gr. Sisk-Express	34.0 grs. 3031	4,389 f.s.
40-gr. 8S	24.0 grs. 4759	3,938 f.s.

Note: All loads in the above group are maximum loads.

Note 2. Above velocities taken at 25 feet from muzzle and chronograph checked with .220 Swift loads at same time and date and was found to be reading 60 f.s. *high*. Assuming the Swift cartridges were giving exactly their advertised velocities, a minus reading in accordance with that knowledge, should be made from each of the above figures.

Further figures supplied for Blue Streak by J. Bushnell Smith

45-gr. W-M 8S	20.0 grs. 4759	3,300 f.s.
45-gr. 8S	22.0 grs. 4759	3,455 f.s.
47-gr. 8S	20.0 grs. 4759	3,255 f.s.
47-gr. 8S	22.0 grs. 4759	3,320 f.s.
50-gr. 8S	22.0 grs. 4759	3,310 f.s.
50-gr. 8S	28.5 grs. 3031	3,575 f.s.
50-gr. 8S	28.5 grs. Hi-Vel No. 2	3,465 f.s.
48-gr. Swift	31.5 grs. 4320	3,441 f.s.

Winchester No. 115 N.M.N.C. Primers used in above loads.

LOADS TESTED BY TARGET SHOOTING FROM BENCH REST
.22 MARCIANTE BLUE STREAK

Fired targets supplied with data; all fired at 100 yards range, in 10 shot groups, except two mentioned, at 130 and 225 yards.

Rifle: Marciante .22 Special Blue Streak Winchester S. S., fitted with 10-X Lyman-Litschert Telescope Sight.

Bullet	Powder	Charge	Case WRA	Primer WRA	Range	Group Size Hor. Vert.
55-gr. Sisk Exp.	4064	31.0 gr.	,,	115	100 yd.	10 shots 1.20" x 1.50" 12 shots
50-gr. W-M 8S Cadm.	4759	22.0 gr.	,,	115	100 yd.	1.35" x 1.20" 10 shots
45-gr. Hornet WRA	Pyro	29.0 gr.	,,	115	100 yd.	1.50" x 1.10" 10 shots
55-gr. W-M. 8S	4350	35.0 gr.	,,	115	130 yd.	1.35" x 1.00" 11 shots
55-gr. Sisk-Niedner	4064	31.0 gr.	,,	115	100 yd.	1.20" x 1.22" 27 shots
55-gr. Sisk-Niedner	4064	30.0 gr.	,,	115	100 yd.	1.38" x 1.40"
67-gr. Sisk-Express	4350	35.0 gr.	,,	115	225 yd.	1.58" x 1.55"

Chap who shot last group was Nick Papernak, who for a time was in the hands of the Germans, as his plane was shot down by anti-aircraft fire in a raid over that country.

All groups were measured by the author with engineer's scale. Measurements were center to center, of shots farthest apart. First horizontal measurement, then vertical measurement. Most groups, about two-thirds given size, if worst two shots be eliminated. Target was 5" black with white cross-hair aiming center, 225-yard target shot on regular bullseye.

WRA No. 115 Primers used in all above loads.

Chapter 10

THE .219 DONALDSON-WASP

DURING the summer of 1945, a great deal of semi-confidential comment was in circulation among rifle cranks, custom gunsmiths, and woodchuck hunters regarding the .219 Donaldson-Wasp .22 wildcat cartridge; to the probability that one of the large rifle manufacturers would put out a commercial rifle for this cartridge, or one very similar to it; and the contention that here in this comparatively moderate size .22 wildcat muzzle velocities were being obtained which were fully equal to those obtained with the .22-250 or .22 Varminter type of case, which is materially longer; and that they were almost equal to those obtained with the .220 Swift. Some claimed they exceeded the Swift in muzzle velocity and in flatness of trajectory.

There was also considerable Gun Editor and other comment appearing in print which concerned the appearance of a .22-250 rifle by a large commercial manufacturer. For this and other reasons the author of this book made a special trip through New England about August 1, 1945 to check up on the very latest developments in .22 rifles of all kinds.

Samuel Clark, of Oakland, Maine, agreed to write up the .219 Donaldson-Wasp, from experiments he knew of or had performed with this cartridge; the work of Vaughn Cail, small bore shot of New Haven; and from what he knew of Harvey Donaldson's development with this cartridge. His story, which covers many phases of .22 wildcat experiments is given here, after very slight editing to agree with certain known ballistic results. The author of this book will only add here definite comparisons of the size and other characteristics of the .219 Donaldson-Wasp cartridges with a number of other most excellent and highly efficient .22 wildcats of comparable shapes, origin and size. From these comparisons, the reader may be able to form interesting deductions and conclusions.

Harvey Donaldson's second case—the .220-25—or original Donaldson-Wasp was made from the .25 Remington rimless case. It compares with the .22 Lindahl Rimless Chucker cartridge and the .22 Kilbourn K-Magnum Junior cartridge. Both are made from the same case as shown in tabulation on opposite page.

It will be seen from this that these three cartridges are almost identical in length to shoulder, in case length and the first two in over-all length, and all three have about the same neck size and length. The Donaldson-Wasp is smaller in diameter at the shoulder than any of the other two, and is materially shorter than the Kilbourn K-Magnum Junior in over-all length as loaded. The neck slopes are so near the same you will have to measure them very carefully to tell the difference. It will be seen, therefore, that the first two cartridges will be found almost identical in ballistic results,

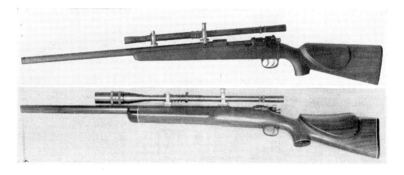

A HEAVY BARREL .220 SWIFT MAUSER

This rifle was made by Lovell for his own shooting. It is Mauser action fitted with heavy barrel, .220 Swift caliber, with .227″ groove and 12″ twist. This rifle killed first five crows in six shots, in two instances left feet and tail still sitting on limb while front half of crow went sailing off into distance, a few feet. Crows seemed rather surprised.

LOWER—A HEAVY BARREL SPRINGFIELD

A typical very heavy barrelled varmint rifle fitted with long, large and heavy target telescope of high grade, having about 2″ eye relief. This rifle is owned by H. V. Noble, and has an R-2, C. C. Johnson barrel on a Springfield action. Stock by Milford Fones, Gibbstown. N. J. Unertl 10X scope, in Fecker mounts, Unertl recoil spring. This rifle weighs 12¾ pounds, without sights, and about 14¼ pounds as shown. Most suitable for shooting out of automobile, over fence rail, prone with sling. It is not an outfit to carry casually, for 10 miles, on a hot August day. when after chucks. It is extremely accurate at 200 yards, and groups very consistently, with a variety of loads.

.25 RIMLESS REMINGTON NECKED DOWN

Cartridge	Shoulder Slope	Diam. Head	Diam. at Shoulder	Length to Shoulder	Length Case	O.A. Length	Neck Length
Original Donaldson-Wasp .220-25	30°	.422"* .4172" Actual	.3864"	1.23"	1.65"	2.05"	0.28"
.22 Lindahl Chucker	28°	.422"* .4225" Actual	.404" to .403"	1.20"	1.605"	2.07"	0.255"
Kilbourn .22 K-Magnum Junior	25°	.422"* .4185" to .4190" Actual	.4019"* .397" to .398"	1.275"	1.70"	2.20"	0.25"

and the Kilbourn K-Magnum Junior should show a very slight increase in muzzle velocity and energy over the other two when all are loaded to capacity, or to relative load-levels. All three are beautifully designed cartridges.

Now let us go to the latest .219 Donaldson-Wasp and compare it physically in cartridge dimensions with other .219 Zipper neckdowns or other cases of very similar powder and bullet content. We can, from this comparison, form an idea of what to expect ballistically from the .219 Donaldson-Wasp as compared with other cases designed by different custom gunsmiths or rifle cranks and made up in other shops; and what to expect from others as compared with the Donaldson-Wasp. We will give the Winchester test on the latest .219 Donaldson-Wasp with Mr. Clark's data in the tabulation on next page.

A most careful comparison of the tabulation will show that the .219 Donaldson-Wasp case differs principally in having a longer neck than any of the others.

Its diameter at the shoulder is much the same, except for the Pfeifer. It averages 0.21″ shorter from face of head to the shoulder. It has just about the same powder capacity, up to the neck, as the .224 Pfeifer. The Wasp is shorter than any of the others except this Pfeifer. The Wasp over-all length, when loaded, averages 0.15″ less than the others, except the Kilbourn. The latter case is longer by another 0.1″.

Approximately 300 rifles of the .224 Pfeifer caliber were in use by the late summer of 1945, with no complaints reported. The Donaldson case is loaded to contain a thin grease wad, which was not regularly used in any of the others. This occupied a small amount of powder volume and imparted a slightly greasy result to the powder residue.

If, as suggested in the manuscript by Mr. Clark, the .219 Donaldson-Wasp cartridge has very exceptional ballistics, as compared with various other cases, although not these mentioned here, to what is this due? The only dimension in which it varies very much from numerous others listed is in having a materially longer neck and a materially shorter body to the shoulder. On the other hand, you will note by comparison, that its length to shoulder is almost identical with that of the Kilbourn K-Magnum Junior. The same is true of the cartridge length and it is only 0.10″ longer than the Lindahl Rimless Chucker or the Lindahl Rimmed Chucker, the latter made from the same case as the Donaldson-Wasp.

This all brings us back to the conclusion which you can easily

COMPARISON OF SIZE OF .219 ZIPPER CASES NECKED TO .22 WILDCATS

Cartridge	Shoulder Slope	Diam. Head	Diam. at Shoulder	Length to Shoulder	Length Case	O.A. Length	Neck Length
Latest .219 Donaldson-Wasp	30°	.506"* .4952" to .4962"	.4045"	1.30"	1.75"	2.25"	0.325"
No. 7 .22 Lovell Improved Zipper	30°	.506"* .4925" Actual	.393" to .395"	1.50"	1.92"	2.43"	0.27"
Kilbourn .22 K-Zipper	25°	.506"* .4925" Actual	.4075" to .4085" Actual	1.52"	1.89"	2.50"	0.20"
.22 Ackley Improved Zipper	28°	.506"* .4965" Actual	.400"	1.50"	1.92"	2.38"	
.22 Ackley-Vickery Improved Zipper (by W. F. Vickery)	28°	.506"* .4965" Actual	.400"	1.54"	1.92"	2.40"	
.224 Joe Pfeifer Rimmed Magnum (.30-40 short case)	28°	.545"* .5385" Actual	.4125"	1.275"	1.660"	2.23"	

In February 1948, Lyle Kilbourn suggested to the author that his Kilbourn K-Magnum Junior and the .219 Wasp were both relatively high pressure loads, although both very accurate and uniform.

prove for yourself, that this cartridge, although beautifully proportioned is, for practical purposes, possibly a good mean of many of the others except for its greater length of neck.

The author regards it unlikely that Mr. Donaldson has seen many of the other cartridges mentioned here, consequently the ideas incorporated in the Donaldson-Wasp are likely quite his own, and any happy results obtained ballistically suggest that most of these cartridges would give ballistic results very similar indeed, and by changing the grain size of the powder, or its coating, or both, could be made to give identical results, or, at least very close to the same results.

One thing is certain—that the .219 Zipper Improved cases have given most astonishing results in the way of both accuracy and high velocities for the powder burned. This whole chapter should be of great interest to woodchuck and coyote hunters who are looking for a .22 wildcat cartridge which shoots nearly as flat as the .220 Swift, gives much better accuracy, does not give either the erosion or cartridge elongation of the .220 Swift, uses less powder and costs less to shoot. Now read Mr. Clark's comments:

THE DEVELOPMENT AND PERFORMANCE OF THE .219 DONALDSON-WASP

by Samuel Clark, Jr., Oakland, Maine

In the year 1935, Harvey A. Donaldson, of Fultonville, New York, began experiments which 10 years later were to result in the development of a very efficient small-capacity, high velocity .22 caliber rifle cartridge now known as the .219 Donaldson-Wasp.

In '35 Donaldson had just completed a long series of tests with the .22 Niedner Magnum which were recorded in *The American Rifleman* of July, 1936. These tests gave him some ideas and theories and a number of conclusions in regard to better chamber design which interested him and which drove him on to further experiments in the development of an ideal .22 caliber cartridge for varmint shooting. It was not with the idea of "improving" any particular cartridge but more that of producing a small, convenient, high intensity cartridge of great accuracy, economy and very flat trajectory without going to the realm of long, heavy cases which often gave high erosion and, at times, considerable pressures near the head. The line of thought was practical, at least when used with a moderate degree of throating.

Possibly a few words in regard to Donaldson and his background will add interest to a discussion of the development of the .219 Donaldson-Wasp.

H. A. Donaldson began shooting at the time of the introduction of the .30-30 Winchester and Marlin rifles—back in the 1893-94 era. By this date he has rounded out 52 full years as a rifle enthusiast and experimenter. He fires on the range and at varmints and other game, in a normal year, more ammunition than many fire in a lifetime. He is a keen observer, according to my observations, and has a remarkable memory. These qualities are backed up by a mass of most carefully kept records such as have been recorded by few and he has, in addition, a wide acquaintance and correspondence with the rifle clan of this country, particularly the experimenters and custom gunsmiths. He has been the designer or co-designer of such notably successful .22 caliber varmint cases as the .224 Donaldson-Krag Lightning and the R-2 Donaldson. He has spent his lifetime in the development of better rifle ammunition.

So, in 1935, after completing tests on the .22 Niedner Magnum previously mentioned, Donaldson realized that an ideal varmint case should develop higher velocities than was possible with this case and steps in this direction were immediately taken.

The .25 Remington rimless case, with its greater capacity, was selected and a preliminary design was worked out, resulting in a case with a body slightly longer than the .22 Niedner Magnum and holding about 8.0 more grains of powder, or 34.0 grains in all.

A medium heavy 27″ barrel, having a 16″ twist and groove diameter of .223″ was selected, fitted to a M/30 Remington bolt action and chambered for the new case, and testing was immediately commenced.

It was a simple matter to form cases for this rifle, as they were not cut off but left a full 2″ in length, after being necked to .22 caliber and the forming was completed by simple firing in the rifle with a forming load.

Work had hardly commenced on this rifle when it was discovered that the results desired were not being obtained. To begin with, the added powder capacity of this new case did not result in the expected increase in velocity over the .22 Niedner Magnum and, in fact, the pressures were increased all out of proportion to the very slight increase in velocity. Lacking a chronograph, the velocities were checked against the .22 Niedner Magnum by shooting into steel plates.

By Donaldson's notes, taken at that time, it was apparent that the cause of the trouble was clear and the next step obvious. The difficulty was that, while more powder was being loaded into the case, it did not follow that the entire mass of the powder was being consumed. In other words, the design of the case was not perfect and so experiments with this barrel ceased and it was discarded, having served its purpose.

Now, concluding from these experiments that a case of small body diameter in relation to neck diameter was a step in the wrong direction, Donaldson deemed it advisable to again return to a case of smaller capacity, but with a shorter, fatter body in proportion to the diameter at the neck of the case. The same .25 Remington rimless was retained for forming the new case.

Therefore, the second design of case was soon drawn up and turned over to Vernor Gipson, who in due time completed the chambering reamers and case forming dies. A heavy 16″ twist Savage barrel, having a groove diameter of .223″ was sent to Gipson and he soon completed the fitting of this barrel to an ordinary Krag action, working over the bolt head and extractor for the small rimless case and chambering the barrel for the new design of case. In changing the design, the length of the case had now been reduced to 1⅝″ over-all and had a short, fat body, with little body taper.

Tests had hardly commenced with the new rifle, using this altered case, when it became apparent that the conclusions reached from experiments with the longer case were correct.

Donaldson now felt that he was on the right track. The new case was developing accuracy finer than any he had ever seen, from a .22 varmint rifle. The entire secret seemed to lie in the very small change in the shape of the case which had been made. The greater body diameter, in relation to the size of the neck, working with a rather abrupt shoulder slope, was now causing every grain of the powder to be fully consumed. The result was that extremely high velocities were being obtained with such small charges of powder that Donaldson could hardly believe the evidence. Checking carefully, by firing into steel plates of different thicknesses, it was apparent that this small capacity case was producing velocities as high as some other .22 varmint cases loaded with 8.0 to 10.0 grains more of the same powder and utilizing identically the same bullet.

Using 45, 50 and 55-grain bullets, it was discovered that a great variety of loads gave almost identically fine accuracy. The improved shape of the case seemed to be correct for many of the common powders adapted to .22 varmint cases of this description. Pressure troubles encountered while using the former, longer case seemed to be entirely eliminated. On one occasion, while testing was being done, five consecutive 10-shot groups were fired from this barrel, using the new short, fat case with three different loads of powder. The groups, although consecutive, were fired on different days and resulted in five 10-shot groups, every shot of which could be contained in a 1″ circle, shooting being done at 100 yards from a bench rest. The well-known bullet maker Charles H. Morse, witnessed and signed these targets.

About this time the question of correct twist, which had frequently arisen, became so important that it was decided to put the matter to the test and so another rifle was assembled for the purpose of fully determining this question.

The barrel selected was a Savage make; it had four grooves .223″ diameter and a 14″ twist. This barrel also was sent to Gipson and he fitted it to a Model 20 Savage bolt action and chambered it for the short 1⅝″ (1.625″) case.

The reader will see that it was now possible to obtain a wide variety of tests with three rifles at hand, one for the original long 2″ case, in 16″ twist; one for the new short, fat case of 1⅝″ length in 16″ twist; and another for the same short case but having a barrel using the 14″ twist.

At this point, an interesting experiment was tried which will illustrate clearly the value of improvements to date. Using the two 16″ twist barrels, one chambered for the long 2″ case and the other for the short 1⅝″ case, it was possible to shoot through more steel with the short case than with exactly the same case, only left its full 2″ length and using *identical* power charges and bullets (this will be obvious—Author; it is also true of other cartridges). Also, using the short, fat 1⅝″ case with a load of 24.0 grains of No. 3031 duPont powder and the 50-grain Wotkyns-Morse bullet, greater velocity was obtained than with 34.0 grains of No. 4064 and the same bullet loaded into the longer 2″ case. This is hard to believe, but nevertheless was conclusively proved. This again clearly illustrates the point that it is one thing to design a case that will hold a heavier charge of powder and another thing entirely to design it so to consume all of the powder. Unless this efficiency is attained, by the design of the case, nothing much has been accomplished. Another very interesting thing that was brought out in the experimenting at this time was the fact that materially higher velocities could be obtained from barrels using the 16″ twist, than from barrels chambered for the identical Wasp case but of 14″ twist.

Now, about three years having been consumed in testing the above three barrels and conclusions carefully drawn, Donaldson was still not satisfied that some of the extraordinary facts turned up had been sufficiently checked and nothing would do but the matter should be gone over again.

At this time, his attention being called to the Winchester .219 Zipper case, which is exceedingly well made, with heavy brass, he decided to duplicate the tests already explained with the first two Wasp cases, in order to see if his findings would still prove true with the Zipper case.

Without loss of time, therefore, a design of case was made up from the Winchester .219 Zipper on identically the same plan as with the original .25 Remington case. In other words, it was left its original length and the only change of the shape of the regular factory Zipper design was to make the slope of the shoulder a little more abrupt. In this way, cases could be formed simply by firing in the new chamber without case forming dies of any sort.

Rifle No. 4 was now assembled for this test, which was to double check on results to date. This rifle was made up on Donaldson's Winchester Model 54 bolt action .30-30 rifle which was used to avoid extra work on the bolt, bolt head, extractor and magazine. In this respect, therefore, it was unnecesssary to make any change where the Zipper rimmed case was to be used.

The barrel of this rifle had also a 14″ twist, was 27″ long, heavy, of .2235″ groove diameter and was fitted and chambered for case No. 4 by Gipson.

When completed and cases were formed by firing with a forming load, they held, with bullets seated in case neck, 34.0 grains of duPont No. 3031 or 37.0 grains of No. 4320. This rifle was then fitted for scope and no time was lost in putting it to the test.

Accuracy at first proved poor and it was decided to make a change in the throat, which seemed to be rather short, as received from Gipson. This operation improved the groups obtained, but when all testing of this rifle was completed, it might safely be said that the results were parallel in every way to those obtained from Rifle No. 1 with the original long 2″ .25 Remington case, necked to .22 caliber. In other words, by increasing the capacity of the case to hold powder and changing the slope of the shoulder, the velocities with heavier charges of powder were not materially increased over those obtained from the standard Winchester .219 Zipper case. Again the fact had been proved that by simply increasing the capacity of a case, it does not follow that this added powder will all be consumed and velocities increased. In fact, this double check was just what had been expected, but Donaldson considered the point not established until proved beyond the shadow of a doubt.

While it will readily be agreed by riflemen that no great amount of thought or time is necessarily lost in the design of an entirely new wildcat case, of any caliber, it may be seen from the foregoing that such methods were not employed in the years that elapsed while the .219 Donaldson-Wasp was undergoing constant changes and improvements and during which time a number of rifles were made up, with which complete and conclusive tests of these changes might be made.

Considering now that the necessary facts had been gathered together, which would enable him to design an ideal .22 caliber varmint case, Donaldson went to work, using this data gathering from some years of the most painstaking work and it was not long before drawings of the completed and final .219 Donaldson-Wasp design were finished.

It is a striking fact that one which shows the clarity of his thinking that this final design, with one minor exception, was never changed in any way, nor did it need any changing, since the results originally desired had been fully obtained.

Before discussing the actual performance of the new case at the target and on game, and explaining the results of chronograph tests of the .219 Donaldson-Wasp with various loads, it will be well to again point out the reasons for the very unusual and satisfactory results that were to be obtained from the design of this case, in relation to that of other .22 varmint cases.

Considering, for instance, the .224 Donaldson-Krag Lightning, which is mentioned for purposes and comparisons, this case was very successful indeed but with this design it was not possible to get top performance with anywhere near the great variety of loads which worked perfectly with the .219 Wasp. The large capacity Lightning case, which held a good 41.0 grains of duPont No. 4064 when full, was originally designed by Donaldson for use with very heavy 60 and 70-grain bullets. For this purpose, the more abrupt shoulder of the .219 Wasp was not necessary, as the heavy bullets caused sufficient pressures to be built up, so that the powders used were efficiently burned. When, therefore, the lighter 45, 50 and 55-grain bullets were used in the .224 Donaldson-Krag Lightning case, it was necessary to carefully balance the load, in order to obtain a combination of bullet and powder where the correct pressures were built up to efficiently burn all the powder. This necessarily reduced the number of loads and types of powder that could be successfully used, and the same factor is true of many of the new high-speed cases that have been designed since the .22 Hornet, especially the larger ones.

This factor is, however, not in the least true in regard to the .219 Wasp which is designed particularly for bullets of 40, 50 and 55-grains weight. The .219 Wasp design was worked out by Donaldson with the idea of having both bullet weight and powder charge so balanced that a case full of powder could be used without exceeding safe pressures, or without having it fail to reach adequate burning pressures.

This latter point is of great value to those using the .219 Donaldson-Wasp, since it is practically impossible, where properly throated barrels are used, to get into the Wasp case more powder of the brands normally used in it than can safely be burned. This applies to all powders adapted to medium and large capacity cases, with the exception of duPont No. 4198 which should *not* exceed 25.0 grains in the Wasp case.

In other words, no feature of this new case was left to chance, everything had a definite purpose and, when the final drawings were completed and sent to Gipson for making up the chambering reamers, Donaldson felt certain that the case would be more than successful.

Now that the chambering reamers were finally made up by Vernor Gipson for the completed .219 Donaldson-Wasp case, Wasp rifles were made up for a number of expert riflemen and varmint shooters in all sections of the country and Donaldson was able to get a clear idea of its fine performance in the hands of others. However, since the very first, this case had labored under an extreme handicap, due to the fact that riflemen who had not seen the results which Donaldson and others were obtaining, positively could not believe it possible that so small a case could develop the velocity and accuracy which it actually was developing, in the hands of riflemen who were familiar with the methods Donaldson was using and who were therefore able to get similar results.

However, word gets around with remarkable rapidity among shooters and when it was learned by some that it was possible to exceed .22 Varminter velocities and equal or exceed .220 Swift velocities with this tiny case, using the same bullet and from 6.0 to 10.0 grains less powder, letters began to come in asking how such excellent results could be obtained. This was all very interesting to Donaldson himself, who was able back in 1936 to obtain velocities from the little Wasp case which were close to the .220 Swift, but at that time no one would believe it possible.

Another handicap was the lack of a chronograph to make these velocity tests. Many informed riflemen claimed that shooting into steel plates was no test of velocity at all. There is, of course, only one way to correctly determine the velocity of a bullet and that is through the use of an accurate chronograph; but since, for reasons of expense the best chronographs are only in the hands of the Army or the larger arms companies, it was not until 1945 that, by actual chronograph tests, the fact was established beyond a doubt that the claims which Donaldson had made of velocities in excess of 4,000 f.s. from the .219 Donaldson-Wasp case were correct.

During this year, Vaughn Cail, the small bore shot from New Haven, who owned both the .22 Varminter and .220 Swift rifles and used them extensively at varmint shooting, heard of the remarkable velocities being obtained from the small Wasp case and he determined to own one of these rifles and to ascertain the facts for himself. As Cail is a remarkably fine rifle shot, as well as being a careful experimenter with the varmint rifle, his experiments will be interesting and valuable.

Learning that his close friend, Al Marciante, the well-known Trenton, New Jersey, gunsmith had become sufficiently interested in the .219 Donaldson-Wasp to decide to tool up for the purpose of chambering rifles for the new case, he wrote to Marciante and learned that he was at that very moment, in process of making up the chambering reamers to Donaldson's specifications and that Donaldson had decided to make an addition of 1/32″ to the length of the neck of the Wasp case in order to accommodate a graphite wad in all loads, without in any way reducing the powder capacity of the case. He further learned, that, if he wished, he might have the very first rifle ever chambered for the slightly lengthened case.

Upon learning through further correspondence that Donaldson's own pet varmint Wasp was in 14″ twist and also that the 14″ twist would handle the very sharp Wotkyns-Morse 50 and 55-grain bullets, for long range shooting to better advantage than would the 16″ twist .219 Donaldson-Wasp rifles, Cail lost no time in obtaining a fine heavy .220 Winchester-Swift barrel and sent this at once to Marciante together with his own fine Model 70 Winchester action and Marksman target stock. This barrel was 30″ in length, 1¼″ at breech and 15/16″ at muzzle, having a groove diameter of .224″ and a 14″ twist, and was in new condition.

Cail learned from Donaldson that a variety of cases could be

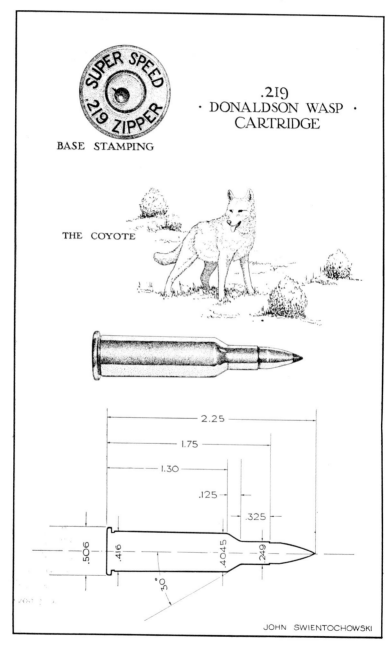

BASE STAMPING

.219
· DONALDSON WASP ·
CARTRIDGE

THE COYOTE

JOHN SWIENTOCHOWSKI

used for forming shells for the forthcoming Wasp, among them the .219 Winchester Zipper, .30-30 Winchester, .32 Winchester Spec., .25-35 Winchester, and .22 Savage HiPower—the .219 Winchester Zipper being the most desirable on account of its fine, heavy construction, and also because of the simplicity of forming the cases in a single operation. In this way, it was only necessary to have a single case forming die and into this die the Zipper cases could be pushed with an ordinary press. This left a section of the neck of the case protruding from the die and this could be cut off with a hack saw and the case filed off smooth within the hardened die, with a file, and finally beveled inside lightly with a sharp knife. This completed the simple, case-forming operation, using the .219 Winchester Zipper, whereas, with cases like the .30-30 Winchester, it was necessary to form the cases more gradually in two operations. Donaldson offered to furnish Cail with a few .30-30 Winchester cases, formed for the Wasp, as these held a bit more powder than cases formed from the Zipper brass and would be worthwhile to have while experimenting with heavy loads.

While this was going on, Marciante, with his usual speed, had completed a perfect chambering job with the new Wasp reamer, having first fitted the Swift barrel to Cail's fine Model 70 action. He had also completed case sizing dies and bullet seating dies to fit Cail's Pacific loading tool and the rifle was ready for trial.

Before leaving for Maine where he expected to spend a week's vacation in testing out the new Wasp and in varmint shooting, Cail could not resist a brief trial of his new rifle, so he fired a few rounds loaded with a forming load of 23.0 grains of duPont No. 4198 in order to form some cases and then fired two witnessed groups at the Lyman range in Middlefield, Connecticut, using a load of 31.0 grains of duPont No. 4320 with the 48-grain Winchester-Swift bullet, No. 115 Winchester primers and .046 IPCO Graphite wad in the mouth of the case. The first 10-shot bench rest group at 100 yards gave a 1 1/16″ group from center to center of bullet holes furthest apart, and was followed by a 1¾″ five-shot 200 yard group.

Cail knew that Donaldson and others had, using the .219 Donaldson-Wasp and loads of 29.0 grains of Hi-Vel No. 3, actually penetrated more steel than was possible with regular custom and factory loads in .22 Varminter and .220 Swift rifles using the same bullets of 50 and 48-grains weight, respectively. Therefore, he was anxious to make this test himself against his own .22 Varminter and .220 Swift rifles. However, upon firing his .219 Donaldson-

Wasp rifle with 28.0 grains of Hi-Vel No. 3 and the 48-grain Winchester-Swift bullets, signs of extreme pressure were noted and further testing with this load was temporarily discontinued.

When his friends heard of this they stated that they were positive that the little Wasp case was not able to develop anywhere near the velocities that Donaldson had claimed for it and offered to back up their judgment in a substantial way. A wager was made by two of them that it would be impossible to obtain 4,000 f.s. velocity on a good chronograph using the 48-grain Winchester-Swift bullet and any load that could be loaded into the Wasp case. Cail accepted the wager.

A few days later Cail left for his vacation in Maine and there joined a friend, who was at the very time engaged in testing a 16″ twist Wasp belonging to Dr. E. W. Paine of that state. Cail was at first much concerned by the indications of high pressure which he had encountered with the load of 28.0 grains Hi-Vel No. 3 behind the 48-grain Winchester-Swift bullet, and he felt that because of this his chances of attaining 4,000 f.s. with this bullet and the little Wasp were slim indeed.

He had, therefore, brought with him from New Haven some steel plates into which he had fired bullets from his own Wasp, as well as some from his .22 Varminter and .220 Swift rifles. In the case of the Varminter the load was a custom load as put out by J. B. Smith, using the 50-grain Wotkyns-Morse bullet; with his Swift he used the regular factory .220 Smith load with the 48-grain Winchester-Swift bullet, which gives a velocity at muzzle of 4,140 f.s.

Now, since Cail's own Wasp rifle had shown indications of high pressures with 28.0 grains of Hi-Vel No. 3 and the 48-grain Swift bullet, it was decided by the two shooters that the barrel required throating by the method Donaldson had used for some years and which had been explained in detail by Fred Ness in the October 1944 *American Rifleman*. Therefore, the 16″ twist Wasp belonging to Dr. E. W. Paine was selected for test. This rifle had been chambered by Gipson for the slightly shorter Wasp case and had showed no pressure troubles, with heavy loads.

The same steel plates were set up into which bullets had been shot from the .22 Varminter and .220 Swift rifles in New Haven. A load of 29.5 grains of Hi-Vel No. 3 was loaded up for the 16″ Wasp behind the 48-grain Winchester-Swift bullet and on trial this bullet penetrated considerably more steel than had been penetrated using the .22 Varminter rifle and slightly more than had been penetrated with the .220 Swift. With the 50-grain Wotkyns-Morse bullets and 29.0 grains of Hi-Vel No. 3 also, considerably more steel was penetrated than with the custom 50-grain Wotkyns-Morse load in Cail's Varminter rifle. No indications of excessively high pressures were present with the above loads, although they must have been close to maximum loads and Wasp users should approach them with caution, especially if the barrels have not been properly throated.

There was now, in the minds of the experimenters, no doubt about the outcome of the wager which Cail had made with his friends in New Haven, and further velocity tests were discontinued in favor of developing some fine varmint loads and determining the accuracy of Cail's new 14″ twist Wasp with the slightly lengthened Marciante chamber.

Since it now seemed certain that Cail's 14″ twist Wasp would need to be throated in order to handle the heavy loads of powder without encountering pressure troubles, it was decided to continue tests with the 48-grain Winchester-Swift bullet, using a load of 20.0 grains of duPont No. 4759, which had proved to be a very accurate load with other Wasp rifles. The primer used was the Winchester No. 120 and the usual .033 IPCO Graphite wad was placed in the mouth of each case loaded. Neither bullet nor powder was weighed, except to check the measure, the powder being loaded into the case as thrown from the Ideal Powder Measure. As the shooters had on hand a few 45-grain Wotkyns-Morse bullets, 25 of them were loaded, using a load of 31.0 grains of duPont No. 4320, No. 120 Winchester primers, .033 IPCO Graphite wad, and cases for all loads were formed from Zipper brasses.

At this time a five to seven mile, 8 o'clock wind was blowing, which did not affect the shooting with its full force, as the range was somewhat protected by a bank along its entire length of 100 yards.

After a couple of fouling shots, Cail settled himself at the bench rest and fired the five-odd shots, using the Wotkyns-Morse 45-grain bullets and 31.0 grains of duPont No. 4320 powder. These grouped well into ¾″. Feeling that this combination was inclined to shoot, Cail continued, using the same load, with a 10-shot group which measured 27/32″ and is No. 1 of the five 10-shot groups illustrated.

Changing now to the load of 20.0 grains of duPont No. 4759 and the 48-grain Winchester-Swift bullet, Cail fired Groups No. 2, No. 3 and No. 4, which measured respectively ⅞″, 1 1/32″ and 11/16″.

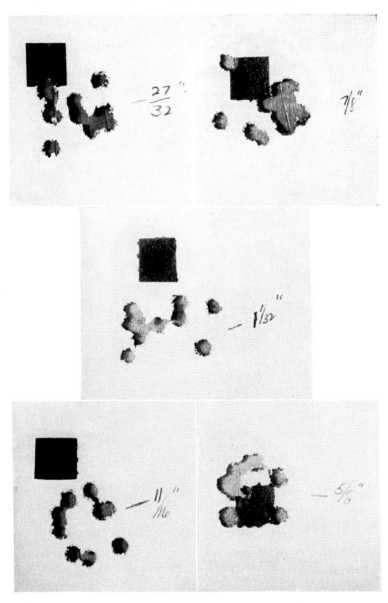

Five consecutive ten-shot rest groups, fired at 100 yards with the 14″ twist .219 Donaldson Wasp rifle, by Vaughn Cail, New Haven, Conn. Reading from L to R #1 and #5, Wotkyns-Morse 45-grain bullet, #2, #3 and #4, 48-grain Winchester-Swift bullet.

What a pleasure it is to lounge in the warmth of a fine summer afternoon, propped comfortably against the shooting house, watching the performance of a finely accurate rifle in the hands of an expert shot, speculating with friends on the merits of the components being used and placing a bet of a trifling sum on the outcome! What moments in life can truly be said to be so free of care, or so pleasant to remember, as these!

A good bench rest had been placed outdoors so that the wind might disperse the mirage which rose off the barrel of the rifle as it was directed through the port of the shooting house. As the rays of the sun began to take on their evening slant, the wind had dropped and conditions for fine shooting could hardly be improved. The spectators, wanting just one more group, urged the shooter to hold them a little closer. He reached for his loading block containing the remaining loads, using the little 45-grain Wotkyns-Morse bullets, settled on the bench rest and began his string. One after another, they cut together. After five shots, they must be within a ½″ circle, —eight—nine—all in close! Can he put the "tough one" in there? A sharp "crack" from the heavy Wasp rifle—and the scopes are trained on the target frame. "It is in there!" Everyone got up, someone picked up a steel rule, and all headed up the path, through the trees, to see what the groups measured. The last one was only ⅝″ on centers, for the 10 shots. Of the 50 shots, the average is only 13/16″.

Cail was praised for his fine holding, and someone wanted to buy his Wasp. Diplock, Turner and Clark hastened to witness the targets. Rifles, scopes, cleaning rods, shooting kits, everything was gathered together, and shooters and experimenters followed one another in single file down the path, leaving the range to its customary quiet.

On another day, it was decided to develop a fine crow load, using the 55-grain Doering bullet, as a raid on the wily crow was planned soon.

A load that had worked perfectly with the 16″ twist Wasp, consisting of 27.0 grains of duPont No. 3031, behind this 55-grain Doering bullet, using the Winchester No. 120 primer and the usual .033 IPCO Graphite wad, did not give fine groups in this particular 14″ twist barrel and the load was increased to 28.5 grains of No. 3031, which narrowed the groups down again, giving accuracy similar to that shown by the 48-grain Winchester-Swift bullet.

It was decided to test this load, to determine its path, if possible, over the 300 yard range, which is about the limit at which crows and chucks can be shot in the comparatively small fields where they can be found in Maine.

After carefully sighting in with the above load at 200 yards, the bench was moved to a neighboring location, targets set up at 100, 208 and 308 yards and Cail settled himself at the rest for the 30-shot test. The conditions of light were good and a gentle four to six mile wind was blowing from 9 o'clock.

Shooting commenced at 208 yards, giving a perfectly centered group at that range and, without any change of elevation or windage on the 20X Super-Targetspot, another 10-shot group was fired at 100 yards, which printed only slightly high. Now, again, without changing position or sights in any way, another 10-shot string was fired at the 308 yard range and the test was complete.

Upon inspection of the targets, some very interesting facts were turned up. The group at 208 yards measured 2⅞", from center to center of bullet holes furthest apart and is perfectly centered for both elevation and windage. The group shows the effect of the four to six mile 9 o'clock wind, as it covers 2½" horizontally and only 1¾" vertically.

Cail's 100 yard group measured 1¼", with nine shots in 11/16" and prints exactly 1" high and ¾" to the left. This is a surprise since the Winchester trajectory tables for the .220 Swift give the 100 yard height of the group, when sighted at 200 yards, as being 1½" high with the 55-grain bullet (but, of course, that was from the line of the bore, not the line of the sights—Author; in this article measurements were taken above or below the line of sight).

The fact of the 100 yard group printing ¾" to the left with the wind blowing from that direction, when the rifle was supposedly zeroed correctly for 200 yards, could have been due to various causes, such as yaw, the drift of the bullet from causes other than wind, the condition that the line through the optical center of the telescope might not have been exactly parallel to the line of the bore. In any event, it shows the small difference between the 100 and the 200 yard zeroes in a light wind.

Next the 308 yard group was inspected. This was fired with the sights perfectly centered for 200 yards. This group measured 4⅝" between centers of widest shots. This was also the horizontal dispersion. The vertical variation was only 2⅜" and shows that this load really shoots, as nine of the 10 shots went into 3". The group printed 2¼" to the right of the center and showed that the four to six mile wind blew the 55-grain bullet but that much between 200 and 300 yards. This is very little indeed.

The drop of the bullet between 200 and 300 yards was shown to be 7½" which Cail says is the drop of his .220 Swift between those distances.

To summarize, therefore, when using the 14" twist, .219 Donaldson-Wasp rifle, 55-grain Doering bullet, 28.5 grains of duPont No. 3031 powder, Winchester 120 primers, .033 IPCO Graphite wads and Zipper cases, and sighted in dead center at 200 yards, the group prints only 1" high at 100 yards, and with the scope sight about 1.6" above the line of the bore that will give a trajectory over 200 yards of 1.80" measured from the bore of the rifle. The rifle shot but 7½" low at 300 yards, when scope-sighted to shoot 1" high at 100 yards, zero at 200 yards. Windage when shooting in a four to six mile cross wind, using 200 yard sighting, is ¼" left at 100 yards and 2½" right at 300 yards, wind blowing from left to right.

In the Ideal handbook, we note that, with the .22 Varminter 36.0 grains of duPont No. 4320 behind the 55-grain bullet gives a muzzle velocity of 3,630 f.s.; also in the .220 Swift a load of 37.0 grains of duPont No. 4064 and a 55-grain bullet gives a velocity of 3,500 f.s. However, from the .219 Donaldson-Wasp 14" twist rifles, a velocity of 3,631 f.s. is shown on the Winchester chronograph, with only 28.5 grains of duPont No. 3031 powder, actually about 8.0 grains less powder and the same weight bullet being used.

This load certainly leaves nothing to be desired for crow and chuck shooting, so the experimenters discontinued further shooting, in favor of preparing ammunition for the crow hunt planned for the following day.

Now, in discussing this matter in the gun room, is was agreed that one need have very little concern whatever about the barrel life of Wasp rifles if three factors are considered and followed: first, the throating of all .219 Donaldson-Wasp barrels; second, the use of graphite wads in all loads; and, third, the fact that from 6.0 to 10.0 grains less powder are used than in cases of the Swift and Varminter class to get equal velocities.

This matter of throating is very important, and, in order to get the best results, a bullet should be used having a diameter of from .001 to .0015 larger than the groove diameter of the barrel in which it is to be used. If the throating is properly done, by the method previously mentioned, the bullet does not slam up against a rather abrupt shoulder when fired, but the gentle taper allows the bullet to move forward into the barrel without being deformed and, most important of all, without building up excessive pressures, as is the case in barrels not so throated. Again, when the explosion occurs, there exists in barrels so throated a gas seal, since the bullet is larger than the hole into which it will enter and the throat is so made as to perfectly fit the bullet and the bullet is seated into the case so as to exactly fit into the throat. It is well to note that, in this throat, the bullet contacts the throat all the way round and not just where the lands touch it as is the case with the conventional throat. In this way, I (Clark) believe it is impossible for gas to escape by the bullet and damage the lands by erosion. When a .223″ or .224″ bullet is fired in a .224″ barrel not so throated, some gas does escape by the bullet, before it upsets and this causes the damage. However, using Donaldson's methods of oversize bullets in conjunction with proper throating, any gas cutting whatever is seemingly impossible. This throat must also increase velocities, since the gas which escapes in conventional throats is, in this way, retained back of the bullet, for a useful purpose.

In the second place, many believe the use of Donaldson's graphite wads also materially increase barrel life and, for a full explanation of this principle, the reader is referred to the March 1936 *American Rifleman,* wherein Donaldson is the first to call the attention of shooters to this fact.

Lastly, it goes without saying that, everything else being equal, the less powder that a case requires to develop a given velocity, the longer will be the barrel life where that case is used. In regard to developing high velocities with small powder loads, the .219 Donaldson-Wasp case is so efficient as to be in a class by itself.

The following day a crow hunt was in order and, accompanied by Dr. E. W. Paine and his Varminter, the experimenters visited a beautiful section of country along the Kennebec River, between Waterville and The Forks. This route follows the so-called Arnold Trail, where in 1775 Benedict Arnold and his expedition, alternately dragged and rowed their heavy bateaux up the Kennebec River on their expedition against Quebec.

The weather might be considered impossible, as it rained almost constantly. Nevertheless, crows offered themselves as targets with reasonable frequency and good sport was had, all shooting being done from the car since, in this country, crows will fly if within 350 yards if a man is seen to get out of a car and, in fact, the shooter has to get his shot off from the car within a few seconds after it is brought to a stop or His Honor, observing what is likely to occur and loudly inviting his friends to accompany him, is off to a safer land.

With the good Doctor, a seasoned crow killer, having a slight advantage from his perch on the back seat, 16 crows were dispatched and in every case very little was left to identify the carcass by the speedy Wasp and Varminter bullets. Is was estimated that 80 per cent kills had been made at distances from 125 to 225 yards and on returning home, it was voted to be the best way possible to pass a rainy day.

The two remaining days were spent in developing additional accurate loads on the range, most of which appear in connection with chronograph tests; Cail was obliged to return to New Haven with his Wasp after having spent a most enjoyable vacation and again after having clearly demonstrated his known ability to "hold 'em in there" from the bench rest as well as the prone position. He is also the kind of rifleman who can hold 'em in there when the money is down on the table, as has been told in another chapter of this book.

After his return he had hoped to be able to have some of the better Wasp loads chronographed at the Winchester plant, as well as to determine Wasp velocities, in connection with the wager he had with friends who contended, it will be recalled, that it would be impossible to attain 4,000 f.s. velocity with any load that could be loaded into the .219 Donaldson-Wasp case using the 48-grain Winchester-Swift bullet.

The results of these tests, on such an accurate chronograph, were awaited with the greatest interest, since they constituted the very first trial of velocities from the little Wasp case, that would establish or disprove, beyond the question of a doubt, claims which Donaldson had made for his case design years ago and which had been thought by many to be too good to be true.

The following velocities with loads used, as taken on the Winchester chronograph, speak for themselves:

ESTABLISHED .219 DONALDSON-WASP VELOCITIES

Chronographed on Winchester Range

Bullet	Powder	Charge	Average Muzzle Vel.
	With 16" twist		
48-gr. Win.-Swift	Hi-Vel #3	29.0 grains	4,064 f.s.
45-gr. W-M	Hi-Vel #3	29.0 grains	3,874 f.s.
50-gr. W-M	Hi-Vel #3	29.0 grains	4,039 f.s.
35-gr. Sisk	Hi-Vel #3	30.0 grains	4,018 f.s.

Bullet	Powder	Charge	Average Muzzle Vel.
With 14″ twist			
63-gr. Sisk	#3031 duPont	27.5 grains	3,485 f.s.
55-gr. Doering	#3031 ″	28.5 grains	3,631 f.s.
55-gr. Sisk	#3031 ″	29.0 grains	3,715 f.s.
48-gr. Win.-Swift	#3031 ″	29.0 grains	3,689 f.s.
45-gr. W-M	#4320 ″	31.0 grains	3,600 f.s.
48-gr. Win.-Swift	#4759 ″	20.0 grains	2,990 f.s.

In inspecting these velocities, established on the Winchester Company's chronograph, it should be noticed that the first four were obtained using the 16″ twist .219 Donaldson-Wasp, on Winchester S.S. action, with Gipson chamber and *without throat* and the remaining loads were fired from Cail's Model 70 Winchester 14″ twist .219 Donaldson-Wasp after it had been throated. Now, this fact should bear special attention, since from the very first Donaldson had established the fact by repeated trials on steel plates with his own Wasp rifles that, with identical loads, quite considerably greater velocities were attained from 16″ twist Wasp barrels than from 14″ twist barrels. Also, in 16″ twist barrels, with equal velocity, the pressures were less than where the quicker twist was used. Again, in throated barrels, very much greater velocity is obtained without pressure troubles than in barrels not so throated, regardless of twist. Hence, referring again to the Winchester chronograph tests, had the same 16″ twist Wasp been used and had it been throated and used the new longer Wasp case, all tests shown could have developed higher velocities, if desired, without the slightest increase in pressures.

Again, the loads shown in the chronograph tests are not in a single case maximum loads, *but* it must be noted that some might become maximum loads in: (1) 14″ twist barrels; (2) barrels not properly throated; (3) tightly chambered barrels; (4) with bullets of excessive diameter; and (5) with barrels of unusually small groove diameter.

The handloader should here note well that the five conditions stated above are not peculiar in a single respect to the .219 Donaldson-Wasp, but each of these factors should be noted well and carefully checked, in reloading for any new or unfamiliar barrel of the high-speed varmint class.

Now, returning again to the chronograph tests and the velocities that may be obtained from the cases under discussion, I repeat, had there been a throat in the 16″ Wasp barrel which developed 4,064 f.s. with the 48-grain Winchester-Swift bullet and had it been chambered for the longer .219 Donaldson-Wasp case, for which Marciante recently chambered, even greater velocities could have been obtained without exceeding the pressures developed in this load. Similarly, where duPont powders are concerned, we note that where the 55-grain Sisk bullet is used, with 29.0 grains of No. 3031 powder in the 14″ twist .219 Donaldson-Wasp rifle, a velocity is obtained of 3,715 f.s. at the muzzle. This is exactly five f.s. less than the velocity of the .220 Winchester-Swift with 55-grain bullet, as noted in advertising put out by the Winchester Company and 215 f.s. more than recommended 55-grain Swift loads, listed in the No. 34 Ideal handbook.

The writer has gone into some detail to bring out these facts, not because a reasonable handloader wishes to obtain from a given case every last foot second of velocity possible, but first to illustrate to shooters again the very remarkable efficiency of this wonderful little case, where the velocities of the fine .220 Swift rifle may actually be exceeded, with about 8.0 grains less of powder; and, second, to establish that Harvey Donaldson's claims, in regard to Wasp velocities are essentially correct.

After experiments here described, the writer is of the firm belief that an accurate load, which will drive a 55-grain bullet at between 3,650 f.s. and 3,750 f.s. from the .219 Donaldson-Wasp rifle is a most excellent load to use in all ordinary varmint shooting. This might be obtained with between 28.0 and 29.0 grains of duPont No. 3031 and either the 55-grain Doering, Sisk Express or Wotkyns-Morse bullets. If greater velocities were desired, a 45 or 50-grain bullet could be used, preferably with a design of point similar to the fine Wotkyns-Morse bullets, but the 55-grain bullet will, in every case, hold up its velocity, shoot flatter and kill better at the longer ranges. Thus, a 55-grain bullet, going at say 3,700 f.s. at the muzzle, will shoot flatter out at 200 yards and beyond than, say, the 45 or 48-grain bullets that give 200 f.s. more velocity at the muzzle.

It is well to note, however, that the 14″ twist will more effectively handle the very sharp pointed bullets, of 50-grains weight or over, and the .219 Donaldson-Wasp rifle should be made up in

14″ twist, if these particular sharp pointed bullets are to be extensively used. The 14″ twist will also handle perfectly, lighter bullets of any shape, and heavier bullets up to 63-grains weight.

On the other hand, if extremely high velocities are desired, or if it is planned to used sharp pointed bullets of less than 50-grains weight, like the 45-grain Wotkyns-Morse, or bullets over 50-grains weight with points more rounded than the 8S, the 16″ twist would be entirely satisfactory.

Both 14″ and 16″ twist Wasp rifles give wonderful accuracy with the very fine and inexpensive 45-grain Winchester Hornet bullets, using 20.0 grains of duPont No. 4759 or 27.0 grains of duPont No. 3031. For group shooting, at the target, it would be hard to beat this fine little bullet, although in a wind, it would shoot second place to a bullet of equal weight, but having a sharper point. Another wonderful shooting load, using the 45-grain Wotkyns-Morse bullet is the one Cail used in making his ⅝″ 10-shot group, namely, 31.0 grains of No. 4320. This group is No. 5 in the illustration of Wasp groups.

Furthermore, if the shooter desires a fine squirrel load, or one exceedingly well adpated to offhand practice, he may use in his .219 Donaldson-Wasp rifle 7.0 to 10.0 grains of duPont No. 4227 powder, behind the Ideal Hornet Loverin gas-check bullet No. 225438. This bullet was designed by H. Guy Loverin, of Lancaster, Massachusetts, along the lines of the best .22 caliber rim fire bullets and will give fine rim fire accuracy in Wasp rifles. This excellent bullet may be purchased custom made from Mr. Loverin. The proper temper is 1-20 and no graphite wad should be used. This offhand load is inexpensive and is just another illustration of the endless number of combinations of powder and bullet that give fine results in the Wasp design of case.

For the information of those desiring to have .219 Donaldson-Wasp rifles made up on any of the better single shot actions, such as the Winchester Hi-Sidewall, Sharps-Borchardt, Stevens Ideal No. 44½, Farquharson, et cetera, or any good bolt action, such as the Winchester Models 54 or 70, Remington Model 30 or Krag, the following gunsmiths are able to do excellent work in chambering and fitting barrels for the Wasp case and numerous others will probably soon be tooled up, when the merits of the new case are known:

Al Marciante, 1216 Princeton Ave., Trenton, New Jersey.

Vernor Gipson, Worth, Illinois.

Robert Keel, 1 Delafield Drive, Albany, New York.

Floyd Butler, R. No. 2, Poultney, Vermont.

At present, however, Marciante is the only one of the list tooled up for the very latest Wasp case, which Donaldson in the summer of 1945 decided to extend about 1/32″ in order to accommodate a graphite wad in each load without reducing the powder capacity.

In the selection of a suitable barrel to be chambered for this new case, varmint hunters would do well to obtain a fine heavy 14″ twist Winchester .220 Swift blank. This blank measures 1¼″ x 15/16″ and is 31″ long. This length is reduced to 30″ when the barrel is chambered and the barrel is then of ideal weight for varmint shooting. Of course, this length may be reduced, if desired.

When the stock work is done, it will be found advantageous in varmint shooting, whether a one or two piece stock is used, to make the forend as nearly as possible to the shape of the Winchester Marksman target stock. The bottom of this forend is almost flat and is so wide that whatever the rest of the forend may be, in shooting, a firm, steady hold is assured, without the least tendency to tipping. If the varmint shooter will follow this suggestion, his percentage of hits at all ranges will be much improved over that obtained from any type of narrow forestock or one in any way rounded at the bottom (on the other hand, a flat-bottomed forend is clumsy to carry, and homely, for hunting, makes the rifle feel heavy, and is not so satisfactory for hunting as a baseball bat shape forend—Author).

There are a number of expert rifle shots and varmint hunters personally known to the writer who have proved to their own satisfaction that the .219 Donaldson-Wasp case in a fine .22 caliber barrel, will produce the most consistent accuracy and the smallest individual groups, with a greater variety of different loads, than any other case design known to them. It is a fact that some of these men have owned as many as three individual rifles, chambered for the .22 Varminter, .220 Swift, .22 Niedner Magnum, R-2 Donaldson, or some other of the popular .22 caliber varmint cases and formerly believed these to be the very finest obtainable from the standpoint of accuracy. And yet they have been obliged to concede first place to the .219 Donaldson-Wasp case, after a thorough trial.

Perhaps some of the very finest groups at 100 and 200 yards ever fired from Wasp rifles are now in the files of Harvey Donaldson himself. The writer, having had access to these files, can testify to this fact, but believes Mr. Donaldson would much prefer to have the wonderful accuracy of the little case left to the testimony of others now that his own work of design and development has been so successfully consummated.

LOADS FOR THE .219 DONALDSON-WASP

31 grains	duPont	#4320	45-grain	Wotkyns-Morse bullet	
29	"	Hercules	Hivel #3	45	"	Wotkyns-Morse bullet
27	"	duPont	#3031	45	"	Win. Hornet	"
20	"	"	#4759	45	"	Win. Hornet	"
28	"	"	#3031	48	"	Win. Swift	"
27	"	"	#3031	50	"	Wotkyns-Morse	"
29	"	Hercules	Hivel #3	50	"	"	"	"
29	"	duPont	#3031	50	"	"	"	"
31	"	"	#4320	50	"	"	"	"
28.5	"	"	#3031	55	"	Doering	"
27	"	"	#3031	55	"	"	"
29	"	"	#4320	55	"	"	"
27	"	"	#3031	55	"	Sisk Express	"
28	"	"	#3031	55	"	Wotkyns-Morse	"
27.5	"	"	#3031	63	"	Sisk	"
7-10	"	"	#4227	45	"	Ideal Hornet Loverin gas-check #225438
23	"	"	#4198	45, 48,	50-grain bullet for case forming load

Primers: Winchester #120, #115; Remington #9 1/2; Western #8 1/2; F. A. #70.

IPCO Graphite Wads used with all loads.

Approach all loads with caution unless barrel be properly throated.

Samuel Clark, Jr.
Oakland, Maine
7-30-45

Chapter 11

CANADIAN DEVELOPMENTS
.22 CALIBER RIFLES AND .22 WILDCAT CARTRIDGES
SUPPLIED BY G. B. CRANDALL

G. B. CRANDALL has been recognized for many years as the No. 1 Custom Gunsmith of the Dominion of Canada. To understand his importance to Canadian, and especially to Ontario riflemen, imagine for a moment that it were possible to combine the business and personal ability of Hervey Lovell, Charles C. Johnson, C. A. Diller and Jerry Gebby into one firm and gunshop. That would represent G. B. Crandall, of Wellington St. N., Woodstock, Ontario, Canada, particularly in the matter of .22 wildcats. Remember, we are speaking not of business volume but of *relative importance* in the two countries, population differences being borne in mind.

It is a big country, north of New York, Michigan and Montana, with a population a million more than in Pennsylvania, but it contains in that portion of Southern Ontario, within comfortable motoring distance of Mr. Crandall's Woodstock shop, more woodchucks than any other part of North America, and more of the rare black woodchucks than any other portion of the globe.

Out West, where his wheat country and British Columbia customers live, Canada extends from Idaho and Washington to the southeastern boundary of Alaska, where the Alaskan highway cuts through the Arctic mountain valleys of the Yukon Territory, on its way to Fairbanks, Alaska, 1,500 miles northwest of the Peace River wheat country of British Columbia and 2,100 miles northwest of Edmonton, Alberta, the most important air base center in Northwest Canada and some day one of the air centers of the Western Hemisphere.

To refresh your memory, Canada contains eight or ten large, modern cities like Toronto, Montreal, Ottawa, Vancouver, Winnipeg, Hamilton, Quebec, Halifax and numerous others all slightly smaller, but the remainder of its population is often found in settle-

ments widely scattered throughout the Dominion, and many of its
people depend largely in winter on game and hides for a living. Its
shooting seasons are earlier and longer than ours, and much of it
is rifle game.

Woodstock, the scene of Mr. Crandall's endeavors, is a busy
little city rather convenient to Detroit, Buffalo and Toronto, and
for all of its earlier and greatest efforts in the shooting world was
the home of *Rod & Gun in Canada,* the Dominion's leading and
largest sporting magazine.

G. B. Crandall began turning out .22 Hornet rifles when they
were first developed, by using the Parkerifled steel tubes supplied
by Parker-Hale of Birmingham, England, the principal subsidiary or
affiliate of the Birmingham Small Arms Co., the largest makers of
sporting and target firearms in Great Britain and which firm corresponds to the Winchester Repeating Arms Co., were that fine
firm located in England.

Mr. Crandall lined or re-lined many rifles with these tubes. In
this work he supplied a service almost identical with that provided
for many years by C. A. Diller, of Dayton, Ohio, to the .22 rifle
cranks of the United States. Many of these rifles so re-lined by
Mr. Crandall were single shot rifles—there have been for many
years a great many single shot Winchester Schuetzen and sporting
rifles in Southern Ontario. Also, in this work, Mr. Crandall supplied a service very similar to that furnished by R. F. Sedgley, Inc.,
in Philadelphia, Pennsylvania, for years and up until Mr. Sedgley
passed on to his considerable reward. Mr. Crandall also re-lined
many B. S. A. No. 12 and similar rifles, including such as the
Greener, Martini and various Winchester bolt action repeating rifles.
Eventually, as Winchester and Savage .22 Hornet rifles appeared on
the market in numbers, this demand for re-lined .22's of Hornet
caliber began to slacken and then materially diminish.

Fortunately, just about that time, the .22/3000 Lovell came into
prominence and Mr. Crandall took that up, producing at first a
chamber a bit after his own ideas, and not just a copy of the original
Hervey Lovell development. This was a plan, said to have been
followed somewhat by most of the experimenters at first, but as the
fame of this fine little cartridge grew, and its adaptability to Ontario
woodchuck and crow shooting became better known, it became more
and more apparent that some sort of standard chamber and cartridge
dimensions would have to be agreed upon, adopted, and used by
everyone, if such rifles were to be 100% effective. Situations could
arise, unless such be done, in which charges intended for use in

fairly long cases with gentle shoulders might be used in chambers made for shorter cartridge cases having very sharp shoulders, the immediate and inevitable result of such occurrence being greatly increased and undesirably high pressures.

Mr. Crandall felt that R. S. Risley, of Hubbardsville, New York, had devised the most practical and useful shape of .25-20 case conversion to .22, and that it was the most nearly correct for powders available. Mr. Risley appears to have done the wildcat specialist a service out of proportion to the very modest acclaim he has so far received.

Crandall follows the Risley .22/3000 dimensions so closely with his .22/3000 R-2 Lovell that the Crandall rifle chamber of this size will interchange ammunition with the R-2 Lovell and also with the C. C. Johnson R-2 chamber.

The Crandall K-Hornet

Crandall has also been making a chamber known as the Improved Kilbourn K-Hornet. "G. B." mentioned that Kilbourn first designed this chamber with a square shoulder, whereupon some shooters and riflemen in Galt, Ontario, a short distance north of Woodstock, came down and asked Mr. Crandall to re-chamber their rifles for that cartridge. He did so but the square shoulder did not suit Crandall so he altered it to a 20° shoulder taper. When completed and tried out he sent a sample of the case to Kilbourn, who is said to have replied that he was just then in process of making reamers to produce the same formation of chamber, and asked for samples of Crandall's cases which were forwarded. Writers soon described this case, or the Kilbourn form of it, as the new Kilbourn cartridge, the new Improved Kilbourn K-Hornet. It was apparently developed on both sides of the International line at approximately the same period. These two custom gunsmiths are, it seems, close friends and both are careful about detracting from credit to the other. Crandall is supplying today, as brass is available, what he describes as the "Standard Kilbourn K-Hornet Chamber."

One of the variations of .22/3000 wildcat production and individual efforts is that some experimenters constantly try to outdo each other by stretching commercial cartridges by firing loaded cases in longer chambers, until they obtain a case sometimes stretched beyond the elastic limit of the brass. Mr. Crandall has suggested that, in his opinion, a few of the more radical designs of .22 wildcat cartridges are not too practical or desirable, because they result in the destruction of too much cartridge brass, weakening the case

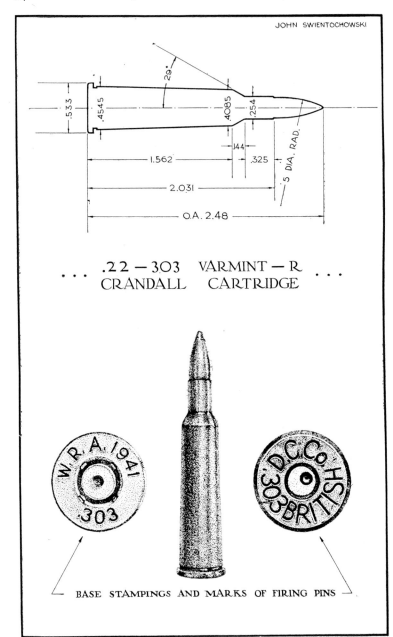

JOHN SWIENTOCHOWSKI

.22 — 303   VARMINT — R
CRANDALL   CARTRIDGE

BASE STAMPINGS AND MARKS OF FIRING PINS

due to excessive elongation and abnormally abrupt shoulder and that at present there is no easy means of replacing such loss of cartridge brass.

The Crandall .22-303 Varmint-R

Two or three Canadian rifle enthusiasts have developed special .25 and .22 caliber wildcats by necking down and then cutting off .303 British service cartridge brass cases. It should be remembered by readers, that in Canada, South Africa and other British possessions, including New Zealand and Australia, the .303 British Lee-Enfield service cartridge is as important and occupied the same relative place in British-designed military ammunition, as does the .30-1906 cartridge in the United States.

There have been many military camps in Canada, those for the training of Canadian troops, those for British Air Corps Cadets and various other camps in and around which much shooting has been done, and at such camps plenty of .303 British service brass is present, and if some of it *is* picked up for practical use elsewhere what better use could be made of it. After World War II equipment is thrown open to sale to the public, military ammunition will be such a drug on the market that what was left over from World War I will seem scarcely a drop splashed into the bucket.

Gunsmith Crandall has stated that his .22-303 Varmint-R cartridge is in no particular similar to the first design produced by W. B. Elliott, of St. Catharine's, Ontario. Mr. Elliott, B.A.Sc. is Manager of the Engineering Tool & Forgings Limited, of St. Catharine's. Elliott advised the author in a letter written May 15, 1939, that his first design (of which he sent a blueprint as of 5-19-1938, and another corrected as of 5-27-38 and of 8-31-38, and also a blueprint of his .25-303 cartridge as of 12-31-37 and of 5-10-38) had the same capacity and shoulder angle as the .220 Swift. Then, J. Bushnell Smith's .22-250 came out and Mr. Elliott re-designed his cartridge to duplicate Smith's cartridge, essentially, with slightly reduced capacity and with a 25° shoulder angle. Smith was said to have preferred a slightly longer neck on his design if such were possible and the .22-303-B has that along with other desirable features. This was mentioned to the author in 1939 correspondence with Elliott.

The .22-303 cartridge, according to Elliott, was a useful case for single shot actions and for certain bolt actions such as the Krag, but for the latter only when underloaded below the maximum capacity of the case. Unfortunately, the case required a magazine alteration in the Lee-Enfield and for that reason the conversion in that arm was not as simple as for the .25-303 case, which required only a slight turning-in of the lips of the Lee-Enfield magazine.

At that time, Elliott believed that a sharp shoulder angle was the better, although the *British Textbook of Small Arms* was quoted as saying that the shoulder angle was immaterial. Some wondered if equal results could have been obtained with equal capacities regardless of shoulder angle.

It has been mentioned by Crandall that Mr. Elliott re-formed a .303 British by necking down the neck of the case and sent a blueprint to Earl Leach, very expert custom gunsmith who later went into war work, but at that time was at Stratford, Ontario, where he is now located. This case was altered somewhat from the first design. Leach sent it down to Crandall, suggesting that Crandall work it out.

Crandall had been thinking along the same lines for a new cartridge, which was natural, and which occurs often in many lines of endeavor in which two, three or four men, operating in widely separated areas or fields of research produce, often entirely unknown to each other, designs for this or that which are practically identical but which are actually the result of individual effort.

Crandall worked out his design and in due course completed the rifle and tested it with excellent results. At that time, a few sample cases were sent around, some to Elliott. It is reported he replied that he was very much pleased with the result.

In 1937 Crandall made up a few of these rifles for customers in the Far West, mostly for coyote hunters and ranchmen or wheat farmers who had coyotes or lobos to deal with. For some years thereafter he did little with the caliber, being busy otherwise. He could have obtained blanks to make the barrels but business happened to be more pressing in other lines.

Eventually, G. B. Crandall became re-interested and finally obtained a number of .219 Zipper barrel blanks from Winchester. Others demanded these rifles, so he obtained additional supplies of the Zipper barrels. Others sent him Hi-Side Winchester S.S. actions and he made up .22-303 rifles on these. At a recent writing to the author, he had put out many of these, and had seven different orders for .22-303 rifles then on hand.

Mr. Crandall does not make up and stock these .22-303 rifles. Each is a special job and is made especially to the rifleman's specifications. He usually obtains Stoeger stocks but fits, shapes, refinishes and reblues the actions, if needed, and among them are some very good-looking rifles. He is at present using Ackley barrels, getting the blanks from P. O. Ackley and Company of Trinidad, Colorado, and fitting and chambering same for the rifle on which blank is to be used. Both Crandall and Epps say these Ackley barrels being sent them to Canada are fine looking jobs of barrel-boring.

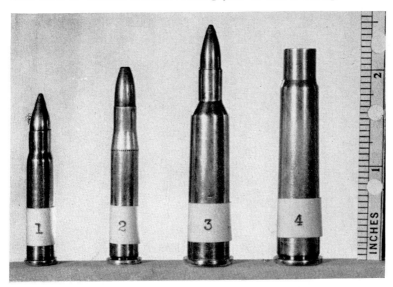

THE VERY FINE G. B. CRANDALL .22 WILDCATS

These are the best Canadian .22 Wildcat cartridges. Each is designed for maximum effectiveness for each grain of powder consumed. Left to right: .22 Crandall Improved K-B Hornet, with 41-grain Sisk bullet; No. 2, .22 Crandall R-2 Lovell, made from .25-20 s.s. case and interchangeable in Lovell and C. C. Johnson rifle chambers; No. 3, .22-303 Crandall Varmint-R, made from .303 British case at right which is shown before cutting off and necking down. This is a good heavy, strong case, as easily obtained in Canada, as our .30-1906 is here, and is better adapted to .22 wildcats due to being slightly smaller than .30-40 Krag case. This .22-303 Crandall Varmint-R develops regularly, 3,864 f.s. with 40-grain Sisk Express, 3,732 f.s. with 50-grain Lovell, and 3,530 f.s. with 55-grain Sisk-Niedner Magnum bullet without excessive pressures. Also, it is ideally adapted to Hi-Side single shot actions. All three Crandall wildcats are *rimmed* cartridges. Note scale on right side of photo to show lengths.

At last accounts Crandall & Son had blanks on hand and more on order. "G. B." has turned out but few .22/3000 Lovell or R-2 jobs since he has been making up the .22-303 rifles, for the good reason that brass cartridge cases for it are practically unobtainable in Canada, while the .303 British cases are being made more plentiful every day. Also, the greater velocity and size of the .22-303 Varmint-R makes it a better long range coyote, woodchuck and crow cartridge. In the Far Northwest coyotes have increased considerably, are becoming a nuisance, and are extremely detrimental to nesting wild ducks all over Central and Northern Canada and to other game in Northwestern Canada.

Charles Welch, of Beachy, Saskatchewan, once killed 19 coyotes with 20 shots from one of these .22-303 Varmint-R Crandall rifles. If you doubt that, it is a fact that the late Ed. Howard killed 20 straight coyotes in the winter of 1910-11, which is 35 years ago, using a .22 Hi-Power rifle made for him by the late Charles Newton, and the cartridge was almost the same as the Gebby Varminter Junior cartridge, less powerful than the .22-303 Varmint-R. You will read of that shooting in *Hunting with the Twenty-two,* a companion book.

Another of the .22-303 Varmint-R's is owned and used by Dr. J. G. Kirk, the former Canadian International Pistol Team Captain, more recently Regimental Surgeon of the 7th Canadian Field Artillery Regiment. A late rifle of the .22-303 Varmint-R caliber was made up by Crandall for Jack Hone, of Rockcliffe, Ontario, a Squadron Leader in the Royal Canadian Air Force. This rifle shot exceptional groups, and when someone wrote to Hone for a number of these for this work, it was found that he had been sent on a trip to Baffin Land. A nice quiet place to spend a weekend, and where you and the mailman do not often meet. Philip Wismer also uses this caliber of Crandall rifle.

Crandall's Metal-Cased .22 Caliber Bullets

For a time G. B. Crandall made up 41 and 46-grain .22 caliber metal-cased hunting bullets. He made up around 40,000 for customers during 1943-44. However, this took time from his gunsmithing and this work was then taken over for him by B. F. Mannen, of St. Thomas, Ontario, who has developed considerable large-capacity equipment for making jacketed bullets. Mannen is making .22 bullets in .22 Hornet and in .22-303 Varmint-R calibers and in different weights. He has developed his own bullet press, which Crandall reports is mechanically quite ingenious. The author saw the press on a visit to Mannen's shop in 1946. Mannen also has a chronograph for determining rifle bullet velocity. He is a tool and die maker by trade.

B. F. Mannen's .22 Caliber Expanding Hunting Bullets

Some further time was spent in obtaining, examining and measuring a complete line of the B. F. Mannen bullets, as the lack of good jacketed bullets has been the most serious drawback of both U. S. and Canadian .22 wildcat shooters during and shortly after World War II.

Most of these Mannen jacketed bullets are made, apparently, from copper or gilding-metal jackets obtained from Dominion Cartridge Company's copper rim fire cases or bullet jacket material, as nearly all of them contain the very small D which is the Dominion trademark. Imagine Western, Winchester and Remington combined into one ammunition company in the United States and you have a proper conception of the relative importance of Dominion to all Canadian shooters.

All of the first-mentioned bullets below have a flat base with sharp edge and a very small indent in the center, while the cases mentioned farther along lack this indent. It appears of no special importance except in the making of the bullet, probably to center it.

50-grain soft point; was discontinued generally in favor of 50-grain hollow point; had sharp base, edge slightly cupped; diameter measures 0.2240″ to 0.2245″. Should have shot and gone to pieces well on earth so as to not cause ricochets on misses; would still be a good bullet.

41-grain flat base with hollow indent in center; F.M.P. with hollow expanding point; measures 0.225″ in diameter; for 0.224″ rifles.

55-grain flat base, soft point; very small lead tip exposed; given as 0.224″ but measures 0.2245″ to 0.225″; for 0.224″ rifles.

50-grain open point, flat base expanding bullet; measures 0.224″ to 0.2245″; for 0.224″ rifles.

45-grain open point, flat base bullet; made in small diameter, medium diameter and moderately large diameter, open or hollow points—three styles—you should specify type wanted; measurements 0.2235″ to 0.225″ for 0.224″ rifles. All the same except type of point for game shooting.

"0.223″-ST 45" a very sharp-pointed, long pointed, soft point 45-grain bullet with flat base; has straighter sides to ogive of point than 8S bullet, and longer point as well; base, perfectly flat with sharp edges and side perfectly straight, up and down, but rather short bearing; this bullet measures 0.2232″ to 0.2238″.

"0.224″-ST 50" the same bullet as above but weighs 50-grain

and has longer bearing due to higher sides; should have *very* flat trajectory over 150 yards or so; measures 0.2235″ to 0.2238″.

"0.224″-ST 56" same bullet as both previous ones except has longer bearing surface up sides; supplied on special order only; measures 0.2241″; soft point with an even sharper point than the 8S bullet.

Larger Diameter .22's

.22 Savage H.P. caliber and size; 63-grain (and also made in 70-grain) with considerable lead exposed at the point; measures 0.227″ in diameter. A very fine looking bullet for woodchuck or deer shooting in rifles of this diameter and sufficient twist to spin a 63 to 70-grain bullet. Has a wide but very shallow crimping or seating groove in copper jacket.

.22 caliber Savage H.P. 55-grain S.P. bullet; same as above just described except very much less lead exposed at the point; a good looking game bullet but will probably not expand as suddenly as above two; measures 0.227″ in diameter.

Mannen also supplies .25 caliber, 61 and 87-grain bullets, .256 Newton and 6.5mm, 120-grain bullets; .30-1906, 150 and 170-grain bullets; and .303 British 150 and 170-grain bullets. These are mentioned here as bullets are a bottleneck to shooters nowadays.

Mannen has also made lead slugs electroplated with copper jacket 0.025″ thick, and also very long, .22 caliber, solid copper turned bullets and also medium length, solid copper turned bullets with boat-tail base weighing probably about 60 grains for the latter. These boat-tails seem to have shot much better than the other two experimental jobs. They are not supplied at present, at least not on regular order.

Mannen prefers to sell his metal-cased, expanding hunting bullets through dealers, in lots of appreciable size, rather than in small lots ordered direct from him. Through such dealers as Charley Parkinson and others who advertise in *Rod & Gun in Canada,* in the same manner that bullet makers in the United States advertise in *American Rifleman,* in classified advertisements. That is the place to look for such supplies.

Full details are given here so that this bottleneck of lack of .22 jacketed bullets which will shoot accurately may be fully overcome. Being non-explosive they may be shipped by mail or express.

Mannen also supplies a custom chronograph service so that rifle cranks can determine the muzzle velocity of any load for any of the .22 wildcats or other cartridges in which they may be interested.

.22 Mannen Super-H.P.

He also has produced a good looking special .22 H.P. cartridge for which a number of good shooting rifles have been made up. This is made from the .22 Savage H.P. case, has moderate case taper, measures 1.48″ to the shoulder, has a shoulder slope of 15° according to my measurement, and a long neck of 0.30″. Shoulder is also moderately long. Cartridge case length is 2.03″ and over-all length of loaded cartridge is 2.575″.

The case looks like a Crandall idea, to whom nearly all Canadian cartridge designs seem to be referred for approval. It contains no radical measurements or slope. Contains a long, gentle-slope point, soft point bullet of good weight and should give good velocity as compared with pressure developed. Mannen says that when the shoulder was altered from 30° to the present, more gentle slope of 15° the velocity rose 200 f.s. A number of fine rifles have been made up in this caliber.

Charges are 32.0 grains of No. 4320 with 63-grain soft point bullet developing 3,425 f.s.m.v., and another of 34.0 grains of No. 4064 with same bullet of 63-grains, giving 3,650 f.s.m.v. These are very good velocities for the 63-grain bullet, and the cartridge is adapted to use in Winchester Hi-Side single shot actions and similar and should be adapted also to Model 70 bolt action Winchester. It is a custom job of ammunition design.

The Crandall Reloading Tool

The Crandall Precision Lever-Loading Tool is 14″ long, 2¼″ wide and 3½″ high when folded and boxed, and weighs approximately seven pounds. The base is a metal casting that will stand up to the heavy lever pressure when in use. The lever applies 20 to 1 multiple power, so that 50 pounds pressure on the lever will apply 1,000 pounds on the head of the shell and this one-half short-ton pressure will easily full length re-size any rifle cases. Full length sizing and decapping of the .303 or the .22-303 case is possible at one operation. The sizing die lies in a semi-circular trough in the base of the tool. The tool can be set up for seating the new primer and expanding the case neck to hold the bullet.

The re-loading tool re-primes the cartridge case by a straight line movement, seats the bullet, and thus finishes the loaded cartridge.

This Crandall tool is made for the .22 Hornet, .22/3000 R-2, .22 Varminter, .22-303-B Varmint-R, .220 Swift, .22 Hi-Power and also for various larger size high power cartridges. Price is $20.00

for any one cartridge and $9.00 additional for extra parts for another cartridge.

Crandall Powder Measure

The powder chamber only shows some similarity, exteriorally, to the Lyman or Ideal measure, but not otherwise. The new patented device is rather simple. The tool body is made of aluminum and steel. When the operating lever is in the vertical position the charge cup is forward in plain view and separated from the powder in the reservoir. Throwing the handle back as far as it will go and then bringing it back to vertical position brings the charge cup into full view filled level full with powder, so the shooter sees each charge before it is dropped into the empty cartridge case. A further move forward brings the charge out and over the charge spout, where it then drops directly into the case. This charge spout is short and open at the top, so that the shooter can look through it and see that the powder has all gone into the shell or cartridge case, making accidental under-loading or over-loading just about impossible. The spout has, at its under end, an inside and outside taper so that all cases from .22 to .455 will fit either inside or outside.

In use, the ordinary principle of powder measure is reversed; the charge cup enters under the powder but does not stop until it has traveled over twice its length under the powder and then reverses and travels back and out and is in long, continuous contact with the powder and that not in one position only. This is claimed to make for uniform accuracy of charge throwing and dumping. Since 1940 the price of this measure has been advanced from $7.00 to $9.00, its present figure. With these two tools any of the Crandall wildcats can be properly loaded, and all of them can be loaded with it by having proper additional parts.

The author has had reports from magazine subscribers concerning Mr. Crandall's work for more than 25 years and during that time has never had one serious complaint. So long as he can get the work out it always seems to be satisfactory. He has customers throughout the whole of Canada and elsewhere.

His main work is fine gunsmithing, rebuilding rifles, supplying and fitting of new barrels, in various .22 and other calibers. He used to fit many Watson sights, before the death of Mr. Watson, and probably still has some on hand. He fits scope mountings— Redfield, Weaver, Stith and Turner mounts. He sells the Crandall hammerless shotgun; makes guns and rifles to order. Because of the urgency of war work in Canada, which lasted about five years, he supplies .22 metal-cased bullets, now of outside make, as mentioned. In normal times, at least, he can supply Parkerifled tubes for .22 rifles. He has supplied some special .22 rim fire rifles but today rarely does so. His work now includes a wide range of rifles and reloading tools and supplies for same.

Elmer McConnell and His Gunsmithing

Another Canadian of outstanding skill in the arms line is Elmer McConnell, of Delhi, Ontario. He is particularly clever with rifles. McConnell is the first man for whom Crandall Parkerifled a 44½ Stevens single shot and then converted it to a .22 Hornet. He is one of the unusual type among the skilled craftsmen who do a bit of gunsmithing quietly, for friends. This is like any other habit and before one knows it he is working at that line professionally. McConnell has turned out some of the finest gunsmithing Crandall has seen, and here in the States that is like having Harry Pope say something nice about your barrel work. McConnell deals in guns and the author examined his extensive collection of high grade rifles and shotguns in 1946.

Maurice Atkinson's Rifle Stocking

Maurice Atkinson, of Streetsville, Ontario, is a young mechanic with unusual ability as a rifle stocker. He is said to be able to do King's presentation quality stocking; this is reported by both Crandall and Ray Weeks. He did that stock on the Winchester single shot Hi-Side R-2 rifle of Weeks' which you will see pictured in one of these .22 books. Atkinson is regularly employed by a radio equipment plant but does some very fine stocking as he has time and is apparently the most expert in Canada on that sort of work.

Those Canadian Party Woodchuck Hunts

This is probably pretty much on the q-t but every month, once or twice, whenever they can slip off, or could get gas, four to six of the Ontario rifle cranks who use .22 wildcats, including Crandall, go woodchuck hunting together and try out new rifles or cartridges, one against the other. It is a most excellent way to compare rifles, ammunition, different loads, scopes and whatnot.

Story is that one day a certain gunsmith hung a sign on the door which read: "Be Back After Lunch." Shortly after the sign appeared it is said that a customer from one of the rural districts thereabouts came to the shop and, seeing the sign, figured that the gunsmith would be gone about an hour or less, consequently, he stepped over to Clancy's and had something to bring down his temperature.

After waiting quite some time, he came back, found the soft side of whatever there was to rest upon, and remained there patiently. About 3 P.M. as no one had showed up, he arose, yawned, and then accosted a passerby: "That gunsmith surely seems to enjoy his meals for a man of his years; I've been sitting here waiting for him to return from lunch since 1 o'clock."

"He isn't out to lunch now," said the passerby. "He and that bunch of rifleshooters, from down the line, with whom he goes woodchuck hunting, have rushed off up the Province after another day's sport; he might be back by late tonight or he may be gone for two or three days."

Comment is that when these worthies step on the gas they pull down their hats so that no one recognizes them slipping out of town. After they reach the district close to their shooting area, they look at each other and grin, after which nothing more is known of them until the rifles began to crack. On the way, they drive over to Delhi for McConnell; they stop for Charley Parkinson, at London; and maybe, if there is time, drive to Tillsonburg, for Ray Weeks. The sporting goods trade being what it is, and people being curious in the wrong way, sometimes Charley Parkinson hangs a sign something like: "Be Back Soon—Attending Toronto Hardware Convention." Then he steps out. During the 1944 shooting season Ned Roberts, of .257 Roberts fame, hunted with Weeks and was back again for the 1945 hunt. This year the author had an invitation to be one of them and Lysle Kilbourn asked him to be a house guest while we had a woodchuck hunt there. Then George Schnerring insisted that the author share his woodchuck hunting in Northern Pennsylvania. Harvey Donaldson invited the author to come up for a hunt. So you can see the temptations that lie in the path of a virtuous gent trying to finish a book like this.

Those Canadian shooters hunt in groups. By shooting one rifle and cartridge directly against *all* the other wildcat combinations in the bunch, with identical ranges, light, wind drift and temperature changes, the combination of rifle, cartridge and bullet which actually produces, given the right man behind it, will very easily demonstrate its superiority and every combination will show its every weakness. You do not have to depend upon what someone *says* the .22 Super-Super will do at 300 yards. You either ring the bell or the ineffective outfit and its owner "eat crow."

Ray Weeks' Work with His New .22-303 Special

On June 30, 1945, Ray Weeks, of Tillsonburg, Ontario, wrote the author concerning his new .22-303 Special rifle. This letter contained so much information about what is possible with this new caliber, and about how to size and form the cartridge cases for this cartridge, that much of it is given verbatim:

"My bag of crows for the first half of 1945 has mounted to 313; I have a rifle now which is pure poison to crows. It is the same old rifle, the Hi-Side Winchester S.S., which had that very fine C. C. Johnson R-2 barrel which gave the 2″ average groups at 200 yards—many much better than this.

"The new tube is a selected Savage barrel which Harvey Donaldson sent me. I had it fitted up as a R-2 last fall but May 5 this year Charley Meredith re-chambered it for the .22-303.

"I have a fine target-weight Winchester Swift barrel, un-threaded and un-chambered, but finish ground, which I had intended to fit up for this caliber but thought I would try the cartridge in the Savage barrel first. The Savage barrel was only 0.2225″ groove diameter but I lapped it out to 0.223″. It is as smooth as silk inside; Meredith throated it for 0.224″ bullets according to my instructions, so that a 50-grain 8S bullet is seated out of the case for about one-half of its cylindrical length or portion.

"For cartridge cases we use .303 British brass from cartridges for aircraft synchronized machine guns. These are heavier than normal cases and no better brass is to be had. The case is 1 15/16″ long, has a neck 0.25″ long and a 28° shoulder—practically the Gebby Varminter in rimmed form with slightly less powder capacity, as the .303 British case is almost 0.017″ slimmer at the head.

"It is quite a chore to make the cases, but as finished they are extremely uniform. They go through *five* forming dies, a cut-off die and an inside neck-reaming die. I have 250 cases finished. The neck tolerance in the chamber is only 0.001″ with a length (mouth) clearance of 0.0012″. It is necessary to keep a close watch on them for lengthening, due to the small tolerance, but none has shown signs of stretching as yet, despite the fact that I have fired 25 of them quite a few times as a test. Meredith did a precision job on the chambering and throating.

"This Savage barrel was just an ordinary good performer as an R-2 but has really gone to town in its new form. I do not know where the credit mostly lies, whether the 'selected' part, the lapping, the fine general workmanship in throating, the merit of the cartridge, or a combination of all of these. Today it is a real tack driver!

"N. H. Roberts was in Southwestern Ontario recently and was at my place for three days. I took those three days off work and we spent the whole time hunting crows or shooting from my bench rest. He had a .219 Wasp with him—a Vernor Gipson job on a beautiful factory engraved Winchester Hi-Wall action with double-set triggers. It shoots very well indeed but not nearly as well as my .22-303 Special—(Single shot—Author). While the Wasp has not anywhere near the killing range of my outfit I shot several 100 and 200-yard groups with it as a comparison with my own rifle. I also killed 47 crows with my own .22-303 Special during my hunting expeditions—some of them at ranges around 275 and 300 yards.

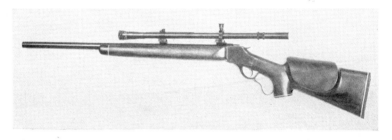

An R-2 .22/3000 Crandall-Winchester S. S. made for S. J. Weatherly of Winnipeg, Manitoba. This arm has a short. rigid barrel, and a very long, splendidly proportioned forearm which is rounded on the sides without being excessively flat on the underside. The finger lever is made with a full loop so that a mittened hand can be slipped through without binding. Stock is of a plain type, with very high comb and cheek-piece, and long, hand-filling grip, a style that is very popular in some parts of Canada, although a style proportioned more like the forearm would look somewhat neater. The rifle telescope is a Lyman Targetspot Junior, in Lyman mounts.

N. H. Roberts Bullets

"Roberts had a supply of bullets made by himself with the RCBS dies for the Pacific Tool. New, un-headed, .22 rim fire hulls formed the jackets and 13/64" lead wire the cores. They weighed 50-grain each, had 7-caliber points and a narrow-rimmed base. To my astonishment they shot practically as well as the Wotkyns-Morse 8S bullets. I fired five groups with them while he was here, as well as two with the 8S's. Exact duplicates of the groups are outlined below.

"The 100-yard 8S group was shot at a rifleman's picnic which

friend Elmer McConnell staged at the Provincial Forestry Station
for N. H.'s benefit. There were about 15 high-velocity rifles in
action but mine was decidedly the best. The shooting was done
prone from an inclined platform with a cushion for a forearm rest."

Groups and the Loads Which Made Them, Rifle .22-303 Special
Shot by Ray Weeks

No. 1. Fired at Rifleman's Picnic June 9, 1945; no wind; range
100 yards; charge 35.0 grains No. 4320 and 50-grain 8S
bullets 0.224″ diameter; group measured 0.22″ vertically
by 0.43″ horizontally. Five-shot group, four in one hole.

No. 2. Date, June 20, 1945, late evening; no wind; range 200
yards; charge 35.0 grains No. 4320 and 50-grain 8S bullets;
group measured 0.68″ vertically by 0.69″ horizontally.
Five-shot group.

No. 3. Date, June 17, 1945, late evening; no wind; range 100
yards; charge 35.0 grains No. 4320 and N. H. Roberts
50-grain R.C.B.S. bullets; group measured 0.38″ vertically
by 0.50″ horizontally. Five-shot group.

No. 4. Range 200 yards; same charge and bullets; group measured
0.98″ vertically by 1.15″ horizontally. Five-shot group.

No. 5. Date, June 17, 1945; range 100 yards; charge 36.0 grains
No. 4064 and 50-grain R. C. B. S. bullets; group measured
0.65″ vertically by 0.20″ horizontally.

No. 6. Date, June 23, 1945; range 100 yards; charge 36.5 grains
No. 4064 and 50-grain R.C.B.S. bullets; group measured
0.34″ vertically by 0.36″ horizontally. Five-shot group.

No. 7. Date, June 18, 1945; range 100 yards; charge 36.5 grains
No. 4064 and 50-grain R.C.B.S. bullets; group measured
0.86″ vertically by 0.63″ horizontally.

No. 8. Date, May 25, 1945; range 200 yards; charge 35.0 grains
No. 4320 and 50-grain B. F. Mannen sharp-taper bullets;
group measured 1.00″ vertically by 0.97″ horizontally.

No. 9. Date, May 31, 1945; range 200 yards; charge 35.0 grains
No. 4320 and 50-grain B. F. Mannen sharp-taper bullets;
group measured 1.35″ vertically by 0.90″ horizontally.
Five-shot group.

All groups measured center to center of shot holes farthest
apart; measured by author.

Weeks reported that, strangely enough, it does not do as well
with No. 3031 powder in any loads as yet tried.

He mentioned a peculiarity of his sighting for crow shooting. He always keeps his rifle sighted 1½" to 1⅝" high and uses what might be described as a modified 6 o'clock hold on the birds. This sighting invariably gives a high percentage of hits—higher than with dead-on sighting—probably because it uses a longer arc of the trajectory. On very long shots he holds dead-on or a trifle over.

Ray says that he finds this .22-303 rifle much less sensitive to wind than the R-2 rifles and his percentage of hits has increased accordingly.

He had only 400 of the 50-grain 8S bullets on May 23, 1945; he kept an account of the hits and it was 77% on crows, on all shots attempted. This covered 26 days, shooting in all kinds of weather, from all sorts of positions, but usually with a rest of some kind and he took shots at 275 to 300 yards.

It also includes crows called to trees directly overhead. The number of crows killed during the 26 days was 157, the best day's bag being 18 on June 16, 1945 and 18 again on June 23, 1945.

Everything considered, this is the highest average for a large number of shots at crows of which the author has record. Mr. Weeks is probably the best known crow shot in Canada, if not in North America. He has shot crows by the thousands and more detailed accounts of his work with two R-2 barrels will be found in *Hunting With the Twenty-two*.

It will give an idea of the great accuracy of this .22-303 Special cartridge at 150 to 200 yards. On woodchucks the percentage of kills would be much higher as the mark is definitely much larger, even on skull shots, neck shots or shoulder shots. Further, the woodchuck permits more prone shooting.

Remember, the powder charges were 35.0 grains No. 4320 with 50-grain 8S bullet; 35.0 grains No. 4320 with Roberts' 50-grain R.C.B.S. bullet; 36.0 to 36.5 grains No. 4064 with 50 grain R.C.B.S. Roberts bullet; and 35.0 grains No. 4320 with Mannen 50-grain sharp-taper bullet. These loads shot like the Franklin W. Mann base band bullets at 100 yards many years ago.

Many years ago, *everlasting* cartridges in .32 Ideal, .32-40, .38-55 and .40-70 calibers were made and sold at 10 cents each. These .22-303 aircraft cases should last just about as long.

Cooperation of Canadian Riflemen

This cooperation of Canadian gunsmiths, riflemen, woodchuck and crow shooters is a very helpful condition to the improvement of .22 wildcat rifles and ammunition. By shooting together they get com-

petition, get to know each other, and avoid much of the jealousy
which at times crops up between rifle experimenters in areas which
are widely separated and in which they do not get to know each
other.

This .22-303 Varmint-R caliber quite obviously ranks with the
Lovell No. 7—the .219 Zipper Improved—for accuracy, if it does
not exceed it. It seems to shoot just as well as any of the .22 Varminters or .22-250 rifles or the .22 Kilbourn Magnum, and the
groups are better than the author has so far received as made with
the .220 Marciante Blue Streak, the .220 Arrow and similar good
shooting rifles.

If able to obtain the .22-303 British cases there is no good reason
why anyone living in the United States should not do just as well
with one of these super-accurate and long-range coyote, woodchuck
and crow outfits. Two hundred to 300 necked cases would likely last
a careful rifleman five to 10 years. Any of the United States firms
normally make good commercial .303 British cases and Sisk and
others could supply 0.224″ bullets. This is a 0.224″ proposition all
the way through, normally, but can be used with a carefully lapped
0.223″ barrel.

CHARLES PARKINSON'S BALLISTIC DATA ON .22-303 VARMINT-R

(Tested Upon Ballistic Range and with Chronograph of B. F. Mannen)

Charge	Powder	Bullet and Weight	Muzzle Velocity
30.0 grs.	3031	55-gr. Sisk-Niedner Magnum	3,379 f.s.
34.0 grs.	3031	50-gr. Lovell	3,532 f.s.
35.0 grs.	3031	50-gr. Lovell	3,656 f.s.
36.0 grs.	4320	50-gr. Lovell	3,732 f.s.
38.0 grs.	4320	40-gr. Sisk-Express	3,864 f.s.
34.0 grs.	4320	63-gr. Sisk-Niedner Magnum	3,373 f.s.
34.0 grs.	4320	55-gr. Sisk-Niedner Magnum	3,493 f.s.
35.0 grs.	4320	55-gr. Sisk-Niedner Magnum	3,530 f.s.

Parkinson tested some loads which gave higher velocities than these
but they were not standard loads of powder and special bullets were
used, so he thought it best not to mention them. He claims that he
obtained over 4,000 f.s. with a 50-grain bullet, but 0.2225″ bullets
were used and a special charge of a slow burning powder which is
not at present available to the shooting public.

He mentioned recently, in a letter to a mutual friend, that the rifle with which he had obtained the unusually accurate targets was his old rifle which had then shot over 4,000 rounds. Fred Johnson had it at that writing. Johnson shot some very fine groups with it in the Fall of 1944. He still had copies of these groups, which were something like ⅜″ for a five-shot group at 100 yards and ⅞″ or less for the same group at 200 yards, according to Mr. Parkinson. These were shot with some special sample Mannen bullets weighing 50 grains and before Mr. Mannen could get a supply of those bullets made up, he damaged the dies, and has just very recently made up another set of dies. Parkinson mentioned obtaining three-shot groups of less than 0.50″ at 100 yards; he seldom shoots more of his difficult-to-get bullets, as he merely sights his rifle to find out where it is grouping its first shot from a cold barrel, and can do this with three-shot groups.

He reports having killed crows at 316 yards, and several over 275 yards and also a number of chucks over 350 yards. He killed one chuck at 510 paces with the third shot fired. This was with a Crandall .22-303 Varmint-R rifle. He is at this writing fitting up another of these rifles for himself which he will have Crandall chamber for the .22-303 Varmint-R. He has a late model Winchester S.S. Schuetzen action and a fine Buhmiller barrel for it which did *not* require straightening. This barrel is of chrome alloy steel. He also has a set-trigger Mauser action he is thinking of fitting up in a similar manner for the same cartridge. Remember, this wildcat is the easiest cartridge in .22 caliber for which Canadians may obtain service brass cases to neck down and turn out in proper size. It also makes up beautifully in a .25 caliber cartridge of very similar shape but slightly thicker in the neck. In these times the supply of cartridge cases is the most important single item in making up and keeping a wildcat .22 rifle in ammunition.

Ellwood Epps' .22 Wildcat Rifles

Ellwood Epps, energetic and progressive proprietor of the Ellwood Epps Sporting Goods, of Clinton, Ontario, is a young rifle crank who, in a comparatively short time has built up a most excellent local and mail-order wholesale and retail business in sporting goods and firearms, including at least a dozen calibers of .22 wildcat and .22 commercial rifles, most of which his gunsmith supplies with P. O. Ackley barrels. He also has the services of four stockers located at various points.

Epps himself used to go down into Connecticut to United States small bore tournaments as an active competitor. He has distinguished himself as becoming a Gun Editor of *Hunting and Fishing In Canada,* and recently had, and probably accepted, a similar offer from a sportsman's magazine in British Columbia.

With this story we will show a cut of two very fine .22 Mauser varmint rifles that Epps' gunsmiths turned out in the Spring of 1945. They follow closely the baseballbat shaped forend of the author's 52 heavy-sporter but the pistol grip is a little more massive and curved and extends a bit farther forward at the lower end. I would assume these rifles were made for a rifleman with large hands.

The one Mauser is a heavy-sporter type with single trigger and a particularly handsome design of cheek piece extending well forward and also high up to the face. The stock goes back almost level on top, from comb to within about 2½″ of the heel, where it drops down gracefully in a Monte Carlo effect. There is good flame walnut in this stock, particularly in the part to the rear of the receiver. The stock forearm is fitted with a neat and rather long cap, apparently copied somewhat after the writer's 52; Epps and I used to talk a good deal of this rifle as a model for heavy-sporters. I want to say that this model of .22 Mauser heavy-sporter that Epps and his gunsmiths have designed is deserving of a great deal of praise. The pistol grip is not excessively large, yet will fill the hand of a large man with long fingers, and should hold splendidly for off-hand shooting. Just how well the stock recoil shoulder is fitted cannot be told without having the rifle in the hands and then first taking it apart, smearing the stock with a color material that will register contact, putting together, then taking apart again and examining.

The rifle has small sporting swivel eyes; the stock comes back rather straight on the underside, with little tendency to shadbelly; the butt plate is thin and neat. This rifle is a .22-250, almost exactly similar to the .22 Varminter cartridge, and due to the large and full stock, with full raised cheekpiece, should weigh nine to 9½ pounds, without scope or sling. Epps says this sporter has shot many groups as small as 1″ for 10 shots at 100 yards, and consistently keeps within 1¼″ for 10-shot groups. Many other rifle makers stick to three and five-shot groups, which are almost invariably smaller.

The other Mauser has a heavier barrel, with very little taper, seems to be of about 28″ length, is likely the standard ⅞″ at the muzzle and is fitted with a J. W. Fecker target telescope. Epps says this one has consistently made many 10-shot groups at 100 yards under or approximately ¾″ in diameter. He has used six

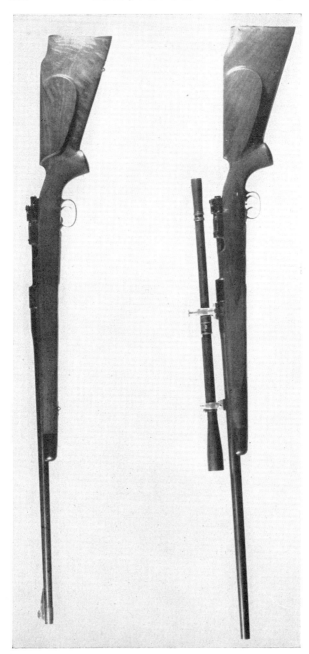

Two beautifully stocked ".22-250 Varmint" rifles turned out by gunsmith employed by Ellwood Epps, Clinton, Ont.

Top rifle is heavy .22-250 Ackley-Mauser sporter which gives $1\frac{1}{4}''$ 10-shot groups at 100 yards, regularly. Note beautifully modeled cheek piece and Monte Carlo stock, long hand-filling nicely checkered pistol grip, swivels and horn cap. Lower rifle is moderately heavy barrel .22-250 Ackley-Mauser fitted with Fecker scope, which gives $\frac{3}{4}''$ 10-shot groups at 100 yards. Stock is plainer wood than in the sporter but fishtail checkering runs clear back opposite receiver. Rifle has double set triggers and groups very uniformly with 6 different loads.

different loads in this rifle and with the six groups of six-shots each, or a total of 36 shots at 100 yards, all grouped in the same cluster 2⅜″ by 3¾″ in size, although the bullets varied from 41 to 63-grain.

Bullets of good accuracy have been probably the most serious difficulty to .22 wildcat experimenters during the latter part of World War II. Almost every manufacturer had trouble of one sort or another, either with metal he had to use for jackets, or with other difficulties. Those who used .22 rim fire cases minus the heads also had difficulty, probably due to poor grade of copper alloy in the cartridge cases, a grade probably good enough for .22 cartridge cases of rim fire persuasion, but not of sufficient purity to work as bullet jackets at very high velocities. Brass .22 cases do not do at all.

The Epps .22-250 heavy Mauser has a stock quite similar to the heavy-sporter by the same maker, but the pistol grip is plainer in outline, the checkering does not appear quite as fine, and the wood is less elaborate in grain. The cheek piece lines are less fancy and do not extend up to the comb.

The accuracy of this rifle has been repeatedly reported to the author by Epps as being really astonishing. It shot a great many groups, according to the owner, of ¾″ for the 10 shots at 100 yards. These groups were largely made by British Kynoch powder which was listed in the table of loads sent to the author. In this, 28.0 grains of Kynoch, with 50-grain bullet; 26.0 grains with 55-grain bullet; and 25.0 grains with 63-grain bullet gave 4,005, 3,940 and 3,775 f.s.m.v. He also had a charge of 38.0 grains of No. 3031 to give 4,155 f.s.m.v. These are all fast loads for this cartridge, which normally gives its most accurate results with 3,750 and 3,250 f.s.m.v. Those Ackley barrels must shoot very well with fast loads in the .22-250 caliber. The charges of Kynoch will be of special interest to Canadian readers who can obtain British products easier and with less expense, due to duty differences, than American goods made south of the International border.

The set-triggers on this heavy Mauser of Epps' enables him to do fine shooting. The rifle probably weighs around 10½ pounds, without scope or 12 pounds with it.

Loads follow which Epps supplied and which were chronographed in Canada. However, they can be used anywhere the materials are available. Most of these loads are fairly fast, particularly for the .22-303 Varmint-R, the .22-250 and a charge of 16.5 grains of No. 4198 with 41-grain bullet in the R-2 Lovell, giving 3,500 f.s.m.v. in this little case.

A photo is also shown illustrating a very long line of different

.22 commercial and wildcat cartridges for which barrels or rifles are supplied by Epps, which photo shows graphically the size and length of the different .22 center fire cartridges, compared directly one with the other. Too bad he did not place a small steel scale along one side of the photograph.

Epps has the good business judgment to reply with reasonable promptness to business correspondence. That is helpful to the rifleman. During the latter part of World War II, his gunsmiths rebarrelled a large number of ordinary 4½ to 5¾ pound .22 Long Rifle singleshot and light repeating rifles of sporting and shooting gallery

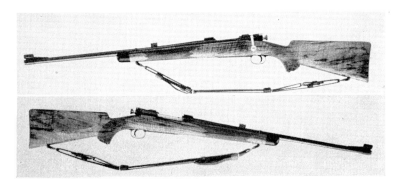

THE SOUTH PAW COMES INTO HIS OWN

Here we have a Springfield Sporter with left handed bolt action, made up to fit a South Paw. Any of the .22 center fires could be made up in this manner, fitted with fancy Circassian walnut stock, sling swivels and scope blocks. Note cheek piece on right side of stock, for left shoulder shooter.

type, and many of these were reported shooting very nicely. The author has had commendatory letters from his Gun Department correspondents about the Epps gunsmiths' quality workmanship. It is logical to expect that as his gunsmiths get this line of heavy varmint and heavy-sporter rifles perfected and different contours compared, one with the other, considering also that Epps is himself comparatively a young man, his line may have considerable future.

In the summer of 1946 Epps moved into his new building and hundreds attended the formal opening. The new quarters are streamlined and his arrangement of display and sales rooms, offices and workshop is an ideal setup for a guncrank sporting goods-gunsmithing operation such as Ellwood Epps carries on at Clinton, Ontario.

ELLWOOD EPPS RECOMMENDED LOADS INCLUDING THOSE
WITH KYNOCH BRITISH SMOKELESS POWDER

*For Use in Epps Rifles with P. O. Ackley Barrels and Other Rifles to
Which These Loads Are Suited*

Cartridge	Bullet Wgt. Grs.	Powder	Chg. Grs.	F.S. M.V.
.22 Hornet	35	2400	11.6	3,020
	40	2400	11.1	2,825
	45	2400	11.1	2,750
K-Hornet	35	2400	11.6	3,020
	41	2400	11.6	2,835
	46	2400	12.5	3,120
.22 Lovell	35	4227	16.0	3,200
	41	4227	15.0	3,050
	45	4198	15.0	2,950
R-2 Lovell	41	4198	16.5	3,500
	45	4227	15.5	3,225
	50	4198	17.0	2,990
.219 Zipper	40	3031	29.5	3,500
	50	Kynoch	20.0	3,300
	55	Kynoch	18.0	3,050
.219 Imp. Zipper	40	3031	30.5	3,650
	50	Kynoch	22.0	3,550
	55	Kynoch	20.0	3,275
Varmint-R	50	4320	37.0	4,129
	63	4320	34.0	3,373
	40	4320	40.0	4,320
.22-250	45	3031	38.0	4,155
	50	Kynoch	28.0	4,005
	55	Kynoch	26.0	3,940
	63	Kynoch	25.0	3,775
.218 Bee	41	2400	15.0	3,200
	50	4227	15.0	3,080
	55	4198	15.0	2,900
Imp. .218 Bee	41	2400	15.8	3,320
	50	4227	16.0	3,150
	55	4198	16.0	3,040
.22 H.P.	40	2400	14.0	3,350
	55	4064	30.0	3,000
	63	Kynoch	23.0	2,900
Swift .220	45	4198	32.0	....
	55	4064	38.0	3,605
	63	Kynoch	30.0	....
.228 Mag.	See Ackley's list for loads for it.			

Mr. Epps added additional information on July 11, 1945, after he had recovered from the results of an automobile accident while on a business trip. These comments add material information to some of his interesting data.

"The two .22 Lovells we have are the original .22/3000 Lovell with 5° shoulder angle, which we made back when E. V. Leach (one of the very top-flight gunsmiths in Canada and who is now very busy and in business for himself as E. V. Leach, 168 St. Patrick Sts., Stratford, Ontario.) used to do my gunsmithing. It is the first Lovell we ever made up, but recently only a few of this style have been made as they all wish the R-2 Lovell. Our .228 Ackley is the large or Magnum Ackley although we have the reamers and everything all ready to make up the shorter .228 Ackley Magnums but have not as yet had opportunity to build and test the lower velocity .228's.

"About the butt plate on the medium barrel .22-250 Mauser sporter: This has a composition type of butt plate; we usually try to install the butt plate which contains a trap, but our supply of these became exhausted and we have not, as yet, had time to build more.

"Your estimate as to the weight of the rifle is perfectly correct; it weighs nine pounds and three ounces. The wood we used is real heavy walnut but the rifle appears to handle equal to the average rifle weighing around seven or $7\frac{1}{2}$ pounds (the author judged that to be so by the splendid design and the heavy weight of stock, back of the pistol grip—such results tending to produce a rifle which feels as though it weighs a pound to two pounds less than its actual total weight). The heavy Mauser .22-250 is $\frac{7}{8}''$ at the muzzle, barrel is 28″ long. The bullets used in testing for the 36-shot group were all made to our specifications with the exception of one load of 55-grain Sisk bullets. I find Mannen's bullets do equally as well with the exception that he uses a very flat base for his bullets and if one is loading a quantity of ammunition it takes a little longer to start the bullets into the case, unless the necks are slightly neck-reamed. Our line of bullets have a slightly rounded base for easier insertion in the case mouth.

"I might add that I (Epps) consistently coat the bullets with microfine graphite which I believe assists greatly in the accuracy and in the condition of the bore. I have shot this rifle about 1,500 rounds, at this writing, and to date have not cleaned the barrel and the accuracy, when I shot it on the range yesterday, was still equal to the first groups I shot with it.

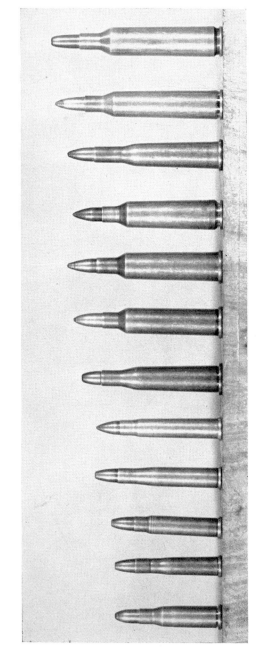

.22 CARTRIDGES FOR WHICH BARRELS ARE SUPPLIED BY ELLWOOD EPPS

Left to Right: 1. .218 Bee; 2. .22 Hornet; 3. .22 K-Hornet; 4. 5° slope .22/3000 Lovell: 5. R-2 .22/3000; 6. .219 Zipper; 7. .219 Zipper Improved; 8. .22 Varmint-R; 9. 22-250; 10. .22 Savage H.P.; 11. .220 Swift; 12. .228 Ackley. Barrels for these bored mostly by Ackley. Some chambered by them, some by Epps' gunsmith.

Grease Wads in the .22-250 Mauser

"I also use a grease wad behind the bullet (this is contrary to the experiences of Hosea Sarber with the .220 Arrow cartridge in heavy-barrelled Wilson-Model 70 rifles, as detailed elsewhere, who could not get accuracy in the .220 Arrow with grease wads—Author). This grease wad is of our own make. I do not know whether it is of an approved formula, but it works. It is a mixture of microfine graphite, beeswax, dictaphone cylinder wax and petroleum jelly. It seems to do an exceptionally good job for us, and although we do not have it commercially available at this time, we make enough for our own use and for any special customer who may wish a small quantity.

"The reason the heavy barrel .22-250 Mauser was plainer in design and not as finely checkered as the other, is that I designed it for my own use and wished to have coarser checkering on a varmint rifle that I could bang around without its showing every little mark. The reason the cheek piece was not carried so far forward is that I am medium height, 5'8", and have a very short neck and do not 'crawl the stock.'

"The loads in the .22-250 work through almost the whole velocity range and I find accuracy in all of them exceptionally good. In fact, the rifle has shot so well that I have not so-far picked out any set load as being the one best bet. Except for weighing the initial charge, the charges are all thrown with the Ideal powder measure making sure, of course, to keep a fairly constant level of powder in that measure. The barrel is one chambered by Ackley and the rifling extends right back to the cartridge. An odd bullet, with not much taper, will pull out of the case and stay in the bore when you try to eject without firing. I expect to open the throat a trifle to eliminate this. Also, thought I would relieve the neck a trifle but have not had opportunity. This short throat and tight neck does apparently raise the pressures some, as I have had approximately a half a dozen punctured primers with the extreme full load.

"The weight of my heavy .22-250 Mauser rifle with the 28" barrel, ⅞" at the muzzle, is a few ounces over 12 pounds, with the Fecker scope. The top loads we have been recommending are satisfactory but we advise our customers that they always begin a grain or two grains under these loads for safety and to take care of any differences in the weights or size of charges they may throw. The two styles of rifles take the same load with very slight differences to adapt the load to the individual barrel. I am working on another sporter for myself and if it shoots as well as did the last sporter I am afraid that my heavy barrel job will be used mainly for targeting and checking purposes."

Epps' .22 Bullets

In the way of bullets Ellwood Epps is handling 41, 46, 50 and 55-grain bullets in the 0.224" and in 0.223" diameters, and is selling the same weights plus a 75-grain bullet in the 0.228" diameter for the .228 Ackley jobs. He also carries numerous other bullets larger than .22 caliber and of metal-cased expanding type. Before the year is out Epps expects to be selling a full line of expanding, jacketed bullets, using new material. He has also made up rifles in .257 Roberts and a special one in .30 Newton caliber for a guide in Northern Ontario, who reports it the finest shooting rifle he has ever used and better than any of the target arms he has fired. This was the well-known guide, Lee McClelland.

The metal-cased expanding bullet situation is so difficult in the United States, that the author has given considerable space to detailing results with Canadian makers of .22 caliber and other small metal-cased expanding bullets, and just how they load them, with or without microfine graphite and the results obtained.

Friends of the author have reported some formerly good shooting bullets, made in the United States, as sometimes failing to hit the target entirely at 100 yards using the ordinary N.R.A. .22 small bore target. Such reports have come from scattered correspondents in New York, Ohio, Alabama and other places and the knowledge that bullets which will shoot can be gotten in Canada and shipped through, will be welcome knowledge to many on both sides of the line.

Many of these Canadian custom gunsmiths and dealers are rifle cranks of the first water, nearly all of them are confirmed woodchuck hunters, and the author has been acquainted, probably better than any other resident of the United States, with what they have been doing for the last 25 or 30 years. This has made a most interesting chapter. He has always found these Canadian riflemen sincere, trustworthy, helpful and friendly and quite willing to pass on their information to others. They seem much less affected with jealousy with each other's efforts than many others who could be named, much of this probably being due to hunting together at every possible opportunity and to exchanging ideas and information with the utmost candor. It is a condition which could be copied to advantage in many other areas. After all, the other fellow is usually a pretty good scout when you once get to know him and discover the subjects upon which he is experimentally inclined and is well grounded by experience.

The idea that some cartridge or rifle is "hush hush," mysterious, is exceptionally accurate because the rifling, chambering, throating or stock bedding of it is a deep secret, is ridiculous. Anyone with proper tools and some experience in their use, can take necessary measurements within a very few minutes, or hours, at the most. Anyone else, then, who is equally skilled, can build another rifle or cartridge which should shoot just as well, and if he has greater skill, which is probable, it will shoot better.

Babe Ruth was the greatest batter of them all because he was of powerful build, especially across the shoulders, had keen eyesight, courage and would stand up there in front of the best of them and take a good healthy cut at the ball.

It is like that in designing rifles and cartridges, in building them and in making metal-cased bullets. Results do not depend upon hocus pocus but upon sound principles of design and expert ability and courage in putting these principles into practice. Public and private tests of both rifles and ammunition have proved this time and time again.

CHAPTER 12

NIEDNER RIFLE CORPORATION'S
.22 CALIBER CARTRIDGES

THE Niedner Rifle Corporation, of Dowagiac, Michigan, is a
firm of fine custom gunsmiths who, 20 or 25 years ago, acquired
a reputation for making very tightly chambered special rifles. With
base band or commercial bullets these worked, provided the bullet
diameter from bullet to bullet was even, and provided also the case
neck thickness did not vary, but when one or the other or both
varied, pressures ran up. The company has advised the author that
they have regularly made no tight chambers for the past 15 years
or so, will not make a tight chamber except to special order, and
they do not apparently want such orders.

In recent years, due in part to the rush of war work, most of
their .22 caliber rifles have been of commercial sizes. Some years
ago the author saw a goodly number of .22 Long Rifle heavy
Niedner barrels, many of them in the shop of Griffin & Howe, as
one instance. G & H were using them on fine custom-made target
and match rifles. Niedner also made then a good .25 caliber wildcat
by necking down the .30-1906 to .25 and using 87 and 100-grain
bullets. This cartridge shot well at 600 yards, as the author has
seen it do in testing at Frankford Arsenal range. Niedners have,
of course, made up custom rifles to many commercial calibers.

The .22 Niedner Wildcats

Thomas Shelhamer, the firm's former expert stocker, gave the
author something of a resume of their .22 caliber wildcat activities
in a letter dated June, 1945. When Mr. Shelhamer went with
Niedner Rifle Corporation, in 1924, the Corporation was furnishing the .22 Baby Hi-Power which was designed and originated by
Emil Koshollek, of Stevens Point, Wisconsin, who happens to be a
gunsmith with very fine ideas and real skill in steel working.
Koshollek had a ".22 Koshollek" made from the .32-20 case necked
down to .22. I do not have the exact dimensions of that cartridge

269

at hand as this account is being prepared but have approximate dimensions as used for Baby Niedner, but understand the charge used by Koshollek was 12.5 grains of duPont No. 50 (at that time an experimental powder) and he used it with a special bullet of his own design weighing 49 grains. The diameter of this bullet was then 0.223″. The muzzle velocity developed was determined by numerous tests to be a trifle over 2,600 f.s.

.22 Baby Hi-Power

This cartridge was made from the .32-20 Winchester H.V. case and made up into a very attractive and husky looking little cartridge. It is suited to developing moderately high velocity and is very easy to load. It was also made up from W.C.C. cases. The author has both. Insofar as he can recall there is no appreciable difference between the cartridge as made by Koshollek and by Niedner, except in the design of the bullet.

PHYSICAL MEASUREMENTS

Shoulder Slope	Length to Shoulder	Length Cartridge	O.A. Length
14°	1.00″	1.30″	1.675″

These measurements of the loaded cartridge were made by the author. Diameter of case at beginning of shoulder is 0.300″ and neck 0.20″ in length.

This cartridge should have been an excellent one to load in quantity by machinery and would have been convenient to carry in small number on belt or in pockets. It would have packed 50 to the box.

As compared with the K-Hornet the head of the Baby Hi-Power is much larger in diameter, the cartridge is larger around, it appears heavier and stronger, the cartridge case is close to 0.10″ shorter, the shoulder is by no means as abrupt. As compared with the .22/3000 Lovell and the R-2 Risley-Donaldson, the length of the Baby Hi-Power is only 0.05″ greater than the distance up to the shoulder on the other pair of .22/3000 cartridges. The Baby Hi-Power is 1.675″ over-all loaded, and the Maximum Lovell is 1.64″ to the end of the empty cartridge, and is 2.16″ when loaded with the bullet before me.

While this cartridge did not give very high velocities with powders then in use, when put out, it could probably have been speeded up over 2,600 f.s. with certain more recent powders. Some how, I like the looks of that little Koshollek and always have liked it. It could be *underloaded* successfully, and this should be better adapted for velocities under 2,200 f.s. than later and more highly touted cartridges.

For one thing, it appears to be a cartridge case that could be fooled with and reloaded fairly safely by a chap with a good deal of imagination but not too much ballistic or explosives knowledge, and who in addition could be classed as something of a muttonhead when it comes to successful cartridge loading. Let me whisper something very "hush hush" and very sacred in your pearly ear; there are more than two or three such handloaders roaming at large. The author of this work has received some terrible looking jobs of cartridge and bullet assembly from gents who apparently thought they were pretty hot as amateur small cartridge designers and assemblers. When you place some of these loads beside precision cartridges put together by a man like Lindahl, you pray nightly for more men with Lindahl's skill in making ammunition that looks like International Match Ammunition yet made for woodchuck hunters.

Shelhamer says, and he is a gun crank, that Niedner preferred to develop a different bullet design from the early Koshollek .22 bullets which were sharp pointed or rather made with a straight taper point in 49 or 50-grain weight, so Mr. Stolley, who owned or controlled the Niedner Rifle Company or Corporation, decided to make a different contour on their bullet. The result was their 45-grain round nose, soft point bullet, of which Shelhamer says he personally made between 300,000 and 400,000. They were used in this Baby Hi-Power and also experimentally in a special small, rather short, rimless cartridge Niedner was thinking very seriously of putting out in the early 1920's.

Shelhamer says that this cartridge was made from the .30 Remington case. Another report was that it was made from a case almost equal to the .22-250, or .250/3000 necked down; in other words, something like the .22 Varminter standard case but with the neck pushed back a good deal farther. A load was mentioned somewhere as of 22.0 grains of duPont No. 25 to give just over 3,300 f.s.m.v. with what was probably a 45-grain bullet.

This cartridge could have been made with less work from the .25 Remington rimless case and probably so far as the author knows, most likely was not so much different from the Kilbourn .22

K-Magnum cartridge of today, except that Niedner always used a much more gentle shoulder slope and the cartridge was probably little, if any longer than the .22 Lindahl Rimless Chucker and the Kilbourn K-Magnum Junior cartridge, both of which are approximately 3,500 f.s. cartridges with 45 and 47-grain bullets, and, be sure to remember this, with modern powders, which Stolley and Niedner did not then have.

This .22-250 cartridge was to be used in a .22 Niedner-Mauser rifle to be made by Niedner and to weigh about 6½ to 7 pounds, with 24″ barrel. The author had been told about it along about the time they were working upon it, and has heard about it since, but the information differs in no important particular. One source said they made up one pilot rifle; another mentioned two. Mr. Shelhamer wrote the author June 13, 1945, that, as he recalls, they made up four model rifles. It is presumed they may have differed somewhat in details. There was no existing Mauser or other short enough bolt action available then to Niedner for such use. They were all made for much longer cartridges.

It is unfortunate that Niedner Rifle Corporation never put out such a rifle for about $75.00 at that time, or priced even more, if they had to have it to pay sales promotional and tooling-up expenses of considerable amount before they could obtain sales in good volume to make the rifle pay for itself. Remember, it takes a good country-wide jobber and traveling salesman organization before you can sell *any* rifle in quantity in this country. They may also have been handicapped by not having and not being able to import to that Dowagiac neighborhood enough good gunmakers to produce such a rifle in quantity. If you have ever tried to hire and *move* a couple of dozen, or maybe a couple of hundred Yankee rifle makers, with their families, from a locality, even if it be homely, where they have become rooted four, six or seven generations since they slipped down off Plymouth Rock on their panties, you will discover that you have to flash more folding money than you must flash to get yourself elected to just about whatever office you want. But we are digressing.

The Early .22 Hornet Bullets

Shelhamer says that about that time, around 1924 probably, Wotkyns and Woody began working on the Hornet. They obtained bullets from Niedner, as at that time there was nothing else available except the full jacketed Velo-dog bullet which had to be sized down. All of such bullets were made 0.223″ in diameter and used in the same diameter barrel as the .22 Long Rifle. Niedner formed these bullets on a hand press and Shelhamer says that he spent many a day operating the lever of said press. Everyone who has had to make many bullets by using a small hand press, or even a power press, complains about the work of it. It is usually hard work, or at least making enough such bullets wears a fellow down by quitting time. He wishes he could take the alarm clock the following morning and hurl it out the window, then turn over and go right back to sleep.

A direct Shelhamer quotation June 13, 1945, follows:

"When the cartridge companies started to make ammunition for the .22 Hornet all four of the large concerns sent to us for sample bullets and as far as I know Western and Winchester still make the identical soft point bullet that we originated."

This seems to be a more modern version of the old saw about wearing a wide and deep path to the door of the chap who makes a better mouse trap. I never shot a better .22 bullet than those Winchester soft point Hornets.

The .22 Niedner Magnum

There are two versions of this cartridge; one is a rimless and the other a rimmed case. They are not alike in diameter at the shoulder nor in angle of slope on the shoulder. My own measurements of sample carrtidges vary slightly from the official measurements, provided by L. G. Anderson of Niedner, for shoulder slope. The diameter of case at shoulder agrees with my measurement, at least approximately.

THE .22 RIMLESS NIEDNER MAGNUM

Slope of Shoulder	Length to Shoulder	Length of case	O.A. Length
22°	1.40″	1.90″	2.38″

As a handy comparison, the Kilbourn K-Magnum *Junior* cartridge has a length of 1.275″ to shoulder while the Lindahl Chucker is 1.20″ to the shoulder. The K-Magnum Junior has a case length of 1.70″ which is 0.20″ shorter; and 2.20″, or 0.18″ less, in over-all length.

The Kilbourn K-22 Magnum was made to hold 7.0 grains more powder than this Niedner cartridge. Obviously it had to be longer. The Kilbourn Magnum measures 1.65″ up to the shoulder, or an additional 0.25″; the cartridge length is 1.90″. It is, of course, made from the same length Remington cartridge. The Kilbourn Magnum

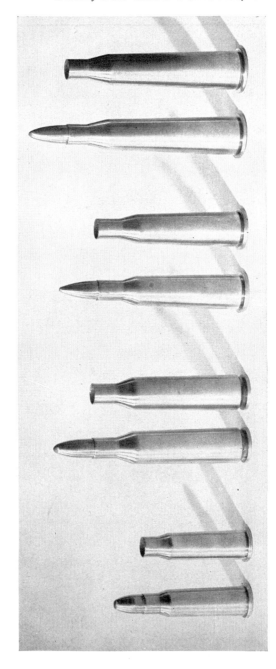

NIEDNER CARTRIDGES

.22 Baby Hi-Power; .22 Rimless Niedner Magnum; .22 Niedner Magnum and .224 Lightning.

and Magnum Junior each have 25° shoulder slopes, which makes the powder burn faster. Being made from the .25 Remington case (it could also be made from the .30 Remington or the .32 Remington case, but with more work) its head diameter is 0.422" and its outside diameter at shoulder is 0.391" which is fairly generous. It has comparatively little taper and, due to the gentle slope of shoulder, looks more like a commercial cartridge than a .22 wildcat. Remember, it was designed before the public went haywire on sharp shoulder slopes and also before the present series of I.M.R. powders were announced.

The slope of the .25 Remington cartridge is 23° and that of this .22 Rimless Niedner is 22° however, remember it is necked down to .22 caliber, the other to .25 caliber, and the neck length of this Dowagiac invention is rather long, 0.29". Not many of the .22 wildcats have longer than 0.25" neck.

NIEDNER .22 RIMLESS MAGNUM LOADS

Bullet	Powder	Charge	M.V.
45-gr. S. P.	3031	26.0 grs.	3,035 f.s.
63-gr. S. P.	3031	25.0 grs.	2,919 f.s.
63-gr. S. P.	4064	25.0 grs.	2,687 f.s.
55-gr. S. P.	3031	26.5 grs.	3,305 f.s.

Mr. Anderson suggests that these loads could be increased somewhat, which is obvious when the cartridge is compared with the Lindahl Chuckers or the two Kilbourn cartridges. Also, the velocities are low. However, these are the loads used in testing by the Niedner Rifle Corporation.

The author doubts that the pressures with that 45-grain bullet and 26.0 grains of No. 3031 are over 42,000 pounds per square inch, but this is conjecture. The standard load for the Kilbourn K-Magnum Rimless is 35.0 grains of No. 4320 with 55-grain bullet to develop 3,700 f.s. This would suggest that 28.0 grains of No. 4320 would develop possibly 3,460-3,500 f.s. with the 55-grain bullet in this Niedner case, but the author does not suggest making this jump. He would increase the charge about 0.2 grain at a time and very closely observe results. This cartridge will give, apparently, about the same velocity to a 55-grain bullet as the Lindahl Chucker, which is materially shorter, will impart to a 45 or 47-grain projectile.

It is the old story of you pay your price and take your choice. Short, medium or long cartridges, each greater length using more powder, stepping up the velocity a few hundred feet per second higher, producing a flatter trajectory and longer killing range; but each step-up cutting down the accuracy life of the barrel, sometimes very sharply.

A choice should largely depend upon how far your *average* target is away from you and its vitality. In Southern negro idiom, it would probably be expressed: "Is yo! or is yo' aint willin' to pay de price?" As the cartridge increases in length and charge, up and sharper and more ear-splitting goes the report. Down goes the curve of accuracy life, sometimes rather sharply. The 4,000 to 6,000 shot barrel may give way to the 750 to 1,500 round tube. You can not have your cake and eat it! A middle-of-the-road policy suggests a medium length of cartridge case and Niedner supplied it.

The .22 Rimmed Niedner Magnum

As compared with the Niedner Rimless Magnum case, this cartridge is more sharply tapered from head to shoulder and of course it is rimmed. It is made by necking down the .25-35 Winchester case. George Schnerring writes the author every now and then that his special .25-35 rifle (with the case not necked down) and using Western Cartridge Company's 87 and 100-grain bullets will more consistently shoot 1″ or better groups, and right where he wants them at 100 yards, than any other cartridge and rifle he has used. He has a special .250/3000 Winchester which also does most remarkable work and is more powerful, this also being a special rifle and is made on the Model 70 action.

The Niedner Rimmed Magnum could also be made from the .22 Savage Hi-Power case or from the .219 Zipper cartridge, as all three have the same head diameter, but this Zipper was not around when the Rimmed Magnum was designed.

PHYSICAL CHARACTERISTICS
.22 NIEDNER RIMMED MAGNUM CARTRIDGES

Cartridge	Shoulder Slope	Diam. Case at Shoulder	Length to Shoulder	Case Length	O.A. Length
.22 Rimmed Niedner Magnum	17°	0.362″	1.35″	1.84″	2.30″

As will be noted by a comparison of the dimensions of the two, the rimless case is 0.05″ to 0.06″ longer from the face of the head, due to the rimless construction. Ballistics are about the same, or a small trifle better, with the moderate Niedner loads when used in the rimmed cartridge. Neck of cartridge is 0.30″ long. All these Niedners have long necks.

This is a moderate size, good looking, well designed cartridge without any features to cause high pressures. The loads could be stepped up some using more modern powders, or those given. It should have many of the characteristics of the various "Zipper Improved" .22 wildcats but less range and power, as it is slightly smaller in case capacity. It would appear that charges of 28.0 down to 27.0 grains of No. 3031, with 55, 50, 47 or 45-grain expanding bullets, should work out, if developed not over 0.2 grains at a time, to see how things go and to discover where the top limit is on *accuracy* as well as pressure. These are not recommendations, they are suggestions; watch changes in primer with faster loads.

The .224 Niedner Lightning

The .224 Lightning cartridge was made up by Niedner at the request of J. Bushnell Smith who furnished Niedner with sample cartridges. These are made by necking down the .30-40 Krag case to .22 caliber. It makes a good strong case and some 20 years back, when the case was more popular among rifle club members who had many Krag rifles and plenty of free ammunition most of which was not worth much except for the cases, the .224 Krag was a logical cartridge. A .25 Krag cartridge was even better because it did not have quite as much taper, hence it was not necessary to neck it down as much.

There are two ways to neck down a .30-40 or a .30-1906 case to a .22 wildcat. One is to sharp taper the body of the case up to the shoulder, a fairly long, gentle slope to the shoulder, and a neck at least 0.25″ to 0.30″ long. You get a sort of wedge-shaped cartridge in this manner, but the pressures stay down. The other method is to do what is usually the procedure today, run the case up fairly straight to an abrupt shoulder, make that very sharply drawn-in to .22 caliber neck, cut off some of the front end to cut down "boiler capacity" and make the finished .22 cartridge with a sharp and short, very abrupt shoulder and rather short neck. P. O. Ackley has three different .228 Ackley Magnums made like that; three others made from the rimmed Krag case and he can make them also from the .303 British case, and the best of those cases are made for airplane or anti-aircraft machine guns. Lovell has one made up by a combination of ideas of McCrea, himself and another shooter, which has a very abrupt shoulder.

The principal advantages of such cases are that the case head is heavy, strong and tough; the developed cartridge, especially if short, is always definitely butt thick and heavy and, in theory at least, plenty of brass for cases is always available. The long, tapered, gentle slope .224 Lightning case is not as likely to crack at the neck, or break off there or at the shoulder, as the sharp shoulder abrupt jobs. On the other hand they do not burn the powder as quickly. They probably have materially lower pressures and should also have a longer barrel life.

PHYSICAL DIMENSIONS OF .224 LIGHTNING

Shoulder Slope	Diameter Head	Diam. at Shoulder	Shoulder	Case Length Full	O.A. Cartridge Length
14°	0.545″	0.375″	1.675″	2.166″	2.61″

The case neck is 0.25″ in length, the usual Niedner case length.

LOADS FOR THE .224 LIGHTNING

Bullet	Powder	Charge	M.V.
40-gr. pointed	4064	39.0	4,165 f.s.
55-gr. pointed	4064	38.0	3,830 f.s.
45-gr. pointed	4064	39.0	4,095 f.s.

Assuming that the latter two charges are not overly high pressure, which is improbable, then the 40-grain bullet should work out with 39.5 to 40.0 or even 40.5 grains of No. 4064 to develop a muzzle velocity approaching T. K. Lee's .22 Varminter Senior cartridge, although with this light bullet it will not hold the velocity so well. The Lee job turned out by Gebby uses the .257 Roberts case. It has more boiler room and is not so tapered.

In obtaining brass to make up cartridge cases for the .224 Lightning Rimmed cartridge, it should be borne in mind that most of the old Krag ammunition given out free to rifle clubs and individuals is now in the neighborhood of 30 years old; and the later issue of .30-40 Krag ammunition which was sold to rifle clubs is now about 20 to 25 years old, but it was worth a great deal more than the original free issue. It would, in fact, even shoot accurately at 500 yards, which is only mid-range distance for a Krag with *good* ammunition.

The best brass for the .224 Lightning conversions would likely be arsenal stuff made as late as possible, and commercial .30-40 f.m.c.

ammunition made to government specifications, as late as that could be obtained. Real old brass should be looked over very carefully for splits and cracked cases. There is no sense in spending real money for a good rifle and a special wildcat case for a Hi-Side Winchester action, or a Krag action, or others which will handle a long, tapered rimmed case and then use poor brass. Matter of fact, the best .303 British cases will make up into a better .224 Lightning than the .30-40 because they are smaller—the .303 part of it only refers to the neck to hold a .303 British bullet and the case itself has less capacity, which in a .22 wildcat is desirable. Whenever you select a .30 caliber case larger than the .30 Remington you are getting more volume or powder capacity than is desirable and the efficiency of the load is cut down. Also, it is considerably more work to trim down and swage down these large cases to a more desirable size for a .22 wildcat.

Hervey Lovell got around this extra work, so it was reported, by slipping out the back door of his shop and going over in the nearby 40 acre woods to feed nuts to his pet fox squirrel until the call was completed. But you cannot so well do that around Dowagiac. There is the matter of the Michigan State Police who might "view with alarrum" any citizen wandering out in the woods feeding his pet fox squirrel. Down around the more ritzy Indianapolis and its famous race track, they are accustomed to almost anything. In fact, people who have bet on the wrong hay burner say: "Sure I can recognize my horse coming in away down there; I know his walk!" With automobiles they recognize its wheeze and its rattle. Unfortunate bettors must have some consolation.

During 1945 Niedner was busy converting to peace time business from war jobs, rearranging rifling machinery and barrel turning lathes and otherwise getting ready for post-war rifle cranks. They have recently been advising the .218 Bee instead of the .22 Baby Hi-Power, because you can also get factory ammunition for the Bee, in normal times, and that saves a lot of reloading worry for rifle cranks who are short of brass, primers and their pet powder.

Chances are that Niedner may come through with a Zipper Improved one of these days for Hi-Side actions, and a cartridge a little longer than the Rimless Magnum, made from either the .25 Remington or the .30 Remington case, necked down and the shoulder put where they want it. And some day they might even get out a .22 and a .25 bolt action for short, rimless cases. I do not say they will do this, but they might to advantage, because one of these days the whole public will wake up to the condition that a nation the size of ours can not get along indefinitely on a budget unbalanced so ridiculously that each day it spends three times what it takes in. When sanity returns to the masses, if ever, then manufacturers and custom gunsmiths alike will suddenly discover that to sell something to the public it has to be what the public wants to buy, and it has to be worth what it costs the public. Then business will again boom.

Niedner is a firm which can do one of the very best and finest fitted re-stocking jobs obtainable in this country. They do good metal work; they can bore a barrel and unless you insist upon a cockeyed set of specifications, can chamber for a good sensible shell, without frills. To these could be added a few wildcat designs which are right up to those which other firms have put out in the last 12 years. It is a good firm to put out a rifle of special type for a commercial cartridge and which would then be dolled up with fine stocking, a scope and engraving. But lay off special close chambering, which went out, practically, with Mann base band bullets, and pick something which really shoots with 8S, Sisk, Mannen or Western Cartridge Company's very fine commercial bullets in .25 and .22 caliber. Then you will have a practical varmint rifle or a woodchuck gun, and Niedner can build you such an arm or a squirrel rifle with Farquharson, Sharps-Borchardt, Hi-Side Winchester, Winchester 52, 70, 20, 30-S, 1917 or Springfield or a Mauser action, you to supply Item 1, same being the action. They also make many .22 Long Rifle barrels, most of them fairly heavy barrels.

They have had enough experience to turn out a good job. Niedner is a practical match rifleman of the old days; however, he retired about six years ago. Shelhamer knows stocking and fitting of recoil shoulders for super-accuracy. It is not a fly-by-night firm and they answer correspondence which, as compared with some gunsmiths not too well fitted for that, is comforting to the chap who is waiting impatiently for the rifle of his dreams and who proposes to do something besides dream about it.

At last accounts the Niedner Rifle Corporation was going through a period of reorganization. At press time the future was open and possibly uncertain.

Shelhamer is in business for himself near Dowagiac.

CHAPTER 13

SOME OF "THE OTHER FELLOWS"
CHARLES C. JOHNSON'S .22 WILDCATS

Charles C. Johnson, of Thackery, Ohio, is a gunsmith who for many years regularly supplied both solid barrels and re-lined tubes for a varied line of .22 caliber cartridges. He works very closely with C. A. Diller, of Dayton. Today he is supplying only solid barrels. Mr. Johnson is a very expert custom gunsmith but is not primarily a rifle shot and should not be confused with either Charles H. Johnson, of Upper Darby, Pennsylvania, an outstanding small bore rifle shot with Frankford Arsenal Rifle Club, of Philadelphia, nor with Eric Johnson, of New Haven and Hamden, Connecticut, also an outstanding small bore rifle shot and a maker of super-accurate .22 Long Rifle match barrels.

Charles C. Johnson probably came into greatest repute about 1935-38 when the R-2 .22/3000 cartridge was in its zenith of popularity. Mr. Johnson made or chambered barrels for many outstanding riflemen and for some years appeared to have probably the No. 1 position as a maker of R-2 .22/3000 wildcats. Possibly no little of his acclaim was due to the remarkable crow shooting and interesting writing of A. R. Weeks, of Tillsonburg, Ontario. He had a Hi-Side Winchester single shot rifle fitted with heavy C. C. Johnson R-2 barrel which consistently shot 2″ groups at 200 yards and many groups were actually materially better. It also had an accuracy life of 6,600 to 6,700 rounds which was equally outstanding and gave Mr. Weeks many years of extremely satisfactory shooting.

For 10 or 15 years Johnson supplied high grade chrome nickel steel barrels for .22 Hornet, R-2 .22/3000, and in .218 Bee calibers. Two of these were wildcats and the others used commercial ammunition. At the present writing he is developing a .22 cartridge from the .25-35 case which is probably very similar to Hervey Lovell's .22-25/35 Improved or No. 9 in his list, a very flat shooting cartridge over 200-300 yards. Lovell's case has a 30° shoulder angle; an

281

outside diameter at neck of 0.393"; is 2.03" in length; and 1.580" up to the shoulder. If the Johnson case is finally turned out as having a sharper shoulder slope, a smaller diameter at the shoulder, or is shorter up to the shoulder than the Lovell case, it will then take less powder than the 34.0 grains of No. 4064, suggested by Lovell for the Lovell cartridge. At any rate, such cases can use two grains more No. 4064 than the Improved Zipper cases unless made with a very short length up to the shoulder. The case can also be made up from the Savage .22 H.P. cartridge.

If the barrel twist is 16", bullets from 41 to 46-grain can be used; 50-grain does fine and 55-grain is tops. If made with 14" twist the heavy bullets shoot best. Powder charge should, in each case, depend upon primer selected, bullet weight and length, and case capacity. Use less powder instead of more in working up your trial charges. The long case made from the .25-35 is just about as large as is extremely efficient for a .22 in velocity developed as compared with the powder consumed. It is a good selection for coyotes and long range shooting on woodchucks. It can also be reloaded nicely with reduced loads of powder from the K-Hornet to the .22/3000 Lovells, or even less for squirrels.

Charles C. Johnson has also made .22 Long Rifle barrels, both solid tubes and re-lined Diller jobs, fitted and chambered by Johnson, but these have not so far received as much acclaim as the R-2 Johnson rifles, although there is no logical reason why they should not give equally good results and probably do. The Diller barrels usually shot well in .22 rim fire calibers. The .22 Long Rifle Johnson jobs were made from high grade manganese steel, not so hard as the center fire barrels, but this is customary with .22 rim fire barrel stock as slightly softer steel machines to better advantage and with fewer soft and hard places throughout the tube. The even texture steel always bores to much better advantage, gives a more even and straighter barrel.

At one time Charles C. Johnson was turning out 250 barrels a year of the .22/3000 and the R-2 calibers, the latter being with the 12° shoulder angle, according to comment, and these were about equally divided as to numbers. These in addition to his other barrels. Lovell recently spoke very favorably to the author of the grade of workmanship and the volume that the Diller-Johnson combination was turning out. Diller bores and rifles the barrels and Johnson does the work from then on. In the Far West, Buhmiller and another gunsmith in Eureka, Montana, are working in an exactly similar combination or team, and with just as good success.

In the way of comment, in addition to Ray Week's notes in the companion book *Hunting With the Twenty-two,* which comment was worded very favorably to his Johnson barrel, is the following by J. Leroy Baker, of Mechanicsville, New York: "The first 10-shot group measured 1⅜" at 100 yards, using 17.0 grains of Hi-Vel and the 50-grain Sisk bullet. Have fired many 5-shot groups of 1" and

Charles C. Johnson. Thackery, Ohio with .22 Wildcat rifles. Rifle he is holding is a Swiss Martini. First one in rack is a Ballard.

two that were under 1". I also had a 2½" group at 200 yards. I have shot 250 rounds within a week and it is the most accurate rifle I have ever owned." This was a Winchester singleshot in .22/3000 caliber.

V. E. Layne, the well-known rest shooter and experimental rifleman, of Halfway, Oregon, wrote: "The accuracy of the rifle, a very fine Winchester single shot, is so extraordinary as to be amazing. I have now fired over 800 rounds from bench rest, and the average group size for 10-shot groups, at 100 yards, is 1⅛". A great many of the groups have been 1" and under. On August 7, I fired 50 consecutive shots, all of which were 10's. These targets were a possible with 7X's, another possible with 7X's, a possible with 8X's, a possible with 9X's and a possible with 10X's. This is 500 x 500 with 41X's. This .22/3000 had the R-2 chamber."

W. H. Meister, of Fargo, North Dakota, wrote: "Maurice's .22/3000 has executed 14 crows and one cat, and mine is now in action. Killed four crows yesterday, one at 140 yards, and later shot three in five minutes, at ranges of 150 to 165 yards. These were killed in as many shots—four shots, four crows! Yesterday morning at 6 A.M. I shot a 1.75" group at 175 yards." The rifle has a Krag action with a solid barrel, 26" long and is in a stock hand-made by Meister himself, upon which he spent 93 hours inletting the barrel and another 30 hours in finishing the outside.

The C. C. Johnson workmanship has been repeatedly reported to the author as being of very high grade. Normally he seems to devote his efforts mostly to small and medium size cases.

JOE PFEIFER'S .22 WILDCATS

When rifle cranks in the Los Angeles district want to get away from it all, yet lack the money to drop into the Brown Derby for a succulent steak, they next think of Joe Pfeifer who has his custom gunshop at 7837 Sancola Avenue, Roscoe 3, California. Even if the Los Angeles city limits do extend—according to some—from just above Tia Juana to Seattle and, on clear days when the visibility is high, practically to Vancouver, British Columbia, the town of Roscoe has, thanks to Joe, managed to preserve its rugged individuality.

Joe Pfeifer is more at home in front of a lathe or a rifling machine than as an author, which is no help when you are marketing .22 wildcats, but it has fortunately, resulted in six cartridges of splendid design, and a quality of workmanship which very closely approaches that of the precision ammunition making of Leslie Lindahl. Pfeifer does not do stocking or engraving. He is a custom gunsmith and barrel maker, as well as a fine tool maker. The combination always goes well together and results in A-1 workmanship—in steel. His shop is reported to be very well equipped with Reed & Prentice 16" tool room lathe, Pratt & Whitney deep hole driller, Pratt & Whitney No. 3 rifling machine and General Electric precision grinding equipment. He uses Red Elliott's reaming and chambering equipment exclusively and is another who speaks well of F. K. Elliott chambering reamers. He says he tries to keep his standards of precision workmanship fully equal to the Elliott level. He has gunsmithed as an amateur since 1930 and professionally since 1939.

He uses Buhmiller rifle barrels for .22 wildcats, plus, of course, whatever else he may find time to rifle for himself.

The Pfeifer .22 Cartridges

There are six cartridges all very well designed, precision jobs; shoulder slopes are very moderate in the smaller sizes and much sharper in the larger cartridges.

No. 1. The .22 K-Hornet: This Pfeifer job is made as designed originally by Lysle Kilbourn. Chambering and dimensions are the same as used by Kilbourn. Ammunition for one is usable in the other. This cartridge measures 1.13″ up to the shoulder, is made by expanding the .22 Hornet case, has a 35° and very short shoulder slope, and is extremely accurate. For load see the table of loads given under the K-Hornet in the Kilbourn data in this book.

No. 2. The .22/3000 R-2 Donaldson: Dimensions interchangeable with other R-2's of that style and as made by reliable workmen, according to Pfeifer. However, the case looks more like the G. B. Crandall R-2 than any of the others, to this author. Loads, same as those for the R-2's of about 12° shoulder slope and made from the .25-20 S.S. cases necked down. This is not one of the *Magnum* .22/3000 cases, like the .22 Maximum Lovell or the .22 Kilbourn K-Lovell. These use two grains more powder.

Pfeifer also chambers barrels for the factory .218 Bee cartridges. Load and ammunition is interchangeable.

No. 3: He likes to make up a barrel now and then for the .218 Mashburn-Bee cartridge, which is a fatter .218 Bee, with a much sharper shoulder slope and with somewhat increased powder charges. Uses loads intended for the .218 Mashburn-Bee.

No. 4. The .224 Pfeifer Rimmed Magnum: Made from .30-40 cartridge brass, necked or swaged down, and then cut off. Probably takes quite a few operations to shorten it this much and reduce same to .22 caliber neck. It is a much shorter case with materially less powder capacity than the .224 Niedner Magnum and the .224 and .220 Donaldson and J. Bushnell Smith cartridges. This .224 Pfeifer Magnum very much resembles the .219 Wasp cartridge developed by Harvey Donaldson, even though made up by Donaldson from the .25 Remington rimless and then from the .219 Zipper.

Pfeifer says that he has made up more than 300 rifles for this .224 Pfeifer in either .30-40 or the .303 British brass, without any complaints. It was formed on these cases shortened to the length of 1.660″ with a rather steep body taper from head to shoulder, and measures but 1.275″ up to the shoulder, which is the same length as for the R-2 .22/3000 and Lovell cartridges made from the .25-20 case. The shoulder slope is 28°, the same as for the Varminter, and as compared with 29° for the Crandall Varmint-R. The latter case, however, has considerable more powder capacity.

The .224-30/40 Pfeifer is loaded with 30.0 grains of No. 3031 or the same or a corresponding charge of No. 4320 or No. 4064 and either the 50-grain Sisk-Lovell, the 50-grain Sisk Express, or the 50-grain 8S Wotkyns-Morse bullet. Charge ignited by the Remington 8½ primer or the Winchester 115 primer. Pfeifer has chambered rifles for this case using both 14″ and 16″ twist and he says it does fine in either; apparently there is very little, if any, difference in accuracy. This cartridge would also do well with 48-grain Swift bullets, or 45 or 46-grain .22 Hornet bullets, the latter if not speeded up too much; and with the 45-grain and 47-grain 8S bullets. With 55-grain bullets it should not be speeded too much or pressures might rise rather quickly, as the case is short. For 55-grain and 60-grain bullets the slightly longer cases may be better. In fact, almost surely would be.

Pfeifer says this case has done a fine job in supplying a moderately short case for single shot falling block actions like the Stevens 44½, Winchester Hi-Side single shot, Farquharson and the Sharps-Borchardt. He says also that prior to its development, about the best the boys had for the single shot was the R-2, which, while being a superb cartridge in its class, was hopelessly outclassed by the larger Magnums in bolt action styles.

No. 5.   The .224-303 British Pfeifer Magnum: This is for the Canadian carriage trade, generally, which can obtain either the .303 service brass or the special heavy, .303 British anti-aircraft empties, for necking down and cutting off. The .224-30/40 and the .224-303 British Pfeifer are as much alike in appearance as the two Lindahl Chucker cartridges. They are of a size which holds four to six grains more powder than the two Lindahl cartridges or the Kilbourn K-Magnum *Junior* cartridge. The Kilbourn K-Magnum case (the longer one, not the Junior) holds about two grains more powder than this Pfeifer .224 Magnum.

This case would likely do well with No. 3031, but not too many maximum loads of 3031 and also with No. 4320 and No. 4064. If you want to use 55-grain bullets, try the 4064.

Lindahl now has a .22 Lindahl Magnum made from the .219

Zipper case which would also have 30.0 to 32.0 grains of No. 3031 capacity. This Pfeifer case is an easy one to make up, having proper swaging down and trimming tools of course, by those having .303 British cartridges. It has 28° shoulder taper; is 1.275″ to shoulder; and 1.660″ over-all case length.

No. 6. The Pfeifer .22-250: Dimensions of this .22-250 are similar with those of the .22 (standard) Varminter or the .22-250 made by other reputable custom gunsmiths, according to Pfeifer. This means a 28° shoulder taper; a length of 1.50″ to the shoulder; and 1.92″ over-all empty case length. The loaded case sent the author was 2.480″ over-all with a long, rather sharp pointed Sisk bullet seated, as compared with 2.38″ for the Ackley .22-250 as supplied, and 2.43″ for the .22 Gebby Varminter. This depends a lot on the length of point of the bullet and how deep the reloader wishes to seat. Also the position of the front end of the bearing surface of the bullet as it enters the throat.

Pfeifer says that, contrary to popular opinion in some places, this .22-250 was developed by J. B. Sweany, Wotkyns and Red Elliott.

Joe Pfeifer is one of the few remaining custom gunsmiths who says he still has a large demand for fine, soft steel barrels in .28-30, .32-40 and .38-55 Schuetzen rifle calibers and for the old Sharps Straight calibers, and that he made up one rifle on a Farquharson action for a chap in China who wanted to do a bit of shooting (guess against whom) with a .22 Pfeifer Magnum.

With true California modesty he maintains that Los Angeles is a small suburb of Roscoe, rather easily found if you once reach the metropolis of Roscoe, and then receive directions from the nearest traffic officer. You can also locate the main stem, if you have to walk home from Tia Juana. All one has to do is to sit on the nearest concrete headwall until two fellows drive by armed with Pfeifer .224 Magnums. You "Hi" them, and they mention that L. A. is easy to find. All you have to do is to walk straight ahead for 250 miles to Roscoe, then turn at right angles, and almost before you know it there you are! Or, Red Elliott's shop is so many miles slightly in a different direction, and after you drop in to see Red you turn South, then West. You will not mind the few extra rods of California sunshine.

As you plod along you will recall many, many interesting incidents. First, that you bought three tipster sheets and bet on the "Daily Double" because a bang-tail with that name could not possibly lose. Neither would he—but another horse shoved him! So it went and finally, after you had tried to recoup your losses by putting $50.00 on Sure Shot to place, Sure Shot had a heart attack right in the stretch. Almost, so had you.

So, there you are, trudging along, most awfully thankful that you are a .22 wildcat fan and are not lugging a 16-pound .32-40 Ballard-Pfeifer. You were a wonderful picker of winning horses but your luck just did not break right! Better luck with Brother Pfeifer. He has six numbers for you to choose from. Do not let anyone shove you!

M. S. RISLEY'S .22 DEVELOPMENTS

Most of you have often heard of the famous Bob Owen Sporting Springfield rifles. The handsomest sporting rifle the author has ever seen was one that Owen took to Camp Perry, Ohio, to the National Matches about the year of 1922. M. S. Risley is the man who is credited with having done most of the fine metal work on these Owen Sporter Springfields. In other words, Owen was one of the finest stockers this country has ever seen. Combine that with Risley's metal work and you have a knockout in custom gunsmithing.

Risley has lived for a good portion of his active custom gunsmithing sort of off the beaten path, at Hubbardsville, New York, which is about 20 miles south of Utica, where the Savage Arms Corporation's main plant was built. The Risley shop is located along New York State Highway No. 12. Risley is a lover of setter dogs, is a woodchuck hunter and is located in good shooting country.

Risley came to the notice of riflemen generally somewhat more prominently about the time that the .224 Krag Lightning rifle first came into wider use. He made the first chambering tool for this caliber after J. B. Smith and Harvey Donaldson swapped ideas; after Smith made up a .22 Magnum from the Springfield case and Donaldson thought the Krag case would do just as well and handle loads with lower pressures to better advantage especially in single-shot rifles, which appears to have been the result. However, more than 33 years ago, back in 1911 or 1912, Charles Newton made up a .22 from the Krag case for the late C. E. Howard, rancher-rifleman of North Park, Colorado, and he used that rifle to kill a large number of coyotes, lobo wolves and some antelope and deer.

Previous to making his home and having his shop next door at Hubbardsville, Risley was a gunsmith for about 22 years in Utica. Another of his major creative jobs was when he made up the first R-2 .22/3000 chambering reamers and was responsible for the first R-2 .22/3000 after talking the matter over with Harvey Don-

CORNER OF RISLEY'S RIFLE SHOP

Note the fine, heavy barrel, bolt action, sporter in vise and the fancy Winchester Schuetzen singleshot standing vertically on bench. Risley's shop contains bench rests and loading room.

aldson and Fred Ness, who wanted a case with a little more powder room than the original 5° slope Lovell. The new shape burned the I.M.R. powders like No. 4198 to better advantage and then, somewhat later, Hervey Lovell came along with a 15° degree slope .22/3000 Lovell as compared with the 12° slope of the Risley. Ackley uses a 12° 30" slope on his, R-2; Milhoan 13° 30", and Johnson had a J-19 of 19°.

For many years Risley turned out .22 varmint and woodchuck rifles on Model 54, Model 70 and Hi-Side Winchester S.S. actions. He made .22 Hornet caliber single shots, R-2's and .224 Lightning calibers, all on the Hi-Side action. He also put them on Stevens 44½ and on Farquharson actions and these jobs have spread around considerably, especially in New York State.

At last accounts Risley was not boring .22 barrels, but used Winchester, Savage and C. A. Diller blanks and probably some Buhmiller's—Risley chambering, fitting, blueing and otherwise completing the rifle. He made his own design of double-set triggers for Winchester S.S. rifles. He re-bores and rifles barrels for Kentucky flint lock rifles. He also stocks with high grade walnut.

Risley's specialty for years appeared to be woodchuck rifles in the R-2 and .224 caliber Krag cartridge, the first a 3,000 f.s. and up case and the latter a 4,000 f.s. job. Fine metal work has been his outstanding characteristic in custom gunsmithing.

ROBERT U. MILHOAN'S GUNSMITHING OF .22's

For a number of years, Robert U. Milhoan, of R. F. D. No. 3, Elizabeth, West Virginia, became well known as a custom gunsmith in a region in which one does not ordinarily expect to find such talent, but where you do find many native hunters and riflemen. Milhoan has specialized in very close fit of stock to receiver and barrel. One of his talking points used to be that his re-stocked rifles would give as good accuracy as the stripped barrel and action, which was, of course, a good deal to claim and which required quality stocking to fulfill.

At last accounts Milhoan was prepared to chamber and fit barrels for four different center fire .22 caliber varmint rifles; the .22 Hornet; the .22/3000; also a special case made up from a necked down .25-35, much like Hervey Lovell's No. 9 case, but which may have been of less powder capacity but of very similar ballistics—that being a very flat shooting case; and another special wildcat made from the .30-40 Krag case necked to .22. This would be much like the .224 Lightning.

Milhoan has also made a good many re-modeled .22 Long Rifle caliber sporters of many kinds. He has made these up on Winchester S.S. actions, on Stevens 44½, on Farquharson and on some bolt actions. He also has fitted light repeaters of the 5¾ pound type with heavier 26″ barrels and special stocks which make a very practical, fine-holding and very handsome little sporting rifle of seven to 8½ pounds as is preferred. Milhoan guaranteed his best match barrels in .22 Long Rifle caliber to make 1⅜″ groups at 100 yards and with after-the-war ammunition running uniformly, they may do even better. He also makes *speed actions* on Ballard, Stevens 44½ and higher numbered grades, with hammer fall of less than ⅜″. These last two specialities are rather unique among most custom gunsmiths and are something to remember when you want work this gunsmith is prepared to do.

On one occasion Milhoan rebuilt a Model 1906 Winchester, the little-top-ejector action repeater which followed the Model 1890, by fitting it with a 26″ barrel for the .22 Long Rifle, then he restocked it with a man's size stock having a full pistol grip and a large forend which extended back over the magazine and action like the extension slide handle of a trap shotgun, except that it was in size proportioned to the little .22 rifle. All told, he appears to be an unusually clever and original gunsmith, capable in both wood and metal working. He stocks with fine walnut and also with myrtle wood. He can make almost any design of sporting, varmint or match rifle the shooter may wish and in a location to which a large volume of business is not ordinarily sent. This should suggest that he might be helpful when many other gunsmiths are overstocked, as he is quite capable in his own right.

A letter received from Mr. Milhoan just before going to press, said that he was back in his shop and converting same rapidly to his commercial business with riflemen; that he is turning out individual orders and will soon be able to turn out many more. At the time of writing he was tooled up for .22 Hornet, .22/3000 M-1 (which is the Milhoan version of the R-2), the R-2, the .22 Niedner Magnum Rimmed and the .22 Niedner Magnum Rimless cartridges, also the .218 Bee and the .220 Krag. He intends to shortly tool up for an Improved .219 Zipper.

The firm is now composed of Robert U. and Patrick E. Milhoan, known as Robert U. Milhoan & Son, same address and shop as before, R. F. D. No. 3, Elizabeth, West Virginia.

Milhoan advises that the shoulder slope he uses in the R-2 he makes is about 13° 30″. He says this seems to fit about all chamber- ing in that caliber. He has checked quite a number of chambers and finds them to vary from 13° 30″ to 17° as turned out by various makers if one takes a sulphur cast of the chamber and then measures the sulphur cast. The author wishes to add here that riflemen will find, if they investigate, that most shoulder slopes are made with a rounding curve at the beginning of the slope, the main slope, and then a curve in the opposite direction out to the neck. A sort of reverse curve with a longer straight tangent or line joining the end of the first and the beginning of the second. In addition, as many custom gunsmiths make them, this line will be a curved line and not a straight line and, especially on Ackley jobs and on the various .30-1906 conversions, will be considerably curved, so that measuring the slope of the shoulder of a cartridge is difficult to do with absolute and definite accuracy and results. The line is short, *very* short, on small cartridges like the K-Hornet and the .22/3000 jobs and you may be undecided after much eye strain and measuring whether it is a certain figure within a range of about 2° 30′ both ways. In other words, you may get results varying 5° from what someone else, equally careful, makes it. That does not prove you are stupid; it merely demonstrates that the shoulder is a combination of curves and lines and may be either convex or concave, as well as being smoothed off at both extremities.

Milhoan suggests that he has found a splendid load for small game in the .22/3000 cases to be 11.0 grains of No. 2400 and the 35-grain, full metal-jacketed bullet. Remember, he lives in a district in which squirrels, turkeys and ruffed grouse would be the small game likely to be shot with a rifle.

EMIL KOSHOLLEK RIFLES AND CARTRIDGES

Emil Koshollek, of 517 South Michigan Avenue, Stevens Point, Wisconsin, is probably the most ingenious custom gunsmith on metal work of rifles and the design of bullets and small cartridges in the Wisconsin area of the Middle West.

Emil's expertness in this line goes back a long time. It must have been 25 years ago when this author first received word from Mr. Koshollek that he was working on one or two .22 caliber center fire rifle cartridges. In one of the 1923 issues of *Arms & The Man* there was an article about the old .22 Hornet, data for which came from a man in Nebraska, which suggested the use of 9.5 grains of duPont

No. 50 powder and a 49-grain metal-cased expanding bullet designed and made by Koshollek, which bullet had a straight taper point very similar in general contour to the later W-M 8S bullets which have given a very creditable account of themselves. There may, however, have been no connection between these designs. Such bullet point design had been used in both metal-cased and cast or swaged lead bullets of other calibers many, many years before. There is really not so much in bullet shape or design which cannot be traced back through the work of generations of previous ballisticians and riflemen.

About the year 1922 Emil Koshollek sent the author one of the original Koshollek .22 center fire cartridges. The powder charge was 12.5 grains of duPont No. 50 and his 49-grain bullet. The bullets were of 0.223″ diameter, with muzzle velocity about 2,600 f.s. I think he found somewhat lower muzzle velocity in those earlier experiments with this cartridge, a condition entirely natural. The .22 Koshollek made 10-shot groups the size of a half dollar at 100 yards, in favorable weather. The author had this information then and had it recently confirmed from Mr. Koshollek.

Various letters dated 1922-23 mentioned efforts were being made by Niedner to bore a barrel with 15″ twist for Mr. Koshollek, presumably for this cartridge. Niedner made up barrels for .22 rifles cut with 12″ and also with 14″ twists, which twists, I believe, the .22 W.R.F. was then using. Niedner tried their Baby Hi-Power cartridge in those twists, as well as in the old reliable 16″ twist. In those days the .22 Savage Hi-Power was sometimes called The Imp, a name which was no more appropriate than was the name Kleanbore as it has been used most frequently. The Imp was made with 12″ twist because it used a 70-grain bullet and needed a fast twist to spin it and some thought The Imp could be made to shoot with a 49 or 50-grain Koshollek bullet measuring 0.227″ in diameter. One of the earlier loads for the .22 Imp was the 0.227″ Koshollek bullet and 23.0 grains of duPont No. 50 powder, although 25.0 grains of the same powder caused the cases to swell in the lever action rifle.

Today the Koshollek cartridge is practically duplicated in the Winchester .22 caliber .218 Bee cartridge, except that a more blunt point bullet is used. The .218 Bee caused the abandonment of the .22 Baby Hi-Power because the cartridge under the other designation was available in factory loaded ammunition—during and after the year of 1939 when it was first announced generally in ammunition catalogs. Hubalek made some target weight barrels and mounted them on Hi-Side Winchester single shot actions and, when bushed and tuned up, groups reduced some 50 per cent from those obtained from the standard lever action sporting rifles in .218 caliber.

Koshollek today does a fine, custom gunsmithing general firearms rebuilding and repair business and apparently has all he can handle most times. He does not, however, appear to be going into the .22 wildcat business anew just at this time. However, he played such an important part, practically, in the development of the early .22 wildcats and their bullets that an appreciation of his work along such lines is due.

The .22 Koshollek, as originally made, and those most recently received from the Niedner Rifle Corporation in 1945, may have had very slight differences in shape or shoulder but they cannot be recalled or noted. It was made from the .32-20 case necked down to .22 caliber, and used with a 49-grain bullet of Koshollek design. The cartridge was approximately 1.65″ in over-all length, loaded, was 1.30″ in case length and was an even 1″ up to the shoulder. It was a thoroughly practical cartridge made from the .32-20 Winchester and Western cases, usually the W.H.V. type, which had good thick heads. It could likely have been made just about as well from the .25-20 Repeater case, although in that instance it might have finished up with very slightly reduced powder capacity.

Emil Koshollek is one of the few remaining custom gunsmiths of the old school, to whom good design and quality of material and fitting are very important and who has a degree of expertness peculiar to his type.

CHAPTER 14

PROBLEMS OF RIFLE AND CARTRIDGE DESIGN

PROBLEMS in rifle breech, receiver length and strength, bolt cross section, and thickness; compressibility of rifle bolt and expansiveness or stretching of receiver walls due to breech pressure upon explosion of cartridge; relative desirability and extractivity of long straight-taper, slightly tapered .22 varmint cartridges as compared with more sharply tapered rifle cartridges, are all vital matters in the design of a varmint rifle or a varmint cartridge. Comments and arguments, pro and con, on these matters are given in this chapter.

It should be understood that a rifle bolt can be compressed slightly, and the receiver stretched lengthwise to an even greater extent, because it is longer and a greater length of it is under tension, when a high pressure, small caliber rifle cartridge is fired. How much of this compression and expansion is eliminated from permanent set, by the elasticity of the steel used in bolt and receiver wall, and how much of the elongation and compression is a permanent set, thus increasing the head space of the cartridge, is of vital import to the owners and users of .22 varmint rifles, and obviously to everyone designing high pressure, small caliber rifles and cartridges.

Also, the ease or lack of it, with which a fired .22 varmint cartridge can be extracted and ejected from the rifle, has much to do with the ease and speed with which a rifle of this type may be reloaded. This subject is also commented upon.

The reason the head space of a rifle increases with use is not only because the metal wears but also because the bolt lugs are gradually reduced in thickness by impacted blows due to firing, and because the receiver walls stretch and set in the greater length. These all add together in their total effect. Some riflemen believe this increase is considerable. Others, that it is immaterial. Better read this comment to find out what actually does happen.

295

Obviously, hard, nickel steel receivers and carefully fitted bolts will stand up better than poorly fitted bolts and rifles made of soft, poor grade machine steel. An old, badly worn and stretched rifle action should be head space checked and refitted before being made up with a new barrel for a high velocity, high pressure, .22 varmint cartridge of large size. This is one of the problems of the custom gunsmith who supplies your new rifle. Meantime, you will find it advisable to read these comments on a situation which should always be taken into consideration when purchasing or building a new small caliber, high speed varmint rifle.

Some pertinent comments follow:

Action Changes Under Stress

Some time ago Lysle Kilbourn, in trying to prove to the author that long, even diameter .22 wildcat cartridges made with sharp shoulder slope forward portions, were much easier to extract and eject than sharply tapered .22 wildcat cartridges, brought up the stretching and compression of metal in the rifle action and breech block, bolt or other holding and bearing parts which, in his opinion, permitted the bolt or breech block to move back a considerable distance, comparatively, and then almost immediately drive forward on the rebound, driving the wedge-shaped, sharply tapered cartridge forcibly into the front portion of the chamber, jamming in there, and thus it was bound to be difficult to start—as extraction began. The comparatively straight and slightly tapered cartridge with a shoulder angle of 25° to 40° would presumably not drive forward any harder and, having a wide, flat faced front bearing surface, would not stick even if it were shot forward by the bolt rebound and would and did, in his opinion, then eject more easily.

An idea is one thing but proving it is another. Nothing like taking a try at mathematics and engineering.

So, *Machinery's Handbook* was hauled out—the most recent edition which the author used for a time while designing jigs to hold parts of Martin Bombers while these were being worked upon in the Bellanca Aircraft Plant. This *Machinery's Handbook* is the Bible of the mechanical engineering fraternity which has to work in steel.

Regarding the elongation of steel bars under stress, *Machinery's Handbook* says:

"When external forces act upon a material (as the steel in a rifle bolt—Author), they produce tension, compression, bending, shearing, or torsional stresses within the material. In most instances, a combination of two or more of these stresses is produced. All stresses to which a material is subjected, cause a deformation in it. If the stress is not too great, however, the material will return *to its original shape and dimensions* when the external stress is removed."

"* * * The Modulus of Elasticity of a material is the quotient obtained by dividing the stress per square inch by the elongation in 1″ caused by this stress. * * *" The Modulus of Elasticity of machine steel is 30,000,000. Now, how are we going to find the amount of stretching or compression if we are working with a breech pressure of 50,000 pounds per square inch?

$$\text{``E (or Modulus of Elasticity)} = \frac{50,000}{0.0017''} = 30,000,000.$$

"Or, e (the amount of elongation) = 50,000 ÷ 30,000,000 = 0.0017″."

Joseph Stuart, Jr., Mechanical Engineer, who has designed much of the fine, special powder-making machinery for Hercules Powder Company says he uses the same figure for both expansion and compression of steel under, of course, normal temperatures. This is the usual practice.

Upon inquiry Edwin Pugsley, who at latest reports was in charge of the large special development department of Winchester Repeating Arms Company, replied to a query on the matter as follows: "The *Machinery's Handbook* which you mention is perfectly reliable in the figure of 30,000,000 pounds square inch for the Modulus of machine steels and your calculation of 0.0017″ stretch per inch of length for a 50,000 pounds square inch pressure is essentially correct (as cartridge heads vary in area that item was not considered for the moment—Author).

"From receiver stress and measurements and elastic theory, however, we like to arrive at the bolt compression in the following manner: we estimate the maximum force on the bolt face by multiplying the gas pressure by the area of the shell or cartridge base. For the caliber .30, or .300 Savage for example, this would be about 50,000 pounds square inch times an area of 0.17 square inch which equals 8,500 lbs. Now this will be absorbed by the face of the bolt, whose area is approximately 0.37 square inch. Dividing 8,500 by this area gives us a compressive pressure of about 23,000 pounds square inch. Dividing this result into the Modulus shows a compression of about 0.0008″ for *each inch* of the bolt back to the locking lugs. As you point out, the length of the bolt to the locking lugs is only about 0.6″, so the compression there would be but 0.6 of the above amount estimated for the 1″ length—(Author's comment—this would then be 0.6 x 0.0008″ = 0.00048″ compression in the bolt to the lugs—less than five ten thousandths of an inch compression of the bolt).

"We certainly agree with you that there is very little to be found anywhere concerning the compression caused by an impacted blow. We do know that local compressions or elongations set up by impacts may be of much greater magnitude than the more slowly applied forces. The time intervals involved and the length of the stress path play a much larger role in impacted forces.

"The compression in rifle bolts has been too small to record actual amounts, but the measurements on the receiver have shown local elongations of the order of 0.001″ stretch per inch during an explosion having a gas pressure of about 50,000 pounds per square inch.

"Our experience has not included direct measurements of the effect of body taper on extraction force. Your friend brings up an interesting point which we would like to investigate directly, for we do not agree with him theoretically. When the time comes that we can convert to the study of peacetime problems, we will try to set up the proper apparatus and determine the difference in starting force."

So that is that: This suggests that to date all that can be proved is that a measurable stretch of 0.001″ elongation has been noted in receivers handling cartridges like a .22 wildcat made from a .30-1906 case necked down, such as the Ackley .228 Magnum, for instance, or the Lovell .22-30/1906, and the others will give less stretch because the cartridge heads of most of them are smaller. The .22/3000 jobs made from .25-20 cases necked down, have much smaller head face areas than the larger cases, consequently, the total pounds of pressure on the bolt face are much lower with these smaller heads. Stretching, thus would be materially less.

However, all this presumes that we are working with a rifle which is made of good material, the bolt and other parts are properly fitted, and stresses are taken and absorbed by the parts which are intended to absorb such stresses, and are given a proper factor of safety in cross section of bearing surfaces.

But when some chap with a bright idea and not much mechanical engineering knowledge or experience decides to fit a good old fashioned pot metal action made 50 to 70 years ago, with a 0.224″ barrel and insists upon having it chambered for the .220 Swift

Improved, and loads said Swift with all the No. 3031 or No. 4064 he can get in back of the bullet, it is time to enter the bomb proof and carefully close the door before it all goes bang!

It is possible to be careful and moderate in all things—or at least in some of them, but when it comes to overloading antiquated actions made two generations before high intensity wildcats became common, the suggestion is definitely, *do not!* Use a very strong action or an action made of modern alloy steel.

The writer has a friend who was hit below the right eye, about 20 months ago, by a block of wood which flew out of a lathe. He has had four operations since that time and still does not see a great deal. Suppose this had been a block of steel—like a bolt, or a part of the receiver, which had been propelled into his face by a force of 50,000 pounds per square inch? Still think you want to trade places with him? The only person who gets any real enjoyment out of these face and eye operations is the surgeon, and it is not *his* face!

Do not overload a weak action and do not overload any wildcat cartridge, because *you* are working without a pressure gun—even an extra 100 feet per second just is not worth it! Flattening the trajectory an extra 0.10″ can also flatten the whole front of your face—in which instance, *you* may never even see that cherished ballistic improvement.

Relation of Case Taper to Extraction

The general opinion among shooters, and also in most ammunition plants, seems to be that the rather sharply tapered and not-too-long cartridge extracts and ejects—and also can be inserted in the chamber and the bolt closed—to much better advantage, and with fewer jams, than the long, straight, or straight-taper cartridge with very little taper.

There are two sides to every question: Lysle Kilbourn strongly favors cartridges with little taper, for easy extraction. He commented to the author as follows:

"I have gone into the matter of case taper very carefully and feel that I have proved the following: The straighter case will extract easier than the more sharply tapered one. I had a case made up, a sample of which is being sent you for examination, which cartridge is very much like the .218 Mashburn Bee. In fact, I can shoot .218 Bee in it, as you will see from the sample. Other cases were made from the .32-20 cases.

"This case holds about the same amount of powder as the R-2

but as you will note its case slope or taper is much sharper. But it would not extract nearly as easy as the R-2. It was hard to start. After tearing loose from the chamber it comes out easily, but the start was a distinct snap due to sticking. The reason puzzled me for a time.

"Finally, I came to the conclusion that the more tapered case, on being fired, forced the bolt back and even compressed the steel, to some slight extent, and steel is likely more compressible and springy than we realize (to the theory that steel is considerably compressible at 40,000 to 60,000 pounds per square inch, the author does not agree—but we may have more about that later on; such springing is probably due much more to excessive head spacing).

"At any rate, as the case goes back until it reaches its limit, and then expands to the full size of the chamber, the pressure is relieved, the bolt or springiness of the steel—its resiliency—causes the bolt to push on the case with its enlarged base, and jams it ahead. The driving ahead of this enlarged shell head, it being solid brass, acts like driving a taper pin in a taper hole, and wedges it pretty tightly. This takes a sharp tug on the extractor to break it loose. After the first movement, of course, it comes away easily.

"To prove my theory on this, I took a perfectly good Hornet and made a reamer for it, with no taper at all. In other words, I had a K-H reamer without taper. I chambered the Hornet with this straight reamer, and the results were that no matter how heavy a load you fired, you could not make this case stick. I fired one case over and over with heavy loads, and the results were always the same. No necessity to snap to break it loose. It pulled just as easily to break loose as after it started. Of course, without any taper at all, it pulled rather snug all the way out. No matter how far back this case was jammed upon firing it could not swell out any larger, and it pushed ahead again after firing, just like a piston in a cylinder.

"So I figured that if I had a little taper, say about 0.010″ to the inch, it would be all that would be needed for easy extraction. You see, with a small amount of case taper, if the shell be pushed back a little on firing, the difference in size of chamber would not be very much, but with a sharp taper it would be considerable, at least it would be considerably more.

"Harry Jackman, of Potsdam, New York, had an R-2 that extracted very hard, but after I re-chambered it for the K-Lovell, it flipped the shells out like nothing. Reverend Raycraft, of central New York, had the same condition with a Low Wall Hornet and after I re-chambered it to K-Hornet, his trouble was over. Virgil Masters, of 119 Pleasant St. Utica, New York, has my .22 K-Magnum I mentioned. He has shot his shells over and over and never any sign of having to snap them to start them. The taper is about the same on all my cartridges, 0.080″ to 0.10″ to the inch. I feel that I can definitely prove that the lesser taper of my K-designed shells makes them easier to extract than those made with more taper."

How Powder Gases Act

It is a principle of physics that a gas exerts pressure in *all* directions equally. This means not only forward against the bullet, and back against the inside of the head of the case, thus against the face of the breech block, but outward against the side walls of the cartridge and thus indirectly against the walls of the rifle chamber. Cartridge cases which are drilled to be tested for chamber pressure developed in a rifle are drilled close to the shoulder, and those not drilled have the gage hole blown over that point, and the pressure upward against the lead or copper crusher is the same as against the base of the bullet, against the breech block, and against the sides of the cartridge. Whether a gas will rise or fall, in air, depends upon its specific gravity, as compared with that of air. But powder gases, ignited and working under pressure, move very quickly. It is true that the bullet, or that portion of it in the cartridge, is longer than the distance from outside of case head to set-back end of bolt travel, and the case may move back against the breech block before the bullet gets completely out of the case and up through the throat. But a closely head spaced rifle will not let a cartridge move back very far.

Rifles which are very loosely head spaced will of course permit greater cartridge movement to the rear, upon firing, and the cartridge would then rebound and drive forward into the chamber. But we are supposing here that the rifle chamber is in perfect condition, slightly oiled, very highly polished, perfectly round, and that it contains no unburned powder grains or residue between case and chamber wall. As a matter of fact, not all of these conditions are present in the firing of many rifles. The chamber is dry, and in many cases it is scarred or it contains both depressed and raised rust spots. It is probably also hot if firing is going on. The rifle has been shot and has not been cleaned. Residue occasionally works back into the chamber and stays there. That cartridge is being fired in a chamber in *anything* but perfect condition. In such case, the author believes that considerable case body taper is helpful, provided the head spacing is not abnormal in amount of play allowed for the cartridge case to drive back and forth.

We all know that the use of Mobilubricant used in considerable amount in .30-1906 and .30-40 rifles, mostly the former, was unquestionably responsible for most burst Springfields and most broken and cracked Krag bolts. The author has seen numbers of both, also split Krag bolt heads.

He knows of not a single instance in which a .30-1906 Springfield rifle was blown up which was shot dry, and which was not blown

Jerry Gebby giving a preliminary checking of head space with several cartridges before barrel is removed from lathe after chambering operation.

up by an overload or on purpose. In a dry chamber the cartridge case grips the chamber walls, if those walls are not smooth and highly polished it grips them very hard, and there is then no reason to assume the cartridge would start easily or pull readily if the cartridge be very straight taper, or if it be considerably tapered. It would, in any case, tend to adhere to the rough chamber because the raised rusting would indent into the cartridge case, or burrs or scratches in the chamber may tend to be engraved in the cartridge. The author has seen plenty of fired cases in which an unburnt powder grain was indented into the outer surface of the cartridge, showing it has been imprisoned between cartridge and chamber.

When rifles· are made for rifle cranks, we have one favorable condition—(although all the ballyhoo about non-corrosive priming has made many rifle cranks less careful of rifle cleaning than they used to be) and when a rifle is made and used by a shooter who is *not* a rifle crank, and who does not regularly clean, and/or oil his rifle barrel and chamber, the cartridge used has to operate smoothly, or else stick, in a condition which the rifle crank seldom if ever presents to a cartridge—that of much rust and a dry chamber wall.

There is another condition to consider. Neither slide action, hand-operated rifles, nor lever action, tubular magazine repeating commercial rifles exert the extractor pull that is developed by a closely head spaced powerfully cammed bolt action rifle like the Mauser of good grade—or the Springfield, the 1917 Enfield, the 720 Remington, or the 54 or 70 Winchesters.

Commercial cartridges must be designed to operate under any conceivable condition in the field. This often precludes the use of too-straight cases, at high pressures, with excessively sharp shoulders, because that obviously puts more strain in the brass, which has been swaged down, and there would then be greater likelihood of a cartridge case bursting at the neck, at the shoulder, or along the side near the shoulder, or even for the neck and shoulder to tear off. Such condition would almost certainly occur only in a rifle with excessive head space. Or, one excessively head spaced and also chambered too large in diameter, or having had the chamber cut too deep at the shoulder.

Most military rifles are fitted with cartridges having considerable taper, especially at the front end. Other shapes of cartridges would be much more liable to jam in the magazine in hurriedly loading by clip. Mr. Kilbourn would only have to get out on a 200-yard firing line, with many men shooting, most of them reasonably nervous, and all of them trying to get off all 10 shots, (two clips full) in the allotted time limit. He would be surprised how many different things can make a cartridge fall out of the clip, get jammed in the top of the magazine and especially when being inserted in the well of the chamber, and also how many things can distract a man from drilling 10 V's into that bullseye.

Most of Mr. Kilbourn's work is with single shot Winchester

Hi-Wall and similar rifles, and with Model 54's and 70's, and with a class of shooters much above the average found in common everyday commercial hunting fields or military commands—places in which quite often less than 5%—in fact, less than 3%—could actually be truthfully called "riflemen."

However, it is an intensely interesting discussion. One thing should be noted—modern smokeless powders designed for rather sharply bottlenecked cases, most of them .30 caliber, are not equally adapted to long, very little tapered, very small cartridges, like the .22 wildcats of *that* type. One reason why these straight cases of .22 caliber started to extract easily was likely because the pressures developed in cartridges of this type, are *lower* than normal unless raised by an excessively sharp shoulder. Also, such sharp shoulder makes the front end of each cartridge have a blunt bearing against the forward chamber walls. One thing we do know from the action of water in nozzles of different shape, that a very blunted front shoulder wall will cause the powder gases to churn around and be raised in pressure materially, and be retained longer in the cartridge case.

A short, fat cartridge case will develop higher pressures, most times, than a long straight case holding the same amount of powder. The primer ignites the powder quicker in the short case. There is lacking the long, usually *cold* or cool column of air, or powder grains, or air and grains found in the longer case. The powder grains heat up all through in a shorter interval of time, and should be expected to burn faster after the powder is ignited in a bottle-shaped cartridge than if ignited in a tube-shaped cartridge. The author would expect more prompt and *uniform* ignition in a cartridge case which is not too long or too straight.

If a rifle be chambered so closely the cartridge case adheres to the chamber walls in a *push fit* he would expect trouble in extraction if the wall became the least bit rusted, especially if the case be straight, or both straight and long. If it were still more tightly chambered, so that expanded shells could only be forced home in what amounted to a drive fit, unless first resized full length and in a fairly small size resizer, he would expect some instances of the extractor pulling over the head of the case. How often this used to happen in the old days, with .22 rim fires, in rifles with badly corroded or rusted chambers, and not too carefully fitted extractors.

As long as a cartridge fits a chamber reasonably close, is head spaced tightly, and this head spacing is not permitted to enlarge materially, and the cartridge also has a real sharp shoulder slope, of 25° to 40°, he would not expect it to wedge into the chamber so as to be difficult to extract, because the sharp shoulder would prevent such wedging unless the chamber be cut so deeply ahead of the case at that point, as to fail to provide a bearing surface. This presupposes the bullet is not loaded so far out of the case as to cause the lands to touch or bite into it, causing high pressures and often blown primers, as cautioned by Hervey Lovell in the instance of loading the .22/3000 Lovell or R-2 types of cartridges. Much cartridge case sticking with many calibers is caused by that type of loading.

The author sees very little chance for back and forth movement of a cartridge in a close fitting chamber, regardless of the case taper, if it is head spaced closely. We shall see what others have to say on this question.

The long straight case is not a cure-all, neither is the idea new. Nearly all the old Sharps, Ballard, Winchester single shot, and Ballard & Marlin cases, and most of the Stevens single shot rifle cases, were excessively long and straight, so as to hold much black powder. When smokeless powders came along, those like Schuetzen were so hygroscopic they absorbed moisture readily, and daily variations in center of impact were large, comparatively; ignition was often not too good, especially with other than full charges; powders made for bottleneck cartridges, such types as No. 75 and No. 80 did not do well in these long straight cases; and only the fast, double base, easily ignited powders like Sharpshooter did do well in those cartridges in those early days of smokeless.

Of the recent I.M.R. military powders, No. 4227 is the only one primarily made for small capacity cartridges; No. 4198 was made for medium capacity cartridges and for short range loads; No. 3031 for medium size sporting and military cartridges, and for mid-range loads; No. 4320 was produced for large capacity sporting and military cartridges; and No. 4064, for Magnum capacity cartridges. You can verify this for yourself, by consulting Page 5, of *Better Loads for Better Shooting* put out by du Pont in August, 1936.

That many of the .22 wildcats shoot splendidly with such larger powders can be put down to the restrictive action of a sharp shoulder case which causes the powder gases to whirl and be retained longer and undergo just about the same action as water shot with force into a hose nozzle having a very abrupt front wall and a small hole of exit. Or, if shot into a bottle with a hole in the bottom for its entrance, and a close, abrupt neck and only a small orifice for the cork. That water will swirl around in there and you can prove this for yourself any time you may feel like it.

It should be remembered that in the United States the center fire sporting cartridges which have the largest sale are those such as the .30-30, .32 Special, .30 Remington Rimless, .30-1906, .250/3000 Savage, and that compared with these most all .25 and .22 caliber center fire cartridges have a small sale in comparison. The .25-35 rifle, for instance, is hardly 1, 2, 3, in sales, compared with the .30-30; neither is the .257 Roberts. The .25-20 repeater had a good sale for years, and the .22 Hornet has a good sale, but the volume of powder sales, for other than .22 Long Rifle and .22 Shorts, is mostly in the larger cartridges, consequently the powders were designed *primarily* for their use.

As a matter of fact, the really extraordinary accuracy of the various .22 wildcats must have surprised a lot of commercial people. It may astonish many riflemen to know that the ordinary .30-30 cartridge was not such a hot number in the matter of accuracy in lever action rifles (nor is the .30 Remington in slide actions) but the same .30-30 in the Model 54 Winchester, for which it was also made, shot *very* accurately at 100 yards in the bolt action; the recoil was moderate, in fact low, in that rifle; the muzzle blast was soft, and the rifle was easy to clean, compared with a .30-1906. But the public would *not* buy the Model 54 in .30/30 caliber.

Today, we can credit the development of .22 varmint rifles almost entirely to developments by private rifle experimenters, private gunsmiths, and to the happy accident that recent sporting brand, commercial size powders just happened to shoot like a house afire in them, when they had enough confinement caused by sharp shoulders in the front end of medium size and small size cases which had been cut off and necked down, or necked down and blown up to chamber size.

A few of these cartridges will take a wide variety of powders and charges while others will have to be suited by an individual charge for the individual rifle. Those with small heads deliver small total pressure on the bolt head. Those with heads of the size of the .22 H.P., 219 Zipper, .25 Remington and .30 Remington and larger will deliver considerably more total pressure on the bolt face.

But the chamber pressure in pounds per square inch is likely to be fairly high in nearly all of them if the shoulder is sharp and the load is a maximum load or close to it. So, when working up your charge, go easy, and begin with *less* powder than the recommended full charge for another rifle of the same named caliber, until you find out how things seem to be working in the rifle you own and are experimenting with, when using the primer and case at hand. Remember, cartridge cases of different makes often have different powder capacity, even though marked as the same caliber on the head of the cartridge. Primers fit *tighter* in some cases than in others. If your cartridge cases have not been resized the full length, they will then have a slightly greater capacity than if full length resizing has been done. In the latter case, keep down your powder charge a few tenths of a grain.

All through the .22 wildcat and loads portion of this book you will see, now and then, such differences mentioned. Pay attention to it for such remarks are put there for your protection. Always remember too, that because some cartridge is called the .22 Mama Wildcat *improved,* it does not mean that you should throw all cautions out of the window, and give old Mom a powder charge that will really make her howl! It is your good right eye which will be behind that primer when it fires! Be satisfied with just a trifle less than Mom Wildcat's full capacity. The accuracy will turn out to be very much better, invariably.

Hard Extraction of Cases

J. George Schnerring made these comments in a recent letter to the author: "Hard extraction of fired cases may be due to several factors. In the Springfield rifle and ammunition, we found that the hardest cases gave the easiest extraction. A soft case will give hard extraction in the Springfield chamber, U. S. Standard limits.

"In the Commercial chamber, one may not have the same dimensions. According to my experience the tapered case should extract more easily than a straight case or one with less taper than the standards used.

"The theory that a tapered case will cause the action to rebound after the pressure is reduced is probably true in a lever action rifle but does not apply to bolt actions. I had the same trouble, that you speak of, in a Sedgley Hornet barrel. I think he chambered the Hornet too tightly. Also, that the Hornet cases were too soft as I found many that had oversize primer pockets after firing the 2,600 f.s. loads.

"The cases like the .25-35 cases (from which the .22 Savage Hi-Power case was first made), are all strong cases. We weaken cartridge cases about 20% of their strength by cutting away the brass to make the extractor cannelure in a rimless cartridge.

"If gasoline and tires ever get plentiful I will drive up to Wayne

County for several days of woodchuck hunting. I often think of the many good times Dr. Given and I had up there. On a chuck hunt last year, using the .250/3000 Model 70 standard barrel Winchester, and 35.0 grains of duPont No. 4320 and the 100-grain Western bullets, I had nine shots and picked up eight chucks. Nearly all were at 100 to 225 yards. This rifle and ammunition, like my .25-35, shoots 1″ groups at 100 yards and holds its zero day after day. In the .25-35 I use 32.0 grains of 4320 and the same 100-grain Western O.P. bullet."

The author's experiences with sticking cartridges are the same as those of George Schnerring, with whom he has spent many a pleasant day.

DIMENSIONS OF CARTRIDGES FROM WHICH .22 WILDCAT CASES ARE USUALLY FORMED

Caliber	Head or Rim Diam.	Diam. Under Head	Diam. at Shoulder	Shoulder Slope Factory case
.250/3000	0.473″		0.4137″	26° 30′
.22 Hornet	0.350″		0.278″	5° 38′
.218 Bee	0.408″		0.3334″	15° 0′
.219 Zipper	0.506″		0.3649″	12° 0′
22 Sav. H.P. ...	0.506″		0.369″	14° 0′
.220 Swift	0.473″		0.402″	21° 0′
.25 Remington .	0.422″		0.4019″	23° 0′
.25/35 W.C.F. ..	0.506″		0.3715″	11° 34′
.30 Remington .	0.422″		0.4019″	23° 0′
.30 -1906	0.473″		0.441″	34° 32′
7mm Mauser ...	0.473″		0.431″	20° 45′
.257 Roberts	0.473″	0.4711″		20° 45′
.348 Winchester .	0.610″	0.5530″		19° 10′
.25/20 W.S.S. ...	0.380″	0.3186″		
.25/20 W.C.F. ..	0.408″	0.3492″		16° 34′
.32/20 W.C.F. ..	0.408″	0.3535″		5° 42′
.30/40 Krag	0.545″	0.4573″		21° 6′
.303 British	0.533″	0.4545″		14° 36′

This data, while incomplete, shows the very wide variation in shoulder slopes in different factory cartridges, giving rise to the thought that possibly not quite as much careful scientific calculation has been made in the design of factory cartridges as some have been led to believe. That, or there have been as many different ideas among ballisticians as there are among members of the UNRRA.

The first table will show the head sizes which will give a variety of measurements which will disclose, more or less at a glance, a cartridge that will fit your rifle action and bolt head and extractor.

We are indebted to Merton Robinson, Ballistic Engineer of Winchester Repeating Arms Company of Olin Industries, for this information taken from factory blue prints or specifications.

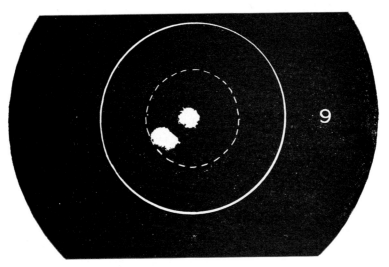

WHO SAYS—THE HORNET WON'T HOLD ITS ZERO?

Despite the loud wails of a few who claim the .22 Hornet won't hold its zero, the author was present when his son, C. S. Landis, Jr., shot this group at 50 yards, March 25, 1939, as his FIRST group at 50 yards, when sight checking for our first woodchuck hunt of 1939. Range was 50 yards, rifle was Savage .22 Hornet Sporter fitted with Marlin 4 power scope, in Marlin mounts. Hand loaded ammunition containing 10.5 grs. No. 1204 and 45-gr. bullets.

Rifle had not been fired for several weeks previously. Two chucks were shot at, and both killed instantly, with one shot each. This 5-shot group measures less than ⅜″ in diam. center to center, and first two shots were pin-wheels.

CHAPTER 15

THE SELECTION OF WILDCAT ACTIONS

THIS is a subject of extreme importance to riflemen, both in the matter of convenience and also in the matter of safety. The rifle selected for alteration must be of a type which is, or can logically be converted, so that it is safe and practical when used with the more powerful cartridge for which it is to be adapted.

The actions most commonly used for making up with .22 rim fire target barrels and heavier sporting barrels are the following:

Ballard

Winchester 52—with new and old actions, speed action and slow type, rounded top and with flat top receiver.

Remington Model 37—best with Miracle Trigger.

Winchester Single Shot

Stevens 44½ Single Shot

Actions for .22 Commercial and .22 Wildcat center fire rifles:

Mauser Bolt Action

1917 U. S. Enfield

Enfield actions used on 30-S and 720 Remingtons

Model 70 Winchester

Model 54 Winchester

1903 Model U. S. Springfield—with nickel steel receiver and nickel steel bolt; and with older receivers, either as originally made or with heat-treated receiver, or with nickel steel bolt fitted in old time and low number receiver.

Krag-Jorgensen, as the 30/40 U. S. in models 1892, 1896 and 1898 is commonly known.

Single shot actions for possible use for .22 Wildcats:

Farquharson—British made action, supplied by Holland and Holland, Westley-Richards, Gibbs and other firms.

Haemmerli—an action often used by Swiss for International Free Rifles, including the .30-1906 ctg.

B. S. A. Center Fire Martini sporting and military action.

B. S. A.—Martini for .22 rim fire only. Not to be used for center fire wildcats.

Sharps-Borchardt hammerless action

Winchester Single Shot—made in a number of different styles in past years, including the following:

Thick or heavy wall High-Side-blued

Thin wall High-Side-blued

High-Side heavy action, case hardened

Winchester Winder Musket action

Low-side, light S. S. action for No. 1 barrel

Stevens 44½ actions, including those made on 45, 47, 49, 51, 52, 54, and 56 rifles. Also 44½ and 044½ Models.

Remington-Hepburn No. 3—a single shot of heavy construction made about 1890 by Remington Arms Co.

Remington-Rider action—not as strong as the Hepburn but was used in some quantity, for South American trade mostly in 7mm caliber. Simple and convenient but not sufficiently strong for most fast wildcats.

The following comment is by the author, from personal experience and his reactions to the suitability and appearance of above actions, and also from comment by other riflemen to him. Futher along in this chapter we will have separate comment by a number of well known riflemen and custom gunsmiths, upon their preferences as to actions for different cartridges and the relative strength and desirability of each action.

Some of this comment may conflict, due to different opinions and the variation in experience of different men. A small amount of it may be duplicated in other portions of the author's books on the .22 rifle and its use, but this is unavoidable because the relative strength and suitability of different actions is a subject which touches almost every phase of small game and varmint shooting.

The reader will do well to study this chapter very carefully, as it has been prepared after exhaustive research and study by riflemen, and after many months of correspondence.

For rim fire rifles, particularly for .22 Long Rifle match rifles and with match ammunition, or standard velocity ammunition, and for hunting rifles using such ammunition, the speed action Model 52 Winchester in a weight suitable for the barrel you will use—

standard barrel or heavy barrel, and with either Winchester speed action or the Hart speed action is probably No. 1 in the author's opinion.

Equally good, or almost so, is the Model 37 Remington with Miracle trigger. This action feeds the cartridge directly into the chamber in practically a straight line. It is a heavy, positive action.

Ballard is the choice of many of the custom gunsmiths for a .22 single shot match rifle. The split breech block makes it *entirely unsuitable* for most .22 wildcats. The rocking motion seating the cartridge upward and forward, in the more desirable Ballards, is a movement which gives very accurate seating of the bullet in line with the bore, and results in good groups and consistent accuracy and no buckled cartridges.

Stevens 44½ action gives splendid accuracy. Upward and forward action of the breech block in seating the cartridge and locking home on the head of it gives uniform accuracy. The Stevens frame is

A PAIR OF .22 HORNET RIFLES OWNED BY THE AUTHOR

Top is a super-accurate Model 54 Winchester, fitted with Malcolm scope in Mann-type Malcolm mounts.

The lower rifle is a Hi-Side Winchester single shot Sedgley .22 Hornet fitted with 52 Winchester barrel chambered for Hornet cartridge. Scope is a 5-A Winchester on Pope rib.

The top rifle is the most deadly rifle, on the first shot fired, the author has ever owned.

made of poor grade metal and will show wear of pins in frame after long use. When well made and well finished it is, in the author's opinion, the handsomest of the .22 single shots for a .22 Long Rifle caliber match or sporting arm. The stocking on the old Stevens Schuetzen rifles was superbly done.

Winchester single shots do not give quite the accuracy with .22 Long Rifle cartridges as do Ballard or Stevens 44½ actions. Breech block is strong, but comes up too straight, tending to buckle cartridge or make a bend or distortion in case in seating cartridge in chamber. Action should move up-and-forward more. When bushed, it is a very strong action, one of the best. In calibers like .22/3000 Lovell and R-2, it is often superbly accurate when fitted with heavy barrel. That with center fire firing pin and breech block; same should always be bushed. Winchester Winder musket appears to be a rather soft action, or rather the frame is soft and, to the author, never appeared equal in quality to regular Winchester S. S. actions of sporting and target grades.

There must be tens of thousands of these actions in the hands of shooters. The author has fired a goodly number of these various rifles in .22 Long Rifle caliber; they all shot fairly well, they all wore well, but none of them which he has shot, grouped like a 44½ Stevens or a Ballard, and very definitely not like a 52 Speed action.

Actions for Center Fire .22 Wildcats—Mauser Actions

The Mausers which come through well made, early World War I Mausers, Sauer-Mausers, the author regards as about the strongest of the bolt actions and the safest, when worked over properly, for .22 wildcats, especially those giving more than 3,500 f.s. muzzle velocity to 45 to 55-grain bullets. The trigger pull is usually not equal to that on a National Match Springfield action. Not equal, as a rule to the best of the Model 70 and 54 Winchesters in smoothness of pull; can be fitted with double set-triggers to advantage, but then has very heavy pull when unset. Note P. O. Ackley comment further along in this chapter, and also about blowing up different styles of action.

The Mauser action, when properly stocked, and used with a good American bored .22 wildcat barrel is superbly accurate. Its shooting has no relation whatever to German bored war barrels of 7.9mm caliber when used with American ammunition which does not fit them; which same barrels often shoot very well with German ammunition which does fit.

1917 U. S. Enfield

The 1917 U. S. Enfield is second in strength to the Mauser. Its principal claim to fame is that a telescope sight can be mounted very close down to the receiver. This, obviously, is an advantage, especially when hunting through brush. Of these rifles made during World War I those Winchester made were the best finished, as a rule, especially as to blueing; those by Remington were next; and the others usually were a poor third.

This rifle has a stock which fits only very large, long armed men —the rifle should be re-stocked to fit the shooter; the trigger pull usually has a good deal of preliminary slack and takeup, and often feels as if it has a double pull as well. The rifle cocks on the closing stroke of the bolt instead of on the opening movement like the Springfield, and this should be reversed, which it readily can be.

It makes a good rifle for the more powerful long range, woodchuck and coyote cartridges if you can get the trigger pull under control. Its principal disadvantage is a tendency to unevenness of trigger pull. You press the trigger until the rifle almost fires; then it sticks a moment, then it moves again and just about the time you wonder why it has not fired it does so most unexpectedly. If that does not upset you, and you can stand the looks of the 1917 action, you will like it very much. If both bother you, as they do the author plus the cocking on the closing movement of the bolt, you will prefer a Springfield, or a Mauser, or a Model 70.

A man has to be a very liberal minded chap to consider the Enfield a handsome rifle.

The Models 720 and 30-S Remington Actions

Remington had plenty of 1917 actions in various stages of dress and undress left over from World War I, so the Model 30 rifle appeared for high power sporting cartridges. It had various small variations in design or stocking, the 30-S being the most popular. The author had one of these for years in .257 Roberts caliber and it was a very fine shooting rifle. However, the trigger pull was rather uncertain, and its appearance was against it with those who do not like the looks of the 1917.

Then the 720 Remington came along, which is materially better looking and the stocking job is much superior. Essentially it is the 1917 with some variations mechanically and in appearance. Of the Enfields, this is the best one and the finest looking job. Pick it, if possible, if you want to have a .22 varmint rifle on that action.

The 54 Winchester

This was the first of the two bolt action Winchesters to take modern cartridges. The author has this action in both .22 Hornet and .220 Swift. He has never had any trouble with the .220 Swift showing excessive pressures or leaking gas, either out through the gas port in the right side of the bolt, forward, or back through the bolt or receiver and down through the magazine. The .220 Swift cartridge is probably the most difficult one to hand load, successfully, of any on the market. Particularly is it liable to give trouble in the hands of those having had no previous reloading experience with high intensity ammunition. The shoulder is so gradual that when extreme loads are used, or even full charge normal loads, the cartridge case lengthens and then, after two or three shots, there is trouble. The case then needs trimming off at the front end.

For this and other reasons, probably because they thought of a better design all-around, Winchester put out the Model 70 which costs between $2.50 and $3.00 more than the 54. It probably is not worth any more, except for cartridges like the .220 Swift, but it is somewhat more pleasing in outline, especially of the forend and, because the gas port was made larger and will handle more gas without permitting a breech rupture, it is safer. It also, in theory, has a better trigger pull than the 54 and a much worse safety. In actual fact, both of my 54's have a slightly better trigger pull than my Model 70.

For cartridges like the .22 Hornet, K-Hornet, .22/3000, .219 Zipper-Improved, and the like, the 54 is just about as good as the 70. For cartridges from the .22 Varminter on up the 70 is better, but unless you want to crowd the roof all the time on pressures with super-loads, probably unnecessary. It is a well-made, good strong action; be satisfied if you have one.

The Model 70 Winchester

The Model 70 is the most modern and best Winchester action for modern high-intensity .22 varmint or high velocity, high pressure, .22 commercial cartridges. It is a bolt action, about 10% stronger in the bolt fastening than the Springfield, according to a statement once made to the author by a ballistic expert of Winchester. I know of none which has blown up.

This is a fine action for the .220 Arrow, the .22/4000 Sedgley-Schnerring and for any of the smaller .22 wildcats. It has a good, smooth trigger pull, cocks on the opening movement like the Springfield, the trigger pull can be changed if desired, but the safety is in the way of low mounting of scope sight. There are a dozen or more different types of safety made for the Model 70, all of which seem to work, but some of which are unmarked so that you cannot tell whether the safety is on or off unless you happen to

recall for instance, whether moving the safety to the left puts it
"on," or puts it "off." Others are properly marked.

The .30-1906 Springfield

It is best to get a "high number" National Match Springfield
action—over 1,257,767 for Springfield Armory or 285,587 for Rock
Island Armory—nickel steel bolt, if at all possible. Saves worry,
and you have the satisfaction of knowing that then you have the
latest and best Springfield. See P. O. Ackley's comments farther
on in this chapter, for reasons.

The late, high number National Match grade Springfields, with
star-gaged barrel are made with bright bolt and bright bolt handle.
Those with blued or other dark finished bolts are usually service
grade action, which is generally not as smooth and the trigger pull
is seldom as good.

The Springfield Model 1903 is a rifle with a very long action
when used for a short length .22 varmint cartridge and this fault
will occur to you after you have the rifle for a time. Also, the
Springfield is a good deal harder to clean in .22 caliber, especially
with a .22 cartridge which is long and rather thin or straight-sided,
because patches persist in slipping off the tip of the rod as it enters
the chamber. The wood of the stock will generally, these days, be
very, very ordinary, open pored, and not fitted to the action any
too closely.

To anyone who "grew up" on a .30-1906 Springfield, there is
no substitute for the National Match Springfield and excessive
ballyhoo about some other rifle or action merely makes such a rifleman angry. The rifle shoots and it is a shooting piece with any
good .22 varmint cartridge suited to this action. What few Springfield actions the author ever saw blown up were fractured by
shooting service loads with Mobilubricant grease on the bullet. Do
not use it and you will avoid this danger.

The Farquharson Action

The quality rifle makers of England produce the Farquharson
rifle action. These include Holland and Holland, who in the author's
opinion turn out the best looking and the best designed shotguns
and rifles made in England; Westley-Richards, another very fine
firm of rifle makers; and Gibbs, the third British firm making the
Farquharson, is also a quality concern.

The Farquharson is an extremely strong action. It is of hammerless type without any open channel in back of the firing pin, and

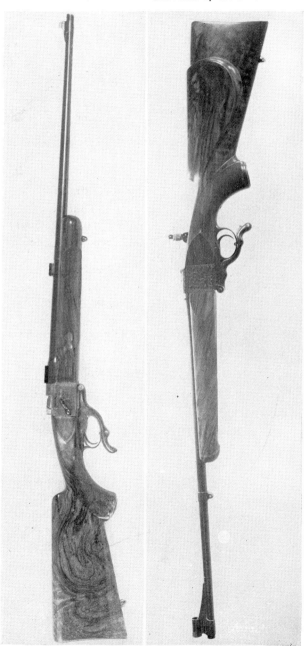

ABOVE: GIBBS-FARQUHARSON-NIEDNER .22 MAGNUM

This is what can be done with one of the very fine English Gibbs-Farquharson actions—singleshot, drop lever type, with Niedner barrel in .22 Niedner Magnum Wildcat caliber. Shelhamer-Niedner stock. Special curly walnut stock and extra fine engraving.

WESTLEY RICHARDS-FARQUHARSON-NIEDNER R-2 LOVELL

Below: Left side view of fancy singleshot sporting rifle made up by Niedner Rifle Corp. from Westley Richards-Farquharson singleshot action, and Niedner barrel in R-2 Lovell caliber. Shelhamer-Niedner stock, with cheek piece. Stock is along lines of British sporting stock such as put out by Westley Richards, but of Niedner workmanship and design. Special ramp front sight and British peep which looks like Parker-Hale sporting type. Sling swivels to take sporting sling.

it is also without cracks or interstices through which gas could escape back into the shooter's face. Some claim this action is somewhat better and safer than the best Hi-Side Winchester or the Sharps-Borchardt action. Its shape and underlever may appear peculiar to some who are accustomed to more prosaic American actions. It is what is called a falling-block action. The breech block drops downward when the action is opened. It is made of most excellent material and splendidly finished. None of the firms that produce it make other than quality firearms which are handsomely finished.

Niedner Rifle Corporation, of Dowagiac, Michigan, has made up quite a number of special rifles using the Farquharson action. Most of these have been for commercial cartridges. Shelhamer has stocked quite a number of such rifles. It is not a cheap action, but then your good right eye is not refillable or replaceable, being a one-time proposition.

The Farquharson, like all the single shot actions, works best with rimmed cartridges. The Farquharson has better extraction than the Winchester S. S., and quicker lock time, unless the Winchester has been worked over and the hammer-fall shortened.

The ability of gunsmiths or individuals to obtain Farquharson actions from England will depend upon a number of things; the willingness of the manufacturers to sell only the action, and their rapidity of complete reconversion. Having the price can also be an item with some of us.

The Haemmerli Action

This is an action used considerably for Free Rifle matches by the Swiss and other European nationals and has been introduced into this country in very limited numbers by some members of U. S. International Free Rifle Teams who have gone abroad. Hartmann and others have rebarrelled this action for the .30-1906 and similar cartridges and it seems amply rugged and strong for the .22 wildcats.

In general exterior appearance and lines it slightly resembles the large Martini action, but is probably stronger than the center fire, full size Martini.

It is possible that American soldiers may bring home or ship home a few of these actions from Europe but the numbers available here will probably be too small to be an important feature in the .22 wildcat production market.

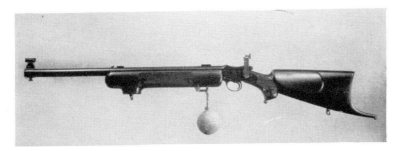

A very finely made Martini action single shot rifle, with custom stock. This rifle was designed for offhand shooting, but is so splendidly stocked that this model, fitted with a much smaller forend and hunting sights, would make a very fine varmint rifle. The stock dimensions are for use with a very high sight line, even the scope sets up high on this one.

A heavy, rigidly constructed single shot rifle, using Martini, Farquharson, Winchester Hi-Side, Stevens 44½, or Ballard action, or the Sharps-Borchardt, which is less handsome, can be custom built, using these stock lines and a hunting forend, and make a very deadly .22 wildcat rifle, of any one of many .22 center fire calibers of moderate power, and turn out to be a remarkably fine shooting rifle for firing out of a car, or for still hunting where long range, deliberate shots, and not too much walking are the rule.

The B. S. A. Martini Actions

The models 12 and 15 B. S. A. Martinis have, in a few instances, been used to action rifles for the .22 Hornet cartridge, but they are not suggested for that use.

The larger receiver center fire type Martini action, used in England and Canada for military cartridges, including the .30-1906 and the .303 British, would obviously handle small and medium .22 wildcats, preferably in rimmed style. But those using a Martini action should have a large hand and very long fingers, because anyone with a short, pudgy hand with short fingers will not find the action comfortable to shoot, as the "reach" is too long from grip to trigger. To run the pistol grip sufficiently far forward on the underside of the tang will look unsightly. It appears to be more in the class of a "usable" action than a desirable one.

The Sharps-Borchardt Action

This action was designed and made in this country but has been off the market for many years. It has been rumored repeatedly, of late, that it would again be manufactured or that a very similar action would be made by a firm in Huntington, West Virginia, and if it is so put out, will be in an improved form for modern wildcat ammunition.

There seems to be some difference of opinion as to the relative desirability of the Sharps-Borchardt action. It appears to be at least as strong, or possibly even more rigid than the Hi-Wall blued Winchester S. S. action. Fred Ness is quoted as saying he believed it would hold the .220 Swift or the .22 Varminter but whether it would extract them properly in all cases is another matter which he mentioned. The drawback of most of the stronger single shot, drop lever actions is lack of extracting ability.

There appears to be little or no likelihood of gas spurts back into the eyes with this type action, if properly made with bushed firing pin. But it has no firing pin retractor. Consequently, it is often only a question of time until someone very carefully snaps on an empty chamber and breaks off the firing pin point upon opening the action. This of course can be remedied if the custom gunsmith knows how, and the customer is willing to pay to have the work done. Trigger pull is rather poor on the average one picked up, but can be improved, but the author has heard of no especially good smooth pulls claimed for this action.

One method of keeping the Sharps-Borchardt working was recounted by Fred Ness in his "Dope Bag," who recounted the comment of O. A. Wagner whose method follows:

"Unless your Sharps-Borchardt has already been revamped by a good gunsmith, including the installation of a firing pin retractor, Wagner suggests drilling a No. 39 hole through the top of the breech block about 23/64" back from the face. Then he also made up a piece of drill rod for a firing pin pry, and placed a chisel point on a piece of No. 45 drill rod, made a hole or a loop in the other end and this can be fastened to your key ring. Then, you will always have the pry with you. It is useless of course, if you leave it at home, and then get hung up with a sealed rifle in the field.

"Before making such pry rod, Wagner had to occasionally take down the Sharps-Borchardt to remove a primer-stuck firing pin. The best way to do this is to drive out the trigger-pin in the rear of the breech block and remove the mainspring plug, keeping it under control with the thumb. Hook out the spring. Force back stuck firing pin with chain-nose plyers to permit opening action. Remove breech block before reassembling spring and plug it in for greater convenience. Reassemble block and trigger in rifle."

In *Sports Afield,* for October 1945, Col. Townsend Whelen, well-known arms writer and rifleman, commented upon various features of the Sharps-Borchardt action for use as the basis of a medium power .22 varmint or wildcat rifle as follows: "The most accurate pair of R-2 rifles known to me are built on Sharps-Borchardt actions and both have averaged about 0.90" groups at 100 yards, and only slightly over 2" at 200 yards, this for 5-shot groups.

"Having an old Sharps-Borchardt action in good condition, I thought I would see if I could obtain an equally accurate rifle. George Hyde fitted a 27" barrel of Remington make to it, the groove diameter being 0.2235" and the twist 1 turn in 15". He also fitted a new firing pin, altered the action to retract the firing pin at the first downward movement of the lever, and extended and shaped the lever to follow the curve of the pistol grip. My friend William L. Humphrey made a stock of such elegant lines and figure that I have never cared to "disfigure" it with checkering.

"I have thus far tested this rifle quite thoroughly with two powder charges: 17.0 grains of duPont No. 4198 and 15.4 grains of duPont No. 4227 powder, the 47-grain 8S bullet being used in both loads. The two charges appear to be equally accurate, although the 4198 powder probably gives slightly higher velocity. With the 4227 load, 10 consecutive 10-shot groups fired from bench rest at 100 yards with 8-power scope averaged 1.08" extreme spread. This is at least as good as a 0.90" average for 5-shot groups. This is the most accurate rifle I have ever owned.

"Although a well tuned-up Sharps-Borchardt action appears to contribute to superfine accuracy, I am not prepared to say that it is superior to a first class bolt action with an equally good barrel and stock. In fact in one way I find that the Sharps-Borchardt action is rather inconvenient. When you push the loaded cartridge fully home into the chamber, and then reach for the finger lever to close the action, before you can do so the weight of the lever has caused the extractor to pull the cartridge slightly out of the chamber so that the breech block cannot rise. Thus two hands often are necessary to load, one to push the cartridge home and hold it there while the other closes the lever. All this is rather inconvenient, particularly when the tube of the telescope sight, extending low over the breech, keeps you from getting your fingers handily into the breech."

Frankly, I do not want that sort of action on a hunting rifle. Further, I have always regarded the Sharps-Borchardt as being an unusually homely rifle action and it makes up in a firearm that, to me, does not look like a rifle. It is strong, safe, rigid, and gives great accuracy with cartridges of the energy and light recoil of the .22/3000 and R-2. Many have been used for these calibers and for the K-Hornet. Certain other riflemen regard this as a handsome action. Tastes differ. That it stocks easily, quickly, and rigidly, is a help in maintaining accuracy.

The author is a hunter who likes to spend part of the time in the field and woods, when there is no game in sight and little in immediate prospect, in resting and admiring the rifle and scenery. I want that rifle to look like a rifle to me. The fancy Stevens Ideals, the Hi-Side Winchester single shot, the Springfield sporter and the 52 Winchester custom sporters, all look like rifles to me. I enjoy simply handling them and looking them over in the woods, between squirrel shooting chances. But if I have to sit there and try to admire a Sharps-Borchardt or an Enfield action, I would just as soon stay home.

Maybe a homely rifle action does not affect you that way, and possibly you do not regard the Sharps-Borchardt action as being homely, in which instance you are lucky, but there are a few actions which do annoy me by their lines. If a person is allergic to the sight of any rifle or rifle action, it is better to get rid of it than to use that action simply because it is strong, or will handle a certain cartridge without letting go. There are other strong actions which you may prefer to sit and admire. Very definitely I do!

The Winchester Single Shot Lever Actions

This is regarded as one rifle by the public but actually it is a collection of quite a number of rifles which vary considerably in strength and finish of metal and wood.

There are at least the following variations:

Thick or heavy wall, Hi-Side S. S. with blued finish.

Thick or heavy side wall, Hi-Side S. S. with case hardened finish.

Thin wall, Hi-Side S. S. with blued finish.

Low Side, S. S. light action for No. 1 sporting barrel. Blued.

Winchester Winder musket, blued finish.

Obviously, these could not all have had the same strength of frame. Fred Ness recently commented to the effect that: "As long as the Winchester is not case-hardened it is very strong and reliable. Even the light action,—the little one, will hold everything up to the R-2 Lovell which is above the .218 Bee in velocity and pressure. The high wall Winchester will hold almost anything, including the .300 Magnum but they are not built to extract such rimless cartridges. However, they will hold the .22 Varminter and .220 Swift class of wildcats (like the .220 Arrow)."

It is believed that the Winder musket action is a comparatively "soft" action as compared with the other Winchester single shot actions, at least its finish, fitting and shooting never seemed to be up to the others and it was obviously an action made only to shoot the .22 Short, .22 Long and .22 Long Rifle ammunition, all of standard velocity in the day of its design.

As there are tens of thousands of the Winder muskets in the hands of shooters and rifle organizations scattered throughout the country, and as this is the least desirable of the Winchester S. S. rifles to reach the public, purchasers of Winchester actions for wild-catting should be certain that they are not being offered a Winder, and if so, pay only its probable worth.

A case hardened frame could, of course, be fractured easier than a blued frame, on the other hand it is much harder, and while more brittle should wear better over a course of years. Normally, if well hardened in good colors, it is handsomer than the average blued action and should most likely, when properly bushed, be safe with cartridges at least up to the .22 Improved Zipper. The author does not suggest the Winchester single shot for the .220 Swift, the .220 Arrow, or similar cases although the best of them will, most likely, handle them without blow backs if properly bushed and fitted with a new firing pin of proper type, and the action well fitted as to the working of the breech block in its grooves. But there will at times be extraction or seating trouble, one or the other, or both, due to the use of expanded and lengthened cases in a tight chamber.

The author feels that the Ballard and the Stevens 44½ actions are better than the Winchester S. S. for rebarrelling for .22 Short or .22 Long Rifle. On the other hand, the Winchester S. S. actions are his choice of the American single shot actions for rebarrelling for larger, longer cartridge cases which are pushed in by the finger and thumb and are seated but a short fraction of their length by the rising and closing of the breech block.

The Stevens 44½ Action

In selecting a Stevens 44½ action for a .22 wildcat, or even for a .22 Long Rifle rebarrelling job, it is better, when possible, to obtain a better model of Stevens single shot rifle than the standard 44½ grade. There was such a grade, the more common Stevens, as well as the action designation of 44½. If a Stevens of No. 49 or higher number is obtained, the breech block itself is much better blued and finished and the outside of the frame is also much better finished, in most instances, but the inside of the frame may be found to contain just as many file marks and cutter grooves and scratches as in the 44½ grade. They routed out the excess metal in a hurry, and without much thought to the feelings of a man who bought a 52, 54, or 56 and looked inside the frame after he had disassembled the action.

Also, it is not advisable to have a number of interchangeable rim fire and center fire barrels on the same frame, because the finger lever pin does not hold equally tight with different barrels, and when hunting or target shooting you will find the finger lever pin working out to one side or the other.

There was a recent instance of a 44½ Stevens action used for years by a well-known rifleman, with a cartridge of the .22/3000 type, and without trouble except from misfires rather frequently, and then for that or other reasons he sold this rifle with its action. The new purchaser may have been unskilled in reloading, and he may have overloaded the cartridge, but at any rate, within a week he blew the firing pin out of its channel and the hammer was reportedly blown completely out of the rifle. This suggests to the author that either the charge was detonated for some reason, instead of being burned; that the charge was very excessive; or that the finger lever pin had become very loose in its holes or bearing points—one in each side of the frame—and that it had partly worked out to one side, when the rifle was fired and the action let go. The author has never seen the results of such an accident and knows of no other reported and rather similar case.

His choice of the 44½ Stevens would be for .22 Long Rifle caliber, due to the excellent manner in which the breech block feeds the cartridge into the chamber and seats home after the cartridge is fully into the chamber. And he would use it only for .22 wildcat calibers up to about the Zipper Improved or the Lovell No. 7 Zipper Improved—Ackley, Vickery, Lovell, Kilbourn and others all have slightly different versions of this cartridge, some vary a trifle in shoulder slope, others in length, or length and slope. It would be a good choice for the .22 Hornet Improved or the K-Hornet, or the Kilbourn Hornet, or whatever you wish to call it, a cartridge by the way which has a great deal on the ball for the powder and bullet it shoots.

In fitting up a 44½ Stevens action the author believes it worth while to have the gunsmith fit the finger lever pin into hardened steel collars or seats (called bushings as most of you know) themselves fitted into the steel frame, especially if you are going to use that rifle for pretty stiff charges. Also, it may be worth while, or necessary, to have a new hammer of tough, tool steel, made by hand,

especially if using a Schuetzen double set-trigger action, because
Stevens have no duplicate set-trigger hammers and some of the last
they had crystallized, and when that happens the hammer spur, by
which the hammer is cocked, may break off in cold weather. Below
freezing temperatures make the metal more brittle and then the
hammer spur either starts to crack and then bend outward and backward from the hammer, like so much peanut brittle, or it cracks
and breaks off entirely. In any instance, you then cannot cock the
rifle. Neither can you let the hammer down safely, if cocked and
your fingers are cold.

In buying and fitting up any of these old rifle actions, most of
them made between 1879 and 1915, you have to take what exists.
None of them was made for *modern* powders and .22 wildcat loads,
and you cannot have a 2½% to 3½% nickel steel frame without
having one made up by hand, which costs plenty of money.

The 44½ Stevens action is splendidly designed to handle .22
Long Rifle target ammunition, the .22 W. R. F., .25 Stevens rim
fire and similar small game loads, but the firing pin should be
bushed if you use high velocity ammunition. The stocking was
splendid, especially in the grades of No. 49 and up. The general
lines of the rifle are the best of any of the single shots. But the
material of the frame and action is only fair and you cannot change
its physical characteristics very much. It can, however, be refinished
on the inside of the frame, and the action parts; the lever pin and
other bearings can be bushed with modern steel bushings and you
will then be greatly surprised at the improvement in the smoothness
or working of the action and in the appearance of the rifle, either
taken apart or assembled. The same can be done, as required, with
a Ballard, a Winchester single shot, or any fairly good action in
which a few fitted bushings would restore an old and very badly
worn action. The custom gunsmith who does this work should
know his stuff and be a good metal worker, so that the result will
be a rifle that works as smooth as a Swiss watch.

The Stevens single shot rifles, especially the Schuetzens, had a
great deal of drop to the stock, and the upper tang sloped down
very sharply toward the rear. Result is that very few tang rear
sights, even when mounted on a block which has been fastened to
the upper surface of the tang, will give sufficient elevation for long
range; they are still so low that with the .22 Long Rifle cartridge
an extreme range of only about 160 yards is possible, often only
125 to 140 yards, even with the highest turning up of the sight
thimble. The very best tang peep sight for the Stevens S. S. rifles

is the tang peep made for the B. S. A. No. 12 and No. 15 Martini rim fire rifles. I had one of these on my No. 52 Schuetzen Stevens 44½ and it worked perfectly. I had it set on a block. The Lyman 103 has too much play and it has been taken off the market recently. A receiver peep of B. S. A., Redfield or Lyman make could also be fitted, in which case the drop of stock makes no difference. But such a peep is too far from the eye for best use with a single shot, drop lever rifle. The tang peep is close to the eye, where you need it.

Remington-Hepburn Actions

This one was common from about 1890 to 1905. Most custom gunsmiths and rifle cranks do not take too well to this action for use as a basis for a .22 varmint rifle. One rifleman friend who has had about a dozen of them, owning one now in .30-40 Krag caliber with 9″ twist, is enthusiastic about their structural strength and locking design. He feels they are stronger than the Winchester S. S. action. The bearing lugs come up even with or above the top of the cartridge head—better coverage than in most other actions. The metal is of the 1890 vintage and molecular composition. The faults of the Remington-Hepburn are that it has a rebound to the hammer and firing pin, resulting in the possible condition that if you get a burst primer, a fused cartridge head, or a bad shell burst near the head of the case, and much gas comes back, its velocity will be such that the inertia of the firing assembly must be reckoned with and some parts may come whistling back into the shooter's face. If wildcatted, the firing pin must be fixed so that it will stay down when the hammer falls, and the firing pin of course must be bushed. The extraction of this action is very weak and unsatisfactory with tight-sticking or long cartridge cases. This condition is due to a combination of the poor side-lever principle plus a small extractor segment. In the .30-40 Hepburn just mentioned, this matter was taken care of by milling out the bottom of the frame and putting in a drop lever action, and a filed trigger guard with finger loop, something like the Winchester finger lever or the Stevens loop lever. Report is that this new action works fine, very very much better than the standard Remington-Hepburn.

Ness has used the Remington-Hepburn for the .22/3000 Lovell and he is quoted as saying he believes it will stand more—when properly worked over of course. This action, when used for a varmint rifle, will probably be found more satisfactory with the .22 K-Hornet, the .22/3000 and R-2 and for the short Lindahl cartridges than for anything longer and much higher, pressured.

There are other actions which may at times be used for rebarrelling with .22 barrels, both for rim and for center fire, which are
definitely on the border line or below it. The best advice possible
in such instances is "better not"! If you are a careful reloader and
do not use maximum charges, you may get along all right, but,
suppose someone else acquires that rifle, who has no such conservative ideas, or suppose a new load comes out or you move to a
locality in which shooting is at longer range or at larger varmints.
What then?

So that you will get an all-around viewpoint of this subject of
wildcat rifle actions and how they will work and what cartridges
they will handle with safety and satisfaction, the author presents
opinions of other riflemen and custom gunsmiths. Read them carefully; they contain much data and comment which is helpful.

(Author's note: G. B. Crandall and E. V. Leach are Canada's
outstanding gunsmiths. Mr. Crandall has had most of the Canadian
and some United States cartridges of .22 wildcat type referred to
him for O. K. or re-design before rifles were built for them. He
also has much the same keen technical skill and judgment of H. M.
Pope and about as much experience. His comments here, therefore,
can be taken at full value. It will be well for you to know what
the different rifle actions will stand and handle successfully before
your enthusiasm for small game and varmint shooting with .22 rifles
leads you to order a rifle for a .22 cartridge which should only
be used on a stronger action. Now read along into Mr. Crandall's
suggestions.)

"*Adapting the Winchester Single Shot Actions:* This comment
applies only to the so-called High-Wall and Low-Wall S. S., lever
actions, so well known throughout America. The Winchester single
shot actions, as a group, will handle all the well known .22 wildcat
cartridges yet conceived, and it would be quite safe to say any likely
to be designed in the near future, using present powders and
bullets. Some forms of these actions are sufficiently strong to resist
any pressures generated by any present-day and practical .22 varmint
rifle. This assumes, of course, that the cartridge cases are of normal
size, thickness, strength, temper, and fit the rifle chamber.

"It should be understood by the reader that it is necessary to
sub-divide the various types of Winchester actions and to indicate
to which cartridges each type is adapted. Therefore, let us begin with
a general discussion of the Winchester single shot action by comparison with all other single shot actions that may be used for such
purpose.

"At the outset it is only fair to say that the Winchester S. S. action as above mentioned is the best all-around action we now have for this purpose and, fortunately for shooters, they are far more abundant, although now growing less so. They are better because they can more readily be fitted up to give satisfactory results in head space, durability and a proper firing pin and extractor adjustment and design.

"Also, they can be conveniently adapted to modern pistol grip stocks and shapely forends with that streamlined beauty effect so coveted by a shooter with aesthetic tastes.

"First, we will consider the thick wall High-Sided Winchester action which has been blued and unhardened. This action is the strongest Winchester S. S. available and will hold pressures up to those developed by the most powerful wildcat .22's such as the .228 Ackley Magnums, the .30-40 and .303 British conversions, and other equally powerful cartridges."

"Second, we will consider the thin wall High-Sided actions which are blued and unhardened. This action is of a type which also is very strong, for it contains sufficient metal properly distributed and it is good steel properly tempered, but I would suggest stopping short of the most extreme loads when using this thin-sided action, as obviously it has a smaller cross-section of metal and is not as strong, structurally, as the heavier-sided Winchester S. S. action which otherwise is much or altogether the same. The thinner-sided high-wall actions were designed to make up in a lighter weight of rifle than when using the thick wall High-Sided action. The thin wall High-Sided action could be used with .22 Varminter, .22-250 and the .22 Varmint-R cartridges in normal charges and it will, of course, be fine for all lesser capacity and lower pressure cartridges and charges.

"Third, we have the thick wall High-Sided case hardened Winchester S. S. action. This action is equal to handling what the above-mentioned would handle, but if the action is annealed by slowly heating to a dull red heat and maintaining the work at that heat for about 30 minutes, then allowed to cool slowly, it becomes much softer and can be used with some of the more powerful cartridges in .22 wildcat calibers.

"Fourth, we come to the low-side-wall light action Winchester S. S. actions. These were generally used with the light, tapered, No. 1 Winchester barrel in .22 Short and Long, .22 Long Rifle, .22 W.R.F., .25 Stevens Rim-Fire, .32 Short, .32 Long and similar calibers in the light Winchester S. S., plain style *sporting* rifles which weighed around 6¼, 7 or 7½ pounds. Most of them had plain rifle butt plates. This description is given to help you identify the rifle and action. Also, the receiver opposite the breech block did not extend up as high and cover the view of the topside of the breech block to the same extent as did the High-Sided Winchester S. S. actions. These actions will handle the standard .22 Hornet, K-Hornet and similar varmint cartridges quite successfully, but I consider it unwise to convert this style Winchester light weight action for the R-2, the .22/3000 Lovell, the .22 Maximum Lovell, the K-Lovell or similar cartridges which are often loaded to give fairly high pressures and to develop 3,300 to 3,500 f.s.m.v. or even higher with the short, light weight .22 jacketed bullets. The highest pressures normally developed in these cartridges are with the 50 and 55-grain bullets. Most of them are not used very extensively with the 63-grain or heavier .22 caliber jacketed weights as these longer bullets require a quicker twist for best results and really are better adapted to the larger cases.

"Then we have the Winchester Musket action, often known as the Winchester-Winder musket, which was made with the thin side, High-Sided, blued action. I believe it was invariably put ouʳ blued 'not hardened.' This action will handle such cartridges as the .219 Zipper or the .219 Ackley Improved Zipper (or the Lovell Improved Zipper, the Vickery, the Vickery Improved Zipper—which has a very slightly increased powder capacity, or the Kilbourn K-Zipper and similar .22 varmint cartridges) quite safely. Of course, as in all the others, the breech block must be properly bushed and a correct size firing pin installed. For the small primer cartridges a firing pin not larger than 0.625″ should be used. For the larger primer a pin about 0.08″—is permissible and is better than the smaller pin."

(Author's Note: The large size rifle primers such as Winchester No. 115, 115½, 120, 35; Western Cartridge Company No. 8½ and 8½G; Remington No. 8½ and 9½; Peters No. 12 and Frankford Arsenal No. 70, Cal. 30, are *all* 0.210″ in diameter. Winchester at one time, and for only a very short period, made a special No. 225 large size primer for some special .30-1906 cases but these are now obsolete. The small size primers for rifle cartridges, including the Remington No. 6½; Peters No. 65; Winchester No. 116 and Western No. 6½, are *each* but 0.175″ in diameter.

(Remember, for the large primers you can use a 0.08″ firing pin; for the small primers the 0.0625″ pin. You will readily see why. The indent made by the nose or point of the firing pin should be proportional to the diameter of the primer, or else the primer may rupture either because the indent may be too deep and too small diameter, or because it is too large and may flatten the primer on edge and pinch it off or make the metal so thin at that point, after striking, that it will burst.

"It is assumed that the breech block in all actions when converted to a .22 wildcat caliber should be properly fitted for head space, if not so found, and correctly bushed (as in *all* cases the firing pins in these actions are too large in diameter at the nose to function at all satisfactorily for any of these modern and recently-developed high pressure .22's from the .22 Hornet up).

"Various methods of converting the breech block and firing pin are in vogue and most of them are satisfactory when expert fitting and precision machine work are done on the small parts used, plus some hand adjustment and polishing in the process, and as required. The writer likes the system of boring out the original firing pin hole clear through the breech block, then counter-boring the face of the block about .312″ to .375″, after which he turns up a plug of quality steel with firing pin hole of the size wanted through the plug. The plug is then turned with a pilot as part of it to enter the original firing pin hole and to dimensions that insure a very tight fit when pressed home under an arbor press. Then the breech block is faced off flush after which the inserted plug is drilled from the rear for the firing pin. The pin has a head which is fluted on one side to receive the original firing pin retaining screw as employed in *all* Winchester S. S. actions.

"The firing pin, with the exception of the point, is made sufficiently large to be practical but not too large to enter freely into a stiff coil spring, used as a retractive instrument to the pin. It applies the force to retract the pin immediately after striking the primer. The flute in the side of the pin at the rear is regulated so that the retaining screw permits the firing pin to recede until it is flush with the face of the breech block. The recoil spring in this case should be sufficiently strong to resist the force of the falling hammer to such an extent that it will push back the hammer so that the firing pin will then be in proper position just flush with the face of the breech block. This does not mean a rebounding hammer in the common acceptance of the term, but one which merely does not press on the firing pin enough to cause it to protrude.

"In all conversions of other types of breech blocks I always endeavor to employ this method of exerting a retracting action upon the firing pin.

The Sharps-Borchardt and Farquharson Actions

"The Sharps-Borchardt and Farquharson actions are sufficiently strong to handle the ultra high speed .22's so far developed but the extractive power developed by these actions is not as satisfactory as the extractive mechanism of the Winchester actions. They are, otherwise very desirable actions. The method of retracting the firing pin and hammer as employed in the Winchester could be adapted to these other actions.

"We also have the B.S.A. No. 12 and No. 15 actions designed originally solely for the .22 Long Rifle. However, I have converted many No. 12 B.S.A. rifles (which are rather common in Ontario and in other parts of Canada, as well as having been used considerably for target shooting in the United States) and I have fitted these with conversions for the .22 Hornet cartridge. This No. 12 B.S.A. action should be strong enough for the R-2 cartridge but that is about its limit. It could be made to handle the K-Hornet.

"However, the No. 15 B.S.A. action is quite unsuited for any cartridge more powerful than the .22 Long Rifle for the reason that the breech block at the rear is supported only by a small pin through the block and receiver frame. In the case of the B.S.A. No. 12 this breech block seats smoothly into the receiver itself and does not depend upon the cross pin at all. Consequently, the former becomes a really strong action up to the limit mentioned. The reader should be careful to not confuse these two B.S.A. actions made for the .22 Long Rifle cartridge.

The Stevens No. 44½

"The Stevens No. 44½ action, as used in the Stevens 44½, 044½, 45, 47, 49, 51, 52 and 54 rifles, and the 56, rather generally, particularly in calibers larger than .22 Long Rifle and beginning with about 1902, is a very nice action of the low side-wall type, quite powerful, of excellent design, the design being better than the material of the frame in which it is contained. It has a limit of cartridge strength and breech pressure around the .219 Improved Zipper class and the medium and shorter lengths of the .22 Hi-Power Improved, but not higher. The extractor is not easily fitted to function properly, as the lever exerts an upward pressure to the extractor before it exerts a backward pressure. The only way to overcome this is to see that the pin through the extractor and frame fits very tightly; otherwise, it will jam the cartridge case up and will seriously increase the difficulty of extraction.

"The 44½ firing pin which goes upward and forward through this 44½ breech block is fitted on such an angle that it strikes the primer an upward blow rather than a direct and sharp tap delivered toward the muzzle and this upward blow at an angle is not so desirable, as a proportional amount of the force of the blow is dissipated against the walls of the lower and forward part of the firing pin channel and it softens the 'percussion' of the blow. It is accepted among engineers that the only time that the full force of a hammer blow, or the striking of a firing pin propelled by a coil spring, can be delivered to the rear face of the primer in the cartridge is when the firing pin is struck fairly on the end and drives forward in a direct line vertical to the face of the cartridge head, or when it is so propelled forward by the coil mainspring in a bolt action.

"It is best to fit the firing pin of the 44½ Stevens action with a nearly flat point slightly rounded on the outer surface or edge. This is better than a semi-spherical point. If well fitted, the Stevens 44½ becomes a good action for the medium-high powered .22 wildcats. The rolling motion of the breech block in closing and in opening is conducive to freedom from firing pin troubles, at least to some extent.

The Remington-Hepburn Action

"The Remington-Hepburn is one of the quite popular and fairly plentiful actions. It is powerful enough for all but the most high-pressure .22 wildcats. As the breech block has no camming action in closing, the firing pin must be fitted with a strong coil spring that will lift the pin with certainty when fired to a just-flush position so there will be nothing to prevent the drop of breech block. If there is it will jam! This firing pin should be stopped in this position in its backward motion, which in turn will prevent possible escape of gas in case of a punctured primer. At least it should reasonably be expected to do so, except possibly in the most extreme cases of abnormally high pressures resulting from a detonation rather than an explosion, or when a charge of such size is used that it is obviously unsuited to shooting in an action of this design.

The Ballard Action and Breech Block

"The last action that we will consider is the fine old Ballard. The writer (Mr. Crandall) has seen some very fine specimens of the famous old Ballard rifles as made by the Marlin Firearms Company, who were always capable of fine workmanship. It was a great old rifle—was the Ballard—in the heyday of the .32-40 and .38-55 target supremacy at all the good old turkey shoots, of which we had so many in Ontario and which were equally popular for many years, and are today, for that matter, in Indiana, Ohio and numerous other states throughout the country. But as a rifle for conversion to the more popular wildcats it occupies a very humble position. Various peculiarities of design and construction of the frame and breech block make it quite unsuitable for any but the lowest power wildcats. The two-piece or split breech block is not good to start with and renders it difficult to get a satisfactory close fit to the firing pin.

"Then the fact that the breech block covers only the head of the cartridge, with no protecting frame around it, is not quite in the category of safe mechanisms against those possible back fires due to a cracked case or other causes. It may be said that the resisting power of the breech block is ample against the most powerful cartridges but it does not cover all of the danger surface around the head of the cartridge. Within this danger surface is where one may expect trouble.

"Too, the shape of the tang does not lend itself to the forming of a shapely pistol grip stock of the kind usually presented on a nice looking varmint rifle.

"It might be added also that the ejector mechanism of the Ballard is weak and unsatisfactory and there is no easy way of securing a good firing pin condition. All in all, the Ballard seems to be out of the running for .22 wildcat conversion in the opinion of the writer.

The B.S.A. Center Fire Martini Action

"The B.S.A. Martini center fire action is a strong rifle action equal to handling any of the .22 high velocity wildcats that can be fed into the chamber. The lock is fast. But I do not consider it a desirable action to choose in the construction of such a splendid weapon as a fine .22 varmint rifle. It has the serious structural drawback of being a muzzle-cleaning proposition. Also, it cannot be examined from the breech. Again, as sometimes happens, if a broken cartridge case becomes stuck in the chamber it is generally then a job of removing the barrel from the action to get out that cartridge. Then again, the trigger is so situated that it is hopelessly out of reach of a man with a normal size hand with fingers of short or average length. It can, of course, be restocked in a way to improve this abnormal condition somewhat but even so, when everything is considered, it is not an A-1 choice for the basis of a fine woodchuck or coyote rifle. The writer has converted many of these center fire Martinis, the majority to use the .22 Hornet cartridge (Mr. Crandall specialized for years in rebarrelling rifles and relining barrels for the .22 Hornet cartridge up until the Savage Sporter and the 54 Winchester became generally available in both the United States and Canada—using Parker-Hale tubes also for relining for the .22 Long Rifle cartridge—Author.) I have also converted a goodly number of center fire Martini actions for the .22-303 British Crandall Varmint-R cartridge, which is a powerful woodchuck and coyote cartridge.

Summary

"Taking everything into consideration, safety, strength of action, excellence of structural design, beauty of rifle after arm is complete and other details, some of which will appear quite important to many customers, I would select the blued receiver, thick wall, High-Sided, Winchester S. S., drop lever rifle action to any other available for a high grade .22 rifle in all other than bolt action style. The best ones are those with single trigger, or with Schuetzen double set-triggers and chosen, of course, as being in a good state of preservation without showing excessive wear or looseness of any of the important parts. The gunsmith can handle the job from there on.

"Obviously, the fitting of such varmint rifle with a first-class telescope sight of a style, mounts and optical power suitable for exact small game and varmint shooting will add greatly to your enjoyment in its use and will add very much to its effectiveness in the field."

ACTIONS, BORE DIAMETERS, BUSHED FIRING PINS
By Henry E. Davis

"My interest in high velocity .22 cartridges and rifles began with the advent of the popular Hornet 15 years ago, and has continued ever since. During this period I have fired thousand of rounds of various cartridges of this type. While my special attention has been given to the cartridges based on the .25-20 single shot case, such as the .22/3000 Lovell, the R-2, and the Maximum Lovell, I have also tested the .22 Niedner Magnum, the Mashburn Bee, and the K-Hornet. My experience with the latter has been rather extensive; the K-Hornet, using 13.2 grains of No. 4227 powder behind the 45-grain Remington Hornet soft point bullet, in a barrel of 0.224″ groove diameter, is the most remarkable cartridge I have ever fired; but do not use it in a standard Winchester Hornet barrel, as the bore is too tight.

"In fact, I strongly advise against using any barrel of less than 0.2235″ groove diameter for any cartridge giving a muzzle velocity of 2,700 f.s. or over. If a shooter persists in using a tight bore, like that of the Winchester Model 52 barrel, for a high intensity cartridge, he is surely headed for trouble. Such bores perform well with light loads, but shooters are never content with light loads.

A Comparison of Different Actions

"In the .22 wildcats, I have used the following actions: Models 54 and 70 Winchester, and Krag in the bolt actions, and Sharps-Borchardt, Winchester High-Wall, Stevens 44½, Farquharson, Nagel (Austrian) in the single shots. To date, I have thoroughly tested 16 different rifles chambered for the three cartridges based on the .25-20 single shot case. The rifles used in these tests were made up on the actions listed above, with the exception of the Nagel, which was a K-Hornet.

"All things considered, the most satisfactory American single shot action is the Winchester High-Wall, with the Sharps-Borchardt a close second. The latter is more accurate, but the Winchester has a better trigger pull, and with Schuetzen double set-triggers, it definitely outclasses the Sharps-Borchardt with single trigger. The

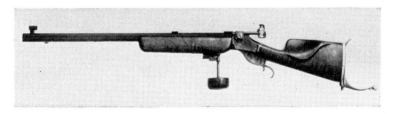

.22 Hornet-Schuetzen. This rifle made many groups of less than 2″ at 200 yards.

best rifle I ever owned was a heavy Winchester High-Wall .22/3000 made by Hervey Lovell with a 0.224″ groove diameter Diller barrel of 16″ twist. With this I killed hundreds of crows and hawks, and shot it until the barrel became eroded. One of the best rifles I now own is a .22 Maximum Lovell built by Hervey Lovell on the heaviest nickel steel Winchester High-Wall action, with coil main spring and Schuetzen double set-triggers. It also has a Diller barrel of 0.224″ groove diameter and 16″ twist.

Vented Breech Blocks Necessary

"Both the Winchester and the Sharps-Borchardt must have the firing pins reduced and properly bushed, and the breech blocks should be vented so as to allow gas to escape. The Niedner Rifle Corporation wrote me some years ago that the proper way to bush the Sharps-Borchardt was to fill the firing pin hole by welding and then drill a new hole for the reduced firing pin. This action can be further improved by installing a firing-pin retractor.

"A decided advantage the Sharps-Borchardt has over the Winchester is that it is much more accurate with a light barrel. I have one of the first rifles ever made by Lovell for the .22/3000 cartridge. It has a light 30″ barrel on a Sharps-Borchardt action, and is second to none in accuracy. I think so much of this action that I am now having a light R-2 rifle made on it for use as a hunting rifle. This is to be equipped with double set-triggers and a retractor. The steel of the Sharps-Borchardt is said to be inferior in tensile strength to that of the Winchester, for which reason it will not stand as high pressure; mechanically, it is just as strong as the Winchester.

"I do not recommend the 44½ Stevens for these high intensity .22 caliber cartridges. Sometime back I had a very accurate Winchester High-Wall R-2 with Schuetzen double set-triggers. It was rather light, and wishing to make a comparison, I had a selected heavy Winchester 52 barrel fitted to a good No. 47 Stevens 44½ action with double set-triggers. The rifle was built by Lovell, but I had it chambered by Leslie Lindahl for his version of the R-2 case. With a load of 15.2 grains of No. 4227 behind the Winchester 45-grain soft point bullet, it proved exceptionally accurate—slightly more so than the Winchester with which it was being compared. However, it frequently gave misfires, so I had Hervey Lovell sell it. Shortly thereafter he reported that in the hands of the new owner, it blew out both firing-pin and hammer. Whether this owner used my recommended load of 15.2 grains of No. 4227 powder, I do not know. This shows, however, that a combination of tight bore and a comparatively weak action is not safe for a high intensity .22 caliber cartridge.

"I now fully agree with the opinion Niedner gave me a few years ago that the Stevens 44½ action is in the same class regarding strength as the Winchester Low-Wall, and I certainly would not recommend the low-wall for use with high intensity cartridges.

"The Remington-Hepburn should be safe for these cartridges if the firing pin is reduced and bushed. I would say that all other American single shots are definitely out.

"The Farquharson is the strongest of all single shot actions, and is the easiest to load. It has a good trigger pull, but can not be fitted with set-triggers and its tangs are so long as to require the use of a rather long scope. With a small properly bushed firing pin, it is perhaps the best of all single shot actions for these cartridges.

"All the bolt actions of Mauser-type are safe for such cartridges, but the Krag is not. The Mauser-type actions, however, are so long as to make single loading a rather slow process. One could load, aim and fire a Farquharson before he could load a Mauser-type as a single shot. I have tried for the past two years to find a Mauser short action, but all in vain. Finally, in despair, I have given up, and am having one made from a Model 1898 Mauser and equipped with a Pike trigger. A short bolt action of this type with a trigger like that of the Model 70 is the greatest need in the field of modern firearms. Such an action properly made would be absolutely safe for all the .22 wildcats, provided barrels of 0.224" groove diameter were used, and would give accuracy comparable to that of the heavy single shots."

CHAPTER 16

PRESSURE TESTS OF MODERN RIFLE ACTIONS

By Parker O. Ackley

JUST PRIOR to completion of the manuscript for this book, the author heard of a most interesting and valuable series of tests being made of various rifle actions at the factory of Parker O. Ackley, the well known riflemaker. These tests seemed so valuable to the varmint shooters, as well as to all riflemen, that arrangements were made for a summary of such testing to be furnished by Mr. Ackley. The material which follows covers such tests as were made up to the time of going to press.

Mr. Ackley reports:

Before taking up the subject of actions—I wish to say, like everyone else, I am a little prejudiced as to which are the best designed, although I might go further than most of the boys by trying to keep these prejudices from being too apparent. I always try to base any personal preference on good points or keep quiet. I have also been criticized from time to time for being too conservative as to the suitability of certain actions for certain uses, especially in connection with the modern, super-wildcat calibers.

No gunsmith can take chances on any action. I refuse a great many jobs which in all probability would be within the limits of safety. After deliberately blowing up numerous actions in extensive tests, I have been able to draw certain conclusions about various makes or designs of actions. As a result of these tests, I have also been able to make some interesting observations on cartridge design.

Since World War II came to an end a great many returning soldiers have brought foreign service rifles into this country with them, either for conversion purposes or as a souvenir. Sooner or later, most of these rifles will find their way into the hands of sportsmen in the form of converted military rifles or as the foundation of a custom-built sporter. Many articles have appeared in the various sporting magazines discussing the merits of various types

338

of actions, including our own military and sporting actions. Because of such wide disagreement among the authors of such articles, I felt it necessary to conduct extensive experimental tests, in order to clear up the confusion.

As a result, some twenty-five or more actions were used and accurate records were kept as to loads used, reactions of the mechanism, pressures and just what happened when each type of action finally blew up. Needless to say, many surprising things were experienced.

The actions most commonly written about or discussed are our own military actions, such as the U. S. magazine rifle Model 1903, popularly known as the Springfield, but actually made by the Springfield Arsenal, Rock Island Arsenal and the Remington Arms Company; U. S. model 1917, more popularly known as the Enfield; the Model 98 Mauser, and the Jap Arisaka in calibers 6.5 and 7.7mm. All of these rifles could be classed as Mauser patterns, but actually there is some difference between the American actions and the other two. In all probability, the outstanding difference between these two foreign actions and our two American military actions is that the forward part of the bolt in the two foreign actions is much better protected than in our own. The Mauser action has a ring inside of the receiver, which encloses the head of the bolt and the head of the cartridge. This action has a stop for the barrel when it is screwed into the receiver—that is, the barrel butts up tightly against this ring when it is in place. At the same time it greatly reinforces the receiver ring.

The Japanese action does not have this ring, but the barrel is recessed deep enough to accept the head of the bolt, so that when the bolt is in locked position the cartridge head and the forward end of the bolt are completely enclosed inside of the barrel. With such features, when a cartridge case is ruptured, the resulting escape of gas is directed away from the walls of the receiver ring and is not as apt to result in rupturing the receiver as the American design is, which does not have any protection of this kind at all. In our own actions the bolt is not enclosed in any way, except for a funnel-like cut in the breech end of the barrel, which in no way reinforces it, but deflects escaping gas against the walls of the receiver. Gas, striking the receiver well at a terrific velocity causes this part of the action to disintegrate and blow up from structural failure. This is not due to any weakness of our own actions, as far as material or workmanship is concerned, but from faulty design.

During this action test we also were able to make some interesting observations on the so-called "reheat-treated actions." Several re-heat-treated Springfield and Krag actions were tested. The NRA supplied quite a bit of information on certain heat-treating companies that had done experimental work for them. They commented on the fact that reheat-treated receivers would stand the same pressure loads as would nickel steel. This is true and it has always been so since we have known about reheat-treated Springfields, but the fact remains that the proof test is not indicative of what they really are.

Reheat-treating may be considered from two angles or two classes of reheat-treatment. One is the reheat-treatment of the actions which are excessively soft, resulting in a harder product; the other is the reheat-treatment of hard actions resulting in a softer product. The latter is probable the more common—especially when certain of the Springfield and Krag actions are considered. The 1903 action, made at Springfield Arsenal with serial numbers under 800,000 were all low carbon steel, case hardened. Actions made at Springfield between 800,000 and 1,275,767 were what is known as double heat-treated actions, but actually were case hardened. All actions made at Springfield over 1,275,767 were of the nickel steel type. All 1903 actions made at the Rock Island arsenal under 285,507 were of the case hardened type. All over that number were nickel steel. The reheat-treatment of these excessively hard case hardened receivers resulted in a lower hardness, thus increasing their ability to withstand heavy proof loads. It is very doubtful whether any reheat-treatment would better the original process used at the arsenal. In fact, our tests tended to prove that these hard actions were in no way improved, but in many instances were actually injured.

An example of the heat treatment of the other type would be the excessively soft Mauser action. Such actions are not made of good material. In this particular, they are somewhat similar to these old hard Springfields, but in contrast to the Springfield or Krag they were left rather soft and sometimes such actions are heat treated to increase their hardness by a special carburizing process. This practice is also probably of doubtful value and instead of trying to reheat-treat actions which are too soft it would be more practical to discard them. Actions which are excessively soft will stand a tremendous proof load or even several heavy proof loads without any apparent injury, but after continued shooting, a very definite set back is developed, which increases the head space to the danger point. It is exactly the same condition that occurs when we strike a piece of malleable iron or soft steel a terrific blow with a sledge hammer. Neither material is fractured nor does it show any tendency to crack, but either material will upset a great deal, leaving a very definite mark where the hammer struck it. If this spot is repeatedly struck several heavy blows, the indentation will become much deeper, which is the condition that we have in all soft actions, such as reheat-treated Springfields, poor Mausers, etc. The lugs of the bolt act in exactly the same manner as the hammer and thus gradually set themselves back into the soft material of the receiver, rapidly increasing the head space to a dangerous point, finally resulting in fractured cases.

On the other hand, if we use a hard piece of steel or similar material and strike it the same terrific blow with the sledge hammer, it is apt to fracture in every direction, but there will be no indentation or definite mark left by the hammer. Such material will not withstand as heavy a blow as the softer material but if the lugs of the bolt do not have a chance to slide back or to get a start, it will withstand a rather heavy blow. In fact, it will withstand a blow heavy enough so that there is no real danger of such an action fracturing, provided the head space is perfectly tight and there is absolutely no tendency for the bolt lugs to set back into the receiver material. In other words, it is the lesser of the two evils to have a hard receiver which will not withstand the terrific proof load that the soft one would take, but one that will withstand a reasonably powerful shock many times over without noticeable set back.

It is obvious what happens when these conditions are found in rifle actions. The continuous hammering of the bolt upon repeated firing sets the lugs back into the receiver, dangerously increasing the head space and as time goes on the head space is much more rapidly increased; hence the real danger from the reheat-treated actions is from this cause. There is also another point in this reheat-treatment, and that is the fact that so many heat treating outfits do not know the score when it comes to firearms and merely give them normal kind of heat-treatment, which allows the unscrupulous dealers to sell such actions as "heat-treated" items and trade on the magic statement. I have contacted some of the better heat-treating companies; for instance one company in New Haven does a great deal of heat-treating of firearms and firearm parts and they have with them one of Winchester's oldest heat treating experts, and they absolutely refuse to touch the old, hard Springfield actions because they say that they can not do any better than the arsenal. Anything they would do would be a detriment rather than an improvement; they also state that the material in the old Springfields was of such poor quality that there would be very little that could be done with it.

Low Number Springfields with Nickel Steel Bolts

Due to all these reasons, I never recommend the use of reheat-treated Springfields actions except for standard loads, such as the ordinary .30-06 or lower pressure ones. When customers ask for definite advice as to the use of, or the possibility of improving these old actions, the only sound advice that I can think of is for them to obtain one of the new nickel steel bolts and fit it properly to one of these old hard receivers. We have made extensive tests with receivers made at Springfield arsenal with numbers as low as 100 but fitted with new style bolts, which gave no trouble at all after repeated firings with government blue pill loads. In fact, we even greased some of the test cartridges and still had no trouble with these old hard actions when left in the original condition and when tightly head spaced.

Here again we come back to the question of head space. These old actions, when tightly head spaced, do not receive the blow from the bolt that they would if excessive head space were present. In other words, the bolt does not get a start and consequently the action does not receive the sharp blow that it would if the bolt lugs could slide back a fraction before they come in contact with the locking recesses. For this reason tight head space is an essential in these old hard actions.

While on this subject, it takes us back to the other extreme, or the soft Mausers. These came over in several forms which are well known to all gun experts. One is the KAR, most commonly made at the Erfurt Arsenal in Germany, and the others without any arsenal marks, although embellished with some crude engraving but of the KAR style. That is, they both have the straight, small receiver ring. These engraved actions, in particular, are very soft and the direct opposite of the hard Springfields. These also have to be very tightly head spaced, because any appreciable head space at all will allow the bolt to get a start and rapidly hammer and stretch the action out, or in other words, set the bolt back so that there is dangerous head space. Nearly everyone of these old actions which came in—and I have hundreds of them every year—showed some set back in the locking recess in the receiver ring. The set back is caused by the soft material and also because of the fact that the Germans during the later part of the World War I did not seem to care about head space. If the bolt closed on a dime they were evidently close enough. Such Mauser actions, although well designed, are definitely to be discriminated against.

As a result of our findings when extensive analysis tests were made of all the actions tested, including all the parts of the actions as well as the receiver and bolt, we are only able to conclude that material is not the only consideration in the construction of an action. It was proven beyond any doubt that a specially heat-treated carbon steel action is vastly superior to an indifferently heat-treated action of inferior design.

As an example, the Japanese Arisaka 6.5 bolt and receiver is made of carbon steel, with a few showing a low content of chromium as compared with our Springfield action or Enfield, which are made of 3½ per cent nickel steel but with a low carbon content. The Japanese actions show an average carbon content of about .80 as compared with our American actions with a carbon content of approximately .40. There was absolutely no comparison between the loads that the Arisaka would stand and those that our own actions would take. Loads which had no effect on the Arisaka would completely blow up an Enfield. Obviously this was not due to superior material, but to superior heat-treating and superior design. From the standpoint of conversion for sporting use, the Japanese actions probably would not compare with our own, but from the standpoint of strong design, the Arisaka is vastly superior. Extensive Rockwell tests showed that the early Arisaka 6.5 actions were very elaborately heat-treated— each part apparently having undergone its own individual type of treatment. In addition, they are so designed that they have the proper distribution of material at the points of greatest stress.

A comparison between the old and new Springfields is also of interest. There is only a small difference between the loads that the old action will take, as compared with the late one, showing that the material is not the only consideration. The good Model 98 Mauser showed an average analysis no better than the original Springfield; in fact, the material in these two actions is practically identical, but due to the general design of the Mauser action it is vastly superior from the safety standpoint than the low numbered Springfield, thus again proving that material is no more important than design.

Bolt Actions

The greatest surprise experienced when running the action tests, after reading all of the criticism on the Japanese actions, was the tremendous pressure that the Arisaka action would stand without any apparent effect. Of all the actions tested, the 6.5 Japanese Arisaka action proved to be the strongest and by a very wide margin.

No. 2 on the list turned out to be the Japanese 7.7 action. We used several of these actions so that we felt that we had made a fairly representative test. It must be noted here that the Japanese Arisaka action is the nearest gas proof of any action tested and that the 6.5 model was the only action that could not be blown up. We were unable to put a barrel on that was strong enough to withstand the loads which would blow the action itself up. It also should be noted here that in designing this action a way was found to protect the head of the cartridge and the forward end of the bolt itself by simply recessing the end of the barrel itself to allow the forward end of the bolt to be fully enclosed. The same result is gained in the Mauser by machining the ring inside of the receiver, but this is an expensive operation and in no way does it seem to be better than the Japanese idea.

As a result of the action experiment we would have to place the military actions tested in the following order, from the standpoint of strength:

No. 1, The Japanese Arisaka, caliber 6.5mm.

No. 2, The Japanese Arisaka, caliber 7.7mm.

No. 3, GEW, Model 98 Mauser.

No. 4, U. S. magazine rifle Model 1917, popularly known as the Enfield.

No. 5, U. S. magazine rifle Model 1903, popularly known as the Springfield, nickel steel type.

No. 6, Mannlicher-Schoenauer.

No. 7, Springfield rifles with serial No. between 800,000 and 1,275,767.

No. 8, Low numbered Springfields under 800,000 (Rock Island under 285,507); also KAR, Model 98 Mauser.

No. 9, Krag; Model 88 Mauser; British Lee-Enfield.

The above list does not mean that the No. 1 would be most desirable for use as a sporting rifle; in fact, it is far from being that. The list is simply to give an idea of the rating of the actions from the point of *strength alone*. The various actions might be rated in the following order so far as gas protection is concerned:

Japanese Arisaka; Mauser Model 98; Enfield; Krag; Springfield.

For sporting use, a different rating has to be used. Just because an action proves itself to be stronger than some other action it doesn't mean it is the most desirable for sporting use. It might not lend itself for conversion into a beautiful sporting rifle. It might be an awkward action to operate or one not capable of smooth operation and trigger pull.

As an example, the Japanese Arisaka, although it has proven to be definitely stronger than some other actions, is not as well adapted as a foundation for a desirable sporting rifle as the Mauser Model 98. It would have a greater safety margin for some sporting cartridges, but this does not mean that the Model 98 Mauser would not have sufficient safety margin for all practical sporting uses. For that reason we have to rate the actions in a different order.

The Japanese Arisaka requires no alteration except to change the form of the bolt handle itself. The safety, in its original form can be used. It is not a particularly handy safety, but so far as it is now known, there is no practical way of altering it so it has to remain in its original form.

From this viewpoint, my own rating of the actions would be about as follows:

No. 1, GEW Mauser Model 98; No. 2, 1917 Enfield; No. 3, High numbered Springfields; No. 4, Japanese Arisaka, 6.5.

From there on, it would simply be a matter of preference. This classification must also be qualified as to caliber: The Model 98 Mauser action is not really as well adapted to magnum calibers as is the 1917 Enfield, so for magnum calibers, we must place the 1917 action No. 1 because of its larger size, thus requiring less alteration and no reduction of the margin of safety.

The Springfield high numbered action is also better adapted to magnum calibers than the Mauser Model 98 because of its greater length. The Model 98 is well adapted, however, for the shorter wildcat magnum calibers, which do not require excessive action cutting.

These ratings do not take into consideration purely commercial actions such as the Magnum Mausers, which of course, would be No. 1 for magnum calibers, nor the popular Model 70 Winchester, 720 Remington, Model 20 Savage, Model 40 Savage, and other commercial types such as these, among which we might find a few of the original Buffalo Newtons.

Many class the Model 70 Winchester action No. 1 regardless. This position is not deserved, but it is nevertheless a very desirable action for general all round use.

Another way to rate actions is from the standpoint of their desirability for use with telescope sights. Here we must place our 1917 action or its commercial counterparts; Model 30 Remington, and 720 Remington in No. 1 place. These actions require no alteration whatever for use with scope sights. The safety is ideally located and the bolt handle, although of questionable design from the standpoint of appearance, is ideal for use with a scope. The Model 70 is also very well adapted for use with a low mounted scope. The factory safety is not desirable, but can be easily replaced with one of several custom made safeties. The Model 98 Mauser requires more extensive alteration. The bolt handle has to be completely reshaped and the safety has to be replaced. Once this is done, it is again on a par with the others.

The Springfield is probably the most difficult of the more popular actions to alter for low scope. So from the standpoint of telescope sights, we might rate the actions as follows: No. 1, the 1917 Enfield type; No. 2, Model 70 Winchester; No. 3, Model 98 Mauser; No. 4, Japanese Arisaka.

From the standpoint of scope use, the Krag can not be considered, because of the top ejection feature. This is also true of the various Mannlichers or their counterparts. All of the Mannlichers require excessively high mounted scopes or a side mount to clear the bolt handle, which passes through the bridge of the action during its rearward travel.

Mannlicher actions are made in a variety of designs. Some were made on the straight pull plan; some have the regular Mannlicher bolt, but are otherwise almost duplicates of the Mauser Model 98; still others are the regular Mannlicher-Schoenauer, which is by far the best of the Mannlicher family. It has the original rotary magazine, and this is one of the most satisfactory magazines ever devised. It may be thought of as a spool, very similar to that found in the Model 99 Savage lever action rifles. However, it is not well adapted to conversion; it is necessary to use a cartridge very similar to the one for which the magazine was originally designed in order to get satisfactory operation. The Mannlicher-Schoenauer is mainly sought after by gun experts for the reason that it was originally made up in a very short, exceedingly light carbine style with full length Mannlicher type stock. These little rifles are about the ultimate in the gunmakers' art. And, although many do not agree with the general design, everyone realizes the workmanship.

The Mannlicher-Schoenauer can be converted to some of the standard modern American calibers, as well as a few of the better known wildcats.

The most popular action for the medium size wildcat calibers is the Model 98 Mauser. This is because of several very good reasons. One is that they are easier to obtain than any other action because of the great number brought over by returning GIs. They make one of the neatest appearing sporting rifles there is and can readily be converted for sporting rifles. They have better gas protection than any other action which lends itself readily for such conversions. They are not as gas proof as the Arisaka, but this action probably never could be made into as neat a rifle as the Model 98 Mauser. The Arisaka also is limited as to the choice of cartridges which it will accept. It will only handle the shorter ones. The Model 98 Mauser would rate No. 1 in desirability for the medium size wildcat calibers.

The No. 2 would be the Enfield, but for the larger wildcat calibers the Enfield is No. 1 action because of its large size, which is sufficient to accept the longer cartridge without excessive alteration. It also has one of the best safeties of all military actions. The bolt handle and safety do not have to be altered in any way. This action is ideal for low telescope sights. It also probably has better gas protection than any other American action. Its strength is sufficient for any of the ordinary wildcat calibers, including the various magnums.

From the standpoint of desirability for sporting actions, the No. 3 action would be the Springfield. Some authorities place the Springfield No. 1, but the reason that it places No. 3 here is from the standpoint of general desirability, because of its lack of gas protection and also because of excessively high line of sight. The Springfield action does not readily lend itself to the use of a low telescope sight because of the high bridge.

There is very little difference in the strength of the above mentioned actions from the standpoint of sporting use. That is to say, there is sufficient margin of safety. From the special purpose standpoint, as an example, there are many shooters who prefer an action to be exactly the right length for his particular caliber. There is a tremendous demand for the so-called "short" actions. The best example of this is the famous short Mauser which has appeared throughout the world in several different designs and our own Model 20 Savage action, which was discontinued several years ago by the Savage Arms Corporation.

The short Mauser action is exactly the same as the other Mausers, except for its length. The Model 20 Savage is of the so-called "Mauser type" but it has the highly desirable characteristics of being exactly the right length for the .250 Savage cartridge and having the tang shotgun type safety, which is undoubtedly the handiest of all safeties.

The Newton action appeals to a great many shooters because of its streamlined appearance and especially its handy low type safety and its low bolt handle. It also had a different locking system which might be termed the multiple lug type or interrupted screw type system, as compared with the double lug Mauser system. The Newton action is suitable for all high pressure calibers, but unfortunately, this action was discontinued many years ago, and some of those found today are in very bad condition. Newtons in poor condition are not suitable for conversion to high pressure calibers because of the fact that no spare parts will ever be found for them.

Single Shot Actions

There is quite a bit of controversy among authors and authorities as to which single shot action is the best. There is probably no great difference between the Sharps-Borchardt and the Winchester High side action. I personally prefer the Sharps-Borchardt to any other American single shot. I would rate the more common single shots in the following order: Sharps-Borchardt, Winchester High Side, Farquharson, Stevens 44½, Remington-Hepburn, Ballard, Stevens 44.

The Stevens 44 and Ballard are not to be considered except for some low pressure cartridges which have been developed expressly for use with them and which are hardly worth considering, except by those who want to play around with these old rifles. We must admit that there are some fine old rifles on these actions and for those who desire to keep them, it is all right to rebarrel or reline them for something like the .25 Hornet, which is nothing more or less than the .22 Hornet cartridge expanded to .25, and which develops low pressure loads.

Rating the Sharps-Borchardt instead of the Winchester High Side action as No. 1 among the single shots will in all probability bring down a shower of criticism upon me. I realize very well that the Winchester does seem to be the No. 1 choice of most of our American shooters. They have many good reasons for this too, which I would not argue with. It is largely personal preference and also the fact that so many gunsmiths do not use the proper method of conversion for the Sharps-Borchardt. The Farquharson is placed No. 1 by some authorities and they also have good reasons. One is that a more beautiful rifle can be built on the Farquharson than any other popular single shot action. It also has sufficient strength for any modern caliber and is very satisfactory in every way.

Sharps-Borchardt

I placed the Sharps-Borchardt first for several reasons: One is because I feel that a rifle can be beautiful as well as useful at the same time, and a neater rifle can be built on the Sharps action than any other American-made frame. It has a relatively fast lock, is more or less streamlined, is made of reasonably good material, has good workmanship, has a separate spring to keep the lever from developing slack, it is more easily stocked, and has sufficient strength for any reasonable load.

On the other hand, it is a victim of circumstances because of the fact that so many gunsmiths fail to get the idea of the proper way to retract the firing pin. Because of this, the Borchardt has always had a "black eye" in all of our magazines and a description of the action is always accompanied by the statement that there is insufficient or faulty firing pin retraction. This is entirely due to the fact that they do not know how to properly adjust the firing pin. There is no better retraction in any action that we find than in the Sharps-Borchardt. There is just positively no better way to withdraw the firing pin than for cocking cams to do it, but of course, if it is improperly set up or adjusted, there is no retraction at all until after the block is well started on its downward travel. When the firing pin is so adjusted that it starts its backward travel as soon as the block starts its downward travel, there is absolutely no difficulty in retracting the firing pin without any trace of sticking in the primer. I will be glad to submit one of our own actions any time to prove this statement.

When the block is removed from the rifle and the mainspring and other parts are out, so that the firing pin is free to travel back and forth in the block, it is easy to see what causes the trouble. As is commonly known, there is a cocking pin which passes through the firing pin and through the block and which engages the cocking cams in the side of the action. The firing pin has to be cut back on the front end of the large portion (through which the cocking pin passes), so that the cocking pin itself comes in contact with the slots in the block at the very forward end. In other words, the cocking pin must go as far forward as the slots in the block will allow it to and this invariably means that the large portion of the firing pin has to be cut back in the lathe to allow the entire firing pin to go farther forward, sometimes as much as 1/16". After this is so adjusted it will be necessary to cut off the striker so that the proper protrusion is obtained, and this should be minimum in the Sharps action, probably not over 0.04" or 0.05" at most. When these actions come to the gunsmith they invariably strike the primer so that the firing pin movement stops with the cocking pin coming to rest approximately 1/16" before it strikes the end of the slots in the block, so it lacks 1/16" of coming in contact with the cocking cams in the side of the action, which means that when the block is lowered as the gun is being opened, the firing pin will not be retracted until the block has started downward a sufficient distance for the cocking pin to come in contact with the cocking cams. This sometimes is $\frac{1}{8}''$ or more, and during this time the firing pin is bound to stick in the primer or score the head of the case. I do not know whether it has been possible for the reader to follow all this, but the fact remains that the Sharps-Borchardt has been the victim of a lot of criticism, when in reality it has been entirely the fault of the conversion jobs themselves.

Winchester Single Shot

The Winchester action should be almost classed as a family rather than individual actions. It was made in two general designs—the low wall and the high wall types. These actions, according to Winchester, were designated as No. 2 and No. 3. The No. 2 action being the Low Side type and the No. 3, the High Side type. Both actions were subdivided into two additional types, namely the panelled type and the straight side type. The panelled type having a rather thin side wall and the straight side actions having rather thick side walls. Both the Low Side and the panelled High Side single shot actions were made with two different thread diameters, the small one measuring .821" and the larger .935". The extremely heavy straight side action of the High Side type was apparently made with only a large thread diameter.

The Low Side action is not to be considered for the more powerful wildcats. It is only suitable for .22 Hornet or at the most the .22/3000 Lovell, but the High Side actions are capable of withstanding almost any pressure that any handloader would ever consider using. The two High Side models were made in calibers from .22 to .50-110 express.

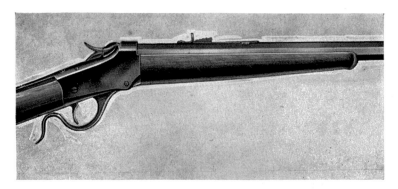

The Low Side Winchester rifle.

According to Winchester, the heavy actions were the original ones and were later changed to the thinner High Side model which has a maximum wall thickness of 0.25″ as compared with 0.30″ for the heavy model. The Low Side also had the same wall thickness as the thin High Side action. All of the early actions were case hardened and were fitted with six standard barrel weights, which went by numbers 1, 2, 3, 3½, 4 and 5. Some of the later actions were made of nickel steel and were fitted with coil springs and light hammer for faster lock time. The Winchester Company advises reheat-treatment of the case hardened actions. This is not supposed to increase the strength materially, but will refine the structure of the metal. This is one instance in which reheat-treatment is recommended. Such actions can be sent to the Winchester Company; they will reheat-treat them and refinish them at a very small cost. When the action is returned by them, it is just exactly like new. The Winchester Company does not recommend the use of the hottest wildcat calibers. However, they do admit that the High Side will withstand any of the modern pressures and we have found by actual tests that these High Side actions will stand almost any load within reason.

The Winder Musket

There is another type of Winchester High Side action known as the Winder Musket. The only difference between this and the others is that the Winder Models were made for .22 rim fire ammunition and were all fitted with the rim firing pin, breech block, and extractor.

I have seen a great many of the High Side .22 Muskets converted to calibers such as the .22 Hornet, Lovell, and Zipper with very good results. These actions are comparatively soft, not being case hardened, but seem to withstand any pressures of the calibers mentioned. With the larger case heads it might be desirable to build up the beveled cut in the top of the breech block, put in there so that the .22 rim fire cases could be more easily seated. They also need a gas vent drilled in the block.

A letter recently received by me from the Winchester Company has the following to say in relation to the Winchester single shots:

"The Winchester single shot rifles were made in two styles, No. 2 and No. 3. The No. 3 or so-called "High Side" was adaptable to all calibers from .22 rim fire up to .50-110 express.

"Some of these early ones had full sides, while later this was changed to panelled sides. Also the early ones were case hardened. Six weights of rifle barrels were adapted to these.

"In adapting any of these case hardened receivers to modern cartridges developing considerable pressures we recommend that they be heat-treated to refine the metal structure.

"This we have been doing, ending up by refinishing, afterwards by bluing.

"These guns were designed for ammunition of the pre-high pressure days, and had ample strength, and no doubt have for much of the modern ammunition.

"However, having made no tests to determine limits of pressure that could be recommended, we suggest the maximum loads of the old pressures as a basis of comparison such as the .35 Winchester, .405 Winchester and .45-70 Government.

"The Winder Musket comes in this category of receivers, but it of course, had the rim fire breech block, firing pin and extractor.

"The No. 2 or Low Side receiver has full sides and small barrel shank and was adapted to all rim fire cartridges and center fire in .25-20 single shot, .32, .38 and .44 Winchester calibers. Many of these have been fitted by gunsmiths with .22 Hornet barrels and for a gun in normal condition we feel that the .218 Bee could safely be used. Incidentally few of either No. 2 or No. 3 frame was made with nickel steel barrels, but instead a strong mild steel was used."

Winchester has also informed me that the supply of components as repair parts for these old actions is almost exhausted. They have only a few of the parts left. They also said that they do not plan to manufacture any additional actions or parts.

There is little fault to be found with the Winchester High Side action. It has good firing pin retraction and is well designed, all the way round. The main fault of both the Sharps-Borchardt and Winchester actions, or for that matter almost any single shot action is the lack of extraction power. Here, the English actions with their double extractors probably have it over our own American made actions.

I feel it is a mistake to speed up the Winchester action by lightening the hammer and installing a coil spring. I am probably laying myself wide open for criticism by making this statement, but I personally prefer the old hammer, with the old flat spring which prevents rebounding of the hammer from the pressure of the primer, resulting in pierced primers unless a very small firing pin is used. In general the old High Side action as made in the old days with a flat spring and heavy hammer is a pretty hard outfit to beat from the standpoint of all round usefulness.

Doubtless the old case hardened variety of Winchester single shot actions were made of some kind of carbon steel, probably more or less of the same type as used in the Farquharson action, which could be classed as similar to our common cold rolled steel. The case hardening prevents wear and the soft core of the steel gives it strength enough to resist any modern high pressure load. I have never personally seen one of these actions blown up. I understand however, that some of the old barrels have developed swollen chambers which resulted in the lower part of the thread portion of the action being cracked away. That is, the thin web, between the lower part of the threads and the opening through which the flat spring extends into the receiver sometimes is ruptured when the barrel is swollen from excessive pressures. Such a rupture is not dangerous to the shooter, but it does ruin the action for further use. Excessive pressures also sometimes result in blowing the firing pin out of the block and also breaking the hammer. This is caused by using a firing pin of too large size, which results in pierced primers and a sudden rush of gas around the firing pin. If the pin is reduced in diameter to about 0.070″ almost any load within reason can be used without danger of pierced primers.

Sometimes the Winchester single shot action is fitted with some type of safety firing pin—the most common of which is the Mann Niedner. In some instances, such pins are very satisfactory, but they are not particularly necessary if the original pin is properly altered and fitted.

The English Farquharson Action

The Farquharson is of English origin. It is similar in operation to the Winchester, except that it has an enclosed hammer and could be called hammerless. It has a falling block similar to the Winchester but does not have as much camming power. The block rises straight up through the action, the same as the Sharps-Borchardt. The lever of the Farquharson action is separate from the trigger guard and has a lock which holds it in place, until the lever is actually separated. This feature is in direct contrast to the Winchester single shot. The Winchester often develops wear in the lever which results in this part not remaining tight when in the closed position. It might be said that the lever sort of flops around. The Sharps-Borchardt does not develop this tendency for the lever to become loose because it has a separate spring which always holds it in position.

There are different makes of so-called "Farquharson" actions. These actions were apparently made under the Farquharson patents. At least, they were made by various different English firms and many versions have come from Germany and Belgium. Almost all of them are fine actions, regardless of origin.

One fault is the apparent lack of standardization of material. They seem to be made of almost anything. We recently imported one from Westley Richards and this is nothing more than a low carbon steel. It is a .577 low pressure action, very heavy and in the white. After a great deal of correspondence, George Vitt of the Holden Company, finally found out that it was made of a low carbon steel and could not be heat treated any way except by carburizing. Of course the great size of the action made it perfectly safe for any load but the fact remains that the material is poor.

Some Farquharson actions are also badly designed in that the hammer is so light that with high pressure calibers the firing pin and hammer are bounced back by the primer when fired, resulting in pierced primers; this being the same condition that we run into now and then with the Winchester single shot coil spring deal or with the Remington-Hepburn. Some models have a different hammer and are much better for high pressure stuff. These actions also have a poorly constructed link and have no camming action whatsoever. There are some nice points about them, however, such as the hammerless, streamlined appearance and the tang safety on some of them. They also have a much better lever lock than any of our American actions. The lever of the Farquharson never gets so that it flops down when the action is closed and a streamlined stock can always be fitted to them, giving them an appearance and feel of a high grade shotgun. Another point is that the firing pin travels upwards at a very acute angle which is probably one more feature that is not too desirable.

The Hepburn

The Remington-Hepburn does not lack anything in strength. It is just as strong or stronger than any of the above actions. Its lack of popularity is due to several things. The slide lever operation never seems to go over with the shooters. There is no particular objection to this feature and it is exceedingly handy for shooting from cramped positions, or for shooting out of a car window. It may be a fact that it is against the law to shoot from car windows, but it is done by almost all of the varmint shooters, and one of the neatest "car" rifles can be made by using the Hepburn action. There is no long, ungainly lever to get tangled up in the steering wheel, door or other passengers. The most objectional features are the rebounding hammer and the complete lack of streamlining. It is nearly impossible to make a good looking rifle out of a Remington-Hepburn because of its pronounced hunch-back appearance.

When the Remington-Hepburn action came from the factory it was probably one of the most ugly appearing rifles ever built in this country. This hunch-back appearance which it has, can be changed by shortening the upper tang and bending the lower tang with a little more curve to get a better pistol grip. The rebounding feature can also be eliminated, and it can be easily adapted to use a coil mainspring, instead of the original flat one.

It must be said here, that there is no danger from the use of the Remington-Hepburn action with any of the hot wildcats when it is properly converted.

The Stevens 44½

The Stevens 44½ is also a very fine action and probably better designed in some ways than any of them. Almost everyone admires the camming action of this Stevens 44½. It is about the only one that we have that gives any real power for seating the case in the chamber. Its main fault is that it is made from castings and poor materials. Even so, it is a good action for most of our Super .22s up to and including the Imp. Zipper. However, it should not be used with calibers heavier than the Imp. Zipper because of the inferior materials. One objection to the 44½ pointed out by many critics is the fact that the firing pin travels upwards at a comparatively acute angle to the axis of the breech bolt.

Ballard and Stevens 44

These two old actions are not to be considered for the high speed, modern super .22 calibers. Owners of these actions are always pestering gunsmiths to rebarrel them for something like the R-2 Lovell or Zipper, or such modern cartridges. *Such a conversion is not safe.* These old actions are only to be considered for the lowest pressure loads. They make a very fine foundation for .22 rim fire target rifles or for extremely low pressure center fire cartridges. However, there is very little use these days for the low pressure loads which would be safe in these actions. For the few who might be interested in such loads, such actions can be safely used with the .25 Hornet, which is nothing more or less than the improved Hornet cartridge expanded to take a .25 caliber bullet or the old original .25-20 single shot. Many of these old rifles still have the original barrel in the original condition—some by our most famous old time barrelmakers, and chambered for calibers such as .32-40, and .38-55. These old rifles are still safe to use in the original caliber, provided only low pressure loads are used.

Chapter 17

BUHMILLER RIFLE BARRELS FOR .22 WILDCATS

J. R. BUHMILLER, of Eureka, Montana, is a manufacturer of rifle barrel blanks who, in recent years, has assumed a very important role in providing bored and rifled, but usually unfinished barrels, to custom gunsmiths and others prepared to fit and finish the tubes. Among his customers have been Jerry Gebby, Hervey Lovell, Hammer & Gipson, Floyd Butler, Jack Ashurst, J. Pfeifer, R. W. Miller, Vard, Mashburn Arms Co., Kenneth Hooper and numerous others. Buhmiller said rather ruefully, to the author, that for some years past he has been so busy boring and rifling barrels that he seldom can find time to chamber and finish a rifle for himself.

A rifled blank is usually shipped out straightened but is unturned, unfitted and unchambered. Most of them are then, of course, not lapped. The custom gunsmith still finds plenty to do after receiving the blank. The extractor slot must be cut and the extractor fitted. The barrel must be inletted into the forearm and the bedding of the stock with the barrel now on the rifle must be checked. It may be necessary to fit or refit a barrel band, or attach a sling swivel. Sights must be fitted and sight slots may have to be cut, or more likely, sight bands be formed and set to place. The whole job must be blued and finished. A barrel blank is only the beginning of a barrel, or a rifle, but it is of course a very important feature of the arm and care and skill in its making must be observed.

Comparatively few custom gunsmiths or expert artisans in steel have the necessary barrel drilling and rifling machines to make barrels, so men like Buhmiller specialize upon this feature of rifle making. With business and industry starting to reconvert to peacetime pursuits, there may be many who have spare time on their hands, and also they will have acquired, due to war jobs, skill in fitting, chambering, finishing or blueing metal parts of machine guns or rifles, so that they can individually purchase a barrel blank which is bored, rifled, and maybe chambered, and from there on make a new rifle. They will do this by fitting the completed barrel to a rifle action and its stock. The caliber can be anything the rifleman wants,

356

and quite likely it will be a .22 caliber commercial varmint or one of the .22 wildcats.

It is entirely reasonable to assume that after the war junk is all shipped home, and reconditioned rifles are assembled at arsenals, Mauser rifle souvenirs sent or brought home by soldiers will begin finding their way to market. The market will eventually be flooded with thousands of Mauser, Springfield, 1917 Enfield, Lee-Enfield, possibly a few Garands and other arms which will supply an unlimited number of suitable actions. Many of you will recall when it was impossible to sell thousands of Krags offered for as low as $3.50 each. Philadelphia store windows were filled with Ross military rifles in excellent condition which were quite unsalable at $5.00 each. At least some twelve or fourteen *million* military rifles and carbines were produced for World War II by manufacturers in the United States. Into such a picture comes Buhmiller and those like him. Men who can drill and rifle barrels in sporting and varmint shooting calibers that riflemen really want.

Today, Buhmiller supplies unturned, unfitted, unchambered and unlapped—but bored, rifled and straightened barrel blanks of chrome molybdenum steel 1¼″ in diameter, 27″ long, for about $17.50 each and the same blanks, made of carbon manganese steel, for $15.00 each, with barrels 1 3/16″ x 27″. Longer barrels can be supplied up to 31″ at an extra cost of about 50c per inch over 27″. These would be special jobs and subject to slight delay. He does no reboring to larger calibers, no barrel fitting, no barrel relining, no woodwork such as stocking because he just does not have the time. He straightens his barrels when necessary, sometimes though a tube comes through so smoothly cut and of such good steel texture that it does not require straightening. In that case, such a barrel is to be preferred to a straightened barrel. It should not "walk" when heating up from firing.

Buhmiller barrels are supplied in .22 Long Rifle; .22 Hornet; .22 Lovell calibers in carbon manganese steel; and in .22 Long Rifle; .22 Hornet; .22 Lovell; .219 Zipper; .22-250; .220 Swift; and various larger calibers in the molybdenum steel. Any of these in 0.224″ diameter can be chambered for any of the .22 wildcats of that groove diameter by custom gunsmiths equipped to do such work, or by private persons skilled in such procedure.

Buhmiller strongly recommends Red Elliott's chambering reamers to chamber Buhmiller barrels. Data on the use and selection of chambering reamers is given elsewhere in this work. Buhmiller pronounces the Elliott reamers "Jewels of Workmanship."

How to Straighten a Rifle Barrel—Turning Down a Barrel—
Lapping a Bore

Buhmiller has cooperated in passing on to you readers some of his methods of finishing and fitting barrels. He feels that it is useless to use a lot of care in boring, rifling and straightening a barrel, and then have someone spoil the barrel for accurate shooting by improper procedure or unskilled workmanship in later steps of barrel making.

In turning down a .22 rifle barrel blank, it is often advisable to use the end of the blank in which the drill started, as the muzzle. That means that the bar is then likely to be well centered at the muzzle end and warpage, if any, is likely to be much less at the forward end, which is the most important part or portion of the barrel, insofar as barrel straightness is concerned. Also, it is the more important part of the barrel insofar as accuracy is concerned, and the more important portion in the matter of keeping a constant center of impact.

In turning down a rifle barrel blank to finished size, the center rest should be selected and a very moderate cut should be made to avoid too much developed heat. In spite of the utmost care, rifle barrels usually warp, more or less, in the process of being turned down. It is obvious, that if a deep cut be taken and much stress set up, also more heat, this warping will be greater, or at least it could be!

A crooked barrel may shoot or group accurately, especially if very heavy and shot very slowly and if, in addition, a relatively light cartridge be used. But most of us prefer a reasonably straight barrel. We do not want to feel that, having done our part, the barrel will not perform according to expectations. No one wants to see his group beginning to walk, with the regularity of a clock, every time he reaches the third or fourth shot; or, maybe the fifth or sixth. A barrel should continue to drive every bullet into the same ragged gash. It stands to reason that a *straight* barrel, other things being equal, has the best chance to do this!

The operation of barrel straightening has at times, been clouded in some mystery, even hocus pocus. Some regard it as a very difficult operation. A recent publicity article claimed that only seven or eight experienced barrel straighteners live in the United States. If that be true, the Axis could have saved their medical corps a lot of work, by disposing of these few men. Speaking of bottlenecks, could you imagine a worse one?

But to get back to straightening a barrel for use on a .22 wild-cat. Many who do much barrel straightening use a barrel-straightening jack (of which Buhmiller has one), which is a heavy, expensive piece of equipment not usually available to the average gunsmith. A moderately heavy bench vise can be made to serve nicely for straightening an occasional barrel. One jaw should be provided with a bar, about 10″ or 12″ long, with a block at each end. A single

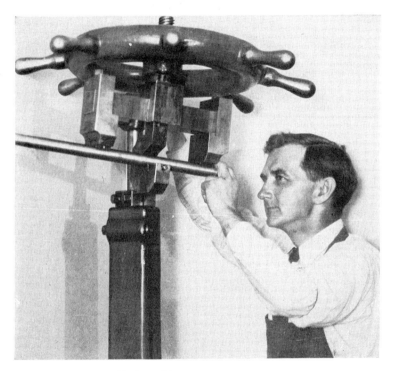

J. R. BUHMILLER STRAIGHTENING A .22 CALIBER RIFLE BARREL

This photo shows how an expert barrel borer straightens a .22 caliber barrel. Note three bearing points of straightening machine.

block is placed in the center of the opposite jaw. A rifle barrel placed in the vise with this arrangement is easily bent as desired, by applying pressure on the screw.

A hollow plug is placed in the opposite end of the rifle barrel, bored so as to show shadow rings in the barrel. If the tube is straight, all the way through, these rings will be concentric, but if the bore is crooked or bent some of the shadow rings will be eccentric. The observer should place a white card or other similar object, which is well lighted, in line with the rifle bore, to make these shadow rings as distinct as possible. The hollow plug to be placed in the end of the barrel should be a push fit in the bore, and for .22 caliber barrel should have a hole in the center about 0.125″ in diameter; for larger calibers, the hole should be correspondingly larger. The plug should be accurately made with the hole in the exact center. The length can conveniently be about 0.75″ in the smaller calibers.

The blocks in the vise should be hung securely so they will not fall out, and should be provided with pins, hooks, or other means for supporting the rifle barrel laid loosely therein. The operator then places the barrel in this arrangement, with the hollow plug in the opposite end, a well-lighted white wall or card, in line with the bore, and he is ready to test the barrel for straightness. Get down so the eye is level with the bore and look through; if the bore is crooked some of the shadow rings will be observed off center. By lightly closing the vise jaws, in different places on the barrel, he can soon find where the bend is, and apply just enough additional pressure to straighten it. After a little practice, one can tell at a glance where the bend is located from the appearance of the shadow rings, but for the beginner it is easier for him to work out the problem for himself, remembering that he does *not* want to apply too much pressure, especially in the wrong place, or just this side of, or that side of, the bend, so that the result is two opposing bends giving a reverse curve or "S" effect. After a little practice, a man generally gets along well enough, or so it appears. In looking through the barrel, most of the shadows he will see will be in the one-half of the barrel next the eye. After this end of the barrel is straightened of all kinks, he will have to reverse the barrel (and plug) and work from the other end. It is then a good idea to recheck the whole barrel, by the light rings, to see that it really *is* straight.

During the progress of the work, when a bend is located exert a little pressure on the vise screw, then release and observe the effect, if any. Continue this process, adding a little more pressure to the vise screw each time, until the bend is straightened. Care, calmness, and patience in making these tests, and applications of slight pressure here and there, is what gives the perfect result. Deftness is more important than strength or speed. The master workman, like the master surgeon, is the one who makes the right move at the right time, and makes his cut, bend, application, or whatnot, with a master's touch. In the boring, rifling and straightening of a rifle barrel it is a good plan, and a wise suggestion, that one should never overdo any one operation.

A great variety of steels are used in making rifle barrels. A soft steel barrel may straighten easily, while another barrel, much harder or tougher, may resist like spring steel. If the operator persists, and is careful, painstaking, and thorough, he can do nicely with a vise.

Lapping

Buhmiller barrels, that is, Buhmiller barrel blanks, are not chambered. Consequently, either end may be used as breech or muzzle. This is only true, of course, of a blank of equal diameter throughout its length, as most of them are. Before chambering, the barrel should be lapped just a little to remove any burrs (which will be few if the barrel has been slowly and carefully bored and rifled) and to smooth and polish and to improve, if possible, the evenness of bore diameter; in other words, to give the last finishing touches that make for perfection. Some barrels contain tight or loose places. Not much can be done for loose places, unless the whole barrel be lapped larger, but tight places can be generally lapped out, by careful lapping and then testing with a lead plug. Usually, the gunsmith or mechanic must depend upon the feel and fit of a round buckshot or other lead gage pushed carefully through the bore, or by other means of gaging the diameter.

Barrels can easily be spoiled by too much lapping; the reason is, of course, one cannot replace metal once lapped out. Lapping is a gradual grinding or polishing out of excess metal. A barrel can also be spoiled by improper lapping. Beware of lapping too much in any one spot; or of applying pressure too steadily on one side of the bore; or of lapping with too coarse an abrasive. The completed bore, after lapping, should shine with mirror-like smoothness, be free of scratches and marks, and be even in diameter throughout the bore. Usually, 15 or 20 passes of the lap are sufficient, then wash out the bore and gage it. When you get a uniform, even resistance all the way through, and cannot find either tight or loose places it is time to quit.

There is usually some choke in each end of the barrel as it comes off the rifling machine. A half inch or more should be cut from the muzzle, after lapping, to make sure the barrel end is perfect. It should be examined carefully under a magnifying glass. The cutting of the chamber will remove all choke from the breech. Provision must, in due time, be made for cutting the extractor slot.

W. A. SUKALLE RIFLE BARRELS

Probably the most completely equipped and one of the best-known barrelmakers in the South West, is W. A. Sukalle, of 1120 East Washington St., Phoenix, Arizona. His shop contains Pratt & Whitney barrel drill, rifling machine and a reaming machine. He bores barrels and barrel blanks in his own shop, and is a barrelmaker rather than a rechambering specialist.

For a goodly number of years, Sukalle had quite a business in supplying other gunmakers with bored and rifled barrel blanks. A "blank" in this sense is a tube or barrel which has been bored and then rifled, but which is then not chambered, does not have the extractor slot cut, and is otherwise unfinished. His counterpart, today, is J. R. Buhmiller of Eureka, Montana. Today Sukalle supplies barrels only—no blanks.

Sukalle, for years, made .22 Long Rifle barrels of most excellent quality and a very high degree of accuracy. He turned them out with 16″, 17″ and 18″ twist, and with groove diameters of 0.222″ and 0.223″, and eventually decided that a 0.222″ groove diameter tube with 17″ twist gave him the best all-around groups, considering the many different makes, brands, velocities and styles of .22 Long Rifle ammunition his barrels might be called upon to shoot. He expected to make some 8-groove barrels in .22 Long Rifle, as there is occasionally some call for them, but all of his barrels for years were 6-groove tubes.

He also bored and rifled a good number of tubes for .218 Bee, .22/3000 Lovell, the R-2, the .219 Zipper, the .220 Swift, and the .22-250. All these gave accuracy comparable to his match barrels, but in the center fires the .22-250 seemed to zero better, with any load, than any other .22 center fire cartridge he ever chambered. The Sukalle .22 center fire tubes were made in 0.224″ groove diameter and with 12″, 14″ and 16″ twists. He also made some barrels for the .22 Hi-Power Savage cartridge and at one time was reportedly making quite a number of .22-250 blanks for Ralph Waldo Miller, of Altadena, California.

Then along came the war. Sukalle became engaged almost solely on war work but that of course is now past tense. In future he expects to devote his efforts to fine sporting barrels rather than .22 Long Rifle match barrels, as in the past he spent so much time on each match barrel that it was unprofitable. He could make up special .22 Long Rifle sporting rifle tubes.

In the past Sukalle has made the Sukalle extension base for

52's and 37's, and special trigger action made to hold its adjustment, with trigger stop and finely fitted parts. He also engine turns rifle bolts, checkers bolt knobs, mats receivers and remodels Enfields so that they cock like a Springfield.

Future Sukalle barrels in .22 caliber will be mostly for .22 center fire commercial cartridges, although he is making .22-250 in heavy .224″ barrels and may turn out .219 Donaldson-Wasp or similar sizes if these cartridges are brought out commercially by one or more of the large arms manufacturers. Sukalle has also made a good many .22 Hornet barrels, and if the .219 Zipper Improved wildcats are standardized in length and shoulder slope this would be a logical number for his shop. Most of the Western and South Western gunshops run to high velocity, long range calibers of .22's, due to the coyote nuisance. You need a rifle that will reach out and smack them at a good distance, and a cartridge that has killing power over 200 to 400 yards. Comment on Sukalle barrels has been very favorable.

CHAPTER 18

MANUFACTURE AND USE OF CHAMBERING REAMERS

IN THE manufacture of super-accurate .22 rim fire, or .22 center fire wildcat rifles, nothing seems to be of greater importance than having accurately-made chambering reamers. These are the fine tools with which the chamber and bullet seat are cut. They determine the size and shape of the chamber in all of its parts and the accuracy with which the cartridge is held in line with the axis of the bore. Also, they determine how the bullet is held in relation to the rifling at the moment the cartridge is fired.

Some rifle barrel makers or custom gunsmiths, who fit and chamber .22 caliber rifle barrel blanks and complete the rifle, make their own chambering reamers. Some make such reamers as they have time, and buy others when they are too much rushed with business. F. K. Elliott, of California, appears to be one of the most expert and experienced rifle chamber reamer manufacturers in this country. His reamers are used regularly, or at times, by many of the most widely known custom gunsmiths.

The Making of Reamers

1. In laying out the design of a reamer it is helpful to have a drawing of the chamber that is to be cut and, if possible, a few samples of the cartridge it is to take. Standard methods of measuring and lettering should be used in making sketches, and measurements should be given to several decimal places. They should, above all things, be given accurately, and the figures closely checked.

2. Chambering reamers are usually made in two general styles, the roughing reamer and the finishing reamer. Roughing reamers are used to rough out the chamber. Finishing reamers are selected to finish a roughed out chamber or to deepen a chamber already finish-reamed, as when a new barrel is fitted to a Springfield.

3. Both roughing and finishing reamers should have a pilot on

364

the front end to center the reamer in the bore. The pilot can be made solid, or it can be made as a separate bushing held by a screw. If of the latter type, bushings of different diameter can be used to fit individual barrels. In any case the pilot must be round, smooth and highly polished, without sharp corners that might scratch the bore.

4. Roughing reamers mostly have four teeth, while finishing reamers are generally made with six teeth. The teeth should be staggered, not evenly spaced, to prevent chattering. A square on the end of the shank affords a convenient method of operating the reamer with a tap wrench. Some reamers are made with a threaded hole in the shank to fit an extension that is screwed in. This extension is very handy when it is necessary to use a reamer on a barrel already fitted to the action.

5. Reamers made for .22 rim fire rifles, such as the .22 Short, .22 Long Rifle and .22 W. R. F., are mostly made without heading counterbore. The Long Rifle reamers can be used for .22 Short and .22 Long, (but are then not cut in as far). The heading counterbore can be made separately, if so wanted, and should be fitted with a pilot that fits the chamber. On some .22 rifles it is not needed.

6. Reamers are turned up from the blank bar in the lathe, and are grooved in the milling machine. The next operation is heat treatment, and after this is done the faces of the cutting teeth should be smoothed, if necessary. The front face of the tooth is part of the cutting edge. If the reamer is to be ground, the cutters should first be lapped smooth. After circular grinding is completed the teeth are ground for clearance. The final cutting edge is put on by hand stoning, and this should be done with skill and care. If the cutting relief is not sufficient, the reamer will not cut; if too much, it is liable to chatter.

Steel Stock for Reamers

7. Three types of steel are commonly used for making reamers. The type employed will depend upon the equipment on hand as well as on the use intended for the reamer. The types are oil-hardening tool steel; high carbon tool steel; high speed tool steel.

8. Oil hardening tool steel offers the advantage that if heat treated properly it will warp very little, if any, when it is hardened. A shop that is not equipped to grind reamers will do well to consider this type. The clearing of the teeth can be done with a file before hardening, and after hardening all that is needed is to stone the edges.

9. High carbon tool steel will usually warp somewhat in hardening. It is customary to make the reamer some 0.030″ larger in diameter than the finished size. After heat treatment, the reamer can be ground to correct size which will straighten out any warping. This type of steel will usually cut better and last longer than the oil hardening type.

10. High speed tool steel has the advantage that it remains hard even when heated to a blue heat, so that it is useful for tools intended to remove metal in a hurry, such as for roughing reamers. It is suitable and satisfactory for finishing reamers also, but since finishing is, as a rule, performed slowly this steel probably offers no advantage over high carbon steel for finishing. High speed steel is more costly than the others, is harder to machine and to grind and most gunsmiths will have to send it to a professional heat treater to have it hardened.

11. All of these types of tool steel are made by practically every tool steel company in the United States, although under different trade names. The makers will supply information as to heat treatment when such is needed.

12. There is still another type of steel used for chambering reamers—tungsten finishing steel. This steel is somewhat brittle, but is possibly the best for finishing reamers as it takes a good edge and is very resistant to wear. It is somewhat difficult to grind without overheating, and the grinding wheel must be dressed often and a plentiful supply of coolant used. When grinding the clearance on reamers made from this steel it seems best to use wheels of green silicon carbide, and it is necessary to use care to prevent burning.

The finished reamer, mentioned in Item 2, is often used to deepen a finished chamber. The Springfield rifle reaming is peculiar in one respect—when new barrels are sent out they are reamed short, so as to make fitting to a worn action produce a tight head space. They then require a touching up by the finishing reamer to give proper head space.

Red Elliott probably has the only stoning jig in capitivity, but L. E. Wilson is reported to also have some such device. A stoning jig takes a long time to build, and is not a fixture that most gunsmiths will require.

Tungsten finishing steel is a very difficult steel to grind. It is almost impossible for men with the tool post grinder used in a lathe to work it properly, at least without great difficulty. It quickly wears a grinding wheel, which makes the wheel burn the steel as it cannot cut it when dull. Unless a man has a great deal of experience in grinding, it can cause a lot of grief. Elliott says he wishes he knew of some easy way to grind it. Its use generally for chambering tool manufacture is not suggested.

Wear of Chambering Reamers

During at least the latter part of the war with Germany, barrel and barrel blank makers had more than their usual difficulty with steel of uneven texture. Barrel bars contained hard and soft spots and many a barrelmaker had to bore his barrels from the steel he could obtain, instead of the smooth, even-textured steel he required for a good, accurate bumble bee barrel. When an uneven blank is obtained, and must be used, the cutter tools tend to follow soft portions of the steel and turn away from hard spots, causing a lack of evenness and straightness in the boring of the barrel, or in the rifling of it. Buhmiller complained to the author of having been furnished irregular stock rather early in the war, but later he obtained a shipment of much better stock which cut evenly and smoothly.

The Use of Chambering Reamers

The pilot bushing should be a *sliding fit* in the bore. It is necessary that the bore turn dead true during the chambering and care should be taken to insure that it does. Possibly the best reaming is done in a lathe, with the muzzle end of the barrel on the live center, and the breech end in the steady-rest where it can vibrate the least. Any run out is liable to cause an enlarged or a rough chamber. A chambering reamer is not something to use carelessly and heedlessly. As there have been many enlarged and also rough chambers, this matter of run out should be considered.

The Chambering Operation

The roughing reamer is run in first and can be held either by the tailstock chuck, or be placed on the tailstock center and held by hand. Those without previous experience should choose the first method. With the finish reamer it is best to let it find its own center, using a blank plate on the end of the tailstock spindle and holding the reamer by hand. The barrel should turn quite slowly while finishing, about 30 revolutions a minute, and the feed, using the tailstock screw, should be smooth and light. Chips should be cleared away often and plenty of sulfurized cutting oil used. About 0.004″ of the chamber *depth* should be left for assembling the barrel to the action, after which operation that tolerance is removed.

Due to difference in texture of steel, toughness and hardness of the metal, and to other conditions, some barrels have a natural tendency to ream more roughly than others. It is suggested that the one who is reaming run the finger nail over the edge of the reamer before finishing, to detect any pickups on the teeth. Any so found may be removed with a piece of copper or brass. If care is used, and the metal is favorable to a good finish, chambers can be completed which will require little if any polishing.

Restoning Chambering Reamers

If the wear on the teeth of the chambering reamers becomes excessive, the reamer can be reconditioned by stoning the teeth on top, back of the cutting edge, so as to leave a narrow land. The edge itself should *not* be stoned; that is, not unless very rough and nicked. When reamer teeth need resharpening, the reamer can be sent back to its manufacturer for resharpening. Such expense is about one-fifth of the original cost of the reamers.

Durability of Chambering Reamers

Elliott has suggested to the author that a properly-made finishing reamer, used for finish reaming only, should finish 100 chambers in hard barrel steel, before needing restoning. It should stand three or four stonings before becoming too small in diameter—assuming the reamer has been made of tungsten finishing steel. The other types may run one-half as many complete barrels. Hervey Lovell recently suggested to the author that, for a commercial gunsmith, making up and chambering many barrels, the average reamer cost is about $1.00 a barrel. For a man making but one barrel, it would cost him the full price of the set of reamers used. Apparently, from his comment, Lovell does not use a set of reamers for this great number of barrels. He probably is very particular about such matters, as he talks of chambering reamers more than any other subject connected with gunsmithing.

The whole subject of the manufacture and use of chambering reamers is important; sometimes full of grief. Barrel steels are tough and hard to cut and this requires very hard steel in the reamers. These are still harder to cut. Persons sending in specifications for reamers, particularly for new and special designs of reamers, should be very certain to have their writing legible. Have each figure so plainly formed that one cannot mistake a 3 for an 8, or vice versa, and be equally certain to give *all* of the required dimensions with great accuracy to several decimal places. Check and recheck each dimension before mailing your drawing. Original ideas are not always too practical, especially when put forth by those lacking machine design experience, and are therefore difficult to put into practice from a production angle. Some demand the necks too tight or the throat too short, both of which run up pressures, especially in the small .22/3000 cartridges.

Anderson and Shelhamer, formerly of Niedner Rifle Corporation, are shying away from requests for the very tight Niedner type of chamber. Hervey Lovell is cautioning against loading .22 bullets in small cases (like any of the .22/3000's) so that the ogive of the bullet is jammed up into the rifling. If the breech is opened, the bullet may remain in the barrel, and if the rifle is fired pressures soar and primers may blow. Seat the bullet to normal depth and have about National Match Springfield tolerances in chambering in your wildcat rifle. Order or make your chambering reamers accordingly; cut accordingly.

Lovell has made a considerable number of very helpful suggestions about reamers to the author, in letters of recent date, some of which are quoted for their helpfulness. He says: "The most efficient and cheapest set of reamers I have found consists of a set of *four* reamers (Hervey insists that there be more than two reamers, as he (Lovell) uses great care in grinding and polishing the bullet seating tool of the reloader, so that a perfect-fitting cartridge may result to be loaded in the rifle; the cartridge should exactly fit the chamber and the bullet be held directly in line with the long axis of the bore; the four reamers are ground at one set-up of tapers on the machine).

"The first reamer is of high speed steel with four flutes. This cuts sizing die for case. Second reamer cuts chambers to nearly correct size and third reamer, kept new and razor sharp, puts smooth finish for easy extraction from chamber. The fourth reamer is held in reserve until the second or finish reamer wears 0.001″. I (Lovell) like the bullet seater slightly larger than the rifle chamber, as finger nails are less strong than extractors and I want loaded cartridge to drop out of the bullet seating die.

"A set of *four* reamers from Red Elliott's shop costs $60.00 to $70.00 (depending upon caliber and size) and will produce chambers at $1.00 per rifle—as previously mentioned.

"The finish reamers of Carpenter's K. W. steel cannot be ground with emery wheels used to grind carbon tool steel, but wear less than common tool steel and do not pick up particles readily, thus preventing rings in chambers so common in many barrels and which

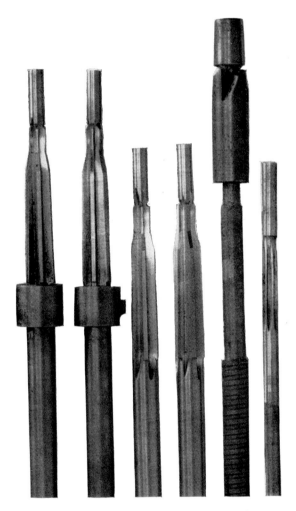

CHAMBER REAMERS FOR .22 H. P.

Set of tools used by Lovell for chambering rifle for short-neck long body, .22 Savage H.P. cartridge. Use 31 gr. charge. Each reamer is one thousandth of an inch larger in diameter, than one used before it. Four tools, not in photo, are used to rough out each chamber before using reamers.

Stops on two reamers are set for chambering Winchester single shot, counter bore for cartridge rim. Small reamer is for throat or bullet seat in bore. Winchester sells a set of three Hornet reamers for $80.00 net according to Lovell.

cause hard extraction of cartridge cases. These reamers are hard to get in war times because of the special reamermakers being fully engaged in war work in reamer and gage manufacture (details omitted—author) but in peace time Elliott supplies most of the better custom gunsmiths with their reamers and head space gages. This amounts to thousands of special and wildcat cartridges per year. Wilson also makes a lot of such fine tools. Both shops are hidden away in small far Western towns but they have built up fine business reputations with most custom gunshops.

"We hope to see all wildcat chambers standardized; (Lovell, Ackley, Vickery, Elliott, and various others have been working on this for some time—author), so that the commercial ammunition factories will be interested in making cases to standard shapes for all of us, to help shooters buy the components through their dealers.

"I have to make dozens of dies for other gunshops' customers as they have just one chambering reamer and it takes three" (Lovell keeps a fourth in reserve—as mentioned above).

Lovell, in his earliest days of making up .22/3000 Lovell cartridges with 5° shoulder slope, and for the "Bell" rifles, told of solving the reamer problem in the following manner—this was about 1930, with business in general going rapidly from bad to worse: "Two taper pin reamers, easy to buy (then) in better hardware stores, were found. They have a taper of 0.25″ per foot. All I needed was to grind the shoulder angles and neck diameters in my friend's machine shop, to enable me to chamber a number of used .22 barrels. One reamer was about the angle of shoulder of the present R-2 (Usually 12° to 12° 30″—author). Other was about 5° at shoulder, or as near to the standard Hornet shoulder (5° 31″) as could be ground. With this angle I could completely size to form .22/3000 and with a steeper angle the shoulder had to be blown (shot) to form by firing necked-down .25-20 S. S. Stevens cases in a rechambered barrel.

"I had a LeBlond reamer grinder with accurate table that could be set to any degree angle for shoulder and body taper and 15° shoulder reamers were ground up. Donaldson lacked a grinder and other tools, so he induced Risley to make a reamer with shoulder angle 0.125″ in length. Tangent tables give this length as, roughly, 12°. My 15° shoulder for the .22/3000 Lovell cartridge is, roughly, 0.10″ in length as set up on an accurate grinder table, where simple rule measure and lathe turned angle was 0.125″. This is the difference between the R-2 Risley-Donaldson chamber and the cartridge dimensions for my .22/3000 Lovell cartridge and chamber.

They are not the same shape case nor are they of equal capacity."

This should make it clear to shooters that a reamer made with shoulder angle of 0.125″ in length will give a shoulder of approximately 12° and one with a shoulder angle of 0.10″ in length will give a shoulder of approximately 15°.

The making, selection and the use of chambering reamers for the finest of .22 rim fire match, .22 rim fire game rifles, for .22 center fire commercial and .22 center fire wildcat rifles is the place for the specialist in such items. We have tried to make this descriptive matter as clear as possible even though compiled from many sources, but in each instance have checked back and forth with the chambering tool makers of greatest experience. Let us hope that you will find these suggestions useful and practical.

CHAPTER 19

THROATING CHAMBERS FOR VARMINT RIFLES

NO MORE important subject faces the custom gunsmith and the purchaser of his manufactured goods—the varmint shooter —than throating chambers for varmint rifles—a subject too, on which personal opinion seems of very little value. Theory has also very little merit in the conclusions which will be formed. A rifle either shoots or it does not. It makes wonderful groups with one bullet, or one load which exactly suits its bore, or which produces vibrations in the barrel which are normal, uniform and properly controlled. It may make miserable groups with some other combination which is normally accurate in many other rifles of presumably the same or a very similar caliber. What are the reasons?

Quite frequently they are very closely related to the seating of the bullet at the start of the rifling.

Comment upon the important subject of throating chambers for .22 varmint rifles has been obtained and will be given here from G. B. Crandall, of Woodstock, Ontario, who is probably the most experienced custom gunsmith in Canada and definitely so in the matter of varmint rifle and varmint cartridge design. Consequently, comment from the Harry Pope of the country of the Maple Leaf should merit careful reading. Says he:

"Among advanced riflemen there is no part of the rifle barrel stressed as of more importance than the chamber, known as that section at the breech which must hold the cartridge for its full length, from the face of the breech block to the point where the bullet first contacts the rifling. While the whole chamber is vastly important, it may be truly said that its throat occupies no minor place.

"Some might stress the throat as the more important point of the whole chamber. It should be and by most riflemen is understood to be that portion of the chamber just ahead of the forward end of the cartridge case and forward to a point where the bullet first contacts the rifling.

373

"It should be, and to most thinking men is obvious that, once cut, a rifle chamber will not measurably increase or decrease its length. Consequently, it should be designed and made to properly handle the length, weight, diameter and shape of bullet which the rifleman will most frequently use—or the one which he finds it most important that the rifle shall shoot accurately.

"It follows therefore that a rifle should not be expected to shoot equally well, that is, it should not be expected to make equally small groups with two bullets which materially differ in length, ogive of point, or in the shape or contours of the sides and the base of the bullet. Most rifles are throated to shoot accurately with a bullet which has a medium length of bearing, has a flat, circular, sharp-edge base, and which has either a fairly "fat" or rounded ogive, or else a quite sharp and pointed nose. In a few instances a barrel had to be throated by custom gunsmiths which would handle a bullet which was fat in the middle, had a short bearing, and which sloped sharply at both ends. In such instance, that rifle might not shoot too accurately with any of the more conventional type of bullets because none of them would fit it properly.

"The above comparisons in regard to bullet types, modern and otherwise, are made to more forcibly impress the truth of later discovery upon the reader, as facts are ever clearer where silhouetted against a background of error. So it becomes necessary in this comment to make certain display of false theories to illuminate facts more clearly. This is the essence of all progress and the author has determined that this book shall be a recital of facts.

"The remarks I intend to make in the remainder or the mid-portion of this story, while applying generally to all sorts of standard designs of rifle cartridges, are expressly written to make observations on what is believed to work best with the ever growing list of varmint cartridges now in use, both commercial and wildcat!

"At the outset, as we consider various matters, we find that the .22 caliber is one size that can be classed as truly a varmint caliber, for even though the .25 and other calibers may be used for shooting varmints, they are not so well suited to that purpose, particularly in the more settled areas, and where the varmints are all of medium or small size, and few if any are dangerous. Also, in areas where rifle report, and the possibility of ricochets is of far greater import than the matter of distributing the carcass of the animal or bird to the four winds.

"There are some, possibly at times of abnormal demands in the matter of accomplishment, or because of inexperience in the matter of what is required in the matter of a wound, or of nervous shock, to produce a kill, who will insist upon having a varmint rifle which will distribute the hawk, crow, or woodchuck for 50 feet in every direction. A bit here, a bit there, torn up turf, a few drops of blood and a blasted spot on the ground where the varmint stood.

"As a man grows older, and as he becomes more experienced, he is not so inclined to demand the complete obliteration of the game, as to insist upon the obtainment of a degree of accuracy, plus a perfection of skill which will permit him to place his bullet with the precision of a draftsman making a fine dot upon a drawing. It must be precisely where it is required and exactly in its place.

"In many districts, and for many men, the larger calibers of varmint rifles *above* the .22 caliber, will be found too expensive to shoot, too noisy to be regarded with indifference by the local landowners and farmers, and too much inclined to let loose with a whining ricochet exactly at the wrong moment and precisely where it is not wanted. Some of them also are more difficult to shoot with the very finest accuracy. Recoil begins to enter in. Blast, jump, barrel whip, all arrive at a point where they tend to destroy that very fine perception which is possible where a sweet trigger pull is pressed off at exactly the right moment when the telescope crosshair intersection exactly quarters the target.

"For these reasons, and because of the small caliber, the throating of the chamber becomes of first importance as it has a very important relation to an extended period of super-accuracy for the barrel.

"To get down to facts and figures, we have to consider first the nature of the cartridge. If it is one of the small type, which will only handle a bullet of limited weight, it follows that the throat must be shorter for a 35 to 55-grain bullet than for a cartridge which will use a 63 or 70-grain bullet. This—the need for throat length—is especially so with a cartridge like the .22 Newton which would handle up to a 90-grain bullet in a barrel of proper fast-twist rifling. The 63, 70, and 90-grain .22 caliber bullets must each obviously be longer, and have a much longer bearing in the barrel, than any of the shorter and consequently lighter weight bullets.

"However, there is a principle of cartridge case design and construction which, if employed makes it possible to use a long bullet, or a short bullet—as desired, in a chamber having a short throat, and this is, generally speaking, the correct principle on which to design a cartridge case. This involves the employment of a medium long *neck* to the cartridge case.

"By adopting such a formation, one can seat a long bullet deeper into the case neck, and so regulate the overall length of the cartridge to no greater length than if a shorter and lighter bullet were used. This formation also has a beneficial effect in protecting the rifling at the breech from erosion in great amount due to the excessive heat developed directly at that spot, due to the rapidly burning and exploding powder which moves up the barrel as it burns, due to the great pressure being developed during combustion and explosion and also because there is but one direction—straight up the barrel—for the powder gases and burning powder grains to move, during the ignition and consuming of the charge. The tremendous pressure developed would blow anything out of the barrel which could be forced up through it.

"A long case neck accomplishes this purpose of protecting the breech ends of the lands to some degree, as well as handling both the light and the heavy bullets. It should be quite obvious that if the cartridge neck is short, a long bullet can not be seated very deeply in the cartridge, because if so seated, quite obviously its base would extend down into the large 'boiler room' of the cartridge body itself, which would certainly tend to cause excessive squirting or flowing of hot gases up along all of the side surface of the bullet.

"This, of itself, would cause much greater erosion and wear on the barrel throat, and the first 4″ of the lands of the barrel at its breech, and would also have a definite tendency to prevent uniform seating of the bullet into the lands, due to excessive oscillation and vibration of the base of the bullet as the front edge of the full diameter of the bullet first struck the hard steel lands of the rifling, which lands would immediately cut into the sides of the bullet and cause the same sort of oscillation exactly, as one can observe when trying to bore, even with a sharp auger bit, into a particularly hard and tough knot in seasoned wood. The effects are exactly the same, the base of the bullet or the shank of the brace bit oscillates or vibrates, kinetic energy—energy of motion—frequently discussed in the study of physics, and daily applied in the work of engineering and construction, is converted almost instantly into excess amounts of heat. There is no other form in which it can readily be dissipated.

"That is the result in the firing of a cartridge having a long bullet in a too-short chamber. When the full diameter of the bullet, just back of the point, strikes the lands in the forward end of the throat, the base tends to wobble or revolve around that forward bearing point as a center of revolution and excessive breech pressure, abnormally high heat and excessive erosion is the result.

"To further explain in perhaps simpler form, the long neck and short throat results in the base of the bullet having a firm and directing hold in the neck of the case when its nose end has gotten a firm hold in the rifling, so that all oscillation is prevented and the bullet is held and started in perfect alignment with the bore.

"Erosion is greatly increased by an increase in temperature, as that softens the steel and tends to permit its smoothing out and pushing forward and then wearing off just as butter, when it is soft, may be flattened and indented with the finger. In spite of all the arguments to the contrary or erroneous opinions held, you cannot increase chamber pressure, build up velocities to high figures, or increase the erosive, rubbing, pushing, abrading effects upon the breech ends of the rifling lands without immediately starting to pay for it with lowered barrel life. It is like flaming youth having its fling—it has its fling, but it does not have a fling at both ends of the life cycle, and the life cycle is thus shortened.

"You can light a box of matches but the once. The only possible way to increase the given total life of a barrel, once it has started to erode materially, is to cut off the breech, rethread it, rechamber it, cut a new extractor slot, and refit it to the receiver. Then and only then do you have a new portion of the lands presented to the bullet as it leaves the cartridge. This rechambering and barrel shortening is an expensive proposition, comparatively, to cutting off and finishing the muzzle of a barrel which has become muzzle worn or burred, and then requires the presentation of a new muzzle bearing to insure continued accuracy.

"When a rifleman outfits himself with a cartridge handling a short bullet, the bullet must have a very short and weak hold in the neck of the cartridge case. It usually jumps a bit before its contact with the rifling and consequently for all of these reasons I (Crandall) prefer any cartridge case to have a medium-long neck. With such a case, the rifling or cone leading to it from the neck of the chamber should be located about 0.125″ from the case neck. I find a cone taper of about 20° to be better than a longer taper, as it cuts quickly into the nose of the bullet, with sufficient grip to start the rotary motion to bullet instantly.

"It is evident that practically as good accuracy can be gotten with a short necked case, provided the throat is comparatively short, but it shortens the life of the barrel and at the same time minimizes the flexibility of the cartridge in using various weights of bullet at varied velocities with uniform accuracy.

"Various varmint cartridges have been developed with short necks only because there was no other resource in the use of the case chosen or worked out by its originator, who admittedly would have preferred a longer neck on his cartridge. Other cartridges have been developed from successful varmint cartridges having long necks. This has been done by having the forward part of the body portions enlarged and moved forward, these two increases in cartridge dimension combining to materially enlarge the case capacity. The change however, often also shortens the case neck.

"These cartridges, if loaded to capacity, must use a fairly long and heavy bullet in proportion to the original design of the cartridge case. They will then require a longer throat in the rifle chamber, and they will always require this longer throat if the bullets are to be seated and held properly in the neck of the cartridge. This is all to the detriment of the accuracy life of the rifle and is also to the detriment of the life of the cartridge, because the heavier bullet and larger charge combine to produce more heat and greater bullet wear, both in seating the bullet in the lands and in moving forward through the barrel.

"You can never increase bullet bearing length past normal without increasing barrel wear—assuming the previous bullet had prevented excessive gas escape up past the sides of the bullet—and you can not increase or prolong the maximum temperature of the charge, without increasing barrel erosion. It is like burning coke for a winter or two in a coal furnace. The increased heat fuses and warps the grate and the fire brick, often to a considerable extent. It is always enough to be observable. It shortens the life of the stove. But it does give a very comfortable heat while the coke is being burned. It is a 'hotter' heat; temperature of combustion is greater.

"Likewise, the new 'super' varmint cartridge gives a flatter trajectory, kills better, usually has just about as good accuracy, and with some powders originally designed for use in larger cartridges or those of greater capacity and with higher pressures of combustion, will give even better accuracy. In other instances, especially in the case of cartridges like the R-2 and the 15° Hervey Lovell .22/3000 cartridges, which were very accurate but also high pressure cartridges to begin with, you will do well to obtain an equal degree of accuracy, with your 300 f.s. or so higher muzzle velocity, although ballistically in all other respects the cartridge is superior.

"In the instance of cartridges like the .219 Zipper Improved and the .22-303 Varmint-R you get better accuracy than with the .219 regular Zipper ammunition because this new shape works to better advantage, it burns the coarser IMR powders to better effect. The

pressure is raised and they require this for complete and even combustion, particularly in comparatively small cases. Even so the pressures developed are sufficiently low that the various difficulties which
attend the firing of very high intensity cartridges with very extreme
loads are absent. Among the drawbacks is paring of the cartridge rim
and sticking of cartridge cases in rifles which are very closely head
spaced—this paring also occurring when the loaded cartridge is
seated in the rifle. The sticking is aggravated by closing the bolt on a
cartridge which fits tightly in a normal chamber, and you have a
rather abnormally tight chamber and, in addition, in it may be some
partially unburned powder grains from a previous shot and the cartridge is jammed forward onto these powder grains, thus immediately
increasing the tightness of cartridge fit, increasing the difficulty of
closing the bolt and resulting in indentations in the outside wall of
the cartridge case by said powder grains—(the author had this trouble time and again with a rather closely chambered and very tightly
head spaced .257 Roberts caliber Remington-Enfield rifle which
would even pare off fine brass shavings from the cartridge heads and
these small shavings would be found in the chamber well and
adhering to the bolt face or extractor and at times would make the
rifle almost impossible to close or to open when used with maximum
factory match ammunition supplied for accuracy tests).

"Thus, close chambering and minimum head spacing are not always
a condition resulting in maximum efficiency and pleasure in the use
of a varmint rifle.

"It is perhaps well to suggest here that a too-tight head space was
the great offender, rather than the too-close chamber.

"As many of you know, and as most of you should know, the
shoulder slope of many varmint cartridges is sharpened or increased
by 10° to 20° of angle, the said angle being measured with the center-
line (CL) of the bore of the barrel. This increase in shoulder slope
has been proved by many experiments to facilitate the complete burning of the charge by causing a higher percentage of the charge to be
consumed within the cartridge case itself.

"The rapid passage of the grains of powder, which are ignited and
flaming as they pass up through and out of the cartridge case is
retarded materially by the increased angle of the shoulder of the case.
Consequently, the flaming grains and ignited gases swirl and churn
around somewhat in the forward portion of the case and more of the
powder charge is largely or altogether transformed from solids to
gases in the cartridge case than formerly. However, it should be
understood that the whole length of the barrel is filled with burning

grains and gases, and some come out of the muzzle, even with so small a bore as a .22 caliber. By looking through a .22 rifle barrel which has just been fired you can see proof of this, by observing the unconsumed particles on the bottom of the barrel bore extending clear to the muzzle. Also, some will be caught by white paper set up before firing in front of the muzzle, and flame can be seen to issue from the rifle muzzle in many instances. Little will be seen at the muzzle with so-called 'flashless' powders but in the main, the larger the charge, the larger the powder grains, the smaller the perforations in the larger powder grains, the more the burning of the powder is held back by chemical or physical deterrents, the higher will be the percentage of the charge which may be found forward of any given point in the barrel or the cartridge.

"No powder is truly 'progressive burning' in the true acceptance and meaning of the word 'progressive.' Some types merely burn slower than others, the pressure is retained at a higher figure at or near the muzzle, but in no instance is the maximum pressure developed by the cartridge just inside the muzzle or at any place near it. It is in every instance, whether single or double base powder, within 1.50″ to 3″ of the front end of the cartridge or even in the front portion of the cartridge itself.

"Double base or nitroglycerin powder—which is powder composed primarily of nitroglycerin and nitrocellulose—ignites faster than single base or nitrocellulose powder, burns more rapidly after it is ignited and while the pressure curve of the explosion is rising rapidly, and recedes much faster as the bullet speeds toward the muzzle. The reason for this is that the 15% to 40% of nitroglycerin in the powder acts like coal oil, fat pine or almost like gasoline in speeding up the burning of the powder. Not only is nitroglycerin an explosive of unusual potentialities itself, but it is also an ignition agent or rather a 'speed-up of ignition' agent to the nitrocellulose. Nitrocellulose is nitrated cotton or nitrated wood pulp, meaning that it has been treated with nitric acid. A cartridge which has 55,000 pounds per square inch at the case neck will only show 3,000 to 8,000 pounds pressure at the rifle muzzle.

"Now another thing to consider in cartridge and chamber and also in throat design is that the firing of a cartridge to fit a chamber which has been made of larger diameter at the front portion, or longer, or both larger and longer, immediately results in the forming of the old cartridge to the dimension of the now longer and larger chamber. This can only result in one condition in the cartridge. Brass can only come from one place, from the walls of the cartridge case itself. These walls, particularly those of the forward two-thirds or three-fourths of the cartridge case, and in some instances probably the whole of the cartridge case, are elongated and thus thinned at the same time. But the head of the cartridge loses none of its thickness. This results in a new cartridge case which has been ironed out, stretched, and made to remain in its new dimensions by gas pressure or gas ironing.

"You now have a cartridge that is thinner in the case walls and which also has been subject to a sudden and violent stress, which action, being in at least two directions and also of a type which might impart a slight twisting motion as well, has undoubtedly affected the modulus of elasticity of the metal and has upset its molecular form. It is useless to expect it to ever be as strong again, and it is quite logical to assume that it may now crack or break, usually in line with the length of the cartridge, and usually also about the junction of the shoulder and the main portion of the cartridge, much easier than before such 'fire-forming' or cartridge expansion. The term fire-forming can be used in another sense and which has little relation to a blow given by suddenly applied pressure—pressure from within the cartridge.

"The causing of a greater proportion of the charge to burn largely within the cartridge case, causes a higher temperature within the mouth of the case, because the primary powder gas column is not so long as if the burning were more continued up the barrel, in a length of 10″ or 15″ instead of in a length of 1.5″ to 3″, plus whatever may be changing from solid to gaseous state as it moves up the tube.

"Erosion from a large sporting cartridge is usually less objectionable because, except in the case of target or military rifles fired extensively rapid fire, there is but little shooting; possibly not over 10 to 20 shots a year. What is that, in the life of a rifle barrel?

"Take the .300 Savage sporting rifle cartridge as an example. This cartridge has a very short neck, due to the effort to get a considerable charge of powder in a cartridge short enough to load through the magazine in a rifle whose receiver is as short as that of the Savage 99 model. But, this is a rifle that will receive but very little use. Seldom is it used for more than one to three weeks on a hunting trip, and rarely is the rifle fired more than five to 20 shots in a hunting season. Such rifle will remain un-eroded to any serious amount, through one to three human generations. It is not shot with sufficient frequency to apply high temperatures to the throat for a length of time to insure the burning or flattening away of the lands at the breech.

"How different is the condition with a .22 high velocity varmint rifle. Its owner may become so enthused with the extraordinary accuracy of the barrel that he may fire 1,000 to 3,000 rounds in a year merely in testing various combinations of bullet, powder and primer and in shooting dozens, even hundreds of groups, simply for the thrill of experiencing such extraordinary degree of accuracy in rifle marksmanship. Give a man a rifle which will group 0.25" at 100 yards, with the same or greater ease than he formerly was able to obtain at 25 yards, and he soon finds himself in the mental condition of the chap who woke up to discover that he had just inherited $5,000,000.00. Such party is not going to be content to merely sit and look at it. He must have action—action, morning, noon and night, he craves; action, morning, noon and tomorrow, he will have, if he has to shoot out five barrels. So long as the primers, powder and bullets hold out, there will come the sound of a varmint rifle being fired, group after group, in the back pasture.

"Therefore, to insure longevity of barrel, yet to maintain flexibility of loading and uniform accuracy, many prefer the rather long-necked cartridge case with the short throat and a fairly abrupt cone in the throat. Chamber and throat tolerances of 0.001" to 0.003" are normal, but those who like to obliterate the X ring, are more likely to be satisfied if the leeway is kept within about 0.002".

"Rifleman, be good to that rifle! Take care of it. Cherish it long after your earthly friends have mostly passed beyond. Your children and your grandchildren may shoot that rifle, and to them as well, it may be an ever source of increasing wonder at the accuracy that man can build in wood and steel. Craftsmanship to the custom gunsmith is usually, and always should be, a matter of professional pride.

"With care, the varmint rifle which cuts out the X-ring today, should be equally reliable tomorrow, or years from tomorrow. Given a true tube, well stocked, carefully chambered, properly throated, and with bullets uniform in core, jacket and in diameter, a man may slowly spend his fortune, and still for many years—be just as well off! He will still be shooting a bumble bee rifle.

"Regardless of wars, atom bombs, politics, international finances, inflation or income tax, a man can still shoot that rifle! Sometimes we think, what more could either a young man or an old man want! So long as he has the sight to see the target through his rifle telescope, he can hit it! Bullet after bullet still lands in the X-ring.

"The throating of the chamber is the one step which has a

greater bearing on the accuracy of the modern .22 varmint rifle, than any other single feature."

Further Crandall comment on neck and chamber clearance:

"I believe that in the case of varmint rifles a tolerance of 0.002″ at the neck is ample and that should be made on the basis of the thicker cases such as made by Winchester and Western Cartridge Company. If one could always be sure of using only Remington cases then the diameter of the chamber, including the neck, should be somewhat less and in proportion to the smaller diameter of such cases.

"With the problem of chambering for the body of the case, the matter of wall thickness does not obtain, at least to the same degree, as each maker aims at making his cases to the same outside dimensions of the body.

(Author's Note: The case heads however, vary in diameter, also in thickness of rim, and as Hervey Lovell has pointed out in his section of this chapter, they are not absolutely round, as anyone can prove to his own satisfaction in a very few minutes, by using an accurate micrometer to measure the cases at rim, shoulder, neck, and by then revolving the case in the jaws of the micrometer just before and during such measurement. These differences are sufficient, not only to be observed and felt, but also to very definitely be readily measured with the micrometer. These variations often run to three and four numerals in the same decimal place. Due to the smaller amount of variation in the diameter of the body of the cartridge cases, and also to the larger diameter of the case, as compared with the diameter of the case neck, the variations in the body diameter are not so vital to accuracy attainment as are neck diameter variations. The case body promptly swells out to and takes the chamber diameter as the powder is being consumed in the case and as the chamber pressure rises very rapidly upon the explosion of the charge.)

"Hence a nearly standard diameter of chamber for varmint rifles can be adopted, and for the finest varmint rifles 0.001 to 0.002 is ample. We all know that the varmint shooter who aims at the zenith of perfection is usually prepared to assume all the trouble of keeping his rifle chamber free of any form of foreign matter, and so he will keep his ammunition when in the field well guarded in a neat, close-covered box or other receptacle, like a small cloth bag. Some make up very clever gadgets to produce this cleanliness and to keep the bullets from being displaced in the neck of the cartridge if not crimped too firmly therein.

"You will not therefore, often hear the real rifle crank complain of dusty, gritty or corroded ammunition or of sticking cartridge cases. It is written, 'Eternal vigilance is the price of liberty,' and so, scrupulous care and cleanliness in keeping a perfect fit, free of outside matter, between cartridge and chamber becomes a hobby as a co-operative part of the whole to make up the rare thrills and joys of the accomplished and properly-outfitted varmint shooter. Comparatively, his numbers are few, but in scientific accomplishment and in precision-made equipment his position is established; it is without precedent except in the Schuetzen game, and is also without competition, and as a result the varmint shooter of today is the rifleman who leads the world in being able to cut the X-ring out of the target, on the range, or in the hunting field. May his numbers increase for the good that they have done to scientific rifle shooting."

Some Kilbourn Comments

Lysle Kilbourn replied as follows regarding chambering tolerances he uses in re-chambering rifles for the K-Hornet, K-Lovell and similar .22 varmint and hunting cartridges for which he converts rifles:

"The Hornet cartridge is about 0.295" (factory case, I mean) at the base, and my reamer is 0.294" at that point. Lapping will take out about 0.002" in polishing the chamber. I do not have to worry too much about the forward portion of the chamber as the cartridge is fired in the chamber and thus formed to its new dimensions. You thus have a perfect fit for the cartridge in the new and longer chamber.

"Throating is done with a tool that is shaped like a Winchester Hornet bullet (Author's note:—which in turn is shaped very closely like the Niedner Rifle Corporation's original .22 Baby Niedner bullet), and this throating tool leaves the first 0.03125" of the bore with no lands for the bullet to rest upon or in, and the bullet should just enter the lands or rest against them" (this agrees perfectly with Hervey Lovell's idea of throating—the bullet of a .22/3000 Lovell, for instance, should not be jammed into the rifling nor have the lands cut into the front portion of the bullet but the projectile should just move forward to, or just touching, the lands when the breech block is home and the rifle is locked, ready for the next shot—Author).

Kilbourn has not tried free-boring. It is a subject in which he shows little or no interest.

Kilbourn's Methods in Lapping Barrels

"In lapping a bore to take out tight spots, which procedure is of course often very important, I cast a lead lap on a steel rod, and right in the barrel. I use a new lap of course for each barrel. This lapping rod has a spade-grip handle and the lap is then run back and forth with oil and flour of emery upon the lap, until the bore appears perfect in diameter and in appearance. The diameter should be uniform throughout most of the barrel, without excessively tight spots.

"By pushing a .22 caliber lead bullet through the bore, one can tell when the barrel is reasonably uniform in bore, and when no tight spots or loose spots are felt, then it is time to stop lapping. Also, in every instance, before the land and groove diameters are enlarged to the point where the available .22 ammunition will not fit the rifle.

"In using barrel blanks, care must be used to determine if the bore is smaller at one end than the other. It often is! It is fatal to accuracy of shooting to install a barrel on an action if the tube is so bored, or bored and lapped, that it is larger in diameter at the muzzle. I find that a barrel that is tight at the muzzle, and about 0.001″ to or even 0.002″ larger at the breech is O. K. In fact, some shooters prefer this proportion to a straight-bored tube."

This seems to bear out in many details the ideas of H. M. Pope and many others, in the matter of a slight amount of choke being O. K. Some few prefer a barrel exactly uniform in diameter, breech to muzzle. In theory such barrel, if cut with shallow and numerous grooves, should deform a bullet *less* than any other system of rifling and boring. Also, any fins which are left either on the side, or especially on the base of the bullet would then be smaller, and also more equal in size and shape, than if the barrel be bored and rifled in any other manner.

Dr. Franklin W. Mann proved time and again that a bullet could be made to print in almost any desired position at 100 yards, when shot from a special Pope barrel, by making a sharp fin on the base of the bullet and placing this in certain relation to the breech—top, right side, bottom, left side, or any other position in relation to the rim of the cartridge as it was placed in the rifle. The number of lands and rate of twist entered in, but you could shoot a hollow group at 100 yards, by placing cartridges loaded with bullets, or seat the bullets by breech seating in the bore, so that the rim of the bullet is so placed that each succeeding shot is fired with a cartridge having the nick on the base of the bullet, a quarter turn or so farther around the circumference. Incidentally, you can get almost the same result by shooting .22 Long Rifle cartridges which have once *misfired,* and have been indented rather strongly on one point as a result, so that this indent is revolved around the circumference of the chamber mouth in much the same manner.

Kilbourn uses the above methods in chambering and lapping on his K-Hornet, K-Lovell, K-Zipper, K-22 Magnum, K-.22 Hi-Power and other calibers, and apparently obtains about the same results from all of them.

It should be remembered by the reader that in no instance should he keep on lapping, even to make the bore brighter and smoother and less likely therefore to lead or metal foul, until the land or the groove diameter has become so large—normally the land diameter will increase more by lapping, than the groove diameter will enlarge—until either or both are larger than the maximum diameter of the average bullet of the ammunition being used.

Today most .22 metal-cased expanding bullets run either 0.2235″ or 0.2245″ in diameter, except those for the .228 Ackley and similar size cartridges in which the bullets will most times be found to be 0.2285″ in diameter, a few 0.2275″. However, the idea is to make the bullets so that the average bullet will be rather uniformly 0.0005″ larger than the groove diameter. In that instance, the smaller bullets in the lot, if noticeable variation be found, will be about the groove diameter of the barrel or one-half a thousandth smaller.

If you should happen to have a 0.223″ barrel and should lap it to 0.224″ (which incidentally, would require but very little lapping—possibly five to ten strokes of the lap) thereafter it would be better to use 0.2245″ bullets in that barrel.

A very hard alloy barrel, nickel steel or chrome-vanadium steel with 1% to 3½% nickel in one or the other, or both, you will have to lap harder and longer to increase the barrel diameter to the same degree desired, as in the case of a softer-alloyed steel normally used in a .22 Long Rifle barrel, such as the standard 52 barrel, or the Remington 37 barrel—other than special nickel steel or other hard steel barrels used sometimes on such rifles. Winchester Proof Steel is a steel easier to machine and bore than 3% nickel steel.

The original Winchester Model 21 double barrel shotguns of

12 gauge were made with frames and barrels of 3% nickel steel, similar to those made on the good looking machine made guns sent over here years ago by the Birmingham Small Arms Company, which shotguns used just about the same type action. Well, those 3% nickel steel Winchesters were very good, remarkably strong and well put together shotguns. But they wore out machine tools about as fast as the patience of a taxpayer wears out on the 14th of March, each Spring. So, along came Winchester Proof Steel which was just as tough and probably as strong but not as hard, and it could be machined with less cost and wear on the gun making machinery and tools. Three to 3½% nickel steel is as hard as the heart of a tax auditor on a Blue Monday when he goes after your report with a grim determination to make it cost you something. However, if you get one of them on a .22 rifle, and which is bored absolutely true without the drill striking hard spots in the metal and veering off to the side—proving that the chap who goes through life avoiding the tough spots is probably only as smart as a barrel drill—you have something which will wear until the cows come home.

In lapping such a barrel, have patience, use care, lap only where you must, because a raised spot is hard metal and difficult to smooth off evenly, and do not make the mistake of digging wallows on both sides of the high point by the use of brute strength plus blind lapping.

Remember that comparatively soft steel cuts rather easily by a lap, it also can be ground out quicker by a set of chambering reamers, or a throating tool, and the amount of time and work it takes to finish a job on a chamber or a lapping proposition will vary not only with the amount of metal to be removed, but the place it is located.

Another idea that may be brought in here to advantage, is that it is *not* a smart idea to buy a Model 52 Winchester barrel for the .22 Long Rifle cartridge and then to try to lap it to larger size to shoot 0.2245″ .22 Hornet or .22/3000 bullets. Result will be that you will have a barrel with the lands pretty well lapped out of it. The grooves will also be enlarged to some degree, but not usually to the same amount of enlargement. Consequently, you could find yourself with a barrel 75% shot out, without ever firing a cartridge. It was also probably a comparatively soft barrel to begin with!

The better plan is to get a Diller or a Buhmiller blank and have your pet gunsmith thread, chamber, and cut the extractor slot, and then fit the barrel tightly into the frame so that the combination is a rigid one-piece proposition with a stock bolt, no play in a take-down, and with enough wood around receiver or tang to keep it rigid. Such a rifle is normally a very accurate .22 varmint rifle. It is made with every engineering problem solved according to correct scientific principles.

THOMAS SHELHAMER ON CHAMBER TOLERANCES

Thomas Shelhamer, the crack stocker and checker of the Niedner Rifle Corporation for many years, and the operating head of that concern from 1930 to 1939, is now in the rifle stocking business for himself, and lives about a mile from Dowagiac, Michigan, where he has some three acres on which to conduct his custom gunsmithing business.

He is the sort of gunsmith who puts in 40 to 60 hours in form-ing, fitting, checkering and finishing a rifle stock, and his reputation as a fine rifle stocker is nationally known. Fred Ness recently listed him as being, in his opinion among the best half dozen stockers in the country. While operating the Niedner Rifle Corporation he had of course full opportunity to investigate and assess the actual worth, if any, of the extremely close type of rifle chambering which was almost universally known as the "Mann-Niedner chamber."

Mr. Shelhamer wrote the author, early in 1946 in reply to various inquiries, that the Niedner type of chambering was so unsatis-factory and heir to so many difficulties that in 1930, when he took over the management of the company, the first thing he did was to abandon this type of chambering entirely. He commented:

"At best they (the bullets) had to be uniform to about 0.0001″ in diameter; only a well-equipped gunsmith could keep working one of the rifles so chambered, or the rifleman got into trouble with many things, including the normal differences in bullets."

He said that nothing was gained by having a rifle with such a closely cut chamber. You either got into trouble with cartridges that would not chamber on the one hand, or that would not hold bullets after firing on the other. Such chambered rifles shot no better, if as well, as a rifle with a chamber with 0.0015″ to 0.0020″ tolerance. He says he proved this many times by testing, both before and after relieving the chamber neck.

Another difficulty with rifles so closely chambered, a difficulty spoken of most bitterly, mostly by ballistic engineers of arms and ammunition companies who would receive all sorts of demands and requests for closely chambered arms from riflemen, was that quite frequently such closely cut rifles gave very excessive and also most erratic breech pressure results when tested with ammunition which showed the least size variation more than the absolute minimum. The greater the variation in bullet fit and bullet seating and the stiffer the charge, the more annoying this variation became.

The whole thing boiled down to the condition that too much ballyhoo by a very few created a condition in the minds of shooters as a result of which the public obtained what Mr. Shelhamer believes to be a very erroneous and unfortunate opinion of the worth, from a practical standpoint, of excessively close rifle chambering at the cartridge neck.

The Niedner Rifle Corporation on their own letterhead, told the author the same thing, essentially, on more than one rather recent occasion. Fact is, that about 1930 the so-called "Mann-Niedner type chamber" died a rather unlamented death at Dowagiac.

This would suggest that today, small caliber varmint rifle chambers should not be cut closer than 0.0015″ to 0.003″ tolerance at the neck, and when you are confronted with a condition of commercial cartridges varying as much as 0.007″ in head thickness, and also a large variation in cartridge neck thickness of brass—which also varies greatly from the desirable diameters, you face a problem in which, to shoot safely, you had better have your close chamber rifle recut to at least ordinary close commercial tolerances. Even then, if the arm be a trifle on the loose side, you are safer and less likely to get into trouble if you are one of those lads who cram the very last grain of powder possible to get into a cartridge case, load up 30 of them in that manner and then drive out to your private range determined to be a rugged individualist and shoot 10-shot groups if it costs a right eye. Could at that—especially if you have a case shed a primer or fuse a cartridge head.

This writer had a .30-1906 service rifle shed a primer on the first shot he had ever fired on the Essington, Pennsylvania rifle range and when he was able to move again and was lifted to his feet, he thought someone had struck him as hard as they could at the base of the skull, with a 2x4 when he was not looking. It is not a pleasant experience. Somehow it dampens your enthusiasm for rifle shooting for the remainder of the afternoon, and you feel neither so rugged nor so individualistic. Incidentally, your head rings like a boiler shop on a busy day.

Theory is all right in its place, and the boys can have a grand time arguing over the relative merits of the excessively close chamber and the first grade commercial or national match type chamber, but it is just as well to remember that most all of these .22 and .25 caliber varmint rifles and cartridges are high pressure jobs, at best, and the idea is always to get a smaller group and higher velocity than everyone else.

It is with today's components, which are not too exact in some instances, just a little too much like investing in a thousand shares of stock in some unknown gold mine. You may make 1001% profit; I said you *may*. You always have the certificate which is usually printed in green or brown ink, and you gain a little experience. Sometimes that is all you do gain. Be a sucker with sufficient regularity and eventually you can paper your gun room with gold mine certificates. But somehow the ordinary commercial job seems to be more satisfactory to the average taxpayer. The best of the custom jobs with normal tolerance, are even better, in varmint rifles!

Under present conditions the author would suggest you *not* order a .22 varmint rifle with abnormally close neck tolerance, nor with such close head spacing, especially with Hi-Side Winchester single shot and Sharps-Borchardt actions that, with abnormal cartridge variations of 1946, you cannot unload a loaded rifle by means of its own extractor and normal functioning. Nor should the assembly be such that you frequently cannot close the action on a normal cartridge.

Cartridge Head Milling

One of the most annoying worries of custom gunsmiths and reloaders of fine .22 varmint rifle ammunition has been the variation in the thickness of the cartridge heads of many commercial rimmed cartridges used in the making of cases for these rifles.

The .219 Zipper has been one of the most persistent offenders in this respect. That has been more than normally objectionable because the .219 Zipper has turned out to be possibly the most useful rimmed cartridge for varmint conversion, due to the strength of the case, the thickness of metal in the head, its excellent design, and the shape of the forward portion of the case so that moderate pressures are developed when the case is used, even after neckdown to a sharper shoulder. The body slope to the shoulder, and the length of neck obtainable, are both desirable.

But, this caliber of cartridge appears to have come through with more and larger variations in case head *thickness,* and diameter also, most likely, than most others. The .30-30 cases have also been very bad offenders in this respect.

Leslie Lindahl, of Central City, Nebraska, has gone after this problem with more effort than many others who have merely expressed their annoyance and let it go at that! Lindahl has secured the services of a precision machinist and toolmaker to help in the production of Chucker and .22 Super-Chucker rifles and ammunition They are adding new machine tools as fast as such can be secured. They are also building such tools themselves—tools designed foi faster production of Chucker cases and also a greater degree oi precision workmanship throughout the job.

They will soon be equipped to mill the heads of the rimmed .22 Chucker cases to a definite and uniform thickness. The thickness of these commercial Zipper case heads varies as much as 0.007". This variation is most unfortunate in Hi-Side Winchester single shot, and in the Sharps-Borchardt single shot actions, because with both the breech block slides practically straight up and down.

The Winchester action requires 0.001" to 0.002" clearance between the face of the breech block and the head of the cartridge case. If this tolerance does not exist, the action will not function, as it was designed so that it will then not let the block again drop down after the action is closed, if this small and necessary clearance is not there.

Consequently, .219 Zipper cases should be regulated in thickness, so that those which are too loose are not used—to prevent excessive head space when the rifle is fired. And so that they are not so tight as to lock the rifle when it has been closed.

If you have ever had a loaded and frozen-shut rifle where you cannot fire it when you want to, or so that it cannot be unloaded, you will realize at once how dangerous this situation can be, and how embarrassing it can be, especially in an automobile, bus, train, or in a city. A man running around with a loaded and cocked rifle these days promptly nominates himself for a free trip to headquarters in the Black Maria, and he is lucky if he can talk his way out when he gets there. Most likely they will take him out to the booby hatch, give him a powerful sedative after dousing him in tepid water for half an hour, with brawny male "nurses" holding him in, and keep him under "observation" for two or three weeks.

These days a man with a rifle is not regarded by the common herd as a big brave he-man out for a lark or about to go hunting. He is too often regarded as a psychopathic case or else some poor chap who has been shell-shocked. After you have cussed out enough commercial cases 0.005" to 0.007" oversize, you are indeed, somewhat "shell shocked" but the good doctor would not understand this. Remember you are case study No. XOP 436701. God help you! I hope they feed you! Also, I hope they do not operate!

Possibly now you will fully realize why brother Lindahl regards this as a *very* serious matter and has resolved to save the brethren all possible embarrassment. Maybe this is another instance of "When more uniform cartridge case heads are made—Lindahl will make them!"

He and his machinist trim 'em, mike 'em, wrap 'em and ship 'em. You shoot em!

All jokes aside, this *is* an important custom ammunition procedure. Remember, that in the main, and as a rule, accurate shooting is dependent upon keeping barrel vibrations uniform and ammunition tolerances within very small limits. To have a bumble bee rifle, you must *always* have bumble bee ammunition. One, without the other, will not produce.

CHAPTER 20

.22 WILDCAT BULLETS

DURING recent years probably the principal source of custom-made metal-cased hunting bullets in the United States, has been R. B. Sisk, of Iowa Park, Texas. There is no question that the Sisk and Sisk-Niedner bullets have been splendidly designed and of most excellent quality. As a general rule, they are designed with a full, quite rounded contour to that portion of the bullet between the straight or base portion and the extreme point. In this, most of them differ from the 8S design of bullet which is made with what is practically a straight-line contour between upper portion of the full diameter part of the bullet and the point.

Many of the Sisk bullets have just as sharp a *point* as the 8S bullets but they do not *appear* to be anything like as sharp pointed as the 8S's which have a point much like that of the average drafts-man's pencil—long, delicate and straight-sided.

Hervey Lovell is a great booster for the Sisk bullets. He claims they consistently and nearly *always* outshoot the 8S bullet in the Lovell rifles at his testing range of 50 yards. Parker Ackley is also a Sisk bullet user, and so is W. F. Vickery.

At latest reports Sisk was at work on a new line of bullets, but to the time of this writing, a full detailed description of all of them was impossible, although various individual samples had been submitted, all loaded in Ackley cartridges of the .22 varmint types.

Such bullets as the following retailed in lots of 1,000 or more, for 1c to 2c each. Later prices will likely be somewhat higher, but that is in any event, much more reasonable than the 5c per bullet charged by some custom bulletmakers.

Among those regularly supplied are the numbers on the two following pages:

393

LOADS WITH SISK BULLETS

Bullet and Cartridge	Wt.	Diam.	Type or Point	Shape Point	Max. Powder Charge	M.V.	Overall Loading L.
.22 Hornet	35-gr.	0.224"	S.P., F.J.	Blunt	11.6 2400	3,020	1.730"
.22 Hornet	40-gr.	0.224"	S.P., F.J.	Blunt	11.2 2400	2,860	1.730"
.22 Hornet	55-gr.	0.224"	S.P., F.J.	Blunt	9.3 2400	2,340	1.718"
.22 K-Hornet	41-gr.	0.224"	S.P., F.J.	Blunt	13.0 2400	3,200	1.810"

Bullet and Cartridge	Wt.	Diam.	Shape Point	Max. Powder Charge	M.V.	Overall Length Cartridge
Lovell .22/3,000 and R-2 Lovell	40-gr.	0.224"	S. P. Sharp	16.5 Gr. 4227	3,400	2.125"
Lovell .22/3,000 and R-2 Lovell	41-gr.	0.224"	S. P. Sharp	16.5 Gr. 4227	3,500	2.125"
Lovell .22/3,000 and R-2 Lovell	50-gr.	0.224"	S. P. Sharp	17.0 Gr. 4198	3,300	2.150"
Niedner .22	55-gr.	0.224"	S. P., F. J.	26.5 Gr. 3031	2,940	2.125"
Niedner .22	63-gr.	0.224"	S. P., F. J.	25.0 Gr. 3031	2,860	2.300"
.218 Bee	41-gr.	0.224"		15.0 Gr. 2400	3,330	1.780"
.218 Bee Super-Lovell	50-gr. Lovell	0.224"		15.0 Gr. 4227	3,080	1.780"

Express	40-gr.	0.224"	Sharp S. P.	43.5 Gr. 4064	4,466	2.680"
Express	55-gr.	0.224"	Sharp S. P.	40.0 Gr. 4064	4,075	2.700"
Express	63-gr.	0.224"	Sharp S. P.	37.5 Gr. 4064	3,600	2.700"

Proportional charges in other good sized .22 wildcat cartridges. The longer Lovells, Kilbourns and the three Gebby cartridges. Longer, 0.224" Ackley, Vickery and similar cases.

.22 Savage H. P.	40-gr.	0.228"	Blunt	14.0 Gr. 2400	3,350	2.357"
.22 Savage H. P.	55-gr.	0.227"	S. P., F. J.	30.0 Gr. 4064	3,000	2.450"
.22 Savage H. P.	63-gr.	0.227"	S. P., F. J	28.0 Gr. 4064	2,900	2.450"
.219 Zipper and						
.219 Zipper Improved						
" 40-gr.	Express	0.224"		25.5 Gr. 4198	3,500	2.400"
" 50-gr.	Lovell	0.224"		28.0 Gr. 4064	3,300	2.415"
" 55-gr.	Niedner	0.224"		26.5 Gr. 4064	3,200	2.400"
" 63-gr.	Niedner	0.224"		27.0 Gr. 3031	3,000	2.350"

New Sisk .22 Metal-Cased and Expanding Bullets

There have been some changes in the designations of the latest 1946 R.B. Sisk .22 caliber metal-cased bullets, as sold by him direct to reloaders, and through dealers in .22 wildcat and .22 commercial metal-cased bullets, and reloading supplies. Each list is given below, so that a direct comparison will enable the reader to note the changes.

Bullets listed in the left hand tabulation of bullets are *not* available today.

Bullets listed in the right hand column, are the Sisk bullets available during and after the year 1946. There will of course, be others added from time to time, as new calibers appear, and as demand changes.

Make a copy of this list for future reference.

Sisk Pre-War .22 Bullets	*Sisk 1946 .22 Bullets*
35-Grain Hornet SP	35-Grain Hornet SP
35-Grain Hornet FJ	35-Grain Hornet FJ
40-Grain Hornet SP	40-Grain Hornet SP
40-Grain Hornet FJ	40-Grain Hornet FJ
55-Grain Hornet SP	45-Grain Hornet SP
55-Grain Hornet FJ	36-Grain Spitfire
35-Grain Spitfire	41-Grain Lovell
40-Grain Lovell SP	50-Grain Lovell
41-Grain Lovell SP	54-Grain Niedner SP
50-Grain Lovell SP	54-Grain Niedner FJ
55-Grain Niedner SP	62-Grain Niedner
55-Grain Niedner FJ	42-Grain Express
63-Grain Niedner SP	49-Grain Express
63-Grain Niedner FJ	63-Grain Express
40-Grain Express SP	55-Grain Express
55-Grain Express SP	40-Grain Savage SP
63-Grain Express SP	40-Grain Savage FJ
40-Grain Savage SP	55-Grain Savage SP
40-Grain Savage FJ	55-Grain Savage FJ
55-Grain Savage SP	63-Grain Savage SP
55-Grain Savage FJ	63-Grain Savage FJ
63-Grain Savage SP	60-Grain 228 Ackley
63-Grain Savage FJ	70-Grain 228 Ackley

The Sisk bullets are well proportioned, have good copper jackets and, in the instance of some of the Express bullets, a 7% antimony core was used to prevent as much as possible, the fusing or melting of the core of the jacketed bullet when the bullet was moving up the rifle barrel.

Sisk is not always too prompt and explanatory in his correspondence but he makes most excellent bullets and sells them quite reasonable. During the latter part of 1945 and early 1946, he spent considerable time in making repeated trips to Trinidad, Colorado, to test his bullets on the chronograph of the custom gunsmithing firm of P. O. Ackley & Co., and its predecessor, and in the developing of new bullets for Ackley 0.224″ and 0.228″ diameter .22 varmint cartridges. It is understood that he also did some work in the development of .170 cartridges of Ackley, Landis, and Hammer & Gipson design. He also worked with Leslie Lindahl on new bullet design for the .22 Lindahl Chucker and Super-Chucker cartridges.

He also presumably worked with Hervey Lovell on bullets for .22/3000, .219 Zipper Improved and .22 H. P. Lovell cases, in the very extensive line of Lovell cartridges. Kilbourn also uses the Sisk bullets to considerable extent, as does Joe Pfeifer, Vickery, and other Western custom gunsmiths.

Altogether, such cooperation takes a good deal of the time of Mr. Sisk, who appears willing to go to extreme lengths to perfect and systematize his bullets, which condition may be ascribed as being largely responsible for the average excellence of R. B. Sisk bullets. No line is better known among .22 varmint rifle users. The only one comparable in popularity is the 8S bullet, largely through the advertising given it by Fred Ness, when he was "Dope Bag" Editor of the *American Rifleman.*

At last reports Sisk had a large number of orders on hand for his hunting bullets for .22 varmint rifles, so it is logical to suggest that the reader make allowance for reasonable delay, at times, in the receipt of bullets ordered. Shortages of lead, tin, and suitable copper or Lubaloy jacketing material for .22 caliber metal-cased bullets, which affected the whole ammunition industry, also a shortage or delays due to strikes, in the making of cartridge brass, introduced factors in ammunition obtainment in the years 1945-46 seldom encountered in the manufacture and use of custom bullets by anyone.

Poor shooting .22 jacketed bullets, due to poor quality and unsatisfactory jacketing material, or cores, in the years 1943, 1944 and 1945, was a matter beyond the control or improvement by custom bullet or also by commercial bullet manufacturers. They should not be blamed too much for the condition for which in most instances, they were but little or of no blame. It is expected that in the years to come such conditions will rapidly improve. The Sisk bullets may be expected to be one of the most rapidly improved lines of .22

caliber jacketed bullets obtainable by our many individual hand-loaders.

Parker Ackley has relayed a number of the most recent Sisk bullet developments to the author just as this manuscript was being packed up for shipment to the publisher. Sisk has been working on a number of new bullets for the last three or four months.

One is a heavily copper-jacketed, hollow point, solid base, .228 Ackley bullet measuring 0.2255″ to 0.2260″ in diameter and with a very long sloping nose. The hole in the point is very small in diameter and the bullet is quite long, with both a long bearing surface and a long point. The other is a very similar bullet but is 78 grains in weight, and is, of course, even longer than the first. The hole in the nose of the latter bullet may be just a trifle larger than the other.

The other two are .170 caliber, both typical Sisk contours, one weighs 25 grains and the other 30 grains. The jackets appear rather thin, but very well made and put on, the soft point in the nose of each is small, and directly in the center of the point. The bases are perfectly flat, without indent in the center. The edges are quite uniform and square cut on the circumference of the base. Bullets measure 0.1715″ to 0.1720″ in diameter. Barrels are .172″.

These latter are for the Ackley and Landis designs of .170 caliber varmint rifle cartridges. Barrels are being supplied by P. O. Ackley & Co., Trinidad, Colorado. The bullets are made by R. B. Sisk, Iowa Park, Texas.

The Milo Hill .22 Caliber Jacketed Bullets

Ever since World War II was well into its second year the obtainment of first class and really accurate metal-cased or jacketed target and hunting bullets in .22 caliber has been a major problem with reloaders. Then too there was also a real scarcity of .22 bullets, caused in large part by the absence of proper Lubaloy or copper jackets for the covering of the lead cores. Beauty may be only skin deep in humans, but in the manufacture of bullets the jacket material is of really first importance.

One of the more recent bullet manufacturers of moderate capacity and production but of really well designed and good looking bullets is Milo Hill, of Caledonia, Ohio.

Hill makes these bullets in 42, 50, 55 and 60-grain weights in 0.224″ bullet diameter, and in 0.227″ in 65-grain size.

In each instance, the Hill bullets of rounded nose form, have about a 6° ogive to the point or nose, and are then very similar to R. B. Sisk bullets in contour and shape, also size, when viewed from a side. However, when one looks at the base, they are different. Each base is indented slightly and very evenly by a complete circular indentation taking in the whole flat base of the bullet, except for a moderate thickness of rim completely around the edge of the bullet base. On one point of this projecting rim is the firing pin mark as made on the empty cartridge case, probably of .22 Short or .22 Long Rifle caliber, which was used as a bullet jacketing material. This indentation is largely obliterated in making up the jacket and assembling same around the core, but some still remains right on the edge, which is not comforting to those who have read Dr. Mann's experiments on putting a bullet exactly where you want it to print at 100 yards by placing a projecting fin so as to make it strike there. However, it should be noted carefully by the reader that this indentation is almost entirely an indentation and not a projection. Other bulletmakers using fired copper cartridge cases for the jacket material will have exactly the same slight difficulty in evenness of outline of the bullet jacket base, and there is no way to avoid this.

Hill claims that remarkably accurate results have been obtained with his bullets even up to and including 4,500 f.s. muzzle velocity —could be—that 1″ groups or better at 100 yards, were normal and were frequently obtained with the Hill bullets. The author happens to know some shooters who had trouble to get better than 4″ groups at 100 yards with many war-time metal-cased bullets of other manufacture.

Hill has a bulletmaking capacity of 15,000 bullets a week by his own or present efforts, but 10,000 bullets a day could be produced with adequate help. He claims that his bullet designs are much more effective on woodchucks than normal factory bullets.

In addition to the conventional 6 caliber or so ogive designs, Hill has also a 42-grain bullet with soft point, very similar to the Wotkyns-Morse 8S pencil point design, except that the Hill bullet has a less sharp slope toward the muzzle. All bullets of the Hill type the author has examined were made from U.M.C.- Remington bullet or cartridge case jacket material, and all bear the U imprint on the indented base of the bullet.

Brass .22 cartridge cases are not suitable for such bullet jackets; brass does not lend itself so well to bullet jacketing material as does copper, which is softer and more ductile. The Hill bullets are all of designs which would aid rapid expansion in game and varmints.

It should be pointed out here, possibly, that in no circumstances should the reloader or varmint shooter attempt to load or shoot 0.227″ bullets in a 0.224″ barrel like on an R-2 rifle.

The Wotkyns-Morse Bullet

A design of .22 caliber metal-jacketed bullet which has aroused a good deal of comment throughout the country during the last few years has been known as the W-M 8S bullet. Primarily, this is a jacketed, soft point bullet having a pencil point outline for the forward portion or nose of the bullet. The point is quite minute, and the angle of taper is direct, without curvature—the sort of point one often sees on a draftsman's pencil.

Quite a number of names have been mentioned in connection with the design and marketing of this bullet, with its making, and with its loading and shooting. Its primary advantage was a claimed higher remaining velocity and a consequently somewhat flatter trajectory in rifles such as the R-2 .22/3000, especially beyond 200 yards.

A FEW .22 METAL-CASED BULLETS

On both ends, Wotkyns-Morse 8S for .22 Varminter; others left to right: 46-gr. Hornet; 48-gr. Swift; 54-gr. Wotkyns-Sweany; 63-gr. Sisk Express Magnum; 55-gr. Sisk Express Magnum; 55-gr. Sisk Niedner Magnum; 40-gr. Sisk Express. All suitable for use in .22 Varminter rifles.

The names of Charles B. Morse, Capt. Grosvenor L. Wotkyns, J. Bushnell Smith, J. B. Sweany, Harvey Donaldson and possibly others, have been connected with the bullet for one reason or another. Most of the 8S's were made by Charles B. Morse, of Herkimer, New York, and much of the publicity and early shooting was on the part of the late Capt. G. L. Wotkyns, so the W-M 8S referred to Morse and Wotkyns and the 8S to the shape of the bullet ogive.

One story of the development of this bullet is that it was designed by Capt. G. L. Wotkyns. Another comment is that the sharp-pointed .22 Hornet hand-made bullet designed and made by Capt. G. A. Woody had attracted the favorable attention of Harvey

Donaldson who wanted a bullet of very sharp point for use in the R-2 rifle. He desired a better retaining of velocity, rather than a higher muzzle velocity, in the R-2 .22/3000 for woodchuck shooting; in other words, a bullet that was going faster out where the woodchuck sat.

Donaldson is said to have urged Mr. Morse to make up a swage to form such a bullet but at the time Morse was doing well with a Sisk shape of bullet swage and seemed satisfied. However, he finally agreed to make up a swage so that Donaldson could make his own bullets to such design and did so, according to the outlines of a small piece of pointed drill rod that Donaldson had turned down and sent Morse after making a half reamer out of it.

Morse made such a reamer which turned out 55-grain bullets of this point shape, and these when tried are claimed to have given superior results at 200 yards; these claims were made by the designers.

Eleven of these original bullets, which were made with the identical swage made by Morse for Donaldson were recently sent to Samuel Clark, Jr., at Oakland, Maine, who used one for a fouler and then shot a 1″ group at 100 yards with the remainder. This group we will try to reproduce. The only difference between these bullets and some other 8S bullets turned out was that Donaldson preferred a base plunger for a recessed base bullet and some others did not; they preferred a flat base bullet. Many were so made!

Charles B. Morse was expert at making dies used in the manufacture of Remington typewriters at Ilion, New York, and it was as easy for Morse to make up the proper swages as it was for Donaldson to suggest a design and comment on the proper swaging of bullets from such dies. This however, Morse would likely have worked out readily for himself, if necessary, that is, the use of the tools after being made.

On the West Coast, Grove Wotkyns shot many of the 8S bullets, gave them unlimited publicity as did Fred Ness and others, including Bushnell Smith, and for a time Smith and Morse worked in some sort of business arrangement in the supplying and marketing of these bullets, or of bullets of a rather similar shape and design. I believe, also, that J. B. Sweany at one time made up a number of thousands of bullets of an 8S design, but as the Bushnell Smith-Morse arrangement was not recently continued, all supply of such bullet appears to have been taken care of, if and when supplied by Mr. Morse. For quite some time such bullets were altogether or largely off the market, and some few, like most other war bullets, did not apparently quite equal the originals, so that with Wotkyns deceased, Smith out of the picture for the time at least on bullet and ammunition supply and loading, and with the riflemen of the country in large measure obliged to resort to their own bullet making, often with the R.C.B.S. swages and with Sisk not too able to take care of shooter wants until along in 1946, the matter of bullet supply in jacketed bullets has been probably the major problem of varmint rifle shooters all over North America. Bullet-making is hard work, laborious to an unusual degree in hot weather, rather monotonous and uninteresting if you have thousands of them to make daily, but something interesting to do if you need but a few hundred. The subject has received probably more attention than would normally be the case during the years 1944, 1945 and 1946. In September 1946 Morse was again supplying 8S bullets.

Frankly, the 8S bullet is the only very sharply pointed bullet the author has ever seen which really was able to shoot very small groups and even those who were most responsible for it agree that much of its accuracy was the result of unusual success in the making of it, and its dies. It does not appear to have been so much a matter of design as of swages and workmanship which made it a splendid little bullet for the R-2 .22/3000 cartridge and others of somewhat similar size and shape—the K-Hornet for instance; the Hornet; the Kilbourn Magnum Junior; the Lindahl Rimmed and Rimless Chuckers, and other small and medium cases. It does not appear to have performed equally well in cartridges of the .220 Swift size, breech pressure and loading. It has done best in 45, 47, 50 and 55-grain weights. Its best groups have been obtained with moderate size cartridge cases.

Hervey Lovell claims that his .22/3000 rifles with 15° shoulder usually shoot more accurately with two forms of Sisk and Sisk-Niedner bullets than with the Morse 8S, when all three are tested together on his range. Numerous others have also obtained better accuracy with the more rounded contour of bullet point. It depends largely upon how this shape bullet fits the rifle throat. The .22 Lindahl Chucker rifles using both rimmed and rimless cases, have done unusually well with 45-grain and with 47-grain Morse 8S bullets.

This bullet appears to have done its most accurate shooting at muzzle velocities of 3,000 to 3,500 f.s. in .22/3000 and Chucker cartridges. While it is true, if the bullet is not tipping in flight, that the 8S bullet should have a slightly higher remaining velocity at

200 to 300 yards than a more rounded shape of bullet started at the same muzzle velocity, there is no logical reason to believe that, given the *same* remaining velocity at the target—and this can be done by using a slightly larger cartridge case like the .219 Wasp, the Kilbourn K-Magnum, the .219 Zipper Improved, the Lovell Nos. 7, 8 or 9, as described in this book—greater laceration of the flesh of the varmint would be assured, but it would require a few grains more powder.

All of which boils down to the condition that no bullet design has all favorable qualities and no unfavorable ones; neither does any one cartridge. The fact remains that commercial ammunition manufacturers today usually choose a bullet with a more rounded point, and this is true of Winchester, Remington, Western and Dominion. Some of them probably still recall the relative popularity and shooting of the 172-grain Thomas bullet in .30-1906 ammunition, and how soon that died out, as compared with the success obtained with the 180-grain flat base bullet and the 173-grain boat-tail bullet.

Varmints are of all sizes, shapes, and degrees of vitality. In the opinion of the author, the question of whether a .22 varmint rifle bullet will *completely* go to pieces upon striking sod or earth, in the case of a miss, or of a varmint cleanly penetrated, is much more important to the shooting of a rifleman, in many localities, than whether the bullet he uses has a pencil point or one of 4° to 7° of slope. A soft point bullet, regardless of the exact shape of point, if made with a soft core and driven at a high velocity, and if of small caliber like a .22, will nearly always be dashed to pieces, but a hollow point bullet, being of stiffer construction, may produce a ricochet. The 8S has cut its niche in shooting history.

B. F. Mannen Bullet-Making Machinery and Facilities

Early in 1946, G. B. Crandall paid a friendly visit to the home and plant of B. F. Mannen, the St. Thomas, Ontario, metal-cased hunting and target bullet manufacturer. Upon his return, while commenting upon other matters, he made the following remarks about the Mannen set-up: "My son and I and his wife drove over to St. Thomas, Ontario, on January 12 for a visit with B. F. Mannen. We found him nicely settled in his new home with his fine wife and two dear little girls. They gave us a royal welcome and we had one of the nicest visits I have ever enjoyed.

"His new bulletmaking plant and workshop is about 50 yards in the rear of his new home and is a well ordered place. He has invented his own bulletmaking machines and other absorbing devices of numerous kinds. He is greatly gifted in this line.

"Mr. Mannen is an employee of the hydro-electric plant there where he puts in eight hours a day. Then he has built up all his bulletmaking business by working long into the night. He also did much of the erection of his own new home, a very modern place indeed.

"He has a bullet press, entirely his own invention and construction. It turns out bullets at the rate of 2,800 per hour. Another recently perfected core-casting machine is forming cores to an accuracy of 1/10th grain, and at the rate of 1,200 an hour. It requires no attention; only once in a while is it necessary to drop in a block of pure lead in the 60-pound tank. It is also run by a small motor. He also has a case washing machine and other clever devices all used to manufacture the B. F. Mannen expanding, metal-cased hunting bullets, accurately and in large quantity."

Making Your Own Metal-Cased Hunting Bullets

Unquestionably the most difficult problem of solution in the attainment of gilt-edged accuracy with .22 caliber wildcat rifles has been the purchase of metal-cased expanding bullets that are really accurate. This was greatly magnified during the last two-thirds of World War II, and for some time thereafter, due to the absence of adequate quantities of first grade bullet *jacket material* and the total lack of commercial bullets and custom-made bullets which would shoot groups smaller than 3″ to 4″ at 100 yards, due to inexperienced help and inadequate supplies of properly-alloyed copper jackets and pure soft lead for cores.

About the time of his retirement from the Ordnance Department, the late Capt. G. L. Wotkyns, and Fred T. Huntington, formed the RCBS Company of 688 High Street, Oroville, California, to supply shooters with equipment with which these riflemen could make their own metal-cased .22 caliber hunting and target bullets. The death of Captain Wotkyns in May, 1945, delegated the work all to Mr. Huntington who has continued and expanded the business. The name "RCBS" is an abbreviation of the Rock Chuck Bullet Swage Co. Huntington says that the idea for making the bullet dies was his own and that it is in process of being patented. This refers to the bullet-forming dies. These were first made about 1941.

The company also makes bullet pullers, these being necessary for the pulling of bullets in the breaking down of factory ammunition to fire-form cases as in the instance of such calibers as the .220 Arrow, the .219 Zipper Improved and other sizes.

Advantages of Bullets Slightly Smaller Than Groove Diameter

Huntington claims that in 75% of the cases, it has been proved by RCBS bullet users that bullets of slightly *smaller* diameter than formerly used are now giving better accuracy in the same rifles. In other words, as most 0.224″ bullets run 0.2245″ in actual diameter, for 0.224″ rifles, it is now thought by some, Huntington included, that bullets of 0.223″ to 0.2235″ diameter are giving smaller groups. He says that he is sending out dies slightly smaller than full caliber, and if the purchaser then does not feel that he is better suited, Huntington laps out the dies to form a slightly larger diameter bullet. This can always be done, just as a muzzle loading rifle barrel can always be "freshed out" to a larger diameter of bore, but the reverse cannot be done—at least without bushing the die, and that might be a problem.

Fred claims that a few dies made slightly on the small side, have been returned for enlargement of the diameter, but only a very few. His theory is that in these small-caliber hi-speed rifles, the smaller diameter bullet starts more easily and with less distortion, and will then *expand* to the correct bore diameter. He feels that this has been proven by free-bored barrels—barrels having free-bored chambers or throats—which give excellent results and act as a guide in getting the bullet started true in the bore. He claims that Wotkyns had a .220 barrel through which 5,000 rounds had been fired and which *then* showed considerable erosion. He then had it free-bored for 0.75″ ahead of the eroded chamber mouth and that this restored the original accuracy of the rifle.

Types of RCBS Bullet Dies

Diameters in bullet dies available run from 0.2225″ to 0.226″—0.228″ for the various .22 Hi-Power wildcats and the 0.228″ Magnums. Three styles of bullet die punches are available. One is the flat base punch which produces a flat base bullet; the recessed face punch produces a slight recess in the center of the base of the bullet; while the Ross type base punch produces a hollow-base bullet with an inverted V-shape in the bullet base. The recessed punch is by far the most popular and is standard equipment with RCBS unless otherwise ordered. Flat face punches are second in popularity, and the Ross type is considerably the least popular style. However, it is most popular with those using long, heavy weight bullets as it puts the center of mass and the center of gravity both farther forward within the over-all form of the bullet.

Where Jacket Material is Obtained

Fired .22 rim fire cartridge cases *made of copper,* or of copper alloy, make very satisfactory bullet jackets, if prepared correctly. This operation takes some time and includes a definite amount of work. However, to a rifle crank, such is usually a small consideration.

RCBS Bullet Dies set up in new Pacific Press.

This press is cast steel instead of malleable iron. All former parts and dies fit in this new tool.

If he has to work hard to get what he wants, the result seems more worth while.

Fired .22 Short and .22 Long empties make good bullet jackets if prepared correctly. As the .22 Long Rifle cartridge is merely the .22 Long case fitted with a 40-grain bullet, obviously the .22 Long Rifle *copper case* cartridges after firing should be found just as satisfactory as .22 Long cases. However, *do not use brass .22 rim fire cases for .22 varmint rifle bullet jackets.* Brass cartridge cases, if used for jacketing material for .22 varmint rifle bullets, will ruin the rifle bore due to scaling. These scales or scalings are forced into the pores of the barrel steel and are impossible to get out. Even a slight coating is extremely difficult or even impossible to remove. So, do not use brass cases and do not use chromium-plated cases for .22 varmint rifle bullet jackets.

De-heading die and extra de-heading punch are furnished by the RCBS Company for bullet jacket-making from fired .22 copper cases. Jackets should be segregated by makes because not all are of the same thickness or alloy. New factory-type bullet jackets are available in normal business cycles—something which we have not had for the past 16 years, remember—and when ammunition manufacturers are not continually being badgered and pestered by government departments of all kinds. No one wants to take a chance on doing favors for friends if he has to make out 11 copies of this and that, and if he might be liable to 14 years in the Workhouse for neglecting some technicality in filling $2.40 worth of shipments. It is quite true that a man can only be hung once (provided the rope does not break) but there are so many unreasonable people who object to walking those 13 steps up the gallows just to satisfy the whims of the, "You have got to do what we say," boys.

What it Costs to Make Jacketed Bullets

Using fired .22 rim fire *copper* cartridge cases, such as you may salvage from almost any .22 rifle or pistol club range, it is possible to make good jacketed bullets for about 35c per 100 bullets. With new jackets, purchased through retailers from the ammunition companies, or others, the cost will be about 75c per 100. The latter will make better and more accurate bullets. Oft-times such jacketing material is *not* available.

Today, one of the big problems is that most of the .22 empties one picks up on the range are *brass*. You must sort out and use only the copper cases. Not part one and part the other, but *all* copper cases. Also, you must separate the U, or Remington cases, from the Winchester, Western or Peters cases. Cases with thick heads should be separated from the thin head cases. Otherwise, as the head forms the base of the bullet and shows the firing pin indentation on the edge (but partly obliterated), you will not obtain bullets uniform as to jacket thickness or exactly uniform as to placing of the center of gravity.

Good jacketed bullets are not made very rapidly. There is a certain routine and a uniformity of procedure, or uniform shooting should not be expected. Professional bulletmakers who have power presses and powerful machines, so that not all of it is hand labor, can make 5,000 to 20,000 or more jacketed bullets per day. Also, they are making them to sell; you are making them for your own shooting.

It is claimed that a rate of 100 per hour is possible with the RCBS dies, but half that number per hour would probably result in more uniform and more accurate bullets. Also, a careful sorting over and segregation of all bullets made, into three or four lots, as to diameters and weights, would not be a bad idea. There is, for instance, little to worry whether a bullet weighs 49, 50 or 51 grains, but you may prefer all 49-grain in one lot, all 50's in another and all 51's in a third lot, if they vary that much. They may vary but half a grain or a grain, but there is always *some* bullet weight variation with any system of manufacture.

A determined bulletmaker can provide himself quite easily with all the bullets he will need, plus some for friends, and if you have a *friend* who is a confirmed bulletmaker, and is generous, that may be regarded by some as even better, assuming he does not sell you all the irregular and slightly deformed bullets. If so, better to set up shop in your own basement distillery.

A lead cutter and a complete set of bullet dies, for use in a Pacific Tool, can be paid for in the saving possible by using discarded cartridges in the making of 2,000 or more bullets. By that time your blisters and callouses will be gone or forgotten, and Monday morning will only be another Monday morning.

Huntington makes bullet dies for forming most of the standard shapes of bullets. He has sent the author quite a collection of different styles. The designs were good, and they were generally well formed. The 8S bullet is, in Huntington's opinion, one of the most accurate .22 metal-cased bullets ever designed. He may have absorbed a good deal of this from Wotkyns whose name is linked with the design of it. He doubts that this accuracy is so much the result of exceptionally good design of the bullet as it is to the very excellent forming dies, and the no doubt "extreme caution" as he phrased it, with which the bullets were made—that is, from even weight cores and very uniform jackets and with uniformity of the swaging process. The author would also add that this shape of bullet could probably be gotten out of the forming die with less deformation of the bullet, than could a bullet with a "fatter" front portion. I never could see any real reason, from the standpoint of design, why this bullet should shoot even reasonably well, as compared with numerous other bullets. The fact remains that no factory ever put out a small caliber cartridge having a bullet with anything like that shape of point which would shoot worth three hoots in a barrel.

Fred comments that "accuracy in bullets is regulated to a great extent by their uniformity, just as in loading powder charges." Another thing he thinks makes the RCBS dies produce better bullets is in the *venting* of them by releasing the head section, not through a vent in the point of the die or by a point ejection type of die. In their method he claims the cores are more solidly formed to the jacket and the bullets are more uniform in density, which is an important and vital factor in accuracy.

Pacific now has a new super-cast frame, to replace the old frame which could be broken if not braced, and all bulletmakers should preferably have one of these new frames if they want to try the RCBS dies and make their own .22 caliber bullets.

The old type Pacific Reloading Tool Frames will stand swaging of bullets in .22 caliber, if braced properly. However, the new Pacific Super Tool is highly recommended for those who feel they can afford the difference in price; it is so much stronger.

Both hollow point and soft point bullets can be made in RCBS dies. Huntington prefers the soft point type of bullet for full streamline shape but the other can also be produced. The H.P. style can be made by adding a smaller core and using a longer jacket and by compressing the bullet enough to squeeze the core out into a longer point. This procedure is best obtained by choosing ogives of about 4 or 5 caliber in the ogive section.

With the RCBS dies, bullets can be made any weight or fraction thereof, from 40 grains to about 65 grains and have them come out satisfactorily. With some types of ogives, you can make 35-grain bullets very nicely. The 40, 45, 50 and 55-grain sizes are the most popular—as they are in the Sisk bullets also—however, 41 and 46-grain bullets are quite popular and quite practical. Some riflemen seem to find that bullets of odd weights appear to shoot best in their rifles, or look best, due to the way the jacket forms around the point of the core. Also, with those dies you can have a large amount of lead exposed at the point, or only a small amount exposed, just as the bullet-maker disposes. This is regulated by choosing the amount or length of the jacket and the amount of lead. A bit of playing with the die will develop many interesting angles and results. Both

Short and Long fired cases are used as jacket material. The .22 Short jackets make bullets of 35 grains to about 46 grains. The .22 Long, or the .22 Long Rifle copper cartridge cases make good bullets from about 47.5 grains to 65 grains in weight. The core of course must also be longer.

Dies to make bullets with about a 4 caliber ogive to the 8S ogive are at this writing, available. Swaging dies complete with forming punch and ram and all parts to form the bullets in a Pacific Reloading Tool are about $25.00 at this writing. If money devalues more, price should be expected to rise. De-heading dies and the extra punch are about $7.50, and are for use in de-heading fired cases for bullet jackets. Lead cutters are another $7.50, but a clever workman reportedly can make his own lead cutter; Fred offers to show the customer how to make such cutter. The lead slugs must be cut uniform or the bullets will not be uniform and thus will not make small groups. Lead wire is available from Huntington in small lots at 25c a pound, and in 25-pound lots or more at 22½c a pound. Lead can often be picked up around plants and so, at times, can small pieces of solder. Remember there is soft lead, which you will want, and hard lead, which you may not want, and which contains about 7% of antimony. However, you may prefer the hard lead for use in cores intended for bullets over 4,000 f.s. muzzle velocity.

Bullet Pullers

These work like a draw-in collet chuck in a lathe. They are made by Huntington to fit only the Pacific Tool and screw right in like the regular dies. They impart considerable leverage upon the bullet. The bullet is held by the collet chuck and the shell holder in the Pacfic Tool pulls the case from the bullet—not the bullet from the case. After the case is away from the bullet, release pressure on the chuck handle and the bullet will drop out readily. The bullets should not be damaged if care be used. Do not forget the powder. It will be in the case if not spilled by carelessness or incorrect tipping of the case as the pulling operation is performed.

A puller is designed so that in any one caliber, it will pull any case in that caliber. For instance, in .30 caliber, it will release any bullet by pulling the case off it, from the .30 Luger cartridge to the .300 Holland and Holland. In .22 caliber, it will pull any case off the bullet from the .22 Hornet to the longest .22-30/1906 necked down, such as the .228 Ackley Magnum, in longest length, or the .22 P.M.V.F. However, one must have the proper Pacific

Shell Holder to grip the case. Chucks and parts are interchangeable. Additional calibers of pullers can be added as desired or as needed.

Obviously, one makes better metal-cased, home-made bullets after some practice and if he happens to be gifted mechanically. The home study course Mechanical Engineer is not likely to do as well at the start as the chap who has pulled everything from an ingrowing toe nail to a 5-ton truck, or who has made bullets, including metal-cased ones, since he was weaned on a .45 Colt.

Experimental .25 caliber bullet dies have been made, but there is today no suitable bullet jacket material readily available which the average chap can make usable. There may be those with a small supply of .25 Stevens Rim Fire *Short* cartridge cases which might possibly be used in a pinch, but who has such?

So, the .22 varmint rifle user is in a preferred position to take the world by the tail and make his own metal-cased bullets, and to town with anyone who does not want to sell him regular copper-casing stock. The chap who can make metal-cased bullets which will really shoot, and has the tools and the "makings," is really sitting pretty.

The down-in-the-cellar bullet manufacturer has another advantage in his favor. If anything goes wrong, he can blame the trouble on non-corrosive primers and everyone will believe him, including the manufacturers of non-corrosive primers—non-corrosive primers being a migraine headache which has backfired so often that just the mention of the name makes some people shiver. With metal-cased bullets of a quality which most of them have been during the last few years, really good home-made metal-cased soft point bullets would do much to improve the cloudy-day disposition of a rifleman to whom the subject of bullets has reached the point where every morning is just another Monday morning.

Operations With the RCBS Tools

The RCBS is attached to the Pacific Loading Tool in the same manner that shell dies are attached, excepting that with the RCBS the hexagonal locking collar is firmly set with a wrench.

The first step in preparation for bulletmaking, is to remove the shell die from the loading frame. Then remove the shell holder from its link and insert the dummy holder with its forming ram or bullet piston which is held in the dummy holder with a set screw and assemble same to the Pacific frame.

The capstan head is then removed from the RCBS and the lower half of the RCBS screwed into the frame. Bring the handle of the loading tool up as far as it will go, and observe the position of the forming piston within the cylinder section of the RCBS. For a 45-grain .22 caliber bullet this position is approximately 0.1875″ from the top face of the cylinder section. You can arrive at this by using a home-made stop of brass that will fit loosely within the cylinder section and rests upon the top of the forming piston. Having made

RCBS Swage Dies for Forming Bullets.
Left to right as you face the picture—Ram or punch holder, forming punch, Swage dies, de-heading Die Punch and De-heading Die.

this preliminary adjustment you firmly lock the hex collar with a wrench and attach the capstan screw head of the RCBS and bring it up firmly with the capstan bar.

A piece of copper jacket with its length of 0.1875″ lead wire which wire has been cut to an exact length so that with its copper jacket it makes a total weight of approximately 45-grains is inserted into the jacket and placed on top of the piston. With the aid of the fingers it is guided to the bottom of the RCBS and the handle of the loading tool is raised to a position *approximately parallel with the floor*. At this point you should stop and lower the handle somewhat and then unscrew the capstan screw head of the RCBS about three-fourths *of a turn* to permit the compressed air to pass from the point of the bullet. Then screw the capstan screw head up snugly and raise the handle until it fully *passes dead center* and comes to a full stop against the back of the frame of the tool.

Then lower the handle fully, unscrew capstan-headed screw completely and place on the table or bench, insert short section of steel rod at bottom of RCBS just as you inserted the bullet portions to be formed and then bring up the handle so that the forming piston will shove the ejector rod and the bullet out of the top of the cylinder sections of the RCBS. You can then catch both the bullet and ejector rod with the fingers and you should be prepared to do so.

A certain amount of what might be called "cut and try" must be used. You may have to develop the adjustment of the tool until you arrive at exact position it will eventually have to have in the frame to assure a perfectly formed bullet of the length, shape and weight desired.

A reloader who wants quick results should never increase the leverage by the addition of a piece of gas pipe or other longer lever. This would likely bend the handle.

Again it may be well to impress that you should always bring the handle of the loading tool which operates the forming piston, so that it *passes* dead center and then comes to a full stop against the back of the loading tool frame. It is possible to form bullets without completing this motion but the bullets so formed will not often be uniform as to density of the completed bullet. Such imperfectly formed bullets are not likely to give good accuracy; in fact, they can not do so.

By trial and error, as above described, you will form a perfect bullet without fins. The Pacific Loading Tool will develop and apply, with its standard length handle, approximately two and one-half tons pressure and still have an ample margin of safety. It requires between a quarter and one half ton pressure to form a .22 caliber jacketed bullet in the RCBS forming tool. With some experience, 50 to 100 properly formed bullets can be expected per hour.

After a reloader has produced 100 or more bullets with the RCBS tool, or is nearly ready to quit for the evening, he should take the capstan head off the RCBS and run the bullets through the cylindrical section of the tool, which acts as a ring die and irons out small blemishes in the bullet. It is these which tend to make minor fliers.

The RCBS tool should be kept clean, even when in use. Both faces

of the dies—head and cylinder sections—should be wiped with a soft
cloth, which of itself is clean and free of grit. This is to remove small
slivers of bullet jacket. Also, there should be no grease or oil at all
in the tool, when being used for forming bullets.

All fired .22 rim fire cartridge cases, to be used as bullet jackets,
should be boiled in clean water for at least 10 to 15 minutes. Use a
good-sized container and agitate the cases. Live steam is better than
boiling water.

The cleaned cases should then be well dried, both inside and outside, and especially should they be completely dried inside each small
case before an attempt is made to de-head the cases. They can be
dried overnight in a warm room, or they can be placed in an oven
and heated, which is faster.

A good white soap, like Ivory or Swan, should be used as a lubricant in the de-heading operation. It makes the de-heading die last
longer. This soaping is applied by rubbing the rim while the fired
case is on the de-heading punch before it is de-headed. A very light
oil may also be used.

All dies and punches should be wiped clean, frequently. Priming
compound which may contain ground glass or other abrasive, is very
abrasive in action on the dies and it must be wiped out frequently or
wear will occur.

In adjusting the de-heading dies the finished jacket should come
just through the top of the de-heading die, when using either .22
Short or .22 Long cases, or the .22 Long Rifle, and on the downward
stroke of the handle the de-headed case is left on the top of the die.
The next jacket pushes out that one and the third jacket pushes out
the second.

Do not mix makes of cases when de-heading. Practically all of the
fired .22 cartridge cases will use the same diameter punch except the
"H" or Winchester cases which require a somewhat smaller punch,
which is supplied by RCBS without extra charge over the regular
size. That means the H cases are thicker, or of smaller inside
diameter. However, this means *two* punches, not just a smaller one.

Annealing Finished Bullet Jackets

After de-heading, the jackets should be annealed as they will then
form more readily and will make a better gas seal in the barrel when
fired. Jackets can be annealed, a few at a time, holding them over
an open flame in a large spoon or they can be placed on a flat steel
plate and heated slowly to 500°-600° F., when they will turn a shade
darker and should then be allowed to cool. They can also be placed

in a flat pan and heated for about 30 minutes in an ordinary oven, at a temperature of 500° to 600° F.

Lead Wire Cutters and Their Use

Fortunately, one can use 0.196″ diameter or 0.203″ lead wire but the 0.1875″ lead wire is best, for .22 bullet cores. The RCBS lead wire cutter works best when held with the short end in a vise which in turn is on a bench or table. It should be held in a horizontal position. Never vertical. The cutter may be accurately adjusted by means of a pair of outside calipers adjusted in fractions of an inch, the bearing points of the calipers being on the cutting side of the operating handle and the outside face of the large stop washer.

Lead wire does not as a rule feed readily and easily through the cutter unless it has first been cut into 10″ or 12″ lengths and rolled between two smooth, flat surfaces, like a flat table-top and a flat board, both of which should be clean. A piece of board, flat on one side and planed smooth should be about 12″ by 6″ and ¾″ or 1″ thick. Nail or screw a small block to the top of the board, to serve as a hand hold.

Forming Pistons

The forming punch must be held loosely in the ram or shell holder. It should never be fastened rigidly by a set screw. The de-heading punch or piston *should* be held securely by the set-screw.

The old style Pacific Loading Tool Frame has at times been broken when too much leverage was applied. Consequently, no additional leverage should be used, and the reloader and bulletmaker should bleed or vent and adjust the dies with caution, as he makes bullets, when using the less-rugged model Pacific with the RCBS. Incidentally, it is only fair to say that the older Pacific Tool was not designed for that purpose.

The handle should be brought up until the pressure begins to build up and then back the head section of the dies off, as you release the handle pressure. Close the head section snugly but do not force the pressure. Do not, in other words, manhandle the tool. Give pressure to the tool a second time and usually the bullet is formed on the stroke however, for good even points, the dies may be vented a second time. Approach the first setting with special care and do not attempt to obtain exceptionally sharp points for the first few bullets, or, until you get "the feel" of the tool and dies. Until then, it is better to use too little pressure than too much.

When resizing large, tough cases, like the .30-1906 and .303

British anti-aircraft brass, to Varminter or .22 Varmint-R cartridges, you may break a Pacific Tool frame. To help prevent this, place a piece of flat steel 0.25″ x 0.625″ on the right side of the frame, tapped or brazed into the head section of the casting and into the base section next to the ram. This tends to prevent springing of the casting. The flat piece is attached by ¼ x 28 SAE cap screws.

In effect, this is a brace across the jaws. The newer Pacific Tool does not require this bracing, but even so do not strain it. If you buy a Pacific Reloading Tool be sure to purchase the newer and stronger model.

General Comment on Making Bullets

The reader should clearly understand that the manufacture of metal-cased soft point or hollow point expanding hunting bullets at home is not always a money saving procedure. It always appears to be, at first thought, but the necessary outlay for dies, punches, tools, and the like is considerable in relation to the cost, for instance, of buying 2,000 or even 5,000 metal-cased bullets. Also, it is hard work, and after a time, to some, not too pleasant work especially in very hot weather or when working in hot, muggy quarters with poor light and little or no ventilation. But it has this advantage: once you have the outfit and a supply of lead wire of the proper thickness for the cores, and fired .22 rim fire *copper* cartridge cases, or empties, you will never be in danger of being out of metal-cased hunting and target bullets. You have "the makings." If you have several bullet dies, you can make bullets with different shape of point, or of a different bullet diameter. One or both may be a real help to you in getting better accuracy. Also, you can make 40, 41, 45, 46, 47, 50, 55, 60, 63, 65 or 70-grain .22 bullets, as you want them, assuming that you have a supply of both Shorts and Long Rifle empties, and the proper bullet dies. One tool or frame will do for all.

Then too, careful workmanship, skill which comes with experience, deftness that is common only to the expert machinist, toolmaker, die sinker, patternmaker, electrician, master plumber, or other mechanic or man who normally works with his hands in making things which require skill with tools, all help in forming bullets better than anyone can normally buy at anything like a low price. By making your own bullets, you can always do more shooting for less money—*once you have the bulletmaking tools and equipment.*

People who are technical experts but who work with their heads more than their hands, are not likely to be mechanically equal in skill to mechanics in the making of bullets, but in designing bullets they often may be far superior. Mechanical and Civil Engineers and draftsmen are the chaps who should be the good bullet designers. Any of them can make a large scale drawing of new bullet designs and have some good toolmaker make up the dies to the new designs.

Generally, professional bullet manufacturers who are custom-makers of bullets in small quantities, comparatively, often quit and drift into easier and better-paying professions, simply because bullet-making on a large scale, eight to 14 hours a day, when someone else is going to have all the fun of shooting those bullets sometimes reaches the point of being not much more interesting than putting bolt No. 34 on a Ford chassis.

Nevertheless, the chap who owns 19 rifles (17 of which he rarely shoots, but buys them to gloat over and look at) or who likes to make and run electric trains, or who "has a shop" in which you can find just about every sort of fine steel tool anyone ever thought of—such are the men who make bulletmakers De Luxe. And De Nuts. They are the boys who really go to town designing and forming bullets by the thousand, and who are usually so busy every evening in the shop back on the lot or down in the cellar that the wife always knows where to find them. In the early stages, such chaps will do well enough with an RCBS outfit. In later stages—well, you know how it is. So why bring that up? It will be every sort of loading tool on the market, half a dozen to a dozen special straight line reloading outfits; three power presses and at least 20 different dies for making every imaginable sort of bullet point and base.

Suppose it all does cost money; did you ever have anything like an equal amount of pleasure in handing it over to Morgenthau? And look what $400,000,000,000.00 worth of it has bought! Just more trouble! Some of this money could have been spent to better advantage, right down in your cellar!

Only by making better bullets than you can buy, can you shoot 0.50" groups at 100 yards.

CHAPTER 21

SMOKELESS POWDERS FOR .22 CALIBER WILDCAT
RIFLES

THE SELECTION and loading of smokeless powders in a
.22-caliber, high velocity, high pressure varmint rifle is a
problem that requires consideration, particularly since the advent
of powerful non-corrosive, non-mercuric primers. These primers
produce hotter and quicker ignition and higher pressures—sometimes
5,000 to 15,000 pounds higher—with certain charges, and thus confront the reloader with problems he did not have to solve a
generation ago.

This situation has produced a condition of universal caution in
the powder and ammunition industries during recent years. The
last reloading booklet of much consequence issued by an explosives
company appeared in 1936. Since that time the concerns which make
the smokeless powders have passed the responsibility for giving out
ballistic information or reloading comment mostly to the loading
companies. The ammunition manufacturers are primarily interested
in making and selling factory loaded ammunition, not reloading
components. Furthermore, they are in a position to test both powder
and primers, individually and in combination, just before they are
loaded, whereas they can not make such tests of components which
have been for a long time in the hands of the reloader.

Everyone in the industry knows that cartridges made by different
ammunition concerns often vary in powder capacity, even though
supposedly of the same size and caliber. Also they are fitted with
primers which vary in composition, thus in strength one company's
primers compared with another company's primers, and a reloader
must use both the powder and the primers he has on hand or can
obtain. This makes it still further complicated when any one
concern, regardless of who they are, attempts to help the shooter
by telling him the primer and the powder charge he should use
with a certain weight, length, core hardness and diameter of bullet.

Each ammunition company has difficulty enough, at times, in
keeping their own primers uniform, especially right after a world

418

war, consequently they are liable to fall back upon the excuse that "information is not available" or "we are unable to keep up with our correspondence." That also *is* a problem.

The author felt that this was a subject, therefore, that had better be discussed by not discussing it at all, but the publisher insisted that to warn our readers, particularly the many who will read this book on .22 varmint rifles who have not had *any* reloading experience at all, it would be safer for all concerned, and a help to thousands of readers to point out which powders are better for this and for that, the effect of different primers on pressures, and the differences in chemical and physical composition of the many brands and sizes of smokeless powders.

As both the author and the publisher have in past years written the ballistic replies to thousands of riflemen seeking information, and so far as we know, without our suggestions causing blown-up rifles or broken actions, and as we have learned from that experience the utter innocence with which many rush into reloading, the author is moved here to make a few remarks which he hopes will be helpful. Just bear in mind however, that we neither guarantee nor recommend the charges, primers, nor combinations which others manufacture. We have on the other hand, compiled here the most carefully selected list of loads tested by the most experienced .22 wildcat shooters in North America, and we have given all of the data pertinent thereto which the informant could supply.

In every instance, when *you* reload, begin two or three grains lower than the charge suggested and develop your load, one or two-tenths grain at a time; never change more than *one* item in the assembly at a time—the primer, the powder (type or amount), the case, or the bullet—and then do that with exactness. If everything appears to be normal, then increase slowly but do not even then load a heavier charge, or a heavier or longer or larger diameter or tougher core bullet on a maximum charge without first reducing the number of grains weight of powder being weighed or measured.

Smokeless Powders

Today there are two primary types of smokeless powders adapted to center fire .22 caliber varmint rifles, with a third type—the ball type of powder—introduced by the Western Cartridge Company only a few years ago. Of the first two important types of dense smokeless, we have the single base powders and the double base powders.

Single Base Smokeless Rifle Powders

Single base powders are made by treating cotton linters or, (in some recent instances) wood pulp, with nitric acid. This results in nitration of the base, hence the name, "nitrocellulose," or nitrated cellulose.

In more recent years, single base powders have been treated or coated with various deterrents to slow down their rate of burning. Such may include diphenylamine, D.N.T., or other products or chemicals, and the powder grains are also usually coated with graphite to make them free running in loading machines.

Powder is normally made in the form of a cake or mass, something like tough biscuit dough, which is rotated in powder mixers that look a little like barrels which are held horizontally. The powder cake is kept moist to prevent it catching fire. At one stage it is dehydrated, ether is added, it goes through various steps, it is formed into round cake, something like a large Lebanon balogna when it comes out of the large horizontal powder press or forming machine, and is then placed in a vertical press from which the powder cake is squeezed in the form of a long, endless string or strings which wind up onto cones. As it comes out of the vertical press in the form of this string, it is pressed around a pin which pierces a hole through the center of the cord—how it gets there is sometimes a mystery and speculation to many, like how they get the last man and bundle down off a high brick smoke stack. The newcomer to the scene often imagines the only thing the man on the stack could do is to let go and drop.

After the tray to hold powder cones under the vertical press is filled with powder, it is shifted to the cutting machines where sharp knives snip off the powder string into small, regular cylindrical pieces of powder, of even length, and of course, also of even diameter, which then have the appearance of broken pieces of lead from a lead pencil. Each of these bits of powder contains the hole in its center to permit the powder to be consumed more uniformly during the combustion of the charge and to help regulate its rate of burning.

After cutting, the powder grains are revolved in drums for graphite coating and sifted and screened, to remove small or large particles and dust and also anything else which accidentally may have been dropped in. Bags selected from different lots of powder, are put together in equal numbers in a new lot, usually of 10,000 pounds, and this is then mixed or blended together so that a finished lot of powder may be as nearly uniform, both chemically and physically, as is possible. Finally, the powder is packed in kegs or canisters for the retail trade, assuming it is to be so sold, and is ready for shipment to the dealer or reloader.

A good many reloaders still have the erroneous belief that a progressive burning smokeless powder develops its maximum pressure at or just before reaching the muzzle of the rifle. This is not so! The maximum pressure in a rifle always occurs within 1.5" to 7" or 8" from the face of the breech block. Its exact position is determined by the size and length of the cartridge, the charge contained within it, and the type of powder being consumed. While the pressure may rise, to, let us say, 55,000 pounds per square inch in the instance of a high intensity case and charge, it is never more than comparatively a small fraction of this amount at the muzzle of the rifle. As the powder gas cylinder lengthens up the barrel, the pressure rapidly falls. Multiple pressure gages, which take the pressure at 1" intervals up the barrel always prove this. The progressive burning powders merely have the rate of fall drop less sharply. In other words, the zenith of the pressure curve is attained somewhat farther forward—an inch or so—and the pressure from that point forward, drops less rapidly. But drop it does, like a sled coasting down hill! If it were otherwise, and the pressure were at the maximum at the rifle muzzle, then obviously the rifle barrel would need to be thickest at the muzzle.

Double Base Powders

Double base or nitroglycerin powders are composed of two bases, nitrocellulose, and nitroglycerin. Usually the nitroglycerin content is 15% to 40% but with later powders containing less than formerly. In appearance they are much like nitrocellulose powders except that the powder grain may be somewhat harder and more dense. The grains are also sometimes cut shorter and stubbier. Such powders are very resistant to moisture.

The author has frequently seen pure nitroglycerin used in the making of double base powder, also in producing nitroglycerin dynamite, and in blasting gelatin, including 100% blasting gelatin. Nitroglycerin—a very powerful and sensitive explosive—is made as a result of the chemical action of nitric acid and sulphuric acid on glycerin. It is not a mechanical process. The pure "oil" is transported carefully from storage to the mixing bowl, and is usually carried when so transported in a nitroglycerin buggy which is handled more carefully than a baby carriage containing twin boys. It is only necessary to stumble but the once, or strike a spark and have it carried to the "oil," and there is an explosion. It may then be a fraction of a second too late to run. The author once arrived on the scene of a $50,000.00 nitroglycerin explosion but a few hours, comparatively, after it had occurred. It smashed plate glass windows *out* of a sporting goods store, four miles away, but the only person hurt in the explosion was a man who was running so fast to get away from there he fell and broke an arm. Sometimes it does not pay to hurry!

A person soon becomes accustomed to having nitroglycerin handled about him but at first it is a bit upsetting. The actual discomfort is mostly from the almost unnoticed fumes which if inhaled may affect some people to the extent of causing most severe headaches at the base of the skull, and which continue for two or three, to even 48 hours.

In high explosives plants, or double base powder plants, most operations are divided so that but two or three persons work in a building at one time. Each small building is surrounded by a barricade. If an explosion occurs, those who knew what might have caused it are there no longer, and those on the outside, although startled, are usually safe. The accident or explosion rate, is not as a rule, so high as to be ominous. It is really surprising the quantity of explosives which can be produced, per man injured.

Nitroglycerin was first invented and produced by an Italian chemist, about the year 1846. When it was first transported in the form of a liquid or "oil," in containers, there were a number of serious explosions, due to its extreme sensitiveness in that form. Some of these explosions were on shipboard. The carrier never sued but often the heirs did.

Then Alfred Nobel, a Swedish engineer and chemist, started mixing nitroglycerin with Fullers Earth, and today it may be mixed, as nitroglycerin dynamite, usually in 20% to 60% strengths (because Interstate Commerce provisions do not permit the interstate shipment of the very high percentage nitroglycerin dynamites) with any one of about a dozen different meals and ground nuthull compounds, any of which makes a suitable absorbent. A stick of N.G. dynamite consists of the nitroglycerin absorbed in its carrier, then wrapped in paraffined paper.

In smokeless powder, nitroglycerin acts much as a speeder-up or added initial igniter of the nitrocellulose. The double base powders ignite and burn faster at the start of the explosion, as the N.G. acts like fat pine splinters in speeding up the kitchen fire. Also, it is of itself a very powerful explosive, alone or in combination. In dynamites it has largely been replaced by the ammonium nitrate high explosives, the blasting gelatins, the semi-gelatins, and the coal powders, which are much safer to handle; many of them give much better (meaning less dense) fumes, but are so much more difficult to detonate that many of them must be detonated by means of primers or booster charges of nitroglycerin dynamite in blasting.

In World War II, while much T.N.T. was used in bombs, especially in small blocks of a half pound or a pound each for demolition work by Engineer units, nevertheless its use was not universal and it was not the most powerful explosive used generally. The tremendous amount of publicity that T.N.T. received was often woefully inaccurate. Many of the demolition bombs were filled principally with ammonium nitrate explosives, which were much cheaper to manufacture in quantity and for which the raw materials were in far greater general supply than those needed for T.N.T. Ammonium nitrate is of itself a powerful explosive and is the principal constituent of most commercial dynamites of the ammonia or "extra" types.

In deep water submarine blasting, particularly where explosives charges had to be kept under and in water for some time the high percentage blasting gelatins were used, usually exploded by booster charges. Where great shattering effect, in certain circumstances, was required, R.D.X. and similar very fast and powerful high explosives were best. In smashing concrete submarine pen roofs, 10′ to 20′ thick, ordinary explosives and bombs are ineffective. You have to employ the real thing and in tremendous force. High percentage blasting gelatin when set off by a booster charge; liquid nitroglycerin or high percentage nitroglycerin dynamite; R.D.X.; and similar high explosives have a speed of detonation of 20,000 to 26,000 feet per second or more, while many ammonia dynamites and coal powders, permissibles particularly, may not develop more than 4,500 to 11,000 feet per second velocity of detonation or explosion. Incidentally, the Japanese made a good deal of R.D.X. and it was quite effective.

It can be seen therefore, that the correct employment of any sort of explosive or powder is a highly technical procedure, as the chap who makes his own according to his own pet formula, or the man who reloads without some outside help and who must use non-corrosive primers to ignite the powder, soon learns. People who have spent their lives developing explosives or testing them continually wish they knew much more on the subject.

Usually double base or nitroglycerin smokeless powders are much

THE MANN V SHOOTING SHED, READY FOR TESTING

The above is an outside, front view of a battery of five Mann V rests located upon and bolted to concrete bases so located that the Mann V rest and the Mann rest operator are both inside the shooting shed and are thus protected from the weather.

If a rifleman who is experimentally inclined, has a range site and proper backstop, he can readily build a small shooting shed of his own, and fit in it either a muzzle and elbow shooting rest for ammunition testing of his different .22 varmint rifles. or he can fit in it, a machine rest or a Mann V rest, or a pressure gage rifle, or all three, assuming he has the room and the means. At times an extra machine rest can be purchased as excess or obsolete equipment from the government or from one of the arms or ammunition companies who may have a few extras due to war work.

The Mann V rest or machine rest bases should be of reinforced concrete, stiffened by small iron rods set in the concrete, and the whole run down 3½ to 4½ feet below ground level so as to be below frost line. Earth should be well tamped around the bases, when completed. Unless the base of the rest be absolutely rigid at all times, a high degree of accuracy of shooting will be impossible.

A rifleman equipped with his own well made and solidly constructed muzzle and elbow rest, and shooting shed, is almost as well equipped to obtain uniformity of accuracy in his ammunition testing as are any of the ammunition companies, all he really needs besides the rest is a home-made chronograph and these have been built and set up by numerous ingenious riflemen.

more waterproof and, under conditions of dampness in storage, are more stable than many single base powders. They develop a higher heat of combustion, which is not desirable, although just how much higher is often a matter of debate. They give somewhat greater erosion in small, .22 wildcat cartridges, fired slowly, as in hunting, than single base powders, but some powder deterrents are of themselves likely to increase or prolong the burning heat. In rapid fire, in large charges, in the instance of large case .22 wildcats, erosion becomes a much more serious matter than in cartridges like the .22 K-Hornet to the .22 Maximum Lovell.

In the use of the nitroglycerin dynamite, because of decomposition, the presence of excessive heat during the storage of the explosive as in a poorly ventilated magazine or storage shed, or for other reasons, it sometimes happens that the nitroglycerin separates from its absorbent carrier and oozes or runs out, assumes then the form of a liquid or an oily mass, and in such condition and form it is extremely dangerous to handle because it is very easily detonated by shock, and is usually set off almost instantly by fire. Never drop, throw, pile anything heavy upon, or carelessly handle such a package and if you attempt to destroy it by burning, do this at least several hundred yards away from buildings, traveled roads, children, livestock or other objects and provide a form of ignition that will permit you to retire several hundreds of yards, to a point of safety, before the fire reaches the explosive.

It is safer to have a Bureau of Mines representative handle any quantity disposal. An instance is known of where a professional waste-powder-burner became confused or turned around and walked into his loosely scattered explosive on a burning ground and died there. This I believe, was with a nitrocellulose explosive which flashed when ignited.

In any explosive in which nitroglycerin is employed, and that includes double base powders, what may occur under abnormal or unusual conditions—particularly if very high or especially below 40° below zero temperatures—is a matter having little relation to what is the normal stability of the explosive under more normal conditions.

In the Yukon, or where it is extremely cold during part of the winter, where temperatures have gotten down to 40° to 70° below zero, a few explosions, which appeared to have been detonations, have occurred, which have wrecked rifles using the comparatively small, short, straight, selfloading cartridges loaded apparently with the -¹d type, high percentage, N.G. powder.

Decomposition of powders, including single base powders, sometimes occurs at very high temperatures, especially when powders in canisters have been stored under hot roofs in the tropics, or during a prolonged heat wave in temperate zones, fumes may be given off and the powder discolors. This is most likely to happen with powders a few years old. In such case extreme care should be used in disposing of those powders and in opening the canister as ignition may occur when oxygen is introduced. Also, be very careful where you throw empty or partly empty cans.

One of the most unfortunate fatalities the author recalls occurred when two young boys found a powder canister containing a small amount of powder which had been discarded. Small boy-like they lit a match and dropped it into the can, to see whether it would ignite. Of course it did and one boy was burned to the extent of second or third degree burns on every portion of his body except the soles of his feet. Nothing could be done for him. As in the instance of the misuse or careless disposal of blasting caps children, and especially boys, are usually the victims.

Powder in canisters should when possible be kept at temperatures of between 50° and 80° F. and in summer it is safer to keep such canisters, with the tops screwed on tight, in a dry cellar than in the upper story of a dwelling. If old powder is to be disposed of, scattering it like wheat kernels in very small portions in an area, and as one walks along, so that no amount collects in a small area, is one convenient method of disposing of it. Do not dispose of it on or along a path.

duPont I.M.R. Powders Suitable for .22 Wildcat Cartridges

The following described smokeless powders were developed and offered by E. I. duPont De Nemours & Company to the retail trade, mostly before the year 1936. There have been some more recent lot numbers, but early in 1946 their Ballistic Station advised the author that no *important* changes had been made in this line, and such changes as had been made represented only such slight chemical or physical differences as may be expected from lot to lot over a time. Each duPont lot has a new code or lot number. These later lots are not at this time being publicly advertised. Each of these duPont powders described here is a nitrocellulose powder.

In the duPont I.M.R. Canister series, starting with the smallest granulation and increasing slightly between each two, are the following brands: 4227, 4198, 3031, 4064, and 4320. IMR 4227 was similar to, and succeeded 1204; 4198 resembled 25½, which incidentally, was never sold universally to handloaders; next came 3031, a very fine powder for the Lindahl Chucker and the .22 Rimless Chucker, the Kilbourn Magnum Junior and similar size cartridges, the .219 Donaldson-Wasp, and so on up. This was similar to duPont No. 17½; 4320 succeeded 1147 in the varmint and military rifle field, and both 3031 and 4320 were and are somewhat similar to duPont No. 16, and Hercules No. 300, which was originally H.P.P. 10 and which the author renamed.

No. 4064 duPont: While this is a coarser powder and slower burning, it is quite similar to the old duPont No. 15½, and also somewhat like duPont No. 15. The weights of charges are not comparable, and the comparison must be regarded as rather general.

Reloaders should bear in mind that no powder is put out strictly as a handloading proposition for .22 wildcats. Not enough would be sold to pay for making the canister label tests. Also, the makers of the powder would not possess any considerable variety of .22 wildcats in which to test it. Many feel that "overhead" is often piled on such tests all out of proportion to the actual work done, especially if other work is slack in the ballistic department just as that work is being prepared. It is unfortunate that there are not more, or at least *some* varmint rifle enthusiasts high up in *key* positions in the powder industry.

No. 4227 duPont: This is the smallest of the five duPont full charge canister brands. The diameter of the small powder cylinder of 4227 is approximately 0.025″ and the length 0.025″. Note the position of the decimal point; this means 1/40″—a very fine grain, tubular grain coated nitrocellulose powder, or at least essentially so. Its best .22 varmint cartridges are the Hornet, the K-Hornet and the K-Hornet Junior. Henry Davis, of Florence, South Carolina, uses 13.2 grains of 4227 behind the Remington 45-grain Hornet bullet in the K-Hornet as his *long* range wild turkey load. It gives about 3,100 f.s.m.v. and will smash a young turkey badly if closer than 150 yards. Any charge from 12.0 grains to 12.8 grains is a good load with 41 or 45-grain M.C. bullet and 13.0 to 13.2 grains is tops; do not go higher.

No. 4227 is a good powder, especially for the lighter weight bullets (remember it is a fine grain, fast powder) in the whole series of Lovells, R-2's and the like, but it is not the best choice with the 50 and 55-grain bullets. That puts up the pressure with the finer cut powders.

It is a good powder for the .22 Hornet. One of the very best. Also, one of the safest, if you do not overload. It can be used for a reduced charge powder in or as a lighter bullet load in many of the larger .22 varmint cartridges, but it is not a good selection for 55-grain bullets in a case like the Varminter Senior or the .22/348, nor for 63 and 70-grain bullets in the .22 Savage H.P.

TESTING A RIFLE IN A MANN V REST

The most accurate-known method of testing a rifle barrel for accuracy, is in a Mann V rest. The rifle is laid in the Mann V, and lies there upside down, while being fired. A stock is immaterial to the testing and usually a rifle is fitted with only a very short piece of the stock, for convenience of the Mann V rest operator.

When fired in a Mann V—which is a heavy steel plate with a deep V in its upper surface, the V having been machined out of the solid steel, the rifle is free to recoil backward in the V and is stopped by the hand of the Mann V rest operator.

It is pushed forward to a stop, for the firing of each successive shot. This insures uniformity of delivery.

Just because you obtained good results with 12.0 grains of 1204 in some cartridge with a certain bullet, and ahead of a given primer, it does not follow that you should use 12.0 grains of 4227 with the same combination. You might need more or *less*. Might even be two grains less. You should develop your charge slowly, one and two tenths grain at a time. You might have a custom rifle with a chamber neck with only 0.001" tolerance and a very short throat. And, you might draw a bunch of empties with very thick necks and so, where would you be? Also, thick heads could happen in the same lot; brittle brass and loose primer pocket; you might get a brass shaving off a previous cartridge head, in the chamber just at that moment; or an unburned powder grain.

You could too, have it happen that you had to open a new box of primers and use a primer from what was, unknown to you, a stronger lot. Thus a hotter primer and a faster ignition of the next charge in a very tight chamber fit. Up goes the chamber pressure by 10,000 or 15,000 pounds! If only 5,000 it could cause trouble if you were crowding the upper pressure limit with an old and weak action or a firing pin which was put in with a sloppy fit!

No. 4198 duPont I.M.R.: This seems to be one of the most generally useful of the duPont I.M.R. series for cartridges which normally take 16.0 to 19.0 grains of powder, or, from 13.0 grains on up to 19.5 grains. This takes in the K-Hornet and up to and including the Maximum Lovell and the Kilbourn K-Lovell. Originally this powder was produced principally for use in such fairly good size, medium power deer cartridges which have a heavy sale, like the .32 Winchester Special and the .300 Savage, and is also used extensively in the .32 Remington rimless. Nevertheless, in the varmint line, it seemed to exactly suit the various numbers made from the .25-20 S.S. case necked down to .22, and to the .218 Bee case swaged down to the same .22 varmint cartridges. The .218 Bee case can be used for the .22/3000 Lovells if you can not get .25-20 S.S. cases, and most likely in many places, you can not.

The 4198 I.M.R. has a fairly long grain—0.085″—and nevertheless a diameter but little more than that of 4227. One writer gives it as the same, but the duPont diagram gives it a definitely larger diameter, about 0.030″. The perforation center is also included; it is in all of the I.M.R.'s used for canister trade.

These cartridges and charges are, almost all of them, extremely accurate up to 250 yards or more, give around 3,000 to 3,300 f.s. and sometimes slightly higher with the lighter bullets, and give a small cartridge a really high rating as a woodchuck killer. It is fine for crows and hawks. However, over-enthusiasm has caused these cartridges to be over-rated on range, lack of wind drift and long range killing power. Accuracy life may be up to 7,000 rounds.

The .22/3000 type of cartridge does not have as much advantage in range and killing power over the .22 Hornet or the K-Hornet as some claim, *provided both use the same ogive and weight of bullet.* A good part of that extra 300 or 400 f.s. is lost in traveling the first 125 yards, and to shoot a 45-grain open point bullet with a wide mouth and a good air chamber, in one, and to shoot a solid pencil-point bullet in the other, is not and never has been a fair comparison. The open point bullet loses velocity faster, for the wind resistance is greater, and the pencil-point bullet never kills as well, other things being equal. Also, you are shooting a custom job against a factory job. That is another advantage in *some* cases.

Nevertheless, 4198 is a *very* useful powder in .22 varmint rifles, especially for crows, hawks, prairie dogs and woodchucks inside 250 yards, and for any place where they have $1,000.00 cows and people with "tetchy" feelings. In other words, for medium size and smaller stuff, and in neighborhoods where it is not good form to shoot a 10 gauge shotgun or a 40mm gun on a Sunday morning.

No. 3031 duPont I.M.R.: Believe it or not, this was made to sell by the ton for loading the good old .30-30. Powder companies talk of the .30-30 in a subdued voice, even those to whom a .22 Super-Varmint is merely a pain in the neck. It means plenty of powder sales over a year, when it is a good loading year; the game commission claims there are 1,250,000 deer in Pennsylvania, and there are no government bureaus to talk out one side of the mouth and whisper something else out of the other—(what they say out the other side is "no"). You could use 3031 in some cartridges which used Lightning No. 1, duPont Nos. 17½, 16 or Hercules 300. Among others it is very good in the .257 and the .348.

No. 3031 seems to be made to order for the 45 and 47-grain Wotkyns-Morse 8S bullets in the Lindhal Chucker, the Rimless Chucker, the Lindahl Super-Chucker and a host of other medium length .22 wildcats, or with 50 to 55-grain bullets and lighter, in the larger wildcats. In other words, it is a "medium burner." The grain size is approximately 0.085" long and about 0.035" in diameter—0.010" larger in diameter, than 4227 for instance. It is a very flexible powder—*if the pressure is not too high;* or the bullet not too heavy in weight.

For instance, it will do fine in loads of about 23.0 to 25.5 grains in the medium fat, medium short .22 wildcats like the Lindahl Chuckers and the Kilbourn Magnum Junior and the short-stubby Pfeifer's—the .30-40 and .303 cut-down cartridges. And it will do just as fine work with 29.0 to 32.0 grains, or a trifle more, in the next larger size cartridges like the Super-Chucker and the various not-too-long wildcats made from the .22 Savage H.P. and the .25-35 and the .219 Zipper cases. Also, up to 35.0 to 37.0 grains in the Supers of those cases. But you better quit with 45 to 55-grain bullets, and do not *up* your charges too fast; feel your way along!

No. 4320 duPont I.M.R.: Chaps who like to shoot medium weight bullets in the larger or medium size .22 varmint rifles think this powder was made to their special order. Actually it followed along after duPont No. 16 and its variations, duPont No. 1147, and Hercules 300. It is a volume seller for the .30-1906, the .270 Winchester, would do in the .276 and .280 cartridges of moderate length and capacity, and in the .220 Swift, especially with 48-grain bullet—in high intensity cartridges in other words—and with not too *much* boiler room or not too heavy bullets. Powder grain is rather short and stubby and you can begin to see the perforation in the grain rather easily.

In the cartridges of the size of the .22 Varminter, .22-250, the longer specials made from the .22 Savage H.P., .25-35 and .219 Zipper cases, and 50 and 55-grain bullets, this powder is a fine selection. It seems to take 50 to 55-grain bullets to make it burn properly, and you can get almost as high velocities with these as with 45-grain projectiles—using 4320.

The author has seen a few remarkably good targets made with this powder in the .220 Swift, and that is not a cartridge to produce super-200-yard targets in many instances. Its talking point (the .220 Swift) is flatness of trajectory and splattering the game, rather than extreme accuracy.

No. 4064 duPont I.M.R.: This is a duPont I.M.R. Powder designed primarily for Magnum type cartridges—the big fellows with plenty of "boiler room." Actually, it was designed primarily for the .375 Holland and Holland Magnum, the .35 Whelen (for which the uses would be very limited because so very few rifles of this caliber were ever manufactured), and the .250/3000 Savage. However, it was found that it did splendidly in some of the larger .22 wildcat rifle cartridges, like the .22 Varminter and .22 Senior Varminter for instance, and .22 cases made from the .348 Winchester cartridge case.

Actually, 4064 was listed in the duPont diagram as being slightly smaller in diameter, than the very similar powder, 4320. But in actual use a slightly greater weight of charge is needed to give comparable results. Specific gravity of the powder is probably less than that of 4320.

Especially with the longer and heavier bullets, this powder can be used to great advantage in a very wide range of cartridges, including the .300 Holland and Holland, .375 Holland and Holland, .220 Swift, .257 Roberts, .250/3000 Savage, .270 Winchester, .275 or .276 cartridges like the British Service experimental cartridge,

.30-1906—including the whole range of bullets from 110 to 220-grain—.30-40 Krag, .303 British, .348 Winchester, the 7.92mm and the special Mausers. Also the 6.5mm Mannlicher-Schoenauer, and 6.5mm Mannlicher-Steyr and the 7mm Mauser, the 7.62mm Russian, the 7.65mm Belgian Mauser, the 9mm Mannlicher—to name but a few. A reloader therefore, is not "stuck" with this powder.

Somehow, it has never become quite as popular as the better known 4320 for use with 50, 55, 63 and 70-grain bullets in .22 varmint rifles but it has its field where you want to fire up the old boiler back of heavier bullets. Like the other duPont I.M.R.'s it is a modern nitrocellulose powder of low erosive qualities.

No. 4759 duPont: This powder is a sporting propellant intended for less than full charges in a long line of cartridges; duPont ballistic men have told the author that it was not intended for full charges in *any* cartridge. It replaces duPont No. 80. It is also not intended for use in pistol or revolver cartridges.

The powder, as extruded from the press in manufacture is black, tubular grain type, about 0.03″ in diameter and 0.06″ in length. It is said that this powder produces a fouling which is not strictly non-corrosive, which means the rifle in which it is used should very definitely be cleaned as soon as possible after firing. Any really good .22 varmint rifle barrel should be so cleaned regardless and cleaned carefully. I have looked through many rifle barrels claimed to be in "perfect condition," although never cleaned, and none of them in my opinion was in perfect condition. All showed a gray cast to the steel and often very minute spots like small pits.

The author has owned since 1923 a Smith & Wesson 10″ fancifully engraved and specially stocked target pistol, which was made in 1909, and has been shot very hard ever since and has been cleaned very carefully and thoroughly every time it has been used. In August, 1945 the Sales Manager of Smith & Wesson stated that its barrel was in the best condition of any single shot Smith & Wesson he had ever looked through. One of the last 10-shot strings fired out of it at this writing scored either 92 or 93, indoors, slow fire, at 20 yards, on the small bullseye, in Match 9 of the USRA Team Matches of 1945-46. It was followed in Match 10 by a 91 and the last five shots of the season were a 48 x 50. So much for the idea that proper cleaning of a .22 barrel will wear it out in short order. Needless to say, this is the original barrel. It has been shot probably in excess of 100,000 rounds.

No. 4759 may be used in charges of approximately 7.5 or 8.0 grains in the .22 Hornet; 8.0 to 12.0 grains in the R-2 and .22/3000;

10.0 to 29.0 grains in the .22 Varminter, and in the .22-250 rifles; 10 to 20 grains or more in the .219 Zipper improved; 16.0 to 25.0 grains in the .220 Swift; and in other calibers in proportion.

Capt. P. H. Wilcox, of Marcus Hook, Pennsylvania, reports that it does exceptionally well in the .28-30 Stevens and in the .32-40 Schuetzen rifles, of which he is a fancier. He is also an enthusiast in the use of .22 and .25 caliber varmint rifles and a co-shooter with George Schnerring. Those stuck for powder and who use the .28-30 and the .32-40, should try 4759 in the following combinations: 10.0 grains in the .28-30 with 125-grain bullet and 14.0 grains in the .32-40 with the long, heavy Pope bullet which weighs about 195-grains. This load in the .32-40 is extremely accurate at 200 yards.

No. 4350 duPont: This was a fairly coarse powder with rather long grains—diameter 0.038″ and length 0.088″. Seems to have been most applicable to use in the .220 Swift, .22 Varminter, .22 Senior Varminter, and similar large and long varmint cartridges with much powder capacity. It worked well in .300 H & H and .375 H & H and is best adapted to use with bullets of 55 to 70-grain weight, and of still heavier weight with faster twist to spin same. It is unlikely that duPont will supply this in quantity as a canister lot. Also, it is unlikely that they will have additional canister powders in the near future.

All in all, these duPont canister powders represent a very considerable addition to the list of handloading powders and are the best ones to choose for the medium and larger size .22 wildcat cartridges at this writing.

Western "Ball" Powders

The Western Cartridge Company, now merged in Olin Industries, is a much more experienced firm in the manufacture of high explosives and smokeless powders than the average reader might imagine. The taking up by them of the manufacture of "ball" or granular powder was therefore not as much of an innovation as is generally supposed.

Ball powder is a single base or nitrocellulose propellant made by immersing nitrated cotton, or nitrocellulose in 10 times its own bulk of water, and in the water is reduced to a liquid by chemical means, one of the chemical agents being ethyl acetate.

Gelatinized nitrocellulose is less heavy than water, therefore will rise in it, and comes to the top in the form of a somewhat creamy lacquer. Stirring the mixture causes the lacquer to form into globules. Additional chemicals are added to keep the globules from attaching, one to the other after the stirring is finished. It has been claimed that the speed of stirring regulates the size of the balls of powder which result.

One feature of the manufacture of ball powder is that it can be made with comparatively inexpensive equipment of a rather crude type. This is an advantage to a new and small company, which lacks other powder-making equipment, but it is no special advantage to a large powder company which already has complete powder making equipment very little of which could be used in making ball powder.

Very extraordinary and, some say, exaggerated claims have been made as to the speed and cheapness, comparatively, with which the ball type of powder is produced. People who have made and sold powder for generations and who have, incidentally, been given opportunity to make the ball powder without availing themselves of this plan (possibly not a very wise rejection, as it put others into competition with existing companies), have known that in the making of the ball type of powder, only a fair percentage of the powder is of any one size. As an example, let us say that 60% of the globules formed, are of sizes which can be used in loading a given caliber, incidentally the desired size. That leaves 40%, which either must be used in other calibers—for which powder a manufacturer might have little or no demand or, it would have to be reworked. Getting 60% of the 40% would be 24%. In two workings you would have 60% plus 24%, or 84% of the powder. In three workings, 60% plus 24% plus 60% of 16% which is 9.6%, or a total of 93.6%. In four workings you would get 97.44%, omitting losses. So that five workings would in theory be necessary to reduce most of your powder to the desired size. Where is the saving in time, money or labor in that procedure? A loading company, loading a wide variety of cartridges, could probably take care of most ball powder granulations in one or two workings, but people who make and sell powder want to be able to make approximately 100% of it of a given size, chemical exactness, and uniformity of grain, so that they can sell the lot of powder to one company for one or more uses. Also, the exact cost of making any sort of powder could be overestimated or mistakenly estimated. Many things enter, and few things are made today that do not have material drawbacks to manufacture or use, as well as virtues and benefits.

So far and to date, "Ball" powders have not been offered reloaders in canister or keg lots; but they may be in time. Much of this powder was made by Western for loading in the .30 caliber carbine cartridge. Much of it was made at a time when speed was more important in getting considerable quantities of powder to a loading company, or to a multitude of them, than the questions of cost, relative superiority, waste, and keeping qualities. To the reloader, or to the powder manufacturer, all of these things are important. During World War II, cost was often of little object in the building of plants or the turning out of munitions, be it explosives, powder, ammunition, rifles, machine guns, airplanes, bombs, rockets, uniforms or what have you? Much went on, in the rush of production that the long-suffering tax-payer will never hear, and it is probably just as well. Even the American Taxpayer must have his rest, so that tomorrow he can take it—again! In the war the many advantages of politicians being compelled to mind their own business and to keep their collective traps shut, in all the cigarette smoke, was lost sight of; it cost plenty.

So, the powders of tomorrow should be the best of today, plus the innovations, the changes, the developments, and the improvements which science and the skill of man, have all brought to pass. Had the author had just *one* of the better .22 varmint cartridges of today, 40 years ago, plus modern powders and primers, with the opportunities he had then for year-round varmint shooting, life would really have been a paradise of rifle shooting. The Happy Hunting Ground would have been something that could have been enjoyed, here, in our lifetime—and enjoyed at a time when the enthusiasm and fire of youth, would have made it seem most worth while.

Townsend Whelen once said, "'that of the many things which have contributed to the betterment of varmint rifles, modern powders probably contributed most,'" or words to that effect. I would add to this, the very real improvements in the design and manufacture of custom-made .22 caliber metal-cased, expanding bullets.

Hercules Canister Powders

When by Court Order, duPont was split up into three explosives manufacturers in 1912, the new companies were E. I. duPont De Nemours & Company, Hercules Powder Company, Inc., and Atlas Powder Company.

The duPont Company came out of the division with the nitro-cellulose rifle powders. It should be clearly understood however, by the reader, that the bulk or volume of sporting powder business, which for duPont is less than 2% of their total business, is in powder for shotgun shells and for .22 caliber rim fire cartridges. The powders for .22 center fire commercial cartridges, and for the .22 caliber wildcats, are very important to those who use such ammunition; to the explosives companies, and to the ammunition loading companies, the volume is much less than in the other lines mentioned.

The Atlas Powder Company does not manufacture sporting powders although they have at times jobbed Hercules Powders, principally to South American and other foreign trade. They are not therefore, an important part of the sporting powder picture in the United States.

The Hercules Powder Company started manufacture in January 1913, with the old duPont and Laflin & Rand lines of double base powders. Hercules had 1908 Bear, Stag, Sharpshooter Nos. 1 and 2, Lightning Nos. 1 and 2, HiVel No. 2, Unique, Bullseye, and various other double base powders all very early in their career. Over a period of 33 years the development and operating divisions and personnel have failed to produce a satisfactory line of nitrocellulose rifle powders. So today, we have a rather sharply defined division in the *types* of powders sold for canister use by riflemen. Nitrocellulose rifle powders by duPont, nitroglycerin or double base powders by Hercules.

No. 2400 Hercules: This is the brand of Hercules Smokeless sporting rifle powder which most users of *gentle shoulder slope* .22 varmint cartridges will find most useful. It has seemed to be best adapted to the medium and smaller size varmint rifle cartridges. It is definitely not so well suited to those cases having 28° to 35° shoulder slope and considerable powder capacity. The combination causes more rapid burning of the powder and also because of the quantity of powder in such type case, a high breech pressure with powders which ignite and burn quite readily.

It is entirely possible for a shape of cartridge case to be ideally suited to one type of powder—in this case the coated nitrocellulose powders—or in the instance of the short or long very straight cases, or those with very gentle shoulder slopes, to be perfectly suited by some of the commercial double base powders. Such powders burn readily without the constriction to their gases, caused by sharp pitch shoulder slopes. Sharply bottlenecked cartridges in small caliber therefore are not well suited to any powder which is easily ignited and which burns more rapidly. This was known as far back as the early days of Sharpshooter powder, in other words, about 1900.

No. 2400 is a double base powder which contains considerable nitroglycerin. Chemically it has some resemblance to nitroglycerin dynamite, due to the importance of its nitroglycerin content.

Nitroglycerin, which is a very powerful explosive of itself, is an oily, viscous fluid commonly called "oil." It is very easily detonated and it detonates at an extremely high velocity. Nitroglycerin, in the form of nitroglycerin dynamite, normally made in 15% to 60%

strengths (the Interstate Commerce Commission will not permit the railroad shipment of higher percentage N.G. dynamites) will often detonate when such dynamite is burned. Also, dynamite, including nitroglycerin dynamite, often deteriorates rather rapidly in strength, with age; even when a few months old, especially if not stored under perfect storage conditions. It is always possible, although not always probable, that some of the nitroglycerin may separate and flow off in liquid form, from the dynamite and be absorbed by the packing cases in transit or in storage.

When this occurs, the nitroglycerin again becomes practically pure nitroglycerin and is very easily and readily jarred into detonating. It is *very* dangerous to handle, should not be kept on hand in such condition, and should be removed and disposed of—be destroyed by someone skilled in such disposal. This liquid N.G. will soak right through or escape by the paraffined paper cartridge wrappings and is difficult to contain, and is always readily absorbed by wood, cardboard or paper packing cases.

The double base, dense, nitroglycerin powder grain, on the other hand, is a hard, almost bone-like material or substance which normally is quite stable and easily transported. But it does contain nitroglycerin in considerable quantity, with all of its latent possibilities.

A double base powder contains *two* bases both of which are highly inflammable, both of which are highly explosive, and the nitrocellulose base or portion is a product which normally has *two* widely different rates of explosion or detonation, a low and a high rate; and the high rate is quite high although not as high as the detonation rate of nitroglycerin.

Even in the hands of experts, long accustomed to making such powders and with all modern equipment, both single base and double base powders can be exploded or detonated most unexplainably with emphatic results. About 1942, the Kenvil Plant of Hercules had a detonation of war powder, mostly single base, in process of manufacture, which snuffed out 53 lives, almost destroyed two powder lines, and delayed the manufacture of powder for the British Government by months. They never found out what caused it. In the winter of 1945-46 duPont had a detonation of 4,000 pounds of single base or nitrocellulose powder. It woke up the author in the middle of the night, although he was asleep in his bed some five or six miles west of the scene of the explosion, yet the explosion wave was so strong, even at that distance, that he felt drawn strongly toward the front window of his bedroom as if he were being pulled irresistibly out of the window. Because of being asleep, he never *heard* this explosion, but the explosion wave was very pronounced and felt like an earthquake. It also broke some 25 or 30 windows of large size some four or five miles northwest of the explosion. No one was killed.

Normally, double base powder is quite waterproof, almost like high percentage blasting gelatin; in fact it is not ruined by getting

TESTING A BOLT ACTION RIFLE FOR PRESSURE

The arrangement on top of this Springfield rifle, is a standard pressure gage used to determine the breech pressure in thousands of pounds per square inch, developed during the firing of a cartridge. The chamber has been drilled through the top, a plunger is fitted in the gage, and a lead slug is fitted against the plunger.

When the charge is fired, the lead slug is shortened by the impact of the plunger against it, and the measurement of this amount when compared with a table previously prepared gives the relative breech pressure developed by the cartridge just fired.

Any .22 varmint rifle cartridge may be tested for breech pressure in this manner, but to do so, the barrel must first be drilled, and thereafter the rifle will be useless as a rifle barrel but it will always be available for a pressure testing device of a relatively fair degree of accuracy, for that cartridge. It will be obvious that any one pressure gage can only test a given degree of clearance between cartridge and chamber and for one length and style of throat. It does not permit determining the relative difference in pressures given by tight chambers vs. loose chambers, or for long throats vs. short throats. But it does permit testing different weights of charges, and different lengths and weights of bullets, in one type of chamber.

The rifle when tested for pressure, is held rigidly on top of the base of a Mann V rest or a Frankford Arsenal type machine rest, or a cradle rest. It is never used by holding in the hands when fired.

it damp, it does not readily absorb considerable quantities of moisture from the air, as did Schuetzen rifle powder, and under normal conditions it may keep without much deterioration and maintain velocity well for periods of 20 to 40 years. These are qualities definitely favorable to its use by reloaders.

Then again, something might in time, or with poor storage facilities such as are common with present-day housing conditions, or because of stupid fire department or police regulations which necessitate the keeping of small canisters of smokeless powder in heavy, thick, hardwood magazines in homes, and which magazines immediately make a dangerous *bomb,* these may result in premature decomposition of some of the powder.

When smokeless sporting powder of any type becomes discolored, when small globules of a honey, oily, or molasses-like liquid have formed, or the nitrocellulose turns green, brown, gray, or flakes off in fine powdery particles or looks like oxidized material, the powder should be gotten rid of immediately and very carefully. Even a Scot should not try to save $1.60 by quickly loading it up and shooting it before it gets worse. If it deteriorates further, it may probably do so at a velocity of about 10,000 to 24,000 feet per second, and the first second will be very interesting in your rapidly closing life period. Some powder chemists have suggested great care in opening a canister of powder which is going bad, especially single base powder, because such action will introduce a fresh supply of oxygen which always promotes combustion, and it also liberates ether fumes which of themselves might result in an explosion if flame be present. Never have a lighted cigarette present when examining or loading smokeless or black powders.

These things are mentioned, not to frighten you about the use or storage of any kind or type of powder but simply to point out for your own safety the chemical constitutents of smokeless powders, their characteristics, especially under decomposition, and what to avoid to eliminate every possible source of preventable danger. You can be right 10,000 times, but if you are very wrong just once, with either nitroglycerin or with decomposing nitrocellulose it may then be too late to prevent trouble.

Needless to say, a small quantity of powder left over from reloading, and which one might wish to dispose of, should not be tossed into the kitchen range or the cellar furnace for burning. A range or furnace fire box does not make good "burning ground" for waste powder. The powder will surely flash; if at all confined it may explode violently, blow open or blow off the lids or the furnace door, or even wreck the stove or the furnace and probably cause a serious fire. Powder should be carefully scattered on bare ground and in widely separated areas apart from persons.

No. 2400 Hercules has been used principally in such cartridges as the .22 Hornet, in which it has performed very well indeed as this cartridge has a very gentle neck taper perfectly adapted to this powder. It has also done well in the K-Hornet, in the 3″ or long .410 caliber shotgun shells (in which immense quantities of it have been loaded). It has also been used successfully in the .357 Smith & Wesson Magnum cartridge, which is regarded by some uninformed persons as a very high power cartridge, but actually it has almost exactly the ballistics of the .32-40 black powder and .32-40 low velocity smokeless loads. It cracks sharply due to the short barrel of the revolver, and seems loud merely in comparison. The case is medium length, straight, and 2400 burns well in such case. Oddly enough these rifle, revolver and shotgun cases vary in length, powder capacity and breech pressure developed, but they all have one thing in common necessary for proper action by a fine grain double base powder; the case is straight or has a very gentle taper at the shoulder, and thus in such cases 2400 is not confined too much during initial combustion. Put it in a sharply bottlenecked case like the .219 Wasp, use a heavy bullet, and an immediate sharp rise in pressure would result.

Purely as a matter of safety to the reader, it should be said that some of the earliest No. 2400 canister label charges were too liberal; they were too high, especially with some of the later and stronger non-corrosive primers, and some such loadings gave trouble. Later charges recommended were far more satisfactory as they were within normal pressure limits for the arms in use, with any of the commercial primers sold to reloaders. Thus, if you have No. 2400 you have had for 10 to 13 or more years, cut down the recommended charges by 3.0 to 5.0 grains, and then develop your loads very gradually, changing but one factor at a time, until you find a proper maximum.

A number of powerful non-corrosive primers came on the market after this powder was introduced in canister lots and this brought about trouble.

No. 2400 Hercules is made in the form of a small, black disc, of a diameter of approximately 0.03″ and a thickness of 0.015″. It contains about the same percentage of nitroglycerin as HiVel No. 2, and of HiVel No. 3—reportedly around 20%—and should be used with modern primers to cut down corrosion and erosion, and to help preserve the barrel of a fine .22 varmint rifle.

As pointed out previously, unusual care should be taken to prevent overloading when priming with strong, non-corrosive primers. No. 2400 seems to be a powder which is uniform in its combustion under normal conditions and in proper loads, but it has shown that it can be quite uncertain under exceptional circumstances not favorable to it and develop high pressures.

It does not appear to be suitable for full charges in very long, large, and maximum capacity .22 varmint cartridges, especially if these cartridges are made with very sharp shoulder slope.

Due to its quick ignition and easy burning No. 2400 works to best advantage with 35, 40, 41, 45, 47 and 50-grain bullets in .22 varmint rifles. Considerable bullet weight and resistance is *not* required to make it burn.

Hercules HiVel No. 3: This double base powder was introduced about 1926. It had the same nitroglycerin content, approximately, as HiVel No. 2, better known to the public, and so exactly suited the gentle slope .22/3000 Lovell cartridge that Hervey Lovell selected it as his favorite powder for that cartridge.

HiVel No. 3 contains approximately 20% N.G., and the black tubular grains measure 0.035" in diameter and 0.080" in length. It first appeared in canister form in 1935, at which time non-corrosive primers started to become popular. One fault developed with No. 3, which was that at temperatures *lower than* 30 to 40 degrees below zero, Fahrenheit, pressures mounted rapidly and it might possibly detonate with strong primers. This is not a temperature level that bothers most of us, but it occurs rather often in January and February in upper Ontario and Quebec, and is very common in Saskatchewan, Manitoba, British Columbia, and in Yukon Territory. Up in the Yukon temperatures of 30 below at times seemed fairly warm in mid-winter and the old bulb went down to 50° to 70° below zero, for as much as 10 days at a time. Around Whitehorse and up toward the mouth of the Mackenzie River where they got out the oil to supply the Whitehorse refinery for the airplane traffic following the Alaskan Highway, it sometimes got down to 75° below zero.

Right at that temperature but in other neighborhoods, HiVel No. 3 folded up, and as there were too many who seemed inclined to take it out to shoot this or that, at such levels it was very quietly taken off the market and lost to the canister trade. It seems that not only does heat stir up non-corrosive primers, but also intense cold gives unusual results when a very hot primer and a very cold charge of double base powder form a union which might, possibly result in detonation. So, HiVel No. 3 is no more.

The author had letters from a fox-trapper friend in the early winter of 1945-1946, reporting daily temperatures of 30° to 50° below zero in Central Ontario, when most of us had real mild weather farther South, so it is probable that manufacturers will be more careful to test primers and powders at temperatures to 80° below zero, before they sell them either in the form of components or in factory ammunition to riflemen who might go hunting by plane to areas to which in the past, most white men did not go. Central Siberia, for instance, might be one of the great hunting areas of the world, 20 or 30 years from now, when things quiet down and airplane routes around the globe are established. It gets *very* cold, in some areas in Siberia and wolf hunting is great sport. Page the .22 varmint rifle shooters of 1975!

HiVel No. 2: This double base Hercules Powder made a remarkable accuracy record in International Match ammunition, and special commercial match ammuntion, of .30-1906 caliber. The black, tough, tubular grains are approximately 0.04″ in diameter and 0.085″ in length. It is the slowest burning of the Hercules double base commercial powders which have sold the public for canister trade, and while it was a top performer in large cartridges of a size of the .30-1906, it does not follow that it would and will do equally well in .22 varmint cartridges. Lindahl, I believe it was, reported that it was apparently unsuited to cartridges of small and medium capacity in .22 center fire wildcats, because a hard, black, gummy deposit was left on the lands and this was difficult to remove. Also, this seemed to interfere considerably with accuracy; apparently the powder was not being properly consumed.

Just another case of too coarse-grained a powder being used in a small case. Even the 20% or so of nitroglycerin in HiVel No. 2, was not sufficient to cause complete combustion under existing circumstances. If it does well in any of the .22 varmint cartridges, it is most likely to be in the .228 Ackley large size Magnum, the .22/348, the .22 Varminter Senior, the P.M.V.F. type and others of considerable size and powder capacity. It is not a good choice for the R-2 and similar size cases—too much like trying to burn sections of log in a small size cook stove with very limited fuel capacity. You might get a long, slow heat and plenty of smoke, but be unable to cook a meal for the old man when he arrives home half starved and roaring for dinner.

Hercules No. 300: You may recall, at the time of World War I, duPont No. 16 was the most popular canister powder for military rifles. It was and is today, when available, a very good powder for 150 to 170-grain bullets in the .30-1906. The first time the Democrats had to be saved, Russia was dragged in with her suspenders down and her socks full of holes. Russia needed rifles and ammunition. It was a ground war, in those days. Wholesale bombing of war prisoners, forced labor in war plants, women and kids and old people, had not as yet become an heroic proceeding. Some do not like it now!

As duPont was making most of the smokeless small arms powder for the United States troops, Hercules took over the job of making cordite for the British forces and H.P.P. 10, for the Russians for the 7.62mm Russian military cartridge with 150-grain bullet.

They needed just a little more bulk than was possessed by 16, so H.P.P. 10 came out a bulkier single base or nitrocellulose powder. It took more of it—1.0 to 3.0 grains more—to produce the same velocity, or if you looked at it another way, one found the powder filling the case clear to the base of the bullet, or maybe compressed a bit, when loading, as compared with a charge of No. 16 which was enough, only being sufficiently bulky to fill a .30-1906 case, for instance, up to about the end of the shoulder, or a bit higher; that left some air space.

Suddenly the Russians were badly mauled in the Masurian Lakes area and folded up, and the world found itself with H.P.P 10 scattered all over way stations from Mt. Arlington, New Jersey to Siberia and Moscow, and then Hercules 300 was born, shortly after the boys got home, as there was a lot of powder making equipment lying around ready to make it.

In our cartridges the story was a bit different. Being rather bulky, it filled up the case nicely in cartridges like the .33 W.C.F. and the .35 Winchester Model 95, and these two really went to town with 300.

But in the .22 Varmint cartridges, if you have any 300 on hand, it will probably be found uniform in accuracy only in the large case jobs and the bottlenecks like the .228 Ackley Magnums; not in either medium size or small .22 center fire cartridges. I would not be surprised if it did fairly well in the .220 Swift and in the .220 Wilson Arrow—a lengthened Swift. However, it arrived at a time when non-mercuric, non-corrosive primers had not as yet been conceived, and it is not always too safe to place bets on what may occur in the matter of weather, if the weatherman happens to change his brand before he looks over the day's highs and lows. He could be wrong, here and there!

Hercules Lightning No. 1: Back in 1899 Laflin & Rand brought out Lightning; it passed with that company to duPont, was inherited by Hercules via court proceedings in 1912, and for more than 30 years a great many more tons of it have been shot than the public imagines.

The black perforated discs of Lightning No. 1 are about 0.02″ by 0.08″ in size, and it is a powder which should do nicely in cartridges like the .22/250 and larger, in charges of 15.0 to 30.0 grains, possibly a bit less on the upper portion, for many which are not too large. This was with the older type smokeless primers and so with modern corrosive primers one would need to reduce the charge 2.0 to 5.0 grains—and keep it reduced.

If the nitroglycerin content of this powder were cut down to 10% or 12%, the size of grain changed to make it ignite and burn faster, and it was then put out under some such name as "Hercules 4000," it, with modern primers, would likely prove to be a very popular propellant for .22 varmint rifles. If made with wood pulp nitrocellulose base it could be advertised as super-improved and super-developed and the public, which has proved it will believe anything, particularly any idea which is set forth attractively, would probably go for it 100%. I am not sure wood pulp would be a help, but it sounds more modern. Lightning is still a good powder but it has never been modernized, especially in name, and until it is, and the public knows it as something else, it will not generally be used by many varmint shooters who reload.

Sharpshooter No. 1: The public does not remember, and most shooters did not know that 5.5 to 5.8 grains of Sharpshooter would give 1,500 to 1,560 f.s. muzzle velocity in the .22 W.C.F. with cast bullet of 45-grains and a pressure of less than 11,000 pounds per square inch and in the .22-15/60 single shot Stevens, the same charge would drive a 60-grain bullet 1,410 f.s. with only a bit over 9,000 pounds per square inch pressure.

In the .22 Savage H.P. 19.0 to 19.6 grains, *with the old primers,* would drive a 70-grain M.C. bullet 2,813 f.s. and be within normal Krag pressures. A modernized Sharpshooter No. 1, with 15% to 18% of nitroglycerin and correspondingly increased percentage of other ingredients, and named "Hercules 3900" or something as modern, if properly cut as to grain size and shape for burning in 28° to 35° neck slopes, would likely be found a most satisfactory powder for cartridges like the .22/250, .22 Varminter, .22 Super-Chucker, .219 Donaldson-Wasp and a host of others. It has too much N.G. for the very sharp shoulder .22 wildcats and, also, it has been too long on the market and has been damned by too many men, to ever be of top notch popularity for varmint rifles under its boyhood christening and with so many people knowing what it would do in the .32-20 and the like, with old time primers, in corrosion and erosion—rusting and wearing—to those who do not understand the larger words.

Sharpshooter No. 1, has given excellent accuracy with very low pressures in long straight cartridges like the .45-70, .45-60, .45-90 et cetera; that is, the straight and comparatively straight ones, and it ought to do well in varmints like the Gebby .22 Varminter Junior, which is the .32-40 necked down, and is a long case in proportion to its velocity.

When a powder manufactured by Laflin & Rand from 1897 to 1902, by duPont from 1902 to 1913, and by Hercules from 1913 to 1946—a tenure of 49 years during which we have deteriorated from Burnsides to radio ballyhoo, and from Free Silver to almost no silver and definitely no gold—a powder that has weathered all that deserves a face-lifting job and a chance to square itself with the Supreme Court, which is the American people. The public is not always so dumb. Frequently it just acts dumb because it does not know any better!

Sharpshooter could, maybe with a little ingenuity, be developed into a real fair or even a very good powder for the gentle neck slope .22 varmints that did not produce more constriction than about 5° in the small sizes and 12° to 15° in the large cases, because with less N.G. it would not burn so fast and would not run up in pressure so fast, upon meeting the normal resistance of a gentle sloping neck.

Hercules Unique: This powder is a very old one, having been on the market for the last 46 years. It is the rifle adaptation of a dense shotgun powder with discs of a thickness of 0.005″ and 0.06″ in diameter, and black in color. It is a high percentage, nitroglycerin powder, and quite fast burning and powerful, even in very small charges.

This is the Hercules rifle powder to use for short range gopher and squirrel loads in .22 caliber varmint rifles. Be sure that you do not use too much Unique and obtain much higher velocity and very much higher pressure than appears likely.

From 3.0 to 3.5 or 4.0 grains, is quite ample for use with cast bullets or gas-check bullets, and 3.5 to 5.5 grains is plenty for metal-cased bullets. Such charges will develop ample velocity and good killing power and might even be on the high side for squirrels.

Some time back a prominent custom gunsmith stated that he was *through* trying to develop reduced loads with sufficiently low velocity for squirrel shooting in the .22/3000 Lovell rifle, because even the lightest ones tore up the squirrel. He was using 50% too much powder with his lightest loads and if he had used 40% as much of the reduced load powder he was experimenting with, he would still have had a snappy charge.

Nearly everyone makes the same mistake with very dense powders like Unique or Bullseye—the latter a pistol and revolver powder— and they also at times overload unthinkingly with Sharpshooter a high percentage nitroglycerin powder, being very quickly ignited and a fast burner and one which has very low pressures with straight-sided cases but very quickly develops quite high pressures with very sharply bottlenecked cartridges. No powder is adapted to all shapes, sizes and tapers of small caliber rifle cartridges.

Readers should very sharply differentiate between the characteristics of double base powders which, when ignited, are a quick hot fire, with plenty of kindling; and coated single base powders which require a bit more coaxing along. No one who has ever seen a bad nitrocellulose fire in a building, will agree that there is much that is slow about it. I once stood within 200 yards of a bad one, of an evening, and watched it throw pieces of wood, the size of a half shingle, for 2½ miles and a half mile or more high, and it set fire to a telegraph pole which was fairly wet, about a third of a mile away, just from the heat of combustion of the cellulose in the building. But a nitroglycerin fire is a race horse in comparison. If exploded, it may travel some 22,000 to 26,000 feet per second up the column, especially when started by a booster charge, and it will likely detonate if not handled carefully and may do so anyhow. Therefore, when switching from powder to powder, you may find more physical and chemical differences than when changing from almost any other product to a somewhat similar product of the same general appearance.

And in conclusion, just one more thought: Do not be so foolish as to try to make your own smokeless rifle powder, just to save about $3.00 on a year's expenses in rifle shooting. Do not pay too much attention to these theories that a tyro can make better powder than he can buy, and that the cellar workshop is a suitable place to mix such things as cotton linters, nitric acid, and with the product of that, treated with ether and other chemicals you put in a seventh to more than a third of nitroglycerin. Maybe you can pick up a quart of liquid nitroglycerin and walk across the cellar and not slip on anything and pour it in a mixing bowl and go to work on it, while you hum to yourself, "Gathering in the Sheaves," and "Silver Threads Among the Gold." You will do fine, until something goes wrong, and then there may be the same sort of bang, but on a reduced scale, that there is in a mixing house or a block press in a regular powder plant, and with the same result.

Some very smart chemical engineers and others just as quick thinking have gone to heaven suddenly, when making powder, and when protected with all of the safety devices that are common in the industry. The fatality rate is not very high in most plants, but the chap who experiments with explosives must understand that he is experimenting with *explosives* and before that with *inflammables,* and it is always safer and usually much cheaper in the long run, to let others more experienced, do it for you. Your fire insurance company, for instance, might not like it!

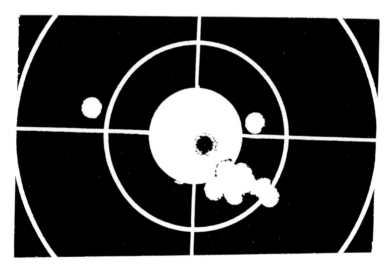

A 200-yard group shot by Gebby, during the summer of 1945. Shot in a quarry in a head wind and with two interruptions by trucks pulling into quarry and stopping. Nine of the shots in 0.77″ x 0.75″ center to center. .22 Varminter.

CHAPTER 22

PREPARATION OF WILDCAT CARTRIDGE CASES

THIS chapter has been prepared and written jointly by Leslie M. Lindahl, of Central City, Nebraska, and the author. Mr. Lindahl has designed and loaded some of the best .22 wildcat ammunition the author has seen. His workmanship is superb; his methods are practical. As no rifle is better than its ammunition, it was felt that this book would be incomplete without a chapter detailing the various steps and processes in the putting together of the very finest .22 wildcat ammunition it is possible to manufacture in quantity. Mr. Lindahl has a similar opinion of the importance of this subject. His data follows:

"In designing my .22 Chucker cartridges I did everything possible to secure and to insure accuracy. The only manner in which uniform neck wall thickness can be obtained is to line-ream the necks of the cartridge cases. This must be done by the use of precision-made dies and reamers, if the case necks are to be uniform. Doing this on a production basis, so that the cases can be sold at the same price as is charged for factory ammunition, is not possible.

"In making cases for the regular 'Chucker' cartridge, the .219 Zipper case is first necked down to a diameter of 0.275″ for the largest portion of the neck. In the second operation the cases are cut off to an overall length of 1.605″. In this operation the case necks are reduced to a diameter of 0.2515″ to 0.252″, and are also sized to the correct cone-to-head length. The third operation on the rimmed version of the Chucker cartridge is to line ream the necks and that is where precision workmanship counts.

"The line reaming die must be accurately made, so that the pilot hole for the reamer body fits to the closest tolerance that is possible when doing the work with a machine. Also the case necks are left such size from the third operation that they are of correct size for the seating of 0.224″ bullets without any further sizing being required. The fourth operation consists of chamfering the inside and outside of the mouth of each case."

448

Different Cartridges May Be Used for Sizing Down

Most of the readers know that it is possible, fortunately, to use several different calibers of cartridge cases for the .22 Chucker cartridges. In the rimmed version, the .22 Savage Hi-Power, the .25-35 W.C.F., the .30-30, the .32 Winchester Special and the .32-40, can each be used. However, both the rim thickness and the head thickness vary somewhat and for that reason the .219 Zipper cases are generally found to be most satisfactory. There are various reasons why it is the best selection. The Zipper is a well-made, strong case. The larger caliber cases require more work to neck them down properly and they do not always make up into neat, uniform cases as is true with the Zipper case.

The Zipper cartridge case requires only a minimum amount of swaging down of the brass for .22 Chucker caliber.

Size of Zipper Cartridge Case

The regular Zipper case runs about 0.370″ diameter at 1.1875″ forward of the head. The sizing die for the first operation is therefore chambered to such size that it fits the original body taper of the Zipper case and the neck part of the die reduces the largest part of the neck to a diameter of 0.275″. This leaves the neck of the case of proper size for seating a 0.224″ bullet, resulting in an outside case neck diameter of 0.248″ with the bullet seated. The Lindahl Chucker chambers are cut to a diameter of 0.2495″ in the neck, thus leaving a neck tolerance of 0.0015″ which is ample clearance.

With precision line-reamed cartridge cases it is possible to use the small neck tolerances. With a precision-made case that is uniform in its neck wall thickness, you should secure a definite improvement in accuracy.

What Could Be Done with the .22 Varminter

Take the .22 Varminter—or the .22-250, which is so popular. It is an extremely accurate cartridge, but could still be materially improved by the use of precision-made neck-reamed cases. Some makes of .250/3000 cases when necked down would not permit much if any removal of brass from the neck, because they are already very thin in the neck wall thickness. The use of cases made from the .257 Roberts and the .30-1906 cases necked down permits the necks to be accurately line-reamed and this operation also leaves sufficient wall thickness in the necks to secure and to provide maximum case life. With a very thin case neck you do not have this assurance.

Advantages of Chamfering Cartridge Case Mouths

The fourth operation on the rimmed Chucker case is chamfering the mouth of each case, both inside and outside. The bullets thus seat more readily and also seat easier. It is especially important that the case mouths be properly chamfered in using bullets that have sharp, square bases. Lindahl uses a specially-made cutter which cuts both the inside and outside chamfer at the same operation—much like the cutter used on the Smiley Super-case trimmer.

Preparing the Rimless Chucker Cases

The foregoing applies altogether to the rimmed version of the .22 Lindahl Chucker caliber of cartridge. The same methods are used by Mr. Lindahl in the making of the rimless Chucker cases. The best case for the rimless version is the .25 Remington autoloading cartridge. This cartridge of itself is an extremely accurate commercial cartridge and it is odd that it has never become more popular with the public. It is used in the making of numerous rimless .22 wildcat cartridges, almost all of them quite accurate.

The .25 Remington rimless case has less body taper and a longer neck than the .219 Zipper cartridge. For that reason, the rimless case requires three necking-down operations prior to the cutting-off operation or trimming the case to length. It requires that number of operations if you wish to obtain good, uniform brass and not lose any cases in the reforming process (a well known Ohio shooter uses as many as six necking down operations in reforming and necking down .32 Remington rimless cartridge cases to make a .22 varmint case very similar to the .22 Rimless Chucker but which is different mainly by being only slightly longer—Author).

Case Life

It has been found that cartridge case life is very good without having to resort to heat-annealing of the case necks in reforming them. Mr. Lindahl is still using some rimless Chucker cases made more than five years before this chapter was written. These cartridge cases were originally made up for the case that used 0.040" taper for its body length. They were all fired several times each in the original design. The improved version as now made has a body taper of 0.015" for its length. These cases were then used in a rifle with the improved design of chamber and are still good cases. For the three necking-down operations on the rimless Chucker case Lindahl uses a special press of very heavy construction. The cases are pressed into the die with a flat plunger. They are removed by a plunger that goes inside the case and presses it out. The rims on the .25 Remington rimless cases are none too heavy, being only 0.046" in thickness. With the conventional type of cartridge case holder, like on a Pacific tool, it tends to bend and mar the rims and bases on the cases in putting them through three necking down operations. More will have a still greater tendency to do this.

Due to such result, it is difficult to maintain uniformity in the succeeding reforming operations. For the cutting-off and neck-reaming operations, Lindahl made up a special cartridge case holder, or shell holder, to the closest possible tolerances. It is perfectly flat on the face portion that presses against the head of the case. The regular Pacific shell holder having the primer arm slot milled into it, as above-explained, will deform the rim of the case when used on several operations on the .25 Remington rimless cartridge case.

How the Cases Are Cut Off

The cutting-off operation, or the shortening of the cases to proper length, is a machine operation. Lindahl uses a specially built frame that mounts into the vise on the milling attachment of a lathe. This frame makes use of the regular Pacific Loading tool, shell holder and toggle assembly. The frame is threaded to receive the 0.875" by 14 thread dies. Various methods of cutting off the necks in the shortening of the cartridge cases, have been tried. The best method, according to Mr. Lindahl's experience, is by the use of a two-lipped end mill ground for cutting brass. A regular Pacific type shell holder is used to push the cases up into the die.

The carriage of the lathe is then advanced forward, which brings the case-neck in contact with the rotating end mill and does a beautiful job of cutting the neck to proper length. A micrometer carriage stop is used on the lathe bed to act as a stop and to control the length to which the necks are cut. It has been found, in this operation, that it is possible to maintain a uniformity of about 0.003" in overall length in running hundreds of cases during a day's work. For the finest finish and the smoothest cutting, the end mill should be driven at a fairly fast speed.

On Lindahl's South Bend 1" collet lathe, the best speed is 700 RPM which is the lathe's top speed with regular gearing. The second operation cuts the cartridge cases to length and reduces the neck diameter to 0.2515"-0.252". The die is of such length that the cases only protrude from the face of the die about 0.010" after being cut to length. It is possible to trim from 300 to 500 cases per hour, using the above method. The frame holding the shell holder and die must be securely held in the milling attachment. In turn, the milling attachment must also be fastened solidly. Otherwise one cannot secure uniform results in production runs of trimming rifle cartridge cases to a given length. The reason for holding the frame in the milling attachment, is because it is then an easy matter to align the neck of the case with the cutter. The milling attachment has micrometer control for the elevation and the cross slide of the lathe for horizontal correction.

The Third Operation on the Cases

The third operation on the *rimmed* version of the Chucker cases is also done on the lathe, using the same frame as in the second operation, to hold the line-reaming die. The pilot hole of the die is the same size from the shoulder to the end, the body of the reamer fitting the pilot hole in the die with a tolerance of 0.0002″. Lindahl has tried many kinds of reamers and also broaches for removing the excess brass from the case neck in the line-reaming operation. The reamer must have all the room possible in the flutes. Therefore, the flutes in the reamer must be as wide and as deep as can be used and still retain sufficient strength for the job it must do. Reamers of two, three and four flutes will all work nicely. Flutes can be from .04375″ to 0.50″ in length. In the case of a four-fluted reamer the flutes can be cut with a 70° or 80° cutter. The reamer should be sharpened like an end mill, square or 90° on the face. The blades of the reamer must be ground for clearance and to correct size. Using a line-reaming die with pilot hole of 0.246″, cases with a neck diameter of 0.252″ prior to reaming and a reamer with cutter ground to a diameter of 0.222″, the cases will come out with an outside neck diameter of 0.247″-0.2475″. Inside neck diameter will run 0.223″-0.2235″.

Fire Forming of Cases

Many riflemen using the .22 wildcat calibers prefer a reduced or medium charge load for the initial firing of the cases, or what shooters call "fire forming." In the instance of the .22 Chucker caliber in the rimmed version and using the reformed .219 Zipper cases, the cartridge has a body diameter of about 0.370″ at the shoulder and 0.413″-0.415″ at the base. A fully formed fired case thus expands in the initial "fire forming" from a diameter of 0.370″ to 0.401″-0.402″ at the shoulder. Lindahl always uses a case full of powder (—full, that is, to the base of the bullet), in the initial or fire forming of the cases.

A new unfired cartridge will hold 23.0 to 23.5 grains of No. 3031 powder. After firing, the same case will hold 25.0 grains of 3031. Lindahl and others have shot some very excellent targets with the initial firing of the cases. The fire forming operation, that is, the expanding of the cases, does not appear to hurt the accuracy very much, if appreciably any, and of course after fire forming the cases fit the chamber.

Lindahl says that he has used the .22/3000 Lovell caliber considerably, he makes up or in the past has made up rifles for a cartridge of this general type, and his pet load for the initial firing as well as for subsequent firings was 15.0 grains of No. 4227 and the W-M 8S 45-grain bullet.

Lubrication of Cases

Lubrication of the cases in the reforming operations is a very important feature—more than many imagine. Lindahl has tried different oils, graphite, soaps and plain lard—just ordinary white lard. The lard has proved to be the most successful of all the lubricants for use in reforming Chucker cases. Also, in full length body sizing of other calibers from the Hornet up to the .30-1906.

Lard, so used, is not as messy as many will assume it to be, provided it is properly applied. Putting it on the cases in the right amount is the secret. Here is a description of the better method. Take a piece of good quality felt of 0.25″ to 0.50″ thickness, and tack it on a board. Punch or cut a hole through the felt (with a hole in the board back of it large enough for the case) and with the hole in the *felt* cut small enough so that the edges of the felt around this hole will rub on the neck of the case. Apply the lard to the felt pad by melting a very small amount in a spoon and pour it around the edges of the hole in the pad. Only a small amount is required.

One application of lard on the pad will serve for 100 cartridge cases or more. Run your case through this hole in the felt, up to the base, holding on to the base with your fingers. This method puts just the right amount of lubricant on the cartridge and does the sweetest job of providing the proper lubricant that Lindahl so far has tried.

Cases go in and out of the dies much easier than with the use of powdered graphite as a lubricant. When graphite is used, it is rubbed on the cases. Graphite is slow to apply and hard to remove. Under pressure it also builds up in the dies.

The lard method of lubrication has been found very effective for full length *sizing* of the .220 Swift, .257 Roberts, .270 W.C.F. and similar larger cartridge cases. Many riflemen will be pleasantly surprised how very easy it is to size these heavier cases when lard and a tool such as the regular Pacific tool are used.

In the necking-down operations required in case forming, the use of too much oil or lard will cause lubricant pockets on the shoulder of the case. To prevent this and to avoid getting too much lubricant on the cases, is the reason for the use of the felt pad. It is a simple and inexpensive gadget, yet it applies just the right amount of grease in a most convenient manner.

A Selection of Bullets

Lindahl reports that he has tested just about all of the different makes and styles of bullets the ammunition companies and the custom makers produce. For the type varmint shooting he does in Nebraska, he prefers bullets of 45 to 50 grains weight in the Lovell and the Lindahl Chuckers. Flat trajectory is one of the essential requirements if you are going to be faced with the problem of making consistent hits at the ranges at which crows, prairie dogs and jack rabbits are shot in Nebraska, which is essentially a comparatively flat or gently rolling area with plenty of space in the distance. It is mostly prairie country.

Accuracy is the first requirement; second, comes trajectory; and third, is windbucking. The best accuracy has been secured by Lindahl with Wotkyns-Morse 8S bullets in 45, 47, and 50 grains weight. This type of bullet—one having a very long, sharp, needle point practically, has in his opinion, given quite a little more remaining velocity at 200 yards as compared with the conventional shaped bullets. The 8S shape of point in 50-grains weight has proven to have higher sustained velocities at the longer ranges as compared with the more conventional shaped bullets.

The 50-grain 8S bullet Lindahl has found superior in windbucking to the 50-grain bullet with six caliber radius nose. Most excellent accuracy has been obtained by Lindahl and his customers with .22 Hornet caliber 45 and 46-grain factory bullets, which have a point radius of three to four calibers. They give accuracy practically as good as any he has tested, but are not equal to the 8S type of bullet in flatness of trajectory and windbucking qualities. Other things being *equal* they should, however, prove to be better *killers.*

The Sisk 41-grain Super-Lovell Bullet

The Sisk 41-grain Super-Lovell bullet has given most excellent performance in some of the .22/3000 Lovell and Chucker rifles.

The 50-grain Sisk-Lovell is another bullet that is preferred by many shooters and has proven to be extremely accurate in most of the rifles that Mr. Lindahl has tested. He says he expects a wide and varied assortment of .22 jacketed bullets to be available as a basis of selection from 1946 on.

The Vernon Speer Bullets

Vernon Speer, of Lewiston, Idaho, is one of the newer custom bulletmakers. Lindahl reports that he had not tested any of the postwar Speer bullets, as not many of them had been made by the time Lindahl's report was received. Mr. Speer, so Lindahl mentions, has had many years of experience in the design and building of precision tools. The Speer postwar bullets that Lindahl has seen are very fine in appearance and quality.

Lindahl feels that Morse, Sisk, Speer and others have made a really worthwhile contribution to the .22 varmint rifle, in their lines of metal-jacketed bullets and should receive the plaudits of the riflemen of America for their products.

The Better Bullet Diameters

Recommended practice calls for a bullet diameter within 0.001" of the groove diameter of the barrel. With bullets made for Hornet velocities, like the regular factory 45-grain Hornet bullet the groove dimensions can be made as small as 0.002" less than bullet diameter, in the opinion of Mr. Lindahl, and still secure excellent accuracy. The Model 54 and Model 70 Winchester .22 Hornet barrels will run very close to 0.222" in groove diameter and 0.217" in bore diameter. The factory Hornet bullets are 0.224" diameter, but in spite of their being 0.002" oversize, they do give most excellent accuracy. Some of the finest groups Lindahl has secured with his .22 Chucker rifles have been made with a Model 70 Winchester Target weight Hornet barrel and bullets of 0.224" in diameter. The bullets were made and designed for the .22 Hornet, Lovell and similar velocities.

Lindahl feels that for the very finest accuracy, the bullets should be no larger than the groove diameter of the barrel. In the case of a barrel having a groove diameter of 0.224", the bullets should be from 0.223" to 0.224". His own preference for his personal shooting and barrel is to have bullets that would be no larger than 0.2235". Tests have shown that bullets of as much as 0.002" to 0.003" undersize, swage up so as to nicely fill the bore, without deforming, while a slightly oversize bullet does deform somewhat and boosts pressures (it is the author's recollection that the best shooting lots of .30-1906 International Match ammunition, especially the 2,250 f.s. stuff, were loaded with bullets measuring 0.3085″ to be used in barrels of a 0.300″ bore and 0.3080″ to 0.3081″ groove diameter and that this was also true of International and National Match ammunition giving around 2,600 f.s. with 172 or 180-grain bullets and 2,730 f.s. with 150-grain bullets.)

Tension of Bullet in Case Neck

Tension of the bullet in the case neck, or what is known as "bullet pull" is an important step in the precision loading of the .22 wildcat and standard calibers. The size of the expanding plug depends upon how much the sizing die necks down the neck of the case. As a general rule, the neck of the case need not be necked down more than 0.002″ to 0.003″ smaller than bullet diameter (this refers to the inside of the neck). The expanding plug will open the neck up to correct size. Cartridge cases of the Lovell and Chucker calibers should have an inside neck size, after resizing and expanding the necks of 0.223″ to 0.2232″ for use with 0.224″ bullets. Thus the required expansion of the case neck for proper bullet tension runs from 0.0008″ to 0.001″. In the seating of a bullet in the cartridge case, Lindahl prefers a seating depth within 0.015625″ of touching the rifling. Lovell also has warned of immediately excessive pressures caused by seating a .22/3000 Lovell bullet up against the lands, or of forcing it slightly into the lands, when closing the breech block— the result is excessive pressure.

Proper Firing Pin Protrusion

A firing pin protrusion of 0.050″ to 0.055″ is about right, though on certain types of actions and primers the protrusion must be cut back to as little as 0.035″. Both the Ideal and the Belding & Mull Handbooks contain reliable information on how to reload safe and satisfactory .22 wildcat ammunition.

Making Accuracy Determinations

Lindahl reports that he makes the initial load and accuracy tests with 5-shot groups fired at 100 yards. Loads that show most promise are then tested in 10-shot groups. The usual indications of maximum pressures in the *smaller* .22 wildcats are primer flatness, extraction difficulties and trouble to start the case from the chamber, expansion of the body of the case just forward of the base, and roughness around the firing pin indentation on the primer.

Excessively flattened primers, pierced primers, excessively expanded cases, reamer marks on the case or blown-out primers should be immediately heeded as being unmistakable signs of excessive pressure. When such occur, further shooting with that load should stop until the trouble is located and *corrected*. Pierced primers are sometimes the result of too much firing pin protrusion or the point of the firing pin has become rough and pitted or is too sharp.

Neck Tolerances

Mr. Lindahl regards a neck tolerance of *0.0015"-0.002"* as giving the best results with .22/3000 or .22 Lindahl Chucker calibers of .22 varmint rifles. Less than this may result in excessive pressures with tight bullets and more than that will give a lower degree of accuracy. Finally, accuracy and tight groups are largely a result of *uniformity* of ammunition and of uniformity of shooting that ammunition. To this end, the .22 wildcat rifle and its precision ammunition has been designed.

The Making of Precision .22 Ammunition

The making of precision cartridge cases for the .22 wildcats is not too difficult once you have the necessary tools required for such work. Building of the line-reaming dies and reamers is the most important part and must be very carefully and to exact tolerances. At the time this was prepared Lindahl was making up special reamers, tools and dies for the .22 Super-Chucker cartridges for the rifleman who wants velocities in the 3,900 f.s. bracket and with the use of the smallest practical amount of powder. Lindahl has secured the help of a real guncrank who is also a careful and precise workman in metal—the best, he says, that he had ever seen. Along with the sale of reloading supplies the Lindahl set-up will do precision barrel fitting, chambering and the furnishing of cartridge cases for the various .22 Lindahl Chucker and Super-Chucker calibers.

Seating Commercial Bullets in Un-reamed Cartridge Cases

Possibly it will be well to point out here something about the best methods of seating commercial or custom bullets in .22 varmint calibers of cartridges which have not been reamed at the neck and for which the rifleman does not intend to ream the necks, regardless of the amount of variation in neck-wall thickness. He will not have the equipment to do this and possibly will not want to bother.

In such instance, it is better to mike the case necks when possible and separate them into piles which are as nearly uniform as possible in neck diameter and in neck wall thickness. Cartridge cases varying by as much as 0.002″ in thickness had better either be discarded, especially if exceptionally tight when loaded and chambered, or, those of within closely the same thickness kept in the same lot of ammunition, those varying considerably higher or lower being placed in separate boxes, or piles. The advantage of reaming the necks is that then the bullet fits in a neck of approximately the same inside diameter—as each of the others in that lot. Remember, when measuring, that few cartridge cases are perfectly round and the heads especially are measurably oval.

Developing Loads for a .22 Wildcat

Lindahl's idea in determining the most suitable load for a .22 wildcat rifle is a matter of a series of tests for accuracy, carried out with all the attention to detail that this requires. In developing loads for an entirely new .22 wildcat, one should start with loads that are within what you think is an amply safe margin and then very slowly increase the load changing but *one* component at a time. Judgment of where to stop comes with experience, unless one has elaborate testing equipment. It should be remembered in this regard, that testing can at times be done through the powder companies.

Some years before World War II both E. I. duPont de Nemours & Co. and The Hercules Powder Company offered to conduct certain ballistic tests for velocity at $5.00 per test; the rifleman to supply the rifle and ammunition. This work had to be passed up during the war, but if it is resumed eventually, the cost is likely to be somewhat higher than $5.00 per test and the following situation should be clearly understood by the shooter.

Neither duPont nor Hercules possesses an elaborate collection of .22 *wildcat* caliber rifles. Their tests rifles are chambered for standard commercial calibers of cartridges. That means the shooter will have to supply the .22 wildcat rifle and its .22 wildcat ammunition, complete.

It is possible for either of these companies to test for velocity only, if they wish to do so, but to test for pressure it would first be necessary to drill the barrel of the rifle and fit it with a pressure gage and that drilling of a hole into the upper portion of the breech of the barrel, specifically into the front end of the chamber of the rifle, would completely ruin that rifle barrel for either hunting or target work. It would be necessary then to fit that rifle with a new barrel for anything else than pressure work determination.

As the private experimenter is handicapped most in developing new loads by not having a pressure barrel and as he, in most instances, is better equipped by both training and range facilities to test for accuracy outdoors than either of the powder companies or their laboratory personnel, unless he wishes to provide a spare barrel for pressure tests exclusively he would gain nothing except velocity data by having such tests made. Also, Ackley, Mannen, and others are equipped with chronograph to make velocity tests at less expense than the larger corporations.

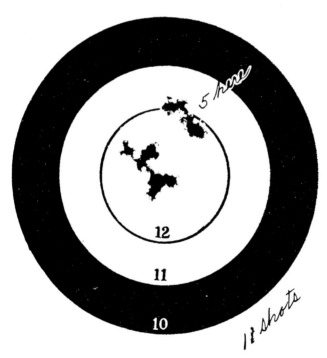

The .219 Donaldson-Wasp, at 100 yards. Eleven shots, fired from bench rest, by N. H. Roberts, on July 25, 1945. The 50-grain RCBS bullet was used with 19.0 grains of #4759. Bullets made with new copper jackets by Fred T. Huntington.

CHAPTER 23

THE EXPANSION OF CARTRIDGE CASES TO FIT WILDCAT CHAMBERS

Q UITE A number of .22 wildcat cartridge cases are formed by firing loaded commercial cartridges of standard calibers in the wildcat rifle chambers, during which firing the case expands to fit the full length and size of the new chamber. In a good many instances, cases are formed in this manner for many of the .22 "improved" wildcats, which means, in most cases, wildcat cartridges which are assumed and claimed to be improvements ballistically over the original cartridge, due to the new cartridge having both a longer case and a different shoulder. This, when first fired.

When a cartridge is fired in a chamber either longer or larger in forward diameter than the original type chamber, obviously the cartridge case is not and can not be supported by the chamber walls in the forward portion of the chamber which has been enlarged, due to having been bored out.

Anyone who has had, or who has seen others have, experience with .22 Long Rifle rim fire cases spit back to the rear, or with gas-escape incidents due to cartridges split along the neck, or split along the side of the cartridge case (the split extending longitudinally), or who has had a primer leak gas, or for any other reason has had a rifle spit out hot gas at high pressure and to the rear, cannot help but wonder whether this method of obtainment of cartridge cases by firing smaller or shorter commercial or wildcat cartridges in the new and enlarged chamber will cause similar bursts, and likely he often wonders whether such practice is advisable.

There is also the matter of wasted cartridge brass to consider, if many cases split and are rendered useless in such firing.

Fred Ness has commented quite a number of times in "The Dope Bag" on the matter of cartridge expansion by such means, and also on the wastage of brass, whether great or little, by such shooting. It seems to vary. Lovell, Kilbourn and others have been consulted on this matter and asked for a frank statement of their

460

experience in such situation. Among the cartridges which are normally made in such manner are the K-Hornet, the Maximum Lovell, the Improved Zippers and some of the Improved Swifts.

Lovell commented as follows: "I like to expand shoulders of cases with slowest burning powders such as Pyro D.G. (not particularly slow burning, but slower than some powders generally used in these cartridges—Author) in large, and No. 4198 in small cases. Yesterday, I fired 40 Zippers with 27.0 grains of No. 3031 and 50-grain bullets, without a crack. Part were Remington .25-35's necked to Zippers, and the Remingtons are the worst to split shoulders. I think they are often made of the extrusion alloys. Some probably were of the old mercury primed, or fired with factory loads containing the early Kleanbore mercury formula. Primers are a darned sight more of a problem than twist, the number of grooves, or the make of barrel.

"Yesterday, a Winchester light No. 64 barrel in a Hi-Side would string its shots up and down, for 2″ at 50 yards, with my favorite No. 115 primer. No. 8½ Western primers cured the trouble; made dime-sized groups using same loads. But this Western 8½ often does the same thing in other rifles when W.R.A. make won't shoot right. Don't ask me why; I have no idea. I am merely stating what happens!"

Lysle Kilbourn's Comments Upon Case Expansion

"In regard to the possibility of a blowback, flashback, or some sort of spitting, when firing commercial or shorter cartridges in special maximum or improved chambers: This I know to be without foundation of fact as to my own cartridge (the .22 K-Magnum Rimless). In shooting any standard factory shell in a K-chamber, you will, from time to time, have a case that is brittle (or one showing evidences of enduring fatigue of metal—Author) split in the side instead of expanding properly. This would surely cause a flashback if it was possible ("likely," would perchance, be a better word—Author), but I have never seen the case where I or anyone else was aware the case had split until the empty had been extracted.

"The process of expanding a .25, .30 or .32 Remington case that has been necked down to .22 caliber, to a K-shoulder, is the same as firing factory Hornet, Zipper, or .22 Hi-Powers in a K-chamber and the action is the same. I have never seen any evidence that it was unsafe." (Excerpts from letter to author, dated May 12, 1945.)

In further comments Kilbourn mentions that in the instance of the K-Hornet, that the shoulder of this little cartridge, formed by firing in the elongated Hornet chamber, "has never given out. The cases sometimes split lengthwise on forming if the brass is old or brittle and, also, heavy loads are less liable to split cases than light loads.

"Very light loads of 7.0 or 8.0 grains of powder, in old cases being formed, caused quite a few splits; but snappy loads rarely do!"

This seems to be rather opposed to the Lovell theory, but they were speaking principally of two different sizes of cases, the Kilbourn-Hornet being a small case, the Zipper a fairly good-sized one. The smaller case being made of thinner metal, and easier expanded, might have a tendency to cling to the walls of the chamber when expanded with a good stiff load, and to spread out and crack and then spring back, when expanded with only a moderate pressure. However, the author cannot do other than feel that there is some cause for caution, for concern, and for being very careful when firing cartridges for expansion, in any chamber which was cut large opposite the main or middle portion of the cartridge. Particularly, in instances of sloppy chambering, and in cases where cartridge brass is being used which was once fired with mercuric priming or in which there is obviously brittle brass, or very old brass weakened by being under tension in loaded ammunition. In such cases, certainly the rifleman who forms his cases by firing in a rifle, when the rifle is not up to his cheek, is following a safety first procedure which would seem sensible.

Merton Robinson Speaks on Such Matters

Merton Robinson is the dean of active, professional ballistic engineers in this country; not only is he experienced but he is frank and candid in his comments. Writing to the author upon whether it is safe to shoot from the shoulder cartridges for expansion to different shape in larger chambers, is included in the following, as of June 5, 1945: "Concerning the transforming of center fire cartridges by shooting in larger or longer chambers for the purpose of reforming for subsequent hand-loading:

"We have never had an accident from that cause. If the shells are properly annealed and if the cases are made of good metal, free from slag and impurities, there should be no difficulty. But you will note there are many 'ifs.'

"I would not wish to go on record as approving of this practice."

You will observe from this that over the years, "we"—meaning presumably himself and those in the Winchester Repeating Arms Company's ballistic laboratory—have not had an accident from this cause. On the other hand, he is unwilling to assume the risk of approving the practice—knowing there are risks, even though these risks may not be frequent nor excessive. Like every ballistic expert he knows that you only have to have one bad gas leak, to have trouble. Unfortunately, there is no way in which a shooter can tell in advance, or protect himself from a cartridge which does give a bad gas leak, if same be shot from the shoulder with the eye directly back of the firing pin.

Results of An Actual Burst

June 8, 1945, the author received an empty .219 caliber Zipper factory full charge Super-Speed case from Kilbourn which contained an oval-shaped orifice 0.20" long and 0.03" wide in the center. The case was gas blackened for about 0.30" to the rear of the puncture. The remainder of the case, farther to the rear, apparently was not gas marked. The cartridge appeared to have sealed the chamber from there backward. I am wondering what would have happened had the cartridge burst in a chamber cut with considerable more tolerance? This burst extended forward through most of the shoulder of the case and backward from the shoulder well into the main body of the case.

Quite obviously this rifle was closely and carefully chambered, but how about Zipper Improved, or similar size cartridges fired in other chambers *not* so closely fitted to the cartridge case? Would there not be more gas escape? Take a case fired in a chamber no better breeched than the average Krag chamber, for instance; what then?

The author is not trying to cast doubt upon this method of obtaining cartridge brass of the proper size. He is simply thinking of the two or three men he has seen hauled off to a hospital when a Springfield blew up in their face; and he is thinking of the time a Springfield fused a head, shed a primer, gave gas leakage down through the magazine and practically knocked *him* insensible, temporarily, as from a blow at the base of the skull, due to having had his head snapped back suddenly, and then of necessity having been helped to his feet by friends. It was *not* a pleasant experience.

A man can come through safely 1,000 times, yes, 10,000 times, but—the question a shooter should ask himself is: *"is it worthwhile taking the chance?;* would it be better to make the expanded cases firing from a mechanical rifle rest?" The reader will have to form his own conclusions and make his own decision. The publisher of this book is apparently of the same opinion on this subject as the author. The publisher's very considerable experience as a hunter and rifleman is not generally known; incidentally, he was for many years in charge of the old Rifle Smokeless Division of the duPont Company.

As commented upon briefly elsewhere, C. F. Hober, of Belmont, New York, reforms his cases for use in his K-Lovell by firing with a charge of 15.0 grains of I.M.R. No. 4227 and does it on his easier shots on woodchucks, at the closer ranges of 100 yards or less. Then he uses 17.0 grains of No. 4198, which is a coarser powder than No. 4227, which suggests he prefers to expand cases with a charge of fast powder which springs them out very rapidly to full chamber size. His rifle is a Winchester S.S. with the high, heavy frame. The bullet he prefers is a 45-grain Hornaday.

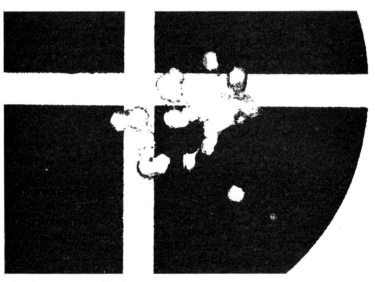

Marciante's Blue Streak at 100 yards. Group of 27 shots, fired on June 6, 1940 by Al. Marciante, the riflemaker. Fired from machine rest, using the 55-gr. Sisk-Niedner bullet, with 30.0 grs. #4064 and the Win. 115 primer. Witnessed by Ernest Baldwin.

CHAPTER 24

THE DEVELOPMENT OF SPECIAL LOADS FOR .22 CALIBER RIFLES

By Hervey Lovell

T HE development of special super-accurate and very high velocity loads for .22 caliber rifles is a most interesting pastime. Thousands find it intensely absorbing. However, it contains almost innumerable ballistic and physical problems which must be overcome, sometimes accidentally, before super-accuracy is obtained.

In recent years a good deal of trouble has developed in the obtainment of *accurate* .22 caliber metal-cased bullets. Some lots will shoot the center right out of the X-ring. Another lot from the same bulletmaker may not do a bit better than a 4.00″ average at 100 yards and some few lots will not even stay on the target paper. This when shot from a barrel and rifle which previously just ruined the X-ring and will again do so, once a perfect shooting combination is obtained. This always requires good bullets.

The comparative size of any defect in bullet-base (the .22 caliber being so small in diameter, and having such a small bullet-base area) ; the difficulty of obtaining a good grade copper for bullet jackets; good brass for cases; good lead and sufficient tin, and antimony for bullet cores; all combine to cause trouble, if any one of them is below normal in quality or texture—especially in the matter of proper jackets. Hervey Lovell thought that special comment should be made in this book in regard to cartridge loading as he was having to make up a great many special loading tools and dies to help out riflemen who each had a good shooting rifle but no means of making proper ammunition; not having in their possession, and not having been supplied with a proper bullet-seating tool, by whoever made up their custom rifle. Maybe the rifleman never ordered such, or would not take good advice and do so when he first bought his rifle.

Lovell comments include the following: "My method of working up a super-load when rifle ammunition components are so scarce, is

465

as follows: I take a bullet, primer, powder that has been known to work in similar calibers and styles of rifles and load just three cartridges, slightly under full charge; for such a case as the No. 7 Lovell Zipper Improved I would set the scale for 29.0 grains of 3031 duPont, and use 8½ Western primers, and 55-grain Sisk bullets. Set the bullet-seater so that the ogive *barely touched* the lands in the throat of bore when bullet was blacked with smoke of a match. With scope bore-sighted to start, I am ready to adjust sight and test the load with great saving of time, effort and components.

"A pad is placed under the forend so as to place the rifle at a comfortable height, so steady that the pulse does not move crosshairs on target. Shop target is 50 yards from rifle. I can easily hold three shots where 10 would include a couple of wild ones. These first three shots, usually off center, make one of two patterns. If underloaded by one grain of powder the three string up and down. Next three loads will be half-grain more and triangle pattern will result but will be as large as the X-ring of the target—an open center group. Next I load three with full 30.0 grains charge, adjust scope and should get three bullets cutting same hole or slightly larger.

"When I have time and want to shoot I will take three expanded cases each with Sisk 55-grain Niedner, 55-grain Express and 55-grain Morse bullets; and usually the 55-grain Sisk wins, although all these groups will be under a dime at 50 yards.

"Next I change just *one at a time* of the various components. Suppose this time we change the powder. I put 4064 duPont or 4320 duPont in powder measure. Without change of adjustment this will throw a couple of grains more weight than 3031, while 4064 requires that increase in weight, not bulk; 4320 takes still more weight.

"This may be the load I crave, but if not further test is made by changing to Winchester No. 115 primer, or softer primer suited to such powder charge. When I get a half a grain too much powder charge a high flyer will show up on the target. One type bullet ogive may cause the higher one. (The author adds here: A primer may not be seated to the bottom of the pocket and that will likely cause a low shot or dirt may be pinched between the primer pocket bottom and the primer and that may cause slow and poor ignition, also causing a low shot, or a wild shot, off in the direction of the rifling, probably).

"When fired cases start sticking in the chamber, cut the load half a grain of powder for a case of this size or back the bullet away from the lands, seat it deeper by 1/32". That is, deeper in the cartridge case, not deeper into the rifling.

"Uniform seating depth is most important part of the cartridge loading and in accuracy of shooting. It is more important than most other operations. The bullet seater is more important than the make of barrel; it costs as much to cut it as to chamber the barrel, and should be a real duplicate.

"It is important that shooters be able to load their ammunition with proper over-all length, and sufficiently tight—bullet held tight in case—case held properly in chamber, for modern primers.

"A large part of my work is making dies for other chap's rifles when said rifles were made up by someone who had nothing but a home-made chambering reamer and they could not duplicate that reamer to save their life. Any garage mechanic can dig a hole in a barrel breech that will permit a cartridge to enter. That is just as easy as digging a hole in the ground in which to bury a not-to-recently deceased cat but the dimensions of the two holes need not necessarily be designed with equal accuracy. Making a California man's chamber that will fit a Washington man's fired case is a horse of another color. One-tenth of the diameter of a human hair difference, may cause the fired case to stick in the California-chambered rifle.

"* * * If the shooter wishes to discover how many different variables in ammunition loading can interfere with the immediate obtainment of super-accuracy, let him cut enough paper and pencils, and carefully sharpen extra pencils so he will not be interrupted, and then have him multiply the five makes of cases by the three types of primers by each maker, then by five kinds of powder (which is 5x3x5 equals 75) and just now, by 50 makes of war-time bullets (that makes 75x50 equals 3,750). If the pencils are still usable, build up the total variables by the numbers of powder measures, scales, bullet seater variations, sizing dies, neck tension, head space, mainspring strength, shape of firing pin, ad finatum, ad finatum."

(The author adds here: Odd bullet sizes like scattered lots of .223", .2235", .224" et cetera bullets which come to hand or which the rifleman may have been carefully hoarding for a rainy day; we have now had about five years of rainy days in bullet obtainment and the end is not in sight. There are also bullets of different jacket thickness and jacket toughness, different weight of bullet, differing bullet-bearing distances, different cores—do not forget the Sisk cores with 7 per cent antimony, which are harder cores than ordinary bullet cores and all other variables).

Then, just to add their bit, there is the matter of primer pockets of different diameter, looseness and depth; cartridge case brass of varying toughness or brittleness, all of which contributes or takes away neck tension; powder which is practically non-hygroscopic and powders which absorb a small percentage of moisture more readily. A change of weather comes along, and your powder either absorbs a one per cent or two per cent or more increase of moisture or loses

Lovell's Precision Bullet Seater on left.
Sizing die to neck down case on right.

it, and its strength, and chamber pressures for identical loads, go down or go up. Your walnut rifle stock absorbs or loses moisture at the same time and to greater percentage than the powders, except possibly the old Schuetzen types, today practically unobtainable generally; also neither necessary or desirable for modern and comparatively short, sharply bottlenecked wildcats. As your rifle stock swells or contracts it definitely affects accuracy, and you may have a fine shooting load under development which is apparently off-color due to stock variations in fit with barrel and stock bands or barrel bands.

All these things enter into the matter of making a rifle shoot like a bumble bee rifle should shoot, and should *continue* to shoot. A table of loads is, therefore, and can be only a starting point, and usually a very reliable and helpful guide in making up ammunition. But as Lovell has pointed out here and above, start your load a grain or so *below* the full charges recommended and do not load up too many cartridges without testing a few of these already loaded. Take along to your range five different loads of three to five charges of each kind, as a preliminary test, rather than 15 to 25 cartridges made up with identical charges. Then load up more of that which appears to be about right in *pressure* and accuracy. Remember, you are working without a pressure gage to guide and help you, without a chronograph in most instances and to make a pressure gage out of your rifle would ruin it as a rifle, because you would have to drill the barrel just back of the shoulder of the cartridge.

It is also advisable, if possible, to shoot on days which are about or close to 70 degrees in temperature, dull, a bit cloudy, not windy and neither extreme in any other characteristics, such for instance, as barometer readings, and you should then be able to start off your ammunition loading with confidence. Also, with the minimum loss of ammunition, precious metal-cased bullets which really shoot, and with minimum expenditure of gasoline and wear on tires. Remember also, that a new rifle, a new barrel or a newly-chambered barrel may take a bit of breaking-in and settling into the stock, before giving maximum accuracy and greatest uniformity of grouping one group after another.

Be *certain* to check your rifle for the following before trying to test ammunition: That the tang screw, or screws, are tight. That the screws in the scope sight *blocks* are tight and the blocks are quite rigid. If even one screw has loosened or will not go to the bottom so that screw head bears properly and the threads grip, your rifle can not be made to shoot accurately. Then see that the scope mounts are rigidly attached to the bases or blocks. Remember, the blocks can loosen on the barrel, the mounts on the blocks. Next, see that the scope lenses are clean, free of gun oil or dust; that none of the lenses are loose so they can revolve in the scope tube. See that the scope barrel is pulled back and upward against the mount bearings before firing of *each* shot. If the stock is one-half inch or even a quarter-inch too long for you, cut if off or have it cut off and the buttplate reset before wasting good ammunition.

After all this is done, and your own digestive tract is freed of too much toxic material, your eyes and nerves have rested and you have had at least one good night's sleep, you are ready to begin firing. Not before; not with 96 per cent of these things attended to, and the other four per cent driven out to the range all ready to enlarge the groups. The worst little "nigger in the woodpile" is loose scope sight mount bases, or loose iron sights. Often you will not observe that condition exists until after the most careful check-up. Merely a change in weather conditions, or a prolonged wet or prolonged dry spell, may have caused sufficient expansion or of contraction in both wood and metal to give trouble.

Above all else, do not mix different lots of powder; do not mix different makes or lots of bullets and especially do not use bullets of two or three diameters; and do not load five cartridges with one primer and five cartridges with another primer, and expect to put all 10 shots under a postage stamp or a dime, at 100 or 200 yards. Good shooting depends in every instance upon uniformity of materials and operations and uniformity of aiming and firing, all the way through the test period.

If this book has impressed this upon you, in that respect, at least it has been a useful book. If you want to make 10-X possibles at any range, re-read this chapter and try to keep as much as possible of this information *under your hat.*

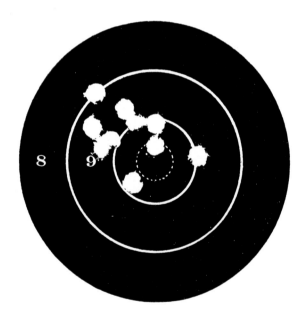

Here is one of Hervey Lovell's groups after the proper combination has been reached and properly put together. Ten shots at 100 yards, with 16.8 grs. of #4198 and the 50-gr. bullet in the "Big Lovell" case.

CHAPTER 25

TESTS AND OPINIONS

TESTING THE WASP AND DONALDSON'S EARLY
EXPERIMENTS WITH THE .22-250

By Samuel Clark, Jr.

IN THE REALM of shooting it has always been interesting to me to note how, when the thread of any particular bit of knowledge is followed backward through the maze of half-remembered events of the past, the trail will, more often than not, lead to some particular personage who has made the shooting game, either his life's work or his lifelong interest. Dr. F. W. Mann and H. M. Pope for instance, have in their day been connected with so much that is vital in the shooting game, that we often find in them the beginners of improvements for which younger men at times claim full credit.

The .220 Varminter is an excellent example, and its history goes way back to 1911 or 1912. At that time, Charles Newton, H. A. Donaldson, and others were using rifles chambered for the .30-40 Krag case, necked to .22 caliber. A picture of one of these rifles, as used by Donaldson, is shown on Page 24 in the March, 1936, *American Rifleman*. At this date, both men were deeply interested in the possibilities of the high speed .22 rifles for use in varmint hunting.

At about the same time, there were, in different sections of the country, several hunters and experimenters who became interested in the idea of the .30-1906 case, since it was not possible then to obtain the velocities desired from the .30-40 Krag case, necked to .25 caliber and using the 100-grain bullet. Experiments along these lines eventually resulted in the shortened .30-1906 case, necked to .25 caliber, using the 87-grain bullet which we now know as the .250/3000 Savage case and which with the lighter bullet gave the velocities desired.

471

Now, Donaldson had several of these .30-1906 cases which had been cut off and necked to .25 caliber about his shop, and one day he reduced the neck still farther to a .22 caliber to see how it would look. This case had the same angle at the shoulder as the .250/3000 Savage case which came out in the Spring of 1914, and in reducing the neck to .22 caliber, the same angle was retained and simply brought down to .22 caliber.

Donaldson was impressed with the lines of this case, and thereupon formed several more and sent one of them to Charles Newton. Newton was also impressed with the appearance of the case, so much so in fact, that he had the Savage Arms Company fit a heavy 26″ barrel of 0.226″ or 0.228″ diameter to one of their lever actions (this barrel had a twist of 1 turn in 12″). Chambering reamers were soon made up by a toolmaker and Newton then chambered the barrel for the new case.

The rifle was a success from the start and some time later Newton sent the rifle to Donaldson for testing. It was thoroughly tried out on the range during part of the season of 1915, and the results that Harvey obtained from it with the 70-grain Savage bullet and Pyro powder, convinced him that it was superior to the .22 Savage High Power case, which had previously been put on the market and which was in considerable favor at that time.

Later that same year, Newton asked for the return of this .22-250 rifle, and it was consequently shipped to him at Buffalo, New York, and thereafter Donaldson lost all track of it.

However, the good shooting qualities of this .22-250 case so impressed Donaldson that he later wrote to Newton asking for the chambering reamers that had been used in chambering the rifle, but at this time, Newton was busily engaged in producing his own line of rifles and he replied that the reamers were somewhere about, but could not be located.

Nevertheless, samples of the case were retained and it is interesting to note that the principal difference between this case and our present day Varminter lies in the fact that the early version sent to Newton had a body taper only slightly greater than the case which many shooters consider one of our most recently developed varmint cases.

Twenty years then elapsed, during which Donaldson was engaged with other rifle experiments, but he never forgot this fine case design and in 1934 he dug up some of the original cases, and being more interested than ever in varmint rifles, decided that his original case might be improved by a reduction of the body taper.

This was immediately done and samples of the case made up and marked with a steel die on the head, ".220 Don. 1934." If samples of these 1934 Donaldson cases are compared with the present Varminter case, it may be seen that they are alike.

In the Fall of 1934, still hoping to interest someone in producing rifles for his case, Donaldson made a trip to the Savage Arms Company, of Utica, New York, obtained an interview with W. D. Higgins of that concern. Mr. Higgins called in Mr. Pierce and Mr. Hickey, also of the Savage Arms Company and to those men, Donaldson exhibited samples of the .22-250 case, but was unsuccessful in persuading them to commerically produce rifles chambered for the new case. They stated that inasmuch as they had scrapped all their cartridge making machinery, it would not be practical for them to place on the market a rifle chambered for a case which was not being manufactured by any of the various arms companies.

So again, 20 years after Newton lost interest in the matter, his co-experimenter was still as far as ever from persuading anyone to produce rifles chambered for the .22-250 case.

However, despite the lukewarm reception his idea had so far received, it was still felt that this case had great possibilities and so on a visit to Vermont, he gave a sample of the case to J. B. Smith, of Smith's Custom Loads. Smith was impressed by its appearance and stated that he might go ahead and have a rifle made up to use it.

Later, in collaboration with J. E. Gebby, the rifles were produced, Gebby doing the chambering work and Smith the custom reloading.

This was announced in the May 1938 *Rifleman* and by the following month the case had been named the Varminter, and under this name was described on Page 47 of the June 1938 *Rifleman*. The name Varminter was copyrighted and it is now one of the most popular .22 high velocity cases.

This is one view of the history of the evolution of the .22-250 or .220 Varminter case design and its connection with H. A. Donaldson, now of Fultonville, New York.

It will never be known how many experimenters had the same idea of necking down the .250/3000 Savage case to .22 caliber, nor how far they carried it. As far back as 1935, it is recorded in the May issue of *The American Rifleman,* that Captain Wotkyns had experimented along these lines.

In this article it states that Captain Wotkyns' idea was to neck the .250/3000 Savage case to .22 caliber, but since Donaldson's original experiments were over 20 years before that time, and occurred even previous to the actual design of the .250/3000 case itself, it appears to him should go the credit for the original design of the case which we now know as the .22-250. (This is Mr. Clark's theory—Author)

To illustrate how far in the past may be rooted the beginnings of events generally considered quite modern, I cite the following: while investigating in order to obtain a copyright of the name .219 Donaldson-Wasp, Morgan & Cail, of New Haven, learned that the name "Wasp" had been copyrighted 34 years previously, in 1912, by a man living in Ireland and at that time he had also copyrighted the name .22 Hornet. (Odd, because the old Ideal Handbook No. 6 also lists a .22 "Hornet" and this book came out about 1894—Author.)

Having described events leading up to the final development of the case known as the .22-250 or .220 Varminter, I would like to relate some later experiences with the .219 Donaldson-Wasp, especially how my friend Diplock lost his money and saw the light, and how the Wasp performed at 200 yards with the aid of a lantern.

In describing the results that we have obtained with these fine shooting Wasp rifles, it should again be emphasized that the .219 Wasp case is definitely not an Improved Zipper case in any sense of the word. This case was developed from experiments with the .25 Remington rimless case, and all dimensions were worked out by Donaldson, through a trial and error method, with the sole object being to eventually arrive at a peak of efficiency where the smallest possible powder charge could be used to give velocities from 3,700 to 4,000 f.s. with 50 and 55-grain bullets.

The simple fact of altering a case by increasing its capacity to hold powder, without increasing the ability of that case to burn more powder, in no way constitutes an improvement. In the course of his experimenting, Donaldson made various changes in the .219 Winchester Zipper case, giving it a greater powder capacity without increasing the efficiency or the velocity obtained from the factory case.

The shooter who is interested in this matter should select some of the numerous versions of the Improved Zipper case and using identical powder charges and bullets, test the velocities against those from the .219 Donaldson-Wasp, either on a chronograph or on steel plates, and he will soon discover how high a degree of efficiency is packed into this little Wasp case.

During the latter part of 1945, Vaughn Cail and the writer were engaged in developing loads to be used in the .219 Wasp rifle at the target and on game, and obtaining the velocities of these loads as revealed on the chronograph.

The range where most of this testing was being done was a very good one, equipped with a fine shooting house containing well-made bench rests, and machine rest and heated by an oil stove so that shooting might be conducted in any weather. Due to these conveniences, it had been common during the course of the year for a number of well-known shooters and experimenters to pay the range a visit and possibly stay for several days or a week, during which interesting tests of accurate target and varmint rifles were conducted.

The writer had often remarked how frequently it is that we read of rifles capable of shooting into a "minute of angle" or how often we hear of ¾″ or even ½″ groups shot from rest or machine rest at 100 yards, or 2″ or less than 2″ groups shot at 200 yards. It has also been frequently noted that although shooting, as just described, causes no great stir among the shooting fraternity, nevertheless, such shooting even at the hands of well-known experimenters, equipped with the most accurate rifles obtainable, has not been the rule on the range described above—in fact far from it—actually, quite the contrary, and if all groups fired by each individual shooter were averaged, the result would indicate that progress along the lines of accuracy was a very dubious matter indeed.

Among visitors to the range who had not neglected to observe this point, was the writer's good friend and genial shooting companion, John Diplock. In fact, Diplock had so often been disappointed when rifles which were described as tack drivers failed to shoot in the vicinity of the tack, let alone shooting group after group measuring 1″ or under, that he had lost a great deal of faith in the expressed opinions of his fellow man.

Another illusion which Diplock had learned to discount about 99%, was that of the dependence that could be placed in the 5-shot groups as a test of accuracy. The whole matter had been discussed from all possible angles and the opinion was firmly held that a group of 10 shots fired from any rifle from bench or machine rest at 100 yards, which measured 1″ from center to center of bullet holes farthest apart, was still a mighty fine group and, despite claims to the contrary, that the rifle and rifleman, who could sit down and do such shooting when the chips were down, with spectators present, and continue to do it for 10-shot group after 10-shot group, just had not come along to date.

The writer had become more than usually enthusiastic about the accuracy possibilities in the .219 Donaldson-Wasp and had plainly stated to Diplock that this rifle would, day in and day out, shoot consistently smaller 10-shot groups than any rifle that had been tried out on his range.

So, on a certain Sunday in December 1945, when six or seven good varmint shooters were gathered at the range, the usual discussion came up and Diplock, sensing an opportunity to turn the weekend into a pay day, pounded his fist on the loading bench and stated that he had listened to all this 1″ talk he wanted to, and he had seen all the selected groups he wanted to see, but what he did want to see was a shooter who was man enough to demonstrate before witnesses and with money on the board, what he could do about this 1″ business. It should be done, he stated, with components loaded then and there, and not selected from something known to be "hot," and under weather conditions taken "as is" which should be reasonably good but not necessarily perfect.

Peeling a big bill off his roll, Diplock laid it on the loading bench and announced that he had had his say.

Now surprisingly enough, on this occasion, with the honor of the varmint rifle at stake, there was no hesitation and no hedging, and amid a loud chorus that here was a bet worth watching, Cail covered the bet for his Wasp and seated himself at the loading bench.

Having fired all of his own bullets, he borrowed twenty-three 50-grain Wotkyns-Morse cadmium-plated bullets from Dr. Paine and proceeded to fit these to loads consisting of 31.0 grains (weighed) of duPont No. 4320, ahead of the No. 120 Winchester primer. This loading was soon completed, despite a clamor of speculation as to the outcome. A last minute formulation of rules was briefly as follows: The shooting was to be done at 100-yards bench rest, scope sights, 10 shots to count for one group only, which must measure 1″ or less from center to center of shots farthest apart, no alibis of any sort once the shooting commenced.

The loading completed, all shooters repaired to the nearby range, where Cail selected an outdoor bench in order to take advantage of a 3 to 4 mile 6 o'clock wind which was blowing, so as to disperse the mirage that soon would rise off the barrel of the Wasp.

Cail selected a target with an aiming point consisting of a ½″ black square, and after firing the three foulers on another target, announced that he was ready to fire for record.

In addition to Cail and Diplock, the witnesses consisted of Dr. E. W. Paine, Peter Hill, Samuel Clark, Sr., Capt. Ed Morgan, and Samuel Clark, Jr., and it was generally conceded that Cail had rather stuck out his neck, to say the least. Scopes were trained on the target and the shooting commenced.

Cail set his sight for his group to form at point of aim, regardless of what might happen to his ½″ black aiming point. Shot No. 1 was

within the ½" square, not cutting the edge, Nos. 2 and 3 were in
the same hole, Nos. 4 and 5 were out but still did not cut to the edge
of the ½" black squeeze, Nos. 6 and 7 made the groups perfectly
round within the ½" center, and Nos. 8 and 9 were in the center of
this circle and did not cut paper. The nine shots were therefore, in
less than ⅜" center to center and not one of the nine cut outside the
0.50" square aiming point.

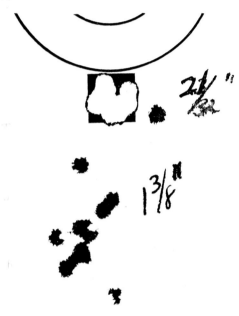

20 shots from Cail's WASP at 100 and 200 yds, fired to settle the
Cail-Diplock wager, as described.

Let the reader place himself in the shooter's position in order to
estimate the pressure under which he was performing. A substantial
sum of money was up, his reputation and the reputation of his Wasp
rifle had to be upheld, a group of skeptical witnesses milled about,
speculating on each shot, as well as the outcome, and at the target,
he had a group of nine shots in *less than 3/8"*. This is a situation in
which few of us will ever find ourselves.

However, Cail squeezed the required 3 pounds on the trigger and
shot No. 10 settled in the target, giving a group just 21/32" to be

exact. Everyone voted this the closest shooting they had ever seen when the chips were down and I imagine many who read this will agree.

Most shooters, after this exhibition, would have been content to take their money and the honor and let the matter stand, but Cail was not made up this way and stated that he still had 10 shots left and lest anyone should think that this might be a freak group, his money was on the table that he could, then and there, shoot 10 shots into less than 2″ at 200 yards.

On this occasion, however, everyone declined and as no bets were forthcoming, Cail stated that he would "show them" anyway, and setting a target with a 1″ black square aiming point at 200 yards, he fired his last 10 shots into a group measuring 1⅜″ center to center of bullet holes farthest apart and eight shots were within ¾″.

If the reader should attempt to duplicate these groups under identical conditions he will soon learn to appreciate the fact that this particular .219 Donaldson-Wasp rifle belonging to Vaughn Cail is a most unusually accurate one and a careful inspection of the cuts of the witnessed groups shown will, I feel, further serve to bear out this point. It should be noted that at the time these groups were shot, Cail's rifle had been fired something over 2,500 rounds, using for the most part, duPont No. 4320 powder and graphite wads, although no wads were used in the groups mentioned. Both Cail and the writer have been unable to attribute any improved accuracy to the use of these wads.

To some, should they inspect these groups and in addition, see the scores of other 10-shot groups fired from it at 100 yards rest, which measured less than 1″ in diameter, it would seem that this rifle must be a freak and could seldom be duplicated, and this is exactly the expressed opinion of a nationally known gun writer and authority on varmint rifles when he had inspected some of these groups.

About this time, Dick Morgan, of New Haven, entered into a partnership with Vaughn Cail with the object of a general gunsmithing business and in particular the chambering of rifles to order, for the .219 Donaldson-Wasp case, and this particular gun editor stated that after Morgan and Cail had chambered 20 Wasp rifles, he would be surprised indeed, if *one* of them produced any such superlative accuracy as this original Wasp chambered by Al Marciante, of Trenton, New Jersey, and throated later by Cail.

Nevertheless, the author was convinced that much of this fine accuracy was due to the superior efficiency of the design of the .219 Wasp and so he placed an order with Morgan and Cail to make up a duplicate of the Cail rifle. It was specified that a Model 70 action should be used, and to it should be fitted a heavy Swift blank and heavy Marksman stock and the barrel carefully chambered for the .219 Donaldson-Wasp case. Furthermore, its loading dies should be made for the Pacific tool.

An order was also placed for a similar rifle to be made up by the *new* firm for Dr. Paine, who, it will be recalled, was a witness to the Diplock-Cail wager, and we shall now see what took place when these rifles were received and tested.

Early in January of '46, the first of these .219 Donaldson-Wasp rifles was received and in fact it was brought to Maine by Cail himself who was at that time returning for a short visit. When friend Cail arrived, he found the range house empty but he determined to load up some cases and give the new rifle a try nevertheless. However, he was unable to locate either the Ideal powder measure generally in use, or a pair of powder scales, so, since no cases had been formed for the new rifle, he loaded up 23 cases, pouring the powder in by guess and using both the 45 and 55-grain Doering bullet. When the loading had been completed, he repaired to the range and despite the unformed cases, guessed powder charges, and an 8 to 10 mile 10 o'clock wind, which was blowing, he was able to shoot two groups measuring 1 3/16″ with the 45-grain bullet and 15/16″ with a 55-grain bullet.

When the writer returned to supper and saw the results of this preliminary shooting he was much pleased and no time was lost in reloading the fired cases and, after a hearty supper, the shooters lighted two gasoline lanterns which come in handy for such testing and prepared to give the new rifle a thorough try-out on the 100-yard range. Unfortunately, the wind had failed to go down by 9 P.M. but as it was not effective over the entire range, it was decided to continue shooting.

The next bullet to be tried was the Rardin 51-grain with 31.0 grains duPont No. 4320 and using the same type target consisting of a ½″ black square printed on a piece of tagboard and lighted at the 100-yard point by a single gasoline lantern. Shooting commenced from the outdoor bench rest. The first 10-shot group using the above bullet measured 15/16″, No. 2 group using the 45-grain Wotkyns-Morse, measured ⅞″, No. 3 with the 55-grain Doering, measured 1 7/16″, horizontally, but was plainly caused by the wind, as the vertical measurement was less than ½″ with an 8 to 10 mile 10 o'clock wind blowing, No. 4 group using the 55-grain Wotkyns-Morse measured ¾″.

The lantern was then shifted to 200 yards. We used a 1" black square for an aiming point. Group No. 5 at this range measured 1 31/32" with the same 55-grain Wotkyns-Morse bullets, and group No. 6 at 200 yards measured 1 17/32" with nine shots in ⅞".

It will be noted that the same powder load was used for all bullets shot, regardless of weight and both riflemen participated in the shooting.

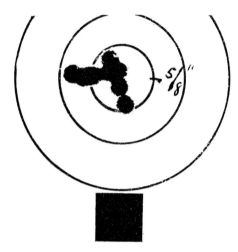

10 shots at 100 yds. B-R shot by Clark with his own .219 Donaldson-WASP rifle.

After each 20 shots were fired, the experimenters returned to the shooting house to load up the 22 empty cases, leaving the rifle outdoors on the bench in weather which was around 20° above zero. Upon returning each time, the barrel would be white with frost and after shooting warming shots, the group would be commenced. It was especially interesting to note, that the fact that the barrel was extremely cold and actually white with frost, before each 22 shots were fired, and had apparently no harmful effect upon the groups, although the barrel would be hot before the 22 shots were completed.

It should also be mentioned that these eight groups, fired with five different bullets, represented the first 80 shots fired from this .219 Donaldson-Wasp rifle with Morgan chamber. Conditions could be termed very poor, although on the last two 200-yard groups, the wind had dropped to three miles per hour. The last six groups were fired at night by lantern light to temperatures approximately 20°

above zero, from an outdoor bench rest, by two different shooters. However, despite these handicaps, if we reduce the two 200-yard groups to their equivalent, at 100 yards, the average of the entire 80 shots is slightly under 1″ per 10-shot group at 100 yards. It will be recalled also that 20 of these 80 shots were case forming loads when powder was poured in the case by sight alone.

10 shots at 100 yds. B-R, shot by S. Clark. Sr., with the Paine-WASP.

This fine shooting under difficult conditions certainly indicated that the new rifle would prove to be the equal of Cail's No. 1 Wasp and the two experimenters decided that this had indeed been a day well spent.

As a matter of fact, subsequent events proved that this particular Wasp rifle was in every way the equal of Cail's rifle in accuracy, and this fact will be apparent by an inspection of the accompanying groups, fired by the writer.

It will be noted that in practically all accuracy tests with this rifle, the powder charge consisted of 31.0 grains of duPont No. 4320 powder, using either 45, 50 or 55-grain bullets and there can be little doubt that of all powders tested, this particular powder will give the finest accuracy in the Wasp case. It is, however, true that the velocity is not quite as great as that obtained from duPont No. 3031, but nevertheless, the writer is convinced that the average accuracy is better and also the wear on the barrel is considerably less where the No. 4320 powder is used. In the case of the writer's original Wasp rifle, on a Winchester S.S. action, there was some slight discoloration in the throat after firing 1,360 rounds, the majority of which used 29.5 grains of duPont No. 3031, but in the case of Cail's rifle, the throat was apparently as new after 2,500 rounds, the majority of which used 31.0 grains of duPont No. 4320.

The actual chronographed velocity obtained with this load of 31.0 grains of duPont No. 4320 is 3,600 f.s. and it is doubtful if there is any material difference in velocity where bullets of either 45, 50 or 55-grains are used. The average velocity obtained on the Winchester chronograph where the 45-grain Wotkyns-Morse bullet was used with 31.0 grains of duPont No. 4320, was 3,600 f.s. and since from the same source we learn that in the .219 Donaldson-Wasp rifle the 55-grain Sisk bullet attains a velocity of 3,715 with 29.0 grains of duPont No. 3031 and the lower velocity of 3,689 with the same powder charge behind the 48-grain Winchester Swift bullet, we may well assume that slightly higher velocities are attained where 50 and 55-grain bullets are fired with 31.0 grains of No. 4320, than with the same powder charge and a 45-grain bullet having the same shape of point. This is of course, due to the fact that the heavier bullet causes the same powder charge to burn better, giving higher efficiencies, and the writer firmly believes that 50 and 55-grain bullets will give even finer all-around satisfaction in the Wasp case, than will bullets of 40 and 45-grains.

There is, of course, no doubt, whatever, that all muzzle velocities being the same, the heavier bullet will hold its elevation better at long ranges, to say nothing of the fact that it will be less affected by wind and consequently it will bag more game. If the Wasp shooter wishes to obtain higher velocity with No. 4320 powder, the charge can be increased to 33.0 grains with 50-grain bullets by tapping the powder charge into the case, but the hand loader should work up to this load very carefully, as the size of the bullet, diameter of the bore, dimensions of the throat, and several other factors will influence his ability to use this load. However, considering only Wasp rifles where 33.0 grains of duPont No. 4320 can be safely used, it will be found to be a very accurate varmint load, although 31.0 grains of this same powder will probably prove better at the target. The 33.0 grain load will give velocities of from 3,700 to 3,750 f.s.

For most varmint shooting, velocities between 3,600 and 3,700 f.s. are very satisfactory indeed, as they answer all practical purposes for certain kills up to 250 yards, which is about the limit at which certain hits can be made, under conditions of resting that exist in the field. There is no appreciable recoil where these velocities are used in heavy Wasp rifles, and the report of the shot is not materially greater than that of the R-2 Donaldson, in fact it is surprising to note how little difference there is in the report from rifles using these cases.

In short, the writer having tried out most available powders, is inclined to agree that duPont No. 4320 is the finest powder for use in the .219 Donaldson-Wasp case.

After preliminary tests had well established the accuracy of the writer's own Model 70, .219 Donaldson-Wasp rifle, with Morgan chamber, he had an opportunity to make the first test of Dr. Paine's Model 70 Wasp rifle which in due time was received from Morgan & Cail.

By this time Samuel Clark, Sr., had acquired a set of Fred Huntington's R.C.B.S. dies for the Pacific loading tool and was engaged in making, by hand, his own .22 caliber jacketed bullets. These handmade bullets had produced more small groups and finer average accuracy than any other bullets tried, up until that time, and therefore, they were selected for the first trial of Dr. Paine's new Wasp rifle.

Weather conditions were very satisfactory for the test, although not perfect, and the load that had been selected was the old reliable 31.0 grains of duPont No. 4320. The previous night, cases had been cut off and formed by firing in the chamber of the rifle at the expense of some sleep in the neighborhood and the results from the new rifle were anxiously anticipated.

Twenty-five rounds were taken to the range and the extra five rounds used to foul the bore and bore-sight the rifle. This was accomplished and shooting for group commenced. The first 10 shots at 100 yards bench rest fired with this S. Clark, Sr., 50-grain R.C.B.S. bullet and 31.0 grains of duPont No. 4320 gave a group measuring 13/16" from center to center of widest bullet holes, and the next 10-shot group measured 11/16".

Here the writer could not resist the desire to try out his own personal Wasp rifle under these identical conditions, and deciding that he could ill afford to let work interfere with pleasure, he returned to the gun room and loaded up 12 rounds with exactly the same S. Clark, Sr., 50-grain bullets and 31.0 grains duPont No. 4320 powder.

Transferring his 20X scope from the Paine Wasp to his own rifle and using the extra two shots for foulers, the resulting 10-shot group at 100 yards bench rest measured only 11/16". Here were 30 consecutive shots, fired with identical conditions, averaging approximately ¾" with no groups larger than 13/16".

In rifle shooting it is not always too easy to determine with certainty which factors contribute most to progress made over any considerable length of time, however, if the writer were asked to

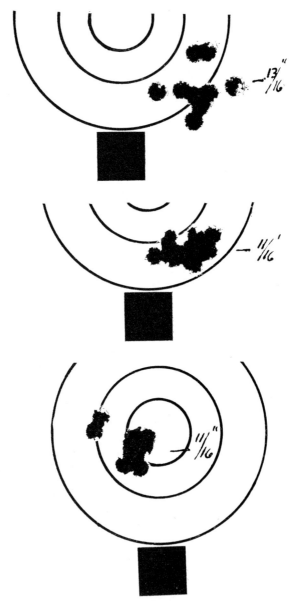

30 consecutive shots at 100 yds. B-R from two WASP rifles, shot by S. Clark, Jr., while testing the Paine-WASP rifle.

name the three factors, which, more than any others, had assisted him in improving accuracy with his varmint rifles he would list them as follows:

1. The ability to produce or obtain accurate shooting bullets and especially bullets of uniformly fine accuracy from lot to lot. This is exemplified by the 10-shot ½" 100-yard group shown with this chapter which was shot by Samuel Clark, Sr., with the Dr. Paine Wasp rifle. The bullets used were his own handmade 50-grain R.C.B.S. bullets and by exercising ordinary care in the swaging of these bullets and selection of their component parts, such extraordinary groups can occasionally be obtained by an expert rest shot, and day-in and day-out average accuracy of 1 minute of angle has been obtained regularly.

2. The selection of a rifle such as the .219 Donaldson-Wasp where the case has been especially designed to efficiently burn the maximum amount of powder contained in the case. This is illustrated by the high velocities that are obtained from Wasp rifles with comparatively small charges of powder.

3. The decision to use only rifles having fine bolt actions such as the Winchester Model 70, with heavy one piece stocks, such as the Winchester Marksman. This is illustrated by the fact that of twelve .22 caliber varmint rifles on single shot actions which the writer has owned or tested thoroughly, not a single one will closely approach the superfine accuracy that was obtained from any of the bolt action Wasp rifles here described.

VARMINT RIFLES—THE R-2 AND THE .22 MAXIMUM LOVELL

By John E. Sullivan

John E. Sullivan, of Bothwell, Ontario, a well-known Canadian rifleman and varmint hunter, who owns a collection of some 25 Schuetzen and varmint rifles and actions, has some interesting ideas on .22 high velocity rifles. He is in the construction business for a firm of industrial engineers and at present is on industrial leave from the Canadian army. He wrote the author as follows:

"I have a Stevens-Pope Ballard .28-30 muzzle-loading outfit, nicely engraved and fitted with Pope gadgets. I also have a Pope-Niedner-Winchester .32-40 with Schuetzen double set-triggers, special stock and other features, and a Remington-Hepburn in .32-40 *Remington* caliber. Also have a 44½ action No. 49 Stevens .32-40 Walnut Hill single shot with fine engraving, and a 44 Stevens .32-40 with fancy stock, the walnut of which is very curly. This rifle also is engraved, has Schuetzen double set-triggers, walnut knob in lever and so forth. The Ballard and this Stevens have palm rests.

"Besides the above I have a very fine shooting but plain .38-55 Stevens with 44½ action and heavy barrel, that is the best-shooting .38-55 on preliminary tests I have found in that caliber to date. However, I have not as yet had time, since coming out of the army, to really give it a complete tryout. The groove diameter of this Stevens is several thousandths smaller than the Winchester .38-55 barrels and I have never found a .38-55 to shoot well if fitted with one of these big bore barrels, which give loose bullet fit with many designs of bullets. My .32-40's will outshoot them. I consider the .32-40 the best Schuetzen caliber I have ever shot, but have never used the .25 caliber or the .40 caliber in the Schuetzen type of rifle. The .28-30 Stevens is the most uncertain rifle I have ever tried to use—0.75″ groups at 50 yards is the best I have had with the .28-30 and could not depend on that. Best load tried was 8.7 grains of No. 4759 and a 138-grain Pope bullet.

"I like the bulk shotgun smokeless, after sifting, for Schuetzen rifle loads, as it seems to burn uniformly and gives better accuracy for me than No. 4759 duPont in most rifles.

"Regarding .22 varmint rifles, I started out with the .22 Long Rifle cartridge as most of us did. In the early 1930's the Hornet appeared and I bought a Model 54 Winchester shortly after they came out. Mine was an early model, with a fine stock and equipped with No. 438 Lyman in ¼ minute mounts, and a ⅜″ height Rowley pad. This was a fine shooting rifle, with the only load I used, the factory loaded Remington Hi-Speed cartridges. It did well for me, for several years. I killed a great many chucks, some large owls, jack rabbits or hares, hawks and probably 150 crows with it. I found the .22 Hornet sensitive in the wind when the breeze was blowing strongly. Otherwise, I have no fault to find with it nor with its ammunition. I wish I still had that rifle today. In a weak moment I traded for a Winchester duck gun using 3″ shells, which I still have.

The Early .22/3000 Lovell

"About 1935, as I recall, Hervey Lovell brought out his first .22/3000 cartridge. I became interested in this rifle and size and finally got hold of W. K. McCurdy's 44½ No. 52 Schuetzen Stevens with 14″ twist, Parker liner tube, 0.224″ groove diameter with 28″ heavy barrel. This is the rifle mentioned by McCurdy in the booklet by B. L. Smith on the .22/3000 cartridge, (incidentally, a very interesting booklet—the author had an early copy). This Lovell job was chambered for the old sloping shoulder case (B. L. Smith chamber we called it). I used 17.0 grains of HiVel No. 3 with Remington No. 6½ primers in Winchester and U. S. cases, with 45-grain Hornet bullets of U. S. and Remington makes. This load shot really well for me, and outclassed the Hornet because the case was larger and held more powder and of course the muzzle velocity was higher.

"When the R-2 chamber came out, McCurdy made a similar reamer and I had him rechamber my rifle for the new shape of cartridge case. I *then* found that 16.0 or 16.5 grains of No. 4198 powder, with the same cases, primers and bullets worked somewhat better than HiVel No. 3 (which was the almost universal experience, because HiVel No. 3, which was a dense, double base powder, ignited very easily and more quickly reached full combustion and maximum pressure, than 4198, and therefore did not require the sharper shoulder slope to make it burn, and did not do so well in the very sharp shoulder type of case, especially in small size, as that had a tendency to make its burning time speed up too much—Author).

"I always found this rifle—now chambered for the R-2 case—to be extremely accurate; it was with all three cartridges, but was slightly more accurate with the R-2 case with 4198. I have fired some 3-shot and 5-shot groups under 1″ at 100 yards but regret I never bothered to save the targets. I used a 6 power Unertl small game scope on this rifle. I later had a ¾″ Lee dot installed in the scope, and now use this glass on a .224 Express (another name for the Maximum Lovell) relined and chambered and fitted to a case-hardened Winchester single shot.

"I still have this fine Stevens Lovell and also an R-2 rifle, but it needs some new pins in the action to bring the head space back to minimum head space adjustment. But I have not had opportunity to have this done as yet. I have a strong drawbolt in the stock in this 44½ action Model 52 rifle *and I have concluded this is one of the reasons why it always shot so well.* It never gives any trouble with its zero shifting. I used it for several seasons without any change in position that I could detect. The zero remained constant to a remarkable degree (this also showed the advantages of a well seasoned stock and a through stock bolt—Author). This of course, when I used the same load over a period.

"I used a few 41-grain Sisk and 50-grain Lovell-Sisk bullets and it shot them very well. This Lovell was the only Lovell that gave me fine accuracy with the 50-grain Sisk bullet. I think it was because of the 14″ pitch of the rifling. My other two Winchester Lovells have 16″ pitch and they did not do so well with the 50-grain bullet as with a blunt 55-grain Sisk-Niedner bullet. This has been a good bullet in all of my rifles which were chambered for the Lovell Cartridge."

(Possibly the author better point out here that the present .22/3000 Lovell has a 15° shoulder pitch, which is materially sharper than the Smith design of "Lovell" chamber and is sharper than the R-2 shoulder which is normally a 12° job, although some have put out a so-called R-2 with 11.5° to 12.5° shoulder—usually the latter, and one or two have put it out with 17° shoulder. For a while it seemed that nearly every custom gunsmith had his own ideas and tried them out, which was interesting and often instructive, but certainly did nothing to standardize the R-2 chamber which should be accurately standardized so that loading companies can be induced to put such commercial ammunition on the market. When this is done, the slope of shoulder preferred by the majority of varmint shooters should be used, and not some design determined by commercial ammunition maker's employees who in most instances are not even riflemen and certainly not crow or woodchuck hunters. Because if they do determine the shoulder slope it will not be sufficiently sharp and the results will be less satisfactory than they should be to satisfy the average varmint hunter or experimental rifleman. Past experience proves this to be so in dozens of instances. There have been any number of commercial cartridges marketed in past years many of particularly stupid cartridge design—consequently few of them were really accurate, as we judge accuracy among riflemen.)

"The .224 Express rifle is on a Winchester single shot action. It has 0.224″ grooves with 16″ pitch. It is 27″ long, is a heavy weight barrel and gives very fine accuracy with nearly any load and bullet.

"I use up to 19.5 grains of HiVel No. 2, (—remember this in the .224 Express or Maximum Lovell cartridge case—Author) with 55-grain Niedner bullet but I like 19.0 grains of HiVel No. 2 with this bullet.

"I like the .224 Express very well, and find it gives no extraction trouble with any load I have tried to date. Cases will nearly drop out when the lever is opened. Primers do not show signs of high pressure, although this is not a sure indication of low pressures, but cases have lasted well, and extraction is very smooth. The accuracy is fine with 41-grain Sisk, 45 and 46-grain Hornet bullets or 55-grain Niedner bullet. The 50-grain Lovell bullet gave about 1½″ to 1¼″ groups at 100 yards. Not as good as the 55-grain Niedner or the Hornet bullets.

No. 4198 in the Maximum Lovell

"I use 18.5 grains of 4198 with B. F. Mannen's S.T. 45-grain bullet and had a fine hunting load for chucks and crows. This bullet gave about 1″ groups at 100 yards from the car, with rest, for 5-shot groups, so I quit target shooting with it and killed around 100 woodchucks, several crows, about a half dozen jack rabbits with this rifle and load while on furlough late in June of 1945. Shooting was in Southern Ontario. I used Western No. 6½ primers, U. S. Cartridge Company's cases. The cartridge I used was probably a rather extreme capacity version of the Maximum Lovell case, as the rifle was chambered by a Canadian source.

"I certainly like this .224 Express rifle and its fine workmanship but could not say it is superior in accuracy to another rifle like the R-2 of equal workmanship. It is probably just as accurate, if not slightly more so; is a trifle better adapted to HiVel No. 2 powder, due to the longer, larger-capacity case; and is eminently satisfactory. It does very nice work with 4198, which is O.K. with this size case, as well as the slightly smaller capacity cases.

"*With light bullets* the R-2 cartridge may be slightly superior—have a fine 'edge' on the .224 Express, in efficiency and in accuracy, but in my opinion it is a toss-up between these two calibers—the R-2 and the Maximum Lovell—they are both right there as a chuck or crow rifle, at 50 or 100 yards beyond the .22 Hornet rifle. The Maximum Lovell naturally has an edge on the R-2 on the very long range shots, being a faster combination.

"I have had no cartridge case troubles with any of my three rifles, but the .224 Express seems to give the smoothest extraction of the three rifles I own of these sizes. I use our Dominion No. 1½ primers in cases after the primer pockets become *enlarged* from long use, (readers should understand this occurs; when it does occur, the normal diameter primer will then no longer fit snugly in the primer pocket, and gas escape may occur upon firing; also, in extreme cases there may be the danger the primer will even drop out of the primer pocket, having nothing to hold it in place—Author).

"The Dominion No. 1½ primer is definitely larger, and seats very tight in *new* cases, so for this reason I use American primers in all R-2 and .224 Express or .22 Maximum Lovell cases until the pockets become enlarged to somewhat above normal size from continued use. Then the Dominion No. 1½ primer gives good primer fit again, for continued use of the case, which is still in good shape in other respects.

Loads for the R-2 Case I.M.R. 4198 and 4227

"In R-2 rifles I use from 16.0 to 16.5 grains of No. 4198—this is all my Winchester cases will hold readily, with 41-grain and with 45-grain Hornet or 50-grain Sisk bullets. These loads all give good accuracy, and are consistently good shooting charges. I also use from 16.4 to 16.7 grains of 4227 with the 41-grain Sisk for a good load (this 4227 is a finer grain and faster powder than 4198; it does well with the light weight bullets which have a short bearing in the rifling—thus need a fine grain, fast powder to burn cleanly and rapidly behind them—Author).

"In my R-2 Winchester with 16″ pitch, 15.0 grains of 4227 with Hornet bullets is heavy enough; 15.5 grains of this powder (4227) give much higher pressures and give also hard extraction, due to the higher pressures tending to seal the cartridge case in the rifle chamber. Consequently, I use 15.0 grains of 4227 and 45-grain Western Hornet bullets with Western No. 6½ primers. This load does better than charges of 4198 in this particular rifle and with these comparatively light weight bullets (this is exactly what one would expect—Author). This 15.0 grain load of 4227 and the Hornet 45-grain bullet is a very good and inexpensive medium range woodchuck load.

Actions for Rimmed Cases

"As to my choice of rifle actions for rimmed cases, I prefer the Winchester Hi-Side with blued receiver if possible- or the 44½ Stevens. I use both actions and like both of them but the Winchester has the better ignition and with a positive ret' action of the firing pin while the retractor is only found in *later* 44½ actions. I have 44½ actions with and without the firing pin retracting feature. I think it should be installed in all 44½ actions. The breech block also needs a gas vent drilled into it for the escape of gas in case of a primer puncture, gas escape past the primer, or a case head failure.

Sights for the .22 Varmint Rifle

"For sights on varmint rifles I prefer from 6 to 8 power telescope or possibly the 10 power target type scope and like the larger objective and a Lee Dot or similar dot to cover about ¾″ per hundred yards. I also want the ¼ minute mount for my own use. I use scopes by Lyman, Fecker, Unertl and Litschert and they are all good, if of the best grades and suited to the job at hand. I like the Lyman 438 best on my Ballard .22 Long Rifle rim fire target-hunting rifle as it is all the scope needed to get all of the range of the .22 Long Rifle for hunting purposes. This scope would do a fine Hornet or Lovell justice.

Stocks—Two-Screw Forends Undesirable

"Regarding stocks for the R-2 and Maximum Lovell types of single shots for varmint hunting: I like the Monte-Carlo style cheek piece stocks with full combs, the good husky type of stock pierced by a full length rigid and substantial bolt to prevent vibration or bending of the stock, especially through the grip. I am using only one screw in the Winchester single shot rifle forend, and think now, that the forend is best bedded snugly to a point just ahead of forend screw. Then let the barrel float from this point to the tip of the forend.

"I am now making forends smaller than the large beavertail type of forend which sort I had made up several years ago. I think the smaller, lighter forend is better, as it is not so likely to warp due in part to its own mass and weight. (Author's note:—Readers should note that mass and weight are not synonymous; mass is the property of a body to which its inertia is ascribed—its bulk or substance; weight is the quality of being heavy—of its being acted upon by the force of gravity. When the large forends warp, if rigidly fastened to the barrel, they tend to bend the barrel with the new direction of the forend.)

"I had one forend with two screws holding it to the barrel. This was on the first Winchester R-2 and I never liked this forend with two screws. The rifle gave trouble with fliers, and all loads gave them. It shot best with the front screw rather slack. This of course permitted more movement.

Regular and Short Hammer Falls on .22 Varmint Rifles

"I also do not care for short hammer falls on Winchester single shot rifles. I had just one of these, and the result was bullets stringing up and down at the target. I also had some misfires. The same primers shot their charges well enough in the Winchester .224 Express and on my No. 44½ Model 52 Stevens Schuetzen R-2 rifle. I installed a standard hammer and got the single set-trigger back with the regular hammer fall, and the same rifle is now satisfactory and is fitted with the regular hammer fall. Some of the trouble was caused by the half cock notch but I simply do not go for a shortened hammer fall, as the standard hammer gives complete and prompt ignition and does well enough for me. A lightened hammer and a shortened hammer fall nearly always requires a stiffer mainspring.

"I am now having a coil-spring Winchester Hi-Side restocked for the .22-303 with latest type chamber by Parkinson. I consider this .22-303 cartridge a fine case for long range shooting at varmints. But I do not consider it as making up into the all-around rifle, but rather as a specialized job to start in where the Lovell leaves off. I think the R-2 perhaps the nearest cartridge to the ideal case for the all-around varmint rifle, under all conditions, including of course, shooting at times in settled areas. I fully intend to keep on using the Lovells for a large part of my shooting.

Buhmiller Blanks

"I am using a pre-turned, lapped Buhmiller blank, 26.5″ long, with 0.224″ grooves, 14″ pitch, 1.125″ at breech and 0.875″ at muzzle. I had a similar rifle nearly ready over two years ago, but sold the Zipper .219 Winchester barrel as a friend wanted it. I let the dies and cases go to another customer for whom Mr. Crandall was making a rifle. I was then going into the Canadian army, and felt I had best let someone else have the use of that rifle, as I could not use it then anyway.

"I have never had any experience with the .218 Bee, .219 Zipper, .219 Wasp, .22 Niedner-Magnum, .22 Varminter or the .220 Swift, or similar cartridges, but feel that the .22 Varminter and the .22 Niedner-Magnum would show the best accuracy of the above calibers.

"I am also going to have a .25-303 rifle soon, in fact as quickly as I can come around to getting the material to start the job. I think this caliber has possibilities. I have another coil-spring Winchester saved up for this job.

The Secords and the Sullivan Rifles

"My friend Jim Secord, Jr., and his father have shot my rifles quite frequently (Mr. Sullivan has one of the finest collections in America and likely the best in Canada), and Jim Secord shot a ½″ three-shot group for check, with my .224 Express—at 100 yards. This was while using my regular hunting fodder. I do not recall which load I had along at that time. I think maybe it was the 19.0 grains of HiVel No. 2 and the 55-grain Sisk-Niedner. Perhaps he still has the target! Jim Secord and his father are very fine rifle shots, the father having won the local championship with rifle and revolver years ago, in Saskatchewan—the rifle one year, the revolver the following season. I understand he did not shoot the rifle the second year.

"Before closing perhaps I should mention a fine .22 Long Rifle conversion job by G. B. Crandall, which he turned out for me several years ago. This was on a 44 action 49 Stevens .38-55. This rifle is closely chambered and head spaced for Dominion ammunition, and does its best work with Dominion cartridges. It is an extremely accurate .22 target job with Parkerifled tube in a 28" medium heavy barrel. No iron sights. It was stocked and converted entirely by Crandall. It has the reputation of being the finest shooting .22 rim fire rifle in this section of the country. It has beaten all comers in matches until the boys lost interest; this was in Schuetzen territory where the riflemen really knew accuracy. Lloyd Secord used it until most of the others stopped shooting against it. He then had to use another rifle to get in a match.

"I have a 5-shot 50-yard target shot in practice at Secord's range, with a 438 scope, which looks like a single .28-30 bullet hole. Secord saw me shoot this target from rest but I hardly like to show it because it seems too good to be true. Crandall said it was the best he had ever seen. It was made with our ordinary .22 Long Rifle Dominion Super-Clean. The rifle has double Schuetzen triggers. My AI mid-range Ballard by Addicks and Diller does not seem nearly so hot, but I think it would do best with Super-Match ammunition as the head space is just about right for those thick head cartridges. The Crandall job does not like Super-Match. It probably is too closely head spaced to use very thick-head ammunition without pinching the rim.

Summation

"To sum up my experiences to date, I find the .22 Lovell rifles, by any good maker that turns out fine workmanship, to give finer accuracy from day to day for varmint or target shooting, winter and summer, with less sight change and adjustment than any other combination I have so far tried. I know Schuetzen rifles have given remarkable groups in the past, and I have a very nice collection of such rifles, as mentioned earlier in this communication, but in my experience the Lovell type of rifle will outshoot them without any special trouble in reloading, due to the efficient case shape—in some instances, extremely efficient shape—so as it is, the

.22 varmint rifles have some advantages not possessed by the Schuetzen rifles.

"The fine copper-jacketed custom and factory bullets in .22 varmint rifle sizes are another big help in making the .22 varmint rifle efficient. I think that today, the .22 varmint rifles are giving the finest accuracy of all the calibers, within of course their normal range for the cartridge in question. These .22 varmint rifles are not 1,000-yard target rifles but they do not need to be. That is not what they are intended for. One reason I believe the .22 varmint rifle is giving the best accuracy is that the other sizes suitable to varmint rifles have not received an equal amount of attention in recent years. They have not recently had the same number of tests by experienced and practical riflemen, due mainly to the fact that nearly all riflemen interested in such rifles, especially east of the Rockies, were turning to the .22 caliber varmint rifles.

"Custom bulletmakers have been so busy grinding out good .22 bullets (however there was a slip in the accuracy and quality of these during 1944 and 45—Author), that these bulletmakers will not even use the valuable time to design and test other sizes, particularly the .25 caliber. The .25 caliber today is handicapped by lack of a variety of really fine, efficient varmint bullets (the Western Cartridge Company's 87, 101 and 117-grain bullets in this caliber are probably the most accurate and uniform on the market—Author) and consequently they do not average as well in smallness of groups. True, we have some custom .25 caliber bullets, but none in my (Sullivan's) opinion, equal to the Sisk and Wotkyns-Morse in the .22 caliber field. I have been unable to get the W-M 8S bullets for my own use, but others have found them, beyond a doubt, to be among the finest yet produced.

"The writer wishes to thank the readers for their interest in Canadian varmint shooting and riflemen, and their experiments, and trusts that this letter, or such part of it as may be reproduced, may be found practical and helpful to all those who may read this book."

The author (Landis) believes the above to be one of the most thoroughly practical, sensible and complete coverages of .22 varmint rifles and cartridges which have been received from outside sources. He would suggest, while you think of it and have the subject in mind, that you read the above communication a second time with the idea of picking out and remembering the suggestions you inadvertently overlooked on the first reading. John Sullivan is one of the most experienced varmint hunters in Canada, has probably the most complete collection of rifles of Schuetzen and .22 varmint type in the Detroit-Toronto-Montreal-Rochester area and in this there are probably more really fine shooting rifles of greater than .22 Long Rifle caliber, than in any other similar area in North America. These riflemen hang on to their fine old single shot rifles, and fix them up to use either the best Schuetzen loads or the more modern metal-cased charges. They happen to be, most of them, but with a few exceptions, one of the most friendly and affable groups in North America and are always willing to share their knowledge with others.

The author feels particularly indebted to Mr. Sullivan for his complete coverage of his subject, supplied at a time, when Mr. Sullivan really needed the time in the construction business. The author has experienced the position of being so swamped with different things needing attention in engineering and construction endeavor, and with trying to write in all his spare time, that he doubly appreciates Mr. Sullivan's contribution.

LOADS FOR THE R-2

By H. V. Noble

H. V. Noble, of R. D. 2, Mt. Healthy, Cincinnati 31, Ohio, Chief Transmitter Engineer, Crosley Radio Corporation, and more recently of Wright Field, Dayton, Ohio, and for years the star individual and team shot on the Wilmington Rifle & Pistol Club's first teams has come to definite conclusions regarding desirable loads for the R-2 Johnson cartridge. He shoots this cartridge in a C. C. Johnson barrel fitted to a Springfield action.

Noble prefers the Remington Hornet .22 metal-cased pointed bullet and 16.4 grains of duPont No. 4227 powder for calm weather shooting and in windy weather hunting he recommends and uses the same charge with the Sisk-Lovell 50-grain bullet. He believes that Winchester primers do a bit better with these loads in his rifle.

Another of his favorite loads is either the 45-grain flat nose, or pointed gas-check bullet, with 11.0 grains of No. 4227. He uses it at 100 yards with the 200-yard high power scope sight settings. This makes what is obviously a very convenient combination, any one of three 200-yard loads, and the gas-check loads, usable with either of two bullets, yet all five charges shooting closely to center with the same sight setting.

Noble usually does most of his rifle shooting in Ohio and in Indiana, which is his old home state, at crows, hawks, woodchucks and squirrels. They have both fox squirrels and gray squirrels. He is a heavily built, powerful man of calm, cheerful, pleasant and even temperament, and this all helps to give good work, and even shooting with a 14¼ pound "bull" gun. Incidentally, Ohio and Indiana are the center of many beef, turkey and other target matches, in winter, and a 14 pound rifle making 2" groups at 200 yards should, every now and then "bring home the bacon" to the Nobles.

COMPARISONS OF .22 WILDCATS

By V. E. Layne

One of the most experienced and enthusiastic rest shooters and rifle experimenters in the far western part of the United States is V. E. Layne, of Halfway, Oregon. The author has been familiar with his shooting for possibly 20 years; in 1938 he supplied some interesting data on the smaller .22 wildcats. A letter written in March, 1945, gives some very interesting comparisons and comments on different .22 wildcats and additional remarks regarding wildcats and Schuetzen rifles.

Numerous shooters are claiming that the .22 wildcats are outshooting the old Schuetzens, few of whom, however, seem to have had any considerable experience with Schuetzen rifles or even Schuetzen double set-triggers; consequently, some comment on the other side of the question might be worth reading. Mr. Layne wrote:

"Since 1938, when I sent you those notes, I have experimented with the .22 Varminter, several wildcats in necked-down rimmed cases of a powder capacity to cause them to just about equal or perhaps surpass the standard .220 Swift, and I have also had fine results with the Zipper Improved. This is the case with steeper shoulder and shorter neck, but otherwise the regular Zipper.

"This last cartridge was used with a fine Westley Richards Farquharson action having the side lever safety. The record I have of experimental work with these calibers and cartridges is not, unfortunately, in tabulated form, and my business management cares are such that I have even been forced to curtail my own rifle shooting to some extent.

"It may be of interest that some five years ago I became intrigued with the possibilities of Schuetzen rifles, using cast bullets and modern components. Success in this field proved difficult. This experimenting has taken almost my entire rifle work time for the past three years. At last I reached a point, with the .38-55 and the .32-40 Schuetzen rifles and loading ammunition for them right at the rest shooting bench, where I averaged 10-shot groups, dead on the 10-ring that measured 1¼″ on centers; this is an average, mind you. Dozens of groups ran ¾″ on centers and some smaller. My lifetime record is a 10-shot, 10-V possible, measuring 7/16″ on centers with a Pope barrelled Winchester Schuetzen .38-55; dozens more were well under 1″; the range was 100 yards.

"This led to a most amazing and interesting correspondence with several fine riflemen, collectors and shooters. I found that my groups were about as good as the best of the late Charley Rowland, of

THE OUTDOOR SHOOTING BENCH

This is the well known rifleman, V. E. Layne, of Halfway, Oregon, firing from his home made muzzle rest testing bench. Mr. Layne is very partial to the R-2 varmint rifles.

Colorado; that is, my selected groups, and that my average groups were also comparable with his, with consistent accuracy slightly above his, as he shot in a day when components were not quite as good as mine.

"Last year some of my correspondence and some selected targets shot here on my range, were posted in the clubhouse at Walnut Hill, Massachusetts, by a Captain O'Neill, one of my correspondents.

"To sum up the matter, my taste for bench rest rifles changed. I found I liked the old timers best, and could get just as good results with them insofar as small groups were concerned and in the matter of *consistent* accuracy, as I could with the best modern small caliber rifles, and I could reload them and test them with the finest large objective scopes, work out a fine load and stay with it. For real fun I will take a perfect Schuetzen every time, on a bench rest.

"Conditions here have changed; the chucks and other varmints have become scarce; hence, I am in the position of following the bench rest rifle shooting game, or nothing.

"It may be helpful for the .22 rifle cranks to know that with the center fire .22's and .25's that cases had to have about a 40° shoulder taper and a comparatively large powder capacity in relation to caliber, if efficient combustion was to be secured. Also, that the groove diameter of the barrels must be about bullet diameter, perhaps 0.001″ smaller, better still if neat bullet size; custom-made, sharp-pointed bullets being best and most uniform.

A Direct Comparison of Results

"To sum up the accuracy, with hand loads entirely, bull barrels, set-triggers and big objective target scopes on all rifles, and all of them shot from the same rest under just about the same conditions:

"I found the .22 Varminter the most accurate and the most flexible as to loads; the standard .250/3000 Savage almost equalled it; the original Lovell, the R-2 Lovell and the standard .218 Bee were so even one could not tell much difference.

"It is also true, as may be surprising to some, the .25-20 repeater case and the .25-20 S.S. case almost equalled them. With hand loads the old .25-35 W.C.F. case was better than a 10-ring rifle combination *all the time*.

"Then still another comparison! I used a fine .30-1906 bull gun with Adriance set-trigger, used reduced loads of No. 4759, and found that strangely enough even with unselected F.A. 172-grain match bullets, I equalled in group size, and impact consistency, *any* of the above. This proves nothing, possibly, yet it does show that accuracy is composed of, or the result of, many factors besides case shape or caliber alone.

"Sheer accuracy is one thing; accuracy with high velocity is another. Our modern .22 wildcats give us accuracy with very high velocity. If I had to pick two, and these the best, I would take the R-2 Lovell and the .22 Varminter, against the field. I would know that then I would have the edge in speed, accuracy, flexibility and ease of loading."

These help to set at rest the fears of some riflemen that they are hopelessly outclassed if they do not happen to have some one rifle or cartridge in their cabinet. Accuracy is not a matter of one individual caliber, bullet or cartridge, but a combination of things which fortunately are working smoothly together.

To show that accuracy is not a matter of any one single caliber, make, barrel bore, or charge, the author includes here data from Mr. Layne in a letter March 16, 1945:

"My testing range is exactly 100 yards long, rifle muzzle to face of the target frame, measured with steel surveyor's tape and four assistants.

"It may be of interest to you, or your readers, to know that in addition to the fine accuracy shown with the various .22 wildcats, and with my Schuetzens in .32-40 and .38-55 caliber, that I was also able to attain an *average* of $1\frac{1}{2}''$ 10-shot, 10-ring groups, with an original Sharps Buffalo rifle in .45-70 caliber. This fine rifle has the original stock, the good old double set-triggers and the big side hammer. The groove diameter is large—0.460″—so that I used a special-sized bullet, one of 0.463″ diameter and in a 450-grain weight. I use fully expanded Remington cases, the same being factory loads originally, fired once in this rifle, and then used without any neck resizing. These are the regular factory smokeless loads. The 0.463″ cast bullets fit the necks perfectly. One pushes them in with the fingers and then seats the assembled cartridge in the barrel, whereupon the breech block completes the seating. The bullet fit is so good that when it is withdrawn from a case neck it makes a little 'pop' like drawing a cork from a bottle. No. 80 powder I find the best propellant, with MX shotgun powder an extremely close second.

"I bought this rifle from the widow of the original owner, an old lady then in her late 80's. The rifle had an interesting history, as it had killed seven men. At the battle of Horse Thief Cave its owner shot on the side of law and order in an untold battle of honest men against cattle thieves. I have been at the spot many times; some of the old stone foundations of the buildings around the cave can still be seen with the desert 'bunch grass' overgrown around them. This famous hang-out of that wild bunch was on the banks of the Snake River. I have been on the spot alone in the fading shadows of a summer evening. There is a haunted atmosphere about the place with the long shadows creeping across the glistening basalt boulders and the murmur of the big swift river. One can see in the mind's eye that long ago scene. Dead men and smoking rifles and the roar of the big Sharps under the blazing sun of a summer afternoon, back in the days of long, long ago.

"I get a thrill out of shooting this old rifle and making it perform better perhaps, than old Christian Sharps, its maker, ever dreamed. A touch of its delicate double set-trigger fires it as easily as in the days of old. The massive old rifle slides back in the barrel

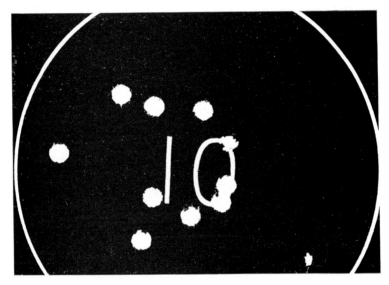

A VERY FINE 200-YARD GROUP

V. E. Layne shot this one with an R-2 .22/3000 Johnson barrel at 200 yards. Group measures $1\frac{1}{2}''$ x $1\frac{7}{8}''$ center to center.

rest and gives my shoulder a slow but powerful push and the heavy bullet spins down the range and punches a clean hole in the 10-ring. A puff of wind or half a gale makes no difference, at least not of over $\frac{1}{2}''$ at the point of impact 100 yards away. I usually use a big $1\frac{1}{2}''$ Fecker target scope when group shooting, and get much the same result in group size, with any one of the good calibers in the best of rifles."

"We all know it is easier to obtain very small groups with .22 or with .25 caliber rifles due to lower recoil of the smaller calibers, using lighter and shorter bullets. But what the author of this book wants to drive home here, is that there is no *"secret"* formula for

obtaining accuracy or consistent accuracy except *uniformity* of loading and of shooting. No barrelmaker has much of an "edge" on
the best of his competition. There is no great "secret" of getting
accuracy with any given cartridge, or caliber, or rifle. If someone
will not tell what chamber clearance or slope of shoulder he uses
there is no reason to worry. They will all shoot, if properly assembled in any reasonably designed case, and the bullets, powder
charges, priming and then the aiming and trigger squeezing are
uniformly accomplished shot after shot.

"Particularly in .22 caliber, a shooting combination of bullet,
charge and barrel should not be changed. It takes real precision
riflemaking—barrel boring and fitting, breeching, stock fitting,
sighting—and then ammunition loading to get accuracy. This can
be obtained, in just about equal degree with any size bore; the
only difference is that the large calibers give much more recoil,
which not all persons can handle to advantage, while the .22 with
short, light bullets, gives a minimum of recoil and greater enjoyment of shooting. On the other hand, in windy weather, the bullet
drift will be more noticeable, and the rifleman will have to develop
into what is known as a good "wind doper."

"What I particularly want to again stress here is that you can
make almost any good .22 rifle shoot, provided the rifle is in good
condition, the stock is not binding at the wrong place, you have a
bullet that suits the rate of twist and the size of the bore, and your
ignition is *good.*" Mr. Layne's observations should help to convince
you that accuracy is a result of many things all working together
to a perfect combination.

THE .22/3000 R-2 CARTRIDGE

By V. E. Layne

"The writer's interest in and experience with the .22/3000 R-2
(Risley-Donaldson) cartridge began in January 1938 at which time
glowing accounts began to appear from many shooters as to the remarkable performance obtained, both as to accuracy and general
suitability as a target and varmint load.

"In deciding on a rifle suitable for the foundation for the new
cartridge I was fortunate in having in my gun cabinets a very fine
Winchester Schuetzen S.S. rifle in practically new condition, with a
beautiful stock, double set-triggers and a heavy No. 3 octagon barrel,
matted on the top three flats. Accordingly, this fine rifle was sent to
Gunsmith Charles C. Johnson, of Thackery, Ohio, with instructions

to reline the barrel, bush the breech block and in general alter as required to handle the new cartridge.

"In due time the rifle returned fitted with a tapered, chrome-nickel steel liner, rifled with a 16″ twist, six grooves and having a diameter of a scant 0.223″. The bore and chamber were perfectly finished and carried a glass smooth polish very pleasing to a rifleman's eye. A case forming die of hardened steel was included with the job, making it a very simple matter to press the .25-20 single shot

A 9-X POSSIBLE AT 100 YARDS WITH AN R-2

Another fine 100 yard group shot with a single shot Winchester Schuetzen fitted with a Johnson R-2, .22/3000 barrel. The work of V. E. Layne.

case into the die which partially reformed the shoulder of the case and constricted the neck to .22 caliber.

"A supply of Winchester .25-20 S.S. cases of late manufacture having been obtained, as well as a shipment of R. B. Sisk's excellent 50-grain Lovell bullets, no time was lost in preparing a generous batch of handloads for trial. A charge of 16.5 grains of No. 4198 powder was used behind the Sisk bullets which were seated to touch the lands. Powder charges were carefully weighed.

"A Fecker 8-power target scope with 1.5″ objective was mounted on the rifle and after a few sighting shots the bullets began to print in the X-ring of the small bore target at 100 yards. Five targets were then placed on the frames and very careful firing begun from bench rest. The result was very gratifying as 50 consecutive 10's with 41 X's resulted from this test.

"Truly my new rifle was a complete success. Since that day some 2,000 shots have been fired from this superb weapon with uniformly excellent results.

"The accompanying targets show two typical groups made at 100 yards bench rest and two exceptionally good groups made at 200 yards. When one has a rifle that will make 1.75" and 2.125" groups at 200 yards he really has something.

"The .22/3000 is very effective and deadly on all types of small and medium-sized game at ranges up to and including 250 yards. The report is sharp but not objectionably loud so as to alarm game. The execution of the load is excellent and the accuracy is almost unbelievable—a really perfect varmint and target cartridge and one well worth any rifleman's unstinted praise.

Reloading Data

"The .22/3000 R-2 cartridge is quite simple to load. Winchester cases should always be used as they are more uniform, thicker and withstand pressures better than other makes. The case is first forced into the die and partially reformed thereby. After firing once the case shoulder snaps out under pressure and forms itself to the contour of the rifle chamber. After the first firing, neck resizing only is required, or full length resizing may be performed by the use of the very excellent custom-made Pacific Gunsight Company's dies.

"In my particular rifle best accuracy is obtained by the use of No. 4198 powder in charges of from 16.5 to 17.0 grains behind the Sisk 50-grain Lovell bullet. In assembly of this load it is necessary to place the empty case in a die and funnel the powder into the die. The die is then tapped smartly a few times with a small mallet and the powder settled by pressing a small steel rod on top of the load. This leaves no air space and the bullet is seated to press directly against the powder charge.

"Another method recommended for rapid assembly of cartridges and one which gives almost as good results as to both accuracy and power is to use No. 1204 powder in charges of from 14.5 to 15.0 grains with above bullet and to measure the powder with a Belding & Mull visible powder measure or any other good measure. This method is less tedious and is perfectly satisfactory for field loads and ordinary target shooting.

"In preparation of loads for the very finest accuracy in bench rest shooting, extra selection and inspection of components is required. Bullets should be passed through a die or carefully drilled hole in a piece of steel to insure a uniform size of 0.224". Cases should be inspected as to uniform thickness of brass at the necks and inside neck reamed to a uniform size if necessary. Cases also vary considerably as to inside thickness of the heads, variations here causing some cases with thick heads to hold less powder than those with thin heads. Variations in this respect may be checked by dropping a depth gage made from a 0.1875″ stove bolt into each case and the ones with thick heads separated from those with thin heads. Case head thickness makes little difference with loads using No. 1204 but does introduce a factor of non-uniformity when the tightly packed loads of No. 4198 are used.

"Pressures in this case with loads of No. 4198 are on the low-side and primer pockets show no tendency to stretch; however, cases do lengthen out somewhat and should be trimmed to a uniform minimum length by use of the Wilson Universal Case Trimmer or some other suitable device.

"Continued use of the .22/3000 R-2 cartridge has convinced me that it is one of the few really worthwhile cartridges of the present day, suitable for finest bench rest shooting and varmint hunting. At the present time it is not available in commercially loaded ammunition but notwithstanding this fact it is well worth the attention of all riflemen.

"It appears that the finest results attained to date have been secured in heavy barrelled single shot rifles, either with relined barrels or with fine new six groove barrels having dimensions of from 0.222″ to 0.223″, and with 16″ twist."

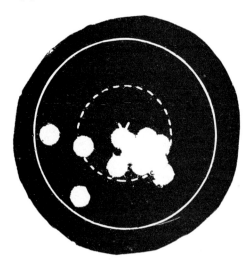

APPENDIX

TABULATION AND SUMMARY OF .22 CALIBER WILDCAT
CARTRIDGE DIMENSIONS

This is the first time that an accurate and scientific comparison has been
made of the many common .22 caliber wildcat cartridges which are
made today.

Obviously no list can contain all the cartridges of any caliber which have
ever been designed, but this list contains most of those which, up to this
time, have been given a fair degree of public approval and popularity.

The two dimensions which should always be compared in estimating the
relative powder capacity of any two cartridges, or their probable relative
velocities with a given bullet, are: 1. The distance from the rear face
of the rim or head, to the shoulder; 2. The outside diameter at the shoulder.

The degree of shoulder slope is important in determining the manner
in which the powder is confined in the case as it is being ignited, and how
it is funneled out of the cartridge into the barrel, as it burns. The sharper
the slope, in degrees, the more the powder will be confined, bullet weight,
neck tension, throating, and other conditions being equal.

Cartridges will, at times, be found which are not cylindrical at the rim
or head, or at the shoulder. In that case, the greatest diameter is given.
You can prove this for yourself by revolving a cartridge between the jaws
of an accurate micrometer.

Bullet diameter and length are measured in the same manner.

Special Note: When an asterisk * is shown back of the dimension, it
means that the figures are the standard agreed-upon dimension among
commercial manufacturers for some one diameter, as for instance, the rim
or head diameter. Other figures are for carefully measured dimensions of
selected cartridges, usually those supplied by the custom gunsmith as
representative examples of the cartridge in question.

Measurements were taken very carefully, were checked and re-checked
by two experienced draftsmen, using fine draftsman's scale and a Brown
& Sharpe micrometer, selected for its accuracy and which had an 0.000"
zero reading.

It should be carefully noted by the reader. that center fire rifle cartridges
will be found to vary in length and diameter, one from the other, the
rim or head will often be found considerably out of round, in which case
the maximum diameter is given, empty fired cases will be found, at times,
to have more than one diameter at the shoulder, when revolved in the
micrometer, due to having been irregular in form, or to having been fired
in a chamber not perfectly round. Cases will be found to vary considerably in thickness of metal in the neck, and cartridges of different makes
will vary in size, especially in rim diameter. Bear these variations in
mind when comparing measurements taken from a cartridge in your
possession, with the carefully computed calculations given here.

505

A very careful examination of the measurements of .22 wildcat cartridges as developed by various custom gunsmiths and set down here, will show the variations which you may expect to find, and which indicate the value of standardization of chamber and cartridge specifications and dimensions for all of the common .22 wildcats.

In comparing any two .22 wildcats, set down their respective diameter at the shoulder, length, rear face to shoulder, length of case, and length of neck and you can then tell, almost at a glance, the relative powder capacity of each and their comparative muzzle velocities, range and flatness of trajectory. If one has a standard load of 25 grains of 3031, for instance, you will know it is a short case, if it uses 29 to 32 grains, it is a medium case, if it accepts 35 to 40 grains of 4064 or some similar powder, you will know it is a large case and probably quite long.

If the suggested charge is 10 to 18.3 grains, you should then know that it is probably a K-Hornet or a .22-3000 Lovell of one type or another, especially if using 4198, 2400 or 4227, and its maximum universally effective range is normally 150 to 225 yards.

Generally, small cases measure 0.90″ to 1.273″ from face of head to shoulder. Cartridges used up to 250 yards, measure between 1.10″ and 1.30″ rim face to shoulder. Medium large cases, 1.35″ to 1.60″, and the very long range cartridges of Super type, 1.55″ and up to 1.80″.

Cases swaged down to .22 and cut off, from .30-1906, .30-40 or .303 British brass, are usually made about 1.50″ to 1.60″ to shoulder, as the case is large diameter, must be necked down very sharply. and holds a large charge of powder even if relatively short in "barrel" length.

As a general rule, a small or a medium size .22 varmint rifle case has a higher ratio of efficiency, if not over 1.50″ to 1.60″ from head to shoulder, than if longer. The very high efficiency cartridges are usually around 1.12″ to 1.30″ in this dimension. Then 1.50″ for the next larger size. From 18 to 35 grains of powder is all you normally require to shove a 45 to 55-grain .22 bullet out to 300 yards with extremely flat trajectory and maximum accuracy. It is better to have a super-accurate rifle give 6,000 rounds of bumble bee accuracy than 750 rounds, by which time you are just getting accustomed to your rifle and its normal sighting for each distance.

Remember that accuracy and even, moderate pressures with not too excessive velocities, go hand in hand.

SUMMARY OF CARTRIDGE SPECIFICATIONS AND DIMENSIONS

Lysle Kilbourn .22 Wildcats

Cartridge	Shoulder Slope	Diam. Head	Diam. at Shoulder	Length to Shoulder	Length Case	O.A. Length	Neck Length
.22 K.-Hornet Junior	35°	.350"* .345"	.2915"	0.83"	1.06"	1.46"	0.18"
.22 K.-Hornet	35°	.350"* .3455" Actual	.2885"	1.13"	1.38"	1.81"	0.22"
.22 K-Lovell	35°	.380"* .377" to .3792" Actual	.3082"	1.380"	1.640"	2.125"	0.21"
.22 K-Zipper	25°	.506"* .4925" Actual	.4075" to .4085"	1.52"	1.89"	2.50"	0.20"
22 K-Magnum Rimless	25°	.422"* .4180" to .4185"	.4075" to .4085"	1.65"	2.05"	2.56"	0.23"
.22 K-Magnum Junior	25°	.422"* .4185" to .4190"	.4019"* .397" to .398" Actual	1.275"	1.70"	2.20"	0.25"
.22 K Hi-Power	25°	.506"* .492" to .493"	.407" to .4075"	1.59"	2.00"	2.58"	0.28"

Hervey Lovell .22 Wildcats

Cartridge	Shoulder Slope	Diam. Head	Diam. at Shoulder	Length to Shoulder	Length Case	O.A. Length	Neck Length
1. .22 Lovell K-Hornet	30°	.350"* .3475"	.2875"	1.13"	1.38"	1.88"	0.27"
2. .22 Lovell R-2	12°	.380"* .377"	.2925"	1.275"	1.633"	2.125"	0.26"
3. .22/3000 Lovell	15°	.380* .374" to .378"	.296"* .295" to .2955"	1.275"	1.633"	2.125"	0.27"
4. .22/3000 Lovell (Original)	5°	.380"* .375"	.2945"	1.12"	1.633"	2.12"	0.18"
5. .22 Short Necked .22/3000	15°	.380"* .374" to .378"					0.21"
6. .22 Maximum Lovell	30°	.380"* .377" to .3792"	.3024"	1.380"	1.633"	2.175"	0.18"

Cartridge	Shoulder Slope	Diam. Head	Diam. at Shoulder	Length to Shoulder	Length Case	O.A. Length	Neck Length
7. .22 Lovell Improved Zipper	30°	.506"* .4965" Actual	.393"* .395" Actual	1.50"	1.92"	2.43"	0.27"
8. .22 Lovell Hi-Power Improved	24°	.506"* .495" to .4965" Actual	.370"* .3795" Actual	1.58"	2.00"	2.46"	0.30"
9. .22 Lovell 25-35 Improved	30°	.506"* .498" to .4985" Actual	.393"* .393" to .3935" Actual	1.58"	2.03"	2.53"	0.27"
10. .22 Super Lovell or, Mann-Lovell	30°	.506"* .492" to .497" Actual	.370"* .354 to .356" Actual	1.70"	2.03"	2.52"	0.20"
11. Lovell-Sweany .22-250	28°-30°	.473"* .471"	.4128"	1.50"	1.92"	2.44"	0.24"
12. .22-30/1906 Lovell	37°	.473"* .470"	.430"* .440"* to .441"	1.50"	1.82"	2.35"	0.25"

Dimensions of Harvey Donaldson Cartridges

Cartridge	Shoulder Slope	Diam. Head	Diam. at Shoulder	Length to Shoulder	Length Case	O.A. Length	Neck Length
Original Donaldson-Wasp (.25 Rem. ctg.)	30°	.422"/* .4172" Actual	.3864"	1.23"	1.65"	2.05"	0.28"
Present .219 Donaldson-Wasp (.219 Zipper case)	30°	.506"/* .4952" to .4962" Actual	.4045"	1.30"	1.75"	2.25"	0.325"

SUMMARY OF LINDAHL .22 WILDCAT CARTRIDGE SPECIFICATIONS AND DIMENSIONS

Cartridge	Shoulder Slope	Diam. Head	Diam. at Shoulder	Length to Shoulder	Length Case	O.A. Length	Neck Length
Lindahl Cartridges							
.22 Lindahl Rimless Chucker	28°	.422"* to .4225" Actual	.404" to .403"	1.20"	1.605"	2.07"	.255"
.22 Lindahl Rimmed Chucker	28°	.506"* .493" to .4945" Actual	.4035" to .403"	1.20"	1.605"	2.07"	.255"
.22 Lindahl L-4 (R-2)	25°	.380"* .375" to .378" Actual		1.280"			
.22 Lindahl Rimless Super-Chucker	28°	.422"* .4195"	.400"	1.420"	1.820"	2.285"	.255"
.22 Lindahl Rimmed Super-Chucker	28°	.506"* .493" to .945"	.400"	1.420	1.820"	2.285"	.255"

Joseph Pfeifer's .22 Wildcats

Cartridge	Shoulder Slope	Diam. Head	Diam. at Shoulder	Length to Shoulder	Length Case	O.A. Length	Neck Length
.22 K-Hornet	35°	.350"* .344"	.285"	1.11"	1.38"	1.92"	0.23"
.22/3000 R-2	12°	.380"* .379"	.2925"	1.28"	1.63"	2.12"	0.25"
.218 Mashburn-Bee		.408"*					
.224 Pfeifer Rimmed Magnum (.30-40 case)	28°	.545"* .5385"	.4125"	1.275"	1.660" to 1.68"	2.23"	0.23"
.224 Pfeifer Rimmed Magnum (.303 British case)	28°	.533"* .528"	.4125"	1.275"	1.660" to 1.67"	2.23"	0.23"
.22-250 Pfeifer	28°	.473"* .4685" .467"	.4165" .4155"	1.50"	1.90"	2.47" 2.48"	0.24"

B. F. Mannen .22 Wildcats

Cartridge	Shoulder Slope	Diam. Head	Diam. at Shoulder	Length to Shoulder	Length Case	O.A. Length	Neck Length
B. F. Mannen, Super .22 H.P. (Savage H.P. case) (3,650 f.s. with 63-gr. S.P. bullet)	15°	.506"* .5025" .503" Actual	.383"	1.48"	2.03"	2.575"	0.30"

SUMMARY OF .22 CARTRIDGE SPECIFICATIONS AND DIMENSIONS

Niedner Rifle Corporation's .22 Wildcats

Cartridge	Shoulder Slope	Diam. Head	Diam. at Shoulder	Length to Shoulder	Length Case	O.A. Length	Neck Length
.22 Baby Niedner (.22-Koshollek)	14°	.403" to .4052" Actual	.321" to .322"	1.00"	1.30"	1.675"	0.20"
.22 Rimless Niedner Magnum	22°	.422"* .4155" to .4185"	.393"	1.40"	1.90"	2.38"	0.28"
.22 Rimmed Niedner Magnum	17°	.506"* .4915" to .495"	.362"	1.35"	1.84"	2.30"	0.28"
.224 Lightning	14°	.545"* .5375"	.375" to .3765"	1.675"	2.166"	2.61"	0.25"
G. B. Crandall .22 Wildcats							
.22 Crandall Improved K. B. Hornet	20°	.350"* .347"	.2872"	1.10"	1.38"	1.78"	0.23"
.22 Crandall R-2 Lovell	12°	.380"* .376"	.2925"	1.18"	1.633"	2.05"	0.27"
.22-303 Crandall Varmint-R	29°	.533"* .5295" Actual	.4085" to .4105" Actual	1.562"	2.031"	2.48"	0.325"

Marciante, Wilson and Sedgley-Schnerring Cartridges

Cartridge	Shoulder Slope	Diam. Head	Diam. at Shoulder	Length to Shoulder	Length Case	O. A. Length	Neck Length
Al. Marciante Cartridges							
.22 Marciante Blue Streak	25°	.506"* .4935" to .494" Actual	.3575" to .355" Actual	1.70"	2.025"	2.56"	0.22"
L. E. Wilson Cartridges							
.220 Wilson Arrow	28°	.473"* .485" Actual	.402"* .401"	1.74"	2.25"	2.70"	0.30"
R. F. Sedgley Cartridges							
.22/4000 Sedgley-Schnerring		.473"* .471" Actual	.431"* .432" Actual	1.75"	2.24"	2.70"	0.35"
Comparison and Tabulation of Jerry Gebby .22 Wildcats							
.22 Senior Varminter (.257 Roberts case)	25°	.473" .472" Actual	.4695"	1.66"	2.20"	2.73"	0.275"
.22 Varminter (.250/3000 Sav.) case	28°	.473" .467" Actual	.4155"	1.50"	1.92"	2.43"	0.25"
.22 Junior Varminter .32-40 case	30°	.4905" Actual	.359"	1.70"	2.03"	2.50"	0.21"

P. O. Ackley .22 Wildcats

Cartridge	Shoulder Slope	Diam. Head	Diam. at Shoulder	Length to Shoulder	Length Case	O.A. Length	Neck Length
1. .22 Ackley Improved Hornet	30°	.350"* .342" Actual	.290"	1.18"	1.375"	1.80"	0.16"
2. .22 Ackley Improved .218 Bee		.408"* .4015" to .402"	.335"	0.93"	1.33"	1.72"	0.22"
3. .22 Ackley Improved Lovell	30°	.382"* .377" to .3792"	.300"	1.380"	1.633"	2.13"	0.20"
4. .22 Ackley Improved Zipper	28°	.506"* .4965"	.400"	1.50"	1.92"	2.38"	
5. .22 Ackley-Vickery Improved Zipper (By W. F. Vickery)	28°	.506"* .4965"	.400"	1.54"	1.92"	2.40"	
6. .22 Ackley Improved .22 Hi-Power	28°	.506"* .495" to .4965"	.400"	1.50"	2.00"	2.46"	

No. / Cartridge	Angle						
7. .22-250 Ackley	28°	.4667″ Actual	.420″* / .4135″ Actual	1.50″	1.92″	2.38″	0.27″
8. .220 Ackley Improved Swift	30°	.473″** / .468″ Actual	.430″** / .4315″ Actual	1.73″	2.18″	2.625″	0.28″
9. .228 Ackley Medium (Standard)	35°	.473″** / .4695″ Actual	.445″** / .4695″ to / .447″ Actual	1.50″	1.90″	2.61″	0.25″
10. .228 Ackley Short	35°	.473″** / .4695″	.440″	1.38″	1.78″	2.40″	0.25″
11. .228 Ackley Magnum	28°	.473″** / .4695″	.445″ / .445″	1.68″	2.21″	2.88″	0.25″
12. .228 Ackley Rimmed Medium	35°	.545″** / .540″	.445″ / .465″ to / .447″	1.50″	1.92″	2.63″	0.25″
13. .22-250/06 Ackley	35°	.473″** / .4695″	.445″ / .465″	1.50″	1.90″	2.61″	0.25″

NOTE: In regard to No. 6, *recent* lots of factory .219 Zipper cases are found to vary as much as .002″ thicker in the neck of the case. Same trouble has been found in .250/3000 cases and in .22 Savage H.P. cases, which sometimes is so excessive as to necessitate freeing of chamber of a close-chambered rifle to admit loaded cases. In such instance, especially with very tight case neck in regular chamber, immediately *reduce* load as much as 2.00 grains of 3031 or similar powder, in 25 to 40 grain case.

INDEX

Index

Samworth Books on Firearms

Above are listed the Samworth Books on Firearms now offered for sale or in process of publication. Some of these titles are described in detail on the following pages and on the jacket of this book. Any of these books may be obtained from your dealer or from

THOMAS G. SAMWORTH
Small-Arms Technical Publishing Company
Georgetown, South Carolina
U. S. A.

February, 1952

Hunting With the Twenty-Two

By Charles S. Landis

For years, the many devotees of .22 caliber rifles have been demanding an authentic and comprehensive work on the hunting of small game and varmints with these popular arms. Landis' *Hunting With the Twenty-Two* amply fills this need.

Charlie Landis has spent more than fifty years in the active use of various .22 rifles: Twenty-twos of all types using the many different cartridges which have been available to American riflemen since the turn of the century. In this book he gives you the benefit of his lifetime of experience in the small game hunting field. Then, to supplement his own extensive personal experience, he has turned to those of his many friends who, through occupation or location, have been more fortunate in their opportunities to hunt and shoot larger or more inaccessible game with rifles of this caliber.

The result is a book of 27 chapters comprising 425 text pages which are filled with instructive data and information on the hunting of the small game and varmints of the North American continent with the various .22 caliber rim and center fire cartridges. It covers all sections of these United States and Canada—Eastern hunting in heavily settled communities—Western experience in the open ranges and mountains—Northern trapping and hunting fields extending from British Columbia to the Hudson Bay country—and Southern shooting in the dense swamps and pine forests.

The habits and histories of many game animals and birds are included, with much information as to the best means of hunting them. Here are many chapters on hunting the various species of tree squirrels—gray, black and fox; grouse, prairie chickens and ptarmigan with rifles; wild turkeys and other game. Then come the varmints—crow and hawk shooting; coyote, wolf and fox hunting; some lynx or wildcat also are treated and several chapters are devoted to that old standby—the woodchuck.

All suitable hunting cartridges and loads for rim and center fire .22 rifles are covered with respect to their use in the hunting field —and when used as the main or as a supplementing rifle. Proper ammunition is discussed, as well as those pertinent factors of sight setting and aiming points.

Here is a contribution of definite value to the riflemen of America —hunting information of a type not previously existent. *Hunting With the Twenty-Two* fully warrants the attention and reading of every owner and shooter of the more powerful, flat trajectory .22 rifles as well as the rim fire devotees.

This is truly a practical book on hunting—not one man's theories or hearsay "b'guess and b'gosh" stories. Well illustrated with numerous plates and drawings. Price $4.50.

The Book of The Springfield

By Edward C. Crossman
and Roy F. Dunlap

If you are a bolt-action rifleman—and most of us are—you will need this book in your library. Although written around the 1903 Springfield rifle and its 1906 cartridge, this is the most complete and attractively written work on modern rifles and their ballistics that is available today. Its text and teachings will stand for another generation or so.

Book of the Springfield was originally written by the late Captain Edward C. Crossman—the foremost writer-rifleman of his day and an author whose style of writing has never been surpassed. The first edition was published in 1931 and has been out of print for several years. Continued and insistent demand has necessitated reprinting in toto the original material compiled by Ned Crossman plus some 160 additional pages of text written by Roy F. Dunlap, a firearms authority and writer of ability equal to that of the original author. His new material brings all subject matter up to the year 1952.

This 1952 edition is a volume of 567 pages, well illustrated throughout. It is the most exhaustive and thorough work in existence on modern bolt-action rifles—military, target and sporting models. The 16 lengthy chapters differentiate at length between the rifle—the cartridge—sights—and on technical tolerances, adjustments, and care.

Its rifle text consists of some 153 pages covering the various military, target and sporting models.

The chapters on metallic sights comprise 65 pages—treating fully all types of military, target and hunting sights.

When it comes to the subject of the modern telescopic rifle sight there is actually a book in itself in the 152 pages in three chapters of up-to-the-minute material on military, target, hunting and varmint scopes—with special emphasis placed upon these last two types. Included also are comprehensive instructions for the proper fitting and adjustment of the many various makes and models. The practising gunsmith will find this material of particular value in his daily work. To the custom gunmaker it will prove a *must* work of reference.

The ammunition section is particularly complete; military, target and hunting ammunition is fully analyzed and discussed, with many illustrations of sectioned bullets included for classification and study.

Roy Dunlap took up where Crossman left off and their combined effort is a work no rifleman or ballistic student can afford to pass up. The hundreds of thousands of owners and users of Springfield rifles will find in this book everything that is today known in practical experience and ballistic science relative to .30 '06 rifle and cartridge matters. *Book of the Springfield* has long been one of the classics in firearms literature and this revised and greatly enlarged edition will assure its top position for years to come. **Price $6.00.**

African Rifles and Cartridges

By John Taylor

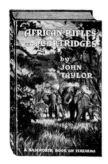

John Taylor is a professional ivory hunter who has spent some 30 years in the African Bush engaging in his chosen vocation of elephant hunting. His total bag runs better than 1,500 elephant, almost as many buffalo, innumerable rhino, hippo, lion and leopard, besides the larger antelope and countless "small buck" that have fallen to his rifles during these years and which were, of necessity, shot to feed his camp retinue and followers.

During this 30 years of continuous hunting he has owned, experimented with, tried out, and otherwise used all of the various suitable British, German and American big-game cartridges, from the 6.5mm to the .600 Nitro. Some of these calibers he acquired two or three times for use on extensive safaris. Single-shots, doubles and magazines; he has tried them all; black powder to smokeless; soft lead bullets to "solids."

The practical aspect of his work is foremost on every page in this book. Here, for the first time, is an actual analysis of the suitability and killing power of *all* modern big-game rifles when used on game ranging from the mighty African elephant on down to the tiny dik-dik antelope. Every question on hunting ballistics that the rifleman can think of has been answered in this book; with much of it never before having been put in type.

This volume sets a new high for actual gun and cartridge suitability, performance and killing effect. There has never been a book before which contains the amount of real, down-to-earth gun and hunting data such as John Taylor herein gives. He takes up every caliber, cartridge by cartridge, and discusses each individually. With his opinion of each cartridge, he tells the value and effect of each bullet available for that cartridge—solids, soft-point, split jacket, hollow-point, or plain lead—and this in all the various weights. Interspiced throughout the text are authentic hunting incidents, quoted from his voluminous notes and given solely to prove some ballistic point in question.

Our staff artist, Ned Smith, has turned out a new style of technical cartridge illustration, fully in keeping with the style and originality of the text of this book. Here are the cartridges reproduced full-size, with case and bullets laid open and analyzed visually for your inspection and knowledge; with jacket construction, turn-in, thickness and coverage shown; all supplemented by elaborate explanations as to the suitability and action of each cartridge and type of bullet.

Whether you intend to hunt in Africa or in Arizona—for lion or for white-tail deer—you will find this book of extreme value in the selection, handling and shooting of your modern big-game rifle. 426 text pages, profuse with accurate and original technical drawings and plates. Price, $6.00.

A Rifleman Went To War

By Capt. Herbert W. McBride

This pioneer work on sniping and battle marksmanship was written by one of the outstanding American riflemen of all times, the late Captain Herbert W. McBride, whose name appeared high up on the lists of prizewinners at Sea Girt and Camp Perry for many years before the First World War. At the outbreak of that war, he enlisted in the Canadian Army and spent some 18 months in Belgium and France with the 21st Battalion, Canadian Expeditionary Force. The greater portion of this period found Mac (as he was known to thousands of us), actually in the front line trenches, with German infantrymen only a matter of yards away.

His book, first published in 1936, is still an applicable and authoritative work on the use of the modern military rifle and telescope on the battlefield. In World War II it was of incalculable benefit to American and British forces in the training of their men in rifle marksmanship and the principles which McBride taught therein were very favorably commented upon by high ranking officers who observed and fought both in Europe and the Pacific.

McBride served with the Canadians as a machine gunner, his work as a rifleman being confined largely to sniping, though he used the rifle in repelling enemy attacks on more than one occasion and writes all about it. He carried a pistol, used it, and tells you what he thinks of it. He made something of a reputation on patrols and raids—having been decorated for work of this sort. There are chapters on each of these several subjects, dealing not only with his experiences but with his observations and conclusions. But the outstanding features are the chapters devoted to sniping and the rifle in battle. Captain McBride was one of the best qualified snipers in the Allied Army and he made a reputation in the Canadian Corps on his shooting ability. In his narrative, he goes into full details regarding the many tricks of the sniper—sniping equipment and its care and use—observation with the big telescope—concealment—range finding—counter sniping—and battle firing. No sob stuff and no dramatics—just a complete and truthful statement of facts, telling you how to "get your man" and get him "fustest."

The instructions given, and the tricks Mac tells of, can be applied on any battlefield of today and in any static position where modern rifles and ammunition are used. His teachings are in no way obsolete; they still stand. Material and extracts from this book have been widely copied and quoted in many more recent domestic and foreign works and it is acclaimed as an outstanding contribution to our shooting literature. 412 text pages and frontispiece. Price $3.50.

Gunsmithing

By Roy F. Dunlap

A 1950 work on gunsmithing—the most complete ever written, containing information on every phase of gunwork from selection of the stock blank on through to the metal engraving and blueing. It is *thorough!*—with not only the "what" and "how" but also the "why." This work was instigated by the publisher and written at his request by Roy Dunlap with a view of replacing Baker's *Modern Gunsmithing*, which was written back in 1927. Everyone who has read Dunlap's manuscript says it is "better'n Baker."

The average user of firearms will find this book to be of value in its technical information on barrels, action bedding, accuracy adjustments and trouble corrections. The shotgun information is exceptionally complete and practical. One can read exactly how the job he wants should be done and how to have the guns fitted properly to himself so that he can get the most out of them.

The targetshooter will be interested in the chapters on modern target rifles, their bareling and chamber work, their special furniture and fittings. Dunlap is a hard-boiled, competent rifleman and his information on rifles of precision is backed by trial, experience, quite a few medals and trophies, and many a head of big game.

The general gunsmith will gain information he has never been able to find except through trial and error. Individual shotguns, rifles, revolvers and pistols are covered in detail, their weak points mentioned, and instructions given as how to fix them without the use of a fully equipped shop and special, expensive machinery.

For the first time, complete and official cartridge and chamber specification drawings are published, with headspace data and barrel threadings, on modern cartridges from the .22 long rifle to the .375, including the more popular wildcats. All barrel shank and thread data is shown by drawings as well as dimensions. Barrel specifications and rifling information in all calibers is listed and analyzed.

Above all—although complete and thorough—this book is not written over the shooter's head. Written and published with the definite aim of turning out the most possible up-to-date information and instruction under one cover—*Gunsmithing* is the best one-book buy that can be obtained today. Its pages are crammed with instruction and formulae necessary in all phases of the gunsmithing art. Professional, amateur, or just plain shooter—this Dunlap work is by far the best shooting-buy offered at the start of the half-century. It has been four years in the making and will prove a milestone in gun literature equal to Baker's famous work of three decades back.

Gunsmithing is sold under the guarantee that it is better and more applicable today than any other published work on that craft. 800 pages—200 illustrations—36 chapters of the most modern, most complete, best all-around book on gunwork published. Price $7.50

Professional Gunsmithing

Gunsmithing methods and textbooks, like everything else, are matters of evolution and change for the better. This is particularly true of the many technical books on gunsmithing now in existence—each in part records or augments the gradual but positive progress of the craft as time goes by.

Here is a recent work written entirely from the professional outlook and devoted mainly to the repair and modification of existing stock weapons. *"Professional Gunsmithing"* approaches the subject from an entirely new angle, supplementing and enhancing all other previous Samworth Books on Firearms treating of this vital matter of gun repair and upkeep. It combines both business and technical phases of gunsmithing, in that matters such as time, ethics, price estimation, how to deal with shooters as customers, and the idea of doing the job exactly as someone else demands and not as the gunsmith himself might want to do it, are given paramount consideration throughout the text.

How to best set up a gunshop and what is more important, how to keep it going on a profitable basis is included in this volume. Subjects such as business set-up and customer relationship are presented in a clear, understandable manner. Several speciality lines which will provide a satisfactory source of revenue are included and the listing of sources of supplies for all gunsmithing materials is the most extensive yet published.

Anyone entering the gunsmithing field, either as a means of livelihood or merely to work on their personal firearms, will find a mass of applicable material herein. The subject of commercial gunsmithing is taken up by Howe in a broad and comprehensive manner, approached from the angle of basic principles and logical reasoning. He tells how to diagnose gun troubles when the weapon is brought in for repair and explains the general reasons and causes for necessity of such repairs. By applying Howe's "approach" to the problem in hand any gunsmith will be enabled to correctly and profitably remedy the fault or repair the defective part.

Walter Howe's instruction is concise and practical because he knows whereof he writes. Specific jobs and types of repair work which have proved to be most frequently brought into the gunshop during his experience as a practicing gunsmith, are treated in detail. The amateur will appreciate this instruction as the advice of a master craftsman; the professional will be impressed with its clarity and practical application to the problems which daily confront him.

"Professional Gunsmithing" is today's outstanding textbook for the gunsmithing profession, and is now being used as such in colleges and training schools which include gunsmithing in their curriculum. 520 pages, 120 special drawings, 21 plates. Price $6.00.

Gunstock Finishing and Care

By A. Donald Newell

This is an extensive and thoroughly complete contribution to the art of modern gunsmithing, a work equally valuable to either professional or amateur craftsmen. It includes materials, suitability, methods of application, and the history of ancient and modern protective and decorative films. The author of this timely book is a technician in the laboratory of one of the largest American paint and varnish manufacturers; then, to further qualify in the preparation of so definitive a work he is a rifleman and amateur gunsmith of several years' standing.

In this most thorough work, Newell sticks entirely to his vocation in that he treats solely of gunstock finishing. In some 16 elaborate chapters, replete with heretofore unpublished trade data and technique, he tells everything known today by the people who make these finishing materials, so that they can be properly applied by the individual gunsmith seeking the most beautiful and thoroughly practical stock finishes for both modern and antique firearms. The greater portion of these procedures and formulae will provide virgin knowledge for the majority of our guncraftsmen.

Herein is given authoritative and qualified information regarding all modern and early wood finishes which can logically be applied to gunstocks—as known to a professional technician and manufacturer. He gives the final word on bleachers, fillers, sealing compounds, water and moisture repellents, stains, driers, drying oils, varnishes, lacquers, shellacs and plastic finishes, with chapters also on waxes, polishing, cleaning and rubbing compounds. And, of course included is that old standby of the profession—the London Dull Oil Finish.

Extensive chapters on primary and advanced treatments for all suitable gunstock woods outline selection, bleaching, sealing, graining, staining, waterproofing and all other necessary pretreatment data that will enhance or improve the natural beauties of the wood, plus an extensive assortment of all types of formulae that will enable the reader to select and compound his own finishing mediums, the like of which never previously have been available to shooters. More than 100 such formulae are given.

The scale of treatments covered by this outstanding textbook ranges from the application of various solutions and solids by means of a rag or brush, or with pressure or spray gun systems, on through to the most modern technique of "baked finish" by means of a three- or four-tube bank of infra-red lights.

The text is written in non-technical form and all subjects discussed are presented simply and understandably in an interesting manner.

Well illustrated throughout. 437 pages of text. Price $4.50.

Checkering and Carving of Gunstocks

By Monty Kennedy

Gunstock ornamentation has been a subject of compelling personal interest to most owners of firearms for the past five centuries and has ranged from the practice of hammering-in lines and whorls of brass nails on up to the meticulous inlaying of mother-of-pearl and semiprecious stones into the wooden stock. Such decorative tastes have leveled-off in the past 100 years and now are confined mainly to the checkering and carving of the gunstock, with a minimum of inlays.

During the past decade American gunmakers have been hard put to meet the increasing demand for more artistic ornamentation to grips and forearms, yet, at the same time, meet the necessary requirements prescribed by usage in hunting fields and on target ranges.

Checkering and Carving of Gunstocks meets the demand for a treatise covering this art of gunstock ornamentation. It is an extensive and specialized work of 244 text pages and some 300 technical illustrations that covers its subject fully from both utilitarian and decorative standpoints. The author, Monty Kennedy, is a top-flight professional gunstocker with several years of steady work at the checkering cradle to back him up, and he tells herein all he knows.

In addition to the author's comprehensive instruction, this book gives the methods, procedures, tools and patterns of such top-ranking craftsmen as Tom Shelhamer, Leonard Mews, John Hearn, Leighton Baker, Keith Stegall, Hal Hartley, Roy Dunlap and many others. Each describes at length his distinctive checkering methods and illustrates his personal choice of actual patterns.

There are some 75 of these checkering patterns shown—each in full size with basic starting lines located—all ready to be used as a template of sorts for transfer to your own gunstock. Notes and comment as to its application by the beginner accompany each pattern. Patterns range from easy ones to some that will take many, many jobs before experience enough has been acquired to start in on them.

The past few years have seen an increasing demand for carved gunstocks, so to help meet this growing trend we present, in full size, some 40 applicable and highly attractive carving patterns—forearm, grip and buttside—of big game, game bird, animal, and leaf-and-seed designs. Nothing conventional here; these are definite, easily recognizable patterns from nature's storehouse, highly original in conception and done by leading American artists. The beauty and appeal of these splendid patterns must be seen to be appreciated and this feature will set a new milestone in custom decoration by American gunmakers. Accompanying these patterns is the essential basic instruction on carving and suggestions as to the application of these particular designs.

Monty Kennedy's great work will prove of equal value to the experienced gunmaker with years of practical experience to his credit, as well as to the man or boy out in the hills with his first standard grade of gun and a bit concerned about that smooth, unfinished look to its grip and forearm. Either of these extremes will find something in *Checkering and Carving of Gunstocks* that can be applied to the gun-in-hand at the particular moment. **Price $5.25.**

Shots Fired in Anger

By Lt. Col. John B. George

Johnny George is remembered by Illinois riflemen as a State Team member at Camp Perry; as the youngest .30 Caliber champion the State ever had; and as a many-times-winner in various local and regional rifle competitions. He knew plenty about the peace-time use of rifles. He got into World War 2 early, as a lieutenant in the 132nd Infantry, American Division, on Guadalcanal. This was the first Infantry Division to be used aggressively against the Axis Powers in any theatre. After the Guadalcanal Campaign, he volunteered and went through Burma with "Merrill's Marauders." Subsequent wartime assignments took him more than twice around the globe. He saw *plenty* of shooting.

"Shots Fired in Anger" is a book covering George's rifle shooting experiences up to and including his platoon-leader and sniping ventures on Guadalcanal. He wrote it particularly for other riflemen.

Half of the text of this work is in narrative form, giving a shot-by-shot account of Lt. George's part in the Battle of Guadalcanal and the events leading up to it. He discusses rifleman training and tactics first, then tells the actual stories of how he and his fellow Infantry-men killed the enemy with rifles and other Infantry weapons. Throughout the book George disclaims being a warrior, but he seems to remain somewhat this side of those who condemn War as a monotonous bore, devoid of thrills. His account sometimes takes the slant of a good big game hunting story as told by one alive to the dangers, as well as the thrills, of the chase. One thing he makes clear is the fierce pride he takes in having been a doughboy and a rifleman. He believes ardently in the traditions of the foot soldier—and more than ever before he believes in accurate rifle fire.

The second half of this book, entitled "The Tools Used," gives a gun-nut's description of the weapons used and encountered in the field, relating their manners of performance. This presentation almost brings the Japanese and American weapons to life; George shows here that he certainly regards guns as much more than inanimate bits of metal and wood.

Every American rifleman and member of the National Rifle Association should read this book. Aside from its entertainment value, it contains a world of practical information which will prove of worth to the younger members of our shooting clan, who may well be called upon to use our American military rifles in another war. It tells you just what to expect of the modern military rifle when shooting "for keeps"—and also what to look out for from the rifle of the other fellow. The sketches illustrating this work were done by one of the best artists in Japan. 421 pages. **Price $4.00**

Ordnance Went Up Front

By Roy F. Dunlap

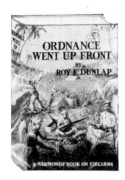

In reality, this book is the elaborated technical diary of an American gun nut who served as an enlisted man in the 27th Ordnance Company of the United States Army and whose duties consisted mainly of going over practically all types of the rifles, pistols and machine guns of World War II, both enemy and allied.

The author's services in both Eastern and Western theatres of war puts him right up into the "been everywhere and seen everything" classification. He really did get around a bit; Aberdeen Proving Ground; Egypt; Mississippi; New Guinea; Leyte; Luzon and Tokyo.

Working on all types of small arms, usually right in the combat area, was Roy Dunlap's job during most of the war, and he consequently describes and treats these various arms within the light and knowledge of his own first hand experience—plus that of the men up on the firing line. When a particular weapon is described, it is actual performance you are reading about—those details of suitability, report, recoil, feel and actual results, known only to practical shooters—and the type of knowledge so desired by other shooting men. These are the facts *you* want to know.

To the owners of these foreign military weapons—the veterans who brought them back as trophies or the individuals who have since purchased them—*Ordnance Went Up Front* is the book to tell you *everything* about that weapon; its specifications; the cartridge it shoots; its limitations; and in particular, what can be done with it to make it up into a top-grade sporting rifle or target arm.

Herein are the most detailed and informative descriptions of German, Italian, British, American and Japanese small arms that have so far been published, with much additional data given on the ordnance of many of the smaller nations. Weapons and cartridges are treated extensively, and in their proper relation to each other. This is the book many shooters thought they were getting when they purchased earlier works on these subjects. It is the first such work really written from the practical-user and not the catalog-reader standpoint, with Dunlap's previous training as an experienced gunsmith and Camp Perry marksman standing him in good stead. He *knows* what *you* want to know—and *writes* it. Here is a trained rifleman's qualified opinions, formed after having examined, dissected, repaired and fired all types of modern military weapons used in the past war. 414 pages, with 44 plates. **Price $4.00.**

Samworth Prints on Firearms

Concurrently with the preparation and editing of the *Samworth Books on Firearms* over the past several years, it became necessary to devote much time and study to the composition and arrangement of the special illustrations and paintings to be used along with our books. This, in most instances, turned out to be no small job.

Fortunately, we made contact with Gayle Hoskins, the famous artist of Wilmington, Delaware. Mr. Hoskins has an especial aptitude for historical scenes and outdoor subjects involving firearms, and to our critical demands for accurate weapons-and-period correctness he has given a most satisfying degree of interest and study. As a result of several of his paintings which we have so far used, there has been created a steady and insistent demand from our book buyers to furnish them, in proper form for framing, certain of the rifle shooting scenes he has so accurately and interestingly depicted.

Consequently, we are now offering *Samworth Prints on Firearms*— a series of attractive and authentic pictures, reproduced in the very best and most modern process of this day—six and seven colors done in color-gravure—which will prove highly suitable for the walls of the rifleman or sportsman's home.

Here is "Trade From the Monongahela," depicting a party of backwoodsmen in from the headwaters of the Ohio, who have a pack-load of deer hides to barter for new rifles and a supply of powder and lead. The smithy shown is also the riflemaking establishment of Phil Lefevre, of Lancaster County, Pennsylvania, time is around 1750. Print surface is 17 x 25 inches in size, plus wide margins. **Price $5.00,** delivered suitable for framing.